Norse Revival

Studies in Critical Research on Religion

Haymarket Books is proud to be working with Brill Academic Publishers (www.brill.nl) to republish the *Studies in Critical Research on Religion* book series in paperback editions. This peer-reviewed book series offers insights into our current reality by exploring the content and consequences of power relationships under capitalism, and by considering the spaces of opposition and resistance to these changes that have been defining our new age. Our full catalog of *SCRR* volumes can be viewed at https://www.haymarketbooks.org/series_collections/6-studies-in-critical-research-in-religion.

Series Editor
Warren S. Goldstein, Center for Critical Research on Religion (U.S.A.)

Editorial Board
Christopher Craig Brittain, University of Aberdeen (U.K.)
Heather Eaton, Saint Paul University (Canada)
Titus Hjelm, University College London (U.K.)
Darlene Juschka, University of Regina (Canada)
Lauren Langman, Loyola University Chicago (U.S.A.)
George Lundskow, Grand Valley State University (U.S.A.)
Kenneth G. MacKendrick, University of Manitoba (Canada)
Andrew M. McKinnon, University of Aberdeen (U.K.)
Sara Pike, California State University, Chico (U.S.A)
Dana Sawchuk, Wilfrid Laurier University (Canada)

Advisory Board
William Arnal, University of Regina (Canada)
Roland Boer, University of Newcastle (Australia)
Jonathan Boyarin, Cornell University (U.S.A.)
Jay Geller, Vanderbilt University (U.S.A.)
Marsha Hewitt, University of Toronto (Canada)
Michael Löwy, Centre National de la Recherche Scientifique (France)
Eduardo Mendieta, Penn State University (U.S.A.)
Rudolf J. Siebert, Western Michigan University (U.S.A.)
Rhys H. Williams, Loyola University Chicago (U.S.A.)

NORSE REVIVAL

Transformations of Germanic Neopaganism

STEFANIE VON SCHNURBEIN

Haymarket
Books
Chicago, IL

First published in 2016 by Brill Academic Publishers, The Netherlands.
© 2016 Koninklijke Brill NV, Leiden, The Netherlands

Published in paperback in 2017 by
Haymarket Books
P.O. Box 180165
Chicago, IL 60618
773-583-7884
www.haymarketbooks.org

ISBN: 978-1-60846-737-2

Trade distribution:
In the U.S. through Consortium Book Sales, www.cbsd.com
In the UK, Turnaround Publisher Services, www.turnaround-uk.com
In Canada, Publishers Group Canada, www.pgcbooks.ca
All other countries, Ingram Publisher Services International, intlsales@
perseusbooks.com

Cover design by Jamie Kerry of Belle Étoile Studios.
Cover photo: Rett Rossi (Godafoss, Iceland)

This book was published with the generous support of Lannan Foundation and the Wallace Action Fund.

Printed in Canada by union labor.

10 9 8 7 6 5 4 3 2 1

Library of Congress Cataloging-in-Publication Data is available.

Contents

Acknowledgements VII
Series Editor Preface IX
List of Figures X
Notes on Translations XI
Notes on Previously Published Material XII

Introduction 1
  Initial Encounters 1
  Transformations and Key-Questions 4
  Twisted Terminologies 9
  What Others Say 11
  Complicated Involvements 13
  Receptions, Adaptions, and Goals 15

1 Creating the Paradigm: Historical Preconditions of Modern Asatru 17
  The Search for a National Mythology in European Romanticism 18
  The Search for a German Religion in Fin de Siecle Germany 28
  German(ic) Faith and Ariosophy in the Early Twentieth Century 37
  Post-War Revivals 48
  Witchcraft and the Celtic Revival 51

2 Creating a Religion: The Emergence and Development of Late Twentieth Century Asatru 54
  In Search of Religiosity: Germanic Neopaganism 1970–1990 55
  In Search of Respectability – Asatru after 1990 62
  Asatru International 77

3 **Believing and Doing** 88
  Finding Asatru 88
  Heathen Beliefs 91
  Heathen Practices 106

4 Contested Fields I: Race and Ethnicity 123
  Asatru and National Socialism 123
  The 'Folkish' Versus 'Universalist' Controversy 128
  An 'Ethnic Religion of Nature'? 133
  Ethno-Pluralism and the European New Right 136
  Cultural Essentialism beyond the New Right 140

5 Contested Fields II: Concepts of Religion and Anti-Monotheism 146

Attitudes Towards Christianity 147
The Question of Anti-Semitism 152
Praising Polytheism 155
Anti-Monotheism in Asatru 167
Religion of Experience 171
Heathenism as Religious Secularism 175

6 Asatru – A Religion of Nature? 180

Nature Spirituality in Asatru 181
Environmental Protection, the *Heimat*-Movement and *Völkisch* Religion in Germany 185
Nature Religion in England and the United States 198
Nature and National Identity in Scandinavia 204
Right-Wing Ecologism and Asatru 208

7 Gender and Sexuality 216

The High Position of Germanic Women 217
Masculinity and *Männerbund* 232
Queering Asatru? The Question of Sexuality 243

8 Asatru – An Academic Religion? 251

How Heathens Relate to their Sources 252
Völkisch Scholarship and Germanic Faith 260
Remnants of *Völkisch* Scholarship after 1945 273
Asatru Uses of Scholarship 286

9 Germanic Neopaganism – A Nordic Art-Religion? 298

Nineteenth Century Concepts of Germanic Art-Religion 299
J.R.R. Tolkien and the Nordic Art-Religion of Middle-Earth 308
Religious and Ideological Art in the German Faith Movement 314
Heirs of Wagner and Tolkien: Asatru Novelists 321
Dark Heirs of Wagner and Tolkien: Metal and Neofolk 336
Art-Religion – An Encompassing Paradigm? 347

10 Instead of a Conclusion 351

Interviews Conducted by Author 361
Bibliography 363
Index 412

Acknowledgements

This book is based on thirty years of research and critical engagement with the shifting scene of Germanic Neopaganism. In spite of my efforts to structure and develop consistent arguments, it still teems with unmanageable details. My hope for my readers is that they will not perceive this as a lack, but will instead find pleasure in getting lost in quirky detail and meandering thought. Sometimes, it is this getting lost itself that holds potential for new insights beyond what is written.

There are multiple reasons that Nordic myth and its reception have occupied my mind for so long. The most relevant of them are laid out in the chapters of this book. Others are of a more personal nature. They have to do with the convoluted threads that tie me, and Germans of my age group, to the thoughts, activities, guilt, and suffering of the previous two generations, whose thoughts and actions shaped the 20th century. It is impossible to do justice to these ties here. But I want to give credit to them by thanking my late grandfather. His erring enthusiasm and later his critical revision of his own passionate thoughts have motivated much of my research without my being fully aware of it for a long time.

During the course of my research, I gradually discovered how similar some a-racist Heathens' struggles with this history are to my own. My most sincere gratitude goes to all of my interview partners, who have made it possible for me to investigate these vexing problems in depth, and thus, to write this book. Without their openness toward a researcher who they must have perceived with understandable skepticism and suspicion, this book would look very different. I would also have missed a valuable opportunity to question my own assumptions about religion, politics, and art. Engaging critically with their positions, questions, and doubts has allowed me to revise my own relationship to not only the discourse on Nordic myth and my own field and interests, but also to religion, spirituality, the aesthetic, and politics in general – questions that I will continue to investigate with the help of other materials. The work with real, unpredictable, illogical, multifaceted, and contradictory people has given me the opportunity to examine tensions and contradictions in my own life as a researcher and beyond, and helped me be more relaxed about them. On the other hand, it has alerted me to the fact that there is a significant gap between the official image or ideology that is projected outward through publications and social media, and the lived experience of contemporary Germanic Neopagans, their self-perception, and their intentions as they become visible in interviews and personal encounters. I hope that this book reflects the fact that my critique is mostly directed at official statements and outward representation, and that gratitude and the pleasant memories stem from the personal encounters with reflective and reflecting individuals who shared their views and knowledge with me.

Beside these subjects of my research, my thanks goes to all those whose critical minds have accompanied my work in the last years: Stefan Arvidsson, Mette Buchardt, Nina Trige Andersen, Florian Heesch, René Gründer, Bruce Lincoln, Catharina Raudvere, Andreas Åkerlund, Horst Junginger, Uwe Puschner, Heinrich Anz, and many others who have given me the opportunity to discuss my theses at conferences, in class, or just in private.

I thank the *Volkswagen* and *Thyssen* foundations and their "Opus Magnum" initiative, which financed an 18 month leave for me to do field-work and write a first version of the manuscript. This grant gave me the rare opportunity to concentrate on my writing, free of the daily obligations of teaching and administration, but also free from the pressure of delivering a specific result at a specific time. If this book turns out to be better than the first version of the manuscript, it is due not only to the critical eye of my first readers but also to a grant with no ties attached, which allowed me the time and freedom to use as much space as was necessary for a thorough revision. Therefore, special thanks goes to Gudrun Tegeder, who encouraged my application from the first phone call onwards and saw me through most of the process, and to Adelheid Wessler and Johanna Brumberg, who took over to see it to the end.

Jana Eder, Jan Schröder, and Heike Peetz assisted with transcribing the interviews, the latter also with background research. Rett Rossi and later Angela Anderson extended invaluable help with transforming the text into a hopefully readable English. Series editor Warren Goldstein's thorough reading and sound suggestions have improved the manuscript to the extent that I heeded his advice. Paul Greiner and Kyle Greenwood braved the tedious work of copyediting. Maarten Frieswijk from Brill publishing house helped with all the practical detail involved in the publishing process.

Finally, I want to thank all those around me who came to share my excitement and suffering during the long research process. Sabine Meyer, who got a close look at my joys and desperation in writing this book as did other friends, family, students, and colleagues at Nordeuropa-Institut at Humboldt-Universität. The deepest and thus inexpressible thanks goes to my fellow traveller in life, Rett Rossi, for being there all along and for other ineffabilities.

Series Editor Preface

Norse mythology has come to be associated with the extreme right in Germany – particularly since its appropriation into Nazi ideology. Stefanie von Schnurbein, who has had a decades-long interest in this topic, engages in an in-depth exploration of Germanic Neopaganism. She examines its roots in the *völkisch* movement of the late 19th and early 20th century as well as engages in ethnographic research of the current movement. While parts of the movement remain racist, anti-Semitic, nationalistic, and xenophobic, other parts of it have emerged which are not. Von Schnurbein's stance toward the movement is critical in that she discerns by separating the regressive elements of Neopaganism from those that are more progressive. With this, she raises the question whether Norse mythology can be freed from its reactionary baggage.

Warren S. Goldstein, Ph.D.
Center for Critical Research on Religion
www.criticaltheoryofreligion.org

List of Figures

6.1 Carl Larsson's first sketch for *Midvinterblot* (1911). Source: Torsten Gunnarson, ed. *Carl Larsson* (Stockholm: Wiken, 1992), 223. Work is in the public domain 206

9.1 Portrait photograph of Guido von List (probably 1909/10). Published with permission from the German Federal Archives (Bundesarchiv). Barch, Bild 183-2007-0705-500/Conrad H. Schiffer 315

9.2 Fidus, *Lichtgebet* (1894/1924). © VG Bild-Kunst, Bonn 2014 319

9.3 Painting by Hermann Hendrich, "*Walpurgishalle*," *Hexentanzplatz*, printed on postcard by Meisenbach, Riffarth & Co., Berlin. Published with permission from Georg Jäger, www.goethezeitportal.de 320

9.4 Peter Nikolai Arbo, *Åsgårdsreien* (1872). Published with permission from the National Museum of Art, Architecture and Design in Norway 338

Notes on Translations

All translations from original sources and other material are mine unless noted otherwise.

Notes on Previously Published Material

Parts of Chapter 5 have been published in Stefanie v. Schnurbein, "The Use of Theories of Religion in Contemporary Asatru," in *Nordic Ideology between Religion and Scholarship*, edited by Horst Junginger and Andreas Åkerlund, 225–246. Frankfurt a.M.: Lang, 2013.

Parts of Chapter 8 have been published in Stefanie v. Schnurbein, "Tales of Reconstruction. Intertwining Germanic Neo-Paganism and Old Norse Scholarship," in *Critical Research on Religion* 3, no. 1 (2015).

Parts of Chapter 9 have been published in Stefanie v. Schnurbein, "Germanic Neo-Paganism – A Nordic Art Religion?" in *Religion, Tradition and the Popular. Transcultural Views from Asia and Europe*, edited by Judith Schlehe and Evamaria Sandkühler. History in Popular Cultures, 243–260. Bielefeld: transcript 2014.

This book has been kindly funded by the Volkswagen-Stiftung and the Fritz Tyssen Stiftung within the framework of the "Opus Magnum" initiative.

Introduction

Initial Encounters

"How could this happen to me?" – It is 1986 and I am sitting in a hall in an old German castle amongst a small, rather diverse crowd: men and women of all ages in ceremonial robes, long-haired, gentle-eyed esotericists, martial-looking young men in paramilitary black, and families in traditional German costumes. Listening to Richard Wagner's *"The Ride of the Valkyries"* on a hoarse cassette player in front of an altar adorned with runes, Easter eggs, and small bread-ornaments along with a clumsily painted image of the goddess Freya, ostentatiously blue-eyed with wavy blond hair, I feel out of place. A tall woman with a charismatic voice stands and begins speaking about the true ancient significance of Easter: a seasonal celebration dedicated to fertility. And then it comes: fertility not only in general, as a celebration of life reborn in nature, but in the service of the Germanic race. I feel a sense of panic. She is actually giving us instructions on how to most effectively breed blond-haired and blue-eyed children and to re-awaken the spirit of the Germanic people. What am I doing here? How in the world did I, a reasonably politically critical, left-leaning albeit a little naïve student in my mid-twenties end-up in a situation like this, where I have to listen to racist ideology couched in esoteric terminology and ritual for an entire weekend?

At the time, it was quite common to search for a mythic world with roots far back before the advent of Christianity – a spiritual world which also reaches beyond established religion. There was a longing for a religion close to nature, a reservoir of ancient truths and a tradition not purloined from Asian, Native American, or other indigenous cultures. Worshipping deities such as Odin, Thor, and Freya, along with the rich world of Nordic myth promising to reconcile green-alternative, esoteric and seemingly non-exploitive, anti-imperialist ideas – all of this vaguely reverberated with the popular Romanticism surrounding American Indian spirituality and Tolkinian worlds. They exuded a seductive appeal to me as a young undergraduate student searching for an authentic spirituality that would not contradict my academic interests. Thus, in 1985, when I first heard about a group that based its religion on Norse mythology, I was slightly intrigued. I arranged an afternoon visit with one of its leaders, the above-mentioned woman who served herbal tea from her kitchen garden. She styled herself as a wise woman of old, and told me stories about living, albeit well-concealed, allegedly ancient, German-Celtic esoteric traditions. As charismatic as the woman was, the afternoon failed to entice me into pursuing the matter further; although at the same time, no alarm-bells were set off either.

This could not be said of the situation that I ended up in a year later, when I decided to re-establish contact with this group in order to do interviews for a class paper. I was admitted to a *Thing*, a weekend of ritual, celebration, song, dance, and lectures, and ended up in the scene described above. I was alarmed by my own naïvety, along with the fact that not only the overtly right-wing extremist activists present, but also the more alternative-minded participants seemed convinced that they were in the presence of 'high initiates,' and that the racist teachings seemed to be accepted by all as deep esoteric truths.

Returning home, I found that my fellow students, my professors and the general public were completely unaware of such right-wing religious groups. My critical spirit was spurred by this experience, and I made it my mission to further investigate the phenomenon of Germanic Neopaganism – an endeavor that resulted in my dissertation, two books and several articles in different languages.[1] All of them concluded that Germanic Neopaganism is a field in which alternative, dissident spirituality and ultra-nationalist, racist, and radical right-wing ideology meet and influence each other.

The association between the radical political right and Germanic Neopaganism can be traced back to common roots in the *völkisch* movement of the late 19th and early 20th century. Core ideas of today's radical right-wing thought were formed within this ideology, which merged nationalism, cultural pessimism, racism, anti-Semitism, anti-materialism, anti-liberalism and an enthusiasm for all things 'Nordic' or 'Germanic' into a heterogenous *Weltanschauung*. Among these core ideas characterizing right-wing radical thought today are:

- the belief in a social inequality based on racial or ethnic categories,
- the belief in the ethnic homogeneity of peoples,
- an anti-egalitarian stance directed against universal human rights,

---

1 Stefanie v. Schnurbein, *Religion als Kulturkritik. Neugermanisches Heidentum im 20. Jahrhundert* (Heidelberg: C. Winter, 1992); *Göttertrost in Wendezeiten. Neugermanisches Heidentum zwischen New Age und Rechtsradikalismus* (Munich: Claudius, 1993); "Fornyet naturreligion eller rasistisk kult. Moderne åsatrogrupper i Tyskland og Norden," *CHAOS. Dansk-norsk tidsskrift for religionshistoriske studier* 22 (1994); "Religion of Nature or Racist Cult? Contemporary Neogermanic Pagan Movements in Germany," in *Antisemitismus, Paganismus, Völkische Religion – Antisemitism, Paganism, Voelkisch Religion*, ed. Hubert Cancik and Uwe Puschner (Munich: K.G. Saur, 2004).

- the priority of community over the individual and the subjection of the individual under a strong state or a strong community and
- the rejection of a pluralism of values as promoted in liberal democracies.[2]

Völkisch, and to a certain degree today's right-wing radical ideology, envisioned the renewal or rebirth of the German people living in unity with its territory, its culture and its racial substance. This "palingenetic nationalism," as Roger Griffin[3] has termed this constellation in his discussion of international fascism, already implies religious connotations, and it comes as no surprise therefore that the *völkisch* movement put religion at the centre of its attention. The search for a religion that was suitable and indigenous for this reborn German *Volk* formed a site of vivid discussion and fierce controversy. While a majority of *völkisch* thinkers favored a Christianity purged of its Jewish roots, so-called Ariosophy and the German(ic) Faith Movement sought to (re-)create a religion

---

2 These core ideologemes are derived from Hans-Gerd Jaschke's definition of right-wing extremism, which he formulated in Peter Dudek and Gerd Jaschke, *Entstehung und Entwicklung des Rechtsextremismus in der Bundesrepublik. Zur Tradition einer besonderen politischen Kultur*, 2 vols., vol. 1 (Opladen: Leske und Budrich, 1984). See also Armin Pfahl-Traughber, *"Konservative Revolution" und "Neue Rechte." Rechtsextremistische Intellektuelle gegen den demokratischen Verfassungsstaat* (Opladen: Leske + Budrich, 1998); Uwe Backes, ed. *Rechtsextreme Ideologien in Geschichte und Gegenwart*, Schriften des Hannah-Arendt-Instituts für Totalitarismusforschung (Cologne/Weimar/Vienna: Böhlau, 2003). More recent culturally-oriented studies of international fascism conducted by Anglo-American scholars, such as Roger Griffin or Roger Eatwell, emphasize the importance of themes like a palingenetic renewal of the nation (or other entities imagined as 'natural' and 'eternal,' such as tribal regions, or Europe), the creation of a 'new man,' and a new state, whereby a key element has been so-called 'mythic thinking.' See for example Roger Griffin, *The Nature of Fascism* (London/New York: Routledge, 1991); Roger Eatwell, "The Nature of 'Generic Fascism'. The 'Fascist Minimum' and the 'Fascist Matrix,'" in *Comparative Fascist Studies. New Perspectives*, ed. Constantin Iordachi (London: Routledge, 2009), as well as the controversial discussions in Andreas Umland, Werner Loh, and Roger Griffin, eds., *Fascism Past and Present, West and East. An International Debate on Concepts and Cases in the Comparative Study of the Extreme Right* (Stuttgart: ibidem, 2006). The terms 'right-wing extremism' and 'right-wing radicalism' have given cause to much controversy and are used somewhat differently depending on the national and disciplinary contexts. For the purpose of this book, I use the terms synonymously in order to emphasize the continuities within the spectrum of the far right. As the main interest of my book lies in exploring continuities of *völkisch* ideology, I limit the use of the term 'fascism' to the fascist regimes of Europe in the 1930s, without denying the continuities with the contemporary right-wing phenomena to which Griffin points. Nevertheless, my approach to such continuities is not dissimilar to Griffin's, as both point out the significance of cultural aspects in the formation of political ideology and action.

3 Griffin, *The Nature of Fascism*.

appropriate for the German people, the Germanic folk-soul, or the Nordic or Aryan race – a religion that is opposed to and goes beyond Christianity, which was seen as racially and culturally foreign, not the least because of its Jewish roots. Contrary to general opinion, this religious movement had little influence during Hitler's regime, in spite of indubitable ideological affinities. However, it was revived after 1945, and in the late 1980s and early 1990s the ideological affinities originating in *völkisch* and fascist ideology turned Germanic Neopaganism into an organizational and ideological link between the political radical right and the esoteric and Pagan scene in general.

By the time my books were published in the early 1990s, there were few exceptions to this rule, though some younger people within the scene had expressed growing concern about this *völkisch* history and its racist implications. There were also a few groups in Scandinavia which seemed to avoid contact with right-wing ideology quite successfully. They promoted something that looked more like the benign religion of nature which had initially attracted me to the scene, and which was based not on the racial-esoteric speculations of Ariosophy, but presumably on 'original' written and material sources.

Many academic researchers of Neopaganism relate stories of how they were changed or even converted through their participation in rituals, festivals and personal encounters with the subjects of their research.[4] My initial experience was the opposite. I entered the field of Germanic Neopaganism with a vague personal interest in and openness to Pagan and esoteric teachings and ritual experience, and left it in the beginning of the 1990s not only with a deep and well-founded scepticism toward such attempts at a Pagan revival, but also with the will to enlighten the public about its problematic aspects.

Transformations and Key-Questions

My own naïve encounter with the Germanic Neopagan scene, along with my own initial ignorance of its right-wing and racist connections, had alerted me to a number of general problems underlying attempts to reconstruct or re-imagine 'ancient,' 'pre-Christian' religions and cults. I became increasingly aware of how deeply ingrained some of the stereotypes of an indigenous

---

4 See many of the contributions in Jenny Blain, Douglas Ezzy, and Graham Harvey, eds., *Researching Paganism* (Walnut Creek etc.: Altamira Press, 2004), as well as Jone Salomonsen, *Enchanted Feminism. Ritual, Gender and Divinity among the Reclaiming Witches of San Francisco* (London/New York: Routledge, 2002), and Helen A. Berger, *A Community of Witches. Contemporary Neo-Paganism and Witchcraft in the United States* (Columbia, SC: University of South Carolina Press, 1999).

INTRODUCTION

Germanic or Nordic spiritual tradition are, not only in right-wing contexts, but also in other alternative circles as well as in mainstream thought, where elements of *völkisch* ideology continue to thrive.[5] Synchronous with my deepening awareness of such mainstream remnants of *völkisch* ideology, the Germanic Neopagan scene underwent a number of changes throughout the 1990s and even more so in the 2000s. New groups emerged in Scandinavia, North America, and Germany. The Internet facilitated the rapid internationalization of the scene, while parts of the community started to develop a critical distance to the right-wing radical and racist ideology in addition to the *völkisch* traditions within their own history.

When I went back in 2010 to conduct the research and interviews that form the basis of this book, my interview partners from these new groups expressed a strong desire for respectability, and assured me that they most definitely did not belong to any right-wing political scene. While these encounters changed my perception of the field and its activists, they still did not cancel out the fact that the basic assumption underpinning the idea of a revival of Germanic

---

5 See for example Stefanie v. Schnurbein, "Gjenbruken av edda-diktningen i 'völkisch-religiöses Weihespiel' rundt århundreskiftet i Tyskland," *Nordica Bergensia* 3 (1994); "Die Suche nach einer 'arteigenen' Religion in 'germanisch'- und 'deutschgläubigen' Gruppen," in *Handbuch zur 'Völkischen Bewegung' 1871–1918*, ed. Uwe Puschner, Walter Schmitz, and Justus H. Ulbricht (Munich etc.: K.G. Saur, 1996); "Mütterkult und Männerbund. Über geschlechtsspezifische Religionsentwürfe," in *Kybele – Prophetin – Hexe. Religiöse Frauenbilder und Weiblichkeitskonzeptionen*, ed. Richard Faber and Susanne Lanwerd (Würzburg: Königshausen & Neumann, 1997); "Kräfte der Erde – Kräfte des Blutes. Elemente völkischer Ideologie in Marion Zimmer-Bradley: Die Nebel von Avalon und Diana Paxson: Der Zauber von Erin," *Weimarer Beiträge* 44, no. 4 (1998); "Transformationen völkischer Religion seit 1945," in *Völkische Religion und Krisen der Moderne. Entwürfe 'arteigener' Glaubenssysteme seit der Jahrhundertwende*, ed. Stefanie v. Schnurbein and Justus H. Ulbricht (Würzburg: Königshausen & Neumann, 2001); "Religionsforskning og religionsfornyelse i 'nordisk' ånd i Tyskland etter første verdenskrig," in *Myter om det nordiska – mellan romantik och politik*, ed. Catharina Raudvere, Anders Andrén, and Kristina Jennbert, Vägar till Midgård (Lund: Nordic Academic Press, 2001); "Religiöse Ikonographie – religiöse Mission. Das völkische Weihespiel um 1910," in *Kunst, Fest, Kanon. Inklusion und Exklusion in Gesellschaft und Kultur*, ed. Hermann Danuser, Herfried Münkler, and in cooperation with der Staatsoper Unter den Linden (Schliengen: Edition Argus, 2004); "Schamanismus in der altnordischen Überlieferung – eine wissenschaftliche Fiktion zwischen den ideologischen Lagern," in *Kontinuität in der Kritik. Zum 50jährigen Bestehen des Münchener Nordistikinstituts: Historische und aktuelle Perspektiven der Skandinavistik*, ed. Klaus Böldl and Miriam Kauko (Freiburg i.Br.: 2005); "Neuheidentum und Fantasyroman," in *Bilder vom Mittelalter. Eine Berliner Ringvorlesung*, ed. Volker Mertens and Carmen Stange (Göttingen: 2007); "Kontinuität durch Dichtung. Moderne Fantasyromane als Mediatoren völkisch-religiöser Denkmuster," in *Völkisch und national. Zur Aktualität alter Denkmuster im 21. Jahrhundert*, ed. Uwe Puschner and G. Ulrich Großmann (Darmstadt: WBG, 2009).

religion is inherently problematic: the persuasion that religious identity can and should be based on indigenous landscape, soil, climate, ancestry and heritage – or to say it short and polemically – on 'blood and soil.' This 'Norse revivalism' is a cluster of ideas taken from an ideological constellation that can be traced back to 19th century Romantic nationalism in Germany and Scandinavia, as well as to Anglo-Saxonism of the same era. It is a politically and ideologically malleable constellation, which has had influence on both nationalist and diverse counter-cultural movements up until today. However, it remains dependent on a certain logic of exclusion. It allows for diversity between nations, religions, or cultures as well as between different traditions, but it requires internal homogeneity. It does not allow for pluralism within these national, ethnic, or cultural holistic entities and thus remains tied in with theories of race and ethnicity, or a cultural essentialism. Furthermore, it has a tendency to 'purify' the respective 'diverse' traditions. It is this aspect which was taken up and radicalized into more violent politics of racial and cultural exclusion by the *völkisch* movement during the beginning of the 20th century.

Such observations motivate the core question of this book: how can we account for discrepancies between a self-understanding of the majority of current Germanic Neopagans as part of a pluralistic, democratic society, and the fact that Germanic Neopaganism carries with it remnants of *völkisch* ideologemes? My thesis is that we have to look at changes both within Asatru and within mainstream thought in order to understand this development and field of tension. On the one hand, Asatru has undergone a reform process during which fantasies of racial or ethnic exclusion and the striving for purity or purification of one's 'own' tradition have become less violent. On the other hand, the reception of the Romantic constellation of a unity between nature, ethnicity, cultural tradition and religion has moved from being perceived as a paradigm of the radical right into being a viable facet of mainstream thought in the 1990s and 2000s.

The shift within Asatru away from racial ideology and into a more critical attitude toward the *völkisch* heritage has of course not been absolute. Rather, it can be described as a shift in the centre of gravity between three main factions within the scene:

(1) A **racial-religious** current that bases religion on a biological concept of race and continues to promote a radical *völkisch* racial ideology along with ideas of racial and religious purity and purification.
(2) A current that has been labelled 'folkish' and that I choose to call **ethnicist** in order to stress the fact that religion here is based on a traditional, homogenous heritage that is to be preserved or restored. This heritage is not exclusively conceptualized in biological terms, but is seen as

rooted in landscape, nature, climate and culture as well. The ethnicist faction thus tends toward a cultural essentialism which sees 'culture' as an immutable and ideally homogenous entity rooted in a deep past – an idea which often carries with it a desire to purify and re-homogenize this alleged essential, traditional culture.

(3) A current that has been called 'universalist' or 'anti-racist,' but that I choose to describe as **a-racist** because it (a) rejects the category of race and goes against conflating biological heritage and religion, (b) is generally inclusive of individuals of all backgrounds, but (c) usually does not go actively against racism, as the term 'anti-racist' would suggest. This faction tends to conceptualize culture in a more dynamic way, as something that is to be created and that is continually transformed through cultural exchange and mixing.

What remains common among all these currents is the close relation which is seen between religion and culture, and therefore, an emphatically culturalist understanding of religion. This common link unites the different factions, which of course never exist in pure forms, but instead intersect in complex and often contradictory and inconsistent ways. As a general tendency, however, we can say that while Germanic Neopaganism in the 1970s and 80s was dominated by racial-religious and ethnicist groups and the controversies between them, the racial-religious groups have been increasingly marginalized throughout the 1990s and 2000s, while the mainstream, most widely accepted, and visible part of Asatru today moves in the field between ethnicist and a-racist.

The shift in mainstream discourse that has contributed to Asatru's gaining of respectability has to do with the perception of religion, culture, and ethnicity. Ideas about the intimate correlation between these entities were perceived as right-wing radical in the 1970s and 80s, but have become more generally accepted after the fall of the Iron Curtain, the end of the Cold War, and even more so after September 11, 2001. This is most visible in the discourse on immigration and Islam, where culture, religion, and ethnicity are conflated into one indistinguishable and immutable entity posited as an antagonist to 'our' cultural identity. Already around 1990, Etienne Balibar had argued that the exclusionary mechanisms of racist thought were not dependent on a naturalist or biological paradigm, but that a cultural essentialism had more or less replaced 'race' in public discourse.[6] This allowed for a circumvention of the

---

6 Racism is traditionally defined as "the idea that human beings could be placed in groups based on physical characteristics, or more deeply, their genetic make-up, and that an individual's personality and likely behavior could be read off from that membership." (Ralph D.

racial biological paradigm that was strongly stigmatized after 1945. In this process, 'culture' or 'cultural identity' became equally deterministic; unchangeable, essentialist foundational entities and anxieties about mixing and exchange permeate such discourses as much as they did classical racism.[7] I would argue that this cultural or 'differentialist' racism, as Balibar calls it, has by now moved beyond the confines of the political and cultural (New) Right's ideology and entered mainstream discourse. Moreover, I would put forth that the central factor in this constellation is religion. Nowadays, there is a general tendency to view 'culture' as a quasi-sacred entity, as well as to perceive religion as a phenomenon that is closely tied not only to 'culture,' but also to specific 'cultures.'

The thesis of this book can thus be specified as follows: The sacralization of culture and simultaneous culturalization of religion found in both Asatru and in mainstream discourse contribute to the increased respectability of Asatru, while at the same time renewing interest in 'Germanic' or 'Nordic' religion and pre-Christian cultural heritage in high and popular culture alike.

The intertwined developments of Asatru reform and the change in mainstream discourse, with regard to the sacralization of culture and culturalization of religion, motivate the double perspective of this book. The first part provides the historical genealogy (Chapter 1), the further development of Germanic Neopaganism and its organizational progression (Chapter 2), and the core beliefs and practices (Chapter 3). This encompassing description of the international, alternative, spiritual subculture or cultic milieu[8] of Asatru

---

Grillo, "Cultural Essentialism and Cultural Anxiety," *Anthropological Theory* 3, no. 2 (2003), 162). However, as I will show in Chapters 4 and 5, 'classical' racism has never existed without strong references to 'culture' and religion either.

7 Cf. Étienne Balibar, "Is there a 'New Racism,'" in *Race, Nation, Class. Ambiguous Identities*, ed. Étienne Balibar and Immanuel Wallerstein (London/New York: Verso, 1991).

8 The concept of 'cultic milieu' was first elaborated by Colin Campbell in 1972. It describes 'fuzzy' constellations held together loosely by a "bundle of ideas and practices related to other ideas and practices in the cultural underground of society" (Jesper Aagaard Petersen, "Introduction: Embracing Satan," in *Contemporary Religious Satanism. A Critical Anthology*, ed. Jesper Aagaard Petersen (Farnham/Burlington: Ashgate, 2009), 4) – milieus which spurn the emergence and decline of "ephemeral and highly unstable" (Colin Campbell, "The Cult, the Cultic Milieu and Secularization," *A Sociological Yearbook of Religion in Britain* 5 (1972), 120) groups, whereas the general milieu and field of discourse from which these groups emerge are relatively stable and cohesive, although not coherent and consistent. The concept has been fruitfully applied to the study of modern esotericism, occultism, and "Satanism" (cf. Wouter J. Hanegraaff, *New Age Religion and Western Culture. Esotericism in the Mirror of Secular Thought* (Leiden/New York/Cologne: Brill, 1996); Petersen, "Introduction: Embracing Satan").

INTRODUCTION

lays the groundwork for the in-depth investigations that follow. In the latter part I examine:

- the interactions and flow of ideas between this religious sub-culture and more general developments in history;
- the history of ideas, ideology and aesthetics;
- the history of the humanities in general, and of religion and Scandinavian studies in particular.

In summary, I closely analyze the 'fields of discourse' and 'shared concerns' that constitute Germanic Neopaganism and tie it to surrounding societies.[9]

In this lengthier second part, the micro-phenomenon Asatru is used as a prism through which to focus on discourses and concepts that have been predominant and contested in what we call 'Western societies' since the 19th century, and which play a central role in the processes of a culturalization of religion and sacralization of culture. They comprise contested fields such as race and ethnicity (Chapter 4), concepts of religion (Chapter 5), and discourses developed in relation to social movements, such as ideas about nature (Chapter 6) and gender (Chapter 7), and their relation to religion. Last but not least, they include the areas of academic thought (Chapter 8) and art and aesthetics (Chapter 9), in which ideas about the relations between religion and culture – as well as about Nordic myth – have been systematically developed and popularized.

Twisted Terminologies

The inner contradictions, changes, and transformations of this religious phenomenon, which I have thus far called Germanic Neopaganism, are mirrored in the shifting terminology used by the groups themselves as well as outside observers. In the first third of the 20th century in Germany, it was called 'German,' 'Nordic,' or 'Germanic Faith,' indicating a mythization or spiritualization of the nation or the 'Aryan' or 'Nordic' race. As we shall see, all of these

---

9 The concepts of "shared concerns" and "fields of discourse" is inspired by the German historian of religion Kocku von Stuckrad, who uses it to account for the "fuzziness" of recent religious movements. Stuckrad bases his investigations on the observation that "religious identities are shaped through communicative processes. They are not found but negotiated." (Kocku von Stuckrad, *Western Esotericism. A Brief History of Secret Knowledge* (London: Equinox, 2005), 86).

terms, as well as the word 'Teutonic,' which has been used in English-speaking contexts since the mid-19th century, refer to constructions of ethnic entities, which by now are strongly contested, and which are based on untenable ideological, for example nationalist and imperialist, assumptions.[10]

Following the terminology of Alexander Rud Mills, an Australian sympathizer with National Socialism and founder of an Anglo-Saxonist version of Germanic Faith, the first American and English post-war groups called their religion Odinism, a term which is still fairly widespread in the UK and North America. As a reaction to the 'monotheistic' connotations of the term 'Odinism,' American groups started to adopt the Scandinavian term Asatru.[11] The term derives from modern Icelandic, and denotes the belief, trust in or allegiance to the Norse gods called *Æsir*.[12] Together with 'Heathen',[13] a Germanic word for Pagan, it is most commonly used today both by adherents of the religion and by outside researchers. The term 'Asatru,' however, is criticized by many for being a relatively young term, having arisen in Scandinavian Romanticism.

A still more recent development is the rejection of terms that were not used in pre-Christian times. This is based on the observation that pre-Christian religions did not identify 'religion' as a separate field within society, and thus did not have words to describe their world-view and religion or to distinguish them from other religions. As a result, names like *'Forn Sed'* or *'Forn Siðr'* (Scandinavian and Old Norse terms for 'the old way' or 'the old custom') have been adopted. This is also a reaction to the fact that both 'Paganism' and 'Heathenism' are terms which were originally coined by the Christian churches in order to separate 'proper religion' from rejected forms of worship. The terms 'Pagan' or 'Heathen' were associated with rural people who adhered to regressive beliefs and lived at the margins of society. Nowadays, when groups or persons describe themselves as Pagans, it can be understood as an attempt to re-signify an originally pejorative term in a similarly complex way as with the term 'queer' for example, i.e. in order to both re-evaluate traditional assumptions and to be provocative.

The prefix 'neo,' which is common within scholarship and the general public, is equally misleading. It presupposes the existence of an ancient, original

---

10   For discussions of concepts of the 'Germanic' see the contributions in Heinrich Beck, *Zur Geschichte der Gleichung "germanisch – deutsch." Sprache und Namen, Geschichte und Institutionen* Ergänzungsbände zum Reallexikon der germanischen Altertumskunde (Berlin: de Gruyter, 2004).

11   Asatru is also spelled Ásatrú, Asatrú or Asatro.

12   The singular for Æsir is Áss and the genitive plural Ása.

13   Equivalents of Heathen are also commonly used in German (*Heiden*) and in Scandinavian languages (*hedning*).

INTRODUCTION

Paganism that only needs to be recovered and revitalized. In fact, the opposite is the case: (neo-)Paganism is a decidedly modern phenomenon, which constructs an idealized religious and cultural past, projecting this imagined past onto sparse sources that tell us very little about pre-Christian European cults. It is not the task of this book however, to dissolve such terminological contradictions.[14] Since they are still most common amongst believers and scholars alike, I shall thus use the terms 'Asatru' and 'Heathen' for the modern groups described here. I will employ the more artificial term 'Germanic Neopaganism' to describe the phenomenon in its broader historical dimension, i.e. for both older German Faith groups and modern Heathen groups.

What Others Say

Due to the right-wing political inclinations and activities in parts of the international Germanic Neopagan milieu, the political and ideological aspects of Asatru and Odinism have attracted the most attention from researchers and more popular writers. The first study conducted was Jeffrey Kaplan's examination of the American scene in a chapter in his *Radical Religion in America*,[15] published in the late 1990s. More recently, the most important study in this context has been Mattias Gardell's *Gods of the Blood* from 2003. Gardell, a Swedish historian of religion, offers an in-depth investigation of the racist, white supremacist, Odinist underground in the USA. Based partly on Kaplan's earlier research, but mostly on in-depth interviews with racial-religious and ethnicist Pagans in North America, this book alerts us to the political radicalism present in parts of Asatru, and brings to light the major significance of the Norse religious revival for a North American context. However, it does not address the international contexts and German origins of such radical thought. Moreover, it excludes a-racist (or in Gardell's terminology anti-racist) groups. Hence, Gardell's investigation is unable to illuminate the more problematic sides of the mainstream discourse on culture and religion, i.e., the intersections

---

14   For a more thorough discussion of terminology from the point of view of a practitioner and researcher see Michael Strmiska, "Modern Paganism in World Cultures. Comparative Perspectives," in *Modern Paganism in World Cultures. Comparative Perspectives*, ed. Michael Strmiska (Santa Barbara, CA: ABC-Clio, 2005).

15   Jeffrey Kaplan, *Radical Religion in America. Millenarian Movements from the Far Right to the Children of Noah* (New York: Syracuse University Press, 1997), for Germany see for example Franziska Hundseder, *Wotans Jünger. Neuheidnische Gruppen zwischen Esoterik und Rechtsradikalismus* (Munich: Heyne, 1998).

of *völkisch*, Germanic Neopagan and contemporary mainstream discourse on Norse myth, which are of central interest in this book.

In the past few years, a-racist Asatru has attracted the attention of younger scholars, who have reacted against the one-sided focus on the racist and right-wing extremist dimension of earlier research. Firstly, studies of national European milieus have been offered by insiders, i.e. researchers with Pagan affiliations themselves, who tend to take an apologetic stance and whose main goal is to actively contribute to Asatru gaining respectability.[16] More importantly, two master theses and two dissertations now provide field-studies of the national Asatru scenes in Iceland,[17] Sweden[18] and Germany,[19] written in the respective languages by students and scholars not affiliated with Asatru or Neopaganism in general. Swedish historian of religion Fredrik Gregorius and Icelandic master's student in the history of religion, Eggert Solberg Jonsson, take historical approaches, situating the respective Northern European Asatru groups in a context reaching back to National Romanticism. Gregorius' conclusion in particular, that Swedish Asatru is driven by a fundamental cultural essentialism, coincides with my own reading of the phenomenon. Both studies are based on first-hand material such as interviews and participant observation, and thus provide material for my investigation as well.

The same is true for the dissertation by German historian of religion René Gründer, who conducted in-depth interviews with German Asatruers. In contrast to the other researchers, Gründer chooses a knowledge-sociological approach and provides insight into individual German Heathens' construction

---

16   The following books on Pagan movements contain comprehensive chapters on Asatru: Graham Harvey, *Listening People, Speaking Earth. Contemporary Paganism* (London: Hurst&Company, 1997), Michael Strmiska, ed. *Modern Paganism in World Cultures. Comparative Perspectives* (Santa Barbara, CA: ABC-Clio, 2005); Blain, Ezzy, and Harvey, *Researching Paganism*. Jenny Blain currently researches British and American Asatru and has already published parts of her results. See Jenny Blain, *Nine Worlds of Seid-Magic. Ecstasy and neo-Shamanism in North European Paganism* (London etc.: Routledge, 2002); Jenny Blain and Robert J. Wallis, "Heathenry," in *Handbook of Contemporary Paganism*, ed. James R. Lewis and Murphy Pizza (Leiden/Boston: Brill, 2009).

17   Eggert Solberg Jonsson, "Ásatrú á Íslandi við upphaf 21. aldar. Uppruni, heimsmynd og helgiathafnir" (Master's thesis, University of Iceland, 2010).

18   Fredrik Gregorius, *Modern Asatro. Att konstruera etnisk och kulturell identitet* (Lund: Lunds Universitet, 2008).

19   René Gründer, *Germanisches (Neu-)Heidentum in Deutschland. Entstehung, Struktur und Symbolsystem eines alternativreligiösen Feldes* (Berlin: Logos Verlag, 2008); *Blótgemeinschaften. Eine Religionsethnografie des 'germanischen Neuheidentums'* (Würzburg: Ergon, 2010).

INTRODUCTION

of their own world-views in late modernity. He focuses on individual perspectives and appropriations along with individuals' attempts to situate their world-view within the conditions of late modernity. It thus alerts one to inner contradictions and ideological problems that circulate within the scene – information and observations which are highly informative for my own investigation on the changes within Asatru in recent years. One of the more stunning findings of Gründer's study is the degree to which the individual believers' religious constructions that he lays out in his book deviate from the official written material the respective groups have published in books, pamphlets, and on the Internet. Gründer, who is interested in reconstructing individuals' world-views in the context of post-modern neo-liberal society, chooses to almost completely ignore such written material. This keeps him from addressing the complicated historical continuities and transformations, as well as the more general significance of the discursive clusters on which my book focuses.

Complicated Involvements

Alerted to the gap between written material and individual beliefs by Gründer's study, my approach to it is the reverse. Since I am more interested in continuities and transformations of a discursive constellation, I pay closer attention to the public image of Asatru as it is presented in diverse published materials (texts, images, music distributed through various media, inside journals, flyers, and not least the groups' homepages, Asatru forums and blogs on the Internet).[20] Here, we find the influences of older ideas. Moreover, it is mainly through these public materials that Asatru interacts with other social and discursive fields, for example academia, the arts and social movements. Such written materials contribute to the transmission and transformation of concepts, ideas and (particles of) ideologies over time and space. However, relying exclusively on published and Internet material brings with it the danger of not being able to judge the factual importance of persons, groups, and individual statements. In order to assess the relative importance and impact of my findings, I established contact with leaders and prominent members of Asatru groups operating nationwide in Norway, Denmark, Iceland, Sweden, the USA,[21]

---

20   In order to respect the right to, and wish for, privacy, I am only using material from public forums, and not from those which have restricted access or require registration. Moreover, I quote without mentioning names or pseudonyms.

21   I limited my field research in Sweden and the USA because the studies by Gregorius, *Modern Asatro* and Mattias Gardell, *Gods of the Blood. The Pagan Revival and White*

England, and Germany. Mainly in 2010, I conducted 25 unstructured qualitative interviews, most in person, although some via e-mail or over the telephone,[22] and attended events of a few German and Danish groups.

My personal contacts, especially with German Asatruers, were complex to say the least. In addition to my books and articles, I had been indirectly involved with the scene for almost twenty-five years through my earlier interviews and participant observation in the 1980s. My research (or rumors and word-of-mouth information about it) had been observed, despised and hailed by different groups, mostly, but not exclusively, in Germany since the 1990s.

Some Asatruers had used my books in an attempt to actively rid the scene of extreme right and racial esoteric influence; others had spent considerable energy distancing themselves from my and others' allegations of the close ties of Asatru to the extreme right. In the process of gaining respectability, Asatruers had taken on the role of interpreters and critical analysts of their sources as well as their own traditional assumptions. In doing so, they also related to more recent texts, such as my own, or books by other critical commentators, such as Kaplan, Gardell, Gregorius, or Gründer. All of this resulted in awkward feedback loops for both sides, which shaped the perception of my questions and the informants' answers. In other words: my writing pre-formed the assumptions my interview-partners had about the stories I wanted to hear, and the stories they told were colored by these assumptions.

Working in the field this time around, I could not deny sympathies and shared interests with parts of the scene that are interested in uncovering the *völkisch* roots of contemporary Asatru and getting rid of shady political associations. I thus re-defined my role as that of a critical observer and interlocutor of these parts of the scene, realizing that through my continuing work with a field that I had studied earlier, I had become an unintentional contributor to the tendency of normalization that I observed within the field. It also has to be taken into account that my current and future work (i.e. my conversations with Heathens, as well as this book) will continue to interact with the scene and contribute to its change. Metaphorically speaking, my position has oscillated between that of being a member of the audience watching and analyzing a play called Asatru, and that of an actor playing the role of adversary and critical companion within the play. Acknowledging that this book will have certain

---

Separatism (Durham/London: Duke University Press, 2003) already provide abundant field-material.

22 These interviews are quoted in two ways: statements made by holders of offices within the groups regarding official group policies are quoted by name; statements regarding individuals' beliefs and convictions are quoted anonymously.

effects on the scene, as a scholar writing on Asatru I am cast in the position of a co-writer of the play as well – a role which becomes amplified and complicated by the fact that Asatruers themselves are making eager use of popular academic writing in order to gain respectability (as Chapter 8 shows in detail).

Receptions, Adaptions, and Goals

As of today, the attainment of respectability for Asatru and the changes within it have not caught considerable public attention. That Asatruers in general have been more heavily subjected to a scrutiny of the right-wing implications of their faith than other alternative-religious communities is certainly due to Germanic Neopaganism's history and the current involvement of several groups and individuals with Germanophile, racial and ethnicist ideology. However, this association has also been exacerbated by a public and by outside observers who are more interested in sensationalist accounts of the political dangers connected with marginal and exoticized new religions than in neutral assessments of their beliefs and practices. The reaction of some friends and colleagues to my tales about the changes within Asatru and the pleasant encounters and good conversations I have had is quite indicative in this respect: "But if they are not actually racists, what is the point of researching them?"

One of this book's goals is to dispel such easy accusations and apologies alike. Asatru today presents itself as a lively micro-cosmos where all imaginable ideas, topoi, and stereotypes about 'Germanic' myth, religion and culture are used, discussed, re-contextualized, and transformed. It is a grateful field of study for anyone who wants to learn about the reception and adaption of such ideas in different historical, political, and ideological contexts. It is a dynamic field of exchange where relations between religion, political and cultural ideology have played a prominent role all along, and where they still lead to controversy and give rise to schisms. It is thus a vibrant field, which can serve as an instructive prism for studies of the complex and contradictory relations between religious subcultures and political ideology.

Instead of singling out Germanic Neopaganism as a weird, marginal, and aberrant form of a political religion, this critical investigation into this small but by now quite diversified subculture offers the occasion to question, discuss and revisit much broader intellectual problems. It is able to shed light on fundamental questions about the relation between modernity and constructions of the past. More particularly, as will be discussed in Chapters 4 and 5, it can illuminate the role that has been assigned to the constructed categories of race, ethnicity and religion in building identities. It can also serve as a prism through which to investigate environmental and gender issues in their relation to modern spirituality, as we shall see in Chapters 6 and 7. Last but not least, it can tell us much about the place and function of the humanities, poetry and art in regard to myth and religion in modern societies, as I will show in Chapters 8 and 9.

Thus, rather than just being an analysis of Germanic Neopaganism as a form of cultural essentialism (which it is), this book strives to provide a critical analysis of traces of such cultural essentialism in different contexts of so-called 'mainstream discourse.' It is not so much a study of the political involvement of individuals and groups (although these play a role and have to be addressed), but rather a more general critical discussion of discursive figures and circulating signs, their history and broader implications which, though much more widespread, crystallize in Asatru in a way that makes for a fruitful field of investigation.

Methodologically, my reconstruction of a Germanic Neopagan discourse in particular, as well as a mainstream discourse on Nordic myth, is informed by the somewhat diverse approaches of the history of ideas and ideology as well as analytical discourse theory. Both approaches have one interest in common: the analysis of the flow and transformation of ideas (not individual or group-policies) over time and space, and their potential political and ideological implications. Both methods are suitable for analytically negotiating between the descriptions of a contemporary social and religious phenomenon, its immediate cultural historical contexts, and its being embedded in contemporary and historical discourse.

This approach requires simultaneous discussions about established intellectuals, philosophers, theorists and Neopagan authors of articles in obscure underground magazines with a minuscule circulation. The purpose of discussing such ideological intersections is not to level out the significant differences in erudition and intellectual complexity between these texts and authors, but rather to reveal the broad distribution of a persistent discursive constellation connected to ideas about Nordic myth, religion and culture, in addition to demonstrating interactions and interrelations between 'high' and 'low' culture, and to put into question the only seemingly clear distinctions between mainstream and aberrant, marginal discourses. Ultimately, this book is concerned with broad questions about the relation between conceptions of myth, nature, tradition, heritage, spirituality, culture and identity. Focusing on a small and manageable phenomenon such as Asatru helps to illuminate the broader fields of discourse which constitute it and which it has helped constitute.

CHAPTER 1

Creating the Paradigm: Historical Preconditions of Modern Asatru

Modern Asatru, as well as the current popular appeal of 'Germanic' or 'Nordic' themes and images, are outcomes of and contributors to a discourse of Germanic myth. This discourse is related to a general tendency to conflate culture, religion and ethnicity, or to culturalize and ethnicize religion and simultaneously sacralize culture. In this chapter I argue that we can identify two prior eras, two points of crystallization, where similar tendencies were prominent and which were formative for later religious and ideological appropriations of Germanic myth: German Romanticism around 1800 and *völkisch* nationalism in the first third of the 20th century.

The first formative moment was defined by the scholarship of Johann Gottfried Herder, Jacob and Wilhelm Grimm, and other intellectuals of German Romanticism. They were the first to systematize ideas about a holistic unity of natural environment, language and history located in a deep past and in rural populations. This unity and its expression in an indigenous mythological heritage were perceived as the necessary foundation for a proper nation or *Volk*. This Romantic constellation proved to be exceptionally malleable, productive and persistent. It influenced both cultural pluralism and exclusionist ideologies with affinities to racism and anti-Semitism. It inspired nationalist movements not only in Germany, but in Scandinavian, Anglo-Saxon and Baltic countries as well. Moreover, it provided the basis for European and North American counter-cultural movements as diverse as Anglo-Saxonism and modern witchcraft (Wicca). It is no coincidence that the years after 1900 – our second point of crystallization – have been characterized as 'neo-Romantic.' Romantic ideas about a unity of the *Volk* were radicalized in the German *völkisch* movement and turned into an alternative religion around 1910.

Thus, it seems relevant to begin our discussions of the genealogy and significance of modern Asatru by briefly introducing the main contributors (persons and organizations alike) to a discourse on Nordic myth in Romanticism, focusing in particular on the names and concepts which will reappear in the following chapters. Furthermore, in this chapter we will consider *völkisch* religion and the German(ic) Faith Movement, and their broader context in several nationalist and alternative movements. Finally, modern witchcraft, or Wicca, will be presented. While the latter takes up the same Romantic constellation as the others, due to its origin in England in the 1950s it gives the constellation a different twist. In many senses, it also contributes a more flexible framework and more malleable ritual practices, both of which prove to be important for contemporary Asatru.

The Search for a National Mythology in European Romanticism

While we can identify German Romanticism as a key formative moment for the emergence of a discourse of Germanic myth, individual elements within this influential cluster of ideas were in place already in European humanism and Renaissance thought. This era extended its interest in the mythologies of Greek and Roman antiquity to imagined national antiquities as well. German humanism contributed with a patriotic interpretation of Tacitus' *Germania* and *Annales* and established the misleading and fateful idea that the German nation was a direct descendant of the Northern tribes on the eastern side of the river Rhine, who were not subject to Roman rule and whom Julius Cesar called "Germani".[1] Consequently, the traits that the Roman ethnographer Tacitus (informed by Aristotelian climate theory and contemporary stereotypes of the ethnic other) had perceived as typical for northern barbarian primitives, now appeared to the German patriots of humanism as timeless, positive national characteristics of a warrior people that:

- is hardened by a harsh climate
- is impressive in its simplicity and authenticity
- possesses a fierce sense of freedom and independence
- is faithful
- is pure
- worships nature
- venerates its women and priestesses
- is prone to excessive drinking.[2]

---

1   Cf. Dieter Mertens, "Die Instrumentalisierung der 'Germania' des Tacitus durch die deutschen Humanisten," in *Zur Geschichte der Gleichung 'germanisch – deutsch.' Sprache und Namen, Geschichte und Institutionen*, ed. Heinrich Beck, et al., Ergänzungsbände zum Reallexikon der germanischen Altertumskunde (Berlin: de Gruyter, 2004).
2   This version of a German ideology is discussed in depth in Klaus v. See, *Deutsche Germanen-Ideologie vom Humanismus bis zur Gegenwart* (Frankfurt a.M.: Athenäum-Verlag, 1970). See also *Barbar Germane Arier. Die Suche nach der Identität der Deutschen* (Heidelberg: Universitätsverlag C. Winter, 1994).

Swedish Renaissance scholars used the Roman scholar Jordanes' *Getica* (or *History of the Goths*, around 551 AD) in a similar way: as a classical witness to the greatness of the Swedish nation as the alleged homeland of the Goths. The acclaimed scholar and founder of Swedish runic studies, Johannes Bureus (1568–1652), identified the antique lost continent Hyperborea as Sweden. He then used this finding to justify prehistoric Scandinavia as mankind's oldest culture. Driven by the contemporary trend to establish Sweden's status as a great European power, the internationally celebrated Swedish historiographer, Olaus Rudbeck, took this idea even further in his 3000 page treatise *Atland eller Manheim* (*Atlantica*, 1679–1702). Both Bureus and Rudbeck, like many of their contemporaries, took a keen interest in occultism and Rosicruceanism, thus adding a spiritual and mystical notion to their speculations about the Nordic origin of culture.[3]

In Denmark, several simultaneous events in the middle of the 17th century spurred the Scandinavian movement of Göticism as well. In 1643, the Danish scholar Ole Worm initiated the academic investigation into the runic alphabet. In the same year, an inconspicuous manuscript was discovered by the Icelandic bishop Brynjolfr Sveinsson. It soon attracted considerable attention and was donated to the Danish king twenty years later. The manuscript contained mythological poems about Norse deities such as Odin, Thor, Frey and Freya, cosmological visions about the origin and end of the world, as well as heroic poetry related to the Nibelungen cycle. The find was all the more sensational as it treated the same mythological materials as another medieval work, the *Edda*, authored by the Icelandic cleric, historian and politician Snorri Sturluson (1179–1241). Snorri had composed this volume as a manual for poets and skalds. Since traditional Norse poetry was based on intricate metaphorical circumscriptions, Snorri felt the need to relate the mythological basis necessary for the understanding of these poetic images, which he feared would not be accessible to Christian poets and audiences. The manuscript identified as being found here was initially (albeit falsely) believed to be the source from which Snorri had quoted the interspersed verses in his *Edda*. Consequently, this untitled manuscript was named *Edda* as well. It became known as the *Elder Edda*, *Saemundar Edda* (after an alleged author) or *Poetic Edda* (most common today).[4] As a result of this false assumption,

---

3 Klaus Böldl, *Der Mythos der Edda. Nordische Mythologie zwischen europäischer Aufklärung und nationaler Romantik* (Tübingen etc.: Francke, 2000), 19.

4 The extent to which these works contain pre-Christian mythological knowledge is disputed up until today. Both works were written in the Christian Middle Ages, more than 200 years after the Christianization of Iceland. In the case of Snorri, rather than relating "authentic"

two lays of the *Poetic Edda*, the *Völuspá* and the *Hávamál*, were included when the first edition of Snorri Sturluson's *Prose Edda* was published in Denmark in 1665. This edition of medieval Norse literature remained the primary source of knowledge about Scandinavian mythology throughout the entire 18th century. Its influence is palpable up until today: the two lays included from the *Poetic Edda* remain the most well known, and are the most quoted in Asatru contexts.

Inspired by Scandinavian scholarship, Renaissance England also developed a variety of Gothicism. 'Gothic' became a common term denoting 'Germanic,' mingling with the Italian use of the word, which associated medieval architecture with the Goths. Also in the English case, this humanist appropriation of Nordic myth was driven by patriotic sentiment. It countered contemporary pejorative Italian stereotypes of the Nordic barbarian with ideas of a 'Germanic freedom.' In all cases, the North–South distinction was thus associated with anti-Catholic affects. In Germany and Scandinavia, this anti-Catholicism was informed by the respective varieties of Protestantism,[5] whereas the English and English colonists in America subscribed to the idea of a pure Anglo-Saxon church along with the myth of the free nature of Anglo-Saxon political institutions (which they based on their reception of Tacitus).[6]

18th century Enlightenment thought contributed additional elements to the discourse of Germanic myth. The French political philosopher Montesquieu's revaluation of Aristotelian climate theory rehabilitated Northerners as industrious, inventive, honest, proud and self-confident individuals, as bearers of nations never subjugated and thus in possession of an original, natural

---

Pagan worldviews, his *Edda* gives an impressive image of medieval European imaginations of one's Pagan "ancestors'" ideas and beliefs. The case of the *Poetic Edda* is even more hotly debated; the age of the individual lays, as well as the materials they are based on, is estimated with great variance by different scholars. Here too, influences of, and engagement with, both classical and medieval Christian ideas are palpable and must be taken into account. Comprehensive research summaries are provided in the introductions by Ursula Dronke, *The Poetic Edda: Heroic Poems* (Oxford: Clarendon Press, 1969), *The Poetic Edda: Mythological Poems* (Oxford: Clarendon Press, 1997), and Anthony Faulkes, "Introduction," in *Snorri Sturluson: Edda. Prologue and Gylfaginning*, ed. Anthony Faulkes (London: Viking Society for Northern Research, 2005).

5   See Böldl, *Der Mythos der Edda*, 67.
6   See Allen J. Frantzen, *Desire for Origins. New Language, Old English, and Teaching the Tradition* (New Brunswick/London: Rutgers University Press, 1990), 31f; Reginald Horsman, *Race and Manifest Destiny. The Origins of American Racial Anglo-Saxonism* (Cambridge, MA: Harvard University Press, 1981), 9–12.

freedom.[7] Montesquieu's republican ideals were a significant inspiration for Paul Henri Mallet, a Swiss who served as a professor at the University of Copenhagen. In 1755, he published the first French translation of Eddic poetry in his *Introduction* to the history of Denmark. It was followed by a second part in 1756 under the title *Monuments de la mythologie et de la poésie des Celtes et particulièrement des anciens Scandinaves* (Monuments of the Mythology and the Poetry of the Celts and Particularly the Ancient Scandinavians) and soon translated into Danish, German and English.[8]

Renaissance and Enlightenment antiquarian approaches to the antique ethnographic and medieval mythological sources thus established Nordic or Germanic myth as an integral part of various patriotic endeavors. Holistic ideas of the late 1700s and early 1800s finally integrated this discourse of Germanic myth with emphatic notions of an organically rooted people. The idea that such an organic unity of landscape, language and history had to be based in mythology soon posed a problem for German thinkers, as mythological sources or information about pre-Christian German religion were practically non-existent. The assumption that language and myth were closely related, however, served as a justification for the appropriation of Scandinavian sources (written in a related language) for the (re)construction of a 'German mythology.'

The Weimar-based theologian and philosopher Johann Gottfried Herder (1744–1803) developed an elaborate, albeit contradictory theory about the uniqueness and equal worth of all the diverse peoples of the world in his four volume *Ideen zur Philosophie der Geschichte der Menschheit* (Ideas for the Philosophy of History of Humanity, 1784–91). He also suggested turning to Norse mythology (as it was transferred to Germany by Mallet's writings) in order to revitalize German poetry using allegedly 'authentic' sources.[9]

Herder's broad and notoriously unsystematic approach led to a number of internal contradictions in his work, which in turn motivated equally contradictory trajectories of reception. His writing revaluated cultural difference, promoted the equal value of vastly different cultures, and criticized the colonial

---

7 Gonthier-Louis Fink, "Diskriminierung und Rehabilitierung des Nordens im Spiegel der Klimatheorie," in *Imagologie des Nordens. Kulturelle Konstruktionen von Nördlichkeit in interdisziplinärer Perspektive*, ed. Astrid Arndt, et al. (Frankfurt a.M. etc.: Peter Lang, 2004), 80f; Böldl, *Der Mythos der Edda*, 27.

8 Thomas Percy's translation *Northern Antiquities* from 1770 was to influence the Victorian reception of Eddic literature to an immense degree. See for example Andrew Wawn, *The Vikings and the Victorians. Inventing the Old North in 19th-Century Britain* (Cambridge: Brewer, 2000), 183–212.

9 Aesthetic appropriations of Germanic myth are discussed in Chapter 9.

endeavors of the European powers of his era, even going so far as tentatively questioning Christianity's right to mission.[10] At the same time, Herder's work was driven by a Christian humanism which sought to integrate this cultural diversity into a universal history of salvation in which the German *Volk* was assigned particularly high status.[11] Simultaneously, Herder formulated negative exceptions to his tolerant and inclusive concept of equality in difference by repeating common cultural stereotypes. Gypsies and Jews were not considered proper *Völker* due to their lack of a homeland and were thus a potential danger to other peoples. Turks and Huns appeared as barbarians, whereas peoples exposed to extreme climates, such as Africans and Greenlanders, were attributed primitive, animalistic qualities. With this oscillatory organicist, holistic concept of a nation or *Volk*, Herderian thought established a field of tension that haunts relativist, holistic and organicist concepts of culture to this day, and still reverberates in the tensions between a-racist and ethnicist conceptions of Asatru today.[12]

---

10 See e.g. Maurice Olender, *The Languages of Paradise. Aryans and Semites. A Match Made in Heaven*, trans. Arthur Goldhammer (New York: Other Press, 1992), 37–50, on the question of mission 42.

11 For such contradictory perceptions of Herder see for example Bruce Lincoln, *Theorizing Myth. Narrative, Ideology, and Scholarship* (Chicago/London: University of Chicago Press, 1999), 52–54 and Zeev Sternhell, "Von der Gegenaufklärung zu Faschismus und Nazismus. Gedanken zur europäischen Katastrophe des 20. Jahrhunderts," in *Die Dynamik der europäischen Rechten. Geschichte, Kontinuitäten, Wandel*, ed. Claudia Globisch, Agnieszka Pufelska, and Volker Weiß (Wiesbaden: vs Verlag, 2011).

12 Herder's scholarship is debated still today. A point in case is Paul Lawrence Rose, *Revolutionary Antisemitism in Germany from Kant to Wagner* (Princeton, NJ: Princeton University Press, 1990) who accused him of laying the grounds for an exclusionary, anti-Semitic, aggressive German nationalism and Pan-Germanism, thus preparing directly for the National Socialist regime. Others have hailed him (slightly uncritically) as the creator of a modern, non-normative, non-repressive concept of culture and aesthetics, the forerunner of an anthropological or cultural turn in the humanities. (Cf. Ulrich Gaier, "Herder als Begründer des modernen Kulturbegriffs," *Germanisch-Romanische Monatsschrift* 57, no. 4 (2007); Wolfgang Pross, "Herder und die moderne Geschichtswissenschaft," *Germanisch-Romanische Monatsschrift* 57, no. 4 (2007), and Renate Stauf, "'Was soll überhaupt eine Messung aller Völker nach uns Europäern?' Der Europagedanke Johann Gottfried Herders," *Germanisch-Romanische Monatsschrift* 57, no. 4 (2007)). For a balanced discussion of these contradictory stances see Karol Sauerland, "'Die fremden Völker in Europa.' Herders unpolitische Metaphern und Bilder zu den höchst politischen Begriffen Volk und Nation," in *Unerledigte Geschichten. Der literarische Umgang mit Nationalität und Internationalität*, ed. Gesa von Essen and Horst Turk (Göttingen: Wallstein, 2000), for a comprehensive discussion of Herder's oscillating work, as well as the controversies around it, see Anne Löchte, *Johann Gottfried Herder. Kulturtheorie und*

While Herder looked to Scandinavian mythology for aesthetic inspiration, the brothers Jacob (1785–1863) and Wilhelm Grimm (1786–1859) gave this search for myth a more cultural, socio-political and scientific turn. They spent their productive lives trying to reconstruct the deep roots of German identity in a pristine pre-Christian German past with the help of diverse sources, ranging from fairy tales to legal documents.[13] Of their works, Jacob Grimm's *Deutsche Mythologie* (*German Mythology*) is the most critical for our context. This collection, however, cannot be separated from the others. The unity of society, its rules and laws, its aesthetic expressions and its religion was foundational for the thought of Jacob Grimm in particular, who read legal sources in a mythological manner, and examined mythology in its social aspects.[14] Jacob Grimm took a twofold approach to solving the problem of lacking mythological sources. Rejecting Scandinavian sources as insufficiently cognate with the German ones, he looked for mythological remnants in various contexts: in rural folk beliefs and customs, fairy tales, place names, language etc., postulating a continuity of folk beliefs, especially in an idealized countryside from pre-Christian times up until his time of writing. Nevertheless, in order to make sense of what he thought to have identified as those remnants, he drew on Scandinavian sources to anchor his finds in a coherent mythology. By way of creating a unity of Germanic sources, he established the image of a coherent Germanic culture in the service of German nation building. Moreover, he contributed significantly to the appropriation of Scandinavian material for not only a German, but by way of the reception of his work, for also English and Scandinavian national ideologies.[15] Like Herder before him, Grimm found the

---

Humanitätsidee der Ideen, Humanitätsbriefe und Adrastea (Würzburg: Königshausen & Neumann, 2005).

13   The Grimms believed fairy tales to be much more ancient than assumed today, and to contain remnants of Pagan German mythological ideas. Legal sources were seen as remnants of an indigenous legal system opposed to the 'foreign imposed' Roman law which must have been the basis of the organization of the original German nation. The results of the brothers' endeavors were published in a number of commented collections of these alleged sources for the German national past starting with fairy tales (*Kinder- und Hausmärchen*, 1812–1815) and legends (*Deutsche Sagen* 1816–1818, 2nd ed.1865–1866), followed by grammar (*Deutsche Grammatik* 1819, 2. ed. 1822–1840), legal sources (*Deutsche Rechtsaltertümer* 1828, 2nd ed., 1854), mythology (*Deutsche Mythologie* (1835, 3. ed. 1854)), and finally, a comprehensive dictionary of the German language which is still in use today (*Deutsches Wörterbuch* 1854).

14   Wolf-Daniel Hartwich, *Deutsche Mythologie. Die Erfindung einer nationalen Kunstreligion* (Berlin/Vienna: Philo, 2000), 51.

15   For a critical discussion of Grimm's reconstructive method and his unacknowledged appropriation of Scandinavian material see Beate Kellner, *Grimms Mythen. Studien zum*

justification for this appropriation in the linguistic proximity between the Scandinavian and German languages. As this proximity also applied to Old English, Grimm claimed Anglo-Saxon literature for his program of a renewal of national German poetry and culture as well: "Anglo-Saxon poems [...] belong to all Germany as much as to England; indeed, they belong to us more than Old Norse poems in so far as their language is closer to ours."[16]

Herder's aesthetic and Jacob Grimms' philological interest in Germanic myth was supplemented with yet another dimension in the late 19th century by Wilhelm Mannhardt (1831–1880). Inspired by Grimm and contemporary ethnologists, for example E.B. Tylor's thesis of 'primitive tribal cultures' survival in modern eras, he turned to contemporary German folk customs and rituals in search of remnants of pre-Christian Germanic myth in his two volume *Wald- und Feldkulte* (Forest and Field Cults, 1875 and 1877). Together with another highly significant medium of popularization, Richard Wagner's aesthetic stage imaginations of Norse gods and heroes,[17] these scholars firmly established an idealized image of a mythic national past, rooted in landscape, folk literature and customs, which was formative for the later religious reception of a discourse of Germanic myth. More importantly though, Herder, Grimm, Mannhardt and others set the standard for modern methodologies in the emerging academic disciplines of philology and folklore, as well as studies of religion.[18] Although Grimm's approaches and results regarding his *German Mythology* and Mannhardt's ideas about contemporary survivals of ancient rituals have both since been proven wrong, their impact cannot be underestimated.[19]

Mythosbegriff und seiner Anwendung in Jacob Grimms Deutscher Mythologie (Frankfurt a.M.: Peter Lang, 1994).

16 From Jacob Grimm's preface to his 1840 edition of *Andreas and Elene*, translated by and quoted in Eric Gerald Stanley, *The Search for Anglo-Saxon Paganism* (Cambridge: Brewer, 1975), 13.

17 See Chapter 9.

18 Cf. Bernhard Maier, *Die Religion der Germanen. Götter – Mythen – Weltbild* (Munich: C.H. Beck, 2003), 53; Hans Gerhard Kippenberg, *Die Entdeckung der Religionsgeschichte. Religionswissenschaft und Moderne* (Munich: Beck, 1997), 120–125.

19 Modern folklore and religious studies highlight the fact that many of the customs observed by Mannhardt are playful modifications or reversals of Christian rites. Some of them might even originate in 19th century theories inspired by Mannhardt and other scholars. Cf. e.g. Maier, *Die Religion der Germanen*, 53 and 85. For the use of Grimm's and Mannhardt's theories in modern Wicca see Ronald Hutton, *The Triumph of the Moon. A History of Modern Pagan Witchcraft* (Oxford/New York: Oxford University Press, 1999), e.g. 113. For a critique of Grimm's methods see Kellner, *Grimms Mythen*.

With their emphasis on creating the German *Volk* by rooting it in a national mythology, Herder's and the Grimms' ideas were also formative for the emerging German cultural nationalism. Paradoxically enough, these nationalist agendas had a strong international impact. The philological method offered by the Grimms promised access to the "concealed origins, the problem of detecting pure, native culture hidden beneath layers of Christian teaching."[20] Its adoption became crucial for the conceptions of pre-Christian mythology and culture in the Scandinavian countries, and – in the case of Anglo-Saxonism – England and America, as they all saw their roots in Germanic culture as well. The early 19th century 'discovered' Old English literature in the wake of the Grimm brothers' and other German scholars' works, hoping to recover "half-veiled remains of pagan poetry,"[21] not least from *Beowulf*.[22] Through English scholarly and literary works (especially by Walter Scott), and through the studies of leading American intellectuals in Germany, German Romanticism and Anglo-Saxonism were also dispersed throughout North America. Whereas in the English context theories of Germanic, Indo-European, or Aryan industriousness, adventurousness, and expansionism were used to justify colonialism, in the American case, the same features served to vindicate the westward expansion.[23]

In the Scandinavian countries, the reception of the German scholars' theories constituted an even greater paradox. Danish scholars and intellectuals such as Nikolai Frederik Severin Grundtvig (1783–1872) and Rasmus Rask (1787–1832) harshly criticized what they considered the illegitimate appropriation of Scandinavian material in the service of a German national mythology. In order to affirm a Danish tradition countering the dominant German scholarship, they simultaneously employed the self-same aesthetic and philological methods. By looking for an alliance between the Icelandic and Danish sources, they created a synthetic view of the Old Norse mythic material in Danish literature. Grundtvig's ideas in particular had a major impact on later

---

20 Frantzen, *Desire for Origins*, 68, cf. 62–71.
21 Stanley, *The Search for Anglo-Saxon Paganism*, 12.
22 Cf. ibid., 67. *Beowulf* consequently came to be considered an original expression of the ancient Germanic national character in both England and Germany.
23 At the end of the 19th century, such Indo-European theories constituted a "potent strain of the New Imperialism," emphasizing Anglo-Saxon supremacy and providing the foundation for the ideology of a "joint destiny" which was to secure British and American world domination. Cf. Jan Nederveen Pieterse, *Empire and Emancipation. Power and Liberation on a World Scale* (London: Pluto Press, 1989), 264f.

Danish popular imaginations of Norse myths and tales, through their wide dispersion in the influential folk high schools initiated by him.[24]

A parallel attempt to renew literature through the use of Norse mythology was carried out by Swedish poets of the late Romantic era. Translations of Erik Gustaf Geijer's and Esaias Tegnér's works had a significant impact on the French and English conceptions of the Viking world.[25] Their poems reconfigured the Vikings as a purifying social force, creating hope for a regeneration of the Occident from the North, downplaying their brutality and emphasizing their heroic violence, as well as their spirit of adventure and discovery.[26] In the Victorian era, Anglo-Saxonism was thus vitalized with a veritable flood of images and theories on Vikings and Norsemen that were utilized for a variety of political, intellectual and aesthetic agendas.[27]

Herder's and Grimm's ideas also spurred an interest in folklore in the Scandinavian countries, as demonstrated by the successful recorders of fairy tales, folk tales and songs (i.e., Peter Christen Asbjørnsen and Jørgen Moe in Norway as well as Gunnar Olof Hyltén-Cavallius in Sweden). Another collector and editor whose work was eagerly received, not only in his native country of Finland but also internationally, was Elias Lönnrot. He compiled folk tales and songs into what was to become Finland's national epic, the *Kalevala* – a central source of inspiration for contemporary popular culture and Neopagans alike.[28]

Productive as they were for nation building and the development of the modern humanities, the Romantic searches for a deep past, a lost ethnic authenticity and unmediated unity as a necessary basis for contemporary national cultures have inherently problematic aspects. First and foremost, they are dependent on operations of exclusion. They tend to neglect or devalue the change, cultural mixing and blending which comes with all cultural development. At the same time, they frequently align regional differences and

---

24 Cf. Flemming Lundgreen-Nielsen, "Gundtvig's Norse Mythological Imagery – An Experiment that Failed," in *Northern Antiquity. The Post-Medieval Reception of Edda and Saga*, ed. Andrew Wawn (Middlesex: Hisarlik, 1994).

25 Cf. Wawn, *The Vikings and the Victorians*, 117–141.

26 Cf. Régis Boyer, "Vikings, Sagas and Wasa Bread," in *Northern Antiquity. The Post-Medieval Reception of Edda and Saga*, ed. Andrew Wawn (Middlesex: Hisarlik, 1994), 72f, Wawn, *The Vikings and the Victorians*, 99f, 176f.

27 Garman Lord, *The Way of the Heathen. A Handbook of Greater Theodism* (Watertown, NY: Theod, 2000).

28 Cf. Øystein Sørensen, "Drømmen om det storgermanske rike. Pangermanismen i Norge ca. 1850–1945," in *Jakten på Germania. Fra nordensvermeri til ss-arkeologi*, ed. Terje Emberland and Jorunn Sem Fure (Oslo: Humanist forlag, 2009).

historical eras that often lie several centuries apart.[29] Any definition of identity is, of course, dependent on exclusions as well as inclusions. Nevertheless, in theories of continuity of a deep past and of pure origins, these exclusions tend to turn against national minorities and often lead to the promotion of ethnic purity. Romantic constructions pitted the 'Germanic,' 'Nordic' or 'Indo-Germanic' against traditional exterior adversaries: France in the case of Germany, Germany itself in the case of Denmark and, to an extent in the case of England,[30] Rome (as the embodiment of the devalued but dominant south), and with it, Catholicism in most national cases. In all cases however, it was a familiar 'interior enemy' who was targeted, the Jew. This particular Romantic anti-Semitism derogates Jews because of their alleged lack of exactly the elements that form a proper *Volk* according to the Romantic logic:[31] rootedness in a homeland, a proper language,[32] literature, and mythology.[33] It is then not only the distinction between North and South – Protestant and Catholic – but rather a more or less fierce distinction between the 'Germanic,' 'Aryan,' or 'Indo-European' and the 'Semitic' that lies at the basis of the Romantic constellation of Germanic myth and religion. As George S. Williamson has argued, "anti-Catholicism and, increasingly, anti-Semitism were not matters simply of individual prejudice or hatred (although these factors also played a role) but instead structural features of the discourse on Germanic mythology"[34] – features which haunt its reception more or less overtly up until the present day. In these

---

29 Thus Tacitus' ethnographic account of different tribes in central Europe in the *Germania* from the first century, Eddic literature from 13th century Iceland, and contemporary folk customs from Germany and Scandinavia are considered expressions of the same essence and used to illuminate each other in order to form a holistic image.

30 Cf. Wawn, *The Vikings and the Victorians*, 99. Horsman, *Race and Manifest Destiny*, 38 alerts us to the fact that some English were unwilling to accept an all-pervasive Germanic-Norse mystique and adhered to the idea of the superiority of the "free Anglo-Saxons." They used the Aryan or Indo-European myth to give the Anglo-Saxons a deeper past, but played down their links to other Germanic peoples.

31 For a comprehensive discussion of the varieties of Romantic anti-Semitism see Wolf-Daniel Hartwich, *Romantischer Antisemitismus. Von Klopstock bis Richard Wagner* (Göttingen: Vandenhoeck & Ruprecht, 2005).

32 Cf. Léon Poliakov, *The Aryan Myth. A history of racist and nationalist ideas in Europe* (New York: Basic Books, 1974); Ruth Römer, *Sprachwissenschaft und Rassenideologie in Deutschland* (Munich: Wilhelm Fink Verlag, 1989); Olender, *Languages of Paradise*.

33 Cf. Stefan Arvidsson, *Aryan Idols. Indo-European Mythology as Ideology and Science*, trans. Sonia Wichmann (Chicago: University of Chicago Press, 2006).

34 George S. Williamson, *The Longing for Myth in Germany. Religion and Aesthetic Culture from Romanticism to Nietzsche* (Chicago: University of Chicago Press, 2004), 297.

constructions, the alliances on the 'positive' side (i.e. assumptions about who belongs to the 'Germanic' or 'Nordic' peoples, and is thus perceived as a fellow campaigner) can vary, so that we are faced with shifting identifications (e.g., Germany and the Scandinavian countries, England and Germany, America and England), which can change according to the current political situation.

So far, we can conclude that already the earliest (re-)constructions of a Germanic pre-Christian religion are fraught with both methodological and ideological problems, which often, if not always, imply cultural imperialist as well as anti-Jewish and anti-Catholic notions. In none of these early cases, however, did the search for a national past and identity lead to genuine attempts to renew the reconstructed Pagan religion as such. Romantic endeavors saw the alleged Pagan ancestors as sources of aesthetic and national renewal, rather than as serious religious competition to the established Protestant churches.

The Search for a German Religion in Fin de Siecle Germany

The first calls to 'Germanize' religion by rejecting central parts of Christianity, and to orient a national religion toward an allegedly more authentic national mythic past appear in Germany in the latter third of the 19th century. They were motivated by a twofold lack of unity in German history: the lack of a unified nation state up until 1871, and the lack of a unified state religion, since German territories were traditionally split among Catholicism, Lutheranism and Reformed United Protestantism. No individual denomination could therefore be claimed as the faith for a Germany that was to be unified politically, as was the case with the Catholic church in post-Napoleonic France, the Anglican Church in England, or Lutheran state Protestantism in the Scandinavian countries.

The first intellectual to publicly voice the explicit need for Germany to find its own national religion was the Göttingen orientalist Paul de Lagarde (born as Paul Anton Bötticher, 1827–1891). He rejected both Catholicism, because of its internationalism, and Protestantism, which he saw as a degenerate, particularistic organization. In an era when Germany as a whole was seized by the optimism of progress after the foundation of the new empire in 1871, Lagarde deplored the materialism and the lack of an inward or spiritual unity of his country. He worked actively for a religious renewal and understood himself as the prophet of a national rebirth: a fundamental reshaping of German national politics, economy, education, and finally, religion.[35]

---

35   For a brief but comprehensive overview of Lagarde's ideas see Ina-Ulrike Paul, "Paul Anton de Lagarde," in *Handbuch zur 'Völkischen Bewegung' 1871–1918*, ed. Uwe Puschner,

He envisioned the integrative, supra-denominational future religion as a Christianity purged of all influences that he saw as foreign to the German people, in particular all Jewish influence, which he claimed to have found in the teachings of Paul especially. Lagarde's anti-Semitism was not based on a biological notion of race but rather on the idea of a unity of religion and nation. Nonetheless, he employed a radical rhetoric of extinction that was to influence later German anti-Semitism, including leading National Socialists such as Alfred Rosenberg.

Lagarde's efforts to 'Germanize' Christianity were not to take effect until later in the century, when the general optimism that prevailed during the era of state foundation and industrialization gave way to cultural pessimist fears of decadence. Lagarde's ideas were taken up by Richard Wagner's son-in-law, Houston Stewart Chamberlain (1855–1927), who brought French race theory to Germany, in particular Comte de Gobineau's ideas about the expansion and degeneration of the white race. With his two-volume racist and anti-Semitic manifesto, *Die Grundlagen des 19. Jahrhunderts* (*The Foundations of the Nineteenth Century* 1899), Chamberlain became another guiding intellectual force for the *völkisch* movement and National Socialism.[36] The third inspirational force for early 20th century revivals of an alleged Germanic religion was Julius Langbehn (1851–1907), a dropout from bourgeois academic life who became immensely popular with his cultural critical manifesto *Rembrandt als Erzieher* (Rembrandt as Educator, 1890). He championed a new reformation toward an 'original wholeness' on the basis of Germanic art and philosophy.[37]

The idea of a Germanization of Christianity was followed up and further popularized by the theologian and former Lutheran minister Arthur Bonus (1864–1941). In his brochure *Von Stöcker zu Naumann. Ein Wort zur Germanisierung des Christentums* (From Stöcker to Naumann. A Word about

---

Walter Schmitz, and Justus H. Ulbricht (Munich etc.: K.G. Saur, 1996). Cf. also Friedrich Wilhelm Graf, *Die Wiederkehr der Götter. Religion in der modernen Kultur* (Munich: C.H. Beck, 2004), 145.

36   Cf. Hildegard Chatellier, "Rasse und Religion bei Houston Stewart Chamberlain," in *Völkische Religion und Krisen der Moderne. Entwürfe 'arteigener' Glaubenssysteme seit der Jahrhundertwende*, ed. Stefanie v. Schnurbein and Justus H. Ulbricht (Würzburg: Königshausen & Neumann, 2001).

37   Cf. Fritz Stern, *The Politics of Cultural Despair. A Study in the Rise of the Germanic Ideology* (Berkeley, CA: University of California Press, 1961); Bernd Behrendt, "August Julius Langbehn, der 'Rembrandtdeutsche,'" in *Handbuch zur 'Völkischen Bewegung' 1871–1918*, ed. Uwe Puschner, Walter Schmitz, and Justus H. Ulbricht (Munich etc.: K.G. Saur, 1996). *Rembrandt als Erzieher* reached 43 editions in its first three years.

the Germanization of Christianity, 1896)[38] Bonus called for the rejuvenation of a Christianity purged of its "Semitic" and Paulinian notions, one reconstructed with 'native' Germanic elements.[39] More important for our context is the fact that he contributed to the introduction of another body of Nordic sources, the medieval Icelandic sagas, to his contemporaries, and to the then-emerging searchers for religious alternatives.

The sagas are a unique genre, codified mainly in Iceland in the late 12th and 13th century. Their most popular sub-genre, the family sagas or sagas of the Icelanders, treats the activities, politics and violent feuds of the early Scandinavian settlers in Iceland in the 10th century.[40] Their realistic style renders laconic facts and dialogues but no direct information about the colorful protagonists' emotions or motives. Therefore, the sagas were long considered to be reliable, orally transmitted documentation not only of the events depicted, but also of the cultural, social, political and legal structures of pre-Christian Iceland, and not least of its Pagan beliefs and practices. Both the Pagan content and the validity of the sagas' oral transmission have long been disputed.[41] Nevertheless, around 1900, they seemed to Bonus and many others perfect evidence of the inherently "modern", unsentimental and heroic character of the medieval Icelanders, as well as of contemporary Germans – again an example of the well-established identification of the Germans with the Germanic. Bonus was a major force behind the ambitious translation project of the Icelandic sagas, called *Sammlung Thule* (Thule Collection), which promised to provide a basis for the "Germanization of Christianity" and the "heroization of Christ" which he stood for.[42] At the same time, the now accessible saga

---

38 Arthur Bonus, *Von Stoecker zu Naumann. Ein Wort zur Germanisierung des Christentums* (Heilbronn: Eugen Salzer, 1896).

39 Cf. Rainer Lächele, "Germanisierung des Christentums – Heroisierung Christi: Arthur Bonus – Max Bewer – Julius Bode," in *Völkische Religion und Krisen der Moderne. Entwürfe 'arteigener' Glaubenssysteme seit der Jahrhundertwende*, ed. Stefanie v. Schnurbein and Justus H. Ulbricht (Würzburg: Königshausen & Neumann, 2001).

40 For an English language discussion on saga literature cf. the standard work by Carol J. Clover, *The Medieval Saga* (Ithaca, NY: Cornell University Press, 1982).

41 Cf. Julia Zernack, *Geschichten aus Thule. Íslendingasögur in Übersetzungen deutscher Germanisten*, vol. 3, Berliner Beiträge zur Skandinavistik (Berlin: Freie Unversität Berlin, 1994).

42 Cf. Lächele, "Germanisierung des Christentums"; Julia Zernack, "Germanische Altertumskunde, Skandinavistik und völkische Religion," in *Völkische Religion und Krisen der Moderne. Entwürfe 'arteigener' Glaubenssysteme seit der Jahrhundertwende*, ed. Stefanie v. Schnurbein and Justus H. Ulbricht (Würzburg: Königshausen & Neumann, 2001).

literature and the views which Bonus and other leading academics harbored about its pre-Christian context became relevant sources for the emerging Germanic Pagan groups.

It was no coincidence that the saga translations as well as the translations of Eddic literature in the *Sammlung Thule* were published in Eugen Diederichs' publishing house. Inspired by, among others, Langbehn and Lagarde (whose work he published and popularized), Diederichs campaigned for a "new myth born from religious forces;"[43] a second Reformation and Renaissance. His neo-Romantic editing program featured a syncretistic blend of works by the most diverse religious and cultural reformers, as long as they promised a contribution to a spiritual renewal, the regaining of a German cultural identity: Christian as well as *völkisch* Neopagan, anti-Semitic as well as Jewish, socialist as well as fascist.[44]

With this program, Diederichs' publishing company became the "most significant platform for the new-religious movement" of Wilhelminian Germany,[45] an institutional center for a number of alternative movements that established themselves in Germany (and partly other European countries) around 1900 and in turn formed the fertile ground in which the first Germanic Neopagan groups would take root. The most important of these were the

---

43   "einen neuen Mythos, geboren aus religiösen Kräften." Quoted in Justus H. Ulbricht, "Wider das 'Katzenjammergefühl der Enwurzelung.' Intellektuellen-Religion im Eugen Diederichs Verlag," *Buchhandelsgeschichte* 76 (1996), B 112.

44   It should be noted that Diederichs never narrowed his nationalist and cultural critical impulse to a national chauvinist attitude, not even in the heated atmosphere of World War I. See "'Meine Seele sehnt sich nach Sichtbarkeit deutschen Wesens.' Weltanschauung und Verlagsprogramm von Eugen Diederichs im Spannungsfeld zwischen Neuromantik und 'Konservativer Revolution,'" in *Versammlungsort moderner Geister. Der Eugen Diederichs Verlag – Aufbruch ins Jahrhundert der Extreme*, ed. Gangolf Hübinger (Munich: Diederichs, 1996), 337. For Diederichs, his publishing house and his journal *Die Tat* (The Action) see also Friedrich Wilhelm Graf, "Das Laboratorium der Moderne. Zur 'Verlagsreligion' des Eugen Diederichs Verlags," in *Versammlungsort moderner Geister. Der Eugen Diederichs Verlag – Aufbruch ins Jahrhundert der Extreme*, ed. Gangolf Hübinger (Munich: Diederichs, 1996); Edith Hanke and Gangolf Hübinger, "Von der 'Tat'-Gemeinde zum 'Tat'-Kreis. Die Entwicklung einer Kulturzeitschrift," in *Versammlungsort moderner Geister. Der Eugen Diederichs Verlag – Aufbruch ins Jahrhundert der Extreme*, ed. Gangolf Hübinger (Munich: Diederichs, 1996); Meike G. Werner, "Die Erneuerung des Lebens durch ästhetische Praxis. Lebensreform, Jugend und Festkultur im Eugen Diederichs Verlag," in *Versammlungsort moderner Geister. Der Eugen Diederichs Verlag – Aufbruch ins Jahrhundert der Extreme*, ed. Gangolf Hübinger (Munich: Diederichs, 1996).

45   "die bedeutendste Plattform für die neureligiöse Bewegung des Wilhelminismus." Quoted in Ulbricht, "Wider das 'Katzenjammergefühl der Enwurzelung,'" B 113.

densely interwoven youth movement, life reform movement, contemporary occultism, and *völkisch* movement.

The German youth movement emerged from a number of independent small circles, associations and journals, amongst them the famous *Wandervogel*, founded in 1901. It gathered hiking groups run by high-school students and reform-oriented teachers. For these groups, 'youth' represented a more authentic state of being, which was set against the stifled, materialistic bourgeois culture of their fathers, and could be accessed through outdoor activities and allegedly authentic, natural cultural activities such as folksong and dance.[46] The youth movement never developed original political or religious ideas and was open to impulses from various directions. It took up influences from the *völkisch* movement from the beginning, and many of the hiking *Bünde* (associations) were closely intertwined with *völkisch* religious organizations, especially those of the non-Christian kind.[47]

Equally important impulses came from the life reform movement, which shared central goals with the youth movement such as an emphatic focus on 'authenticity,' 'purity,' 'beauty,' 'naturalness' and 'health.' United by such general ideals, and by a bourgeois anti-capitalism critical of blind industrial progress and urbanization gone awry, the life reform movement presented as a heterogeneous network of more or less loosely structured associations, circles, journals, businesses, publishers and individuals. Fears of degeneration were countered with an array of reform efforts regarding body and soul, concepts of nature, and various life practices.[48] Among its branches were movements for

---

46   Cf. Frank Trommler, "Mission ohne Ziel. Über den Kult der Jugend im modernen Deutschland," in *'Mit uns zieht die neue Zeit.' Der Mythos Jugend*, ed. Thomas Koebner, Rolf-Peter Janz, and Frank Trommler (Frankfurt a.M.: Suhrkamp, 1985); Winfried Mogge, "Wandervogel, Freideutsche Jugend und Bünde. Zum Jugendbild der bürgerlichen Jugendbewegung," in *'Mit uns zieht die neue Zeit.' Der Mythos Jugend*, ed. Thomas Koebner, Rolf-Peter Janz, and Frank Trommler (Frankfurt a.M.: Suhrkamp, 1985). See also Uwe Puschner, "Völkische Bewegung und Jugendbewegung," in *Ideengeschichte als politische Aufklärung. Festschrift für Wolfgang Wippermann zum 65. Geburtstag*, ed. Stefan Vogt, et al. (Berlin: Metropol, 2010).

47   Winfried Mogge, "'Wir lieben Balder, den Lichten...' Völkisch-religiöse Jugendbünde vom Wilhelminischen Reich zum 'Dritten Reich,'" in *Die völkisch-religiöse Bewegung im Nationalsozialismus. Eine Beziehungs- und Konfliktgeschichte*, ed. Uwe Puschner and Clemens Vollnhals (Göttingen: Vandenhoeck & Ruprecht, 2012).

48   Cf. Klaus Wolbert, "Die Lebensreform – Anträge zur Debatte," in *Die Lebensreform. Entwürfe zur Neugestaltung von Leben und Kunst um 1900*, ed. Kai Buchholz, et al. (Darmstadt: haeusser, 2001), Diethart Kerbs and Jürgen Reulecke, *Handbuch der deutschen Reformbewegungen 1880–1933* (Wuppertal: Peter Hammer Verlag, 1998).

the protection of nature and landscape; garden settlements; the renewal of architecture and crafts;[49] alternative agriculture; naturopathy and alternative medicine; reform of education, art, music, dance, clothing and nutrition; anti-alcoholism; nudism; social and racial hygiene; and sexual reform. As practical as individual undertakings within the movement were, some of them can be read as interventions into religious discourse as well, since all of these concepts of nature, the body, and health took on a spiritual or transcendental quality. In our context, it is important to note that the North became the location of such desired qualities as light, naturalness, youth and beauty – a fact that linked the life reform movement with equivalent movements in the Scandinavian countries, and allowed the inclusion of racial ideologies of whiteness.[50] Nevertheless, the life reform movement, as with most of the alternative movements discussed in this book, was not politically unified, rather it "connected modernity and counter-modernity, enthusiasm for progress and reaction, a rational world-view and irrational eccentricity."[51]

Religious or spiritual ideas within the life reform movement were based on several contemporary intellectual and popular currents that also became relevant for *völkisch* religion. Modern worldly conceptions of religiosity were based on 19th century theological anticlerical philosophies, historical-critical bible studies, and historical Jesus studies originating in David Friedrich Strauß' and Ernest Renan's ideas of Jesus as both a human and merely an example of an eternal divine essence of humanity.[52] Another strand of influence was contemporary Darwinism, especially in the form of Monism, which the zoologist and physician Ernst Haeckel (1834–1919) promoted in the popular science foundation *Monistenbund* (Monist League, founded 1906).[53] Vitalist philosophers such as Arthur Schopenhauer, Friedrich Nietzsche, Eduard von Hartmann and Ludwig Klages emphasized the irrational and its rejection of intellectualism and mechanism, thus providing many contemporaries with immanent,

---

49 This is an equivalent of the English arts and crafts movement, with which it shared motives and was connected to on many levels.
50 A spiritualization of race was particularly prominent in German nudism, which was dominated by a spirituality of the sun, light, and whiteness and quickly moved into a cult of the healthy, light Aryan body. Cf. Ulrich Linse, "Nordisches in der deutschen Lebensreformbewegung," in *Wahlverwandtschaft. Skandinavien und Deutschland 1800–1914*, ed. Bernd Henningsen, et al. (Berlin: Jovis, 1997).
51 Wolbert, "Die Lebensreform – Anträge zur Debatte," 17: "vernetzt die Moderne mit der Gegenmoderne, die Fortschrittsbegeisterung mit der Reaktion, die rationale Weltsicht mit irrationaler Verstiegenheit."
52 Cf. Arvidsson, *Aryan Idols*, 92–96.
53 For Haeckel see Chapter 6.

activist concepts of religion as well. Vitalism was frequently combined with racial theories attributing 'Aryans' or Germanic peoples a specific propensity for this kind of activist spirituality.

Whereas Ernst Haeckel's scientific concepts played a certain role for racial theories of an immanent religion, a spiritual version of such racial teachings was developed in several varieties of contemporary Western occultism, as in Theodor Reuss' *Ordo Templi Orientis* (O.T.O.), Aleister Crowley's *Order of the Golden Dawn*,[54] and particularly in the international theosophical movement.[55] As a whole, theosophy, as well as the manifold secret orders and lodges by which it was inspired and which it in turn inspired, oscillated between two poles: a liberal faction, which emphasized the unity of mankind and the hope for a New Age in which love and beauty would rule; and a racist, nationalist faction that gained more and more influence throughout the early 20th century, and held strong connections with the European anti-Semitic movement.[56] A German branch of the *Theosophical Society* (founded in New York in 1875, and later relocated to India) took hold around 1900 within the life reform movement, with which it shared its ambivalent political and ideological position. It attracted liberals and progressive bohemians at the alternative spiritual center at Monte Verità near Ascona, but also individuals with conservative and *völkisch* leanings and Wagnerians.[57]

---

54   For an overview over occult orders and secret societies in the era see Stuckrad, *Western Esotericism*, 113–121. For a discussion of Crowley's significance for modern Paganism in general cf. Henrik Bogdan, "The Influence of Aleister Crowley on Gerald Gardner and the Early Witchcraft Movement," in *Handbook of Contemporary Neopaganism*, ed. James R. Lewis and Murphy Pizza (Leiden/Boston: Brill, 2009).

55   Modern theosophy originated within the context of American spiritualism in the last half of the 19th century. It was mainly based on the writings of Helena Petrovna Blavatsky (1831–1891), a Russian-born adventuress who spent parts of her life in India, where she claimed to have had medial contact with spiritual masters who conveyed their ancient teachings to her. Combining traditional occultist elements with popularized Hinduism, Buddhism, and Darwinian evolutionary theory, Blavatsky depicted world history as a continual spiritual progress towards ever-higher spiritual spheres. See Nicholas Goodrick-Clarke, *Helena Blavatsky* (Berkeley, CA: North Atlantic Books, 2004), for a brief summary and for more literature on theosophy see Stuckrad, *Western Esotericism*, 123–132. Claiming that all religion was based on a common esoteric essence, which she 'revealed' in her books *Isis Unveiled* (1877) and *The Secret Doctrine* (1888), she imagined an intricate system of so-called "root races" and "sub races" with the "Aryans" at the very top of the scale.

56   Cf. James Webb, *The Occult Establishment* (La Salle, IL: Open Court, 1976), 213–222.

57   Cf. Nicholas Goodrick-Clarke, *The Occult Roots of Nazism. The Ariosophists of Austria and Germany 1890–1935* (Wellingborough, Northamptonshire: Aquarian Press, 1985), 22–27.

Within this complex conglomerate of alternative spirituality, one person stands out who was to influence later Neopaganism to a significant extent: Carl Gustav Jung, the student and collaborator of Sigmund Freud. Jung turned the focus of depth psychology from early childhood sexual trauma and fantasy to a theory of the collective unconscious, in which myths and tales were seen as foundational for the development of the human psyche. What is less well known today is the fact that he based his reflections about the collective unconscious and its archetypes on theories of land and nationhood, which he saw as foundational for psychological as well as cultural forms. He thus assigned a mythic substructure to not only individual, but also national and racial psychologies. He proclaimed a clear distinction between the 'Aryan' and the Jewish psyche. Germans and Jews thus became complementary 'nations' with complementary psychic and mythic structures.[58]

In their complex structures and often contradictory ideologies, the life reform and occultist movements resembled another integrative network of the era, the *völkisch* movement, with which they overlapped significantly. The *völkisch* movement was characterized by an equally confusing organizational structure, an extra-parliamentarian conglomerate of small associations, circles, journals, etc. Its ideology was far from unified, as it contained contradictory elements of anti-modernism and modernism, nationalism and pan-Germanicism,

---

Rudolf Steiner, a former chair of the German *Theosophical Society*, went on to develop his own version of theosophical thought, anthroposophy. Anthroposophy shifted the emphasis from Eastern to Gnostic-Christian spirituality and was to bring forth a number of alternative reform efforts, the most internationally well-known being biodynamic agriculture and Steiner schools. For a comprehensive recent biography of Steiner see Helmut Zander, *Rudolf Steiner. Die Biographie* (Munich: Piper, 2011).

[58] For discussions of Jung's attitude towards Jews and anti-Semitism see Aryeh Maidenbaum and Stephen A. Martin, eds., *Lingering Shadows. Jungians, Freudians, and Anti-Semitism* (Boston/London: Shambala, 1991); for his role as a "psychologist who lent his authority to nationalism, thereby legitimizing ideas of innate psychological differences between nations" see Andrew Samuels, "National Socialism, National Psychology, and Analytical Psychology," in *Lingering Shadows. Jungians, Freudians, and Anti-Semitism*, ed. Aryeh Maidenbaum and Stephen A. Martin (Boston/London: Shambala, 1991), 188. In his controversial book, *The Jung Cult*, Richard Noll, *The Jung Cult. Origins of a Charismatic Movement* (New York etc.: Free Press Paperbacks, 1994) uncovered the connections between Jung and Jungianism with the *völkisch* movement and *völkisch* ideology. Jung's "post-Holocaust assault on the God of the Jewish people" (Steven M. Wasserstrom, *Religion after Religion. Gershom Scholem, Mircea Eliade, and Henry Corbin at Eranos* (Princeton, NJ: Princeton University Press, 1999), 177) was criticized by Martin Buber as a testimony of gnostic anti-Semitism (ibid). See also Chapter 5.

spirituality and scientism.[59] Based on an outspoken anti-Semitic and racist ideology, the *völkisch* movement promoted an extensive renewal or rebirth of the German people, which was to counteract the widespread fear of a 'racial,' 'cultural' and not least 'spiritual' 'degeneration.' This program of renewal was based on the German ideology discussed above, which conceived of a true *Volk* as a holistic, self-referential, pure, and natural organism. Ideally it was to be structured in an 'organic' feudal, medieval social order, which was antithetically set against the alleged individualism, rationalism and liberalism of Mediterranean civilization and modernity.[60] (Neo-)Romantic ideals thus reappear in *völkisch* ideology in a radicalized and especially racialized form. The desired national and cultural renewal is founded on a program of often violent racial purification and rebirth. *Völkisch* protagonists objected strongly to their ideology being reduced to an exclusively anti-Semitic, pessimistic racial ideology that focused on resistance against negative cultural forces (which they certainly saw in Jewish and 'degenerate racial elements'). Their commitment to 'positive' goals, and to a cultural, mental and spiritual renewal of the German people led to the promotion of a new, positive spirituality. Thus, as Uwe Puschner has aptly remarked, religion became the "archimedic point" of *völkisch* ideology.[61]

Its promotion of a holistic or totalitarian cultural renewal and its peculiar mixture of anti-modernist and modernist elements link the *völkisch* movement to a larger ultra-conservative current in Germany in the early 20th century: the Conservative Revolution. The term was coined by Armin Mohler, the most prominent post-war apologist of this heterogenous extreme right-wing movement, in an attempt to distinguish it from National Socialism proper, which many of its adherents regarded with a mixture of fascination and skepticism.[62] Although it has been considered contentious due to the mythic and

---

59 See Uwe Puschner, *Die Völkische Bewegung im wilhelminischen Deutschland. Sprache – Rasse – Religion* (Darmstadt: Wissenschaftliche Buchgesellschaft, 2001) for a comprehensive investigation of the *völkisch* movement and ideology prior to WW I. An English summary of his findings can be found in "'One People, One God, One Reich.' The 'Völkisch Weltanschauung' and Movement," *German Historical Institute London Bulletin* 24, no. 1 (2002).

60 Cf. *Die Völkische Bewegung im wilhelminischen Deutschland*, 92f.

61 "Deutschchristentum. Eine völkisch-christliche Weltanschauungsreligion," in *Der Protestantismus – Ideologie, Konfession oder Kultur?*, ed. Richard Faber and Gesine Palmer (Würzburg: Königshausen & Neumann, 2003), 96.

62 Mohler's seminal work on the Conservative Revolution, albeit apologetically tainted, has appeared in several editions since 1950. See for example Armin Mohler, *Die konservative Revolution in Deutschland 1918–1932. Grundriss ihrer Weltanschauungen* (Stuttgart: Vorwerk,

idealizing quality Mohler's use gave it,[63] the term has become established. It is useful for our purposes because it captures a central moment that is also constitutive for the *völkisch* religious currents discussed here. While conservatism is traditionally understood as a political movement which aims at preserving existing political, social and cultural structures, Conservative Revolutionaries are convinced that modernization has already proceeded too far, and that there is little or nothing left that is worth preserving. They conclude that what is to be preserved (a new holistic state structure, a new organic culture, and a new man) has first to be created or restored in a violent revolutionary effort which is to destroy the existing structures. These "politics of cultural despair"[64] are not exclusively retrogressive or anti-modern, but combine a rejection of an allegedly 'degenerate' modernity with modernist elements in shifting combinations, which lend them their peculiar dynamic – a dynamic which, as we shall see in the following chapters, characterizes large parts of Germanic Neopaganism and its attempts at religious reform and re-creation as well.

German(ic) Faith and Ariosophy in the Early Twentieth Century[65]

In the first decades of the 20th century, a number of Germanophile religious and spiritual associations began to grow out of the contradictory amalgamation of turn-of-the-century ideas and ideologies of spiritual, national, and racial renewal. Early groups such as the *Deutschbund* (German Union, founded in 1894) and *Deutschreligiöser Bund* (German Religious Union, 1903) promoted a German Christianity. Here journals played a key role in not only spreading German religious ideas but also in establishing groups: for example, the *Deutsche Erneuerungsgemeinde* (German Congregation of Renewal) grew out of the anti-Semite Theodor Fritsch's journal *Hammer* (first published in 1902),[66]

1950); *Die konservative Revolution in Deutschland 1918–1932. Ein Handbuch*, 6. revised and expanded ed. (Graz: Ares, 2005). Historian Stefan Breuer has suggested limiting it to a much smaller faction of interwar right-wing intellectuals. Cf. Stefan Breuer, *Anatomie der konservativen Revolution* (Darmstadt: Wissenschaftliche Buchgesellschaft, 1993).

63 Cf. "Die 'Konservative Revolution' – Kritik eines Mythos," *Politische Vierteljahresschrift* 31, no. 4 (1990).
64 Stern, *The politics of cultural despair*.
65 This sub-chapter follows my brief outline of Germanic Faith groups found in Schnurbein, "Die Suche nach einer 'arteigenen' Religion in 'germanisch'- und 'deutschgläubigen' Gruppen."
66 Michael Bönisch, "Die 'Hammer'-Bewegung," in *Handbuch zur 'Völkischen Bewegung' 1871–1918*, ed. Uwe Puschner, Walter Schmitz, and Justus H. Ulbricht (Munich etc.: K.G.

and a reading circle formed around *Der Volkserzieher* (The People's Educator). The latter was an influential journal, begun in 1897 by the teacher and journalist Wilhelm Schwaner, which focused on reforms in education, culture and religion (mainly in a German Christian sense).[67]

A number of programmatic publications in the first decade of the 20th century suggested thinking beyond Christianity altogether, paving the way for the establishment of Germanic Neopagan groups after 1910. The first public initiative was taken in 1900 by Ernst Wachler (1871–1945), a Germanist and promoter of the open air theater movement,[68] in a booklet titled "Über die Zukunft des deutschen Glaubens"[69] (On the future of German faith) – "the prototype of all later 'neopagan' prophecies."[70] Following Lagarde in his scathing rejection of the Jewish roots of Christianity and "the epileptic fanatic" Paul, Wachler asks: "Who knows if our natural belief, our world-view will not *return*? Has returned and lives amongst us."[71]

"Are you, German soul, not rich enough to build yourself a shrine out of your innermost being?"[72] – With this question, the painter, art professor and

---

Saur, 1996), 358. The co-founder of *Deutsche Erneuerungsgemeinde* (founded in 1904) was the promoter of an Aryan "racial breeding" Willibald Hentschel.

[67] Justus H. Ulbricht, "Völkische Erwachsenenbildung. Intentionen, Programme und Institutionen zwischen Jahrhundertwende und Weimarer Republik," in *Handbuch zur 'Völkischen Bewegung' 1871–1918*, ed. Uwe Puschner, Walter Schmitz, and Justus H. Ulbricht (Munich etc.: K.G. Saur, 1996), 257–262, discusses Schwaner's significance for *völkisch* educational programs. See also Christoph Carstensen, *Der Volkserzieher. Eine historisch-kritische Untersuchung über die Volkserzieherbewegung Wilhelm Schwaners*, Diss. Jena 1939 (Würzburg-Aumühle: Konrad Triltsch, 1941) and Alfred Ehrentreich, "Wilhelm Schwaner (1863–1944) und die Volkserzieherbewegung," *Jahrbuch des Archivs der deutschen Jugendbewegung* 7 (1975).

[68] The significance of Wachler and his theater reform for Germanic Neopaganism is discussed in Chapter 9.

[69] Ernst Wachler, "Über die Zukunft des deutschen Glaubens," *Irminsul. Schriftenreihe für Junggermanische (eddische) Religion und Weltanschauung* 44 (1930 [1900]).

[70] Puschner, *Die Völkische Bewegung im wilhelminischen Deutschland*, 226. This fact has been largely obscured by later protagonists of the movement, who tried to downplay Wachler's significance as a key figure for the early Germanic religious movement after 1913 because of his partial Jewish descent (cf. ibid., 233).

[71] Wachler, "Über die Zukunft des deutschen Glaubens," 13. "Wer weiß, ob nicht unser Naturglaube, unsere Weltanschauung *wiederkehren* wird? Wiedergekehrt ist und unter uns lebt?" [Emphasis in original].

[72] Der Volkserzieher 6 (1907), 42f: "Bist du, deutsche Seele nicht reich genug, dir aus Ureigenstem ein Heiligtum zu bauen?".

playwright Ludwig Fahrenkrog (1867–1952) followed suit in a couple of articles titled *Germanentempel* (Germanic Temple) which he published in 1907 and 1908 in *Der Volkserzieher*. It culminated in the suggestion to form a "German religious congregation" and fight for the official recognition of this German religion.

These appeals resulted in the foundation of the *Bund für Persönlichkeitskultur* (Union for the Culture of Personality) in 1911.[73] In 1912, Ludwig Fahrenkrog, Wilhelm Schwaner and Karl Weißleder constituted the *Germanisch-deutsche Religions-Gemeinschaft* (Germanic-German Religious Fellowship) and consecrated the outdoor altar at Hermannstein, near Rattlar, Hessen, as a place of worship. The community aimed at "leading the German to himself",[74] and hoped to offer a religious alternative on an explicitly racial basis to those who felt alienated from the Christian churches:

> We however want to create a space where physical and spiritual foreign economy is excluded, that is: from our most sacred: the religion. [...] Therefore, we demand from everybody who is to be admitted a clear, unambiguous declaration, that he be Germanic. That, according to the best of his belief, no drop of blood of the yellow, black, or Jewish race is in him.[75]

In 1913, the group was renamed the *"Germanische Glaubensgemeinschaft"* (German Belief Fellowship), united with the *Gesellschaft Wodan* (Society Wodan)[76] and given a constitution.

---

73 Daniel Junker, *Gott in uns! Die Germanische Glaubens-Gemeinschaft. Ein Beitrag zur Geschichte völkischer Religiosität in der Weimarer Republik* (Hamburg: Verlag Daniel Junker, 2002), 47.

74 "den Germanen zu sich selbst führen".

75 "Aufruf: Was will die Germanisch-deutsche Religionsgemeinschaft?," *Der Volkserzieher* 26 (1912): "Wir wollen aber eine Stätte schaffen aus der körperliche und geistige Fremdwirtschaft ausgeschieden sei, das ist: aus unserem Allerheiligsten: der Religion. [...] Darum fordern wir von allen Aufzunehmenden die klare, unzweideutige Erklärung, daß er Germane sei. Daß nach bestem Wissen und Gewissen kein Tropfen Bluts der gelben, schwarzen oder jüdischen Rasse in ihm sei."

76 The background of this association is slightly obscure. In 1906, the German officer Josef Weber (alias Adolf Riemann) had published a book titled *Allvater oder Jehova* (Allfather or Jehova). This book, as well as a number of articles by the same author, Adolf Kroll (who went on to become a leading member of the *Germanische Glaubensgemeinschaft*) and Ernst Wachler in the journals *Hammer* and *Heimdall* seem to have led to

It is not quite clear what relation the foundation of the *Germanisch-deutsche Religions-Gemeinschaft* had with the *Deutscher Orden* (German Order), which was established in 1911 by another important early protagonist of the German Faith Movement, Otto Sigfrid Reuter (1876–1945). It was most probably a competing endeavor, which, however, did not preclude close connections between the organizations, or membership in both. Reuter was the director of the telegraph office in Bremen and had published a book that was much read within the *völkisch* movement. In *Sigfrid oder Christus* (Sigfrid or Christ, 1910), the hero of the Nibelungen story, Sigfrid, is celebrated as a 'light' warrior who leads through victory (*Sieg*) to peace (*Frieden*). The *Deutscher Orden* was soon complemented by the *Deutschreligiöse Gemeinschaft* (German Religious Community), an inner circle for members who had left the church officially. It was renamed as the *Deutschgläubige Gemeinschaft* (German Faith Fellowship) in 1914.[77]

A third important impulse for the spirituality, ideology and practice of German(ic) Faith came from the overtly racial esoteric version of modern occultism, which gave itself the telling name 'Ariosophy.' Like *völkisch* religion in general, Ariosophy originated in an extreme anti-Semitic climate, and an anti-Semitic affect lies at the basis of its philosophy. However, while the German Faith Movement was based in Northern German national Protestantism, the roots for Ariosophic thinking lie in anti-Catholic, pan-German Austrian milieus.[78] While German Faith can be understood as an attempt to 'Germanize' or 'Aryanize' Protestantism and certain forms of the freethinking and free-religious movement, Ariosophy, in spite of its anti-Catholic attitude,

---

the establishment of the *Gesellschaft Wodan* in 1911. The exact date of the foundation is unclear. The "Verhandlungsschrift zur Germanentagung zu Salzburg vom 29. bis 31. Gilbharts 2034" (1921) mentions 1907 as the founding year of *Wodan*. However, this date cannot be verified by other sources, as it possibly refers to a different group. This leads Uwe Puschner, *Die Völkische Bewegung im wilhelminischen Deutschland*, 238f, and Daniel Junker, *Gott in uns!*, 26, to the probably more correct dating, 1911. As the *Gesellschaft Wodan* did not require its members to leave their official affiliations with the Christian churches, it is not always counted as a truly Pagan group.

77   Cf. also Stefan Breuer, *Die Völkischen in Deutschland. Kaiserreich und Weimarer Republik* (Darmstadt: Wissenschaftliche Buchgesellschaft, 2008), 95–97. Daniel Junker, *Gott in uns!* argues convincingly for Reuter's *Deutschgläubige Gemeinschaft* to have been the first major Germanic religious organization in Germany. 1912 is the founding year of two other politically active militant German-religious groups, the *Reichshammerbund* and the *Germanenorden*, the latter of which was allegedly involved in several attempted assassinations in the Weimar era.

78   Cf. Goodrick-Clarke, *The Occult Roots of Nazism*, 10.

adopted Catholic ideas and traits, and can be understood as the 'Germanization' of contemporary occultism, especially theosophy. Ariosophy took one of its cues from the theories of and experiments with sexual magic that were characteristic of magical orders such as Theodor Reuss' *Ordo Templi Orientis* (O.T.O.) and Aleister Crowley's *Order of the Golden Dawn*.[79] This emphasis on sexuality and fertility (both literal and magic) was shared by theosophist Max Ferdinand Sebaldt von Werth (1859–1916), who described a "sexual-religion of the Aryans, a sacred practice of eugenics designed to maintain the purity of the race."[80]

Sebaldt's writings provided inspiration for the first popular author to combine occultism and theosophy with an explicitly *völkisch* ideology: Guido (von) List (1848–1919), an Austrian journalist and author of *völkisch* novels and plays,[81] and an activist in numerous right-wing groups. After a temporary loss of vision in 1902, List claimed to have had visions of earlier incarnations, purported to have access to what he called the ancestral memory (Erberinnerung) of the 'Ario-Germans,' and began to 'reveal' the mystic origins of the runes and language in general.[82] A number of Viennese and German dignitaries (amongst them Ernst Wachler)[83] supported his theories and founded the *Guido-von-List-Gesellschaft* (Guido von List Society) in 1908, which promoted his ideas and financed his numerous publications. List himself never established a religious organization, except for a minuscule circle of initiates called

---

79 For an overview of occult orders and secret societies in the era see Stuckrad, *Western Esotericism*, 113–121. For a discussion on Crowley's significance for modern Paganism in general cf. Bogdan, "The Influence of Aleister Crowley on Gerald Gardner and the Early Witchcraft Movement."

80 See his two works from 1897, *Wanidis* and *D.I.S. Sexualreligion*. Cf. Goodrick-Clarke, *The Occult Roots of Nazism*, 51.

81 As is the case with many religious founders and occultists, verifiable facts about List's life are rare, and speculation abounds. The most reliable summary of his life and work is still Nicholas Goodrick-Clarke's investigation into Ariosophy. Cf. ibid. For a discussion of List's literary writings see Inge Kunz, "Herrenmenschentum, Neugermanen und Okkultismus. Eine soziologische Bearbeitung der Schriften von Guido List" (Unpublished doctoral thesis, Universität Wien, 1961).

82 From then on, List claimed to be of an ancient aristocratic family. Although the claim was refuted by the Austrian authorities, List and his followers continued to use the "von" in his name. Cf. Goodrick-Clarke, *The Occult Roots of Nazism*, 41f. For a general discussion on concepts of a new aristocracy in the *völkisch* movement see Alexandra Gerstner, *Rassenadel und Sozialaristokratie. Adelsvorstellungen in der völkischen Bewegung (1890–1914)* (Berlin: SuKuLTuR, 2003).

83 Cf. Goodrick-Clarke, *The Occult Roots of Nazism*, 43.

Hoher Armanen Orden (HAO, High Armanic Order).[84] However, his theories and speculations about an alleged pre-historic Ario-Germanic high culture and its secret transmission through runic inscriptions and secret societies have had a strong impact on German Faith as well as on Germanic Neopaganism worldwide.

List combined a pan-German nationalism with an interest in Romantic theories of pre-Christian ritual surviving in rural customs and heraldics. Fusing it with contemporary occultist ideas, he hoped to prove once and for all that the ancient Germans and Austrians were not uneducated Pagans, but had instead developed a superior culture that became the origin of "all Aryan cultures up until today."[85] From theosophy and occultism List borrowed the pantheistic and Gnostic concept that the divine permeates the world and mankind in all their dimensions, radicalizing their implicit racist and imperialist notions into an overt racial esotericism. Peoples and races appear as stages of development, with the Germans, Aryans or Ario-Germans figured as the superior and most spiritually developed race, thereby claiming leadership over and enslavement of all others. The main purpose of the Wuotanist religion promoted by List was the preservation of the superior Aryan race and the breeding of an even higher noble race through the succession of numerous incarnations. List's most original and enduring contribution to this racially radicalized theosophic system was his claim to have found a key to the original sacred language of the Ario-Germans in the runes. In his work *Das Geheimnis der Runen* (The Secret of the Runes, 1908), the pioneer of *völkisch* rune occultism developed an intricate system of correspondences, which laid the foundation for most modern versions of rune divination.[86]

From his friend and collaborator, Ariosophy's second 'prophet' Jörg Lanz von Liebenfels, List borrowed some of his ideas about the "occult significance of the Templars, the Manichaean struggle between the master race (the Ario-Germans) and the slave races (non-Aryans) and a theory about the original homeland of the Aryans, a vanished polar continent called Arktogäa."[87] Lanz was a former Cistercian monk who went on to form his own Aryan racial order,

---

84   Cf. ibid., 46f.
85   Johannes Balzli, *Guido von List. Der Wiederentdecker uralter arischer Weisheit. Sein Leben und Schaffen* (Vienna etc.: Guido-von-List-Gesellschaft, 1917), 29.
86   Cf. Puschner, *Die Völkische Bewegung im wilhelminischen Deutschland*, 27–48. For the history of modern rune magic see Chapter 3.
87   Goodrick-Clarke, *The Occult Roots of Nazism*, 55.

the *Ordo Novi Templi*, or Order of the New Templars, around 1900[88] with the goal of purifying and reviving the blond, blue-eyed, heroic god-men of the Aryan race. Lanz promoted his white supremacist ideas through *völkisch* and Social Darwinist journals and, from 1905 on, in his own journal *Ostara*, where a number of members of the *Guido-von-List-Society* published as well.

While List received his inspiration from folklore and archaeology, Lanz based his Aryan Christian ideas on a gnostic theology. In a number of books, most prominent amongst them his *Die Theozoologie oder die Kunde von den Sodoms-Äfflingen und dem Götter-Elektron* (Theozoology or the Lore about the Sodom-Apelings and the Divine Electron, 1905), he elaborated an occultist reading of the Fall. According to him, man at the moment of creation was a divine creature with highly developed electric organs, artificially bred by heavenly races, the Theozoa or Elektrozoa. Lanz gave his theories a strongly misogynist bent by claiming that the unfortunate desire of the females of this "Aryan heroic race" for racially inferior "apelings" led to the "original sin" of racial miscegenation and consequently to the loss of the Aryan electric organs used to communicate with divine entities.[89] Christ's mission according to Lanz was the recreation of this heroic race, the Grail its central 'electric' symbol.[90]

List's and Lanz' systems proved remarkably productive within the *völkisch* religious movement. Some of List's students applied the 'Master's' methods of

---

88   Just as is the case with List, little is known about Lanz' life, as he and his followers were careful to create a legendary biography. Cf. ibid., 90–122. The most knowledgeable investigator into *völkisch* religion, Ekkehard Hieronimus, "Jörg Lanz von Liebenfels," in *Handbuch zur 'Völkischen Bewegung' 1871–1918*, ed. Uwe Puschner, Walter Schmitz, and Justus H. Ulbricht (Munich etc.: K.G. Saur, 1996) summarizes the scarce facts. According to him, the Viennese born Adolf Josef Lanz (1874–1959) entered the Cistercian monastery Heiligenkreuz in Austria around 1893 and left it for unknown reasons in 1899. However, he seems to have considered himself a Cistercian brother all his life. Wilfried Daim, *Der Mann der Hitler die Ideen gab. Jörg Lanz von Liebenfels*, 3. ed. (Vienna: Überreuter, 1994), whose study first appeared in 1958, loses himself in speculations about Lanz' fundamental influence on Adolf Hitler, whereas Rudolf J. Mund, *Jörg Lanz v. Liebenfels und der Neue Templer Orden. Die Esoterik des Christentums* (Stuttgart: Spieth, 1976) wrote an equally unreliable apologetic biography.

89   One of the shifting subtitles of *Ostara* illustrates Lanz' racist and anti-feminist program: *Bücherei der Blonden und Mannesrechtler* (*Library of the Blondes and Masculinists*).

90   For a comprehensive discussion of *völkisch*-religious Grail mysticism see Sandra Franz, *Die Religion des Grals. Entwürfe arteigener Religiosität im Spektrum von völkischer Bewegung, Lebensform, Okkultismus, Neuheidentum und Jugendbewegung (1871–1945)*, Edition Archiv der deutschen Jugendbewegung (Schwalbach Ts.: Wochenschau-Verlag, 2009).

intuitive association and theories of racial memory to other esoteric systems such as yoga,[91] or added esoteric aspects to established antiquarian disciplines, such as historical architecture.[92] These protagonists were also active in the German Faith Movement as leading members or founders of their own groups, lodges, circles and journals.[93] Ariosophy thus became an integral part of German(ic) Faith throughout the 1920s.

However, it did not remain uncontested in a scene that was notoriously split amongst factions and idiosyncratic activists who each had their own personal mythology and claim to leadership. Other contested issues were the necessity of a formalized ritual and institutionalized priesthood, as well as the status of the Old-Icelandic sources. These issues played a role in the controversies between Ludwig Fahrenkrog's *Germanische Glaubensgemeinschaft* and Otto Sigfrid Reuter's *Deutschgläubige Gemeinschaft*. The latter rejected formalized religious practices along with a "cult of Wotan" based on ancient sources.[94] Aside from personal competition and religious questions, contemporary social

---

91 Friedrich Bernhard Marby (1882–1966) and Siegfried Adolf Kummer (1899–?) developed exercises called rune gymnastics or rune-yoga, complete with mudras (hand positions) and runic chanting, practices which are still popular amongst Asatruers today. Cf. Goodrick-Clarke, *The Occult Roots of Nazism*, 161f, and Bernd Wedemeyer-Kolwe, "Völkisch-religiöse Runengymnastiker im Nationalsozialismus," in *Die völkisch-religiöse Bewegung im Nationalsozialismus. Eine Beziehungs- und Konfliktgeschichte*, ed. Uwe Puschner and Clemens Vollnhals (Göttingen: Vandenhoeck & Ruprecht, 2012). For a detailed discussion of rune magic in Asatru, see Chapter 3.

92 Philipp Stauff (1876–1923) imagined hidden runic messages in the beams of half-timbered houses. Cf. Goodrick-Clarke, *The Occult Roots of Nazism*, 131 and 153–155, Gregor Hufenreuter, *Philipp Stauff. Ideologe, Agitator und Organisator im völkischen Netzwerk des Wilhelminischen Kaiserreichs. Zur Geschichte des Deutschvölkischen Schriftstellerverbandes, des Germanen-Ordens und der Guido-von-List-Gesellschaft* (Frankfurt a.M.: Peter Lang, 2011).

93 Rudolf John Gorsleben's (1883–1944) book *Die Hochzeit der Menschheit* (The Zenith of Mankind, 1930) is still read in contemporary Ariosophic and racial-religious circles. Another key figure was Lanz' publisher Herbert Reichstein (1892–1944), editor of the journal *Zeitschrift für Menschenkenntnis und Menschenschicksal* (Journal for the Knowledge of Man and Fate of Man). A comprehensive overview of Ariosophic activities after List can be found in Goodrick-Clarke, *The Occult Roots of Nazism*, 123–176.

94 The connections and controversies between the two associations and their leaders Fahrenkrog and Reuter are discussed by Uwe Puschner, "Deutsche Reformbühne und völkische Kultstätte. Ernst Wachler und das Harzer Bergtheater," in *Handbuch zur 'Völkischen Bewegung' 1871–1918*, ed. Uwe Puschner, Walter Schmitz, and Justus H. Ulbricht (Munich etc.: K.G. Saur, 1996), 222–262, and Junker, *Gott in uns!*.

CREATING THE PARADIGM   45

issues such as sexuality and reproduction also led to splits within the German Faith community.[95] The tendency to split and form new groups was accompanied by continual attempts to (re)unite the movement and to form umbrella organizations.[96] The best-known endeavor in this respect was launched in 1933 by Jakob Wilhelm Hauer (1882–1962) in the wake of Hitler and the NSDAP's rise to power. The internationally renowned Indologist and long-term activist in Germanic Faith contexts had been campaigning for years to unite all non-Christian, German religious splinter groups into one movement, and finally founded the *Arbeitsgemeinschaft Deutsche Glaubensbewegung* (Work Fellowship German Faith Movement). However, Hauer's ambition for his movement to become the official religion of the 'Third Reich' was quickly thwarted. A number of subgroups resigned from membership soon after the movement's foundation because they did not accept Hauer's claim to leadership, or else had their own sectarian agendas. At the same time, Hitler's power politics needed the support of the established churches and had no room for dissenting religious movements.[97] In spite of the fact that *völkisch* religious and Aryan occult ideas

---

95 A case in point is Ernst Hunkel's propagation of an alternative racial breeding program inspired by Willibald Hentschel. Here, the German race was to be actively improved through the foundation of breeding settlements in which one 'pure Aryan' man was to impregnate ten women, who would then raise the children collectively in the countryside. As a consequence, Hunkel was excluded from the *Deutscher Orden* and the *Deutschgläubige Gemeinschaft* in 1923. Cf. Uwe Puschner, "Mittgart – Eine völkische Utopie," in *Utopien, Zukunftsvorstellungen, Gedankenexperimente. Literarische Konzepte von einer 'anderen' Welt im abendländischen Denken von der Antike bis zur Gegenwart*, ed. Klaus Geus (Frankfurt a.M.: Peter Lang, 2011).

96 Together with a number of younger *Deutschgläubige*, whose associations had split off from the mother organization as well, Ernst Hunkel founded the *Orden der Nordungen* in 1924. This order had stronger leanings toward occultism, esotericism, Ariosophy, parapsychology, and psychoanalysis and included theories of Ludwig Klages, C.G. Jung and Friedrich Nietzsche into their system of belief. A new attempt at re-uniting the split groups was launched in 1927 with the *Nordische Glaubensgemeinschaft* which fell apart again already in 1928 due to major disputes between the founders, Otto Sigfrid Reuter and Norbert Seibertz. A more modest endeavor to at least establish a joint working group which could represent the diverse Germanic religious scene publicly was started in 1932, the *Nordisch-Religiöse Arbeitsgemeinschaft*. Cf. Ulrich Nanko, *Die Deutsche Glaubensbewegung. Eine historische und soziologische Untersuchung* (Marburg: diagonal-Verlag, 1993), 44–49.

97 For an extensive discussion of the foundation, rise, and fall of the *Deutsche Glaubensbewegung* see ibid. The only English-language investigation, authored by Karla Poewe, *New Religions and the Nazis* (New York: Routledge, 2006), greatly overestimates

were cultivated in certain National Socialist circles, e. g., in Hitler's 'chief ideologist' Alfred Rosenberg and his *Amt Rosenberg*[98] as well as in Heinrich Himmler's SS,[99] neither Ariosophy nor Germanic Faith groups in general gained widespread positive recognition.

The significance of the whole Germanic religious movement did not lie in the numbers of its adherents, it should be noted. Even in its heyday during the 1920s, the movement as a whole probably never had more than a couple of thousand organized members.[100] However, the movement counted amongst its ranks a considerable number of journalists, writers, artists, illustrators, teachers and scholars – (mostly male) members of an intellectual middle-class who were driven by the fear of losing influence and status in modern society. They proved to be active and effective disseminators of Neopagan ideas. Their imaginations of lost and regained national and cultural greatness fell on fertile ground, especially in the urban middle classes, who were driven by similar fears and hopes in connection to the rapid modernization, industrialization and urbanization of their country. Due to their activities and ideas about the nature of a pre-Christian Germanic faith and its renewal, concepts related to

---

    Hauer's influence on National Socialism. See also the English essay on the German Faith Movement by Wilhelm Hauer, "Origin of the German Faith Movement. An Alien or a German Faith? The Semitic Character of Christianity," in *Germany's New Religion*, ed. Wilhelm Hauer, Karl Heim, and Karl Adam (New York: The Abingdon Press, 1937) as well as the contemporary dissertation by Heinz Bartsch, *Die Wirklichkeitsmacht der Allgemeinen Deutschen Glaubensbewegung der Gegenwart* (Breslau: Ludwig, 1938).

98   The *Amt Rosenberg* promoted research of alleged pre-Christian cults and folklore and used it as the basis to develop non-Christian celebrations, a new German ritual tradition. Cf. Ernst Piper, "'Der Nationalsozialismus steht über allen Bekenntnissen.' Alfred Rosenberg und die völkisch-religiösen Erneuerungsbestrebungen," in *Die völkisch-religiöse Bewegung im Nationalsozialismus. Eine Beziehungs- und Konfliktgeschichte*, ed. Uwe Puschner and Clemens Vollnhals (Göttingen: Vandenhoeck & Ruprecht, 2012), 346, and Esther Gajek, "'Feiergestaltung' – Zur planmäßigen Entwicklung eines 'aus nationalsozialistischer Weltanschauung geborenen, neuen arteigenen Brauchtums' am Amt Rosenberg," in *Völkische Religion und Krisen der Moderne. Entwürfe 'arteigener' Glaubenssysteme seit der Jahrhundertwende*, ed. Stefanie v. Schnurbein and Justus H. Ulbricht (Würzburg: Königshausen & Neumann, 2001).

99   SS leader Heinrich Himmler sported an intense interest in popular *völkisch* historical theories and occult speculation and for a while employed the "magician" Karl Maria Wiligut (1866–1946), called "Weisthor" or "Himmler's Rasputin" who claimed to have direct access to the Aryan ancestral memory, cf. Goodrick-Clarke, *The Occult Roots of Nazism*, 177–191.

100   For an estimate of membership numbers in the individual groups see Nanko, *Die Deutsche Glaubensbewegung*.

Germanic Neopagan religion were able to take hold in other alternative movements such as the environmental movement, as well as in the academy and, most notably, in the aesthetic imagination: in literature, theater, and music.[101] Thus, German(ic) religious thought and a racialized or *völkisch* religion became more established in the 1920s and 30s, and the foundation was laid for the further development of a neo-Germanic religion later on in the 20th century.

A modest international spread of German Faith ideas already in the 1920s and 30s contributed to this as well. The *Deutschgläubige Gemeinschaft*, for instance, established and maintained contacts in the Netherlands and Scandinavian countries through the *Germanen-Ring*.[102] In Sweden, the cultural society *Samfundet Manhem*, founded in 1934, gathered sympathizers of National Socialism and held contacts with the *Deutsche Glaubensbewegung* through pastor Nils Hannerz.[103] Hauer's ideas spread in Norway through the small National Socialist subculture, which opposed the official National Socialist party's leader Vidkun Quisling and promoted a more radically racist and anti-Semitic approach. The circle around Hans S. Jacobsen and his journal *Ragnarok* also fostered a racial Nordic Heathen religion inspired by Jakob Wilhelm Hauer's ideas, which the liberal theologian Kristian Schjelderup had advanced in Norway. The conspiracy theories of the *Tannenberg Bund* were another source of inspiration in Germany.[104] This movement had been started by the psychiatrist Mathilde Ludendorff and her husband Erich, the famous World War I general. Its ideology was based on a fierce anti-Semitism, anti-masonism, anti-Catholicism, and anti-esotericism, which eventually encompassed a rejection of Christianity as well.[105]

---

101 For in depth discussions see Chapters 6, 8, and 9.
102 Nanko, *Die Deutsche Glaubensbewegung*, 46.
103 Anders Gerdmar, "Germanentum als Überideologie. Deutsch-schwedischer Theologenaustausch unter dem Hakenkreuz," in *Die völkisch-religiöse Bewegung im Nationalsozialismus. Eine Beziehungs- und Konfliktgeschichte*, ed. Uwe Puschner and Clemens Vollnhals (Göttingen: Vandenhoeck & Ruprecht, 2012). For a recent gender theoretical investigation of Mathilde von Ludendorff see Annika Spilker, *Geschlecht, Religion und völkischer Nationalismus. Die Ärztin und Antisemitin Mathilde von Kemnitz-Ludendorff (1877–1966)* (Frankfurt a.M.: Campus, 2013).
104 Cf. Terje Emberland, *Religion og rase. Nyhedenskap og nazisme i Norge 1933–1945* (Oslo: Humanist forlag, 2003), "Im Zeichen der Hagal-Rune. 'Arteigene' Religion und nationalsozialistischer Aktivismus in Norwegen," in *Die völkisch-religiöse Bewegung im Nationalsozialismus. Eine Beziehungs- und Konfliktgeschichte*, ed. Uwe Puschner and Clemens Vollnhals (Göttingen: Vandenhoeck & Ruprecht, 2012).
105 Cf. Bettina Amm, "Die Ludendorff-Bewegung im Nationalsozialismus – Annäherung und Abgrenzungsversuche," in *Die völkisch-religiöse Bewegung im Nationalsozialismus. Eine*

The Ludendorffs were also one of the many sources of inspiration for Alexander Rud Mills (1885–1964), who was responsible for transferring Germanic Neopagan ideas into an Anglo-American context. The Australian lawyer had traveled extensively in Europe between 1932 and 1935 and established contacts with British and German National Socialists. Driven by sympathies for National Socialism and a conviction of traditional Anglo-Saxon supremacy, he founded the *Anglecyn Church of Odin* in the 1930s and published his ideas of a racial, anti-Semitic and anti-Christian religion in his main work, *The Odinist Religion. Overcoming Jewish Christianity* (1939).[106] In the same year, a Commonwealth investigation was launched against him. He was briefly interned in 1942, partly because of his membership in the nationalist and racist movement *Australia First*, but mostly because he had a "fanatical regard for the German Nazi system and an equal hatred of the Jews."[107] Post-war attempts to establish the *First Church of Odin* bore equally scant results as his first attempt at founding a church, but as we shall see, his written legacy was to influence modern Odinism significantly.[108]

Post-War Revivals[109]

The very limited efficacy of Germanic Faith and Ariosophic groups in Germany between 1933 and 1945 had a paradoxical effect on the further development of Germanic Neopaganism in the 1950s and 60s. On the one hand, the organizational structures of neo-Germanic groups were largely destroyed, the membership reduced to a few faithful individuals, and *völkisch* ideology in general discredited. On the other hand, in West Germany, *völkisch* religious groups were able to profit from the fact of their persecution and re-organize under the protection of the constitution, which granted freedom of religion.

Beziehungs- und Konfliktgeschichte, ed. Uwe Puschner and Clemens Vollnhals (Göttingen: Vandenhoeck & Ruprecht, 2012).

106 Alexander Rud Mills, *The Odinist Religion. Overcoming Jewish Christianity* (Melbourne: Ruskin Press, 1939).
107 Peter Henderson, "Frank Browne and the Neo-Nazis," *Labour History* 89 (2005).
108 Cf. Kaplan, *Radical Religion in America*, 15f; Gardell, *Gods of the Blood*, 167–170. See also the website for the *Odinic Rite Australia* which hails Rud Mills as one of their prophets and provides information on his life and work: http://www.reocities.com/osred/Rud_Mills_Brief_Biography.htm (last accessed March 03, 2014).
109 The following section is based on my article about the revival of Germanic Neopaganism in post-War Germany: Schnurbein, "Transformationen völkischer Religion seit 1945."

Thus, the remaining members of the Ariosophic *Guido-von-List-Gesellschaft* continued their activities immediately after 1945 based on the 1936 statutes. Already in 1951, Wilhelm Kusserow had founded the *Artgemeinschaft*[110] as a continuation of the *Nordische Glaubensgemeinschaft*, which had split-off from the *Deutschgläubige Gemeinschaft* in 1927. In 1957, the *Deutschgläubige Gemeinschaft* was re-established as well, and in the same year, Hermann Musfeldt founded the *Goden-Orden*, championing a race-based Ariosophy-inspired religion.[111]

Leading members of the *Deutsche Glaubensbewegung*, including its founder Jakob Wilhelm Hauer, gathered into two organizations after 1945:[112] the *Deutsche Unitarier Religionsgemeinschaft* (German Unitarian Religious Community, *DUR*)[113] and the *Freie Akademie* (Free Academy).[114] Whereas the *DUR* was a free-religious organization, the *Freie Akademie* fashioned itself as an academic institution with the goal of (re-)establishing the study of religion. Together with the aforementioned religious groups, these cultural organizations played an integral role as communicative centers where organized right-wing extremism was able to re-group. Here, central ideas of the so-called New Right were conceived – a movement which in turn harked back to the Conservative Revolution rather than to National Socialism and

---

110   The term is hard to translate into English. In German, "Art" is a biological term meaning 'species' and has been used to avoid the term 'race.' 'Artgemeinschaft' thus refers to the community of our kind, our nature, our ways, or, in fact, our race.

111   For an account of the early history of the *Goden-Orden* see their journal *Die kosmische Wahrheit. Kosmisch-religiöse Blätter zur Pflege persönlichen Lebens* [The Cosmic Truth. Cosmic-Religious Papers for the Cultivation of Personal Life], here no. 10 (1964), 4.

112   The post-war regrouping of the former *Deutsche Glaubensbewegung* is outlined in Ulrich Nanko, "Religiöse Gruppenbildungen vormaliger 'Deutschgläubiger' nach 1945," in *Antisemitismus, Paganismus, Völkische Religion – Antisemitism, Paganism, Voelkisch Religion*, ed. Hubert Cancik and Uwe Puschner (Munich: K.G. Saur, 2004).

113   For an account of the German branch of the Unitarian faith, which took a very different path than its liberal North American counterpart, see Wolfgang Seibert, *Deutsche Unitarier-Religionsgemeinschaft. Entwicklung, Praxis und Organisation* (Stuttgart: Quell-Verlag, 1989). Seibert takes an apologetic stance and does not mention the connections between the *DUR* and right-wing extremism in Germany. Peter Kratz, *Die Götter des New Age. Im Schnittpunkt von 'Neuem Denken,' Faschismus und Romantik* (Berlin: Elefanten Press, 1994), on the other hand, is able to trace these connections, however his analysis of the ideological connections is too simplistic and overly influenced by his own anti-fascist ideology.

114   Cf. Ulrich Nanko, "Von 'Deutsch' nach 'Frei' und zurück? Jakob Wilhelm Hauer und die Frühgeschichte der Freien Akademie," in *Das evangelische Württemberg zwischen Weltkrieg und Wiederaufbau*, ed. Rainer Lächele and Jörg Thierfelder (Stuttgart: 1995).

the 'old right' and which emerged at the end of the 1960s in France and Germany.[115]

Another important area in which right-wing extremists re-grouped and networked after 1945 were youth organizations such as the *Wiking Jugend* (Viking Youth) from 1952 or the *Bund Heimattreuer Jugend* (League of Homeland Loyalist Youth, *BHJ*), a *völkisch* nationalist organization which based itself on the ideals of the youth movement.[116] They provided a forum which not only recruited amongst the younger generation, but where later leaders of the *völkisch* religious scene of the 1970s also gained their first experiences and contacts.[117]

---

115   Cf. Dudek and Jaschke, *Entstehung und Entwicklung des Rechtsextremismus*, 1, 42. For a discussion of the New Right and its intertwinement with modern Asatru see Chapter 4. Amongst the organizations is the *Deutsches Kulturwerk europäischen Geistes* (German Cultural Society of European Spirit, *DKEG*) founded in 1950 by the former National Socialist cultural functionary Herbert Böhme, who was involved in the foundation of the *NPD*, the German right-wing party. The *DKEG* was closely connected to the *DUR* and was unique in its ability to gather authors tainted by their involvement in National Socialist politics under allegedly apolitical goals. (cf. Kratz, *Die Götter des New Age*, 294, Dudek and Jaschke, *Entstehung und Entwicklung des Rechtsextremismus*, 1, 44–47). The *Gesellschaft für freie Publizistik* (Association for Free Journalism, *GfP*) was able to strengthen the contacts of the *DKEG* and other cultural and religious organizations to right-wing publishing houses (cf. ibid., 47–50). The *Weltbund zum Schutz des Lebens* (World League for the Protection of Life, *WSL*), founded in 1958, and its conference center, *Collegium Humanum* in Vlotho, have been important links between this scene of cultural right-wing extremism and the green movement as well as anthroposophical circles, especially during the time when Georg Werner Haverbeck was its chairman (cf. Reinhard Opitz, *Faschismus ud Neofaschismus*, 2 vols., vol. II (Neofaschismus in der Bundesrepublik) (Cologne: Pahl-Rugenstein, 1988), 53; Raimund Hethey and Peter Kratz, *In bester Gesellschaft. Antifa-Recherche zwischen Konservativismus und Neo-Faschismus* (Göttingen: Die Werkstatt, 1991), 128–135; Kurt Hirsch, *Rechts von der Union. Personen, Organisationen, Parteien seit 1945. Ein Lexikon* (Munich: Knesebeck & Schuler, 1989), 165; Volkmar Wölk, *Natur und Mythos. Ökologiekonzepte der 'Neuen' Rechten im Spannungsfeld zwischen Blut und Boden und New Age*, Natur und Mythos ed. (Duisburg: DISS-Texte, 1992), 6–19.) See also Chapter 6.

116   Hirsch, *Rechts von der Union*, 130f; Dudek and Jaschke, *Entstehung und Entwicklung des Rechtsextremismus*, 1, 436–480. The national and international networking of right-wing extremists with the help of cultural organizations, publishing houses and journals is also discussed at length in Gert Heidenreich and Juliane Wetzel, "Die organisierte Verwirrung. Nationale und internationale Verbindungen im rechtsextremistischen Spektrum," in *Rechtsextremismus in der Bundesrepublik. Voraussetzungen, Zusammenhänge, Wirkungen*, ed. Wolfgang Benz (Frankfurt a.M.: 1989).

117   Both *Collegium Humanum*, the *Heimattreue Deutsche Jugend*, a split off from the *BHJ* and the *Viking Jugend* have come under the scrutiny of the German Federal Agency for

Witchcraft and the Celtic Revival

As important as the German *völkisch* forerunners are for contemporary Asatru, the stigma connected to them posed a major obstacle for the post-war expansion and renewal of Germanic Neopaganism. Another wave of esoteric and occult Neopagan revival, the Wicca movement, or witchcraft, which started in England in the 1950s and gained momentum in the 1970s, helped shift general attitudes toward such revivals and indirectly also influenced Asatru. Like Germanic Neopaganism, Wicca has its roots in 19th century European attempts to reconstruct ancient, pre-Christian religions.[118] Although non-Anglo-Saxon in its orientation, it emerged from a mixture of 19th century sources very similar to that of neo-Germanic faith in Germany: English and German fictional accounts of Greek, Roman, Oriental, and also Druidic and Norse religion and scholarly studies. These in turn were employed by occultists and mysticists, culminating in Helena Petrovna Blavatsky's theosophy, which combined scholarly claims with religious revelation. In England, these Romantic images were combined with Enlightenment ideas of joyous, liberationist, and life-affirming (Germanic) Pagans – a strand of thought that also influenced German Faith groups, especially through the mediation of liberal 19th century freethinkers.[119] Wicca's 'invention' of an ancient European earth goddess and her companion, the horned god (Pan), can be interpreted as the result of collaboration between poets and scholars. What scholars like Johan Jakob Bachofen, Sir Arthur Evans, Jane Ellen Harrison or James Frazer configured as ancient matriarchies and erotic rites of fertility were in fact projections back in time to what poets had imagined earlier.[120] This type of 'collaboration' between fiction writers and scholars continued into the 20th century, involving authors such as Rider Haggard, Rudyard Kipling, Richard Yeats, D.H. Lawrence and Dion Fortune, who then inspired scholars such as Robert Graves and Margaret Murray. Masonic orders and their European occultist successors (e.g., the Rosicrucians, theosophy, and the *Order of the Golden Dawn*) provided Wicca with a pattern of ritual and organization.[121]

National Security (*Bundesamt für Verfassungsschutz*) in recent years. Cf. for example http://www.spiegel.de/politik/deutschland/0,1518,616421,00.html, last accessed October 19, 2011.

118 The most extensive study of the Wicca movement's inception and pre-history in the 19th century has been offered by Ronald Hutton in *The Triumph of the Moon*. This brief sketch is mainly based on this work.
119 Cf. ibid., 21f.
120 Cf. ibid., 39, and 43ff.
121 Cf. ibid., Chapter 4.

Three lay scholars are of crucial importance to the blending of 19th century academic thought (mostly folklore and anthropology) with the popular folk belief in witches, and thus making them directly involved in the formation of modern witchcraft. The oldest of them, Charles G. Leland (1824–1903), had been directly exposed to the emergent discipline of folklore (*Volkskunde*) in Germany in the mid-19th century and to contemporary radical nationalist ideas. All of these influences were merged in his most influential work, *Aradia; or the Gospel of the Witches* (1899).[122] Also Margaret Murray (1862–1963), a trained Egyptologist, attended lectures at German universities. There she was influenced by theories of 'survivalism' of ancient rites in folklore and customs which had been taken from Mannhardt and developed by James Frazer, the famous initiator of the myth-ritual school in religious studies and theorist of magic.[123] Murray's book *The Witch Cult of Western Europe* (1921) gained some scholarly response and spawned an impressive popular enthusiasm.[124] Her idea that the people burned as witches in early modernity were actually practitioners of an ancient European fertility cult inspired the British civil servant and hobby-folklorist Gerald Gardner to claim that he had been initiated into ancient rites by English witches, which he now, breaking his oath of secrecy, revealed to the English public. Murray's theories are largely refuted and it is by now widely acknowledged, also in Wiccan circles, that Gardner's claims to authenticity are not based on reality (he constructed his own religion out of books and the practices of secret orders such as the *Hermetic Order of the Golden Dawn* and the *Ordo Templi Orientis*).[125] Nevertheless, Gardner's and his later followers' (re-)construction of the alleged witches' rituals led to the formation of a broad movement. Throughout the 1970s and 80s it branched into various subgroups with vastly differing ideas about politics, sexuality and gender, ranging from conservative, male-oriented covens to the progressive, feminist earth-centered *Reclaiming Witches* around Starhawk in the San Francisco Bay Area.[126]

---

122 Cf. Sabina Magliocco, *Witching Culture. Folklore and Neo-Paganism in America* (Philadelphia: University of Pennsylvania Press, 2004), 44f.
123 Cf. ibid., 42f, Susanne Lanwerd, *Mythos, Mutterrecht und Magie. Zur Geschichte religionswissenschaftlicher Begriffe* (Berlin: Dietrich Reimer, 1993), 112–146.
124 Cf. Magliocco, *Witching Culture*, 47.
125 Hutton demonstrates this in detail, and at the same time emphasizes the "extraordinarily novel" form of religion which "concealed innovation under a language of continuity and restitution." Hutton, *The Triumph of the Moon*, 236.
126 For a still-valid comprehensive description of the various strands of Wicca and other Neopagan groups in America, see Margot Adler, *Drawing Down the Moon. Witches, Druids, Goddess-Worshippers, and Other Pagans in America Today* 4. ed. (New York: Penguin, 2006

We can conclude that the basis for the emergence of modern witchcraft in England is a similar mix of Romanticist thought, nationalism, fictional literature and anthropological theory as in the case of the German scene.[127] Moreover, a number of the major thinkers and inventors of this fictional ancient religion were influenced by German thought. There are other parallels as well. In both the English and the German case, adherents of the new pagan religions express alienation from and reject the dominant social order, the particular form their national state has taken. In both cases, there is also a tendency to identify with a defeated idealized group of the historical past (the ancient Germans or the ancient Celts). In the course of such operations, a number of significant dichotomies were invoked: dogmatic belief was rejected in favor of ritual, the cognitive mind in favor of the body and sexuality, the alienated in favor of authenticity, discourse in favor of imagination – and at times, and more so in Wicca than in the outspokenly masculinist German and Anglo-Saxon ideologies – the masculine in favor of the feminine. The main bearers of these movements were middle-class or lower middle-class male intellectuals fearing a loss of influence and status in capitalist and commercialized modernity.

This counter-cultural search for 'authentic' roots, the interest in the creation and execution of new rituals and the organization either in secret orders or in other small initiatory groups facilitated exchanges and sympathetic meetings between English and German forerunners of today's Neoaganism. Nonetheless, the significant differences between the revival of witchcraft in England and attempts to create a German(ic) faith in Germany should not be overlooked. The adherents of modern witchcraft had no interest in creating a new state based on a new (old) religion. Their agenda was less nationalist and more counter-cultural, whereas the German movement took a radical nationalist position from the beginning. The reasons for this can probably be found in the very different situations the two states were in. Britain was a proud imperial power at the time, held up partly by a strong Anglican and Presbyterian state church. The political problems were related to inner differences between several groups, such as the English, the Scots, the Welsh, the Irish etc. Moreover, the political fears of middle-class individuals were mostly related to a loss of imperial power, and later on, a nostalgic mourning for its loss. As has been demonstrated, in Germany, the creation of a nation state and a national religion was of eminent importance for leading intellectuals and had been so for most of the 19th century.

[1979]). For an account of Reclaiming Witches in San Francisco see Salomonsen, *Enchanted Feminism*.

127   See also Magliocco, *Witching Culture*, 5.

CHAPTER 2

Creating a Religion: The Emergence and Development of Late Twentieth-Century Asatru

When and how exactly did Asatru emerge out of the scattered and heterogenous Romantic, neo-Romantic and *völkisch* tradition described in the previous chapter? Many Asatruers tell the founding myth of an astonishingly spontaneous and independent appearance of unrelated Germanic Neopagan groups in different countries: Britain, USA, Iceland, Sweden, and Germany – a phenomenon which some interpret as the re-surfacing of archetypal mythic and religious powers.

This apparently spontaneous emergence of Asatru in different countries was fed by two currents related to shifts within Germanic Neopaganism as well as mainstream discourses. Beginning in the 1970s, older *völkisch* religious groups and ideologies such as German Faith, Ariosophy and Odinism re-grouped and once again recruited a younger membership. At the same time, the growing popularity of Wicca, the New Age, and the esoteric movement in the wake of the hippie era awakened the interest of a broader counter-cultural public in non-Christian religious alternatives. These currents intersected in complex ways. Having had ties to the Western occultist tradition all along, Germanic Neopaganism opened up to new alternative religious ideas. Simultaneously, spiritual counter-cultures harking back to Romantic ideas of survival and revival developed an interest in 'indigenous' cultural and religious traditions. The idea of a faith rooted in pre-Christian Northern Europe did not seem far-fetched any longer.

The emergence and development of Asatru since the 1970s can roughly be divided into two periods: 1) A period of foundation in the 1970s and 80s, during which the first Asatru groups were formed in Iceland, Sweden, Norway, Britain, and the USA, and the *völkisch* religious community in Germany started its renewal. It was during this period that the central concerns and controversies that were to become crucial for Asatru's further development were formulated. This period was marked by a gradual shift from racial religions to ethnicist paradigms. 2) A period of establishment and consolidation in the 1990s and 2000s, when the controversies of the first period peaked, initiating a process of reformation and adaption to the surrounding societies, their changing perceptions, and their organization of religions. During this period, a-racist Asatru started to gain ground.

In Search of Religiosity: Germanic Neopaganism 1970–1990

The continuities between modern Asatru and *völkisch* religion, as well as the later attempts to become emancipated from this tradition and to reform the movement, can be seen most clearly in the German case.[1] Here, the renewed interest in the 'Germanic' version of a new Paganism originated in the previously mentioned *völkisch* and post-war right-wing religious and cultural circles. This milieu's opening up to popular New Age and esoteric currents was initiated by the *Armanen-Orden* (founded in 1976) and its leaders, Adolf and Sigrun Schleipfer (who later called herself Sigrun von Schlichting).[2] The two were long-term activists in the *völkisch* religious and right-wing extremist scene – Adolf in the *Guido-von-List-Gesellschaft*, Sigrun in the right-wing youth organization *Bund Heimattreuer Jugend* (Association of Youth True to the Homeland),[3] and both in the *Goden-Orden*. The racial-religious *Armanen-Orden* is a hierarchical nine-level initiatory order. It promotes a racial mysticism inspired by Guido von List's and other Ariosophists' teachings. In the 1980s, it began to include popular Celtic elements, teachings from the emerging goddess movement and feminist spirituality, and elements of a popularized Native American spirituality. With this, and with Sigrun Schleipfer's

---

1 In the 1980s and early 90s, I did extensive fieldwork and conducted interviews in the then-active Asatru milieu, mainly with the *Armanen-Orden* and related groups. These findings were published in two books (Schnurbein, *Religion als Kulturkritik*; *Göttertrost in Wendezeiten*). Unless noted otherwise, the discussion of the emergence of German Germanic Neopaganism is based on these publications and the sources used there.

2 Earlier, she had gone under the names Sigrun Strauß-Hammerbacher, and Sigrun Schleipfer-Friese. As the daughter of NSDAP-Kreisleiter (district leader) Hans Wilhelm Hammerbacher, she was socialized into the *volkisch* religious milieu. Hammerbacher authored books and brochures such as *Midgards Morgen* (Midgard's morning), *Die Donar-Eiche. Geschichte eines Heiligtums* (The Donar Oak. History of a Sacred Place) or *Irminsul. Das germanische Lebensbaumsymbol* (Irminsul. The Germanic Symbol of the Life-Tree). Some of his books were sold through the mail order book store which Adolf Schleipfer used to run. Currently, they are re-edited by Orion-Heimreiter Verlag, owned by right-wing publisher Dietmar Munier. Munier was also active in the *Bund Heimattreuer Jugend* in the 1970s (cf. Felix Krautkrämer, "Wachwechsel in Coburg. Politische Publizistik: Der Verleger Dietmar Munier hat offenbar das Traditionsmagazin 'Nation & Europa' gekauft," *Junge Freiheit* 42, no. 09 (2009)). For more on Munier see e.g. Ministry of Interior of Land Schleswig-Holstein, ed. *Verfassungsschutzbericht 2008 [Report on the Protection of the Constitution]* (Kiel: The Ministry of Interior of Land Schleswig-Holstein, 2008), Stephan Braun and Daniel Hörsch, *Rechte Netzwerke – eine Gefahr* (Wiesbaden: VS Verlag, 2004).

3 See Jochen Maes, *Dokumentation: 'Völkische' Ideologien und Gruppierungen* (Berlin: PREMA-Presseagentur, 1983).

appearances at events within the esoteric scene, the *Armanen-Orden* was able to attract a significant contingent of younger members not only from the right-wing political spectrum but also from the broader alternative religious milieu. The racial-religious *Artgemeinschaft* entered a phase of renewal in the early 1980s as well. It attracted a younger following, although not from the New Age and occultist contexts it rejected. This was due to the Hamburg right-wing lawyer Jürgen Rieger's activities. Rieger had forced Wilhelm Kusserow out of the organization and taken over the leadership in 1983, which he held until his death in 2009.[4]

The first groups in Germany that promoted a religion resembling modern Asatru were founded in the 1980s by younger members of the *Artgemeinschaft* and the *Armanen-Orden* in Berlin. Out of the several alternately collaborating and competing small regional groups grew two groups,[5] both of which are still active today: *Heidnische Gemeinschaft* and ANSE. The *Heidnische Gemeinschaft* (Heathen Community) was founded by Géza von Neményi in 1985. Neményi eventually left the group and reactivated Ludwig Fahrenkrog's *Germanische Glaubensgemeinschaft* (GGG) in 1991, harking back to one of the first Germanic Faith groups in Germany.[6] These ethnicist groups were the first to turn away

---

4 Jürgen Rieger was widely known in Germany as a lawyer for right-wing extremists, neo-Nazis, and Holocaust deniers. In the 1960s, he was active in the *Bund Heimattreuer Jugend* and later on in the racist *Gesellschaft für biologische Anthropologie, Eugenik und Verhaltensforschung* (Society for biological anthropology, eugenics and behavioral science). In his later years, he used his significant inheritance to finance centers for right-wing extremist organizations and youth groups and served as vice chairman for the right-wing party, NPD. Cf. Juliane Wetzel, "Die Maschen des rechten Netzes. Nationale und internationale Verbindungen im rechtsextremen Spektrum," in *Rechtsextremismus in Deutschland. Voraussetzungen, Zusammenhänge, Wirkungen*, ed. Wolfgang Benz (Frankfurt a.M.: Fischer, 1994), 171; Sven Röbel, "NPD-Vizechef Rieger ist tot," Spiegel Online, 29.09.2009, http://www.spiegel.de/politik/deutschland/prominenter-rechtsextremist-npd-vizechef-rieger-ist-tot-a-658206.html, last accessed January 05, 2015; Ingolf Christiansen, Rainer Fromm, and Hartmut Zinser, *Brennpunkt Esoterik. Okkultismus, Satanismus, Rechtsradikalismus* (Hamburg: Behörde für Inneres, 2004), 149–152, Stefan v. Hoyningen-Huene, *Religiosität bei rechtsextrem orientierten Jugendlichen* (Münster/Hamburg/London: LIT Verlag, 2003), 232f.

5 *Der Hain* (The Grove) the journal of the *Gemeinschaft für heidnisches Leben* (*Community for Heathen Life*), a third group emerging in this context, has remained active as an internet publication (http://www.derhain.de/, last accessed February 26, 2014). Its editor Matthias Wenger is engaged in several Neopagan contexts. See also Chapters 8 and 9.

6 For Ludwig Fahrenkrog and the original GGG see Chapter 1. The foundation of this group, which he wanted to become a significant umbrella organization for all Asatruers in Germany, brought Neményi into conflict with Jürgen Rieger's *Artgemeinschaft*, which also laid claim to being the direct successor to the *Germanische Glaubensgemeinschaft*. However,

from Ariosophic beliefs and aim at reconstructing an allegedly authentic Germanic religion based on Old-Icelandic sources and relevant research within folklore and archaeology. They also installed statutes requiring their members to distance themselves from fascism and racism, holding fast to a strongly ethnicist line. Competing with the GGG was another umbrella organization, the racial-religious *Arbeitsgemeinschaft naturreligiöser Stammesverbände Europas* (ANSE, Working Group of Nature Religious Tribal Associations of Europe), founded by Sigrun von Schlichting in 1990. For a number of years it served as a networking platform for different neo-Germanic groups, including the *Armanen-Orden*, the *Artgemeinschaft*, the *Deutschgläubige Gemeinschaft*, and organized national and later on international meetings.

The international network, to which the ANSE as well as the GGG belonged, also included the ethnicist English *Odinic Rite*, one of the earliest and most internationally influential post-war Heathen foundations. It goes back to the initiative of John Yeowell, who in his youth had been a member of the French Foreign Legion and a bodyguard for British fascist leader Oswald Mosley.[7] Yeowell was inspired by John Gibbs-Bailey, who had been an Odinist since the 1930s (and thus had probably had contact with Alexander Rud Mills' teachings).[8] In 1973, the two men, under the pseudonyms Stubba and Hoskuld, took the initiative of forming a *Committee for the Restoration of the Odinic Rite*, which dissolved and was converted into the *Odinic Rite* in 1979, and then registered as an official charity in 1988. With its slogan "Faith, Folk, Family" and the claim that Odinism is the "organic religion of the Northern-European peoples,"[9]

---

the courts ruled in favor of Neményi. Cf. Schnurbein, *Göttertrost in Wendezeiten*, 42; Katrin Riedel, "Von Gott und den Göttern. Eine komparative Untersuchung der neuheidnischen Germanischen Glaubens-Gemeinschaft(en)," *Zeitschrift für Religions- und Geistesgeschichte* 66, no. 3/4 (2014).

7 This claim was made by an early member of the OR, Stephen Flowers/Edred Thorsson. Cf. Edred, *History of the Rune-Gild*, vol. III (The Reawakening of the Gild 1980–2005) (Smithville, TX: The Rune-Gild, 2007), 103.

8 It is not quite clear how strongly Yeowell was influenced in the beginning by Alexander Rud Mills' writings. Rud Mills is mentioned on the OR website as an important promoter of Odinism, and his book *The Call of Our Ancient Nordic Religion* is for sale on the OR website (http://www.odinic-rite.org/main/the-call-of-our-ancient-nordic-religion/, last accessed February 26, 2014). See also Hengest/OR, "In Memory of John Yeowell – 'Stubba,'" The Odinic Rite, http://www.odinic-rite.org/main/in-memory-of-john-yeowell-%e2%80%9cstubba%e2%80%9d/, last accessed June 03, 2011.

9 Cf. Schnurbein, *Religion als Kulturkritik*, 138. The account given there is based on information material by the OR, amongst others a flyer "Odinists say 'Yes!' to life." Many of the formulations there can also be found on the OR's homepage today. See www.odinic-rite.org.

the tightly structured group, which bases its coherence on a system of life-long oaths, established itself as a leading ethnicist Asatru group early on.

Alexander Rud Mills' 1930s version of Odinism was particularly influential for one of the new groups in the USA, Else Christensen's *Odinist Fellowship*. The inception of the *Odinist Fellowship* is a prime example of the international roots of radical racial-religious Asatru. Else Christensen (1913–2005)[10] was a native of Denmark, where she was involved with both revolutionary unionism and the national Bolshevist wing of the early National Socialist movement at a young age. After her emigration to Canada in 1951, she further pursued "her interest in class-based racial radicalism"[11] and discovered the writings of Alexander Rud Mills. Christensen combined Mills' theories with those of the American anti-Semitic National Socialist Francis Parker Yockey and with Jungian philosophy. From this, she developed Odinism as a racial religion. Initially it was designed as a discreet vehicle to establish her cultural pessimist, anti-Semitic and radical racial agenda in a religious cloak. It was thus not her primary interest to support a polytheistic religious agenda. Rather, she followed a path that is reminiscent of the German Faith Movement of the early 20th century. Christensen was looking for cultural manifestations of the 'Germanic racial spirit' in an idealized Nordic past, which was to be emulated and revived by way of a 'retribalization' of society.

According to his own retrospective claims, the founder of the other influential early North American Asatru group, Stephen McNallen, did not have a racial agenda when he established the *Viking Brotherhood* around 1970, nor did his "pagan epiphany [...] spring from the leftist/hippy/Age-of-Aquarius counterculture of the 1960s."[12] Rather, it was spurred by an anti-clerical affect, "the perception that the God of the Bible was a tyrant and that his followers were willing slaves, and an admiration for the heroism and vitality of the Norsemen as depicted in popular literature."[13] It was once his group was renamed the *Asatru Free Assembly* in the mid-1970s that he started adopting the ethnicist assumption of "an innate connection between Germanic Paganism and the Germanic peoples."[14] The AFA developed a structure of regional subgroups, the *Kindreds*; and interest groups, the *Guilds*; and started devising rituals. Leading

---

10   The information on Else Christensen is taken from Gardell, *Gods of the Blood*, 166–174.
11   Ibid., 167.
12   Stephen A. McNallen, "Three Decades of the Ásatú Revival in America," in *Tyr: Myth – Culture – Tradition II*, ed. Joshua Buckley and Michael Moynihan (Atlanta: Ultra, 2003/04), 205.
13   Ibid., 205, cf. Kaplan, *Radical Religion in America*, 18.
14   McNallen, "Three Decades of the Ásatú Revival in America," 207.

protagonists of later Asatru groups on the American continent, for example Edred Thorsson/Stephen Flowers (*Rune Gild, Ring of Troth*), Valguard Murray (*Asatru Alliance*), and Prudence Priest (*Ring of Troth*, later *American Vinland Association*) began their religious careers in the AFA. Accusations and internal controversies around the AFA's involvement with racists and National Socialists caused considerable turmoil in the 1980s. It remains unclear to what degree these controversies contributed to the dissolution of the AFA around 1986.[15] However, the disagreements around racial-religious and ethnicist versions of Asatru persisted into the 1990s, when former AFA members started the current leading Asatru groups in the USA (*The Troth, Asatru Folk Assembly* and the *Asatru Alliance*).

As we have seen, modern Asatru in Germany, Britain, and the USA had links to *völkisch* religious ideology; either directly, as in the German case, or indirectly through Odinism, in the Anglo-American cases. Early attempts at installing Asatru as a religious alternative in the Scandinavian countries differ from this picture. They seem to mainly emerge out of counter-cultural impulses. This is true as well for the most nationally successful and most internationally important newly founded Asatru group of the 1970s, the Icelandic *Ásatrúarfélagið* (the Asatru Association or *Ásatrúarmenn* – 'Asatru-Men,' as they were called initially), which was formed around 1972. Nevertheless, this counter-cultural, a-racist group was supported considerably by a group called *Nýalssinna* in its years of establishment. This spiritist organization was founded in 1950 based on the writings of geologist Dr. Helgi Péturss. It combined spiritist, theosophical and nationalist ideas with scientific elements, claiming that the spirits who appeared in séances were inhabitants of other planets and communicated with humans through dreams and telepathic means. For Péturss, the Nordic gods were denizens of remote stars who had supposedly reached a higher level of consciousness. They were now active as spiritual leaders of mankind, speaking especially to the supposedly highly developed Icelanders.[16]

---

15   This is the conclusion Jeffrey Kaplan, *Radical Religion in America*, 19, draws, and Mathias Gardell, *Gods of the Blood*, 260, follows. McNallen himself states the contrary: that the AFA's demise "had nothing to do with racial politics," but was due to him and his wife being overworked, and thus "unable to continue putting in the workload required to sustain the group without financial compensation." McNallen, "Three Decades of the Ásatú Revival in America," 208f.

16   Spiritism and theosophy had a unique position in Iceland as the "ideology of the new bourgeoisie and the middle classes," during the second and the third decades of the 20th century. Spiritist ideas were instrumental in the process of nation building and the move towards independence from Denmark, which Iceland gained only in 1944. Medieval Icelandic sources on mythological themes, the Eddas and the Sagas, which held an

According to church historian Pétur Pétursson, it was the support of members of *Nýalssinna*, not least its leader Þorsteinn Guðjónsson, which provided the organizational structure and PR know-how[17] required to attain official government recognition as early as 1973 – a fact which gave rise to the suspicion that the group might have had ties to racist and even National Socialist ideologies.[18] Such allegations were eventually refuted by pointing to the fact that National Socialism was not a Neopagan movement, but rather closely allied with the Christian churches, and also by combining the application for government recognition with a call for "true freedom of religion."[19] The inner coherence of the membership (consisting of heterogeneous counter-cultural, anti-clerical and nationalist circles) and the development of rituals in the 1970s and 80s was the work of one charismatic man: its religious leader, *Allsherjargóði*[20] Sveinbjörn Beinteinsson (1924–1993). Having been attracted to Helgi Péturss' writings in his youth,[21] the farmer and autodidactic poet of the traditional Icelandic genre

---

unquestioned status as foundational elements of Icelandic cultural heritage and thus also of constructions of national identity, were frequently read in the light of theosophical and spiritist theories. Cf. Pétur Pétursson, *Church and Social Change. A Study of the Secularization Process in Iceland 1830–1930*, vol. 4, Studies in Religious Experience and Behavior (Helsingborg: Plus Ultra, 1983), 164 and 169f. See also *Asasamfundet på Island och massmedia*, ed. Religionssociologiska Institutet, vol. 185:1, Forskningsrapport (Stockholm: Religionssociologiska Institutet, 1985), 27 note 2, and 1–3.

17 *Asasamfundet på Island och massmedia*, 185:1, 10.

18 In the 1970s, much of the criticism was directed against Þorsteinn Guðjónsson, who tried to introduce overtly right-wing political issues into *Ásatrúarfélagið*. Although he was briefly successful with one resolution, taking a strong stance against abortion in 1974, he failed to establish this political direction within Asatru. He consequently founded a political organization, *Norrænt Mankyn* (Nordic Race) in 1982, as a forum for his anti-immigrant and pro-life views. Jonsson, "Ásatrú á Íslandi við upphaf 21. aldar," 151–153. Current Allsherjargodi Hilmar Örn Hilmarsson assesses this initiative in retrospect with the following words: "They were deservedly treated as anachronistic clowns." (Correspondence with Hilmar Örn Hilmarsson (Ásatrúarfélagið), 2012) The importance of Þorsteinn Guðjónsson for the international network of Asatru is discussed below.

19 Pétursson, *Asasamfundet på Island och massmedia*, 185:1, 7–12; Sveinbjörn Beinteinsson, *Correspondence with the Icelandic Ministry of Justice and Church* (Reykjavík: Archive Pétur Pétursson, 1972).

20 *Allsherjargodi* (All-warring chieftain) was a title in medieval Commonwealth Iceland for the person who was recognized as the Goði in the district of the first Norse settler in Iceland. It was his task to sanctify the annual assembly of chieftains, the Allthing. The *Ásatrúarfélagið* uses such medieval terms also for other functions within the group, the most important next to the *Allsherjargodi* being the "lawspeaker" (*Lögsögumaður*).

21 Cf. Correspondence with Hilmar Örn Hilmarsson (Ásatrúarfélagið).

CREATING A RELIGION

of *Rímur* was already a well-known character by the time he gained the status of a key figure for Asatruers worldwide.

Due to Iceland's official recognition of Asatru, its community became the most significant internationally. Sweden, by comparison, sported the most lively and diverse milieu in the Nordic countries. It was comprised of a number of small groups representing everything from loose networks to hierarchical initiatory groups, and from a-racist New Age interpretations of the Nordic to strictly ethnicist and nationalist understandings of Asatru. The first attempt to establish an organized group, the ethnicist *Breidablikk-Gildet*, was made in 1975 by Arne Sjöberg (1921–2000). Sjöberg had a background in Sweden's equivalent to the life reform movement, the teetotaling *Frisksportrörelsen* (Movement for Sport and Health). *Breidablikk-Gildet* was organized as an order, with an initial structure patterned after the Good Templars. It had its most successful period in the mid-1980s with an estimated 130 members, but folded after Arne Sjöberg's death in 2000.[22] Its main goal was cultural, rather than religious in the narrow sense. Its focus was the cultivation of national tradition and history.

This ethnicist and nationalist orientation facilitated contacts to militant right-wing milieus, resulting in controversies with an a-racist group that was influential for the formation of later Asatru, the neo-shamanic network *Yggdrasil*.[23] *Yggdrasil* grew out of a small group in Stockholm which cultivated an interest in neo-shamanism in the wake of the Carlos Castaneda's books' popularity.[24] This group launched the journal *Gimle*, and founded a "Network for Nordic Shamanism" in 1982. American neo-shaman Michael Harner's visit to Sweden in 1983, and his courses on "core-shamanism," inspired more practical explorations of shamanism. *Yggdrasil* then went on to collectively design the Swedish version of *seid*.[25]

---

22 Fredrik Skott, *Asatro i tiden* (Göteborg: Språk och folkminnesinstitutet, 2000), 50; Gregorius, *Modern Asatro*, 91.

23 The fact that right-wing extremists were attracted to *Breidablikk-Gildet* was acknowledged by Arne Sjöberg himself. Criticism was raised in an article in *Gimle*, the journal for the shamanist network *Yggdrasil*, written in an attempt to refute alleged ties to *Breidablikk-Gildet*. See Interview with Arne Sjöberg (Breidablikk-Gildet), 1991; Schnurbein, *Religion als Kulturkritik*, 196f; Gregorius, *Modern Asatro*, 91.

24 *Modern Asatro*, 95.

25 A thorough study of the *Yggdrasil* community and their practice of *seid* is presented in Galina Lindqvist, *Shamanic Performances on the Urban Scene. Neo-Shamanism in Contemporary Sweden*, vol. 39, Stockholm Studies in Social Anthropology (Stockholm: Department of Social Anthropology, 1997). For a detailed discussion on different versions of *seid* and neo-shamanism see Chapter 3.

In contrast to Sweden and Iceland, Danish and Norwegian Asatru did not seriously emerge until the 1990s. An exception is a small group in Norway, which started as a counter-cultural student prank at the University of Oslo in 1983 and "grew out of a subculture with general interests in Paganism and the occult."[26] The group went on to found *Bifrost* as an umbrella organization for Asatruers in Norway and tried to achieve official acknowledgement by the Norwegian state as a religious association, following in the footsteps of the Icelanders. The attempt failed, however, and the group went on to celebrate the occasional ritual (called blot), but ceased its activities in 1987.

In Search of Respectability – Asatru after 1990

By the early 1990s, Asatru groups in Northern and Northwestern Europe, as well as in the USA, had established themselves as small and highly controversial participants within the spectrum of alternative religions. With regard to organization, they oscillated between the closed structures of occult orders and initiatory organizations, and those of more open, community-building religious groups. An international network of contacts between the most active leaders and group members was in place as well. All of this was accompanied by a structural pattern which also characterized the *völkisch* religious movement in the first part of the 20th century, and which remains formative for the 'cultic milieu' of Asatru up until today. It is characterized by the frequent emergence of small groups that split as soon as they have reached a certain volume of membership, and by equally frequent attempts to reunite splinter groups and form umbrella organizations. Splits occur for different reasons, most of them not ideological. Instead, they tend to be related to financial or organizational issues and motivated by competing claims to leadership. In spite of these dynamics, there is considerable continuity in the milieu. It remains organized around a limited number of active individuals; core ideas as well as points of contention remain astonishingly stable.

According to Fredrik Gregorius, *Yggdrasil* became part of *Merlinorden* in 1997, *Gimle* continued to exist until 2004 and reported on the new group *Sveriges Asatrosamfund* in 1997. One of its central protagonists, Jörgen I. Eriksson, remains active as an author of books on shamanism as well as on Swedish folk magic and rune magic under the pseudonym Atrid Grimsson (cf. Gregorius, *Modern Asatro*, 98).

26   Egil Asprem, "Heathens Up North. Politics, Polemics, and Contemporary Norse Paganism in Norway," *The Pomegranate* 10, no. 1 (2008), 50.

Nevertheless, the 1990s and 2000s brought a new quality to Asatru worldwide. Most countries saw the rise of new groups. Together with some of the older groups, they followed a course of integration into mainstream society and aimed at different forms of official acknowledgement from the respective state authorities. A stronger emphasis was placed on the inclusion of original sources and academic theory for the re-construction of a pre-Christian religion. A new strategy for the authentication of one's own religion developed. Many groups also started to distance themselves more assertively from overtly political agendas, from racism in particular. This path towards 'respectability' and desire for 'normalization' was motivated not least by the increasing negative media attention that the racist elements in Germanic Neopaganism had started to attract by this time. Books investigating the ideological and organizational right-wing connections of Germanic Neopaganism[27] contributed to this attention, as did the more sensationalist press coverage. The latter was alternately concerned about neo-Nazi and Satanist tendencies in youth and religious sub-cultures, at times stoking up veritable moral panics.[28] At the same time, Norway and Sweden in particular saw the rise of new radical racial-religious groups, such as the *Allgermanic Heathen Front*. Both developments elicited the need for a clearer delineation of Asatruers who perceived themselves as a-racist. Finally, this process of change was facilitated by the technological and communications revolution of the Internet, which the new groups in particular made use of quickly and effectively in order to spread their ideas, solicit members, and carry on their controversies.

Norway

Norway is the most obvious example of such a coincidence of the emergence of new right-wing extremist, racial-religious Asatru groups and the drive for "more mainstream" Asatru communities to "adopt[...] an explicitly anti-racist position."[29] In 1993, black metal musician Varg Vikernes founded the racial-religious *Norwegian Heathen Front* during his stay in prison.[30] In the same

---

27 Kaplan, *Radical Religion in America*; Schnurbein, *Religion als Kulturkritik*; *Göttertrost in Wendezeiten*.
28 See for example Asprem, "Heathens Up North," 44.
29 Ibid., 44.
30 The organization added other national chapters and the international umbrella *Allgermanic Heathen Front* (AHF) throughout the years, but ceased to exist in 2000. Cf. Gardell, *Gods of the Blood*, 307. Two other groups, *Vigrid*, run mostly by Tore Tvedt between 1998 and 2009, and *Det norske Åsatrosamfunn*, claimed to build their religion and worldview on Norse mythology and/or folk customs. A visit to their websites shows that their emphasis on anti-Semitic or anti-monotheist sentiment stands more in the foreground

year, the inactive Norwegian *Åsatrofelleskapet Bifrost* revived the idea to establish a nationwide a-racist Asatru organization, and resumed the process of applying for official government recognition. Two obstacles were to be overcome in this process. Firstly, an earlier application had failed because the group did not manage to formulate an official statement of creed; secondly, Asatru was perceived as a movement dealing with magic, an "antisocial and subversive practice" in the eyes of the authorities.[31] In 1996, *Bifrost* was accepted as the first official Neopagan religious community in Norway and mainland Scandinavia. By 2001, the group had also submitted a marriage ritual to the state authorities that was subsequently recognized officially.[32] *Bifrost* considers itself an umbrella organization for independent individuals and, currently, five regional groups (*blotslag*). Just as *Bifrost* had to formulate their creed within the frames of what is officially considered appropriate for a religion, it structured its organization according to official guidelines. Like any other religious association in Norway, *Bifrost* has a board consisting of a director, here called *høvding* (chief), a treasurer, and a secretary. Their responsibilities include running the association's daily affairs and managing its finances, which consist of membership fees as well as the state and communal support granted by the Norwegian government.[33]

In 1998, disagreements about administrational structures and details of beliefs led to the breakoff of a small faction of *Bifrost* members, who then established *Foreningen Forn Sed* (FFS, Association of the Old Way). The a-racist group continues to exist as an official religious association with a membership of approximately 70. It sports similar views to *Bifrost*, and the members I spoke to see few differences in beliefs and general opinions. However, they experience FFS as more open and experimental regarding rituals and practices. Further, they appreciate the less rigid organizational structure, which lacks

---

than the elaboration of a religion. See e.g. http://vegtam.info/hundensminne/Hvorforaasatru.htm; http://www.vigrid.net/, last accessed February 26, 2014. For studies of Vigrid see also Astrid Espseth, "Stemplingens konsekvens? En studie av nynazistiske grupperinger" (Master's thesis, University of Oslo, 2007) and Lill-Hege Tveito, "Kampen for den Nordiske rases overlevelse. Bruken av den norrøne mytologien innenfor Vigrid" (Master's thesis, University of Tromsø, 2007).

31   Egil Asprem, "Heathens Up North" connects this perception with the mentioned 'moral panics' around "Satanism" which raged in the Norwegian press in the early 1990s. For details see Chapter 9.
32   Egil Stenseth, "Nyhedendom i Norge," *Humanist* 2 (2003).
33   Cf. "Bifrosts lover" (Bifrost's Laws) http://www.bifrost.no/index.php?option=com_content&task=view&id=326&Itemid=104, last accessed February 26, 2014.

formalized local groups, and they reject the practice of having *goder* and *gydjer* as leaders for individual *blotslag*.[34]

Sweden
With the formation of the a-racist *Sveriges Asatrosamfund* (SAS; Swedish Asatru Association) in 1994, Swedish Heathens established their first successful and sustainable national organization. Older ethnicist organizations such as *Breidablikk-Gildet* had only little influence on this group.[35] Its founding members had roots in *Yggdrasil* as well as in the folklore association *Järnåldersföreningen Birka* (Iron Age Association Birka).[36] The group initially consisted of about twenty mainly Stockholm-based members, but numbers grew quickly to 150 in 1996 when SAS started its own journal, *Mimirs Källa* (Mimir's Well), and rose to around 350 by 2000. This necessitated the establishing of regional and local subgroups called *godeord*. Controversies and problems around issues of leadership and finances, as well as a case of embezzlement,[37] caused a number of members to leave the organization around 2004 and flock to two other Asatru associations: *Nätverket Forn Sed* (Network the Old Way), a loosely organized network of individual *blotlag* (ritual groups) with no central leadership, and *Nordiska Ringen* (Nordic Ring). The latter was founded in 2000 and changed its name to *Norröna Samfundet* (Norse Association) in 2003 when it was officially recognized as a religious association.[38] A fierce debate ensued about *Norröna Samfundet's* ethnicist,

---

34 Interview Q and Interview R.
35 An indirect line connects *Breidablikk-Gildet* to SAS, the small group *Telge Fylking* founded in 1987, which had close ties to *Breidablikk-Gildet* initially. *Telge Fylking* shared *Breidablikk-Gildet's* interest for a national cultural tradition, but turned to a more genuinely religious orientation as well, emphasizing its character both as a folk-religion and a religion of nature. Although it never had more than 25 members, *Telge Fylking*, and its journal, *Ratatosk* (1989–1994), was one of the two most significant sources of inspiration for later Asatruers in Sweden. Gregorius, *Modern Asatro*, 93f.
36 Ibid., 100. In an interview with the Danish Asatru journal *Valravn*, Mikael Perman, the former head of SAS contradicts his own involvement with *Yggdrasil*, stating that he learned shamanism in the USA, read *Yggdrasil's* journal *Gimle*, but was never a member, and kept shamanism completely out of SAS (Cf. Valdemar Ravn, "Interview med Mikael Perman," *Valravn. Hedensk tidskrift om samfund og kultur* 12 (2005), 11). The apparent necessity of such a refutation points to the fact that the neo-shamanic practices of *Yggdrasil* remain a point of contention within Swedish Asatru.
37 Cf. Gregorius, *Modern Asatro*, 104f.
38 For a brief history of *Norröna Samfundet* see ibid., 113–115.

genealogical interpretation of Asatru and the leading members' association with right-wing organizations. Shortly thereafter, in 2005, the group ceased its activities.[39] SAS re-stabilized and achieved official recognition as a religious association in 2007. In 2009/10 its statutes and organizational structures were reworked, and the name was changed to *Samfundet Forn Sed* (SFS – Association The Old Way).[40]

In order to gain recognition and acceptance, SFS has followed a similar strategy to, for example, *Bifrost* in Norway. It firmly rejects any racist or xenophobic interpretations of Norse mythology and emphasizes its democratic basis. This unambiguous stance has provoked criticism among other Swedish and Danish groups, who at times blame SAS for being too narrow and exclusionist out of "political correctness."[41]

On the other side of the political spectrum, Sweden has had its share of right-wing extremist, racial-religious groups as well. Most prominent for a while was *Svensk Hednisk Front*, a branch of the *Allgermanic Heathen Front*. It had considerable influence on nationalist movements in Sweden and Norway, not the least through its publishing company *Nordiska Förlaget* and its web-portal for *Nordic Identity, Culture, and Tradition* (www.nordisk.nu). Whereas *Allgermanic Heathen Front* had been in decline since 2003 and stopped its activities in 2006, the publisher and the portal currently still seem to be functioning well.[42]

Denmark

The development of modern Asatru in Denmark is the best example of the paradigm shift that took place within the Heathen world in the late 1990s.

---

39   Ibid., 108–110.
40   http://www.samfundetfornsed.se/om-samfundet-1282525 (February 26, 2014). See also Sveriges Asatrosamfund, "Snart är de nya stadgarna här!," *Mimers Källa* 21 (2009), 5f.
41   Gregorius, *Modern Asatro*, 107. "Political correctness" is used here not as an analytical concept, but as a term which has been used polemically by conservative and right-wing circles to discount emancipatory political positions.
42   Cf. ibid., 115–117. A different approach is followed by *Samfälligheten för Nordisk Sed* (Community for the Nordic Way). Founded in 1997, the group claims to follow a living, unbroken, but constantly changing folk tradition. In contrast to other Asatruers, they adamantly reject being counted among Asatru or Neopagan groups, because they feel that the others' faith is based on modern national Romantic constructions, whereas theirs is seen as authentic and firmly rooted in tradition. The group seems to be fairly small, has little contact with the general Asatru milieu in Sweden or elsewhere, and claims to be deliberately ignored by the media and general public. Ibid., 117 and http://www.nordisksed.se/, last accessed February 26, 2014.

CREATING A RELIGION

During my initial research in Scandinavia around 1990, I was not able to find Asatruers in Denmark, and none of the Norwegian or Swedish groups with whom I was in contact could point me in the direction of any. By the time I started my new research in 2010, the nation-wide *Forn Siðr* (The Old Way or Old Custom) had become one of the most internationally significant and largest Asatru groups, officially acknowledged as a religious community with its own burial site and a fairly solid status within Danish society. What had changed?[43]

Only in 1997, after the arrival of the Internet and the successful establishment of popular history events such as Viking markets, a handful of individual Asatru practitioners, Viking enthusiasts, and 'net-Heathens' had established the organization and its journal, *Vølse*. *Forn Siðr* is a nationwide organization in which individuals can become members. As long as they can list a *Forn Siðr* member as an official contact person, independent *blotgroups* are given associate status. The existence of such an umbrella organization with common statutes and a ritual structure guarantees a fairly strong public support for Asatru in Denmark. A network of independent *blotgroups* on the other hand leaves ample room for a wide variety of sometimes loosely structured, sometimes very tight-knit, regional and special interest organizations.[44]

The early years were marked by the emerging community's efforts to obtain the status of an official religion by the Danish state. This would give them the authority to conduct publicly acknowledged rites like marriages, blessings of newborns, and funerals, as well as educating children about Asatru in schools. Their first official application was turned down by the Ministry of Church because the organizational structure, especially the relation between the *blotgroups* and *Forn Siðr*, was considered too loose and the minimal requirements for official rituals too vague.[45] Because of this failure, *Forn Siðr* codified a more binding ritual structure in a similar way as Norwegian Asatru had done before. This not only demonstrates how Scandinavian Asatru interacts, but also how the interaction between state authorities and a previously loosely organized,

---

43 As I learned later on, a small local Asatru group, *Odins Hird* in Amager, a suburb of the capital Copenhagen, was founded in 1986. Cf. Valdemar Ravn, "Interview med en vølve," *Valravn. Hedensk tidskrift om samfund og kultur* 7 (2003).

44 Among them is, for example, *Asatrofællesskabet Yggdrasil*, a loosely structured group that achieved its goal of buying and preserving a piece of land near Silkeborg in Central Jutland in 2004, and is currently branching out into regional subgroups. http://www.asatrofaellesskabet-yggdrasil.dk/, last accessed February 26, 2014.

45 The process of official acknowledgement and the relevant correspondences are documented on *Forn Sidr's* homepage: http://www.fornsidr.dk/om-forn-sidr/godkendelsesforloebet, last accessed February 26, 2014.

non-committal religious movement can play a major role in the formation of a new religion. In 2003, this formalization of *Forn Siðr's* structures and practices was finally successful. Their official recognition as a religious community led to considerable media attention for the young group, and consequently a significant growth in membership – an effect that was repeated when the group was granted its first burial ground on a cemetery in Odense. In 2014, the group counted around 600 members.

The network of Asatru in Denmark has been supplemented by a number of independent groups with their own media of communication. Former *Forn Siðr* member Morten Grølsted (alias Grølheim), who had been dismissed from the organization, ran the ethnicist *Asatrofællesskabet* (The Asatru Community), and more importantly, edited the journal, *Valravn*. Between 2002 and 2008, this journal provided the only international platform for Scandinavian Asatruers. It provided information about groups in other countries and took up a number of controversial issues over the years.[46] In 2005, a heated debate as to whether Asatru in general, and *Valravn* in particular, was taking a turn to the political right broke out between *Valravn* and another Danish discussion forum, the now-defunct online board *Kindir* run by an informal network since 2004/05 with the goal of educating people about Asatru. *Kindir* functioned, among other things, as a critical platform for speaking out against ethnicist, latently racist, right-wing and cultural essentialist positions within Asatru, and brought some of the controversies within *Forn Siðr* to a broader Heathen public.[47]

Danish Asatru has had no controversies with overtly racial-religious groups in the country, but stormy debates about the significance of ethnicist positions within the self-professed a-racist *Forn Siðr* have shaken the milieu in recent years.[48] The disputes motivated a number of long-term or even founding members of *Forn Siðr* to form *Nordisk Tingsfællig* (NTF, Nordic Ting Community) in December, 2010. NTF aims to develop a clearer a-racist profile than *Forn Siðr*, which in their eyes has made itself vulnerable to political agendas through its

---

46 *Valravn* understood itself as an open and deliberately controversial forum for all varieties of Asatru. Aside from speaking out against right-wing extremist groups such as the *Heathen Front*, and for more progressive sexual politics, it also gave voice to ethnicist and ethno-pluralist positions within Heathenism as well as to pro-Hindu nationalist, anti-Muslim, anti-Christian and anti-Jewish sentiment. On Hinduism, see *Valravn* 1 (2002), 7 (2006), 23 (2007). On underlying anti-Christian and anti-Jewish sentiment see 1 (2002), 25; 3 (2002), 24; 12 (2004), 7.
47 www.kindir.dk, last accessed December 07, 2010.
48 These controversies which circle around 'anti-monotheistic' positions are discussed in detail in Chapter 5.

principle of openness to all political persuasions that are not directly National Socialist. Their first published statements were a codex and a declaration, in which they formulate their allegiance to the ideals of multiculturalism, environmentalism, and the rejection of all those who connect religion to race, blood, genes and ethnicity.[49] The community's long-term goals include its registration as an official religious community and the acquisition of land where Asatru celebrations can be held.[50]

Iceland
As mentioned, the Icelandic *Ásatrúarfélagið* attained official recognition much earlier than any other Asatru community did. Nevertheless, the death of its first *Allsherjargodi*, Sveinbjörn Beinteinsson, in 1993 and the activities of his successor, Jörmundur Ingi Hansen, who had previously taken care of a large part of the official media representation and international liaison,[51] marked a shift in the history of this group. The creation of a burial ground and the purchase of a house in Reykjavík as a center for the group motivated a considerable expansion. The *Ásatrúarfélagið* lost its image as a gathering place for outsiders and made its way into mainstream society. In light of the group's rapid growth, the membership demanded that the increasing institutional and administrative obligations be distributed among other elected office-holders, but Jörmundur Ingi insisted on keeping them under his control. In 2002, the conflict culminated in his removal from office. The following year Hilmar Örn Hilmarsson, the well-known composer and musician,[52] took over as *Allsherjargodi* with Jörmundur Ingi's approval.[53] Since then, the group has expanded continually, and its integration into Icelandic society has been solidifed.[54] On the other hand, international relations, which Jörmundur Ingi Hansen had energetically pursued (also with members and

---

49 Cf. http://www.nordisktingsfaellig.dk/9303/Om%20os, last accessed March 09, 2014.
50 Cf. http://www.nordisktingsfaellig.dk/9703/, last accessed March 09, 2014.
51 In this capacity, I conducted an interview with him in 1991.
52 Hilmar Örn Hilmarsson worked with the 'industrial' groups *Psychic TV* and *Current 93* (cf. Stéphane François, "Les paganismes de la Nouvelle Droite (1980–2004)" (Doctoral thesis, Université de Lille II- Droit et santé, 2005), 211). He wrote the music for the internationally acclaimed movie *Children of Nature*, directed by Friðrik Þór Friðriksson (1991), and a great number of other renowned Icelandic films.
53 In 2006, Jörmundur Ingi formed his own group *Reykjavíkurgoðord*, Jonsson, "Ásatrú á Íslandi við upphaf 21. aldar," 129f.
54 Interview with Óttar Ottóson (Ásatrúarfélagið). Ottósson claims that the membership was 98 in 1990, in 2005 it had gone up to 953, in 2010 to around 1500, by 2014 it had risen to around 2500.

leaders of racial-religious and ethnicist groups such as the *Armanen-Orden* and the *Odinic Rite*),[55] were toned down and the association worked more within its own country.[56] With currently around 2500 registered members (in 2014), the group is still small, but in relation to the total number of Icelanders (approximately 320,000) it constitutes a considerably higher percentage of the general population than in other countries. The somewhat exceptional position of *Ásatrúarfélagið* within its own country has two explanations. Firstly, Norse mythology and medieval Icelandic texts are considered an integral and important part of the Icelandic national heritage and identity, and are well known to most Icelanders from their school years. Hence, the *Ásatrúarfélagið* considers the preservation of an ancient Nordic culture as one of its main functions. Some of its members are not even primarily interested in religious issues, but rather in the preservation of such a cultural identity.[57] Secondly, *Ásatrúarfélagið* has managed to establish itself as an alternative to the Lutheran Icelandic state church and has even attracted a few atheists and agnostics who sought an affiliation with a non-Christian denomination.[58]

United Kingdom
In spite of a temporary split of the organization in 1991,[59] the ethnicist *Odinic Rite* developed into a well-established group and expanded internationally, forming branches in the United States, France, and Germany over the years.[60]

---

55 For these connections see below, chapter "Asatru International."
56 See Interview with Óttar Ottóson (Ásatrúarfélagið).
57 Interview with Óttar Ottósson (Ásatrúarfélagið).
58 Cf. Interview with Óttar Ottóson (Ásatrúarfélagið). *Ásatrúarfélagið*'s status as an established religious community beyond the Lutheran National Church for a time also brought the group some exceptional members: a flock of Russian Orthodox refugees, who did not want to join either the State Church or the Roman Catholic community, but who as foreigners were obliged to be members of an officially acknowledged religious community in Iceland. They inscribed themselves into *Ásatrúarfélagið* and used their space for annual meetings for a while. Cf. Jonsson, "Ásatrú á Íslandi við upphaf 21. aldar" 149.
59 In 1989, John Yeowell resigned from his post as the director of the Court of Gothar, and Heimgest took over the office in which he has been serving up until today. In 1991, an expelled member of the OR founded a rival organization under the same name, which Stubba joined for a brief period. However, he returned to the original OR later, and the new organization was renamed *Odinist Fellowship*. See Hengest/OR, "In Memory of John Yeowell – 'Stubba'"; and http://www.odinistfellowship.co.uk/, last accessed February 26, 2014.
60 For the split of the German branch from the British mother organization see below.

However, some of its members' far-right political associations and sympathies made it increasingly contentious. Some of these controversies had repercussions for the overall Neopagan community in the UK, since Pete Jennings, High Gothi of a competing Asatru group, the a-racist *Odinshof* (founded in 1987 and more strongly connected to Wicca), served as the head of the influential *Pagan Federation* for a number of years.[61] Because of these problems, two former OR members, Mike Robertson and Stuart Prior, left the group and founded *Kith of Yggdrasil* in 2001. *Kith of Yggdrasil* has around 50 members by now; it is counted among the a-racist groups, and is actively networking with Asatru groups in Scandinavia and Germany.[62]

In contrast to other countries, Heathenry in the UK is considered an integral part of the broader Neopagan scene, on par with Wicca and Celtic groups. Asatruers are less likely to be formal members of groups in the UK and tend to practice their religion independently. They connect through mailing lists, Internet forums,[63] and gatherings organized by the general Pagan community. Pete Jennings observes that there is "less need for social networking organizations for Heathens. Greater openness, Internet groups and coverage in the general Pagan press & conferences result in less need for that aspect."[64] At the same time, two groups originating in the USA have established branches in the UK. One of them, the *Rune Gild*, an initiatory organization for runic magic established by Edred Thorsson in 1980, has been headed by musician Ian Read[65] since its founder Freya Aswynn's falling out with Edred Thorsson around 1993.[66] It enjoys a good reputation in the Pagan scene.[67] The other group to have established a UK branch is *The Ring of Troth*, also initiated by Freya Aswynn. After being dormant for a while, it seems to have resumed

---

61 Cf. Correspondence with Pete Jennings (Odinshof), 2010. *Odinshof* was established by Martyn Taylor and John Broughton, and registered as a religious and educational charity in 1989. Honoring all Germanic and Celtic deities as well as local sacred sites and "promoting a mystery cult of Odin," the *Odinshof* had closer contact with Wiccan organizations than with Odinists. See Schnurbein, *Religion als Kulturkritik*, 140, as well as "Odinshof. The Way of the Raven" (http://www.gippeswic.demon.co.uk/odinshof.html, last accessed February 26, 2014).

62 Correspondence with Alan Nash, 2010.

63 See for example http://groups.yahoo.com/group/ukheathenry/, last accessed February 26, 2014.

64 Correspondence with Pete Jennings (Odinshof).

65 For more on Read see Chapter 9.

66 Cf. Edred, *History of the Rune-Gild*, III (The Reawakening of the Gild 1980–2005), 110.

67 Correspondence with Pete Jennings.

some activity.⁶⁸ One of its members is Jenny Blain, an ethnologist and prolific writer on Asatru.⁶⁹

USA

When the *Asatru Free Assembly* faltered in the mid-1980s, two new groups emerged, and have since struggled for hegemony while developing North American Asatru into opposing ethnicist and a-racist directions. Stephen McNallen formally turned over the remains of the AFA to Valgard Murray, who was then heading the *Arizona Kindred*, and to Robert N. Taylor from the *Wulfing Kindred*, who in turn started the ethnicist *Asatru Alliance*.⁷⁰ Another long-term member of both the AFA and the *Odinic Rite*, and founder of the initiatory *Rune Gild*, Stephen Flowers (alias Edred Thorsson), started *The Ring of Troth* in 1987 together with James Chisholm. This organization was eventually to bring new impulses to Asatru not only in North America but in Europe as well. In the early 1990s, accusations of Satanism⁷¹ and racism⁷² led to a number of rapid changes in leadership and structure, the withdrawal of Thorsson and Chisholm from *The Troth* as well as the split off of another group, Prudence Priest's *American Vinland Association* (started in 1995).⁷³ Today, *The Troth* is established as the largest and most active a-racist Asatru group in the USA, led by an elected steersperson and board called High Rede.⁷⁴ Like the *Asatru Alliance*,

---

68   Cf. Correspondence with Pete Jennings (Odinshof); http://www.troth.org.uk/history.htm, last accessed February 26, 2014.
69   See Blain, *Nine Worlds of Seid-Magic*.
70   Valgard Murray had a background in the National Socialist wing of the radical right, where he learned about Odinism, Alexander Rud Mills, and Else Christensen. His *Arizona Kindred* was the first to be officially affiliated with the *Odinist Fellowship*, where Murray eventually became vice president. In 1984 he and his kindred changed affiliations and became part of the AFA.
71   The accusations were based on the fact that Thorsson and Chisholm were members of Michael Aquino's occult order *Temple of Set*. Cf. Kaplan, *Radical Religion in America*, 26. See also Edred, *History of the Rune-Gild*, III (The Reawakening of the Gild 1980–2005), 90–93.
72   These problems had to do with the involvement of Theodism, an Anglo-Saxon version of Heathenism, with *The Troth*. Theodism's ancestral and racial approach caused considerable turmoil. See http://gamall-steinn.org/Gering/gerthist.html, last accessed March 19, 2014, cf. also Garman Lord, "The Evolution of Theodish Belief. Part I," *THEOD Magazine* Lammas (1995), "The Evolution of Theodish Belief. Part II," *THEOD Magazine* Hallows (1995).
73   Cf. Kaplan, *Radical Religion in America*; 29; Gardell, *Gods of the Blood*, 164.
74   Cf. Kaplan, *Radical Religion in America*, 31; Kveldulf Gundarsson, ed. *Our Troth, by Members of the Troth and Other True Folk*, 2. ed., 2 vols., vol. I (History and Lore), vol. II (Living the Troth) (North Charleston, SC: BookSurge, 2006), 119.

The Troth serves as an umbrella under which various regional groups called 'kindreds', 'hearths', 'garths' and 'hofs' gather. In the formative 1990s and 2000s, *The Troth* aimed at creating a training program for clergy within Asatru and put considerable emphasis on and effort into providing knowledge about what they call 'The Lore,' i.e. academic and popular information about Scandinavian, German and Anglo-Saxon myth, religion, culture, folk-customs etc., upon which the reconstruction of a faith can be based. All of these elements have made *The Troth* a forum that is sought out for its knowledge of sources and practices by many Asatruers. This and the emphasis on anti-racist and non-folkish policies have been deciding factors for *The Troth's* international influence within a-racist Asatru.

However, its emphasis on knowledge, theory and sources has provoked critique as well, for example, from the ethnicist *Asatru Alliance* for being overly academic, for "coming from the head" and not being action-based enough.[75] This already highlights the fact that the *Asatru Alliance* in its continuing development put a stronger emphasis on the building of community. The same is true for the *Asatru Free Assembly*, which was reestablished under the new name *Asatru Folk Assembly* in 1994 by Stephen McNallen. He claims he was motivated by his resentment of "signs that the politically correct faction" or "the universalists" in Asatru were "making inroads into territory long dominated by the folkish."[76] Since then, the AFA's activities have fluctuated. In the last few years, McNallen and the AFA have put considerable effort into community building in the virtual word as well as the real, with an active homepage (www.runestone.org), a Facebook presence, YouTube interviews, radio programs, a blog, and a podcast.

Racial-religious Asatru in the USA has been active in prison outreach. Forming prison ministries was an activity which Else Christensen had initiated, and which, up until today, seems to have remained a specialty of Odinist groups, not least the *Odinic Rite*.[77] Prison outreach took on a new dimension

---

75   Cf. Kaplan, *Radical Religion in America*, 30.
76   McNallen, "Three Decades of the Ásatú Revival in America," 210f. During this time, the AFA seems to have had cordial ties with Ron McVan, a visual artist active in the radical racist Odinist group *Wotansvolk* and the *14 Word Press*, together with David and Katja Lane. An editorial in *The Runestone* 9, Fall 1994, 5 hails Ron McVan as "one of Asatru's most prolific and talented artists," whose "drawings are frequently found in THE RUNESTONE." On McVan, *Wotansvolk* and *14-Word-Press* cf. Gardell, *Gods of the Blood*, 205–216.
77   For a discussions on prison outreach see *Gods of the Blood*, vol. 1, 175f; Gundarsson, *Our Troth*, 112; Jeffrey Kaplan, ed. *Encyclopedia of White Power. A Sourcebook on the Radical Racist Right* (Walnut Creek: Altamira Press, 2000), 361.

with the foundation of the white supremacist Odinist group *Wotansvolk*, which was registered as a church under the name *Temple of Wotan* in 2000. Through their professional use of the Internet, *Wotansvolk* and *14 Word Press*[78] succeeded in spreading their white supremacist, Ariosophic and Jungian-inspired ideology internationally.

Germany

In Germany, the direct connection to *völkisch* religion and German Faith became an increasing burden for Germanic Neopagans. While the *Armanen-Orden* decreased its public activities, Sigrun von Schlichting intensified her contacts with Eastern European Pagans such as the *Romuva* in Lithuania, and moved to a castle in Poland where she remained in active contact with Heathen groups and individuals until her death in 2009.[79] Younger Asatruers started publicly distancing themselves from connections with the *Armanen-Orden* and the *ANSE*.[80] Such actions were not only spurred by criticism of right-wing religiosity in the media, but also taken up by the Neopagan community itself. In 1994, the *Rabenclan* (Raven's Clan), an association for different Pagan traditions, was founded. It fought against *völkisch* and racist traditions and activities within Neopaganism. Asatruers in the *Rabenclan* started a working group, the *Ariosophieprojekt*, to actively investigate connections between *völkisch* ideology, right-wing extremism and Germanic Neopaganism.[81] This small a-racist Asatru faction, which today calls itself *Nornirs Ætt* (Kin of the Norns), declared its formal independence from the *Rabenclan* in 2005.[82] It remains a

---

78 According to Gardell, *Gods of the Blood*, 191, the notorious "14 words" which *Wotansvolk* founders David and Katja Lane coined "We must secure the existence of our people and a future for White children" is "one of the very few concepts that has won almost universal acceptance in the notoriously factious milieu of white-racist revolutionaries."
79 Cf. Andrzej Szczudlo, "Schlichtingsheim. Das 'Feenschloss' Rothenhorn der Frfr. Sigrun v. Schlichting," *Neuer Glogauer Anzeiger*, September, 2005.
80 This was not least a result of the publication of my books (Schnurbein, *Religion als Kulturkritik*; *Göttertrost in Wendezeiten*) and media discussions.
81 The *Rabenclan's* early activities on the Internet contributed significantly to the spread of this information. Over the years, the *Ariosophieprojekt* has provided well-researched background material, which has also been used by researchers and journalists. It gave the *Rabenclan* and its Asatru group *Nornirs Ætt* the reputation of a critically informed, politically engaged faction within the Neopagan scene in Germany. On the other hand, its political criticism of some groups has elicited refutations and allegations of slander from other Germanic Neopagan groups. Cf. http://www.nornirsaett.de/doc/ario/ario.html, last accessed February 26, 2014.
82 Cf. http://www.rabenclan.de/index.php/Aktuelles/AktuellesNornirsAett, last February 26, 2014, and Interview with six members of Nornirs Ætt, May 2010, Iceland.

small group, with just over twenty members located in different regions of Germany and Austria. It is still set apart within the milieu through its explicit political positioning. Acknowledging that Germanic Neopaganism since the early 20th century has been closely connected with national Romantic, *völkisch* and racist tendencies, *Nornirs Ætt* feel they have a responsibility to counteract these and to engage actively in the development of a democratic, pluralistic society. Other German Heathens tend to perceive this political positioning as a distraction from religious goals proper, and consider it sufficient to follow a general 'un-political' policy.

Their political line pits the *Rabenclan* and *Nornirs Ætt* against not only the *Armanen-Orden*, the ANSE, and the *Germanische Glaubensgemeinschaft*,[83] it also sets it apart from another new group, the *Odinic Rite Deutschland* (ORD, later renamed as *Verein für germanisches Heidentum VfgH*, Society for Germanic Paganism).[84] The ORD started out as a chapter of the British *Odinic Rite* in 1994, representing an ethnicist wing in German Asatru. Concerns about the mother organization's turn toward the extreme political right were voiced in the ORD's journal, *Ringhorn*, as early as 1995.[85] That, combined with differences in structure, ideology, and practices, led the ORD to declare its independence. Between 2004 and 2010, *VfgH* doubled its membership from around 40 to 80, while developing a number of new regional groups called *Herde* (Hearths) and establishing itself as a small, but influential Germanic Neopagan group in Germany. The *VfgH's* statutes require a fairly strong personal commitment from each member.[86] This idea of collective commitment, combined with the individual freedom to formulate one's own beliefs and design one's own religious

---

[83] The GGG intensified its efforts to become a forum for all Germanic Neopagans in Germany in the 1990s. Géza von Neményi's attempt to proclaim himself as the leader (*Allsherjargodi*) for "all traditional Germanic Heathens" in 2003 is today considered a failure within the community and its observers, cf. Gründer, *Blótgemeinschaften*, 59f, Matthias Pöhlmann, "Streit um Heiden-Papst – Géza von Neményi erhebt Führungsanspruch innerhalb des Neuheidentums," *Materialdienst Evangelische Zentralstelle für Weltanschauungsfragen* 66, no. 11 (2003). In 2007, two former members of the GGG formed their own group, *Wodans Erben* (Wodan's Heirs), which is active up until today as well. Cf. Wodans Erben, *Gemeinschaftsblatt*, vol. Ausgabe 2010 (Berlin: Wodans Erben e.V., 2010).

[84] The *Rabenclan* published a long discussion of the ORD's political position on its homepage in 2005. Cf. Berna Kühne-Spicer, "Der Odinic Rite Deutschland – Neuheidentum im Spannungsfeld neurechter Religiosität," Rabenclan e.V., http://www.rabenclan.de/index.php/Magazin/KuehneSpicerORDKap1 last accessed February 26, 2014.

[85] See Fritz Steinbock's editorial in *Ringhorn* 8 (1995) titled "Ehre" (Honor).

[86] Cf. "Mitgliedschaft im VfgH," http://www.vfgh.de/data/te_2.asp?MLEVEL1=20&MLEVEL2=40, last accessed February 26, 2014.

practice, is the essence of the "Leitidee freies Heidentum" (Guiding Idea of a Free Heathenism), which the *VfgH* promotes as its unique trademark within the international Asatru community. It implies the rejection of privileged religious mediators, spiritual authorities, and leadership, making priesthood accessible to all members and limiting the function of priest-like *Blótmen/ women* exclusively to the conduct of rituals.[87]

The largest and youngest of the new Asatru groups in Germany, the a-racist *Eldaring* (Old Norse "eldr" means fire) differs from both *Nornirs Ætt* and the *VfgH* in its conception of itself as not a tight-knit religious community, but as a contact and service platform – a network for Asatruers who perceive of their faith as a personal and private matter.[88] Like the *VfgH*, it developed out of a foreign Asatru group, in this case *The Troth*, into an independent organization in 2000. According to founding members, the appeal lay in *The Troth's* a-racist agenda and the significance it assigned to reconstructing Asatru from sources and research the *Eldaring* adapted. The central position of the *Eldaring* within German and international Asatru can be attributed to several factors; first, its character as an open platform requiring little commitment from its members; second, its unpolitical approach; third, its emphasis on academic research, which gives it an air of authenticity and respectability; and finally, the existence of active local *Herde* (Hearths), Blót Communities, special interest groups and annual events. The relative openness to elements of general Neopaganism and Wicca make it attractive for the around 200 registered members as of 2014.

Controversies between the different groups continue to exist, in spite of their shared emphasis on reconstructing Asatru from written sources and in accordance with contemporary research. In recent years, disputes have focused on *VfgH* members' ethnicist sympathies and engagement in right-wing extremist parties.[89] Another point of contestation is the small alternative publishing

---

87　See "Allgemeine Konzepte des VfGH im Überblick," http://www.vfgh.de/data/TE_2. asp?MLEVEL1=20&MLEVEL2=10, last accessed February 26, 2014. While a number of ideological parallels can be found to Géza von Neményi's *GGG*, this emphatic rejection of priesthood marks a pronounced difference between the groups – a difference which can be compared to the distinction between Ludwig Fahrenkrog's *GGG* and Otto Sigfrid Reuter's *Deutschgläubige Gemeinschaft* in the 1910s and 20s.

88　Cf. for example Interview with Uwe Ehrenhöfer (Eldaring). It is a statement that I have found in many other interviews as well.

89　*VfgH* member, Volker Wagner (Stilkam), is a controversial figure because of his open embracing of *folkish* Asatru and his translations of Stephen McNallen's articles about metagenetics (see Chapter 4). Furthermore, Thilo Kabus used to be a member of the right-wing extremist party *NPD* (National Democratic Party of Germany) and worked for

company, the *Arun Verlag*, which has supported Asatru and other Neopagan endeavors. *Arun*'s owner, Stefan Björn Ulbrich, has a background in right-wing extremist organizations in Germany, which he later publicly renounced as "youthful indiscretions" (Jugendsünden).[90] Ulbrich himself wrote a book on Germanic Neopagan religion and ritual, *Im Tanz der Elemente* (In the Dance of the Elements, 1990), where he drew upon Germanic Faith and Conservative Revolutionary ideas from the early 20th century. *Arun* started out publishing New Right and NS-occultist titles, but in the mid-1990s turned increasingly toward Neopagan and nature spirituality, neo-shamanism, esoteric self-help, and healing, gradually eliminating right-wing titles such as Julius Evola's *Revolt Against the Modern World* from its book-lists.[91] Within the scene and beyond, the credibility of Ulbrich's recent distance from right-wing organizations and ideologies is a matter of controversy, and accordingly, individual Asatruers' affiliation with *Arun* remains a difficult topic.

Asatru International

Day-to-day, Asatru groups are primarily involved in their own affairs; most contacts and controversies between groups remain limited to their respective national context. At the same time, Germanic Neopaganism has always had an internationally active network at its disposal. Ideas and influences have been routinely exchanged, even though these interactions often happen through individual contacts and the majority of members might not always be aware of them.

Already the key figure for the formation of Odinism in Australia and the Anglo-American world, Alexander Rud Mills received at least some of his core ideas from German *völkisch* religion. After World War II, those ideas were dispersed by Danish-born Else Christensen in the USA and taken up by the British *Odinic Rite*, one of the groups that played a key role in the development of the

---

another right-wing party later on. Cf. Matthias Pöhlmann, "Trügerischer 'Heidenspass'? Das '1. Berliner Heiden- und Hexenfest' im Spiegel interner Kritik," *Materialdienst Evangelische Zentralstelle für Weltanschauungsfragen* 11 (2004); see Kühne-Spicer, "Der Odinic Rite Deutschland – Neuheidentum im Spannungsfeld neurechter Religiosität" for an in-depth discussion of possible right-wing involvements of some ORD members (the article was written before the name change to *VfgH*).

90 The text has since been removed from *Arun*'s homepage, but is quoted here: http://www.taz.de/1/archiv/archiv/?dig=2003/06/16/a0252, last accessed February 26, 2014.

91 Cf. also Gründer, *Germanisches (Neu-)Heidentum in Deutschland*, 55–58.

international Asatru network. Throughout the 1980s, the OR developed a set of rituals eventually codified in the *Book of Blótar*, which was widely distributed throughout the Germanic Neopagan community in the 1990s, providing inspiration for other groups in forming their rituals. Another major contribution of the OR to the international Heathen community was the formulation of the "Nine Noble Virtues,"[92] a moral code widely used by Asatru groups in English-speaking countries and beyond. The OR acquired this key role by admitting foreign members and, through the process of initiation, giving them a status within their own countries' Odinist and Asatru milieus. These include prominent founders of other groups, such as Edred Thorsson from the *Rune Gild* and the early *Ring of Troth*; Freya Aswynn from the *Ring of Troth* UK; Valguard Murray, the early AFA member and founder of the *Asatru Alliance* in the United States;[93] Volkert Volkmann, founder of the *Yggdrasil Kreis* in Germany; and Bernd Hicker (alias Thorbern), one of the founders of the *Odinic Rite* (later *VfgH*) in Germany.[94] The OR also played a significant role in the short-lived attempt in 1997 to unite leading Asatru groups internationally in the IAOA (International Asatru/Odinist Alliance), initiated by Valguard Murray, Stephen McNallen, and Heimgest, the leader of the *Odinic Rite*, and later joined by the French and German branches of the OR.[95]

The Icelandic *Ásatrúarfélagið* had less practical but more symbolic significance for the Asatru movement. After the group's official recognition in 1973, it attracted considerable international attention. One of its founding members,

---

92 The original nine noble virtues, which can be found on the OR website (http://www.odinic-rite.org/virtues.html, last accessed November 03, 2010), read as follows: "Courage, Truth, Honour, Fidelity, Discipline, Hospitality, Self-Reliance, Industriousness, Perseverance." A number of modified versions are currently in use by other groups.

93 Cf. Gardell, *Gods of the Blood*, 263.

94 In the 1990s, the ORD collaborated with the *Yggdrasil-Kreis*, which combines Celtic and Germanic elements into a "European religion of nature." The membership of Volkert Volkmann in the OR is mentioned on a German site on geomantics (http://www.geomantie.net/authors/988/view.html, accessed February 26, 2014) as well as in a critical article on the ORD by Berna Kühne-Spicer, "Der Odinic Rite Deutschland – Neuheidentum im Spannungsfeld neurechter Religiosität." Volkmann's contact with the ANSE and the *Armanen-Orden* in the 1990s is a matter of dispute. Volkmann emphatically denies having been a member of these organizations, and the *Yggdrasil-Kreis* has published numerous refutations of such claims on its homepage (http://www.yggdrasil-kreis.org/html/gegendarstellungen.html, last accessed February 26, 2014). See also the critical reflections on these matters by Lucas Corso on the *Rabenclan's* homepage (http://www.rabenclan.de/index.php/Magazin/LucasCorsoVolkmann, last accessed February 26, 2014).

95 Cf. Gardell, *Gods of the Blood*, 263.

the controversial head of *Nýalssinna,* Þórsteinn Guðjónsson, played a more active role in the international Asatru network. He started the English-language journal *Huginn & Muninn,* which was distributed internationally. He was in close contact with Sigrun von Schlichting from the *Armanen-Orden* and ANSE (whose German-language journal adopted the same name), as well as with Géza von Neményi from the *Heidnische Gemeinschaft* and later the GGG.[96] Both travelled to Iceland in the 1980s and established contact with Jörmundur Ingi Hansen. Together, they facilitated the first international *Flax Harvest Celebration,* held in Iceland in 1988. It was followed by the participation of ANSE and *Armanen-Orden* members at the *Odinic Rite's* National Moot in 1990.[97]

We can conclude that already by the early 1990s, an international network of racial-religious and ethnicist Asatruers had emerged, which expanded into Eastern Europe and in particular to the Lithuanian *Romuva*[98] after the fall of the Iron Curtain. It acted as the taproot for the *World Congress of Ethnic Religions* (WCER), an international attempt to unite 'indigenous' religious groups under one roof.[99] At its official foundation in 1998, *Romuva's* long-term leader, the ethnologist Jonas Trinkunas, became the first head of the WCER. The Icelandic *Ásatrúarfélagið,* Danish *Forn Siðr,* and the German GGG were among its original members.[100]

In spite of the fact that the term 'ethnic' was disputed from the beginning,[101] the *World Congress of Ethnic Religions* quickly gained sympathy among

---

96   In a contribution on GGG's online forum, Neményi emphasizes this connection with Þórsteinn Guðjónsson, his visit to the GGG in 1992, his contribution to its journal *Germanen-Glauben,* and the fact that his son is a member of "our GGG-Ring": http://www.ggg-world.net/forum/showthread.php?tid=290, last accessed February 26, 2014.

97   Schnurbein, *Religion als Kulturkritik,* 218. Sigrun von Schlichting and her ANSE also held contacts with Arne Sjöberg of the *Breidablikk Gildet* in Sweden as well as with Thorbjørn Ragnarsson of *Norges Åsatrolag* in Norway. (Cf. ibid., 211). It also seems to have attracted the early AFA's attention. The *Armanen-Orden* was listed by the AFA among the "more positive groups, and ones more allied with us." Ibid., 132, cf. *Runestone* Spring 1982, 12.

98   Vilius Rudra Dundzila, "Baltic Lithuanian Religion and Romuva," *Tyr. Myth – Culture – Tradition* 3 (2007).

99   For a brief account of the foundation of the WCER see Michael Strmiska and Vilius Rudra Dundzila, "Romuva. Lithuanian Paganism in Lithuania and America," in *Modern Paganism in World Cultures. Comparative Perspectives,* ed. Michael Strmiska (Santa Barbara, CA: ABC-Clio, 2005), 276–278.

100 http://ecer-org.eu/about/, last accessed February 26, 2014.

101 Cf. Gregorius, *Modern Asatro,* 86f. For a discussion of the disputed term 'ethnic' in this organization, initially known as the *World Pagan Congress,* see Strmiska, "Modern Paganism in World Cultures. Comparative Perspectives," 14f. He emphasizes that the concept of 'ethnic' in this context had nothing to do with "ethnic purity" or "race ideology,"

Asatruers, not least due to its early public condemnation of "discrimination, suppression, or persecution based on race, color, social class, religion, or national origin."[102] It was seen as a good forum in which to further the legitimatization of one's own efforts toward public recognition.[103] Throughout the first half of the 2000s, more groups joined, including the German *Eldaring* and the Norwegian *Foreningen Forn Sed*.[104]

Gradually though, more and more groups and individuals voiced a growing unease with the way the WCER was run, with its guiding principles, and with some of the groups involved.[105] The problems came to the surface after the WCER's 2008 meeting, which was held at the castle of Rothenhorn in the village Jedrzychowice (formerly known under the German name Heyersdorf) in

---

but rather denoted "anything that defines a people: its language, customs, daily behavior, food...or spiritual outlook." (15) Conceptions of ethnicity in Asatru are discussed in Chapter 4.

102 Jonas Trinkunas, "Revival of the ancient Baltic religions. Presented at the First International Gathering and Conference of Elders of Ancient Traditions and Cultures in Mumbai, India. Presentation sponsored by the Infinity Foundation," Infinity Foundation, http://www.infinityfoundation.com/mandala/h_es/h_es_trink_j_baltic.htm, last accessed February 26, 2014, 6.

103 Cf. Gregorius, *Modern Asatro*, 87.

104 The WCER's intensifying involvement with Hindu organizations, built on the idea of a common Indo-European religious heritage surviving in India, culminated in the participation of WCER-affiliated groups at the *First International Conference and Gathering of the Elders* in Mumbai (see Michael Strmiska, "Romuva Looks East. Indian Inspiration in Lithuanian Paganism," in *Religious Diversity in Post-Soviet Society. Ethnographies of Catholic Hegemony and the New Pluralism in Lithuania*, ed. Milda Alisauskiene and Ingo W. Schröder (Farnham/Burlington: Ashgate, 2012), 136–141; "Modern Paganism in World Cultures. Comparative Perspectives," 28), an event which was repeated in Jaipur in 2006 (cf. Carl Johann Rehbinder, "Multikulturell andlig konferens i Indien – en omtumlande resa på många sätt," *Mimers Källa* 13 (2006)) and in Nagpur in 2009 (See http://www.indiastudychannel.com/resources/www.indiastudychannel.com/resources/49543-International-Conference-Gathering-Elders.aspx, last accessed February 26, 2014). Occasional criticism that this entailed contact with militant, radical Hindu nationalist groups did not attract significant attention from Asatru groups within the WCER. Gregorius, *Modern Asatro*, 87, mentions the participation of representatives for Vishva Hindu Parisad (VHP) a group known for its involvement in the riots leading to the destruction of the mosque of Babur in 1992. See also the justification in the Danish journal *Valravn* (Sarrinder P. Attri, "Striden om et tempel – historien bag AYODHYA," *Valravn. Hedensk tidskrift om samfund og kultur* 1 (2002)).

105 Icelander Hilmar Örn Hilmarsson recounts that he "became deeply distrustful after viewing some material from the Greek and Italian members. When I hear a mention of Julius Evola I head for the hills..." Correspondence with Hilmar Örn Hilmarsson (Ásatrúarfélagið).

CREATING A RELIGION

Poland, a castle owned by the late Sigrun von Schlichting (*Armanen-Orden* and *ANSE*).[106]
In 2010, the *WCER* changed its name to *European Congress of Ethnic Religions* (*ECER*). Its new homepage features a passage where the organization now distances itself from Ariosophy as well:

> By Ethnic Religion, we mean religion, spirituality, and cosmology that is firmly grounded in a particular people's traditions. In our view, this does not include modern occult or ariosophic theories/ideologies, nor syncretic neo-religions.[107]

The Ariosophic, occultist, and rune magic branch of Asatru has had a significant impact on the internationalization of the movement beyond the *ECER* as well. Although the *Armanen-Orden* in Germany has held a low profile publicly and acted more as a secret society, it had some influence on the young Stephen Flowers (alias Edred Thorsson), who attended *Armanen* gatherings in 1981/82. Thorsson writes that these visits left him harboring "feelings of esoteric respect," but also the sense that he and the *Armanen-Orden* had "different heritages, different destinies." Nevertheless, Thorsson brought Guido von List's and other Ariosophists' ideas and writings to the attention of an English-speaking audience.[108] His *Rune Gild* presents itself as an "initiatory group dedicated toward the serious exploration of the esoteric and innermost levels of the Germanic tradition, as well as the greater Indo-European culture of which it is but a branch."[109] The *Rune Gild* represents an

---

106 This fact, and especially her presence, as well as that of some members of the *ANSE* and the *Armanen-Orden*, caused a heated discussion about the *WCER's* history and politics, especially within German Asatru. The *Eldaring* in particular was heavily criticized for sending a delegation. See http://www.asawiki.de/index.php?title=Benutzer_Diskussion: Robert_Nordlicht, last accessed February 26, 2014. Consequently, an *Eldaring* workgroup investigated further into the *Armanen-Orden's*, *ANSE's* and *GGG's* membership in the *WCER* and tried to inform other European Asatru groups about the problems arising from being associated with the Ariosophic faction within the *WCER*. To the *Eldaring's* chagrin, this educational initiative failed; as a consequence, the *Eldaring* decided in 2009 to leave the *WCER*. Cf. Correspondence with Kurt Oertel (Eldaring), 2010.
107 http://ecer-org.eu/, last accessed February 26, 2014.
108 Edred, *History of the Rune-Gild*, III (The Reawakening of the Gild 1980–2005), 36f, Stephen Flowers and Michael Moynihan, *The Secret King. The Myth and Reality of Nazi Occultism* (Los Angeles: Feral House, 2007), Siegfried Adolf Kummer, *Rune Magic*, edited and translated by Edred Thorsson (Smithville, TX: Runa Raven, 1993).
109 Michael Moynihan, "Wisdom for the Wolf-Age. A Conversation With Dr. Stephen Flowers," *New Dawn Magazine* 77, no. March-April (2003).

international network of select Asatruers, which currently has contact addresses in the USA, England, Germany, Finland, and Australia.[110] As the author of numerous publications on runes and "Germanic mysticism," and as the founder of a number of occultist and Heathen organizations, Stephen Flowers/Edred Thorsson has been one of the most active, outspoken and influential protagonists in the Asatru community in North America, if not worldwide. Having studied Germanic and Celtic philology, he received a Ph.D. from the University of Texas at Austin in 1984, with a dissertation on *Runes and Magic: Magical Formulaic Elements in the Elder Tradition*.[111] In the mid-1980s, Thorsson started publishing more popular books on Runes and Germanic magic aimed at the occult book market.[112] As Stephen Flowers, he continued to publish academic work[113] as well as translations and investigations of German Ariosophists such as Guido von List and Siegfried Adolf Kummer.[114] After having left university teaching, he founded the Woodharrow Institute[115] to further impart his theories to an academically interested audience. In addition, he started his own publishing company and online bookstore, *Runa Raven Press*.[116]

Thorsson/Flowers was also a regular contributor to the journal *Tyr*, which the influential *Rune Gild* member Michael Moynihan edited together with Joshua Buckley. This journal brought ideas of German Germanic Neopaganism and the German Faith Movement to the English-speaking world (e.g., about Géza von Neményi, the *Germanische Glaubensgemeinschaft*, and Ludwig

---

110 http://www.rune-gild.org/contact/, last accessed February 26, 2014.
111 Stephen E. Flowers, *Runes and Magic. Magical Formulaic Elements in the Older Runic Tradition* (New York: Peter Lang, 1986).
112 For example Edred Thorsson, *Futhark. A Handbook of Rune Magic* (Wellingborough, Northamptonshire: Llewellyn, 1984), *Runelore. A Handbook of Esoteric Runology* (Wellingborough, Northamptonshire: Llewellyn, 1987), *The Nine Doors of Midgard. A Curriculum of Rune-Work* (Smithville, TX: Runa Raven, 2003 [1991]).
113 Stephen Flowers, "Magic," in *Medieval Scandinavia. An Encyclopedia*, ed. Phillipp Pulsiano (New York/London: Garland Publishing, 1993).
114 Cf. Guido v. List, *The Secret of the Runes*, edited and translated by Stephen E. Flowers (Rochester, VT: Destiny Books, 1988); Kummer, *Rune Magic*.
115 http://www.woodharrow.com/, last accessed February 26, 2014.
116 *Runa Raven Press* is currently listed as a branch of the occultist Magus Books, http://www.magusbooks.com/category/RUNA-Raven, last accessed February 26, 2014. Thorsson/Flowers, books and other titles from his *Runa Raven Press* are now distributed by the expanding Swedish-British publisher *ArktosMedia* of the New Right (www.arktos.com, see also Adam Carter, "Packaging Hate – the New Right Publishing Network," Online Article, *Searchlight* (2012), http://www.searchlightmagazine.com/archive/packaging-hate-%E2%80%93-the-new-right-publishing-networks).

CREATING A RELIGION

Fahrenkrog).[117] On the other hand, *Tyr* seems to be widely acknowledged as an intellectually ambitious project, and is read and distributed by a number of groups internationally. Thus, the AFA recommends it, and even sells it on its website. Furthermore, Stephen McNallen revived the AFA's journal, *The Runestone*, in a similar yearbook format as *Tyr* and acknowledges Joshua Buckley's "advice and guidance."[118] Daniel Junker, a member of the German ORD/VfgH, makes a strong positive reference to it in the ORD's journal, *Ringhorn*.[119] The format of the German *Heidnisches Jahrbuch* (Pagan Yearbook), which Junker co-edited and published for a number of years, is so close to *Tyr's* that a certain inspiration does not seem unlikely.[120]

Two other authors affiliated with *The Troth* have had significant international influence on the development of Asatru beliefs as well. One is Freya Aswynn, whose book *Leaves of Yggdrasil* (first published in 1990, then published again under the title *Northern Mysteries and Magick* in 2002), along

---

117 See Markus Wolff, "Ludwig Fahrenkrog and the Germanic Faith Community. Wodan Triumphant," *Tyr. Myth – Culture – Tradition* 2 (2003/04); and the article by Géza v. Neményi, "Rune Song or Magic Charms? An Investigation of the 'Hávamál,'" *Tyr. Myth – Culture – Tradition* 3 (2007), transl. by Markus Wolff.

118 http://www.runestone.org/index.php?option=com_hikashop&ctrl=product&task=show& cid=14&name=the-runestone-journal-1&Itemid=557&category_pathway=10, last accessed February 26, 2014.

119 See *Ringhorn* 36, 12.

120 A possible direct connection between the *Rune Gild* and the editors of *Heidnisches Jahrbuch* can be traced as well. Edred Thorsson relates the visit of Thomas Karlsson, from the Swedish occult order *Dragon Rouge*, at the Gild-Moot in Schleswig in 2005 (cf. Edred, *History of the Rune-Gild*, III (The Reawakening of the Gild 1980–2005), 159). The co-editor of *Heidnisches Jahrbuch*, Holger Kliemannel, is the leader of this order's German section (cf. biography Holger Kliemannel in *Heidnisches Jahrbuch* 2008, 493). Kliemannel is also editor of the occult journal *Shekinah*, which published an interview with Thomas Karlsson by Thomas Lückewerth in its issue 5:2009. Lückewerth is a regular contributor to *Heidnisches Jahrbuch*, where he published an article on the German mythological and *völkisch* artist Hermann Hendrich (Thomas Lückewerth, "Hermann Hendrich – Mythenmaler und Tempelkünstler," *Heidnisches Jahrbuch* 1 (2006)). It is unlikely that it is a coincidence that a review of a book about this fairly obscure painter also appeared in *Tyr* (Markus Wolff, "Review of 'Hermann Hendrich: Leben und Werk' by Elke Rohling," *Tyr. Myth – Culture – Tradition* 1 (2002)). It thus does not seem too farfetched to assume at least a loose association between the editors and authors of *Heidnisches Jahrbuch* and the editors of *Tyr*, which may well have been facilitated at the mentioned *Gild Moot*, or through other contacts between *Dragon Rouge* and the *Rune Gild*. (For *Dragon Rouge* cf. Kennet Granholm, *Embracing the Dark. The Magic Order of Dragon Rouge – Its Practice in Dark Magic and Meaning Making* (Åbo: Åbo Akademi University Press, 2005)).

with its German translation,[121] have provided inspiration for many Asatruers worldwide. This is even truer for Stephan Grundy (alias Kveldulf Gundarsson), *The Troth's* academic specialist or "Warden of the Lore." Gundarsson/Grundy initially worked in close contact with Edred Thorsson in *The Ring of Troth*, but took a different path later on. He has published a number of seminal books on Asatru,[122] as well as historical fantasy with Germanic themes. His novels treating the *Nibelungen* material were widely read in German Asatru circles as well.[123]

With the advent of the Internet, the connections within international Asatru intensified. Most of the bigger mailing lists have threads in English in addition to their respective native languages, and a number of international closed and open lists as well as online forums have formed. According to one of my German interview partners, current international Asatru contacts function analogously to the "Facebook principle," i.e. a snowballing system of more or less committed personal or online connections. The Scandinavian groups, which started in the mid to late 1990s, have traditionally been in close contact with each other, which is facilitated by the similarities between the Norwegian, Danish and Swedish languages. Personal contacts and the existence of 'internet Heathens' enabled Germans interested in Asatru to find a forum for their interests outside of the Ariosophically-tainted German scene in the 1990s.

In spite of such international cross influences, these are not always acknowledged by individual Asatruers. Scandinavian Heathens in particular tend to consider American Asatru as somewhat less authentic and more

---

121   Freya Aswynn, *Leaves of Yggdrasil. Runes, Gods, Magic, Feminine Mysteries, and Folklore* (St. Paul, MN: Llewellyn, 1990), *Northern Mysteries and Magic. Runes and Feminine Powers* (St. Paul, MN: Llewellyn, 2002), *Die Blätter von Yggdrasil. Runen, Götter, Magie. Nordische Mythologie & weibliche Mysterien*, trans. Lionel Snell (Vienna: Edition Ananael, 1998).

122   Kveldulf Gundarsson, *Teutonic Magic. The Magical and Spiritual Practices of the Germanic People* (St. Paul, MN: Llewellyn, 1990); *Teutonic Religion. Folk Beliefs & Practices of the Northern Tradition* (St. Paul, MN: Llewellyn, 1993); *Our Troth*; Kveldúlf Hagan Gundarsson, *Wotan: The Road to Valhalla*, E-book www.aswynn.co.uk (s.l., n.d.).

123   Stephan Grundy, *Rhinegold* (New York: Bantam, 1994); *Attila's Treasure* (New York: Bantam, 1996). For a more in-depth discussion of Grundy's literary work see Chapter 9. Grundy currently resides on a remote farmstead in Ireland leading a withdrawn life with his wife, but corresponding with Asatruers worldwide. He is also responsible for the two volumes of *Our Troth*, a comprehensive overview of the history and beliefs in Asatru, which is translated into German by Kurt Oertel, the "Warden of the Lore" of the German *Eldaring*. Cf. Gundarsson, *Our Troth*; Kveldúlf Hagan Gundarsson, *Ásatrú. Die Rückkehr der Götter. Zusammengestellt von Kveldúlf Hagan Gundarsson. Deutsche Ausgabe erweitert und herausgegeben von Kurt Oertel* (Rudolstadt: Edition Roter Drache, 2012).

speculative, arguing that it is not tied to land and traditional culture in the same way as it is in those countries they themselves inhabit. An ethnicist Danish Asatruer, Søren Fisker, contradicts such reservations, invoking a paradigm of shared ancestry:

> Even people who consider themselves so all-embracing universalist are somewhat narrow in their perception of what real Asatru is. And it obviously doesn't include the Americans. The fact that some emigrated to the USA apparently disqualifies them as Asatru. And personally I don't agree. I think they can be as much Asatru as we are even though their ancestors moved across half the globe. Realistically speaking, they have been going much longer than we in Denmark; they have been going since the eighties. So I actually think that they have been through many of the things twenty years ago that we are struggling with today. [...] And therefore I think that their experiences are also very relevant.[124]

As a consequence of such attitudes, Søren Fisker has been actively networking with international ethnicist Asatru groups over the past few years. In 2012, he was hosting the annual ECER congress in Denmark.[125] Fisker was also involved in a controversy that was sparked off by an initiative that has become important for the intensifying network of European Asatru. In 2009, the first *International Asatru Summer Camp* (IASC) gathered around 150 members from nine Asatru associations in Denmark, Norway, Sweden, Germany, the Netherlands, Great Britain, and Spain; individual Asatruers from France and the U.S.A attended as well. The IASC featured blóts and rituals, lectures, workshops, and excursions, and was generally considered an important step in

---

124 Interview with Søren Fisker and Lars Irenessøn (Forn Siðr): "Selv folk, som skulle være sådan meget vidtfavnende universalistiske og så videre, de har en eller anden form for snæverhed i deres opfattelse af hvad der er rigtig asatro. Og den omfatter så tydeligvis ikke amerikanere. Det faktum, at der er nogle, der er udvandret til USA gør åbenbart, at de er diskvalificerede på forhånd som asatro. Og det er jeg så personligt ikke enig i. Jeg mener jo de kan være præcis lige så asatroende som vi er. Selvom deres forfædre er flyttet en halv jordklode rundt. Realistisk set har de jo været i gang væsentligt længere end vi har i Danmark. De har været i gang siden halvfjerdserne. Så jeg synes faktisk at mange af de ting, som vi sidder og døjer med, det er jo sådan lidt en øjenåber for mig, at det havde de jo siddet og døjet med for tyve år siden. [...] Og derfor synes jeg måske at deres erfaringer er også meget relevant for."
125 Cf. http://ecer-org.eu/event/program-for-the-15th-ecer-congress-odense-denmark/, last accessed February 28, 2014.

forming an international Asatru community in Europe.[126] In the lead up to the event, the invitation of outspokenly ethnicist groups and individuals, in particular the American AFA and the British *Odinist Fellowship*, caused considerable turmoil. The board of Danish *Forn Siðr*, which stood for the organization of the camp, had sent out invitations to both groups upon the initiative of two board members, Søren Fisker and Lars Irenessøn who, it later turned out, were members of the AFA as well.[127] The Norwegian *Bifrost* and the Swedish SAS threatened to boycott the event, and then the two Dutch groups followed suit, perceiving the AFA's folkish approach as racist.[128] The issue was eventually resolved, and the summer camp was on the whole considered an enormous success by all involved. In 2012, the camp was reprised, this time organized by the German *Eldaring* and *VfgH*, as well as the Dutch *De negen verelden* and *Het Rad*.[129] Currently, Fisker and Irenessøn are building up a Danish branch of the AFA[130]

The national and international controversies within Asatru are an indicator that a clear demarcation between a-racist Asatru and its ethnicist varieties is difficult to uphold. During the 1980s, there were attempts at actively concealing *völkisch* and racial themes within Germanic Neopaganism, especially in Germany. These have diminished considerably, not least due to an interaction between growing public awareness and media criticism on the one hand, and an equally increasing awareness of such problems within Asatru itself on the other. Asatru today is a politically diverse scene, ranging from leftist environmentalism to New Right ethno-pluralism. Many Asatruers are not involved

---

126 See e.g., the Post-IASC edition of the *IASC Herald*, an online newsletter created for the event (http://www.asatru-summercamp.eu/Docs/iasc_herald_2_print.pdf, last accessed February 28, 2014).

127 The following description is based on the documentation of the correspondences in *Völse* 47, March 2009, 40–52.

128 The origin of *Bifrost's* skepticism of McNallen and the AFA might lie in an event that took place in 2001. According to Asprem, "Heathens Up North," 62, *Bifrost's* head, Harald Eilertsen, published an article in AFA's magazine *Runestone* and was consequently "bombarded by letters and e-mails from enthusiastic American racialist Odinists." Eilertsen's urgent request to publish an article in which he could distance himself and *Bifrost* from any such racialist positions was never answered.

129 See http://www.asatru-summercamp.eu/, last accessed February 28, 2014.

130 See https://www.facebook.com/AsatruFolkAssemblyDenmark, last accessed March 10, 2014. For details see also the unpublished interview between Søren Fisker and Lars Irenessøn which, according to the author, was declined by the journal Vølse and published on the AFA Denmark's Facebook page: http://www.afa-europe.eu/docsys/docsys. php?tag=AFA&docid=261, last accessed March 3, 2014.

with and are in fact credibly appalled by *völkisch*, right-wing or racist ideologies. Hence, if we want to understand the controversies and difficulties inherent in drawing clear distinctions, we need to systematically discuss the history and various transformations of basic ideas, beliefs and practices within Asatru, rather than the more or less problematic activities of individuals, although the latter, no doubt, are of major significance as well.

CHAPTER 3

Believing and Doing

Who are they? What do they believe? How do they make sense of the world? And what do they do? Asatru's path towards public recognition can be traced in the changing make-up of its adherents, in the continuities and changes of its core beliefs and practices, as well as in the attempts to contextualize one's own worldviews and rituals within one's respective social context. We can observe significant overlaps with other varieties of Neopaganism, Western esotericism and Wicca regarding conceptions of the divine; individual deities; the relations between humans, gods, and the world; as well as views on ritual and magic. Nevertheless, the continuities of religious ideas originating in *völkisch* contexts are still significant, albeit often unacknowledged or unnoticed. Such contradictions and controversies around basic beliefs are perceived as insignificant in Asatru today. This is due to the fundamental self-conception of Asatru as a non-dogmatic religion that leaves ample room for individual constructions of faith and allows for the relatively easy adaption of broader sub-cultural and mainstream currents.

Finding Asatru

Asatru is not a widespread phenomenon, with group membership usually ranging in the hundreds, often even less. Even if we allow for a certain extrapolation of individual practitioners or those practicing exclusively in loosely organized local or regional circles, the total number of Asatruers worldwide probably does not surpass 20,000. The lack of reliable hard data makes it difficult to assess the membership's social background. In my interviews, it was not uncommon to hear complaints about social outsiders or misfits dominating other Asatru groups, as well as the claim that their own groups consisted of members from all strata of society. For Germany, Gründer observes that the average class and economic background of Asatruers is lower in racial-religious groups than in a-racist ones. In the case of the latter, more members come from middle-class environments, and hold college or university degrees, although they often work in insecure or low-paying jobs.[1]

1 Cf. Gründer, *Blótgemeinschaften*, 66f.

In comparison, Scandinavian groups seem to consist mainly of members in fairly secure middle-class professions.[2] Typically, the majority of members are between thirty and sixty years old. Many of them have previously passed through a stage of spiritual 'search' via several different religious communities or ideologies. Most groups have older members as well, who have been active in the movement for a longer time and tend to be in leading positions or at least have a degree of authority. The most significant deviation in the make-up of Asatru groups as compared to other alternative religions is gender distribution. Due to its cult of the warrior and Viking heroism, Germanic Neopaganism has traditionally been attractive to men, although the number of female members has been increasing in recent years. Today, the membership of the typical Asatru group is about one-third women.

What then are the stories Asatruers tell about how they came to be attracted to this religion? Almost all of the Heathens that I encountered in the 1980s were motivated by strong affects against their own Christian backgrounds. Anti-Christian sentiments still drive many individuals and group policies.[3] In accordance with a general decline of traditional church life's significance in Western societies, this motive has become less prominent in recent years. It remains in place in areas such as parts of rural Norway or the USA, where fundamentalist Christian churches are influential. Christian background or not, the most common story Asatruers tell is one of "awaking childhood memories."[4] These memories are frequently connected with storybook adaptations of Norse mythology or with popular films and comics. Scandinavian Asatruers invoke school lessons about Eddic poetry and saga literature, which still today form part of the national curricula. For some, recollections of folk customs by parents, grandparents, or other older relatives play a role as well.[5] These accounts indicate that many Asatruers attach great importance to the fact that their faith is connected to what they perceive as cultural roots transmitted through family and childhood experience. These accounts also suggest a sentiment many Asatruers share as well, the sense of "always having been Asatru."

---

2 My Norwegian interview partners reported unanimously that there was a curious predominance of people working in the IT and health sector.
3 For a more in-depth discussion see Chapter 5.
4 This term was used by Kaplan, *Radical Religion in America*, 18, who made the same observation amongst American Asatruers already in the 1990s.
5 Not only my own interviews, but also ones with prominent Asatruers published in the Danish journal *Valravn* over the years, show these results.

Nevertheless, for most Asatruers, as for converts to other non-dominant religions, this feeling of "coming home"[6] occurs only after a longer period of searching and examining other religious, esoteric, and philosophical traditions – a fact which explains the relatively high average age within most Asatru communities.[7] For many, this includes a period within the Wicca milieu, for others, a phase of religious indifference or atheism. Many of the latter have been involved in popular cultural scenes of live re-enactment or role-playing. They are drawn to Asatru through a growing sense that cultural re-enactment and historical interest is not enough, but that spirituality is an important facet of their lives after all, and that "all humans have an inner religious need."[8]

The final turn to Asatru is experienced differently from country to country. In Scandinavia, their 'coming home' is usually perceived as something rather undramatic, as the finding of an 'instinctive certainty'; as something that 'just feels right.' As Norse mythology and Viking history are considered integral parts of Norwegian, Danish, Swedish and Icelandic heritage, the turn to Asatru seems to require less elaborate explanation and feels more like a "natural consequence," as one Icelander put it.[9] In the USA, many Heathens motivate their choice with their German or Scandinavian heritage and ancestry – a generally accepted paradigm in a country of immigrants in which many people are

---

6 In her "classic" presentation of the diverse Neopagan scene in North America from 1979 (revised editions appeared in 1986 and 2006) Margot Adler calls Paganism "a religion without converts." She builds her argument on such experiences of "coming home," of always having "had a religion, I just never knew it had a name" (Adler, *Drawing Down the Moon*, 13). Sían Reid, "'A Religion Without Converts' Revisited. Individuals, Identity and Community in Contemporary Paganism," in *Handbook of Contemporary Neopaganism*, ed. James R. Lewis and Murphy Pizza (Leiden/Boston: Brill, 2009) "revisits" this thesis, distinguishing between a Christian, Paulinian model of conversion as "something that 'happens to' an individual" and a "'new paradigm' of the activist conversion, the prototype for which is the 'seeker'" (173). This model can be used to describe contemporary Pagan experiences of conversion. See also Gründer, *Blótgemeinschaften*, 96f, who observes a certain tension between a processual transformation of worldviews, an interpretive drift towards a polytheistic religious framework, and such "coming home" experiences, which are narrated as singular and concrete experiences.

7 Obviously, this does not mean that Asatru is necessarily the last stage in everybody's religious search, but from the data available to me it is impossible to assess the percentage of long-term versus short-term members. The impression given here – that a larger number of adherents tend to stay with Asatru for at least an extended period of time – might also have to do with the fact that the long-term active members tended to volunteer more frequently to be interviewed than less committed members.

8 See Interview U.

9 Cf. Interview S.

searching for their roots. Germans who choose to join more right-wing Asatru groups already have a fairly secure ideological conviction and understand their adoption of a Germanic religious framework as its logical consequence.[10] For the growing number of German Asatruers who explicitly reject racial and ethnic paradigms, the turn to the Norse gods has not been unproblematic. It is often accompanied by considerable inner struggles resulting from the fact that German neo-Germanic Paganism up until the 1990s was strongly dominated by groups promoting a more or less overt racial esotericism.[11] This might also be the reason why an astonishingly large number of German Asatruers present their being drawn to Norse mythology as a strong, but ultimately inexplicable and irrational inner pull. This is especially the case for outspokenly a-racist, politically critical Heathens who are looking for explanations for their own choices beyond any ethnic or racial criteria.[12]

A similar wish to demonstrate the sincerity and authenticity of one's own religious path might lie at the basis of another common narrative. A good number of Asatruers emphasize their having had liminal or mystical experiences occasioned by accidents, personal crises or similar, in which they directly encountered the presence of a deity. In my interview samples, such experiences were mostly conveyed by German Asatruers. However, Michael Strmiska and Baldur Sigurvinsson provide similar examples among North American Heathens.[13]

Heathen Beliefs

Most of my interview partners offered elaborate personal narratives about how they found Asatru and what it means to them. They were also quite articulate when it came to describing Asatru rituals and their worldview in general. In contrast, the question of how they perceive the Norse gods and their relationship to them proved difficult for many. Answers were frequently emphatic statements that concepts of the divine are so diverse and varied

---

10   Cf. Gründer, *Blótgemeinschaften*, 78f.
11   It is hard to judge the extent to which such narratives are influenced by my position as a critical investigator of the field. My impression is that they emphasized these notions over other motives for my sake and in order to not be grouped among right-wing extremists, but that they at the same time were honest and sincere about them.
12   It is thus a sentiment that was especially shared by all members of *Nornirs Ætt* to whom I spoke.
13   Michael Strmiska and Baldur A. Sigurvinsson, "Asatru: Nordic Paganism in Iceland and America," in *Modern Paganism in World Cultures. Comparative Perspectives*, ed. Michael Strmiska (Santa Barbara, CA: ABC-Clio, 2005), 147, 155.

within Asatru that no outsider could possibly understand them. Some also see it as a very personal and intimate question, which they are reluctant to answer. One German Heathen gave a particularly elaborate explanation typical of these widespread sentiments. It shows the variety of concepts within one person along with those concepts' indeterminability, and points to unresolved contradictions:

> This is the question that I find the most difficult, and I am afraid to not be able to give a really satisfactory answer in this limited space, especially since my ideas about [the gods] are not one-dimensionally constant, but oscillating. Furthermore, it is impossible to communicate numinous experiences without distorting them through the limitations of the possibilities of linguistic expression. A personified concept is of course helpful and makes many things easier, and I often see them like that. At the same time, I am aware that such a limitation, which comes from our limited imagination, cannot do justice to them. In other moments, I see them as abstract, as the forces which hold the cosmos together, which let life germinate in spring and which are remote from human invocation. Then again, I think that I can feel their protective and directive force in my own life. Or maybe they are only aspects of my own psyche, which are inaccessible in normal consciousness, but can be experienced and helpful in liminal experiences and extraordinary situations? In general, I experience the deities as basic characters and basic qualities of the world which appear in the psyche as well as in nature.[14]

---

14   Interview N: "Diese [...] Frage empfinde ich als die schwierigste überhaupt, und ich fürchte, auf dem hier begrenzten Raum keine wirklich befriedigende Antwort geben zu können, zumal meine Vorstellungen über sie nicht eindimensional konstant sondern oszillierend sind. Zudem ist es unmöglich, Erfahrungen des Numinosen wiederzugeben, ohne sie dabei durch die Begrenzungen sprachlicher Ausdrucksmöglichkeit zu verbiegen. Eine personifizierte Vorstellung ist natürlich sehr hilfreich und macht vieles einfacher, und so sehe ich sie auch oft, während mir aber doch gleichzeitig bewusst ist, dass ihnen eine solche Einschränkung, die nur unserer begrenzten Vorstellungskraft entspringt, nicht gerecht werden kann. In anderen Momenten sehe ich sie eher abstrakt als die Kräfte, die den Kosmos zusammenhalten, in jedem Frühling wieder das Leben sprießen lassen und die menschlicher Anrufung fern stehen. Dann wieder meine ich, ihre schützende und bestimmende Kraft auch im eigenen Leben zu spüren. Oder sind sie vielleicht nur Aspekte der eigenen Psyche, die einem im Normalbewusstsein unzugänglich, in Grenzerfahrungen und Ausnahmesituation aber erfahrbar und hilfreich sind? Allgemein aber empfinde ich die Gottheiten als Grundcharaktere und Grundqualitäten der Welt, die in der Psyche ebenso wie in der Natur erscheinen."

This Heathen goes on to explain that for him, humans and gods are inextricably connected to one another, as they are each an integral part of the world. However, when it comes to the question of whether the gods are an expression of a certain cultural heritage, he initially rejects this notion in order to later reaffirm a similar relation:

> About gods and culture: On the one hand, I see the least connection there, because culture is purely a product of human communities. On the other hand, Asatru, as a reconstructionist religion, of course aims at a certain cultural integrity which is limited to the Germanic cultural sphere. But as Asatru for me is not based on theological hair-splitting, I have never found it necessary for myself to work out final answers to these questions. Nevertheless, I think that all humans experience the same forces, although they are modified by landscape and climate and called by different names.[15]

The statement about the lack of theological hair-splitting reflects a very common attitude among Heathens. It indicates that the implicit contradiction between irreconcilable elements, that are nonetheless perceived as equally necessary, are common in Asatru (and of course not only here), but that they are rarely openly addressed and usually evaded. This happens frequently through the almost dogmatic invocation of the notion that the fundamental nature of Asatru is its lack of dogmatism. Therefore, in spite of the variety of images and concepts of the deities, there is hardly any controversy around the 'right' concept.

However, it is possible to discern a general trend about how concepts of the divine have developed since Germanic Neopaganism's 'invention' in the early 20th century. Adherents of a *völkisch* religion found the polytheistic nature of their ancestors' faith embarrassing, but nevertheless in accordance with the general attitudes of their time; they were naïve at best, objectionably primitive at worst. They thus followed different strategies to prove the superior,

---

15   Ibid.: "Zu Göttern und Kultur: Hier sehe ich einerseits am wenigsten Verbindung, da Kultur ein reines Produkt menschlicher Gemeinschaften ist. Andererseits aber bemüht sich Asatru als rekonstruktionistische Religion dabei natürlich um eine gewisse kulturelle und auf den germanischen Kulturraum beschränkte Integrität. [...] Da Asatru aber nicht von theologischen Spitzfindigkeiten geprägt ist, habe ich es für mich nie als notwendig empfunden, mir zu diesen Fragen endgültige Antworten erarbeiten zu müssen. Dennoch denke ich, dass alle Menschen dieselben Mächte erfahren, wenn auch landschaftlich und klimatisch modifiziert und unterschiedlich benannt."

monotheistic nature of Germanic faith.[16] Such negative attitudes toward polytheism changed in the 1970s. All the same, the assumption that the Germanic pantheon is a natural expression of the spiritual forces that guide the Germanic or Nordic peoples, or manifests the folk- or race-soul, remained firmly in place. This racial-religious idea is reminiscent of C.G. Jung's theory of archetypes; it is no coincidence that Jung's thought was and still is frequently referred to, not only by Germanic Neopagans, but in other Neopagan and alternative spiritual circles as well.[17] The archetypal approach is easily combined with the idea that the gods are forces, active within nature and within humans themselves. As the above quote demonstrates, the combination of these three aspects – cultural heritage, psychological principle, and the force of nature – is still prevalent among contemporary Asatruers.

The archetypal approach has lost its dominant position since the 1990s. The German ethnicist *VfgH's* homepage makes this clear:

> Traditional Germanic Heathenism is a polytheistic religion which does not see 'aspects' of an abstract divinity in the gods as do some esoteric systems. It does not reduce the diversity of their personalities to speculative phantoms as 'the god and the goddess' and it certainly does not psychologize them as 'archetypes' or diminish them to mere symbols. Gods and Goddesses really exist and are concrete, personal beings with individual personalities.[18]

---

16   German Faithlers would vehemently refute accusations of wanting to revive a primitive "Cult of Wotan" by making it clear that their religion had evolved from these roots into modern times and included the philosophies of all 'great German thinkers.' In accordance with theosophy and other contemporary neo-Gnostic schools, Ariosophists such as Guido von List avoided the problem of polytheism by distinguishing between an exoteric, polytheist 'Wotanism' for the broader masses, and a secret, monotheist 'Armanism' for the initiated higher warrior, king, and priest elites.

17   For Neopaganism in general, the renegade Jungian analyst and theorist James Hillman's ideas about archetypal psychology being polytheistic in nature had major significance. See e.g. Hillman's afterword in David L. Miller, *The New Polytheism. Rebirth of the Gods and Goddesses*, 2. ed., with a prefatory letter by Henry Corbin, appendix by James Hillman (Dallas, TX: Spring Publications, 1981).

18   "Das traditionelle germanische Heidentum ist eine polytheistische Religion, die in den Göttern keine 'Aspekte' einer abstrakten Göttlichkeit sieht, wie es manche esoterischen Lehren tun, die Vielfalt ihrer Persönlichkeiten nicht auf spekulative Phantome wie 'den Gott und die Göttin' reduziert und sie schon gar nicht als 'Archetypen' psychologisiert oder zu bloßen Symbolen herabwürdigt. Götter und Göttinnen existieren tatsächlich und sind konkrete persönliche Wesen mit individuellen Persönlichkeiten." ("Was sind Götter überhaupt," http://www.vfgh.de/, last accessed March 19, 2014).

Increasingly, and with less obvious embarrassment, Asatruers speak about their gods as "real and mighty beings";[19] as individual, independent entities with different powers and areas of responsibility;[20] as "good friends" one can "relate to" and "ha[ve] a relationship with";[21] as parts of this world; and as complex, wise, and powerful beings who are "not omniscient."[22]

The trend toward a more 'strict' polytheism in recent years serves to delineate one's own religion against three tendencies that are seen as potentially problematic. The first is Christianity and other 'book religions,' which allegedly posit God as "an abstract, otherworldly, eternal, all-mighty being that hovers above the world and rules it from the outside, not a 'pure spirit' or moral authority that exclusively embodies the so-called good."[23] The second is C.G. Jung's theory itself, whose concept of archetypes has come increasingly under attack for being too close to *völkisch* and racial thinking.[24] The third is the more syncretistic Wicca movement, against which Asatru tries to posit itself as authentic and in accordance with original sources.[25]

One concept developed within German and Scandinavian scholarship of the 1920s and 30s has survived up until today: the belief in a *fulltrúi* or patron deity. It can serve as an instructive example for the symbolic continuities as well as the ideological transformations within Germanic Neopaganism over the last hundred years. The term *fulltrúi*[26] surfaces first in Icelandic medieval hagiographic manuscripts, where it is used to characterize patron saints. Later on, it appears in saga literature, describing a man's relation to a Pagan god, with whom he has an exclusive patron-subject relationship. It is likely that the

---

19   Gundarsson, *Our Troth*, vol. 1, 131.
20   GardenStone, *Germanischer Götterglaube. Asatru – eine moderne Religion aus alten Zeiten* (Engerda: Arun, 2003), 43.
21   Interview O.
22   Gundarsson, *Our Troth*, vol. 1, 131.
23   "Was sind Götter überhaupt "(http://www.vfgh.de/, last accessed March 19, 2014): "Eine Gottheit im Heidentum ist kein abstraktes, jenseitiges, ewiges, allmächtiges Wesen, das über der Welt schwebt und sie von außen regiert, kein 'reiner Geist' und keine moralische Instanz, die ausschließlich das sogenannte Gute verkörpert."
24   This sentiment was voiced by a number of my Scandinavian interview partners. In its new edition of *Our Troth* (Gundarsson, *Our Troth*,vol. 1, 100), Jung is even grouped as part of the *völkisch* movement. This change in the perception of Jung has to do with the publication of Richard Noll's controversial book *The Jung Cult* (Noll, *The Jung Cult*), which brought to light Jung's debt to *völkisch* ideology.
25   Cf. Gregorius, *Modern Asatro*, 200.
26   Incidentally, the term has moved into the modern Icelandic language as well, where it now means 'representative.'

fulltrúi is a Christian imagination of what Pagans' relationships to their gods might have looked like. In these texts, it has predominantly literary functions. The popularization of the concept in the 1920s and 30s is related to the desire to prove the monotheistic, and thus superior, character of the original Germanic faith. It was posited as an alternative to Christianity and Judaism, as an "upright" form of religiosity, based not on the "fear of God, but an equal relation between man and god based on mutuality,"[27] corresponding with the freedom-loving mentality of the Germans.[28] The imagined relationship of equality, and its often polemic, antithetical contrast to the alleged relation of submission and obedience ascribed to Christianity, has a significant persuasiveness for Asatruers worldwide.[29]

At the same time, an increasing number of Asatruers are by now aware of the tenuous link between their belief in a *fulltrúi* and the Old Icelandic sources from which the concept is derived.[30] Here, as in other cases in which historical accuracy contradicts lived experience in Asatru, the latter is ranked higher in terms of importance. A participant in the *Eldaring* online forum summarizes this attitude:

> The discussion is unnecessary in practice, because even though x scholars prove that an intimate relationship to a god/goddess is originally Christian, I know what I have experienced and felt. And that is what counts.[31]

---

27   Julia Zernack, "Fulltrúi," in *Reallexikon der Germanischen Altertumskunde*, ed. Heinrich Beck, Dieter Geuenich, and Heiko Steuer (Berlin/New York: Walter de Gruyter, 1996), 244.
28   This summary follows "Fulltrúi," in *Reallexikon der germanischen Altertumskunde*, ed. Heinrich Beck, Heiko Steuer, and Dieter Timpe (Berlin: de Gruyter, 1997).
29   This is probably also due to the spread of the concept by Swedish scholar Folke Ström, whose summarizing presentation of "Nordic Paganism" from 1967 serves, for many Scandinavian Asatruers, as an important source for the construction of their religion (Gregorius, *Modern Asatro*, 209, see also Folke Ström, *Nordisk hedendom. Tro och sed i förkristen tid*, 2. ed. (Göteborg: Akademiförlaget, 1967)). According to the user "Bil" on www.asatrulore.org (last accessed March 19, 2014) American Asatruers have received the *fulltrúi* or 'patron' concept from Harry Harrison's alternative historical trilogy *The Hammer and the Cross*, published in 1993. For the significance of these novels see Chapter 9.
30   See the contributions by "Bil" on www.asatrulore.org (last accessed March 19, 2014), who draws attention to the fact that the concept lacks historical support and is considered a syncretistic construction, influenced by Christian and New Age thought. In Germany, this skepticism is fueled by Bernhard Maier's recent book on Germanic Religion (Maier, *Die Religion der Germanen*), which is widely read in Asatru circles and summarizes the problems of this concept.
31   "Die Diskussion erübrigt sich meines Erachtens für den praktischen Bereich, denn selbst wenn mir jetzt x Wissenschaftler belegen, daß die innige Beziehung zu einem/r Gott/

This, however, implies that the ideological dimensions of the concept of the *fulltrúi* are rarely discussed.

It comes as no surprise that the deities to whom Asatruers relate most frequently are the ones best known from mythology and its various popularizations throughout the centuries, i.e. Odin/Wotan, with Thor[32] being a close runner-up; the love and fertility goddess Freya and her counterpart Freyr; Odin's wife Frigg; and Tyr, who is perceived as a god of justice.[33] In German and Anglo-American Asatru, another goddess, Ostara, ranks highly as well. This goddess' surmised existence goes back to a misunderstanding by Jacob Grimm and became immensely popular in Romanticism.[34] She appeals to contemporary Anglo-Saxon and German Heathens to the degree that they abandon their claims of scholarly-based authenticity and worship this spring goddess around Easter, because it "works for them."[35]

The only controversial case when it comes to the worship of deities in Asatru is that of Loki, the troublemaker and trickster of the Nordic pantheon. Racial-religious Asatruers see him as the spawn of miscegenation (he is the child of a god and a giant); others view him as a destructive force due to his role in the killing of Balder and the demise of the gods in Ragnarok. A few, however, especially those who are interested in 'shamanistic' practices or *seid*, or in questions of gender and the transgression of gender boundaries, see him as a problematic although interesting figure, who deserves attention and careful worship.[36] In addition to these deities, entities from

---

Göttin originär christlich sei, weiß ich doch, was ich erfahren und gefühlt habe. Und das zählt doch wohl." Thread "Fulltrui – was sagen die Quellen?" (http://www.eldaring.de/pages/forum---community.php, last accessed November 27, 2012).

[32] Jóhanna Harðardóttir in Iceland claimed that Thor is (and has been through the ages) most Icelanders' favorite deity, whereas mainland Scandinavians tend to adhere to Odin, cf. Interview with Jóhanna Harðardóttir (Ásatrúarfélagið), August 12, 2010, Iceland.

[33] The quantitative evaluation of Gründer's interviews shows a similar tendency with mentions of Odin leading, followed by Thor (127), Freyja (80) and Loki (72), see Gründer, *Blótgemeinschaften*, 248.

[34] Ostara's worship is related to a passage in Jacob Grimm's *German Mythology*, based on his reading of Bede's account. In *Ecclesiastical History of the English People* (around 731 AD), the Anglo-Saxon monk writes about a Germanic spring goddess, Eostrae, from which the term Easter (German Ostern) is supposedly derived.

[35] See for example MartinM, "Ostara – oder: dem Fest ist es egal, ob eine Göttin so heißt," Nornirs Ætt, http://www.nornirsaett.de/ostara-oder-dem-fest-ist-es-egal-ob-eine-gottin-so-heist/, last accessed June 03, 2015.

[36] See for example Interview L. For a general discussion of Loki's contested nature in Asatru see Diana L. Paxson, *Essential Asatrú. Walking the Path of Norse Paganism* (New York: Citadel Press, 2006), 72.

'low mythology,' e.g. local spirits of nature called *vættir*, play a role.[37] This emphasis on beings known not only from written mythological sources but also from folk religion and customs seems to be an increasing trend in Asatru today.

Relations and interactions between humans, gods, and other (super)natural entities such as the aforementioned *vættir*, dwarves, giants, elves, etc. are theorized more or less elaborately in different countries and groups. Most Heathens refer to Eddic sources regarding Yggdrasil, the World Ash Tree that encompasses the nine worlds (*'níu heimar'*) in which the different species of beings reside. Neither scholars nor Heathen practitioners agree about the nature and significance of these 'worlds' and their respective inhabitants.[38] A number of elaborate theories have been put forth which are particularly influential within Anglo-American Asatru. Every basic discussion by Heathens about their faith, or by outside researchers, will give at least a summarizing account of the location and meaning of the nine-world model. Frequently, the nine worlds are described as levels of individual and cosmic consciousness,[39] a concept which was initially developed by Edred Thorsson in *A Book of Troth*.[40] This concept opens up a variety of esoteric speculations about correspondences between the nine worlds, the runes, and astrological signs, etc.[41]

The idea of the nine worlds corresponds with the postulation of different types or aspects of human 'souls,' or physical, psychic, and spiritual levels of existence. Frequently, this model is used to distinguish Asatru's understanding of an intricate psychosomatic wholeness from the Christian tradition's supposedly simple dichotomic split between body and soul, matter and

---

37   For Danish Asatru author Gudrun Victoria Gotved, *Asatro. De gamle guder i moderne tid* (Copenhagen: Aschehoug, 2001), 30, the gods are "not for daily use."

38   For a scholarly discussion, see for example Margaret Clunies Ross, *Prolonged Echoes. Old Norse Myths in Medieval Northern Society: The Myths*, vol. 7, The Viking Collection, Studies in Northern Civilization (Odense: Odense University Press, 1994), 50–56, who incidentally does not work with a neat system of nine worlds, but alerts to the complex and contradictory spatial structures in eddic literature.

39   Cf. Pete Jennings, *The Norse Tradition. A Beginner's Guide* (London: Hodder & Stoughton, 1998), 26f, as well as the summary in Harvey, *Listening People, Speaking Earth*, 54.

40   Edred, *A Book of Troth. Runa-Raven Yrmin-Edition* (Smithville, TX: Runa-Raven Press, 2003), 22.

41   See e.g. GardenStone, *Germanische Magie* (Engerda: Arun, 2001), 75–77. Such principles of esoteric correspondences between micro- and macro-cosmos are frequent in other groups as well. See Brochure "Åsatrofellesskapet Bifrost," ed. Åsatrufellesskapet Bifrost (2002), 9.

spirit.[42] These elaborations also seem to be limited to the wider context of the American *Troth* and groups influenced by it or by Edred Thorsson's and Kveldulf Gundarsson's writings. The connection of concepts of souls with various forms of rebirth in the kin or clan,[43] or with reincarnation in general,[44] has traditionally been more widespread.[45] Today, most Asatru groups do not make official statements about this issue, but instead leave it up to the individual members.

The concept of the World Tree in Norse mythology in general, as well as Asatru in particular, is tied to the mythological figures of the three norns, Urd, Verdandi, and Skuld, who, according to Eddic accounts, reside at the Urd Well at the roots of Yggdrasil. These figures, which have often been compared to the Moirae or Parcae (the Fates of Greek and Roman antiquity), give cause to much speculation and theorization about the role of fate or *wyrd* in Heathenism and the existence of an alleged characteristic 'Germanic fatalism' (Germanischer Schicksalsglaube).[46] Although the book *Our Troth* claims that "there are not contradictions [with our religion] as there are in other faiths,"[47] many Heathens agree with Graham Harvey's assessment of there being "an ambivalence or oscillation between fatalism and free-will"[48] within Asatru. This ambivalence is illustrated in the following reflections by a Norwegian Asatruer:

> Actually, it is impossible to prove how far there is a fate or a free will. It depends on one's perspective. [...] Shall we believe in both responsibility

---

42   Cf. "Germanischer Seelenglaube und Seelenkonzepte im modernen Seidhr" (http://eldaring.domainfactory-kunde.de/ELDARING_4/board58-artikel-germanisches-heidentum/board62-runen-und-magie/7750-germanischer-seelenglaube/, last accessed September 16, 2014). Cf. also Gundarsson, *Our Troth*, vol. 1, 499–508.
43   See ibid., 508.
44   Gotved, *Asatro. De gamle guder i moderne tid*, 39.
45   The German *Armanen-Orden*, as well as the Icelandic *Nýalssinna*, held the belief that souls undergo various incarnations in different 'lower' and 'higher' races, in order to develop and finally incarnate on other, more highly developed planets. Cf. Schnurbein, *Religion als Kulturkritik*, 50f, and 177–179.
46   In particular, the etymological proximity of 'urd' to the Anglo-Saxon term 'wyrd' (which is again echoed in the modern 'weird'; Shakespeare's "weird sisters" on their part being an echo of the three fates) has motivated most of the prominent English and American Asatru authors to consider the available research on 'wyrd' and reflect about the role of fate.
47   Gundarsson, *Our Troth*, vol. 1, 523.
48   Harvey, *Listening People, Speaking Earth*, 56. Gründer, *Blótgemeinschaften*, 210, comes to a similar conclusion and observes that worldviews of Asatruers are deterministic to varying degrees.

for our own actions and fate? Perhaps, it's difficult to balance. That's the stuff we modern Heathens struggle with.[49]

Authors writing about *wyrd* agree that it is not an immutable, divinely imposed 'fate,' but rather the expression of an interaction between past deeds and their consequences in the present which form the future. This results in a complicated web of cause and consequence, to which all beings, including the gods, are subject. Such a worldview also gives rise to reflections about the significance of past, present and future. Based on the observation that Germanic languages do not have a separate form for future tense, but instead need an auxiliary verb such as 'will' or 'shall' to express it, the conclusion is drawn that the rootedness of the 'folk' in the past takes on an a remarkable significance. This idea can be traced back to Romanticism, and is expressed emphatically in this passage from *Our Troth*:

> To us, that-which-is, 'the past,' is not gone or lost: it is forever living and green, and more, it is the source from which all springs, even as the roots are the source of the tree. New branches can spring forth if the crown is chopped off; but the destruction of the roots is the end: and thus it is with our folk. To lose the ways of our forebears – to lose our foothold in that-which-is, or get too far from their thoughts and beliefs – is to be rootless trees and to die.[50]

This notion of rootedness in the past is often set against either a "Mediterranean" or a Christian perception of a "linear past, present, and future,"[51] which by some is seen as potentially dangerous to the invoked "roots" of Germanic faith.[52] Such reflections on the significance of roots and ancestors also show how easily ethnic arguments enter into the worldview of a-racist Asatruers.

Concepts of *wyrd* (*skæbne*, or *Schicksal*, the terms for 'fate' in Danish and German) are most elaborated in Danish, German, and especially Anglo-American Asatru. This is related to two factors. Firstly, the concept of *wyrd* has

---

49 "Hvorvidt det fins en skjebne eller om man har fri vilje, det er umulig å bevise, egentlig. Det kommer an på perspektivet man har. [...] Skal man kunne tro på både ansvar for egne handlinger og skjebne? Kanskje vanskelig å få til å gå opp. Det er sånt som vi moderne hedninger strir med." Interview O.
50 Gundarsson, *Our Troth*, vol. 1, 487f.
51 *Teutonic Religion. Folk Beliefs & Practices of the Northern Tradition*, 15.
52 Such dichotomies are discussed in detail in Chapter 5.

enjoyed a strong interest within Anglo-Saxon scholarship.[53] Secondly, the popularity of the topic of fate in a broader sense has to do with the attention one particular book has attracted in Danish, German and Anglo-American Heathen communities, the Danish historian of religion Vilhelm Grønbech's *The Culture of the Teutons* (1909–1912). His imaginative summary of the mentality and worldview of "our ancestors"[54] elaborates the concepts of *orlög* (another word for fate), *hamingja* (referring to the 'luck' of a clan or kinship group), and *frith* (an active form for peace within the group, when its *hamingja* is present). The frequency of the use of these Grønbechian key terms is a good indicator for his influence in different contexts.[55]

For everyday ethics, only certain aspects of *wyrd* or fate are foregrounded. With few exceptions, Heathens agree that good and evil are categories imposed by Christianity, and thus apply to Heathen ethic as little as the ideas of sin, punishment, redemption, and judgement. They are replaced by the allegedly Heathen idea that one's deeds are all that count, which influences the web of *wyrd*, and bears consequences for which each individual is responsible. Many Asatruers mention this idea of personal responsibility for one's own actions and a principle of 'honor' as the most appealing aspects of their religion, appreciating it primarily because of its simplicity and straightforwardness. In Iceland, this attitude was codified already in 1972, in the second article of *Ásatrúarfélagið*'s rules: "The main core of this custom [*sið*] is the responsibility for oneself and one's actions. In this matter we make use of the Snorra-Edda and other holy scriptures."[56]

A female member of the Norwegian *Bifrost* put it this way:

---

53   The most influential work in Asatru contexts is no doubt Paul Bauschatz' *The Well and the Tree*, a thorough investigation into the *World and Time in Early Germanic Culture* (Paul Bauschatz, *The Well and the Tree. World and Time in Early Germanic Culture* (Amherst: University of Massachusetts Press, 1982)). Around the same time, the idea was popularized in Neopagan spiritual contexts, e.g. by psychologist Brian Bates, "professor of shamanic consciousness at the University of Brighton" in his fictional account of the spiritual experiences of an "Anglo-Saxon Sorcerer" (dust cover for Brian Bates, *The Way of Wyrd. Tales of an Anglo-Saxon Sorcerer*, 2. ed. (Carlsbad, CA: Hay House, 2005 [1983])).

54   Vilhelm Grønbech, *Vor Folkeæt i Oldtiden*, 4 vols. (Copenhagen: Pios, 1909–12). English edition *The Culture of the Teutons*, 2 vols. (London: Oxford University Press, 1931).

55   For a discussion of Grønbech's significance and a critique of such approaches see Chapter 8.

56   "Helzta inntak þessa siðar er ábyrgð einstaklingsins á sjálfum sér og gerðum sinum. Í þessu efni hófum við hliðsjón af Snorra-Eddu og öðrum helgiritum." Quoted from Jonsson, "Ásatrú á Íslandi við upphaf 21. aldar," 98.

If you make a wrong choice, then you have to deal with the consequences right away, and then it is not God who is angry at you, it is just you who has made a wrong choice, and then you have to learn from it, and then you don't do it another time, right?[57]

The particular interpretations of concepts such as responsibility and honor range from everyday ideas about being "able to look at myself in the mirror in the morning"[58] to calls for a vitalist warrior heroism. An article in the German journal *Herdfeuer* takes up the main themes of such a Germanic *amor fati*:

> To live in the North has always meant to bend to the unavoidable, to make use of the opportunities that offered themselves, and to do what needed to be done as thoroughly as possible. What the nature of the North taught our ancestors, we find in their myths. Fate appears as inexorable as the invading winter. Everything that happens is interwoven, often in a fatal way. One deed leads to the next; everything comes as it has to come. Man is left to do what has to be done. [...] But astonishingly enough, in this world where everything is counted and weighed, we find not a trace of a rebellion against unjust fate, no disappointed turning away from the brutal world. Neither was there a cynical nihilism, no withdrawal into satisfying private appetites as one might expect. The characters who meet us in Germanic mythology fulfilled their fate with verve, they were full of life-energy, active, self-confident. Not that they resigned to their fate, no, they seemed to positively love their fate. [...] A true life-fervor inhabited these people. They were animated by a fighting spirit. Life was sacred to them, and fate, the *wyrd*, that what has become as it is called in Germanic tradition, was life, being, in and of itself. It was given to man at his birth, and he took part in it all his life, was rooted as an individual in the eternal deep ground of being. He knew that something sacred lived in him – that force which gives life to his heart and his loins. This made him worthy of life and his life worthy of living. This was the basis of his courage and his honor.[59]

---

57 "Gjør du et feil valg, så må du ta konsekvensen av det med én gang, og da er det ikke Gud som er vred på deg, det er bare du som har tatt et feil valg, og så må du lære av det, og så gjør du ikke det samme neste gang, ikke sant?" Interview P.
58 Ibid.
59 "Im Norden zu leben hat immer geheissen (sic), sich dem Unvermeidlichen zu beugen, die Chancen zu nutzen, die sich boten, und das, was zu tun war, möglichst gründlich zu tun. Was die Natur des Nordens unseren (sic) Vorfahren gelehrt hatte, finden wir in ihren

This quote, describing a Germanic Heathen fatalism, foregrounds an activist religion of 'deed' which favors heroism in the face of natural hardships and places values such as honor in a position of preeminence. It can be read as a 21st century reflection of the popular Nietzscheanism which permeated early 20th century intellectual culture in Germany and elsewhere in Europe,[60] and which informed the belief in the absolute value of actions of atonement: the *Tat*, action, or deed in Germanic Faith as well. In the first part of the 20th century, GGG-founder Ludwig Fahrenkrog summarized it emphatically in the slogan "God in us – the law in us – 'the self-redemption'"[61] and explained:

> Action became action and lives on in its consequences, and action was mine eternally. Nothing eradicates it, nobody else's action, but the healing, bettering action done by myself – the action that makes any wrong right again or – atones for it.[62]

Mythen. Unerbittlich wie der einfallende Winter erscheint uns hier das Schicksal. Alles, was geschieht, ist, oft auf verhängnissvolle (sic) Weise miteinander verwoben. Eine Tat führt zur anderen, alles kommt, wie es kommen muss. Dem Menschen bleibt, zu tun, was zu tun ist. [...] Doch erstaunlicherweise finden wir in dieser Welt, in der alles gezählt und gewogen ist, keine Spur einer Revolte gegen das ungerechte Schicksal, keine enttäuschte Abkehr von der brutalen Welt. Es gab auch keinen zynischen Nihilismus, keine Rückzug in die Befriedigung privater Gelüste, wie man vermuten könnte. Die Figuren, die uns in der germanischen Mythologie entgegentreten, erfüllten ihr Schicksal mit Verve, sie waren voller Lebensenergie, aktiv, selbstbewusst. Nicht, dass sie sich in ihr Los schickten, nein, sie schienen ihr Schicksal förmlich zu lieben. [...] Eine wahre Lebenswut wohnte diesen Menschen inne. Sie waren vom Kampfgeist beseelt. Das Leben war ihnen heilig, und das Schicksal, das 'Gewordene,' wie es in germanischer Tradition so treffend heißt, war das Leben, das Sein, an und für sich. Es wurde dem Menschen mit seiner Geburt gegeben, und er hatte ein Leben lang daran Teil, wurzelte als Individuum im ewigen Urgrund des Seins. Er wusste, dass in ihm etwas Heiliges lebte, jene Kraft, die sein Herz und seine Lenden belebte. Dies machte ihn würdig zu Leben und sein Leben lebenswürdig. Dies war die Grundlage seines Mutes und seiner Ehre." Peter Walthard, "Die alte Sitte," *Herdfeuer* 2, no. 3 (2004), 5.

60   For an in-depth discussion of the widely varied appropriations of Nietzsche's thought in Germany see Steven E. Aschheim, *The Nietzsche Legacy in Germany 1890–1990* (Berkeley: University of California Press, 1992).

61   "Gott in uns – das Gesetz in uns – 'die Selbsterlösung.'" Quoted from Junker, *Gott in uns!*, 39.

62   Fahrenkrog 1923: "Die Tat ward Tat und lebt in ihren Folgen fort, und immerdar war mein die Tat. Nichts tilgt sie, keines anderen Tat, als nur die heilende, bessernde Tat von mir getan – die Tat, die jenes Unrecht wieder recht macht oder – sühnt."

Such notions are taken up by Theodist Eric Wodening, an early member of the *Ring of Troth*, who gave his frequently cited book the telling title *We Are Our Deeds*[63] – an almost literal quotation of Ludwig Fahrenkrog's famous motto for the *Germanische Glaubensgemeinschaft*: "Deine Tat bist du!" (You are your deed!) Generally speaking, we can note a transformation of the ideals of honor, deed, and self-redemption in Germanic Neopaganism from a racial-biological, Social Darwinist framework in the 1920s to 1940s to an individualized concept, no longer tied to a people, nation, or race. René Gründer aptly calls this process "traditionalizing individualism."[64] Such individualism (including its masculinist, heroicist overtones) seems indeed adaptable to a late modern agenda. However, we should not overlook the fact that *völkisch* religion and German Faith in the early 20th century was also not exclusively dependent on a biological paradigm. The aforementioned religious models also owed much to liberal theology and to liberal and Nietzschean critiques of religion. The quotes also show that remnants of Social Darwinism are still active within parts of Asatru today.[65]

German a-racist *Nornirs Ætt* is the only group that I encountered which harks back to the concept of *wyrd*, yet squarely opposes any cult of heroism and the explicit or implicit disdain for weakness. Instead, the small group stresses the importance of a community based not only on consensus but also on the principle of consideration for its weakest members. One of the early members wrote the following explanatory sentences:

> Nothing has impressed me more from the beginning than the consistent strategy of our initial spokespeople to abolish their own status. [...] *Nornirs Ætt* is a community in which you may show weakness without provoking strength. THAT is OUR strength: We are a home for handicapped people – nothing but totally normal people who have one [...] guarantee – that our speed is determined by those who walk slowest. THAT is what WE call (with some hubris, I know) 'Germanic.'[66]

---

63 Eric Wodening, *We Are Our Deeds. The Elder Heathenry. Its Ethic and Thew* (Watertown, NY: Theod, 1998).
64 Gründer, *Blótgemeinschaften*, 273, cf. his discussion of *Heil* and *hamingja*, 272–275.
65 The example of Anthony Winterbourne, *When the Norns Have Spoken. Time and Fate in Germanic Paganism* (Madison/Teaneck: Fairleigh Dickinson University Press, 2004), shows that the idea of an "all-embracing fate" that "somehow leaves room for pride, dignity, and defiance, rather than an encouragement to supine submissiveness" is interesting for popular philosophy about fate, time, heroism, and action as well.
66 "Denn kaum etwas hat mich von Anbeginn an mehr beeindruckt als die konsequente Strategie unserer anfänglichen Wortführer, ihren eigenen Status abzuschaffen. [...]

Most of these contradictions and implications remain latent though. Asatruers tend to appreciate the relative simplicity and straightforwardness of their ethic of responsibility, and very few intervene critically. A rare voice of concern by a "Heathen academic in the US" is quoted by Jenny Blain:

> Seeing all the 'trailer park philosophies' being peddled, a horrible thought occurred to me: Maybe one of the reasons Asatru is appealing to some folk is because the ethical codex laid out in the Havamal is very 'motherhood and apple pie.'... If you strip away all the mythological veneer and 'far away Iceland in a different age' type mystique, all that remains from the Havamal is a behavioural codex that is about as complex as Fulghum's 'All I needed to know I learned in Kindergarten.'[67]

The idea that Germanic Neopaganism is based on a worldly ethic of action and not on a belief in supernatural beings fueled the debate as to whether Asatru should be considered a religious belief system, or rather a philosophical worldview and cultural tradition based on practices that should be preserved, revived, and transformed.[68] The latter position, as well as the claim that in Heathenism "religious and social community are identical,"[69] is gaining ever more prominence within Asatru. This has led a number of groups to reject the term 'Asatru' and replace it with terms like '*Forn Sed*' or '*Alte Sitte*,' meaning

---

Die Nornirs Ætt ist eine Gemeinschaft, innerhalb derer du dich schwach zeigen darfst, ohne Stärke zu provozieren. DAS aber ist UNSERE Stärke: Wir sind Heimat für Behinderte – lauter stinknormale Menschen, die eine [...] Garantie haben. Nämlich die, dass unser Tempo bestimmt wird von denen, die am langsamsten laufen. DAS nennen WIR (mit einiger Hybris: I know) 'germanisch.'" Correspondence with Duke Meyer.

67   Blain and Wallis, "Heathenry," 242. One might add the question in how far the cautionary and skeptical advice of the Hávamál, a poem originating in a society ruled by an oligarchy and split by violent feuds, can and should be adapted to contemporary conditions at all.

68   This question already led to controversies and schisms between Ariosophy and German Faith, cf. Gründer, *Blótgemeinschaften*, 166, as well as Junker, *Gott in uns!*. However, there have neither been clear borders between the two camps, nor is it possible to say that one of the sides is per se closer to a racial-religious paradigm. Esoteric speculation today can be found both in ariosophic and a-racist groups while a cultivation of tradition is practiced in racial-religious organizations such as the *Artgemeinschaft* in Germany as well as in culturally (but not necessarily politically) conservative groups such as *Foreningen Forn Sed* in Norway.

69   "Religiöser und sozialer Verband [sind] identisch." Asfrid, "Heidnische Grundbegriffe," *Ringhorn. Gemeinschaftsanzeiger des Vereins für germanisches Heidentum e.V.* 51 (2007), 11.

'the old way,' 'the old tradition,' or 'custom.' In doing so, they acknowledge that pre-Christian Scandinavians or Germans did not have a name for their religion, and that the term 'Asatru' is an invention of Scandinavian National Romanticism. They see the emphasis on 'tru' (belief, or faith) as an ultimately Christian notion, which does not reflect the activist and practical nature of modern (and in their eyes also ancient) Heathenism. This increasingly common attitude explains why there is room for so many divergent ideas about deities and other supernatural beings and their relations to humans and the world. Moreover, it places ritual practices at the center of contemporary Germanic Neopaganism, as Fritz Steinbock, of the German *VfgH*, writes:

> Rituals are the traditional core of Heathenism. It is not a dogmatic religion that places the belief in its teachings in the center, but a living relationship to the gods, to nature and to everything holy that realizes itself actively. It is not theory, but practice. Being a Heathen means to practice Heathenism.[70]

Heathen Practices

The above quote is representative of another typical feature within current Asatru. Ritual is seen as an aspect of religion connected to a lived reality and sense of authenticity. There is no general critique of ritual (for example as a stifled, petrified, and oppressive social force) although many Asatruers reject 'dogmatism' with regard to beliefs. I have found no instance where this implicit contradiction is addressed, and many Heathens today indeed agree with Steinbock's assertion that ritual is at the center of, and defining for, their religion.[71] Most groups use the term 'blot' (often spelled blót) for their main ritual activity.[72] There is extensive agreement that the purpose of the blot is to connect with the deities, to communicate with 'the powers,' and, at least in case of communal blots, to strengthen the human community and group coherence.

---

70 "Rituale sind das traditionelle Herzstück des Heidentums. Es ist keine dogmatische Religion, die den Glauben an ihre Lehren in den Mittelpunkt stellt, sondern eine lebendige Beziehung zu den Göttern, der Natur und allem Heiligen, das sich tätig verwirklicht. Es ist nicht Theorie, sondern Praxis. Heide sein heißt das Heidentum auszuüben." Fritz Steinbock, *Das heilige Fest. Rituale des traditionellen germanischen Heidentums in heutiger Zeit*, 2. ed. (Hamburg: Verlag Daniel Junker, 2008), 13.
71 See also Interview O.
72 The term is derived from the Icelandic sagas.

Also in this respect there has been a fluctuation over time. From the 1920s to the 1940s, the communal aspect was predominant, while the 1970s and 80s saw an increasing individualization of rituals. Today, there seems to be a shift back to the emphasis on community celebrations.

In his discussion of Icelandic Asatru, Eggert Solberg Jonsson roughly distinguishes four types of ritual which can be also applied to most modern Asatru groups in other countries: Rituals of the solar cycle, rituals for other occasions (including different types of Heathen historical memorial days), individual rituals of the life cycle, and individual solitary or communal rituals to connect with deities and ask for help or advice.[73]

The basic structures of communal blots in most groups are similar, and usually comprise the following elements:

1. The delineation of a ritual space, usually a circle of the participants around a fire or another sacral center (an altar, statues or images of deities, symbolic objects). This is frequently done by invoking the four points of the compass.
2. The invocation of gods and goddesses.
3. The passing of a horn filled with mead or another, usually alcoholic, drink to all participants, who then drink to the gods, making wishes or boasts.
4. A donation of food, or sometimes objects.
5. The opening of the circle.

This is frequently followed by a communal meal, which in some groups forms the actual ritual itself.[74] The common general structure for the blot varies according to the ideals of the group or the requirements of the occasion. Some, such as the *Vfyll*, include the incantation of runes. The outspokenly anti-racist Swedish *Samfundet Forn Sed* starts its blots by raising a so-called *nid*, a type of banishment or spell against groups who they feel misuse Asatru for political or racist purposes.[75] Danish *Forn Siðr* has incorporated readings of Eddic texts into their official ritual.

---

73 Jonsson, "Ásatrú á Íslandi við upphaf 21. aldar," 159f.

74 English and American groups, as well as the German *Eldaring* that grew out of the American *Troth*, call the latter, i.e. a ritual exclusively devoted to the passing of the horn, praising the gods, making toasts and boasts, a 'Sumbel.' For a more detailed discussion of different tendencies in the ritual practices of German Asatru see Gründer, *Blótgemeinschaften*, 108–112.

75 Cf. Gregorius, *Modern Asatro*, 230. The practice of raising a "Nidstang," a pole of banishment, refers to an event described in the Egilssaga where a horse's head was raised on a pole in order to ward off an enemy.

There is also a somewhat general agreement about the times for the main blots. In most groups, they are held at or around the solstices and equinoxes.[76] Scandinavian and German groups today hold most of their rituals outdoors, a practice that they perceive to be most authentic. Some groups and individuals choose to hold blots at locations that are considered pre-Christian sites of worship. Swedish and Icelandic Asatru groups have succeeded in establishing their own national traditions of annual worship at sites considered national treasures. *Ásatrúarfélagið* celebrates once a year at Thingvellir, the site (today a national park) where the medieval Icelandic legislative and judicial assembly, the Althingi, was held between 930 and 1271. Since 2000, Swedish Asatruers have had permission to celebrate a blot at Gamla Uppsala (Old Uppsala), a site of Iron-Age burial mounds considered a pre-Christian center of administration and worship, which later became Sweden's archbishopric.[77] Both events attract considerable media attention, and are seen as important symbolic events positing Asatru in overt competition with the dominant Christian churches. Both Gamla Uppsala and Thingvellir were used, by Swedish and Icelandic Asatruers respectively, in the year 2000 to mark a reclaiming of traditional Heathen sites – acts which led to some controversy as well as welcome media attention for Asatru groups.[78] In Germany, the Externsteine, near the Teutoburg Forest, as well as the Sachsenhain, the alleged site of the killing of Saxon leaders by Charlemagne in the 8th century, have served similar functions. However, both are strongly contested sites and are today only wholeheartedly embraced by racial-religious

---

76   The Icelandic *Ásatrúarfélagið* celebrates the spring and fall blots at slightly different times in mid-April and mid-October, basing these dates on mentions of different celebrations in medieval Icelandic sagas and Eddic literature. Individual Godis have also established their own traditions of annual blots at different times of the year, cf. Jonsson, "Ásatrú á Íslandi við upphaf 21. aldar," 170–173. Some groups additionally celebrate at other times of the year as well, Easter (Ostara) being popular amongst German groups. Thorrablót, a festival mentioned in some medieval Icelandic sources which marks the last month of winter (Thorri), was re-created by Icelandic students in the late 19th century in the tradition of contemporary student fraternities' drinking rituals. It has become widely popular in Iceland in general, amongst the *Ásatrúarfélagið*, and other Scandinavian groups as well, cf. ibid., 75, 196.
77   For information on the contemporary museum at Gamla Uppsala see http://www.raa.se/cms/extern/se_och_besoka/gamla_uppsala.html, last accessed March 29, 2014.
78   The Icelandic case is discussed in Strmiska and Sigurvinsson, "Asatru: Nordic Paganism in Iceland and America." For *Sveriges Asatrosamfund's* celebrations in Gamla Uppsala see Gregorius, *Modern Asatro*, 103.

groups due to their extensive use by National Socialism, which tried to establish them as German national sacred sites.[79]

The question of proper locations for local, regional and national celebrations is tied closely to debates about the extent to which it is important or appropriate for Asatru to establish temples or halls of worship. Some American groups, as well as the Icelandic *Ásatrúarfélagið*, attempt to build their own halls of worship, often called *Hof*. Others, such as *Asatrofællesskabet Yggdrasil and Nordisk Tingsfællig* in Denmark, or the *Olgar Trust* in England, aim at purchasing land to dedicate to Heathen celebrations.[80] The lack of funds, and the attitude that official temples are not appropriate for a 'nature religion,' caused considerable controversy between different Germanic Faith groups in the 1920s. Ambitious plans to construct such sites of worship, such as those of Ludwig Fahrenkrog and Fidus, were never realized, however.[81] The establishment of temples is a minor issue in current Asatru as well.[82]

In addition to seasonal festivals, Asatruers observe events in the life cycle, such as the birth or naming of a child, coming of age, marriage, and death. For Scandinavian groups, which are or were functioning within state church systems, it became particularly important to be able to officially conduct marriages as well as funerals. Norwegian, Danish and Icelandic groups have attained this right with their official recognition by their respective states, and by now also have their own funeral sites. These aspects are of less importance in countries like Germany and the Netherlands, where official marriages may only be conducted by state authorities, whereas all

---

79   For the Externsteine see Volker Schockenhoff, "'Stonehenge' contra 'Störrische Kuh,'" in *Wir zeigen Profil. Aus den Sammlungen des Staatsarchivs Detmold. Ausstellung des Nordrhein-Westfälischen Staatsarchivs Detmold* (Detmold: NW Staatsarchiv, 1990) and Uta Halle, "'Treibereien wie in der NS-Zeit.' Kontinuitäten des Externsteine-Mythos nach 1945," in *Völkisch und national. Zur Aktualität alter Denkmuster im 21. Jahrhundert*, ed. Uwe Puschner and G. Ulrich Großmann (Darmstadt: WBG, 2009), for a discussion of the Sachsenhain as a National Socialist and German Faith site of worship see Justus H. Ulbricht, "'Heil Dir, Wittekinds Stamm.' Verden, der "Sachsenhain" und die Geschichte völkischer Religiosität in Deutschland, Teil 1 und 2," in *Heimatkalender für den Landkreis Verden: Verdener Sachsenhain, Jahrbuch 1995 und 1996*, ed. Landkreis Verden (Verden: Landkreis Verden, 1995/96).

80   For a discussion of this strategy, see Chapter 6.

81   Cf. Rainer Y, *Fidus, der Tempelkünstler. Interpretation im kunsthistorischen Zusammenhang mit Katalog der utopischen Architekturentwürfe*, 2 vols. (Göppingen: Kümmerle, 1985).

82   For such debates on temple building in Germanic Neopaganism see also Chapters 1 and 9.

religious ceremonies – including Christian ceremonies – are regarded as personal matters.[83]

It is not easy to determine the exact origins of the modern Asatru practice of blot. The first groups to apply the term were the Icelandic *Ásatrúarfélagið*, the British *Odinic Rite*, and the AFA.[84] The international spread of ideas on the blot can probably be attributed to Edred Thorsson's books, (e.g., *A Book of Troth*) and later Kveldulf Gundarsson's writings. Concurrently with the *Odinic Rite* and the *Ásatrúarfélagið*, the German *Armanen-Orden* (especially Sigrun von Schlichting) developed their own rituals.[85]

Since medieval sources are notoriously quiet about Heathen practices, elements of rites can rarely be traced back to or even considered to have been inspired by them. The few accounts of rituals found in medieval saga literature mention a temple (*hof*) where statues of gods are erected and sprayed with the blood of sacrificed animals.[86] The question is rarely asked how authentic these descriptions are, or to what extent they are creative imaginations by Christian minds fantasizing about the 'bloody' and 'primitive' practices of Heathens.[87] Be that as it may, the mentioned practices are not part of modern Asatru rituals.[88] The only aspect from medieval sources that is included in contemporary blots is the ritual drinking and toasting. This is probably a reflection of a 19th century Romantic imagination of medieval drinking rituals, which also found expression in student fraternities.[89]

---

83 In Germany, a burial site for non-denominational as well as *völkisch* religious individuals was erected in 1958 in Conneforde, cf. Gründer, *Blótgemeinschaften*, 116.

84 The *Odinic Rite* started early on to codify the rituals its members designed into the *Book of Blotar* (cf., Stubba, *The Book of Blots. Ceremonies, Rituals & Invocations of the Odinic Rite* (London: Odinic Rite, 1991)), whereas the AFA's rituals were documented by Stephen McNallen in three booklets *Rituals of Ásatrú* in 1985, the first carrying the sub-title *Major blots* (cf. Stephen A. McNallen, *Rituals of Ásatrú. I Major Blots* (Breckenridge, TX: The Ásatrú Free Assembly, 1985)).

85 Cf. Schnurbein, *Religion als Kulturkritik*, 56–61, Gründer, *Blótgemeinschaften*, 169.

86 Cf. Martin P. Hansen, "Blótets liturgi, før og nu," *Vølse* 45 (2008).

87 See for example Rudolf Simek, *Religion und Mythologie der Germanen* (Darmstadt: WBG, 2003), 282.

88 A few Asatruers mentioned that they use animal blood bought from butchers in their private rituals. The only exception I could find is High Theodism, which allegedly practices animal sacrifices conducted by members trained in proper butchering. See Lord, *The Way of the Heathen*, 23f.

89 For a reception of such rituals in circles of Icelandic students in Copenhagen in the late 19th century as well as in 19th century National Romantic Icelandic paintings, plays etc. that make use of the motives of drinking to the dead, the ancestors, and the gods, see Jonsson, "Ásatrú á Íslandi við upphaf 21. aldar" 75–82.

At the same time, there are a number of similarities between Asatru rituals and Wiccan practices: outdoor worship, the circle, the hallowing of the four directions, and the dates for the four main seasonal celebrations.[90] These unquestionable parallels have a number of possible explanations. On the one hand, Wicca is, as mentioned, the largest and most influential faction within modern Paganism, and has thus formed popular ideas about the general nature of Pagan religions.[91] In Asatru, connections to Wicca are frequently despised, denied, or downplayed, either because Wicca is perceived as being too libertarian, permissive, and leftist (this is often the case in North American Asatru), or because it is seen as a fictional religion which rivals the establishment of a 'real,' authentic, indigenous Paganism (as many European, particularly Scandinavian Asatruers claim). In spite of this, many Asatruers have been involved with Wicca, making mutual inspiration likely. This is also true for some of those Asatruers who set out to construct rituals in the 1980s and 90s and dispersed them throughout the Asatru world.[92]

On the other hand, not all of the Wiccan-looking elements necessarily have to be attributed to a direct influence of Wicca on Asatru. Rather, some may also

---

90   In addition to the equinoxes and solstices, which are celebrated in Asatru as well as in Wicca, Wicca has four seasonal celebrations between these dates. In some Asatru groups, an equivalent to these is also celebrated.

91   For an in-depth discussion of Wicca's success in creating a functional new religion and forming perceptions about Paganism in general see Hutton, *The Triumph of the Moon*.

92   This applies to Freya Aswynn (http://www.aswynn.com/about-me.html, last accessed March 19, 2014) and Prudence Priest (*AFA, American Vinland Association*) who is an elder in the Wiccan *Covenant of the Goddess* (cf. Sylvana SilverWitch, "Just 'Wiccatru' Folk. A Word With Prudence Priest," Widdershins, http://www.widdershins.org/vol3iss6/y9702.htm, last accessed November 01, 2011). Theodism started as an split-off from Wicca. The founder and leader of the *Yggdrasil Kreis*, Volkert Volkmann, holds amongst other things, a Wicca Master Degree (cf. http://www.yggdrasil-kreis.org/html/runasongr.html, last accessed March 19, 2014). It should be mentioned that the *Odinic Rite* is one of the groups that most vehemently rejects Wicca. Nevertheless, Volkert Volkmann was a professed member of the *OR* as well. According to former *VfGH* leader Haimo Grebenstein, the collaboration with the *Yggdrasil Kreis* in the early years of the *Odinic Rite Deutschland* played a certain role in the creation of the *VfGH* blots, along with the *Odinic Rite*'s *Book of Blotar*. Edred Thorsson, probably the most influential Asatru author worldwide, has not been directly involved with Wicca, but relates having had an "indirect connection" that made him "familiar with the workings of that system." (Edred, *History of the Rune-Gild*, III (The Reawakening of the Gild 1980–2005), 27). For his instrumental *The Book of Troth* he invented the Hammer ritual, which has definite parallels to Wiccan practices. It is a form of calling the four directions and hallowing the circle for a blot used by many Asatru groups, including Scandinavian ones.

result from their shared background in Western ritual and ceremonial magic,[93] or even possibly from German neo-Pagan influences on Wicca – especially since Germanic pre-Christian religion as a seasonal religion of nature is older than the Wicca movement itself. Some early 20th century German Faithlers already celebrated the seasonal sun cycle and saw Eddic myths as reflections of nature and fertility, and combined these with a belief in the unity of the Germanic race with its nature.[94]

In everyday practice, reflections on the origin of Asatru blots play a fairly marginal role. The question of codifying Asatru rituals is also a point of discussion. Many groups and individuals welcome the lack of sources on 'Germanic' rituals, as it gives them an opportunity to freely create practices of worship that fit contemporary needs and predilections. In Norwegian and Danish Asatru, codification only took place when the process of institutionalization and professionalization i.e., the application for state recognition, required it.[95]

Closely related to this question of codification is the issue of priesthood within Germanic Neopaganism. Three main models of organization have been in place since the early 20th century. The first is an initiatory model, which implies a Masonic system of ascending degrees. It was practiced in, or propagated by, Ariosophic groups and related secret societies or lodges in the early

---

93 The basic Wicca ritual as it was constructed by Gerald Gardner is based on Aleister Crowley's *Book of Shadows*. For the influence of Crowley on Gardner and Wicca see Hutton, *The Triumph of the Moon*, 216–223. In an article about the origin of Danish *Forn Siðr's* blot Martin P. Hansen, "Blótets liturgi, før og nu" points to this parallel as well. Crowley's ideas were also instrumental for the modern occult revival, which Ariosophy and Germanic Faith, theosophy, and a number of occult orders, such as the sex-magic *O.T.O.*, are part of (cf. Bogdan, "The Influence of Aleister Crowley on Gerald Gardner and the Early Witchcraft Movement").

94 This is illustrated in the 'sacred dramas' written by Ernst Wachler and Ludwig Fahrenkrog for the outdoor stage at *Harzer Bergtheater*, which also served as a location for ritual activities of the GGG. Here, the seasonal cycle, along with the hammer and swastika symbols (both read as sexually charged symbols of fertility and a violent national and racial rebirth) were frequently used, cf. Ludwig Fahrenkrog, *Baldur* (Stuttgart: Greiner und Pfeiffer, 1908), *Wölund* (Stuttgart: Greiner und Pfeiffer, 1914), Ernst Wachler, *Walpurgis. Ein Festspiel zur Frühlingsfeier* (Leipzig: C.F. Amelangs Verlag, 1903), *Mittsommer. Trauerspiel mit Chören für die Bühne unter freiem Himmel* (Munich/Leipzig: Georg Müller, 1905), Schnurbein, "Religiöse Ikonographie – religiöse Mission. Das völkische Weihespiel um 1910." For a more in depth discussion see Chapter 9.

95 *Forn Siðr's* first application was turned down because its ritual structures, especially those for public services, such as marriages, were not clear enough. See *Forn Sidr's* homepage: http://www.fornsidr.dk/om-forn-sidr/godkendelsesforloebet, last accessed February 26, 2014.

20th century, and later the *Goden-Orden*, as well as the *Armanen-Orden* in Germany. Today, Edred Thorsson's *Rune Gild* follows a similar initiatory pattern, which is otherwise not very prominent in contemporary Germanic Neopaganism.[96] The second type implies a church-like structure, with an officially appointed clergy ('*Gode*' or '*Godi*' for male, '*Gydja*' for female), an official religious leader comparable to a bishop ('*Allsherjargodi*'), and at least plans for the erection of *hofs*. Ludwig Fahrenkrog's ideas about Germanic ritual practices and temple buildings at alleged sacred sites in Germany dating from the early 20th century can be included in this category.[97] Today, the *Germanische Glaubensgemeinschaft* continues Fahrenkrog's tradition not only in the name of its association, but also in its model of priesthood.[98] Iceland is the only country that has a functioning system of an officially appointed clergy and a formal election process for the *Allsherjargodi* as the national religious leader. The most influential American groups, *The Troth* and the AFA, do not have any national religious leaders, but have both introduced clergy training programs.[99] Swedish *Samfundet Forn Sed* established a training program for Goder and Gydjer in 2010 to ensure the quality of spiritual services offered.[100]

In other respects, *Samfundet Forn Sed*, Danish *Forn Siðr*, Norwegian *Bifrost*, *Foreningen Forn Sed*, along with the German *Eldaring* and *VfgH*, are organized according to the third, least-structured model. It follows an idea formulated already in the early 20th century by Otto Sigfrid Reuter (*Deutschgläubige Gemeinschaft*), who completely rejected a formal priesthood as well as a formalized creed or temple-buildings.[101] In the contemporary groups previously mentioned, the national organizations function as umbrellas or networks

---

96 An exception is Theodism, which claims to reconstruct the full Anglo-Saxon social hierarchy, including the model of sacred kingship, cf. Lord, "The Evolution of Theodish Belief. Part 1"; *The Way of the Heathen*.
97 Cf. Puschner 2001, 252.
98 However, its leader Géza von Neményi's claim to the status of *Allsherjargodi* has not been recognized by any other Asatru group in Germany and has given rise to much resistance and ridicule, cf. Pöhlmann, "Streit um Heiden-Papst – Géza von Neményi erhebt Führungsanspruch innerhalb des Neuheidentums."
99 http://www.thetroth.org/index.php?page=clergyprograms&title=Clergy%20 Program%20|%20The%20Troth&css=style2&pagestyle=mid; http://www.runestone.org/about-the-afa/clergy-program.html, last accessed March 19, 2014.
100 Cf. http://www.samfundetfornsed.se/om-samfundet-1282525, last accessed March 19, 2014. See also Sveriges Asatrosamfund, "Snart är de nya stadgarna här!," 5f.
101 Although the structure Reuter imagined was similar to contemporary groups,' his reasoning was not. For him, the creation of structured "teaching communities" (Lehrgemeinschaften)

allowing anyone who wishes to conduct a ritual to do so.[102] Associated regional or special interest blotgroups may institute their own rules and practices. As state-registered associations (e.g., German *Eldaring* and *VfgH*) or official religious communities (e.g., Scandinavian groups), they are chaired by an elected board, usually comprising of at least a chairperson, their deputy, a secretary, and a treasurer, all of whom have administrative functions, but no religious authority.[103]

The existence of a formal priesthood notwithstanding, Asatru has another, more informal system of religious specialists: members who engage in rune magic or a neo-shamanic practice called *seid* (sometimes spelled Sejd, seidh, seidhr, or seiðr). Both remain contested in Asatru and Odinism. Some see them as dishonorable, inauthentic, foreign, modern occultist, or esoteric practices associated with Wicca. Others consider the study of runic or *seid* practices the core of their religious activity. Rune magic, and to a lesser degree and more recently *seid*, can be seen as Germanic Neopaganism's unique contributions to the modern occult and esoteric revival. They have also become popular practices outside Asatru, and thus their history, context, and present status deserve particular attention here.

The roots of modern esoteric runology are found in Guido List's visions.[104] He 'revealed' the runes as the sacred original language of mankind, or rather of

---

served to create a "pure racial community." Cf. Puschner, *Die Völkische Bewegung im wilhelminischen Deutschland*, 252f.

102 The problem in these groups is more often the lack of individuals willing to and interested in accepting the responsibility for designing and conducting a ritual. In practice, this leads to the same people leading rituals and thus taking on an informal role as religious specialists.

103 Also in this respect, the German *Nornirs Ætt* deviates most. They decided against registering as a society, so that they could institute a principle of consensus and not of elected representatives, cf. Gründer, *Blótgemeinschaften*, 217.

104 The runes are an alphabet used for inscriptions between the 2nd and 14th century, mainly in southern Scandinavia. The older rune-row (called *futhark*, after its first six letters) consisted of 24 letters, the younger *futhark* of 16. Most inscriptions date from the Viking Age. There are some hints in the sagas that runes were used for magic purposes, but not much is known about these practices, if indeed they ever existed. (For a comprehensive overview of theories and scholarship on runes cf. Klaus Düwel, *Runenkunde*, 4. ed., Sammlung Metzler (Stuttgart: Metzler, 2004)). The idea that 'Teutons' actually 'cast runes' for divinatory purposes originates in a specific reading of Section 10 in Tacitus' *Germania* about omens and casting of lots. As the first runic inscriptions to have been found date considerably later, it is not very likely that Tacitus (if his account itself is actually accurate and not just a projection of Roman practices onto the Northern Barbarians) really referred to the runes here. In the modern era, the idea of the runes' magic properties was first taken

its spiritual leaders, the Aryans, and as expressions of the highest cosmic powers guiding the ancient 'Ario-Germans.'[105] In his most influential work, *Das Geheimnis der Runen* (The Secret of the Runes, 1908), List created an allegedly ancient eighteen-letter runic alphabet, and assigned each rune a verse of Odin's spells in the Eddic lay *Hávamál*.[106] For List, this runic system contained the essence of Ario-Germanic wisdom. He claimed that it had been secretly transmitted through the 'dark ages' of Christianity and racial mixing via clandestine brotherhoods: medieval guilds of Masons, Templars, witchcraft, and also the Icelandic skalds, who allegedly preserved the ancient German mythology, albeit in Icelandic translation. The idea that runic wisdom was concealed in various symbolic systems that could be decoded by way of his intuition allowed List to identify traces of this ancient knowledge in all kinds of later sources, be they Christian, heretic, philosophical, or symbolic.

List's system fit with common occult practices of analogical thinking, and proved easily applicable to various systems of esoteric classification. List and Lanz von Liebenfels' follower Rudolf John Gorsleben applied them to astrology,[107] while the Ariosophists Friedrich Bernhard Marby and Siegfried Adolf Kummer created runic gymnastics, or 'rune-yoga.' It bears repeating that such ideas regarding the secret functions of the runes cannot easily be separated from the underlying assumption that cosmic runic energies speak only to those of "pure Aryan blood." It is thus the Aryan's obligation to preserve this

---

up by Renaissance runologist Johannes Bureus, who interpreted them and Norse mythology in the light of Rosicrucian, cabbalistic, astrological, and hermetic theories.

105 Schnurbein, *Religion als Kulturkritik*, 92f; Ulrich Hunger, *Die Runenkunde im Dritten Reich. Ein Beitrag zur Wissenschafts – und Ideologiegeschichte des Nationalsozialismus* (Frankfurt a.M.: Lang, 1984), 316f.

106 This section, sometimes also referred to as *Rúnatal* (Rune-poem), tells of Odin hanging from a tree for nine nights, "finding runes" and listing 18 "songs of power," which describe, for example, how enemies can be beaten and women's desire awakened. It is still debated if this actually refers to the letters or merely to 'secrets,' the literal meaning of the word 'runa.'

107 Rudolf John Gorsleben, *Hoch-Zeit der Menschheit. Das Welt-Gesetz der Drei oder Entstehen – Sein – Vergehen in Ursprache – Urschrift – Urglaube. Aus den Runen geschöpft* (Leipzig: Koehler & Amelang, 1930) designed an astrological chart he called "Tyr-Kreis," claiming that the German word for the zodiac, "Tier-Kreis" (meaning "animal circle"), is a distortion of the original meaning, which refers to the Nordic god Tyr. Sigrun von Schlichting and Géza von Neményi followed this idea and the theory is fairly widespread in Asatru circles (cf. Schnurbein, *Religion als Kulturkritik*, 47; Valdemar Ravn, "Interview med Géza von Neményi den Tyske Allherjargode," *Valravn. Hedensk tidskrift om samfund og kultur* 13 (2005), 11). A Google search for "Tyr-Kreis" gave 41,300 hits in March 2014.

purity of the blood, a task in which runic practices are an indispensable tool. This attitude is summarized in Guido von List's "mystical interpretation" of the *ka*-rune: "Dein Blut, Dein höchstes Gut" (Your blood, your highest possession).[108] Gorsleben embedded his rune esoteric in a theory of "racial consciousness and selective racial breeding," claiming that "God and race are one."[109] Marby, and later his post-war publisher, Rudolf Arnold Spieth, were both adamant that his "Rassische Gymnastik" (racial gymnastics) was to be understood as an "Aufrassungsweg" (path of racial improvement), which was to be strictly reserved for members of the "Germanic Race."[110]

If the runes were discredited as viable icons after the fall of Hitler's regime in 1945, it was not due to rune esotericists' racial theories, but rather to the extensive use the National Socialist state had made of some 'Germanic' symbols, in particular the swastika,[111] and specific runes such as the double *sig*-rune for the SS. It did not take long before an attempt was made to rehabilitate the "Armanen" rune system and purge it of its more overt racial implications. In 1955, Karl Spiesberger (1904–1992), a member of the occult order *Fraternitas Saturni*, started publishing on rune divination and rune exercises while teaching workshops using Gorsleben's, Marby's, Kummer's and most of all List's works as points of reference.[112] He distanced himself from "distortions of runic knowledge by race fanatics" and thought it important to separate the "everlasting wheat grain of eternal values" from the racist chaff.[113] At the same time, he carefully omitted mentioning that the racist content of rune knowledge was actually propagated by the 'masters' of esoteric runology themselves, and could not just be attributed to misuse by National Socialists.

The works by Spiesberger, List, Marby and Gorsleben strongly influenced the rune practices within the German *Armanen-Orden*. Internationally, the post-war runic revival was spearheaded mainly through the activities of Stephen Flowers, alias Edred Thorsson. He founded his initiatory *Rune Gild* in 1980 and launched three influential books on rune esoteric.[114] Flowers/

---

108 List, *The Secret of the Runes*, 53.
109 All quotes from the Table of Contents in Gorsleben, *Hoch-Zeit der Menschheit*.
110 See http://spiethverlag.de, last accessed September 16, 2014.
111 It should be noted, however, that the swastika played a central role as a sign of racial consciousness and life energy in Ariosophy as well.
112 Karl Spiesberger, *Runenmagie. Handbuch der Runenkunde* (Berlin: Schikowski, 1955).
113 Ibid., preface.
114 Thorsson, *Runelore. A Handbook of Esoteric Runology; Rune Might. Secret Practices of the German Rune Magicians* (St. Paul, MN: Llewellyn, 1989); *Northern Magic. Rune Mysteries & Shamanism* (St. Paul, MN: Llewellyn, 1998).

Thorsson has been ambiguous about his being influenced by Ariosophy. On the one hand, we know he discovered Spiesberger's writings in 1974,[115] and that like Spiesberger, he strongly denounced the abuse of runic symbolism by National Socialism. However, he claims to offer a more historically sound take on rune divination beyond early 20th century German rune magic, e.g., by basing his theories not on List's invented 18-part rune row, but on the older, historically informed 24-part alphabet. This, along with his academic background, convinced Heathens worldwide that his rejection of racial readings of the runes was honest and serious, and that his esoteric teachings were based on solid historical knowledge.[116] Nevertheless, in acknowledging the help extended to him by Adolf and Sigrun Schleipfer, of the racial-religious *Armanen-Orden*, Thorsson's second book, *Runelore*, indicated that he might owe more to Ariosophy than what was initially understood.[117] In addition to quoting academic literature in *Rune Might*, he recognizes List and Marby as authors on runology who "shine out above all the rest,"[118] and goes on to present the *Armanen-Orden* as a contemporary bearer of List's runic knowledge.[119] In 1988, Flowers/Thorsson published an English translation of List's *The Secret of the Runes*, and thus initiated a surge of interest for Ariosophy and the 'Armanen-runes' within Asatru in the United States.[120] Up until 2012, his publishing company *Runa Raven Press* distributed his translations of other works by List, as well as by the Ariosophists Lanz von Liebenfels, Siegfried Adolf Kummer, and Rudolf von Sebottendorf.[121]

This runic revival was further supported by a number of others. A former member of Thorsson's *Rune Gild*, the Dutch-British Asatruer Freya Aswynn, published the essence of her runic teachings in 1990 under the title *The Leaves*

---

115   Edred, *History of the Rune-Gild*, III ('The Reawakening of the Gild 1980-2005), 28.
116   Cf. Interview with six members of Nornirs Ætt. My interview partners from Nornirs Ætt mentioned that this initial positive impression was soon disappointed when Thorsson's uncritical references to Ariosophy became obvious.
117   Thorsson, *Runelore. A Handbook of Esoteric Runology*, 'Acknowledgements.'
118   *Rune Might. Secret Practices of the German Rune Magicians*, xiii.
119   Ibid., 29f.
120   Several American Asatruers mentioned being "great fans of List." A Google-search on the key words 'Armanen-runes' in November 2011 gave 4,280,000 hits.
121   The press was closed down in fall 2012. https://www.facebook.com/Asatru.Folk.Assembly/posts/443338919052337. *Runa Raven Press* is currently listed as a branch of the occultist Magus Books, http://www.magusbooks.com/category/RUNA-Raven. Books formerly distributed by *Runa Raven Press* by Thorsson/Flowers and others can now be found on www.arktos.com. For information about the New Right publishing company *Arktos* see Carter, "Packaging Hate – the New Right Publishing Network."

of *Yggdrasil*.[122] The same year, in *Teutonic Magic*, Kveldulf Gundarsson/ Stephan Grundy harked back to List's/Thorsson's rune esoteric. While praising List's *The Secret of the Runes* for its intense depth of understanding and brilliance of approach, he conceded that the text contains some "downright bizarre" elements,[123] although he failed to mention the racial theories behind List's work.

Rune divination, incantation, magic and rune yoga thus became widespread practices in Germanic Neopaganism. Up until today, Thorsson's work on runes continues to be hugely influential, if not the ultimate authority on the subject.[124] At the same time, there is currently a growing resistance to his work's dominance. Quite a few European Asatruers, as well as Pagans and esotericists of other persuasions, have tried to break Thorsson's monopoly and have written their own versions of rune books.[125] Authors affiliated with the Swedish network for shamanism, *Yggdrasil*, started their own tradition of rune esoteric in the 1980s, referencing not only Thorsson but also Renaissance scholar Johannes Bureus.[126] Due to the entanglement of rune magic with occultism, a greater skepticism has taken over within Asatru in recent years, especially in

---

122 Aswynn, *Leaves of Yggdrasil*. A second revised edition appeared in 2002 under the title *Northern Mysteries and Magic*.
123 Gundarsson, *Teutonic Magic. The Magical and Spiritual Practices of the Germanic People*, 180.
124 Most Asatru groups will at least list some of Thorsson's books on their reference lists, and many of my interview partners in all countries had them in their bookshelves.
125 Amongst them are Géza v. Neményi, *Heilige Runen. Zauberzeichen des Nordens* (Berlin: Ullstein, 2004), Jan Fries, *Helrunar. Ein Handbuch der Runenmagie* (Bad Ischl: Ananael, 1997), Igor Warneck, *Ruf der Runen. Eine Einführung in die Welt der Runen* (Darmstadt: Schirner, 2005), and GardenStone, *Germanische Magie*.
126 Their approaches distinguish themselves by using the theory of Sigurd Agrell, *Runornas talmystik och dess antika förebild* (Lund: Gleerup, 1927) (1881–1937), a professor at the University of Lund, Sweden, who in the early 1900s forwarded the speculative theory that the first letter of the runic alphabet, the 'fe'-rune, belonged at its end, so that the rune row should actually be called "uthark," cf. Gregorius, *Modern Asatro*, 256. Meanwhile, Flowers/ Thorsson has discovered and translated Bureus' *Adalruna*, (Stephen Flowers, *Johannes Bureus and Adalruna* (Smithville, TX: Runa-Raven Press, 1998)). The "uthark" theory in its esoteric form is spread to an English speaking audience by Thomas Karlsson, head of the Swedish occult order *Dragon Rouge*, who combined Agrell's theories with his own thoughts on magic in Thomas Karlsson, *Uthark. Nightside of the Runes* (Sundbyberg: Ouroboros Productions, 2002). Through his occult order *Dragon Rouge*, Karlsson's work seems to have a certain influence in international esoteric circles connecting him with Edred Thorsson/Stephen Flowers (cf. Edred, *History of the Rune-Gild*, III (The Reawakening of the Gild 1980–2005), 159), the German occultists and Asatruers.

Germany and Scandinavia.[127] Most groups today take an ambivalent position. They use runic practices sparsely in their communal rituals, but allow for the practice of rune and other magic by individuals.[128]

Runic quests are often accompanied by methods Germanic Neopagans borrow from neo-shamanism, for example *utiseta* (sitting out). While the name of this practice is taken from saga literature, it is more related to neo-shamanic 'vision quests,' in which solitude in nature (mainly at night) is hoped to facilitate communication with gods or spirits.[129] Shamanism has probably been the single most popular magic technique within the alternative religious and esoteric movement; self-help books, seminars, and lectures in the 1970s propagated its practices of expanded or extraordinary states of consciousness, meditation, and healing. Moreover, this neo-shamanic wave was "spawned by the drug culture of the 1960s and 70s, the human potential movement, environmentalism, interests in non-Western religions, and by popular anthropology, especially the Castaneda books."[130]

Neo-shamanism is closely connected to American and European leftist counter-culture, which is one reason it is regarded with suspicion by some Germanic Neopagans. However, this did not stop several groups and individuals in the 1980s from investigating the possibilities of (re-)creating a 'Nordic' or 'Germanic' form of shamanism. In reference to a (usually despised) practice of magic and divination mentioned in medieval Icelandic texts such as the Sagas of the Icelanders, as well as in the Eddas, it is frequently referred to as *seid* or *seiðr*. In order to develop a modern version of *seid* from medieval sources, and on the grounds of 'empirical testing,' the Swedish network of shamanism, *Yggdrasil*, based their reconstructive efforts mainly on two Swedish scholars' works: Dag Strömbäck's famous study *Sejd* (1935) and Folke Ström's

---

127 Gregorius, *Modern Asatro*, 264f.
128 Cf. Correspondence with Kurt Oertel (Eldaring).
129 Cf. Jonsson, "Ásatrú á Íslandi við upphaf 21. aldar," 179; Blain, *Nine Worlds of Seid-Magic*, 63.
130 Jane M. Atkinson, "Shamanisms Today," *Annual Review of Anthropology* 21 (1992), 322. Carlos Castaneda was an American anthropologist who wrote several books about his encounters with the Mexican shaman Don Juan. The accounts were later revealed as fictive, but had a great impact nevertheless. Another anthropologist, Michael Harner, who had done field-work in South America in the 1950s, extracted a method which he called "core shamanism" from various cultures and has taught it in workshops all around North America and Europe since the 1980s. Cf. Merete Demant Jakobsen, *Shamanism. Traditional and Contemporary Approaches to the Mastery of Spirits and Healing* (New York/Oxford: Berghahn Books, 1999), 160; Mihály Hoppál, "Urban Shamans. A Cultural Revival," in *Studies on Shamanism*, ed. Anna-Leena Siikala and Mihály Hoppál (Helsinki/Budapest: Finnish Anthropological Society, 1992), 200.

1967 history of Norse religions, *Nordisk hedendom* (Norse Paganism).[131] Another attempt to revive *seid* was undertaken by Stephen Flowers/Edred Thorsson, who combined runic practices and shamanism in his book *Northern Magic* (1998). Here, he linked Norse shamanism to the genetic heritage of the Germanic peoples, or "Aryans," and suggested that Norse shamanism should be practiced as an expression of an "ancestral path."[132] His former student and prominent *Troth* member, Kveldulf Gundarsson/Stephan Grundy, further developed this combination of runic and shamanic activities in the abovementioned *Teutonic Magic*[133] and popularized them through his novel *Attila's Treasure*.[134] Finally, *Troth* member and fantasy author Diana Paxson and her group *Hrafnar* in Berkeley, California developed a particular form of *seid*: oracular *seid*, or *spae*, in which a seidwoman or man (*völva*) go into a trance with the aid of drumming and chanting, and then answer participants' questions with the help of images they encounter in their trance.[135] Furthermore, it is

---

131 Cf. Ström, *Nordisk hedendom*; Dag Strömbäck, *Seijd. Textstudier i Nordisk Religionshistoria* (Stockholm/Copenhagen: Levin & Munksgaard, 1935). Lindqvist, *Shamanic Performances on the Urban Scene. Neo-Shamanism in Contemporary Sweden*, 39, 133ff, describes the history of the ritual in *Yggdrasil*, from its initial beginnings in a small circle of friends. She evaluates this development as a strategy of authentification. According to her, the material and research on *seiðr* give it an authentic feel. At the same time, the scarce material leaves enough space for imagination and improvisation in the creation of a ritual appropriate to the time and one's own needs. Although *Yggdrasil* by now is defunct, its method of seid and variations of it have survived and entered into at least parts of Asatru practice. Carl Johan Rehbinder head of *Sveriges Asatrosamfund* between 2000 and 2003 and also initiator of *Ratatosk* (another network for Nordic Shamanism), maintained in an interview that the Nordic Way is steeped in shamanistic attitudes and practices, cf. Valdemar Ravn, "Interview med Carl Johan Rehbinder, en svensk hedning," *Valravn. Hedensk tidskrift om samfund og kultur* 15 (2005), 7. However, other leading members of *Sveriges Asatrosamfund/Samfundet Forn Sed* are careful to point out that seid is not considered an official group activity, although individuals practice it and many of the groups' activists over the years have had a "seid perspective" on Asatru. "Interview med Mikael Perman."

132 Thorsson, *Northern Magic. Rune Mysteries & Shamanism*, xii and 4.

133 Gundarsson, *Teutonic Magic. The Magical and Spiritual Practices of the Germanic People*.

134 Grundy, *Attila's Treasure*. Grundy/Gundarsson however rejects the term seid for these magic practices due to its negative valuation in saga literature. He suggests using 'spae' for these divinatory activities – a practice which has been followed by the German *Eldaring*, cf. Correspondence with Stephan Grundy (The Troth), 2011; Correspondence with Kurt Oertel (Eldaring), see also Blain, *Nine Worlds of Seid-Magic*, 59, 97.

135 This oracular *seid* has been made particularly popular by Jenny Blain, a member of *The Troth* and professor of anthropology at Sheffield Hallam University in England, who investigated her own and others' practices of seid as well as its basis in medieval sources in her *Nine Worlds of Seid-Magic*.

quite common for Asatruers to attend seminars on "core shamanism" and experiment with combining these techniques with their own understandings of Norse sources on *seiðr*.[136] Bil Linzie, an Asatruer in the American South-West, was taught shamanic practices by Sami neo-shaman Ailo Gaup.[137] In Scandinavia as well as in Germany, Annette Høst reaches a broader Asatru audience through courses at her *Scandinavian Center for Shamanic Studies*.[138]

Although *seid* has established itself ever more as an important practice, its status remains ambiguous and precarious. By some, it is perceived as dangerous and fear-inspiring,[139] others are suspicious because of its sexual overtones and gender-bending associations.[140] For these critics of *seid*, such 'perverse' activities appear incompatible with a Germanic worldview based on honor and heroism. There is, however, another concern which even some practitioners of *seid* have, and which applies not so much to *seid* as such, but to its combination with neo-shamanism. American *seid* specialist Bil Linzie puts it this way:

> Neo-shamanism in the past decade is resulting in significant changes in the heathen Germanic worldview. These changes are really a distraction and a movement away from Ásatrú as a reconstructed religion, and even though many claim to have found support in the lore for something similar to neo-shamanism, the fact is that the worldview presented by neo-shamanic practitioners remains mostly inconsistent [sic] with the ancient worldview.[141]

The disputes within Asatru about the authenticity of practices like rune magic or *seid* indicate a concern with what some call the need to preserve the 'purity' of Asatru. This leads to questions about the sources Asatruers base their ideas on, how they deal with the precarious status of these sources, and how they deal with the academic theories developed around them. These questions will be addressed in Chapter 8. The debates around authenticity return us to our previous observation: that Asatru prides itself on being a non-dogmatic religion that does not prescribe articles of faith, rules, or regulations. Our

---

136 See for example Correspondence with Kurt Oertel (Eldaring).
137 Blain, *Nine Worlds of Seid-Magic*, 118.
138 See http://www.shamanism.dk/, last accessed March 20, 2014. Cf. also Chapter 7.
139 Interview Q.
140 Interview K. For a fuller discussion of these aspects of *seid* cf. Chapter 7.
141 Bil Linzie, "Germanic Spirituality," Temple of Our Heathen Gods, http://heathengods .com/library/bil_linzie/germanic_spirituality.pdf, last accessed December 06, 2011, 39.

discussion of Germanic Neopagan beliefs and practices in this chapter has indeed shown that Asatru lacks some characteristics considered typical for religions. As Piotr Wiench so aptly notes with regard to Central and Eastern European Neopaganism, it does not have an "elaborate system of religious and moral thought, a mature set of doctrines, [or] refined theology," nor does it offer institutional support to individuals.[142] Instead, many Heathens perceive their faith not just as a spiritual path but also a holistic worldview: religion, culture, and social practices are unified, expressing Germanic cultural or ethnic essence in a specific way. In other words, there is a tendency to focus more on discourses of identity and ethnicity than on religious matters, and to imbue dimensions such as ethnic identity with spiritual meaning. Such perceptions of Pagan religion overlap with political worldviews, a fact that fuels vivid controversies about the 'ethnic' character of Asatru and Germanic Neopaganism's perception of religion – two contested fields which will be analyzed in detail in the following chapters.

---

142 Piotr Wiench, "A Postcolonial Key to Understanding Central and Eastern European Neopaganisms," in *Modern Pagan and Native Faith Movements in Central and Eastern Europe*, ed. Scott Simpson and Kaarina Aitamurto, Studies in Contemporary and Historical Paganism (Durham: Acumen, 2013), 13.

CHAPTER 4

Contested Fields I: Race and Ethnicity

> Contemporary Asatru as a whole is an ethnic tradition, largely stemming from the interest in recovering a forgotten heritage, and our forebears placed great weight on matters of kin and clan [while] prohibit[ing] racism of any sort.[1]

This somewhat anachronistic statement, which suggests that pre-Christian Nordic peoples prohibited racism, can be found in *Our Troth*, the two-volume self-presentation of North American a-racist Asatru. It indicates a dilemma within Asatru that revolves around the categories of race, ethnicity, culture, tradition, and heritage, and their relation to spirituality. The controversies and schisms deriving from this quandary are interesting for three reasons: Firstly, they are an integral part of the path toward respectability Asatru has taken. Secondly, they point to the acute self-consciousness of contemporary Asatruers regarding the racist implications of their faith. Lastly, they are connected to the shifting significance of relations between culture, ethnicity, and religion, i.e., to processes of "neo-ethnification"[2] that have structured discussions on immigration and integration in the Western world over the past twenty years. In this chapter, we will examine these disagreements and ruptures, and consider how they are intertwined with mainstream discourses on ethnicity.

Asatru and National Socialism

From the outside, Asatru is time and again equated across the board with neo-Nazis and *völkisch*-Ariosophic concepts. Asatru is thus constantly in a defensive position and has to face up to the challenge of actively proving its own innocence, so to speak, daily.[3]

---

1 Gundarsson, *Our Troth*, vol. II, 31.
2 Marianne Gullestad, *Plausible Prejudice. Everyday Experiences and Social Images of Nation, Culture and Race* (Oslo: Universitetsforlaget, 2006).
3 Correspondence with Kurt Oertel (Eldaring): "Asatru [wird] von außen [...] immer wieder pauschal mit Neo-Nazis und völkisch-ariosophischen Konzepten gleichgesetzt. Dadurch befindet sich Asatru in einer konstanten Verteidigungsstellung und muss sich quasi täglich erneut der Herausforderung einer aktiven Beweisführung der eigenen Unschuld stellen."

With these words, a German a-racist Asatruer justifies the need to dissociate from National Socialism and racism. According to him, such an automatic association is caused by an uninformed public, in whose eyes the use of Norse deities and symbols such as the Thorshammer, the Irminsul, and the runes – not to mention the swastika – have been associated with National Socialist ideology and propaganda. Furthermore, a number of white supremacist groups claim that their political agenda has to be realized through the belief in the 'ancestral religion' of the 'white race,' the 'Aryans' or 'Germanic peoples.' This forces Asatruers to distance themselves from overtly racist interpretations of their faith.[4] The common association between 'the Germanic' and National Socialism has led the vast majority of Asatruers after 1945, even racial-religious ones,[5] to at least superficially distance themselves and their religion from National Socialism. In 1984, Adolf Schleipfer, leader of the racial-religious *Armanen-Orden*, emphasized that the idea of a German empire, as well as the cult of a *Führer*, stood in stark contrast to the values of the *Armanen-Orden*. According to him, it was time the world finally acknowledged

> that the Germanic and Armanism have absolutely nothing to do with violence, dictatorship, fascism, oppression, concentration camps, war mongering, etc.! That such prejudices are nothing but propaganda meant to veil the 'grand plan of the anonymous' for the annihilation of the Germanic! This is anti-Germanism in its highest power![6]

As mentioned, especially in Germany, my own publications have at times been perceived as generalizing condemnations of Asatru. This has to be taken into consideration, as my interview partners of course reacted to this perception.

4   There are two reasons this has become all the more necessary: Firstly, a number of books in the 1990s and 2000s, e.g. by Jeffrey Kaplan, Mattias Gardell, and myself, have brought to light the overt and, in some cases, more hidden and implicitly racist, anti-Semitic, or white supremacist agendas of such groups. Secondly, more recently established Asatru groups have taken a stance against racist tendencies within Heathenism, cf. Kaplan, *Radical Religion in America*, Gardell, *Gods of the Blood*, Schnurbein, *Religion als Kulturkritik*, *Göttertrost in Wendezeiten*.

5   Only the most overtly religious National Socialist organizations, such as the *Gylfiliten* in Germany, who counted Hitler amongst their deities (cf. *Religion als Kulturkritik*, 174), and some of the American white supremacist Odinist groups investigated by Mattias Gardell, *Gods of the Blood*, refer unambiguously positively to National Socialism.

6   Quoted from Schnurbein, *Religion als Kulturkritik*, 72: "daß Germanentum und Armanentum nichts, aber auch garnichts mit Gewalt, Diktatur, Faschismus, Unterdrückung, KZ's, Kriegshetze usw. zu tun hat! Daß solche Vorurteile nichts als Propaganda sind und den ‚großen Plan der Anonymen' zur Vernichtung des Germanentums verschleiern sollen! Dies ist Antigermanismus in höchster Potenz!"

In fact, this quote does not reveal an anti-National Socialist attitude, but rather an anti-Semitic one. The "grand plan of the anonymous" alludes to the *Armanen-Orden's* conviction that Jews and Christians are behind a world conspiracy encompassing the churches, communism, socialism, liberalism, capitalism, Masonic orders etc., all of which are considered "international exploiters, destroyers of *Volk* and nature."[7]

American Asatru author and occultist Stephen Flowers/Edred Thorsson makes a structurally similar argument, pointing to more concealed anti-Semitic and anti-Masonic implications.[8] He blames the idea that the modern Norse revival and National Socialism are closely related on a specific genre of popular occult literature dealing with National Socialism, which sees the roots of National Socialism in an all-embracing occult conspiracy.[9] Flowers turns to an

---

7 Ibid., 70. "Internationale Ausbeuter, Volks- und Naturzerstörer."
8 Cf. his introduction to *The Secret King*, a book about Heinrich Himmler's alleged magician Karl Maria Wiligut (alias Weisthor). (Flowers and Moynihan, *The Secret King. The Myth and Reality of Nazi Occultism*) Wiligut claimed to have access to ancestral or racial memory in a similar way as Guido List did, but set his idea of an "Irminic" Christianity in competition to List's Armanist system. Schnurbein, *Religion als Kulturkritik*, 113–115.
9 For example Louis Pauwels and Jacques Bergier, *The Morning of the Magicians* (London: Mayflower, 1971), Trevor Ravenscroft, *The Spear of Destiny* (London: Samuel Weiser, 1972). Pauwels/Bergier's and Ravenscroft's works have had considerable influence on the spread of an esoteric Hitlerism. Their theories rely partially on an account by Rudolf Glauer (alias Rudolf von Sebottendorf, 1875–1945), a cosmopolitan adventurer and spy who combined List's teachings with the Islamic mysticism he had encountered on his travels to Turkey and Egypt. In 1918, he founded the lodge *Thule-Gesellschaft* (Thule Society). The *Thule Society* seems to be one of the few *völkisch* religious and Ariosophic associations that for a time attracted leading National Socialists, such as Dietrich Eckart, Rudolf Heß, and Alfred Rosenberg as guests or members. In 1934, Sebottendorf published a book under the sensational title *Bevor Hitler kam* (Before Hitler Came) where he stylized himself and his *Thule Society* as the most important precursors of National Socialism. This publication was not well received by Hitler and the National Socialist establishment, who were eager to demonstrate respectability and thus denied all connections with occultist activities. Sebottendorf's essay was certainly highly unreliable as a historical source and unfounded in most of its claims. However, it became the main source not only for Pauwels, Bergier, and Ravenscroft, but also earlier writers, such as the anthroposophist Joachim Besser, "Die Vorgeschichte des Nationalsozialismus im neuen Licht," *Die Pforte* 2 (1950) and Dietrich Bronder, *Bevor Hitler kam. Eine historische Studie*, 2. expanded ed. (Geneva: Pfeiffer, 1975). For a recent thorough repudiation of theories about occult influences within National Socialism, cf. Ulrich Linse, "Der Chiemsee-Goldkessel – ein völkisch-religiöses Kultobjekt aus der NS-Zeit? The State of the Affairs," in *Die völkisch-religiöse Bewegung im Nationalsozialismus. Eine Beziehungs- und Konfliktgeschichte*, ed. Uwe Puschner and Clemens Vollnhals (Göttingen: Vandenhoeck & Ruprecht, 2012).

anti-capitalist counter-theory of conspiracy. According to him, the anti-Nazis who depicted National Socialism as a demonic, occult endeavor had their own occult agenda in which high-ranking politicians, in particular Winston Churchill, were involved. Flowers goes on to claim that the "Freemason" Churchill believed the true grail would manifest itself "as a global form of finance capital." This belief was supposedly Churchill's motivation in fighting German National Socialism, which was "dedicated to the abolition of usury."[10] Flowers' emphasis on Churchill's involvement with Masonry and his implicit reference (through the loaded term "usury") to Jews, insinuates that these forces might somehow be responsible the occult anti-Nazi propaganda. At the same time, Flowers/Thorsson puts himself into the tradition of *völkisch* occultism by publishing books about and by Ariosophists. For him, National Socialist and SS symbolism contain a "great and dark historical significance, whose cause is now intelligible only to those who have the ability to see beyond good and evil to extract the Noble even from that which is base in the eyes of the mob."[11]

In spite of the fact that Flowers/Thorsson and his *Rune Gild* enjoy a good reputation in large parts of current a-racist Asatru, such veiled anti-Semitic statements have become rare in Asatru. It has instead become more common to ascribe the evils of National Socialism, including its anti-Semitism, to Christian patterns. Whereas protagonists of the *völkisch* religious movement tended to reject Christianity because of its Jewish roots, many a-racist Asatruers take the opposite stance, condemning anti-Semitism by pointing to its origin in Christianity. In 1972, the Icelandic *Ásatrúarmenn* argued successfully against allegations of being racist and National Socialist by stating that National Socialism was not a Neopagan movement, but closely allied with the Christian churches.[12] Géza von Neményi, of the ethnicist German *Germanische Glaubensgemeinschaft*, claims that both anti-Semitism and National Socialist ideology are based in Christian thought. This allows him to downplay the racist foundations of his own historical forerunners, such as Ludwig Fahrenkrog.[13]

---

10   All quotes Flowers and Moynihan, *The Secret King. The Myth and Reality of Nazi Occultism*, 22f.
11   He goes on to argue that "its symbolic quality has little [...] to do with the political aims of National Socialism, or with its criminal behavior," and he maintains that the forms it used remain "fascinating and worthwhile," cf. Edred, *History of the Rune-Gild*, III (The Reawakening of the Gild 1980–2005), 90. The quoted passages refer to a "magical Working" of Edred Thorsson and Michael Aquino from the *Temple of Set* at the SS castle Wewelsburg, where Aquino gave Thorsson an SS dagger – an act that Thorsson interprets as "one of the most powerful rites of passage in the Germanic world – the sword taking." (ibid., 89).
12   Pétursson, *Asasamfundet på Island och massmedia*, 185:1, 7–12.
13   Géza v. Neményi, *Heidentum und NS-Ideologie* (Werbig: Germanische Glaubensgemeinschaft, 1997).

The ethnicist German *VfgH* also sees a "monotheistic-dualistic configuration" at the basis of *völkisch* religiosity and thus salvages modern Asatru from the association with both.[14] *Our Troth* aligns the *völkisch* Germanic mysticism and National Socialism with the Christian enemy, in this case the medieval Christian mission in the North. It thus exculpates itself, or rather, the roots of 'one's native tradition'. It describes "German Mysticism and the Nazi Perversion of the Faith"[15] as the result of a mix of medieval anti-Judaism, Darwinism, and nationalism, considering it the "greatest harm Germanic religion and culture have suffered since the [...] eleventh century,"[16] i.e., the era of Christianization in Iceland. By referring to the medieval Christian roots of anti-Semitism and (incorrectly) claiming that it was exclusively a German phenomenon that did not exist in Scandinavia, the author isolates a continental 'perverted' tradition of a Germanic revival. He posits it against a good, untainted English and Scandinavian tradition of interest in Nordic myth in the 19th and 20th centuries, but fails to mention how entangled these movements are and the common roots and interests that they share.

The fact that the a-racist German *Eldaring* initially sought the proximity of exactly these Anglo-American and Scandinavian traditions in order to mark its own distance from the tainted German *völkisch* mysticism demonstrates how effectively the topos of a 'harmless' Nordic revival and its German/Nazi (and Christian) perversion has been employed. The treatment of Alexander Rud Mills in *Our Troth* is a similar attempt at distinguishing a 'good' Anglo-Saxon from a 'bad' continental tradition. Although Mill's anti-Semitic tendencies are acknowledged, his involvement with National Socialism is largely ignored. He comes across as a person prosecuted mainly for his faith and not for his National Socialist politics and anti-Semitic ideology.[17]

We can draw three preliminary conclusions:

1. The identification of Asatru with National Socialist thought is a problem Asatruers cannot avoid.
2. Asatruers frequently try to evade this problem by aligning National Socialism and racial mysticism with what they perceive as their main enemy, Christianity. In this way, they cast themselves as the 'good' minority persecuted by authoritarian forces such as National Socialism or Christian churches.

---

14 Anonymous, "'Gott in uns.' Völkische Religiosität in Deutschland," *Ringhorn. Gemeinschaftsanzeiger des Vereins für germanisches Heidentum e.V.* 41 (2004). The anonymous author here quotes Henning Eichberg, a protagonist of the German New Right.
15 Gundarsson, *Our Troth*, vol. 1, 99.
16 Ibid., vol. 1, 101.
17 Ibid., vol. 1, 106.

3. It is reductionist to narrow all that is problematic with racial or ethnicist thinking to National Socialist ideology. This is equally true from the opposite perspective. Rejecting Asatru as a racist cult because of its alleged proximity to National Socialism, or explaining National Socialism through alleged Neopagan or occult origins, does not hold up to scrutiny either.[18] Rather, the concepts of ethnicity and cultural heritage employed in Asatru hark back to National Romantic and *völkisch* traditions that seem to surface in modern Western societies on a regular basis, giving rise to the various waves of ethnification in public discourse.

The 'Folkish' Versus 'Universalist' Controversy

Within Asatru, the affiliation of ethnicist positions with *völkisch* right-wing extremist ideas has been the cause of many heated debates. The most internationally high-profile debate has raged since the 1990s between the so-called 'universalists' and the 'folkish' faction in the USA, and has spread to other countries as well. It revolves around the question of who should have access to Asatru. While the folkish faction (represented by members of the AFA as well as the *Asatru Alliance*) maintains that Asatru is the native religion for people with 'Germanic' ancestry, and that it should remain exclusive to them, the universalists (represented by members of *The Troth*) insist the religion should remain open for everyone drawn to it. Such a clear distinction is difficult to uphold even on an empirical level. A number of influential Asatruers[19] have been involved in both folkish groups and *The Troth* and contributed considerably to shaping the latter's worldview without this causing any major disruption. Outspokenly folkish groups have occasionally admitted members of 'non-Germanic' heritage,[20] while even the most inclusive universalist groups acknowledge that they do not have significantly more members with

---

18 Such a thesis was most prominently advanced by Wilfried Daim, *Der Mann der Hitler die Ideen gab. Jörg Lanz von Liebenfels* (first edition 1958) who considered Jörg Lanz von Liebensfels "The Man who Gave Hitler his Ideas." To my knowledge there are few scholars who have taken that route in recent years. One of them, Peter Kratz, *Die Götter des New Age*, identifies the New Age movement with fascism, the other Karla Poewe, *New Religions and the Nazis*, greatly exaggerates Jakob Wilhelm Hauer's and his *German Faith Movement's* influence on Hitler and his followers.

19 This is, for example, the case for William Bainbridge, who has been a member of both *The Troth* and the *Asatru Alliance*. cf. Kaplan, *Radical Religion in America*, 21. Also leading Theodists' active involvement with *The Troth* makes the distinction tenuous.

20 Cf. examples in Strmiska and Sigurvinsson, "Asatru: Nordic Paganism in Iceland and America" and Gundarsson, *Our Troth*, vol. II, 27.

non-European backgrounds than the exclusive, folkish groups. At the same time, the distinction between ethnic and cultural criteria remains unclear. While universalist Asatruers often include ideas about ethnic specificities into their faith, folkish concepts occasionally emphasize cultural difference over ethnic.[21] Differing attitudes regarding the role of genetics, heritage and ancestry cannot be dichotomized easily; rather, they structure a diverse and frequently contradictory spectrum of positions within and beyond Asatru.

Only racial-religious groups with an outspokenly white supremacist or Aryanist agenda, such as *Vigrid* in Norway, the *Armanen-Orden* in Germany, or the ones investigated by Gardell claim that Asatru is a religion based mainly or even exclusively on race.[22] These groups tend to consider the gods as racial archetypes and turn race itself into a religious category. In this way, they justify the superiority of the 'white,' 'Aryan,' or 'Nordic' race and religion, and argue that conserving the race is a religious act and thus an aim in itself. Even in such openly racist groups, race is never conceptualized as an exclusively biological category, but a spiritual and cultural one as well. This was already true for the *völkisch* movement and *völkisch* religion of the late 19th and early 20th century, which, as Uwe Puschner and others have shown, initially rejected a purely biological-racial anti-Semitism as a reductive simplification. Nevertheless, *völkisch* ideology was firmly based on a cultural and religious anti-Semitism and a 'positive Aryanism.'[23] Even the more biologistic concepts, which had an increased influence on *völkisch* religious thought after 1900, relied on the perception of race as a spiritual or cultural category. The same is true for the racial theories of Anglo-Saxonism. "There was never any sharp separation between a precise scientific racialism and literary racial nationalism."[24] Distinguishing between racial-religious and ethnicist groups is a matter of degree, not of principle. Both insist that genetic heritage, cultural tradition, and religion form an indistinguishable unity, and that Asatru is therefore the naturally inherited religion of all people of 'Germanic' ancestry.

American Asatruer Stephen McNallen has frequently laid claim to a

> middle ground on racial issues. On the one hand we were proud of our European heritage, and we actively espoused the interests of European-descended people. On the other hand we opposed totalitarianism and

---

21 Cf. Gründer, *Blótgemeinschaften*, 88, who calls attention to these borderline phenomena, but maintains that the dichotomy 'folkish – universalist' remains an important factor for the self-understanding of differences in Asatru.
22 Gardell, *Gods of the Blood*.
23 Puschner, *Die Völkische Bewegung im wilhelminischen Deutschland*, 54, 71–76.
24 Horsman, *Race and Manifest Destiny*, 159.

racial hatred, convinced that decency and honor required us to treat individuals of all racial groups with respect.[25]

In the early 1980s, McNallen came forward with a scientific-metaphysical theory explaining how biology and spirituality are organically intertwined. This theory of "metagenetics" has made him one of the most controversial Asatruers worldwide. Basing his arguments on Jungian psychology and studies on "reincarnation memories"[26] – which he assumes are recollections coded in the DNA – he comes to the conclusion that "Asatru is the expression of the soul of our race."[27] In a revision of his thoughts in 1999, he elaborates:

> Our religion is a function of who we are, not just what we believe. Since the human being is a holistic entity, our spirituality cannot be considered something apart from our physical ancestry. In terms of both genetics and metagenetics, our ancestors are encoded into our very beings. [...] It seems reasonable, then, to predict that people will tend to be most fulfilled by the religious and spiritual paths of their ancestors. [...] The beliefs of our ancestors are largely confirmed by modern psychology and the biological sciences. Most especially, the Jungian collective unconscious and Sheldrake's hypotheses concerning 'morphic field' and 'morphic resonance' are very close to the Germanic ideas surrounding the Well of Urth, in which orlog or 'fate' is laid.[28]

McNallen's need to revisit his concept in 1999 indicates the impact his provisional reflections have had among Asatruers.[29]

---

25 McNallen, "Three Decades of the Ásatú Revival in America," 208, cf. Kaplan, *Radical Religion in America*.
26 This concept closely resembles the idea of an ancestral memory as was put forward by Guido von List.
27 Stephen A. McNallen, "Metagenetics," Asatru Folk Assembly, http://www.runestone.org/index.php?option=com_content&view=article&id=143:metagenetics&catid=82:articles&Itemid=571, last accessed January 12, 2015. Cf. Gardell, *Gods of the Blood*, 270.
28 Stephen A. McNallen, "Genetics & Beyond. Metagenetics – An Update," *The Runestone* 26 (1999). The article is also available online: http://www.runestone.org/index.php?option=com_content&view=article&id=144:genetics-a-beyond-metagenetics-an-update&catid=82:articles&Itemid=571, last accessed January 12, 2015.
29 Most groups and individuals who are convinced of a biological dimension of their religion at some point refer to McNallen. See also the discussion of metagenetics in Gundarsson, *Our Troth*, vol. II, 31–37.

McNallen and the majority of 'folkish' Asatruers are careful to distinguish themselves from radical racists who claim superiority of their 'folk' or 'race' and its right to subdue other 'races,' a position only the most radical white supremacist Odinists would hold today. However, they make it quite clear that they deem it necessary to keep one's race or tradition as pure as possible. Individuals of non-European backgrounds are thus not welcome in Asatru, and individuals of mixed heritage are considered a grave problem.[30] McNallen even revised his earlier infatuation with the Vikings on these grounds, arguing that they were cosmopolitan and "incorporated a mass of non-native elements."[31]

The question of a relation between race and spirituality also surfaces in European groups. Like McNallen and other ethnicist Asatruers, German Géza von Neményi rejects the idea of a unified 'white race,' instead relying on older theories about various European races, such as the 'Nordic,' the 'Faelic,' and the 'Ostic,' etc. He maintains that race differences are a fact, "albeit unpopular." Moreover, he narrows the definition of racism to apply only to an overt hierarchization of races, stressing defensively that the exclusion of non-Germanic persons does not imply a degradation of others, but ensures "a kind of religious self-actualization of the Germanics."[32] The argument that racism only pertains to active discrimination and that differentialism and separatism are 'non-racist' also arose in the aforementioned controversy surrounding Stephen McNallen's invitation to the International Asatru Summer Camp in 2009. Those opposing his invitation considered the rhetoric around race and heritage displayed on the AFA's website a breach of their own anti-racist statutes. Danish supporters explained this disagreement by pointing to different definitions of racism: In Denmark, they claim, the term 'racism' is used to describe the assumption of racial superiority only, while Norwegians and Swedes allegedly consider the categorization of humans into races as

---

30 Cf. for example Gardell, *Gods of the Blood*, 270f.
31 McNallen, "Three Decades of the Ásatrú Revival in America," 216. In his e-mail newsletter AFA update, McNallen occasionally quotes from blogs on the anti-immigration website vdare.com, cf. AFA update 1-5-11. In 2002, he served as the president of the *European American Issues Forum*, an organization that describes itself as a civil rights and activist organization working on behalf of people of European heritage and warns of 'reverse racism' against whites, cf. for example Adrienne Sanders, "Group Claims White Victims," *San Francisco Examiner*, June 05, 2002.
32 "eine Art religiöser Selbstverwirklichung der Germanen," Neményi, *Heidentum und NS-Ideologie*, 3f. The article is also available online: http://allsherjargode.beepworld.de/heidentum-und-ns.htm, last accessed March 26, 2014.

racist in and of itself.³³ The turmoil was partly motivated by concerns around attracting unwanted media attention, although statements made by some of the groups, who were clearly deeply upset, indicate that it was more than just the fear of stigma from negative press that motivated these European Asatruers (along with members of *The Troth* in the USA) to adopt a broader definition of racism and to perceive all racial categorization as unscientific and based on prejudice.³⁴ One Asatru critic of McNallen's metagenetics writes that, instead of offering "an explanatory rendering of the interface between history, the body, ethnicity, and religion," it is nothing but a "totalizing narrative that attempts to seal the borders and protect itself from contamination from the Other."³⁵

Such a stance has also been taken by Edred Thorsson/Stephen Flowers, who rejects the idea that Germanic culture was ever static or 'pure.' He modified the metagenetic paradigm accordingly, considering its exclusive focus on biological heritage reductive and suggested looking not just at 'ethnic culture' but also at 'ethical,' 'material,' and 'linguistic' culture, as well as their constant interaction with one another. According to Flowers, they need to be reintegrated "into an organic and vital whole in which the individual will stand as a culturally authentic man."³⁶ This model seems less exclusionary and static, but still maintains that physical, biological heritage plays an important role in spiritual traditions.³⁷ It mirrors Romantic and *völkisch* ideals of a holistic unity of ethnicity, language, culture, and spirituality that reaches into a deep past. It reaffirms the significance of biological heritage by emphasizing that

> The body contains a code which bears the essential story of all of one's ancestors. One's cultural myths articulate these, and these myths are re-encoded in actual tales expressed in often archaic languages.

---

33 The controversy is documented in Danish *Forn Siðr*'s journal *Vølse* 47, March 2009.
34 Cf. Gundarsson, *Our Troth*, vol. II, 35–37, as well as Asfrid, "Warum Asatru?" *Ringhorn. Gemeinschaftsanzeiger des Vereins für germanisches Heidentum e.V.* 48 (2006), and Interview F, with a German Asatruer, May 2010, Germany; Interview D, with a German Asatruer, March 2010, Germany.
35 Garadyn McOisdealbhaigh, "Metagenetics: The Fear of Penetration and the Penetration of Fear," Irminsul Ættir, http://www.irminsul.org/arc/008gm.html, last accessed January 12, 2015.
36 Stephen Edred Flowers, "The Idea of Integral Culture. A Model for a Revolt Against the Modern World," *Tyr. Myth – Culture – Tradition* 1 (2002), 11.
37 Ibid., 13.

Consequently, the rediscovery of Norse sources and their employment in cultural and religious contexts constitutes a "whole cultural *reawakening* of dormant or vestigial patterns."[38]

An 'Ethnic Religion of Nature'?

Both a-racist and some ethnicist Asatruers who reject genetic paradigms feel that the term 'ethnic religion' or 'ethnic nature religion' avoids the problem, and is thus better suited to describing their faith. We have to ask whether or not this is a mere strategic shift of terminology. In other words: When is 'ethnicity' to be understood as a euphemized replacement for the stigmatized term 'race,' and when, if at all, does it in fact denote something qualitatively different?

Danish Asatruer Grølheim emphasizes that 'nature religion' not only refers to a faith which sees nature as animated or divine, but also to its 'natural' evolution. He continues:

> By far the most naturally developed religions are simultaneously ethnic religions. [...] It is undoubtedly correct that most of us have chosen Asatru because it is the root of our ethnic identity.[39]

Grølheim uses 'ethnic' in much the same way as 'folkish' Asatruers in America would, but he avoids addressing the question of genetic heritage. *Forn Siðr* officially distances itself from the idea of genetic heritage by stressing "we consider all humans equal. [....] Everybody with a sincere interest in Asatru is welcome independent of descent/form/color." At the same time they admit to a certain form of "ethnocentrism" in "our tradition."[40] Nevertheless, both Grølheim and *Forn Siðr* are in agreement with ethnicist Asatru when it comes to defining an ethnic group or 'folk' not as a nation, but as a smaller entity. In contrast to the US, Danish Asatruers tie ethnicity closely to a territory, to the "area where it originated and therefore usually is suited to the people who live there."[41]

---

38   All quotes ibid., 16.
39   "Det er utvivlsomt rigtigt at de fleste af os har valgt Asetroen fordi den er roden til vores etniske identitet." Grølheim, "Mangfoldighed og tolerance," *Vølse* 11 (2000), 16.
40   "Man kan selvfølgelig ikke se bort fra det etnocentriske i vores overleveringer," FAQ *Forn Siðr* (http://fornsidr.dk/om-forn-sidr/spoergsmaal-og-svar#Nationalisme, last accessed March 26, 2014).
41   Ibid.

This idea of a relation between territory and people is shared by German *VfgH*, the group which has elaborated the concept of Asatru as an 'ethnic nature religion' the farthest. Their definition reads as follows:

> Germanic Paganism is the religion of the gods who are in the nature of Northern and Central Europe and who live in all beings and things this nature has created.
> Germanic Paganism is the religion of the historical Germanic peoples and their culture. It does not make the claim to be valid worldwide and it does not mission.
> Germanic Paganism is the religion of today's people who are members of a Germanic community by birth or association and who feel obliged to their heritage.[42]

Here, the idea of a unity between culture, heritage, descent, and nature is foregrounded and tied indissolubly to deities, myth, and cultic practice, so that religion comes to define a people or *Volk* in much the same way as National Romanticism has:

> A *Volk* in the traditional sense of 'ethnos,' 'gens,' and 'diot' is an association with common gods and cultures who others do not share. A native religion is a constitutive characteristic of a *Volk*, and vice versa, the *Volk* is a constitutive characteristic of religion. [...] *Völker* in this sense, which is also the traditional Pagan one, are founded mythically. [...] In myth that forms the foundation for a *Volk*, that *Volk* recognizes itself – and always, when people recognize themselves together in a myth, they become a *Volk*.[43]

---

42 "Allgemeine Konzepte des VfgH im Überblick" (www.vfgh.de, last accessed March 26, 2014): "Das germanische Heidentum ist die Religion der Götter, die in der Natur Nord- und Mitteleuropas sind und in allen Wesen und Dingen leben, die diese Natur hervorgebracht hat. Das germanische Heidentum ist die Religion der historischen germanischen Völker und ihrer Kultur. Es erhebt keinen Anspruch auf weltweite Gültigkeit und missioniert nicht. Das germanische Heidentum ist die Religion heutiger Menschen, die durch Geburt oder Aufnahme Angehörige einer germanischen Gemeinschaft sind und sich ihrem Erbe verpflichtet fühlen."

43 "Die Religionen der 'Völker,'" *Ringhorn. Gemeinschaftsanzeiger des Vereins für germanisches Heidentum e.V.* 41 (2004), 3f: "Ein Volk im traditionellen Sinn von 'ethnos,' 'gens,' und 'diot' ist ein Verband mit gemeinsamen Göttern und Kulturen, die andere nicht haben. Die eigene Religion ist ein konstituierendes Merkmal für ein Volk, und umgekehrt ist das Volk ein konstituierendes Merkmal von Religion. [...] Völker in diesem Sinn, der

Accordingly, several members of the *VfgH* feel sympathetic toward the AFA and Stephen McNallen's attempts at 'folk-building,' although the majority would still reject the (meta)genetic approach as too narrow.[44] Fritz Steinbock's/ Asfrid's writings illustrate well the ambivalences and contradictions implicated in this approach. Steinbock, the author of several books on Heathenism, is considered the guiding theorist of the *VfgH*, and frequently points out the pitfalls of overly simplistic and straightforward presumptions about cultural and religious continuity. Nevertheless, his point of departure is the assumption of a unity of gods, nature, and men, from which language and culture have developed.[45] He considers a genetically 'pure' 'Germanic' ancestry a potentially dangerous fiction, and goes on to salvage the concept of ancestry and heritage in two ways. Firstly, he claims that anybody can be considered an ancestor, if they contributed to

> creating what is common to us, what defines our common identity: Language, culture, history, the homeland (Heimat) which they cultivated and helped to create, and not least the religion, which for us Heathens probably is the most important heritage of the ancestors that we succeed to. [...] Ancestors are the ones whose heritage we succeed to.[46]

Secondly, he makes ancestry into a matter of active choice, of conscious construction, which remains necessary, however, for the creation of a "stable" and "unambiguous identity":

> We are not in every way and not exclusively heirs of the Teutons (Germanen), but an interplay of factors identify us *fundamentally* as their heirs so that contradictions seem less important. It becomes indeed

---

auch der traditionell heidnische ist, sind mythisch begründet.[...] Im Mythos, der ein Volk begründet, erkennt es sich selbst – und immer dann, wenn sich Menschen gemeinsam in einem Mythos erkennen, werden sie zu einem Volk."

44   An exception is *VfgH* member Stilkam, who published translations of the two articles by McNallen on his (now defunct) homepage "Stilkams Seiten." The German articles were also printed in the magazine *Schwarz&Magisch* (No.1, 2005).

45   Steinbock, *Das heilige Fest*, 222.

46   "[...] denn sie haben all das geschaffen, was uns gemeinsam ist und unsere gemeinsame Identität bestimmt: Sprache, Kultur, Geschichte, die von ihnen bebaute und mitgestaltete Heimat und nicht zuletzt die Religion, die für uns Heiden das wohl wichtigste Erbe der Ahnen ist, das wir antreten. [...] Ahnen sind diejenigen, deren Erbe wir antreten." Asfrid, "Ahnen," *Ringhorn. Gemeinschaftsanzeiger des Vereins für germanisches Heidentum e.V.* 42 (2004), 3.

unsubstantial when such a search for identity has the consequence that we pay more attention to the heritage we consider more substantial. Heritage becomes that which we appropriate consciously, and after which we form ourselves. Thus, the Teutons become all the more 'our ancestors' the more we consider them as such and the more we want to come into their inheritance.[47]

This quote shows again how potential contradictions within such views are avoided in order to maintain the goal of recovering a Heathen religious tradition, which should remain unmixed and unadulterated by foreign elements in spite of evidence to the contrary.[48] On the basis of such implicitly problematic claims, Hans Schuhmacher, from the German *Rabenclan*, has classified Steinbock's construction of an ethnic religion of nature, as outlined in his book *Das Heilige Fest* (The Sacred Feast), as a version of an ethno-pluralist ideology.[49]

Ethno-pluralism and the European New Right

The term 'ethno-pluralism' emerged in the 1980s in discussions within the European radical Right, and owes much to the Romantic Herderian concept of *Volk* (see Chapter 1).[50] It conceptualizes ethnic communities as

---

47 Ibid., 5: "Wir sind nicht in allem und nicht ausschließlich Erben der Germanen, aber ein Zusammenspiel von Faktoren weist uns *wesentlich* als ihre Erben aus und lässt Widersprüchliches unwesentlich erscheinen. Es wird dann auch in der Tat unwesentlich, wenn die Folge einer solchen Identitätsfindung ist, dass wir dem als wesentlich erachteten Erbe größere Aufmerksamkeit schenken. Es wird dasjenige, das wir uns bewußt aneignen und nach dem wir uns formen. So werden die Germanen umso mehr 'unsere Ahnen,' je mehr wir sie als solche betrachten und ihr Erbe antreten wollen."
48 Steinbock, *Das heilige Fest*, 60f.
49 Cf. Hans Schuhmacher, "'Das Heilige Fest' – ein Grundlagenwerk?" Rabenclan e.V., www .rabenclan.de/index.php/Magazin/HansSchuhmacherDasheiligeFest3, last accessed January 21, 2015.
50 It was initially suggested by Henning Eichberg, a German sport sociologist now residing in Denmark, who at the time identified as a national revolutionary and a member of the New Right. Eichberg has been a member of both left-wing and right-wing organizations in Germany and Denmark. He has promoted a 'third way' of bridging the differences between the left and the right through a revolutionary liberation nationalism, cf. Claudia Globisch, "'Deutschland uns Deutschen, Türkei den Türken, Israelis raus aus Palästina.' Ethnopluralismus und sein Verhältnis zum Antisemitismus," in *Die Dynamik der*

homogenous cultural entities bound to, and formed by, a specific territory or nature, and by a common cultural heritage with roots in a deep past. Under ideal conditions, such communities should remain homogenous and identical; they are not overtly hierarchized, rather considered 'different but equal.' Any kind of mixing or migration is considered detrimental to the formation of stable identities and thus to peaceful co-existence. Due to its essentialist view of culture as deeply rooted in tradition and landscape and immutable in its fundamental essence – rather than a meeting place of constantly changing and evolving ideas, mentalities, and practices – the concept bears strong similarities to racist thought. However, ethno-pluralism performs a shift from a primarily biological paradigm to a cultural one.[51] It has therefore been aptly described as a 'new racism,' 'cultural racism,' or 'differentialist racism,' i.e., an ideology that serves the same purpose as racism, while avoiding the stigmatized term 'race.'[52]

The scattered movement constituting the European New Right goes back to an initiative in the late 1960s centering around the French philosopher Alain de Benoist and his organization GRECE (*Groupement de recherche et d'études pour la civilisation européenne* – Research and Study Group for European Civilization).[53] In Germany, a heterogenous network of groups, journals, and publishers took up these activities, among them Pierre Krebs' cultural organization *Thule Seminar*, as well as cultural-political journals such as *Nation & Europa* (which Henning Eichberg wrote for) and *Junge Freiheit* (Young Freedom). The New Right fashioned itself as a reaction against the leftist ideas of 1968. It adopted political strategies and tools from the New Left in order to instigate a 'culture war' (*Kulturkampf*) from the right. These strategies were directed against all international, universalist, capitalist, and socialist forces that allegedly threatened the ethnic substance of European identity by

---

europäischen Rechten. Geschichte, Kontinuitäten, Wandel, ed. Claudia Globisch, Agnieszka Pufelska, and Volker Weiß (Wiesbaden: VS Verlag, 2011), 207.

51 Considering the fact that 'traditional' versions of racism also never relied on exclusively biological paradigms, but always resorted to cultural or spiritual notions, this shift is certainly not absolute. In recent public discussions, at least in Germany, biological or genetic arguments have resurfaced as well.

52 Cf. Balibar, "Is there a 'New Racism'?" as well as Pierre-André Taguieff, *La Force du préjugé. Essai sur le racisme et ses doubles* (Paris: La Découverte, 1988) (Engl. translation *The Force of Prejudice. On Racism and its Doubles* (Minneapolis: University of Minnesota Press, 2001)).

53 For recent English language analyses of the European New Right see Tamir Bar-On, *Where Have all the Fascists Gone?* (Aldershot-Hamshire: Ashgate, 2007) and Roger Woods, *Germany's New Right as Culture and Politics* (London: Palgrave Macmillan, 2007).

imposing a "vodka-cola imperialism."[54] From Antonio Gramsci, Benoist borrowed the concept of cultural hegemony and the goal of influencing the ideological and cultural superstructure in order to eventually gain political power. The concept of ethno-pluralism contributes to this meta-political strategy. In contrast to the traditional extreme right, the New Right is not necessarily antidemocratic, nor does it usually promote authoritarian or autocratic forms of government.[55] However, it perceives democracy as a matter of ethnic homogeneity by claiming that natural organic collectives are the only appropriate expression of a people's will. It rejects representational and parliamentary systems as undemocratic because they impede the immediacy of a direct influence of the *Volk* – hence the critical term 'ethnocracy' for such concepts.[56]

In our context, it is important to note that exponents of the French New Right, Benoist in particular, already relied heavily on Herder's cultural relativist notions of a homogenous *Volk*, and traced his ideas back to German Conservative and National Revolutionaries.[57] From this tradition, Benoist derived his anti-Christian attitude and philosophical Paganism. It is driven by a rejection of Marxism, liberalism, and the idea of universal human rights. Moreover, Benoist sees the roots of these universalist ideas in the Judeo-Christian tradition, against which he sets Indo-European mentality and

---

54   Michael Minkenberg, *Die neue radikale Rechte im Vergleich. USA, Frankreich, Deutschland* (Opladen/Wiesbaden: Westdeutscher Verlag, 1998), 152f.
55   "Die radikale Rechte in Europa heute. Profile und Trends in Ost und West," in *Die Dynamik der europäischen Rechten. Geschichte, Kontinuitäten, Wandel*, ed. Claudia Globisch, Agnieszka Pufelska, and Volker Weiß (Wiesbaden: VS Verlag, 2011), 117.
56   Cf. Globisch, "'Deutschland uns Deutschen, Türkei den Türken, Israelis raus aus Palästina,'" 211f. In a recent interview (Robert Scholz and Mathias Brodkorb, "Über Habitus, Ideologie und Praxis. Im Gespräch mit Henning Eichberg," Endstation Rechts, http://www.endstation-rechts.de/index.php?option=com_k2&view=item&id=4971, last accessed November 11, 2011), Eichberg describes his journey from the (German) right to the (Danish) left in terms that mirror this privileging of the *Volk*. He describes the orientation towards Europe he found in the New Right as an expression of a fascist totalitarianism, because it took its relation to power as a starting point. Focusing on the *Volk* instead means a necessary turn towards democracies. One could also describe this move as a turn from a statist right to a Romantic right. Cf. Diedrich Diederichsen, "Der Anarch, der Solitär und die Revolte. Rechte Poststrukturalismus-Rezeption in der BRD," in *Rechtsextremismus. Ideologie und Gewalt*, ed. Richard Faber, Hajo Funke, and Gerhard Schoenberner (Berlin: Edition Hentrich, 1995), 241.
57   Cf. most recently Globisch, "'Deutschland uns Deutschen, Türkei den Türken, Israelis raus aus Palästina,'" 209f. See also Minkenberg, *Die neue radikale Rechte im Vergleich. USA, Frankreich, Deutschland*, 141f, 152, 161 as well as "Die radikale Rechte in Europa heute. Profile und Trends in Ost und West."

culture. Like his forerunners in the Conservative Revolution, along with C.G. Jung and Mircea Eliade, from whom he drew inspiration, Benoist's Paganism – although philosophical in nature and not meant as a call for a literal revival of a Pagan religion – led to an increased value being placed on myth. Myth is seen as a privileged access to the deep essentials of each culture, i.e., its archetypal roots.[58] While Benoist's Paganism led to the political marginalization of the New Right in the 1990s,[59] it offers a welcome philosophical framework to ethnicist Asatruers who have found it relevant and adaptable to their concepts of ethnic religion.

The reception of New Right thought within Asatru started in Germany in the mid-1980s. Harry Radegeis (alias Harry Schmidt), a member of the racial-religious *Armanen-Orden* and activist of the extreme right, called for a change of direction from the old authoritarian right to the new National Revolutionary right within Pagan political activism. Demonstrating clearly the strategic purpose behind this shift, Radegeis wrote:

> Go to the grassroots! Work with the Greens, Alternatives, National Revolutionaries, etc. Contribute there with your knowledge! [...] That would be true progress! That would confuse the enemy! For then he would no longer know where to look for us and how to survey us.[60]

In recent years, the circles around Stephen Flowers' *Rune Gild* and Stephen McNallen's ethnicist AFA have actively promoted Benoist's and others' New Right theories.[61] The AFA offers the English translation of Benoist's *Being A Pagan*, published by the same press as the journal *Tyr*, with a preface by Stephen Flowers.

---

58   Cf. Göran Dahl, "Den 'nya högern' och nyhedendommen," in *Myter om det nordiska – mellan romantik och politik*, ed. Catharina Raudvere, Anders Andrén, and Kristina Jennbert, Vägar till Midgård (Lund: Nordic Academic Press, 2001), 132–134.

59   Minkenberg, *Die neue radikale Rechte im Vergleich. USA, Frankreich, Deutschland*, 154.

60   *Irminsul – Stimme der Armanenschaft* 1 (1985). Cf. Schnurbein, *Göttertrost in Wendezeiten*, 31: "Löst den NPD-Haufen endlich auf! Was Besseres könnte garnicht passieren! Geht in die Basis! Arbeitet bei den Grünen, Alternativen, Nationalrevolutionären usw. mit. Bringt dort euer Wissen ein! [...] Das wäre echter Fortschritt! Das würde den Gegner verwirren! Dann wüßte er nicht mehr, wo er uns suchen soll und wie überwachen."

61   Flowers has been working on two related book projects, one about "The European New Right and its Meaning for America" another one about "The Pagan Right." See "About the Contributors" in: *Tyr* II (2003–2004), 415.

Cultural Essentialism beyond the New Right

Considering the turn of terminology from racism to cultural essentialism, the claim that ideas such as the ones promoted by the German *VfgH* resemble an ethno-pluralist paradigm is justified. They do not emphasize genetic ancestry as foundational for an ethnic religion, but for an organic cultural heritage. Potential associations with New Right or racial-biological essentialist ideologies are the reason why a-racist Asatru groups reject the epithet 'ethnic.' Nevertheless, the majority remains convinced that the intimate intertwining of cultural traditions with the surrounding natural world is the foundation of Asatru – a unity which is perceived as natural and immediate to people who grew up in the respective area and culture. However, as Egil Stenseth of Norwegian a-racist *Bifrost* asserts, in much the same way as Fritz Steinbock of the ethnicist *VfgH*, it can be appropriated and learned by people with different heritages and cultural backgrounds as well.[62]

Most European Asatruers, regardless of their political convictions, thus base their faith on a sentiment of rootedness and belonging, of the familiar and known, which is tied to landscape as well as childhood memories of stories and songs. The feeling of immediacy is probably strongest in Scandinavia, where it is reinforced by the fact that Eddic myth and medieval literature have been considered integral and unquestioned parts of the national heritage since the 19th century. In countries such as Iceland and Norway, this sense of a national cultural heritage is also closely tied to images of wildlife. Here, the sense of Asatru being rooted in nature, which allegedly has been part of pre-Christian worship for centuries, becomes all the more self-evident. Such ideas of an 'organic culture' permeate Asatru on all levels. Furthermore, Fredrik Gregorius' argument that "concepts tied to cultural identity are often used to avoid touching questions which are related to ethnicity"[63] is valid for more than just Swedish Asatru.[64]

---

62   Stenseth, "Nyhedendom i Norge." The implications of such views are discussed further in Chapter 6.
63   "att begrepp kopplade till kulturell identitet många gånger används för att undvika att beröra frågor som har med entnicitet at göra." Gregorius, *Modern Asatro*, 132.
64   Following the publication of Gregorius' book, many Swedish Asatruers have taken exception to this claim, asserting that they have problems finding their own attitudes towards culture and ethnicity in a generalizing statement like this. Instead, they emphasize the aspect of new creation on the basis of tradition (see, for example, Interview W, with a Swedish Asatruer, August 2010). However, even the most adamant and articulate critics of an ethnic perspective, such as Egil Stenseth of Norwegian *Bifrost*, accentuate that the basis of Asatru could be called ethnic, although the main focus today should be to build something new on this basis, so that the 'doing' of Asatru, i.e. the *blot*, is at its center, instead of ideology. Cf. Stenseth, "Nyhedendom i Norge," 19.

The idea of an immediate connection between culture and nature is neither 'natural' nor self-explanatory. We have to understand it as a recurrence or transformation of the Romantic Herderian idea of an organic unity of people, landscape, climate, language, history, and myth. The fact that it seems self-evident to many Asatruers, and that it can be used effectively as a strategy of justification also indicates that the idea is part of a broader cultural consensus. In today's globalized society, cultural essentialism and the conflation of the categories 'religion,' 'culture,' 'ethnicity,' and 'race' thrive once again. In one interview, a female Danish Asatruer in her thirties, who perceives herself as a-racist, exemplified the contradictions inherent in such a paradigm. She first rejected the idea of a racial Asatru and a 'pure' heritage, but later maintained that she can easily relate to the concept of an Aryan race. She went on to say that she sees conflicts as taking place not between races, but between religions, a position that in her view is all too often confused with racism. In another part of the interview, it became clear that she sees Islam, which she considers a patriarchal, authoritarian *religion*, as the main antagonist. Immediately afterwards, she talked about Islam as a "*culture* that wants to take my freedom away" [my emphasis].[65]

This example does not reflect values and judgments promoted specifically by any Asatru organization. Instead, it represents a widespread attitude in current Danish society[66] applied by an Asatruer to explain her religious attitude. It is a trend that extends well beyond Denmark and has been astutely analyzed by Norwegian anthropologist Marianne Gullestad in her writings about the new "integralist ideologies" in Europe. Gullestad observes that "the anti-racist pact among the general public in Europe after Nazism and World War II seems to be slowly and imperceptibly eroded," and that arguments and ideas from former times," especially a "longing for the warmth of an ethnically-based *Gemeinschaft*" (community),[67] are "reappearing in new forms."[68] Gullestad speaks of a process of 'neo-ethnification,' asserting that

---

65 "en kultur [...], der vil tage min frihed fra mig." Interview H, with a Danish Asatruer, April 2010, Denmark.
66 Cf. for example the contributions in Jørgen S. Nielsen, ed. *Islam in Denmark. The Challenge of Diversity* (Lanham etc.: Lexington Books, 2010).
67 Gullestad here uses the German term *Gemeinschaft* as a reference to German sociologist Ferdinand Tönnies' distinction between *Gemeinschaft* (community) and *Gesellschaft* (civil society). For Tönnies, *Gemeinschaft* is an organic form of society based on emotions of belonging, which he distinguishes from the modern, technical, rational, contract-based civil society. This distinction has played a significant role for the self-understanding of corporatist movements, alternative communities, and nationalist movements in Germany in the first part of the 20th century. For a translation of Tönnies' 1887 work see Ferdinand Tönnies, *Community and Civil Society* (Cambridge University Press, 2001).
68 Gullestad, *Plausible Prejudice*, 295.

the concept of 'ethnification,' with its focus on "specific ideas about language, culture, descent and territory," is "recombined in new ways in the face of extra-European immigration."[69] These "categories, rhetorical strategies, and points of view formerly regarded as extremist" are aggressively promoted by populist right-wing politicians all over Europe. At the same time, they have by now turned into much more deeply ingrained "signs which circulate" and are regarded as "a form of self-evident conventional wisdom."[70] One of the effects is to replace or veil social class or economic inequality as valid categories of social conflict and to mask, as well as implicitly reaffirm, existing privilege.[71]

While Asatru in many ways has moderated and reflected its own roots in and attitudes toward racial and ethnicist ideologies, the European mainstream itself has taken a turn toward culturalist or cultural essentialist thought. Both trends are responsible for the fact that the majority of Asatruers today can no longer be found in radical right-wing environments. Asatru fashions itself as an alternative religion that sides with other allegedly suppressed religions and ethnic cultures. At the same time, it finds increasing support in mainstream ideologies, at least with regard to its views on culture and cultural roots. Heathens connect their ideas about culture, heritage, and religion with the political discussions in their respective countries. A case in point is the difference between Swedish and Danish Asatru regarding some Asatruers' attitude toward immigrants in general, and Islam in particular. Many Danish Asatruers will quite uninhibitedly set 'our religion' and 'our people' against the 'foreign culture' of Islam. This, however, should not necessarily be read as a sign of Asatru in Denmark having become more ethnicist and anti-Islamist in recent years. Rather, it is a sign that the current anti-Islamic climate in Denmark and the restrictive immigration policy make it possible for Asatruers to voice such attitudes more openly. The opposite is the case in Sweden, which has a more open and integrative immigration policy and has officially embraced the idea of multi-culturalism as an identity marker for modern Sweden. Correspondingly, many Swedish Asatruers fashion themselves and their religion as pluralist and multi-culturalist and emphasize the cosmopolitan and diverse nature of Old Norse society, whereas attitudes that betray cultural essentialist stances remain in the background.[72]

---

69   Ibid., 299.
70   Ibid., 302.
71   Cf. ibid., 307. In this sense, we could speak of a success of the New Right's struggle for cultural hegemony, although it is a success that has not directly benefited the circles that promoted these ideas.
72   This is an argument that Gregorius, *Modern Asatro*, 132, is making.

The ongoing discussions within and around Asatru about issues of race, ethnicity, and culture have had an opposite effect as well. Some a-racist groups and individuals have in fact developed a heightened awareness of the problems connected with naïve and unreflective assumptions about heritage, ethnicity, cultural tradition, and their relations to religion that reveal a considerable amount of political astuteness and skepticism toward fantasies of origin. Jenny Blain, an anthropologist and member of a-racist *The Troth*, has noted the danger of possible slippages toward basing religion on concepts of ethnicity and race. They are motivated by the faulty assumptions that the 'peoples' of the past can be identified at all; that their cultures and spiritualities were clearly demarcated and that culture, spirituality, language, and 'race' coincide. While such assumptions are common in Neopaganism, Blain insists that, due to the problematic history of Heathenism, they are more reflected in some Heathen groups than in Neopaganism in general.[73] In fact, interviews with members of a-racist groups such as Norwegian *Bifrost*, Swedish *Samfundet Forn Sed*, and the German *Eldaring* in particular indicate that Blain has a point. Many Asatruers today see the necessity of criticizing what Ann-Marie Gallagher has called "a whole range of misconceptions, and arguably misappropriations, of concepts of history, nation, 'race,' and ethnicity, which seem to exist within popular Pagan lore."[74]

Kurt Oertel, the *Warden of the Lore* in the German *Eldaring*, cautions:

> In the Germanic world, ethnicity wasn't by far as fixed as older models or also some of our contemporaries would like to see. [...] Celts as well as Teutons [*Germanen*] were not homogeneous peoples [...]. One has to always be clear that the term 'culture' in archaeological language exclusively refers to similarities of ceramic forms, styles of jewelry etc. and it is far from sure whether or not this concept of culture corresponds to the social reality of this era.[75]

---

73 Blain and Wallis, "Heathenry," 423.
74 Anne-Marie Gallagher, "Weaving a Tangled Web? Pagan Ethics and Issues of History, 'Race' and Ethnicity in Pagan Identity," in *Handbook of Contemporary Neopaganism*, ed. James R. Lewis and Murphy Pizza (Leiden/Boston: Brill, 2009), 577.
75 Kurt Oertel, "Die Angeln. Teil 2: Die neue Heimat," *Herdfeuer. Die Zeitschrift des Eldaring e.V.* 3, no. 10 (2005), 9f: "Ethnizität war in der germanischen Welt keineswegs so festgelegt, wie ältere Modelle und auch noch gewisse Zeitgenossen das gerne hätten. [...] Sowohl Kelten wie auch Germanen waren in sich selbst ja kein jeweils einheitliches Volk [...]. Man muss sich stets darüber klar sein, dass der Begriff 'Kultur' in archäologischem Sprachgebrauch ausschließlich auf Ähnlichkeiten von Keramikformen, Schmuckstilen

Henrik Hallgren, former chair of the Swedish *Samfundet Forn Sed* (formerly SAS), also argues against a holistic concept of culture, and for seeing "culture [...] as an open system."[76] Others follow Gallagher and insist on asking what attracts so many right-wing groups and individuals to Paganism, and emphasize the importance of making "a positive statement which irrevocably dissociates us from them."[77] For Egil Stenseth, of Norwegian *Bifrost*, this means taking a firm political stance against right-wing extremist, racial, and ethnicist thought within Asatru. He points out how a completely 'unpolitical' attitude within Asatru can lead to fierce infighting and splintering in groups whose membership spans the full political spectrum, from far right to far left.[78] German a-racist *Nornirs Ætt* directs a similar critique against groups that claim Asatru to be a spiritual way that should be considered separate from politics. For *Nornirs Aett*, this unreflective and naïve attitude unintentionally opens up the potential for *völkisch* and right-wing ideologies and individuals to gain influence. For them, the choice of following a 'Nordic' or 'Germanic' spiritual path requires a politically active and critical stance against the *völkisch* and right-wing tendencies within Asatru. *Nornirs Ætt* maintain that they feel inspired by Old Norse texts and artefacts along with fictional and Neopagan readings of them. Nonetheless, they perceive culture and community not as reified entities that can be traced back into a (deep) past or even something that already exists, but as something which must be continually created.

We can conclude that Asatru religion is characterized by a tension that is difficult to resolve. On the one hand, there is awareness of the problems connected to racial paradigms and of the fact that modern Asatru has to be based on new constructions of religion. On the other hand, there is a strong desire for wholeness and authenticity, for rootedness. A German Asatruer stresses that "one nevertheless wants to have something like a feeling of continuity," a sense of – and desire for – something "authentic," which can be found in the realm of the archaic. He acknowledges the reality of constant cultural mixing, while insisting on the necessity of having a mythological basis as a "support which integrates a person into his or her environment."[79]

---

usw. beruht, und ob dieser Kulturbegriff der damaligen sozialen Realität entsprach, ist keineswegs gesichert."
76 Interview with Henrik Hallgren (Samfundet Forn Sed): "Jag ser kultur mer som ett öppet system."
77 Gallagher, "Weaving a Tangled Web?" 587.
78 Interview with Egil Stenseth (Bifrost).
79 Interview D: "aber, man möchte trotzdem noch zumindest so was wie das Gefühl einer Kontinuität haben. [...] Ich denke, eine Mythologie bindet einen Menschen in seine Umgebung mit ein."

Summarizing these controversies, we could say that the field of Asatru religion is formed by a tension or oscillation between the search for community, which is often, but not always, conceptualized as culturally homogenous, and the desire to find an expression for one's own spiritual or esoteric preferences, a desire based on a modern liberal individualism. One possible way to reconcile such differences is to attempt to see the values of individualism and personal spirituality not as modern phenomenon, but to conceptualize them as pre-Christian Nordic values.

What this chapter has shown is the persistence of a neo-Romantic conflation of religion, culture, and ethnicity, which is not limited to Asatru, but can be found in Western societies in general – a conflation which could be described as an ethnification or culturalization of religion as well as a sacralization of culture. In her discussion of neo-ethnification and new culturalism in Northern Europe, Marianne Gullestad also mentions in passing the religious aspects of the problem: "Religion, as a repository of traditions of symbols and beliefs, always stands ready to be tapped by those who wish to develop a new framework of ideas about social order." She makes this point in order to demonstrate how "in Norway, the Christian religion, in the form of the Lutheran State Church, has gained renewed importance as an institution uniting even secularized majority Norwegians in opposition to Islam."[80] While similar arguments could easily be made about the Protestant and Catholic churches in other countries as well, Asatru obviously takes a path diverging from the mainstream in this respect.

---

80   Gullestad, *Plausible Prejudice*, 304.

CHAPTER 5

Contested Fields II: Concepts of Religion and Anti-Monotheism

Positing a 'native,' 'progressive,' Western, Euro-Christian or 'Judeo-Christian' tradition against an 'unenlightened,' 'foreign,' 'Oriental' Islam is a common figure of thought in the discourse of neo-ethnification. Obviously, since Neo-paganism is by definition set in opposition to Christianity, this is not a viable dichotomy within our context. Pagans tend to perceive Christianity itself as 'foreign,' and as a destroyer of 'native' spiritual heritage. An article in the German *Heidnisches Jahrbuch* reacts to this problem:

> The ongoing discussion about Islam, integration, and immigration politics has put the question about our own culture into the foreground. In this context, one likes to emphasize that our society has a Christian-Jewish background. The so-called 'Western values' of the Occident, which include a separation between religion and state, are set in a brusque opposition to a religion of immigrants that does not know this separation and has barely thematized it. The unreflected-upon repetition of a Judeo-Christian understanding of values requires a closer look, because: Is it really true that Germans and Europeans are Christians and derive their orientation for action from religion? Democracy, pluralism and legal equality are some of the bedrocks of European societies, but they cannot be derived from the Bible.[1]

---

1 Christian Brüning, "Zum Unterschied von Monotheismus und Kosmotheismus," *Heidnisches Jahrbuch* 5 (2011), 217: "Die anhaltende Diskussion um den Islam, Integration und Zuwanderungspolitik hat die Frage um die eigene Kultur in den Vordergrund gerückt. In dem Zusammenhang wird gerne betont, dass unsere Gesellschaft einen christlich-jüdischen Hintergrund habe. Die sogenannten ‚westlichen Werte' des Abendlandes, zu denen die Trennung von Religion und Staat gehört, stehen schroff einer Religion von Zuwanderern gegenüber, die diese Trennung nicht kennt und kaum ansatzweise thematisiert hat. Die unreflektierte Wiederholung des jüdisch-christlichen Werteverständnisses bedarf einer näheren Ansicht, denn: Ist es wirklich so, dass Deutsche und Europäer Christen sind und aus der Religion ihre Handlungsorientierungen ableiten? Demokratie, Pluralismus und rechtliche Gleichheit stellen einige der Grundpfeiler der europäischen Gesellschaften dar, doch aus der Bibel lassen sie sich nicht herleiten."

The author initially remains within the common opposition between a modern secularism and an unenlightened Islam. However, he then goes on to associate Islam with the "Christian-Jewish" tradition and answers the questions he himself poses by delving into both traditional, anti-clerical secularist literature, and into recent theories of religion that make a distinction between monotheism and its other, polytheism. In this process, he aligns the traditional anti-Christian attitude of Neopaganism with currently circulating anti-Islamic stereotypes – and, as we shall see, he does so in much the same way as the German Faith Movement's aligning of its critique of Christianity with contemporary mainstream anti-Semitism.

Against such contemporary political backgrounds, it becomes all the more important to ask how Germanic Neopagans have constructed their attitude toward Christianity and other religions, and how they conceptualize their own religion – to look at the theories they draw upon and the traditions in which these attitudes are entangled.

Attitudes Towards Christianity

Attitudes towards Christianity vary considerably among Asatruers today, ranging from more relaxed or indifferent attitudes to a vigorous rejection of the religion as the main antagonist, or as one of the "alien religions that do not truly speak to our souls."[2] The most common allegations against Christianity are directed against its (violent) proselytizing which, in the eyes of Heathen critics, has led to the extinction of Pagan religions in the past, and to a loss of religious and cultural diversity in the present. In addition, cricitisms are aimed against what is seen as Christianity's repressive morality, and its demand to 'mortify flesh' and nature. In areas where Christian fundamentalism or puritan traditions are entrenched, such as in parts of provincial Norway or in some North American contexts, the idea that Christianity is a simplistic, authoritarian religion spreading fear of hell and punishment reverberates through many of the interviews I conducted.

Such positions are offset by other Asatruers, mostly from a-racist groups. Prominent German and Scandinavian Heathens have spouses who identify as Christians, and report no problems with this fact.[3] Only groups in Scandinavia,

---

2 Answer to "Why is the religion of our ancestors the best one for us?" See http://www.runestone.org/index.php?option=com_content&view=article&id=83&Itemid=487, last accessed September 16, 2014.
3 Interview D.

where they are officially recognized as religious communities by the respective states, require members not to be registered in Christian or other congregations. This is not due to ideological reasons, but rather serves to comply with state regulations limiting membership to only one official religious community. A few, such as the former leader of Swedish *Samfundet Forn Sed*, Henrik Hallgren, are open to integrating Christian elements into their beliefs and practices, and perceive them as part of a religious tradition that should be taken seriously, and which may serve as a source of inspiration for Asatru. He claims: "For me the dividing line is not as sharp: Christianity – Paganism; I feel: what is it that inspires me?"[4] Even Stephen McNallen, of the American *Asatru Folk Assembly* (AFA), has put forth a related argument, and has modified what he himself called his earlier "stridently anti-Christian" attitudes. In contrast to Hallgren, he does not put it into the frame of a post-modern cultural bricolage, but one of ancestry. McNallen reminds his followers:

> that (1) Asatru is an ancestral religion and (2) most of our recent ancestors have been Christian. [...] I honor my Christian ancestors just as I do my pre-Christian forebears, because blood is thicker than water – and, specifically, thicker than the water of the baptismal font.[5]

Others tend to emphasize their appreciation of the ethical values of compassion and charity, which they either positively associate with Christianity or interpret as universal human ideals.[6] René Gründer has demonstrated that square rejections of Christianity are not constitutive or instrumental for the construction of individual Asatruers' worldviews and lived religious attitudes.[7] The fairly widespread indifferent or tolerant attitudes towards Christianity and other religions among younger Asatruers can be understood as the result of a diminished influence of Christian churches and doctrines in families and Western secularized education systems.

---

4 Interview with Henrik Hallgren (Samfundet Forn Sed): "[...] för mig är inte gränsen så skarp: kristendom – hedendom, utan jag känner att, vad är det som väcker inspiration inom mig?."
5 All quotes: Stephen McNallen: AFA Update 5-7-10, E-mail Newsletter, also available at: http://asatruupdate.blogspot.com/2010_05_01_archive.html, last accessed December 16, 2012.
6 The now-defunct Danish online forum *Kindir* ran a discussion about positive aspects of Christianity under the title "Compassion and Christianity" in 2008 ("Medlidenhed og kristendommen," http://www.kindir.dk/forum/viewtopic.php?t=3982, last accessed November 14, 2011). Hermann Ritter, "Zaubern ohne Gott?," *Herdfeuer. Die Zeitschrift des Eldaring e.V.* 6, no. 22 (2008) criticized simplistic anti-Christian attitudes amongst Pagans in the German *Eldaring's* journal *Herdfeuer*.
7 Cf. Gründer, *Blótgemeinschaften*, 314–324.

Nevertheless, a general tendency persists within Asatru of all varieties to configure everything in history that harmonizes with one's own perspectives as originally Pagan, while all that one despises is understood as an expression of Christianity's 'foreign' influence. This attitude can take as many different forms as there are political, social, and cultural ideals. A-racist German groups, for example, like to distance themselves from Ariosophy by underlining the monotheistic core and thus ultimately Christian nature of such theosophical ideas.[8] Stephen Flowers, in his version of the story of the "reawakening of the Germanic spirit," celebrates the alleged fact that a unified "Germanic cultural matrix has come to dominate not only Europe but the world" – a claim which implicitly justifies Euro-American imperialism and colonialism as a consequence of an innate spiritual Germanic heritage. In contrast, Flowers does not consider the negative implications of such endeavors, in "Germany in the first half of the 20th century," for example, as "the natural outcomes of Germanic culture *per se*, but rather [as] the eventual results of prolonged attempts at the admixture of ultimately incompatible cultural features" and the "Christian doctrine."[9]

More importantly, anti-Christian attitudes characterize programmatic definitions of Heathenism. This indicates that the opposition to Christianity might not be instrumental for all individual Asatruers' personal beliefs, but that it still forms the basis for group philosophies. An instructive example is a contribution listed under "basic articles" on the German *Eldaring's* homepage, which carries the programmatic title "What is Heathenism?"[10] Here, Heathenism is consistently defined in opposition to Christianity and its alleged oversimplifying ethics of good and evil. Asatru appears as a religion of nature, based in experience and oral wisdom, as opposed to a religion in need of external revelation, blind faith, priestly authoritarian mediators, and codified texts – as a system that seeks salvation ("Heil") in this world and not in the hereafter; a faith that rates deeds higher than abstract values, abrogates the artificial

---

8   See for example Eibensang, "Ariosophie – was ist das und wo kommt sie her? (Basiert auf: "Ariosophie – ein Überblick" von Hans Schuhmacher 1996. Textliche Neufassung samt Erweiterungen von Duke Meyer 2004)," Nornirs Ætt, http://www.nornirsaett.de/ueberblick-uber-ariosophie/, last accessed November 14, 2011. See also Chapter 3, in particular the discussion of *fulltrui* or patron gods.

9   Stephen E. Flowers, *The Northern Dawn. A History of the Reawakening of the Germanic Spirit*, vol. I (From the Twilight of the Gods to the Sun at Midnight) (Smithville, TX: Runa-Raven Press, 2006), XIV.

10 Kurt Oertel, "Was ist Heidentum? Wie kann man den Begriff verstehen," Eldaring e.V., http://www.eldaring.de/pages/germanisches-heidentum/was-ist-heidentum.php, last accessed November 14, 2011.

division between the secular and the spiritual, and rejects the central concept of original sin.

Paralleling the rhetoric of earlier proponents of a 'heroic' Germanic religion, the article's author finally invokes an implicitly Nietzschean framework and grants Christianity in contemporary society a function for those with insufficient moral strength and will:

> From this follows one of the reservations as to why the old Heathen way is not suitable for everybody: People who depend on others or some "holy scriptures" to constantly tell them what they ought to do; people who are not willing to take responsibility for their own life; people who are too weak to develop a persuasive ethic and an individual character on their own; people who need a divine system of prohibitions, e.g., in the form of the biblical Ten Commandments, in order to understand the most natural things; for these people, the Heathen way is indeed the wrong alternative.[11]

The article succinctly summarizes some of the most widespread Heathen attitudes about the evils of Christianity and benefits of a Pagan worldview. At the same time, it demonstrates striking parallels between the concepts of religion within contemporary Asatru and Germanic Faith or *völkisch* religion of the early 20th century.

While a majority of followers of German *völkisch* religion in the early 20th century adhered to a 'purified' version of Protestantism – purged of its 'Jewish,' universalist, and Paulinian elements, and promoting an 'Aryan Christ' – the Neopagan minority in the German Faith Movement set itself apart by combining its anti-Semitism with a pronouncedly anti-Christian stance as its guiding force and strongest motivation. Early manifestos by Ernst Wachler and Ludwig Fahrenkrog, to mention just two, constructed their ideas for the "future of the German Faith"[12] in clear opposition to what they perceived as the central

---

11   Ibid.: "Und daraus folgt nun eine der Einschränkungen, warum der alte heidnische Weg nicht für jeden Menschen geeignet ist: Menschen, die darauf angewiesen sind, dass andere oder irgendwelchen "heiligen" Schriften ihnen dauernd sagen, was sie zu tun haben, Menschen, die nicht willens sind, Verantwortung für das eigene Leben zu übernehmen, Menschen, die zu schwach sind, eine überzeugte Ethik und einen individuellen Charakter aus sich selbst heraus zu entwickeln, Menschen, die z.B. in Form der biblischen Zehn Gebote erst ein göttliches Verbotssystem benötigen, um Selbstverständlichkeiten zu begreifen, für die ist der alte heidnische Weg in der Tat die falsche Alternative."

12   Wachler, "Über die Zukunft des deutschen Glaubens"; Ludwig Fahrenkrog, "Germanentempel I," *Der Volkserzieher* 6 (1907); "Germanentempel II," *Der Volkserzieher* 6 (1908); "Germanentempel III," *Der Volkserzieher* 10 (1908).

Christian and Jewish dogmas. Christianity appeared as an authoritarian religion detached from the world, fixated on the hereafter, promoting a bleak, unnatural gospel of sin, repentance, punishment, and the need for redemption due to the inherent evil of human nature and sexuality. The 'Aryan' or 'German' religion appears as this life-negating Christianity's polar opposite: a religion celebrating (human) nature's goodness, cultivating "a pure view of nature, an affirmation of the world, a self-confident, high-handed view of life and custom,"[13] and the possibility for, as well as the duty of, self-redemption through one's own (heroic) deeds.

German Faithlers ultimately saw the reason for the destructiveness of Christianity in its foreignness, i.e., in its being based on a Semitic worldview that despises "natural differences" between races, classes, and sexes.[14] Under its influence, the Germanic peoples' "faith and myth, poetry and morals, custom and law were annihilated or distorted and deprived of their creative power."[15] While dominant German Christianity can be understood as a radicalization and racialization of Lutheran Protestantism and anti-Catholicism, its Neopagan counterpart in the German Faith Movement integrated elements originating in Catholicism as well. This can partly be attributed to the influence of Austrians, such as the Ariosophists Jörg Lanz von Liebenfels and, in particular, Guido von List, who, in accordance with folklorists in the Alpine area, interpreted local (mainly Catholic) folklore and other Catholic rites as concealed remnants of pre-Christian practices.[16]

---

13 Wachler, "Über die Zukunft des deutschen Glaubens," 16.
14 Cf. ibid., 4.
15 Ibid., 7.
16 Gründer, *Blótgemeinschaften* uses Uwe Puschner's thesis that the *völkisch* movement is a predominantly Protestant affair to distinguish the *völkisch* and racist religion of the early 20th century and its remnants in current *völkisch* Pagan groups from 'universalist' groups that integrate Catholic folk customs and beliefs into their faith. However, Puschner, *Die Völkische Bewegung im wilhelminischen Deutschland*, already alerts us to the fact that the Neopagan minority within the *völkisch* movement was significantly influenced by what can be called crypto-Catholic ideas, in spite of its anti-Roman attitudes and its origin in the Los-von-Rom ("Free from Rome") movement (see also "Katholisches Milieu und all-deutsch-völkische Bewegung. Die Münchner Zeitschrift 'Odin' (1899–1901)," in *Le milieu intellectuel catholique en Allemagne, sa presse et ses réseaux (1871–1960) / Das katholische Intellektuellenmilieu in Deutschland, seine Presse und seine Netzwerke (1871–1960)*, ed. Michel Grunewald and Uwe Puschner (Berne: Peter Lang, 2006)). Thus, a mixture of crypto-Protestant and crypto-Catholic elements can be seen in the anti-Christian Neopagan faction of the *völkisch* movement as well as in modern Asatru. This particular differentiation is therefore not well suited to distinguishing contemporary Asatru from its *völkisch* forerunners.

The Question of Anti-Semitism

The obvious parallels between German Faithlers' outlook on Christianity and anti-Christian attitudes held by contemporary Asatruers can be traced back to a broader critique of Christianity originating in a number of 19th century strands of politico-religious thought. Most prominent among them are the anti-universalist attitudes of National Romanticism, biblical criticism, and research on Jesus' life in the wake of the works of French political philosopher Ernest Renan (1823–1892) and the German philosophers David Friedrich Strauß (1808–1874), Ludwig Feuerbach (1804–1872), and Friedrich Nietzsche (1844–1900), as well as the free religious and free thinker movements. These inspired many later academic theories of religion, and thus lie at the basis of the academic field of History of Religions (or *Religionswissenschaft*). At the same time, they informed both *völkisch* and other alternative religious movements of the 20th century and found their way into diverse Neopagan ideologies.[17]

In his discussion of *völkisch* versions of Nietzschean religiosity, Steven Aschheim maintains that "the ideologies of the *Glaubensbewegung* [...] created a Germanic religion that transposed Nietzscheanism onto a racial-national base."[18] However, he under-emphasizes that these German Faithlers found a fertile ground for their ideas: the pre-existing distinction between Aryan and Semitic languages, myths, and religions. It is important to note that the linguistic differences discovered in the early 19th century were imbued from the beginning with, if not outright racial, then cultural connotations.[19] In Renan's work in particular, Judaism and its offshoots – Christianity, and particularly Islam – appear as static, conformist (monotheistic), nomadic, intolerant, and oppressive religions of revelation, whereas Aryan religion is painted as diverse (polytheistic), rational, immanent, modern, and formed by god-men or

---

17   For a systematic discussion of the interrelations between the study of religion and new religious movements in the 19th and 20th centuries see e.g. Kippenberg, *Die Entdeckung der Religionsgeschichte*. Cf. also Friedrich H. Tenbruck, "Die Religion im Maelstrom der Reflexion," in *Religion und Kultur*, ed. Jörg Bergmann, Alois Hahn, and Thomas Luckmann, Kölner Zeitschrift für Soziologie und Sozialpsychologie, Sonderheft 33 (Opladen: Westdeutscher Verlag, 1993).

18   Aschheim, *The Nietzsche Legacy in Germany 1890–1990*, 227.

19   For a critical discussion of the Aryan-Semitic dichotomy in the study of myth see Arvidsson, *Aryan Idols*. Cf. also Poliakov, *The Aryan Myth*, Maurice Olender, *The Languages of Paradise. Aryans and Semites – A Match Made in Heaven*, trans. Arthur Goldhammer, 2nd revised and augmented ed. (New York: Other Press, 2002).

avatars.[20] This distinction recalls Enlightenment climate theory (cf. Chapter 1) and assigns all the negative traits of a sterile and rootless monotheism to its origin in a nomadic desert culture (hence the catchword 'desert religion'). The positive characteristics of Aryan polytheism are attributed to a climate in favor of a fertile, cultivated nature.[21] The distinction between a life-affirming polytheism or nature religion and a life-denying, unnatural monotheism has been productive in many alternative religious contexts in the 20th century. As later chapters will show, they have all been burdened by this anti-Jewish heritage and criticized within and beyond their respective movements for their overt or implied anti-Semitism.

Anti-Jewish affects of this ilk can be found within contemporary Germanic Neopaganism as well. For racial-religious groups, a more or less outspoken anti-Semitic attitude is foundational. More indirect anti-Semitic arguments are occasionally voiced by ethnicist Asatruers. Garman Lord, the founder of Theodism in the United States, sees the origin of both Judaism and Christianity in "one little nomadic tribe of gypsy traders whose whole tribal economy was based on foreign trade and commerce." He invokes the stereotype of the Jewish usurer, and stresses the utterly different nature of the "Semitic value system of cunning and a guilty conscience." He contrasts it with the "Germanic" value system, which purportedly combined the need for a struggle against a perilous nature with "individual toughness, resourcefulness, and vigor, as well as an abundant flow of the milk of human kindness."[22] On the British *Odinic Rite*'s website, Heimgest writes about the "judeo/christian holocaust" [sic] which "our people suffered."[23] And Jack Jackson claims in the Danish journal *Valravn*:

> [...] we allow ourselves to be at odds with and doubt a basic Jewish self-understanding which is simultaneously humble towards their god-concept, and arrogant, ignorant and self-satisfied in relation to human diversity. [...] Still, after a thousand years, the Semitic religious systems

---

20   In asking the question whether or not the avatar Jesus could be Jewish at all, Renan first brought up the idea of an Aryan Christ, born in the green and fertile Galilee, rather than in the arid desert. Cf. Arvidsson, *Aryan Idols*, 113–115. For a discussion of Renan's attitudes towards Islam see, for example, Mattias Gardell, *Islamofobi* (Stockholm: Leopard, 2011), 66.
21   Cf. Arvidsson, *Aryan Idols*, 102–118.
22   All quotes Lord, *The Way of the Heathen*, 165.
23   Heimgest CG, "Continuing Tradition," The Odinic Rite, http://www.odinic-rite.org/main/continuing-tradition/, last accessed April 18, 2014.

treat their adherents like primitive, half-conscious, stupid animals that have to be kept under control by all means.[24]

Such an (anti-Christian) anti-Jewish attitude appears today as a less important facet of Neopaganism, and represents a minority position within current Asatru. Even within the faction that promotes a strongly ethnicist or even racial attitude toward Germanic religion, 'the Jew' is rarely the first figure of an enemy that is mentioned. This, however, does not mean that stereotypes about Judaism are absent. Some see and sometimes admire Judaism itself as a religion without universalist claims that is based on blood ties, and which is able to integrate religion, culture and ethnicity. They thus perceive it as a nonthreatening 'ethnic religion,' among others. A member of Danish *Forn Siðr* would like to see missionary religions "disappear from the face of the earth" because of their bloody repression of ethnic religions, but emphasizes that he "doesn't distance [himself] from Judaism in the same way. It is not totalitarian in this way. They take care of themselves. And they are not missionary."[25] Such attitudes mirror the reluctant admiration some *völkisch* anti-Semites had for the resilience of Judaism. Moreover, as the quote in the beginning of this chapter has shown, even those who still see Judaism as the root of the despised monotheistic religions are usually quick to mention Islam as the most threatening, non-native foreign religion.

The anti-Jewish and anti-Islamic connotations often implied in a critique of Christianity and monotheism have made the issue of anti-monotheism into a highly controversial topic within Asatru. This has to do with the considerable public attention monotheistic world religions and the conflicts between them have received since the 1990s, when the theory of a "Clash of Civilisations" was launched by Samuel Huntington,[26] and especially in the wake of the events of 9/11, 2001. At the same time, the thinking around the nature of monotheism and polytheism is part of an attempt by Asatruers to conceptualize the specificity of their religion with the help of current theories of religion. In the

---

24 Jack Jensen, "Om æren, freden og lykken," *Valravn. Hedensk tidskrift om samfund og kultur* 12 (2005), 7: "[...] vi tillader os at være på tværs og tvivle på en grundlæggende jødisk selvforståelse, der på samme tid er selvudslettende ydmyg over for deres guds-forståelse, og arrogant ignorantisk og selvtilstrækkelig i forhold til den menneskelige diversitet. [...] Stadig etter tusinde år, behandler de semitiske religiøse systemer deres tilløbere som primitive og semi-bevidste dumme dyr, som for enhver pris må holdes under kontrol."
25 Interview J.
26 Samuel P. Huntington, *The Clash of Civilizations and the Remaking of World Order* (New York: Simon and Schuster, 1996).

following section, I want to use a few instructive examples from Denmark and Germany, where the controversies have been most vivid, in order to tease out some of the more general problems.

Praising Polytheism

The idea that worshipping more than one god is an expression of and contributing factor to diversity and tolerance, whereas monotheistic religions create potentially totalitarian systems, is fairly widespread within Asatru as well as Neopaganism in general. Géza von Neményi, from the ethnicist German GGG, captured this popular attitude in the slogan: "One God creates uniformity and simple-mindedness, multiple gods create diversity."[27] For many Asatruers, this concept expresses an intuitive truth and serves as convincing proof of Paganism's alliance with and suitability for modern democratic and pluralistic societies. Although it has been exposed as a "myth of modernity" rather than a verifiable statement about the politico-religious character of Greek and Roman antiquity to which it was originally applied,[28] the idea has developed a remarkable productivity. Already in early Renaissance thought, a "polytheism of reason" was mobilized against "a military – and perhaps also theologically – superior monotheism." It was combined with the call for a "pragmatic state reform" directed against the "disagreements within the Christian churches."[29] Some Enlightenment philosophers utilized this kind of critique of church power and invoked polytheism as a guarantee of tolerance. In *The Natural History of Religion* (1757), David Hume saw polytheism as the natural and primary religion, claiming:

> The intolerance of almost all religions, which have maintained the unity of God, is as remarkable as the contrary principle of polytheists. The implacable narrow spirit of the JEWS is well known. MAHOMETANISM

---

27 "Ein Gott schafft Einfalt, viele Götter schaffen Vielfalt." The German *Einfalt* not only denotes uniformity, but simple-mindedness as well, cf. Ulrich Andreas Wien, "Interview mit Géza von Neményi, dem Allsherjargoden (Stammespriester) der Germanischen Glaubens-Gemeinschaft," *Materialdienst der Evangelischen Zentralstelle für Weltanschauungsfragen* 60, no. 4 (1997).

28 Joachim Losehand, "'The Religious Harmony in the Ancient World.' Vom Mythos religiöser Toleranz in der Antike," *Göttinger Forum für Altertumswissenschaft* 12 (2009).

29 All quotes Burkhard Gladigow, "Polytheismus und Monotheismus. Zur historischen Dynamik einer europäischen Alternative," in *Polytheismus und Monotheismus in den Religionen des Vorderen Orients*, ed. Manfred Krebernik and Jürgen van Oorschot (Münster: Unrast Verlag, 2002), 16.

set out with still more bloody principles; and even to this day, deals out damnation, though not fire and faggot, to all other sects. And if, among CHRISTIANS, the ENGLISH and DUTCH have embraced the principles of toleration, this singularity has proceeded from the steady resolution of the civil magistrate, in opposition to the continued efforts of priests and bigots.[30] [Capitalizations in original]

In this passage, Hume makes use of traditional concepts of the otherness and despicability of Jews and Muslims to create a backdrop against which the criticism of Christianity first gains its momentum.[31]

Toward the end of the 18th century, German Romanticism revisited the "rediscovery of polytheism"[32] and developed the three closely interdependent aspects which, according to Burkhard Gladigow, recur in all European and American versions of the debate since the Renaissance. The first appears in art theory, where the lament about the de-deification of nature leads to the claim that it is in (the genius of) the artist alone that the disenchantment resulting from monotheism can be compensated.[33] Three works mark the beginning of a new religious paradigm promising to reunite sentiment and reason – polytheism and monotheism – in a "monotheism of reason and the heart, polytheism of imagination and art": Friedrich Schiller's poetic praise of *Die Götter Griechenlands* (The Gods of Greece, 1788) as an alternative to the mechanistic attitude of monotheism, the *Ältestes Systemprogramm des deutschen Idealismus* (Oldest Programme for a System of German Idealism, 1794 or 1796),[34] with its call for a "new mythology" and a "new religion," and

---

30   David Hume, *The Natural History of Religion*. Edited with an introduction by H.E. Root (London: Adam and Charles Black, 1956), 50.
31   Robert S. Wistrich, "Radical Antisemitism in France and Germany (1840–1880)," *Modern Judaism* 15, no. 2 (1995) has analyzed the contributions of French Enlightenment thinkers such as Voltaire, Renan and Proudhon to a modern secular anti-Semitism and argued that modern anti-Jewish "race-hatred" "grew out of the anthropological critique of monotheistic religion." (128) He also points out that neither French nor German anti-Semitic *Weltanschauung* is anti-modernist, ultra-nationalist, and culturally conservative in the beginning, but is compatible with a radical-democratic anti-clericalism, anti-capitalism and secularized humanism. (122).
32   Gladigow, "Polytheismus und Monotheismus."
33   Cf. Williamson, *The Longing for Myth in Germany*, 192f, 223f. These aspects of art-religion and their relation to modern Paganism are discussed in Chapter 9.
34   The authorship of the short programmatic essay remains a matter of debate. It has been ascribed to Friedrich Wilhelm Schelling, Friedrich Hölderlin, and Georg Wilhelm

Friedrich Hölderlin's hymns.[35] This art-religious polytheism was continued by Ludwig Feuerbach and Richard Wagner in the 19th century and connected with a pronounced anti-Jewish attitude in its critique of a "Hebrew monotheism." The second aspect revolves around the idea that polytheism is closer to nature, that it recognizes myths, images, and rituals as forms in which the gods hidden in nature reveal themselves. This leads to the claim that a real understanding of nature is intimately intertwined with the respect for traditional polytheism.[36] Johann Wolfgang Goethe's pantheistic ideals and his organicistic approach to the study of nature, as well as Johann Gottfried Herder's and later Ernest Renan's reception of climate theoretical concepts, are examples of this line of polytheistic revival.[37]

The third aspect calls upon polytheism as an alternative to monotheism's claim of being in possession of an absolute truth.[38] Arthur Schopenhauer, and especially Friedrich Nietzsche, can be seen as the guiding intellectual forces behind this "polytheism of tolerance" or "diversity" after the "death of God" in the 19th century.[39] "Nietzsche's combination of the 'right of individuals' with the polytheism of antiquity becomes the central theme of a new polytheism, which now defines itself as 'post-monotheistic.'"[40] Not least due

---

Friedrich Hegel. An English translation is accessible as an appendix to Nicholas Halmi, *The Genealogy of the Romantic Symbol* (Oxford: Oxford University Press, 2007).

35   "Monotheismus der Vernunft und des Herzens, Polytheismus der Einbildungskraft und der Kunst." Cf. Gladigow, "Polytheismus und Monotheismus," 17, Jacob Taubes, "Mythos und Moderne. Begriff und Bild einer Rekonstruktion," in *Mythos und Moderne. Begriff und Bild einer Rekonstruktion*, ed. Karl Heinz Bohrer (Frankfurt A.M.: Suhrkamp, 1983), 457.

36   Burkhard Gladigow, "Polytheismen der Neuzeit," in *Religion und Wahrheit. Religionsgeschichtliche Studien. Festschrift für Gernot Wießner zum 65. Geburtstag*, ed. Bärbel Köhler (Wiesbaden: Harrassowitz, 1998), 47, "Polytheismus und Monotheismus," 17.

37   These aspects are explored further in Chapter 6.

38   Although the three aspects are often invoked together in contemporary criticism of monotheism, the latter two, the "polytheism of nature" and the "polytheism of the diversity of truths," are contradictory in many ways and can be understood as "competing patterns of reception and options" (Gladigow, "Polytheismus und Monotheismus," 18). In his discussion of the often incongruous lines of reception of Friedrich Nietzsche's thought in different avant-garde circles in Germany, Steven E. Aschheim points to a similar inconsistency between the invocation of a "'masculine' imperative of dynamic and sovereign self-creation and the more 'feminine' submersion into a transindividual Dionysian whole." (Aschheim, *The Nietzsche Legacy in Germany 1890–1990*, 82).

39   Gladigow, "Polytheismen der Neuzeit," 49.

40   "Polytheismus und Monotheismus," 18: "Nietzsches Verbindung des ‚Rechts der Individuen' mit dem antiken Polytheismus wird zur Leitidee eines neuen Polytheismus, der sich nun als ‚postmonotheistisch' definiert."

to their promotion of religious pantheistic or polytheistic alternatives, Goethe and Nietzsche acquired "an aura, an assumed authority"[41] in a broad range of circles yearning for a cultural and religious renewal. The ensuing popularized Nietzscheanism of the late 19th and early 20th century serves as a source of inspiration for numerous Neopaganisms, and not just those of the Germanic variety.

As has been frequently remarked upon, an inherent problem in the praise of polytheism as a religion of tolerance is that it has been polemically conceptualized as an antagonist to an 'intolerant' monotheism. As a result, the tolerance of the self-proclaimed new polytheists quickly finds its limits when it comes to granting tolerance to the religions perceived to be, or rather construed as, fundamentally different, i.e., monotheistic religions.[42] As long as such anti-monotheism is directed primarily against the dominant political, social, and discursive power of the Christian churches, these problematic aspects have little obvious bearing. However, David Hume's and particularly Ernest Renan's theories already demonstrate that this critique of power is too easily directed not exclusively against hegemonic forces, but instead aimed at discriminated minorities, Jews in particular.[43] Seeing the origin of the antagonist monotheism in the Jewish god, the anti-monotheist polemic criticized its target, Christianity, by simultaneously adopting Christianity's own construct of an antagonist. Consequently, a traditional Christian construction of the Jew as 'arch-enemy' is preserved in an anti-Christian form. It is thus no coincidence that most of the aforementioned contributors to the several polytheistic renewals (e.g., Johann Gottfried Herder, Ernest Renan, Arthur Schopenhauer, Friedrich Nietzsche, Ludwig Klages, and Alfred Schuler) have been accused of anti-Jewish attitudes.[44]

The anti-Christian and anti-Jewish elements of Nietzschean critique, especially the accusations he levels against these 'book religions', 'slave morality,' 'humility,' 'oppression,' and enmity toward human nature's dynamism and

---

41 Aschheim, *The Nietzsche Legacy in Germany 1890–1990*, 33.
42 For a differentiating critique of the "myth of religious tolerance in antiquity" see Losehand, "'The Religious Harmony in the Ancient World.'" See also Klaus Koch, "Monotheismus als Sündenbock?," in *Die Mosaische Unterscheidung oder der Preis des Monotheismus*, ed. Jan Assmann (Munich: Carl Hanser Verlag, 2003), 229f.
43 Nietzsche's contradictory attitudes towards Jews and Judaism, his "anti-anti-Semitism" in particular, indicate that he himself was aware of this problem.
44 For Klages and Schuler see Aschheim, *The Nietzsche Legacy in Germany 1890–1990*, 78; for Renan see Arvidsson, *Aryan Idols*, 102–118; for Herder see Sauerland, "'Die fremden Völker in Europa.'"

heroism, were eagerly adopted within emerging Germanic Neopaganism. At the same time, the religious alternatives promoted by them were not outspokenly polytheistic, but rather related to a pantheism inspired by the era's Goethe-cult and a general 'cult of the genius,' who either embodies the transcendent or strives for self-deification. An overt praise of polytheism in the wake of Nietzsche's anti-bourgeois, libertarian, intellectual and aristocratic individualism first became fashionable again in the 1970s, in a variety of national and political contexts. The rise of Neopaganism in general thus coincided with a 'new wave' of philosophical praises of polytheism. The two tendencies were not always directly related, but they indicate a general discursive climate in which Germanic Neopaganism could re-emerge and thrive.

In 1974, American professor of religion David L. Miller published his much-debated book *The New Polytheism*, ascertaining that the appropriate philosophy for modern, pluralistic democracies must be polytheistic. Starting with Friedrich Nietzsche's praise of polytheism's "marvelous art and capacity for creating Gods," he observes "an incipient polytheism" which is "always lurking in democracy," and stresses that polytheism is today both a social reality and a philosophical condition.[45] Relying on historians of religion such as Mircea Eliade and Gerardus van der Leeuw,[46] Miller does not promote any overt anti-Christian, anti-Jewish or anti-Islamic sentiments, but rather identifies polytheistic elements in all of these religions. He thus does not take the step of promoting Neopaganism as a lived religious option, but instead points to the necessity (in his view) to re-connect with the Greek gods in particular. They lie in the depths of "our heritage" and are therefore compatible with "Western consciousness and behavior," whereas the Christian tradition forms a more superficial layer.[47] In his fourth chapter, Miller discusses renegade Jungian analytical psychologist James Hillman's polytheistic psychology as one of the expressions of this contemporary polytheism. Consequently, in the second edition of *The New Polytheism* (1981), Miller includes an older essay by Hillman, augmented with a postscript by Hillman himself, in which he discusses the objections made against his alleged "polytheistic theology whose target is Christianity and Judeo-Christian monotheism."[48] He claims that one of the main problems of the hegemonic monotheistic framework is the impossibility of "an understanding of our cultural foundations," i.e., the polytheism of Greek mythology. This implies that he considers

---

45   Miller, *The New Polytheism*, 26.
46   Ibid., 89.
47   Ibid., 33.
48   Ibid., 127.

"Judeo-Christianity" as less foundational for "our culture." The ensuing debates on Miller's "new polytheism" within an American context did not take up the potential political dangers of such mythologies of the 20th century, i.e., the reversion to cultural essentialism. Instead, critics voiced fears of a privatization of religion, of the emergence of individual wealth accompanied by a diminished social cohesion.[49]

In Germany, the discussion on polytheism was taken up by conservative philosophers and authors, rather than psychologists. The first among them was the philosopher Odo Marquard, who opened a similar debate about the suitability of polytheistic thought for post-modern pluralistic societies in 1978. In his poignant essay "Praise of Polytheism"[50] he delivers an aestheticist, post-modernist critique of grand, unifying narratives which he calls "mono-myths," and which he sees as motivated by the belief in one god, who only has one story. He sets such mono-myths against a polytheism that guarantees "a separation of powers in the absolute,"[51] a system of checks and balances between different gods and their diverse stories, as compared to monotheism, which appears as "essentially tyrannical."[52] Marquard identifies two stages in the demise of the poly-mythic worldview: The first was the end of polytheism through the Christian mission during the Middle Ages; the second, the philosophy of history of the French revolution, which gave rise to the idea of a linear history of progress toward a greater freedom.[53] Marquard makes a direct reference to the "Oldest Programme for a System of German Idealism" and its call for a new mythology and a new era, as well as to Nietzsche, who saw the "end of monotheism" as the beginning of modernity. He thus conceptualizes

---

49   Cf. Robert S. Ellwood Jr., "Polytheism: Establishment or Liberation Religion," *Journal of the American Academy of Religion* 42 (1974). For a more recent philosophical plaidoyer for a polytheistic world-view see the book by John Michael Greer, *A World Full of Gods. An Inquiry into Polytheism* (Tucson: ADF Publishing, 2005), a member of three Druid organizations. The book is reviewed favorably by Diana Paxson on amazon.com and recommended for "the pagan clergy training programs with which I am involved." Cf. http://www.amazon.com/World-Full-Gods-Inquiry-Polytheism/dp/0976568101/ref=sr_1_1?ie=UTF8&qid=1321353383&sr=8-1, last accessed September 16, 2014.

50   Republished several times, e.g. in Odo Marquard, "Lob des Polytheismus. Über Monomythie und Polymythie," in *Abschied vom Prinzipiellen. Philosophische Studien*, ed. Odo Marquard (Stuttgart: Philipp Reclam jun., 1991); "Lob des Polytheismus. Über Monomythie und Polymythie," in *Zukunft braucht Herkunft. Philosophische Essays*, ed. Odo Marquard (Stuttgart: Philipp Reclam jun., 2003).

51   "Gewaltenteilung im Absoluten."

52   "Seinem Wesen nach tyrannisch."

53   Marquard, "Lob des Polytheismus," 99.

polytheism as a "possible political theory for modernity" and promotes a program of aestheticist conservatism.[54]

In 1993, author and dramatist Botho Strauß published a cultural critical essay titled *"Anschwellender Bocksgesang"* (Swelling Chant of Male Goats, an allusion to the literal meaning of the Greek *tragedia* which derives from *tragos*: male goat and *ōidē*: song). Although he does not directly mention polytheism, he delivers an implicit polemic against a "leftist phantasm" which, according to him, merely parodies a Christian history of salvation. He supports what he calls a "right" alternative to a shallow, "economistic and democratistic" modernity and promotes the search for a connection to an (implicitly pre-Christian) "long past," which "in its essence is deep memory, and thus a religious and proto-political initiation."[55] He furthermore calls for a new understanding of the necessity of pain, catastrophe, and sacrifice in order to shock modern Western man out of his superficial, materialistic selfishness. Strauß calls for a deeper understanding of, for example, Eastern European new nationalisms, with the deliberately provocative words: "We no longer understand that a *Volk* wants to assert its moral law against others and is ready to make blood sacrifices for it, and we consider it wrong and abominable in our liberal-libertarian self-centeredness."[56] This cultural critical impulse of a radical aestheticist in the Nietzschean sense found great sympathy among supporters of an intellectual New Right in Germany, who republished Strauß' essay in 1994, followed by a series of articles on the necessity of a new German patriotism bearing the telling title *Die selbstbewusste Nation* (The Confident Nation). The ensuing controversy demonstrated that this kind of aestheticist evocation of myth and a deep past was perceived as particularly useful for the German New Right.[57]

---

54   Cf. Alois Halbmayr, *Lob der Vielheit. Zur Kritik Odo Marquards am Monotheismus*, vol. 13, Salzburger Theologische Studien (Innsbruck: Tyrolia, 2000).

55   Botho Strauß, "Anschwellender Bocksgesang," in *Die selbstbewusste Nation. 'Anschwellender Bocksgesang' und weitere Beiträge zu einer deutschen Debatte*, ed. Heimo Schwilk and Ulrich Schacht (Frankfurt A.M.: Ullstein, 1994), 25.

56   Ibid., 21: "Daß ein Volk sein Sittengesetz gegen andere behaupten will und dafür bereit ist, Blutopfer zu bringen, das verstehen wir nicht mehr und halten es in unserer liberal-libertären Selbstbezogenheit für falsch und verwerflich."

57   On the dust cover of the third edition, some of the negative criticism of the book is quoted in an affirmative sense, such as the verdict: "It shows the intellectual right in Germany quasi in the moment of its self-creation," or "Most contributions are a challenge to parts of the basic consensus of the old Federal Republic." Cf. also Jonathan Olsen, *Nature and Nationalism. Right-Wing Ecology and the Politics of Identity in Contemporary Germany* (New York: St. Martin's Press, 1999), 118f, who mentions this book as a prime example of German right-wing intellectuals' central discursive moves: "the relativization of the

In his intervention in the debate in 1998, novelist Martin Walser attacked the apocalyptic scenarios permeating contemporary media discourses. For him, the ecological, social, and political suggestions for a solution to such global problems appear to be "utopias of salvation" directly derived from Christian "missionary zeal."[58] He combines an anti-universalist critique of Western humanism with a Nietzschean critique of the Christian doctrine, which sees human nature as evil and thus produces this evil in the first place by demanding submission to one jealous god. Walser concludes by praising the 'local' ("das Hiesige") and the 'near,' setting it against the universalist, international, and global in his verdict: "By all means, no ethic for everyone."[59] He combines it with a call for a restorative return to an older, pre-Christian tradition, the "protective screen of a diversity of gods spread over meadows and forests,"[60] which allegedly poses no danger to the planet.

These attacks on monotheism and complaints about the lack of myth and gods in modernity are united by their reference to a Nietzsche-inspired postmodernism that defends individual freedom and difference against universalist claims of equality. The latter are seen as agents of the tyrannical, disciplinarian central power personified in the monotheistic god. They are thus also connected to a post-modern, post-structuralist and post-colonial impulse, which posits a logic of difference against a unifying, colonializing logic of sameness. However, the nationalist implications of Strauß' and Walser's anti-monotheism point to other, not always latent political implications of such tributes to polytheism. Considering this, Jacob Taubes' early critique of Marquard is not as far-fetched or one-sided as it might have seemed at the moment of its publication in 1983. Taubes suggested that Marquard might produce exactly the "mythic atmosphere"[61] it pretends to merely indicate, and drew an implicit parallel to the *Kosmiker* (Alfred Schuler and Ludwig Klages) re-mythologizing project.[62]

---

misdeeds of National Socialism through a comparison with other totalitarian regimes, chiefly communist regimes" and the "reinterpretation of National Socialism as an aberration, a perverted form of nationalism quite alien to traditional German nationalism."

58 "Ich vertraue. Querfeldein," re-published in Martin Walser, *Ich vertraue. Querfeldein* (Frankfurt A.M.: Suhrkamp, 2000), 9–22.
59 Ibid., 19: "Bloß keine Ethik für alle."
60 Ibid., 18: "der Schirm einer über Wiesen und Wälder hingestreuten Göttervielfalt."
61 "mythische Geisteslage", Taubes, "Mythos und Moderne," 464, cf. Gladigow, "Polytheismus der Neuzeit," 57.
62 Taubes, "Mythos und Moderne," 462. For Schuler's and Klages' anti-Jewish polytheism see below, as well as Chapter 6. Even though Burkhard Gladigow, "Polytheismen der Neuzeit," 56, modifies such a critique by pointing to the fact that Marquard's "enlightened

In his critique, Taubes refers directly to French intellectual Alain de Benoist's seminal book, "*Comment peut-on être païen*" (How to be a Pagan),[63] first published in France in 1981.[64] In his praise of "being Pagan" as a religio-philosophical alternative for Europe, the leading political theorist of the New Right in France questions and modifies the totalitarian ideas of the 'old' extreme right and condemns the 'Judeo-Christian' idea of monotheism as the root of all totalitarianism. This take on polytheistic tolerance and diversity motivates his ethno-pluralist approach discussed in Chapter 4: the idea that, in order to grant this desired diversity, cultures need to be preserved in their own areas of origin and kept pure and unmixed in order to thrive and develop. In the context of this chapter, Benoist's perspective is pivotal; he considers the mission mandate and universalism of Christianity originating in the rootlessness of Judaism as one of the main culprits for the demise of cultural diversity and globalization. It comes as no surprise that since the 1980s, Benoist's anti-Christian, pro-Pagan approach has found supporters among Asatruers, and is even sold on the ethnicist *AFA's* homepage with the following commentary:

> In this book, the founder of the profoundly Pagan "French New Right" argues that Christianity has failed Europe, and that only a re-linking with the eternal truths of our pre-Christian heritage can rescue us from the guilt, fear, and rootless nihilism of the present age. This book is highly intelligent, compelling, and designed for men and women living real lives in the 21st century.[65]

Among a-racist German Asatru groups, Benoist's ethno-pluralist, anti-monotheist ideology has not been so well received. Interestingly, the same is true of the anti-monotheist praises of polytheism featured in the aforementioned intellectual and media debates. Its early contributors, Odo Marquard,

---

polytheism" owes too much to the complexity of the "Oldest Programme for a System of German Idealism" to be easily appropriated by a political New Right, Taubes' overall critique of this anti-monotheist formation has become even more valid in the light of the debates surrounding Strauß' and Walser's essays.

63   Taubes, "Mythos und Moderne," 469.
64   A German translation appeared in 1982, an English translation was made available only in 2004 in Joshua Buckley's publishing house Ultra with a preface by Stephen Edred Flowers. See also Chapter 4.
65   http://www.runestone.org/shop-afa/onlinestore/product/show/cid-16/name-on-being-a-pagan-by-alain-de-benoist/category_pathway-10.html, last accessed May 05, 2013.

Botho Strauß, and Martin Walser, are rarely evoked by Asatruers in their attempts to describe, theorize or contextualize their own religion.[66]

In recent years, an internationally better-known German contributor to the debate about the negative implications of monotheism – the Egyptologist, Jan Assmann – has provided international Heathenism with another concept of religious distinctions.[67] In his attempt to explain the deep historical genesis of violent intolerance, religious persecution, and especially anti-Judaism, Assmann identifies a revolutionary, decisive religious shift from "'polytheistic' to 'monotheistic' religions, from cult religions to religions of the book, from culturally specific religions to world religions."[68] Assmann makes use of a distinction between "primary" and "secondary" religions proposed by the professor of missiology, Theo Sundermeier,[69] and explicates the relation between primary and secondary religion as follows:

---

66 The only exception to this, a thread on *Eldaring's* online forum from 2004 on Martin Walser's essay, shows that some German Asatruers are aware of the anti-Semitic potential in Martin Walser's dichotomization of a "Judeo-Christian culture" and the "pre-Christian Germanic" as the "original German culture." Others, Swiss and Austrian participants in the discussion in particular, accused these critics of Walser's positions as intolerant and overly "politically correct." See thread "Martin Walser ist Heide" (Martin Walser is Pagan) started in 2004: http://www.eldaring.de/pages/forum---community.php, last accessed December 16, 2012. "What Walser is up to stands in a long tradition of anti-Semitism which occasionally declares itself anti-Christian, but constantly emphasizes Christianity's Jewish roots by always mentioning both terms simultaneously." ("Was Walser treibt, steht in einer langen Tradition des Antisemitismus, der sich gelegentlich auch als antichristlich deklariert, dabei aber unentwegt die jüdischen Wurzeln des Christentums betont, indem beide Begriffe immer gemeinsam genannt werden.").
67 See Jan Assmann, *Die Mosaische Unterscheidung oder der Preis des Monotheismus* (Munich: Carl Hanser Verlag, 2003), English translation *The Price of Monotheism*, trans. Robert Savage (Stanford: Stanford University Press, 2010).
68 *The Price of Monotheism*, 1. *Die Mosaische Unterscheidung oder der Preis des Monotheismus*, 11: "von 'polytheistischen' zu 'monotheistischen' Religionen, von Kultreligionen zu Buchreligionen, von kulturspezifischen Religionen zu Weltreligionen."
69 Theo Sundermeier, *Was ist Religion? Religionswissenschaft im theologischen Kontext* (Gütersloh: Gütersloher Verlagshaus, 1999); "The Meaning of Tribal Religions for the History of Religion. Primary Religious Experience," *Scriptura* 10 (1992). In contrast to Assmann, and in an attempt to demonstrate possibilities of religious dialogue between contemporary 'tribal religions,' especially in Africa and Christianity, Sundermeier does not see a fundamental difference between 'primary' and 'secondary' religious experiences, but maintains that they form various syntheses. He also stresses the distinctions between different *religious experiences* and avoids speaking of primary and secondary *religions*. See Anja A. Diesel, "Primäre und sekundäre Religion(serfahrung) – das Konzept von Th. Sundermeier und J. Assmann," in *Primäre und sekundäre Religion als Kategorie der*

Primary religions evolve historically over hundreds and thousands of years within a single culture, society, and generally, also language, with all of which they are inextricably entwined. [...] Secondary religions, by contrast, are those that owe their existence to an act of revelation and foundation, build on primary religions, and typically differentiate themselves from the latter by denouncing them as Paganism, idolatry und superstition.[70]

In his attempt to characterize the core idea of this turn, for which he coins the term 'mosaic distinction,' Assmann notes that the crucial difference is not the one between polytheism and monotheism, "but the distinction between truth and falsehood in religion, between the true god and false gods, true doctrine and false doctrine, knowledge and ignorance, belief and unbelief."[71] The claim that this distinction motivates a new kind of religious hatred and violence is crucial for the reception of his theses in contemporary debates.[72]

For our purposes, the differences between Sundermeier's and Assmann's theses are of little relevance, as is the fact that both have been criticized by theologians and historians of religion for their insufficient and anachronistic descriptions of religious distinctions.[73] What matters instead are the ways in

---

    Religionsgeschichte des Alten Testaments, ed. Andreas Wagner, Beihefte zur Zeitschrift für die alttestamentliche Wissenschaft (Berlin: Walter de Gruyter, 2006).

70   Assmann, *The Price of Monotheism*, 1;. *Die Mosaische Unterscheidung oder der Preis des Monotheismus*, 11: "Primäre Religionen sind über Jahrhunderte und Jahrtausende historisch gewachsen im Rahmen einer Kultur, Gesellschaft und auch Sprache, mit der sie unauflöslich verbunden sind. [...] Sekundäre Religionen dagegen sind Religionen, die sich einem Akt der Offenbarung und Stiftung verdanken, auf den primären Religionen aufbauen und sich typischerweise gegen diese abgrenzen, indem sie sie zu Heidentum, Götzendienst und Aberglauben erklären."

71   *The Price of Monotheism*, 2; *Die Mosaische Unterscheidung oder der Preis des Monotheismus*, 12f: "zwischen wahr und falsch in der Religion, zwischen dem wahren Gott und den falschen Göttern, der wahren Lehre und den Irrlehren, zwischen Wissen und Unwissenheit, Glaube und Unglaube."

72   See also his recent essay on the topic titled "Monotheism and the Language of Violence." *Monotheismus und die Sprache der Gewalt* (Vienna: Picus Verlag, 2006).

73   See for example the critique by German theologian Wolfgang Stegemann, "Wie 'christlich' ist das Judentum? Zur Kritik an einigen seiner (protestantischen) Konstruktionen," in *Zwischen Affirmation und Machtkritik. Zur Geschichte des Protestantismus und protestantischer Mentalitäten*, ed. Richard Faber (Zurich: Theologischer Verlag Zürich, 2005), 161: "But seen in the light, the 'mosaic distinction' and its alleged violent consequences are a discursive product of an anachronistic discourse of religion!" ("Doch bei Lichte betrachtet,

which they describe primary and secondary religions, as well as the shift from one to the other. They have been inspiring and productive for the conceptualization of Neopagan religions and their own distinction from Christianity and monotheism. Assmann claims that the turn from primary to secondary religion goes hand in hand with a turn from ritual to text, from cult religion to book religion.[74] This medium shift led to an identification of writing with the transcendent, whereas ritual became identified with immanence. This idea is well suited to the image of Heathenism as an immanent religion based on a unity of practice and community. The same applies to the idea that secondary religion is not fulfilled through the correct performance of ritual but instead leads to the invention of an inner self and needs to be fathomed introspectively, thus requiring faith, belief, and a distinction between truth and falsehood.[75]

Jan Assmann is certainly not a thinker with affiliations to right-wing ideology.[76] His theory of a potentially destructive 'mosaic distinction' does however recall the more radical rejections of monotheism circulating in anti-Semitic and right-wing contexts. Elements of his main argument have, for example, been appropriated by the Hindu nationalist *Council for the Hindu Revolution* or *Hindu Kranti Parishad* (HKP) in order to justify a radically anti-monotheist, anti-Capitalist and anti-Communist, anti-Islamic and anti-Semitic agenda.[77] Accordingly, the theory of the 'mosaic distinction' between 'true' and 'false' religions and other anti-monotheistic ideas has been actualized in quite divergent ways within European Asatru.

---

sind die 'mosaische Unterscheidung' und deren angeblich violente Folgen ein diskursives Produkt eines anachronistischen Religionsdiskurses!").

74 Assmann, *Die Mosaische Unterscheidung oder der Preis des Monotheismus*, 145.
75 Cf. ibid., 156.
76 A more recent contribution by the popular German philosopher Peter Sloterdijk shows the appeal of Assmann's distinction. Veering considerably from Assmann's statements, Sloterdijk makes monotheism and its "holy warriors" into an even cruder construction and blames it for having "attacked the natural and cultural being of mankind [...] their all too secure rootedness in their descent" ("das natürliche und kulturelle So-Sein der Menschen anzugreifen hatte [...] ihre allzu sichere Verwurzelung im Herkommen." Peter Sloterdijk, *Gottes Eifer. Vom Kampf der drei Monotheismen* (Frankfurt A.M.: Verlag der Weltreligionen, 2007), 184f). Sloterdijk aims his attack at what he calls the "paramonotheism" of the Enlightenment as well.
77 Dhirendra Nath Shastri *Monotheism and the Western Pathology. Causes, Development and Impact of the Western Drive for World Domination from the 1st Millennium BCE to the Present*, http://www.hindurevolution.org/01/monotheism-and-the-western-pathology-contents.htm (2009).

Anti-Monotheism in Asatru

At the one end, we find attempts to merge anti-monotheism with the ethnopluralist and violently anti-monotheist theories of the New Right. In 2005, a passionate debate on the topic erupted in Denmark, starting with the publication of a series of articles in the magazine *Valravn*, titled "The Mischief/Terror [*uvæsen*] of Monotheism. A Religious Liberation of Concepts."[78] Author Starkad Storm Stensgaard motivates the need to exterminate monotheism with a set of sharp distinctions:

> The differences between monotheism and polytheism are greater, more important, and more essential than it is possible to communicate verbally. The necessity to make these differences known, however, grows with the pace in which monotheism's intellectual and spiritual pest casts the darkness of chaos over the world, this time armed with modern technology and weapons of mass destruction.

He criticizes the "totalitarian monopoly of existence, a monopolization of all that is sacred" using a rhetoric of poisoning, pollution, contagion, and psychiatric pathology, e.g., when he describes Judaism as the origin of "monotheism's evil obsession." Polytheism, in comparison, appears as the "in all respects superior and natural religiosity."[79] Quite obviously, Stensgaard's objection to monotheism's alleged intolerance, and his praise of polytheism's tolerance of other gods beyond one's own pantheon, mainly performs the limits of this tolerance: It explicitly excludes the tolerance for a monotheism posited as fundamentally irreconcilable with a polytheistic paradigm – hence the author's unambiguous call for open-eyed hatred of and revenge against monotheism.[80] Stensgaard

---

[78] Starkad Storm Stensgaard, "Om Monoteismens Uvæsen. Religiøs Begrebsbefrielse, del 1," *Valravn. Hedensk tidskrift om samfund og kultur* 14 (2005); "Om Monoteismens Uvæsen. Religiøs Begrebsbefrielse, del 2," *Valravn. Hedensk tidskrift om samfund og kultur* 15 (2005); "Om Monoteismens Uvæsen. Religiøs Begrebsbefrielse, del 3," *Valravn. Hedensk tidskrift om samfund og kultur* 16 (2006).

[79] All quotes "Om Monoteismens Uvæsen 1," 18: "Forskellene mellem monoteisme og polyteisme er større, vigtigere og væsentligere, end det fyldestgørende er muligt at kommunikere verbalt. Nødvendigheden af at bevidstgøre disse forskelle vokser imidlertid, i takt med, at den monoteistiske åndspest atter sænker kaosmørke over verden, denne gang bevæbnet med moderne teknologi og masseødelæggelsesvåben." "[...] et totalitært eksitensmonopol, en monopolisering af alt helligt." "Polyteisme er i stort set enhver henseende den overlegne og naturlige religiøsitet."

[80] Cf. "Om Monoteismens Uvæsen 3," 20.

uses the familiar rejection of racial hatred in the spirit of the New Right, claiming that his anti-monotheistic resentment is based exclusively on religious and philosophical grounds. He promotes a societal structure combining Social Darwinist and ethnicist elements, and calls for a revival of the "aristocratic culture of trust" which, according to him, characterized both ancient Greek and ancient Germanic societies.[81] Here, the best prove themselves as natural leaders by inspiring trust in their followers – an ideal allegedly directed against both totalitarian rule and an equally despised egalitarian, 'superficial' democracy of the masses.

Starkad Storm Stensgaard's attacks, which he continued to launch in *Forn Siðr's* journal *Völse* in 2008 and 2010,[82] have been constantly commented on and contradicted by a-racist Danish Asatruers. They see such anti-monotheism as the expression of an unnecessary fixation on the concept of an enemy, and instead advocate concentrating on the building and promotion of one's own faith.[83] Moreover, they point out that anti-monotheists fall prey to exactly the exclusionary logic they project onto monotheism.[84]

The anti-monotheism controversy has not remained purely theoretical within Danish Asatru, but has motivated several leading members who had opposed the radicalism of such positions and their influence on *Forn Siðr's* board to leave the group altogether.[85] This demonstrates the potential for dissent and split which lies in a radical anti-monotheist position. At the same time, meta-political theories such as Stensgaard's anti-monotheism are able

---

81   Steensgaard also offered training in the principles of heroic leadership and a culture of trust on the basis of ancient Germanic and Greek principles in his company *Heroic Consulting*. The company's homepage is now defunct: www.heroic.dk, last accessed December 16, 2012.
82   Starkad Storm, "Politisk Polyteisme og Antimonoteistisk Selvforsvar," *Vølse* 45 (2008), see also *Vølse* 52, 2010.
83   This could be read as a structural analogy to the debates in *völkisch* religion and the *völkisch* movement mentioned in Chapter 1 around the exclusive fixation on a 'negative' anti-Semitism versus a 'positive' national and racial renewal.
84   Cf. Martin P. Hansen, "Politik og religion," *Vølse* 44 (2008), Martin Mørch, "Om politik og religion," *Vølse* 46 (2008). One author, Morten Grølsted, "Den mosaiske skelnen," *Vølse* 55 (2011), also evokes Assmann and his distinction between good and evil in religion to criticize both sides in the debate while simultaneously elaborating on Assmann's point about Judaism's nature as a counter-religion forming the root of anti-Semitism.
85   This was discussed in detail on the threads "Min fremtid i Forn Sidr" as well as "Farvel Forn Sidr," and "Nyt trossamfund – Nordisk Tingsfællig" (all 2010 and 2011) on the now defunct forum www.kindir.dk, as well as in the thread "Anti-monoteisme" on http://www.idasletten.dk/forum/viewtopic.php?f=6&t=300, last accessed December 16, 2012.

to give a religiously motivated framework to the more general and little reflected-upon anti-Islamic sentiments circulating not only within Asatru but also characterizing contemporary European public debates in general. Denmark so far seems to be the only country where such eliminatory antimonotheism in the style of Benoist and parts of the New Right (as well as the anti-Jewish and even more anti-Islamic sentiments connected with it) have been able to dominate the debates within nationally active Asatru groups.[86] This is probably equally related to the overall political climate in Denmark, where populist xenophobic and anti-Islamic positions have entered the parliamentary and legislative spheres.[87]

In Germany, similar radical distinctions between monotheism and polytheism, which rebuke monotheism for its dualistic thinking, have been circulating in Asatru contexts closer to New Right and Conservative Revolutionary thought. One example is Björn Ulbrich, who maintains in his book about the "cult and rite of the Heathen community," *Im Tanz der Elemente* (In the Dance of the Elements), that the opposition monotheism/polytheism requires a debate not about the number of gods, but about their quality:

> Therefore, the central point is the question of whether or not the world and being is to be judged according to dualistic criteria. [...] Paganism rejects the dualism of *good or evil*, of *wrong or right*, it overcomes the separation between god and the world as well as the one between body and spirit. No absolute *either–or*, but a tolerant *both–and*. The antagonistic positions of the Christian faith (obedient–arrogant, weak–preposterous, humble–self-confident, etc.) are replaced in paganism by the communicating pairs *noble–low, honorable–dishonored, ill–healthy, brave–cowardly,* etc.[88]

---

86   A search for the term 'anti-monotheism' (or rather its Scandinavian equivalents) on the most important Swedish and Norwegian Asatru websites and online forums gave no hits, a search for "monotheism" and "polytheism" resulted in a few leading to threads where similar controversies were debated, but in a less inflamed manner.

87   Cf. Lisbet Christoffersen, "Religion and State. Recognition of Islam and Related Legislation," in *Islam in Denmark. The Challenge of Diversity*, ed. Jørgen S. Nielsen (Lanham etc.: Lexington Books, 2010); Brian Arly Jacobsen, "Muslims in Denmark. A Critical Evaluation," in *Islam in Denmark. The Challenge of Diversity*, ed. Jørgen S. Nielsen (Lanham etc.: Lexington Books, 2010); Jørgen Bæk Simonsen, "Denmark, Islam and Muslims. Socioeconomic Dynamics and the Art of Becoming," in *Islam in Denmark. The Challenge of Diversity*, ed. Jørgen S. Nielsen (Lanham etc.: Lexington Books, 2010).

88   Björn Ulbrich, *Im Tanz der Elemente. Kult und Ritus der heidnischen Gemeinschaft* (Vilsbiburg: Arun, 1990), 18f: "Der zentrale Punkt...ist daher die Frage, ob die Welt und das

It remains unclear in this quote what the exact conceptual difference is between the latter hierarchical "communicating" and the former "antagonistic" pairs. But it is obvious that the antagonistic or dualistic logic that monotheism is blamed for is also at work in this quote as well as in Ulbrich's entire book, which is based on a definition of Heathenism as Christianity's other.

Such attitudes also evoke critique because of their proximity to New Right thought. For Asfrid (Fritz Steinbock) of the German *VfgH*, Assmann's paradigm helps to formulate a politically unsuspicious position. He suspects a tendency in (folkish) Asatru to make a dogma out of the idea that "each people" or "each land" should adhere to their own religion. Further, he identifies a trend to "make an ideology out of the relativity of the Pagan 'correctness' – its being tied to land and people, nature, culture, history, social group, fate (whatever one wants)."[89]

Generally speaking, German Asatruers who promote the usefulness of Sundermeier's and Assmann's categories of primary and secondary religion[90] are most attracted by Assmann's description of "cosmotheism." For them, it is characterized by a religious attitude that sees Gods and the world as a unit, puts nature at its center, experiences the divine as an emanation of the world, and is not dependent on a transcendent revelation.[91] Moreover, it aims at anchoring individuals in the world and integrates them into the divine orders of the earth.[92]

Sein nach dualistischen Kriterien zu beurteilen sind oder nicht. [...] Das Heidentum [...] verwirft den Dualismus des *gut oder böse*, des *falsch oder richtig*, es überwindet sowohl die Trennung von Gott und der Welt wie die von Körper und Geist. Kein absolutes *Entweder-oder*, sondern ein duldsames *Sowohl-als-auch*. Die gegensätzlichen Positionen des christlichen Glaubens (gehorsam-hochmütig, schwach-anmaßend, demütig-selbstbewußt, etc.) ersetzt das Heidentum durch die kommunizierenden Paare *edel-niedrig, ehrbar-entehrt, krank-gesund, mutig-feige*, usw."

89 Asfrid, "Warum Asatru?," 4f: "dann machen sie aus der Relativität der heidnischen 'Richtigkeit' – ihrer Gebundenheit an Land und Leute, Natur, Kultur, Geschichte, Sozialverband, Schicksal (wie immer man will) – eine Ideologie."

90 Mainly, the 'theoreticians' of the *Eldaring* and the *VfgH*, Kurt Oertel and Asfrid (Fritz Steinbock).

91 Cf. Asfrid, "Religion der dritten Sorte," *Ringhorn. Gemeinschaftsanzeiger des Vereins für germanisches Heidentum e.V.* 55 (2008), Fritz Steinbock, "Die Freiheit eines Heidenmenschen. Inhalt und Gründe der 'Leitidee freies Heidentum' des ORD," *Heidnisches Jahrbuch* 1 (2006), 149f.

92 E-mail correspondence with Kurt Oertel, *Eldaring*, April 12, 2011: "Primäre Religion zielt auf Beheimatung des Menschen in der Welt und auf seine Integration in die göttlichen Ordnungen des Irdischen."

In spite of the idealized image of primary religions painted here, there is a certain awareness that returning to such a state is neither possible nor desirable. In an attempt to resolve the implicit contradiction between individualist and collectivist strands in Asatru, Asfrid emphasizes the profoundly modern and liberal character of contemporary Heathenism and reminds his fellow Heathens: "We want the church to dictate which gods we should honor and how we should do it just as little as we want a tribe or other society – fictive as they are – to." On the contrary, he continues invoking liberal paradigms of the autonomous individual, whereby modern Heathenism is characterized by an individual choice of a suitable religion based on freedom of choice. From this, he draws the conclusion that the "primary" Germanic religion can only serve as an inspiration, whereas modern Heathenism is of a "new, third kind;" a "tertiary religion which posits a new beginning as a critically thinking 'enlightened' alternative to secondary religion." This emphatic invocation of a new beginning is combined with an avowal of the "cultural fundaments" of the present age: "self-determination of religion, critical philosophy and science, humanism and Enlightenment, democracy and human rights."[93] With this statement, he also aligns Heathenism with a classical liberal democratic modernity – an operation whose significance we shall return to at the end of this chapter.

Religion of Experience

Generally speaking, the majority of German Asatruers would support similar values of enlightenment, religious plurality, and humanism, thus positioning Asatru as a valid choice in a late-modern marketplace of religions.[94] Such notions stand in a certain, albeit unacknowledged tension to another category German Asatruers frequently evoke to characterize their religion: *Erfahrungsreligion* (religion of experience). This term is of course not new, but has been used to describe a variety of religious trends that emphasize personal emotional experience: from mysticism, through pietism and

---

93   All quotes Asfrid, "Religion der dritten Sorte," 11: "So wenig wie von einer Kirche wollen wir uns auch von einer – ohnehin fiktiven – Stammes- oder sonstigen Gesellschaft vorschreiben lassen, welche Götter wir verehren und wie wir das zu tun hätten." "Es ist eine neue, dritte Sorte: Die tertiäre Religion, die als kritisch denkende, 'aufgeklärte' Alternative zur sekundären einen neuen Anfang setzt." "Selbstbestimmtheit der Religion, kritische Philosophie und Naturwissenschaft, Humanismus und Aufklärung, Demokratie und Menschenrechte."

94   This is one thesis of Gründer, *Germanisches (Neu-)Heidentum in Deutschland*.

Christian free-churches, to Buddhism, Hinduism, and Wicca. When invoking this category, German Asatruers seem unaware of this use of the concept, and rather ascribe it to the German historian and "natural philosopher" Reinhard Falter.[95] Obviously, the invocation of the category of experience offers a seemingly self-evident description of Asatruers' perception of the origin of their religious choice. They see it in an immediate experience of divine forces either within themselves, in the surrounding nature, or in their community, and set it against a religious concept relying on revelation and scriptural authority.

In a programmatic article in the first volume of *Heidnisches Jahrbuch* titled "What is Neopaganism?"[96] Baal Müller, a former *Eldaring* and ORD/VfgH member and close collaborator of Falter, sharpens this distinction by derogating the dimension of "faith" and positing "experience" as superior: "A religion which bases itself on faith is worthless. [...] Experience, not faith, is the true religious attitude towards the world."[97] For Falter, as well as for Müller, the "Gods of the religion of experience" are to be characterized as "basic qualities or basic characters of the world," as "seizing or moving atmospheres" in a similar sense to C.G. Jung's conceptualized archetypes.[98]

Falter and Müller aptly place their own attempts at defining religion in the "tradition of a new mythology." They stress the influence of Nietzsche, as well as

> philosophers like Ludwig Klages, Hermann Schmitz, or Kurt Hübner, historians of religion like Walter F. Otto and Mircea Eliade, in some respects also psychoanalysts like C.G. Jung and in an artistic sense poets like Stefan George, Gottfried Benn, Rainer M. Rilke, Theodor Däubler, Alfred Schuler, or Rudolf Pannwitz.[99]

In Walter F. Otto and Mircea Eliade, they refer to two influential historians of religion, who identified religious experience of "The Holy" as the common denominator of all true religion. Similar to that of many other historians of

---

95 Cf. Steinbock, "Die Freiheit eines Heidenmenschen," 152: "Reinhard Falter's concept of religion of experience has become established in the modern 'Heathen scene' like no other academic term." (Reinhard Falters Begriff der Erfahrungsreligion hat wie kein anderer akadamischer Terminus Eingang in die moderne 'Heidenszene' gefunden).
96 Baal Müller, "Was ist Neopaganismus?," *Heidnisches Jahrbuch* 1 (2006).
97 Ibid., 12: "Eine Religion, die sich auf Glauben gründet, ist nichts wert. [...] In der Erfahrung und nicht im Glauben liegt die eigentliche religiöse Welthaltung."
98 Ibid., 20: "Grundqualitäten oder Grundcharaktere der Welt – ergreifende Atmosphären."
99 Ibid., 21.

religion, their agenda can be called religious itself, since they saw their task as saving religion from modern critique, and saw religious feeling and experience as opportunities to reconcile the modern split between concept and reality,[100] a desire Falter wholeheartedly embraces.[101]

The strong reliance of Falter and Müller on both the *Kosmiker* Alfred Schuler and his student Ludwig Klages reveals the potentially problematic implications of this concept of a "religion of experience." The *Kosmische Runde* was a circle of intellectuals in Munich around 1900, which initially stood in close contact with the circle around the poet Stefan George. They developed an irrationalist mysticism of natural essences, in which the "cosmic" truth was supposed to be preserved in the "blood." History, progress, and capitalism all appeared as a conspiracy against this truth of eternal "images" – and the driving force of the despised historicism was seen in Judaism.[102] This antagonism between "imageless Judah" (*bildloses Juda*) and "'cosmic' Germania" (*kosmisches Germanien*) structured their worldview and their attempts to revive a Greek/Roman/Germanic Paganism based on a fierce anti-monotheism. It is this anti-historicism and religiously motivated anti-Judaism that Falter adopts unfiltered, and develops further in his work on an

---

100 For an in-depth discussion of the role of European historians of religions' in creating "a scientific store of world-views and norms to which one could recur in order to provide meaning" see Kippenberg, *Die Entdeckung der Religionsgeschichte*, 266.

101 Reinhard Falter, "Die Götter der Erfahrungsreligion wieder verstehen. Das griechische Beispiel und die heutige Situation," *Heidnisches Jahrbuch* 1 (2006), 95. See also the discussion on Eliade's concept of a "holy," mythic time in Müller, "Was ist Neopaganismus?," 22, where he explains that for Eliade, the mythic event is not something located in the past as a singular occurrence, as the religions of revelation dependent on the Bible have it, but rather something which always happens in an archetypical sense, and which can be made present for example in a ritual act.

102 Cf. Walter Schmitz and Uwe Schneider, "Völkische Semantik bei den Münchner 'Kosmikern' und im George-Kreis," in *Handbuch zur 'Völkischen Bewegung' 1871–1918*, ed. Uwe Puschner, Walter Schmitz, and Justus H. Ulbricht (Munich etc.: K.G. Saur, 1996), 722f. Cf. also Elke-Vera Kotowski, "Verkünder eines 'heidnischen' Antisemitismus. Die Kosmiker Ludwig Klages und Alfred Schuler," in *'Verkannte Brüder'? Stefan George und das deutschjüdische Bürgertum zwischen Jahrhundertwende und Emigration*, ed. Gert Mattenklott, Michael Philipp, and Julius H. Schoeps (Hildesheim: Georg Olms Verlag, 2001), 205–208; Tobias Schneider, "Sektierer oder Kampfgenossen? Der Klages-Kreis im Spannungsfeld der NS-Kulturpolitik," in *Völkische Bewegung – Konservative Revolution – Nationalsozialismus. Aspekte einer politisierten Kultur*, ed. Walter Schmitz and Clemens Vollnhals (Dresden: Thelem, 2005).

ethic based on nature and its laws.[103] In contrast to Asfrid, Falter rejects enlightenment, humanism, and with it "the ideology of human rights which supports the spread of capitalism as well as of the world police,"[104] quoting, among many others, Alain de Benoist. Championing a subjection of humanity under the laws of nature, he attests monotheism a fundamental unnaturalness, replacing the more neutral secondary religion with the biologist term "*Pfropfreligion*" (graft-religion). He combines his anti-monotheistic and anti-universalist opinions with eugenic sentiments, rejecting the notion that all (human) life deserves protection, a concept he feels leads to "making an idol of mere life, in other words of survival, and a levelling of hierarchies [...]."[105] Again, it is Judaism which he sees as the root cause of such a denial of death and sacrifice, and with it, the order of nature. With remarkable cynicism, he deplores an

---

103 Falter distances himself from any kind of racial theory, claiming that his rejection of Judaism is based purely on religious arguments concurring with his anti-monotheism. Ludwig Klages' anti-Jewish invectives are explained in a similar way. In his discussion of Alfred Schuler's anti-Judaism, Baal Müller follows a similar line when he writes: "His anti-Judaism is not a racist anti-Semitism, but an anti-monotheism motivated by vitalism." ("Sein Antijudaismus ist kein rassistischer Antisemitismus, sondern ein vitalistisch motivierter Antimonotheismus," Baal Müller in his preface to Alfred Schuler, *Cosmogonische Augen. Gesammelte Schriften*, Edited, commented and with an introduction by Baal Müller (Paderborn: Igel Verlag, 1997), 10). See also Georg Dörr, *Muttermythos und Herrschaftsmythos. Zur Dialektik der Aufklärung um die Jahrhundertwende bei den Kosmikern, Stefan George und in der Frankfurter Schule* (Würzburg: Königshausen & Neumann, 2007), 193f. Thomas Rohkrämer, *Eine andere Moderne? Zivilisationskritik, Natur und Technik in Deutschland 1880–1933* (Paderborn etc.: Ferdinand Schöningh, 1999), 196, makes a similar argument regarding Klages' anti-Semitism. However, the distinction between an (implicitly benign) anti-Judaism and a dangerous racist anti-Semitism can be understood as an expression of the same "appeasement syndrome," for which Jürgen Ebach criticizes theologians who try to whitewash Christian anti-Judaism by distinguishing it from scientific racism. See Jürgen Ebach, "Amputierte Antike. Über Ursachen und Folgen des Antijudaismus in deutscher Altertumswissenschaft und Theologie," in *Antike heute*, ed. Richard Faber and Bernhard Kytzler (Würzburg: Königshausen & Neumann, 1992), 186.
104 Reinhard Falter, *Natur prägt Kultur. Der Einfluß von Landschaft und Klima auf den Menschen. Zur Geschichte der Geophilosophie* (Munich: Telesma-Verlag, 2006), 165. The book and others by Falter appeared courtesy of Müller's publishing house, Telesma.
105 "Die Götter der Erfahrungsreligion wieder verstehen. Das griechische Beispiel und die heutige Situation," 107: "Vergötzung des bloßen Lebens sprich Überlebens und eine Einebnung der Hierarchien [...]."

inclination which is characteristic for Judaism in every form, i.e., the will for survival at any price or the unwillingness to accept a relation to death as a necessary sacrifice in the sense of Anaximander.[106]

Such attitudes are in dramatic contrast to Asfrid's support of human rights and other Enlightenment ideals on which an optimistic new (Pagan) beginning is to be based. They represent two contradictory ways of culturalizing religion and simultaneously sacralizing culture: an outspokenly anti-modern and a modernist one. It is a contradiction that remains implicit within Asatru and is not openly discussed. These observations warrant the question: how can such unacknowledged inconsistencies and their potential effects be understood?

Heathenism as Religious Secularism

Here, our previous reflections on the origin and contexts of an alleged fundamental difference between monotheism and polytheism, religions of experience and religions of revelation, tribal and universal religions, or Aryan and Semitic religions come into play once again. The conception of such an essential distinction permeates both popular and academic discourse, or, as Friedrich Wilhelm Graf claims for the "new cultural historians" of the 20th century, they "merely reproduce the everyday knowledge which is always already formed by the *Kulturkämpfe* [the struggles between church and state] in the past."[107] In the case of Neopaganism, the academic construction and critique of religion mutates into the formation of new religions. It is, of course, not illegitimate to construct a new religion out of a well-established critical discourse on religion, and I shall discuss the mechanisms behind such constructions of religion from academic knowledge in Chapter 8. However, it is equally

---

106   *Natur prägt Kultur. Der Einfluß von Landschaft und Klima auf den Menschen. Zur Geschichte der Geophilosophie*, 290: "Eine Neigung, die für den Judaismus in jeder Form charakteristisch ist, nämlich der Wille zum Überleben um jeden Preis, bzw. der Unwille, ein Verhältnis zum Tod als notwendiges Opfer im Sinn des Anaximander zu akzeptieren." Falter's ideas on nature conservation are discussed in more detail in Chapter 6. For a critical discussion of Falter's positions see Ulrich Linse, "'Fundamentalistischer' Heimatschutz. Die 'Naturphilosophie' Reinhard Falters," in *Völkisch und national. Zur Aktualität alter Denkmuster im 21. Jahrhundert*, ed. Uwe Puschner and G. Ulrich Großmann (Darmstadt: WBG, 2009).

107   Graf, *Die Wiederkehr der Götter*, 108f: "reproduzieren die 'neuen Kulturhistoriker' häufig nur jenes Alltagswissen, das immer schon von den konfessionellen Kulturkämpfen der Vergangenheit geprägt ist."

legitimate to point to some problems inherent in such critical and creative constructions.

The anti-monotheism of Asatruers like Starkad Storm Stensgaard, or the anti-Judaism/anti-monotheism of philosophers like Reinhard Falter are extreme examples of potential problems that are inherent in constructions of modern religiosity based on theories of essential differences between mono- and polytheism. The anti-Christian prejudices circulating in Neopagan circles do justice to neither the complex and contradictory developments, historical effects of, and lived experiences within Christianity, nor to the equally diverse manifestations of religions grouped together as 'polytheistic'. The logic of such a dichotomization of religious systems also frequently leads to excluding everything associated with Christianity, and thus to a curious division of history into 'good' Pagan eras and elements and 'bad' Christian or monotheistic ones.[108]

In Asatru, but also in some academic contexts mainly interested in reconstructing pre-Christian religion, a similar mechanism leads to a mental exclusion of Christian elements and influences in general. An Icelandic Asatruer professed a vivid interest in history, then added: "I am interested in history except for the latest one thousand years. That is not interesting. I won't be bothered listening to that. It has to be a thousand years or even older."[109] The one thousand years in this quote refer to the history of Iceland and the Northern European areas in general, which were Christianized fairly late in the unification of larger kingdoms. Another effect of such attempts to identify original Paganism and detach it from its Christian interpretations is a rather curious de-Christianization or 'Paganization' of the Middle Ages,[110] an effect which can be found both in scholarship and in its Asatru appropriations.

---

108   Such processes of dividing out adversary tendencies from one's own (idealized) object of study can already be observed in the construction of 'antiquity' in the 19th century. Jürgen Ebach, "Amputierte Antike" has shown that German classical studies and theology systematically excluded Judaism from an academic reception or configured it as a mere minority within the empires of antiquity. He concludes: "In contrast to Greek and Roman antiquity, ancient Israel was not supposed to be recognized and discussed because it was not supposed to be present." (186: "Anders als die griechische und römische Antike sollte das antike Israel nicht rezipiert werden, weil es nicht gegenwärtig sein sollte.")
109   Interview U: "Jeg interesserer mig for historie bortset fra de seneste ettusind år. Det er uinteressant, det gider jeg ikke høre på. Det skal være tusind år gammelt eller endnu ældre, ikke?."
110   Cf. František Graus, *Lebendige Vergangenheit. Überlieferung im Mittelalter und in den Vorstellungen vom Mittelalter* (Cologne/Vienna: Böhlau, 1975); Julia Zernack, "Germanische Restauration und Edda-Frömmigkeit," in *Politische Religion – religiöse Politik*, ed. Richard Faber (Würzburg: Königshausen & Neumann, 1997), 147.

Not every Asatruer or group as a whole would follow these rigorous claims, which merely repeat or mirror the dichotomizing operations for which Christianity or monotheism are so frequently blamed. And not every Heathen would follow Pagan historian Michael Strmiska's thesis that the Viking raids against monasteries starting in the 8th century should be understood as battles in a religious war of resistance against Christian missionary attempts.[111] *The Troth*, in its brief and rather 'matter of fact' overview of Asatru's history, summarizes the Vikings' activities rather laconically: "more land, more gold, more lore, more glory."[112]

Some of these objections to Christianity may pass as justified, albeit one-sided objections to a dominant and repressive social and political force against which a more liberal and open Paganism/polytheism is cast. Frequently though, this disapproval of the Christian churches and their power turns into the vilification of Christianity's own favorite scapegoat: Judaism, which is then seen and despised as the creator of monotheism and its evils. This stereotypical image of an 'arch-enemy' may more or less latently lay at the basis of many of the constructions Asatruers and other Neopagans build their religion on. However, as was demonstrated earlier, 'the Jew' does not figure very prominently, at least not overtly, in these contexts anymore.

Today, Islam has taken its place as the incarnation of the most radical and developed monotheism, the monotheistic religion that allegedly calls most loudly for war against polytheists and Pagans.[113] Not all Asatruers enter into alliances with general anti-Islamic tendencies in Western societies. However, those who do give this Islamophobic discourse a peculiar twist. Within the current mainstream critique of Islam, it has become common to ascribe the capability of modernization and secularization exclusively to the 'Judeo-Christian' tradition.[114] In contrast, Islam is depicted as inherently stagnant and

---

111   Michael Strmiska, "The Evils of Christianization. A Pagan Perspective on European History," in *Cultural Expressions of Evil and Wickedness*, ed. Terry Waddell (New York: Rodopi, 2003).

112   Gundarsson, *Our Troth*, vol. 1, 80.

113   It is striking how many of the traditional anti-Semitic stereotypes are applied in current anti-Islamic discourse. For a critical discussion see for example Ivan Davidson Kalmar, "Anti-Semitism and Islamophobia. The Formation of a Secret," *Human Architecture. Journal of the Sociology of Self-Knowledge* VII, no. 2 (2009), who alerts to the shared Orientalist background of parts of anti-Semitic as well as Islamophobe ideology.

114   For a critique of such Islamophobic secularisms see Talal Asad, "Europe Against Islam. Islam in Europe," *The Muslim World* 87, no. 2 (1997); Judith Butler, "Sexual Politics, Torture, and Secular Time," *The British Journal of Sociology* 59, no. 1 (2008); Jasbir K. Puar, *Terrorist Assemblages. Homonationalism in Queer Times* (Durham/London: Duke University Press, 2007).

pre-modern. Heathens who align with such discourses on religion take them a step further and configure 'secularism,' and with it a somewhat limited understanding of enlightenment and emancipation, as a specific trait of a Northern European pre-Christian tradition and religion. In this sense, Germanic Neopaganism can be understood as a Western secularism that has turned into a religion.

When we consider that one of the sources of inspiration for the early German Faith Movement in fact came from freethinkers and the free-religious movement, this observation is not as surprising as it might seem.[115] This 'religious secularism' can have two related consequences. Parts of Asatru ally themselves with a modernity whose main values and ideals are then projected onto a deep past. In these cases, 'modernity' itself is turned into an atemporal marker of a cultural essence.[116] In other cases, attempts to define a tradition of their 'own' modernist tradition versus the 'alien' Islam can even lead to a reluctant alliance with Christianity. An example is a contribution on the online-forum for the *VfgH* in a thread on "Islam and World Domination":

> I completely agree that we are not dealing with an antagonism between Christianity and Islam, but between a liberal-secular order and a religious dictatorship or theocracy. [...] Nevertheless – after this reprimand against the Christians – we must not blur the borders, not even in a Pagan forum: The separation between church and state had to be wrung from Christianity, but it could be wrung from it because it was already inherent in it ("Render to God the things that are God's, and to Caesar the things that are Caesar's"). In addition – in spite of being a book religion like Islam – Christianity is considerably more multi-layered and more open to different interpretations.[117]

---

115 See Chapter 1.

116 An earlier example of such a-historical readings of modernity is Arthur Bonus' idea that both saga literature and the works by Scandinavian realists and naturalists, such as Henrik Ibsen, are expressions of a timeless Nordic spirit which has always been 'modern.' See Chapters 1 and 9.

117 Entry by 'Etzel' on March 28, 2008, online-forum www.vfgh.de, thread: "Islam und Weltherrschaft": "[...] stimme ich vollkommen zu, daß es nicht um einen Gegensatz zwischen Christentum und Islam, sondern freiheitlich-säkularer Ordnung und religiöser Diktatur bzw. Theokratie geht. [...] Dennoch dürfen – nach dieser Scheltrede gegen die Christen – auch in einem heidnischen Forum nicht die Grenzen verwischt werden: Dem Christentum wurde die Trennung von Kirche und Staat zwar auch abgerungen, aber sie konnte ihm deshalb abgerungen werden, weil sie in ihm bereits angelegt ist ('Gebt Gott, was Gottes, und dem Kaiser, was des Kaisers ist'). Zudem ist das Christentum – obgleich wie der Islam eine Buchreligion – wesentlich vielschichtiger und unterschiedlicher auslegbar."

This alliance of Christianity, Judaism and Germanic Neopaganism is often found in radical Islamophobic circles as well, and has reached its most violent expression in Anders Behring Breivik's ideology. In his "Manifesto," the Norwegian, who killed 77 people (mostly youths) in Oslo and Utøya on July 22, 2011, stylized himself as a Christian crusader while voicing strong sympathies for Odinists, whom he saw as allies in his attempts to extinguish Islam and its supporters. This argument is reminiscent of similar attitudes held by German Christians who perceived Christianity not as a universal religion, but as a German (or European) cultural force based on ethnic Pagan foundations.

We can thus identify two means of culturalizing religion and sacralizing culture in Asatru: an anti-modern one, which rejects enlightenment and secularism as ultimately foreign (and Jewish-Christian) and propagates an ethnopluralist model of different and separate rooted cultures and tribal religions; and a secularist one, which associates itself with modernity and projects its values and ideals onto a deep past. Nevertheless, both assume that such a cultural or ethnic religion is not only more rooted in a deep past than Christianity, but is also closer to the natural world. This central figure of a Heathen religion of nature will be discussed in the next chapter.

CHAPTER 6

Asatru – A Religion of Nature?

Critiques of monotheism, the promotion of polytheism, and the related discourse on Nordic myth frequently work on the assumption that polytheism, and thus Paganism, is closer to nature and more conducive to ecological ideals than monotheisms. In comparison, monotheism and/or Christianity are seen as inimical to both natural human drives and to the natural environment. Such ideas can be traced back to theories of Germanic or Indo-European religion as fertility cults with a more intimate relation to nature than 'desert religions,' which allegedly originate in arid, infertile climates. These theories intersected with Romanticism's revaluation of nature as a metaphor for the primordial, unspoiled, and pure.[1] They were taken up positively in the primitivist neo-Romantic currents around 1900, which in turn inspired new, alternative religions. Since then, ideas about a Pagan and Nordic nature spirituality have developed a remarkable productivity. They have influenced Western perceptions of nature and the natural within ecological and new spiritual movements and beyond. This is evident in the fact that many people today experience nature as a realm for spiritual, or at least uplifting, experiences. Equally widespread is the idea that Christianity or monotheism, with its mandate to 'subdue the earth,' is responsible for the destruction of the natural environment, whereas Paganism sees nature as animated, and thus supposedly treats it with more respect.

Over the last few decades, environmentalism and environmental spirituality have enjoyed a reputation as being progressive. Therefore, the widespread self-understanding of Asatru as a 'religion of nature' is much less controversial than the issues of ethnicity and concepts of religion with which it intersects. This identification with nature religion has contributed to a more general acceptance of Asatru in the 1970s and 80s. Since then, Heathenism as a religion

---

1 Steven Sutcliffe, "Between Apocalypse and Self-realisation. 'Nature' as an Index of New Age Religiosity," in *Nature Religion Today. Paganism in the Modern World*, ed. Joanne Pearson, Richard H. Roberts, and Geoffrey Samuel (Edinburgh: Edinburgh University Press, 1998), 33, reminds us that the concepts of nature active in New Age and Neopagan thought today go back to the 17th and 18th century. Here, nature was conceptualized as "the material world itself," but also personified as a "singular nature," as in "mother nature," on the one hand. On the other hand, it was used for specific locations, such as the countryside, unspoiled places, plants, and creatures other than man. Thus, it came to occupy an oppositional place to culture and was identified with the primordial and authentic.

of nature has been promoted by Asatruers in order to create a self-image compatible with modern, progressive social ideals and values, such as environmentalism. At the same time, some of the underlying concepts of an animated nature and of nature spirituality are fraught with an intellectual heritage going back to Social Darwinist, racist, and *völkisch* traditions. Investigating the relationship between nature and spirituality in Asatru and in general discourse can therefore shed light on the problems and ambivalences of nature-spiritual traditions within ecological movements, while explaining much about Asatru's successful alignment with respectable and powerful new social movements.

Nature Spirituality in Asatru

The 1970s and 80s, the years of contemporary Asatru's inception, coincide with the early heyday of the environmental movement. It is thus no surprise that Asatruers worldwide already then highlighted the environmental aspects of their religion.

In his book bearing the telling title *Heidnische Naturreligion* (Heathen Religion of Nature), Géza von Neményi, of the ethnicist German *Germanische Glaubensgemeinschaft*, emphasized the unity of nature, peoples, and spirituality (combined with a New Age doctrine of reincarnation) in a characteristic way, offering Paganism as the solution to the environmental crisis:

> Each people on this earth had or has its own mythology and variety of nature religion. These have to be revived in order to be able to solve the threatening problems of our age. Because the anti-nature attitude of Christianity has brought us to the brink of self-destruction. The gods work against it: For some time now they primarily have let incarnate individuals who in previous incarnations (previous lives on earth) lived in peoples who were completely in touch with nature. [...] It is the task of these people to rouse mankind to a return to the gods in order to end the destruction of nature.[2]

---

2   Géza v. Neményi, *Heidnische Naturreligion. Altüberlieferte Glaubensvorstellungen, Riten und Bräuche* (Bergen a.d. Dumme: Johannes Bohmeier Verlag, 1988), 17: "Jedes Volk dieser Erde hat oder hatte seine eigene Mythologie und Naturreligionsform. Diese müssen wiederbelebt werden, um die drohenden Probleme unserer Zeit lösen zu können. Denn die naturfeindliche Haltung des Christentums hat uns an den Rand der Selbstzerstörung gebracht. Die Götter wirken dagegen: Seit einiger Zeit lassen sie vorwiegend Menschen sich verkörpern, die selbst in früheren Inkarnationen (früheren Leben auf der Erde) in Völkern lebten, die völlig

Icelandic Asatruers have always seen it as a matter of course that their faith is a religion of nature. According to one of my interview partners, this is the most important aspect connecting Asatruers to other Icelanders: "They are open to different religious points of view and beliefs. Everybody in Iceland is connected to the powers of the earth."[3] A similar conviction is held in Swedish Asatru. Members of the shamanistic network *Yggdrasil* claimed that it was important to connect to "one's own soil, own landscape, own climate, light and darkness, the own animal- and plant-life."[4] The idea that it is mainly Christianity's attitude towards nature that is responsible for the common "ruthlessness against the environment," was prevalent.[5] The Swedish a-racist group *Samfundet Forn Sed* continues this attitude, and devotes part of its self-description to emphasizing that Norse mythology is based on an ecological balance of which humans are a part. An equally common theme is the claim that culture and myth are formed by climate, landscape, and nature; and that religion, nature, and cultural identity are closely intertwined.[6] The American *The Troth* favors a view of Heathenism in which the gods can be encountered in the forces of nature. Its view of 'nature religion' and 'holy earth' tends to emphasize the importance of seeking the wilderness as a way of connecting with the deities – an attitude which they see in accordance with the practices of the ancient Germanic peoples.[7]

An interview with a long-term member of Norwegian a-racist *Bifrost* confirms that this is still a common theme among Asatruers:

> Many [Asatruers] have a romantic relationship with nature, like to be in nature, and like natural phenomena. [...] There is something special about this contact with the forces of nature. It is important.

To the question if there are connections with the ecology movement, he replies:

> For some it is surely connected. Because one likes nature, because one likes unspoiled nature, one doesn't like interference. [...] We don't live in

---

naturverbunden waren. [...] Aufgabe dieser Menschen ist es, die Menschheit aufzurütteln und zur Rückkehr zu ihren Göttern zu bringen, damit die Naturzerstörung beendet wird."
3   Interview S.
4   Schnurbein, *Religion als Kulturkritik*, 200.
5   Ibid., 252.
6   Cf. Gregorius, *Modern Asatro*, 187–189.
7   Cf. Gundarsson, *Our Troth*, vol. II, 5–24.

contact with nature anymore. [...] And then it maybe becomes important to have ceremonies outdoors, because then we somehow get back a sort of link to nature. [...] There is a romantic idea here, I think – not in a bad way, but in a nice way.[8]

This quote refers to the fact that such general attitudes about nature are mirrored in the design of Asatru rituals, which not only take place outdoors but also invoke images of rural life, agriculture, nature, fertility, etc. Many of them are organized according to the cycles of the year and life, and invoke the deities almost exclusively in their alleged expressions of forces of nature, growth, fertility and decay, as well as of kin and ancestry. The close proximity posited between exterior and human nature, between an organic culture, landscape, and perception of nature, is reaffirmed in ritual performances, while other aspects of everyday life in modernity take a backseat.[9]

Few Heathens openly disagree with such common perceptions of Asatru as a religion of nature. Nevertheless, some see it as an anachronism and emphasize the fact that Germanic religion is no longer a religion of nature.[10] Others remind their fellow Heathens that all religion is always already cultural, and that the preservation of nature is in fact a modern phenomenon for which 'the ancestors' had no concept.[11] Still others criticize such general compensatory views of nature religion as superficial and call for more concrete action. In an article in the German *Eldaring's* journal *Herdfeuer*, Marcel Behringer confirms the idea that Asatru is a nature religion based on an exchange between humans and environment. From this he derives the moral obligation to develop an ecological conscience. He harshly condemns thoughtless practices in Asatru, which are "limited to weekend walks in the nearby forest. One consumes the poet's mead in honor of the gods from as big horns as possible, and wallows in impressions of nature which seem to calm our soul." He

---

8   Interview O: "[...] mange [...] har et romantisk forhold til natur og liker å være ute i naturen og liker naturfenomener. [...] Det er noe helt eget med det...kontakten med naturkrefter...den er viktig." "For noen så henger nok det sammen – helt sikkert. Fordi man er glad i natur, og fordi man er glad i uberørt natur så vil man ikke så godt like inngrep. [...] Vi bor jo ikke i kontakt med naturen i noen særlig grad lenger [...] og da blir det kanskje også så viktig for oss at vi har seremoniene utendørs, for da får vi på en måte en slags link ut i naturen igjen [...] Det ligger en romantisk forestilling der, tror jeg, som – ikke på noen fæl måte men på en snill måte."
9   A good example for this is the second part ("Praxis") of Steinbock, *Das heilige Fest*.
10 GardenStone, *Germanische Magie*, 54.
11 Interview I, with a Danish Asatruer, April 2010, Denmark.

ends with an apocalyptic vision: "We stand on Midgard's glowing ashes and celebrate a nature-loving spirituality while that which the gods gave us burns down around us..."[12]

Such attitudes have indeed motivated some Asatruers to embrace environmental activism. One of the first actions of Icelandic *Allsherjargodi* Sveinbjörn Beinteinsson to come to public attention was to erect a *nidstang* (nithing pole) against the stationing of atomic weapons on the American airbase in Iceland – an act which contributed to establishing the image of Asatru as an environmental religion as well as a religion of peace and national sovereignty.[13] Ivar Hille, the leader of Norwegian *Foreningen Forn Sed*, emphasizes his former membership in the environmental youth organization *Natur og ungdom* (Nature and Youth) as well as his membership in the Norwegian Nature Protection Society. He presents environmental activism as an important part of his faith, and espouses a political vision that promotes a return to a society more oriented toward agriculture than industry.[14] Henrik Hallgren, chair of the Swedish *Samfundet Forn Sed*, is one of the most outspoken and differentiated defenders of a view of Asatru as an ecological religion and is author of the book *The Green Change*,[15] in which he accounts for his environmental engagement.

In some instances, landscape conservation and environmentalism are central to the self-conception of entire groups. Pagan ideas of a deified, animated nature and landscape, among which ancient heritage sites are counted as well, have motivated activism among English Pagans of all persuasions in recent years. For many of them, the protection of local landscape and remnants of the past has become an important facet of their religion.[16] Frequently, this kind of

---

12   Marcel Behringer, "Naturreligion und ökologisches Bewusstsein," *Herdfeuer. Die Zeitschrift des Eldaring e.V.* 5, no. 18 (2007), 14; "[...] Naturreligion jedweder Couleur [scheint sich] auf wochenendliche Spaziergänge im heimischen Wald zu beschränken, zu Ehren der Götter wird Dichtermet aus möglichst großen Hörnern konsumiert, und man schwelgt in den Eindrücken der Natur, die unsere Seele zu beruhigen scheinen [...]." "Wir stehen auf der glühenden Asche Mittgards und zelebrieren naturverbundene Spiritualität, während um uns herum das verbrennt, was die Götter uns gaben..."
13   Cf. Jonsson, "Ásatrú á Íslandi við upphaf 21. aldar," 155.
14   Interview with Ivar Hille (Foreningen Forn Sed), February 25, 2010, Norway, and email correspondence from November 11, 2011.
15   Henrik Hallgren, *Det gröna skiftet. Från industrialism till ekologism* (Borås: Recito, 2009).
16   Cf. Jenny Blain and Brian Wallis, *Sacred Sites – Contested Rites/Rights* (Brighton: Sussex Academic Press, 2007), Jenny Blain, "Heathenry, the Past, and Sacred Sites in Today's Britain," in *Modern Paganism in World Cultures. Comparative Perspectives*, ed. Michael Strmiska (Santa Barbara, CA: ABC-Clio, 2005).

nature spirituality finds its expression in practices such as *seid* or 'sitting out,' as they are perceived as ritual activities ensuring a connection to the forces of the earth or nature.[17] A number of groups, especially in England and Denmark, have also developed initiatives to buy land – projects in which two motives come together. On the one hand, there is a desire to own and develop a sacred space on which rituals and gatherings can be held without having to make concessions to state authorities or owners. On the other hand, it is seen as a measure to protect natural spaces.[18]

The quoted statements, as well as the varying group policies, show a strong consensus around ideas of Asatru as a religion of nature. At the same time, this consensus encompasses a wide variety of different concepts of nature and of different ideas about the relationship between humans and the natural environment. However, it often fails to address their inner contradictions. 'Nature' can either mean the present, concrete, immanent world 'as it is'; or a romanticized location of beauty, peace, and authenticity. In some instances, nature religion is a term that serves as a delineation from monotheism. In others, it is connected with a general feeling of being close to nature and seeing humans as part of nature. Pantheist or animist attitudes entail the worship of different beings in the universe or see nature as a bridge to the deities. A closer look at the genealogy of such views and activities in different conservational and environmental movements of the 19th and 20th century in Germany, England, the USA, and Scandinavia can help us understand the discourses on nature and spirituality in which Asatru is embedded as well as the potential political consequences of such attitudes.

Environmental Protection, the *Heimat*-Movement and *Völkisch* Religion in Germany

Germany was certainly not the first country in which nature conservation became a pressing issue in view of the problems posed by a rapid industrializa-

---

17   See chapter 3.
18   An example for this is the British *Ormswald*, which was bought and developed by *Odinshof* as part of a so-called Land Guardians scheme. When the initial land guardians lost their charity status, the *Olgar Trust* was founded. This trust gained charity status by formulating environmental goals, such as the protection of woodlands. Cf. http://www.olgartrust.org/history.htm, last accessed February 03, 2015. The Danish group *Asatrofællesskabet Yggdrasil* pursues a similar goal with its purchase of an area of untouched woodland in Jutland. Cf. http://www.asatrofaellesskabet-yggdrasil.dk/, last accessed February 03, 2015.

tion and urbanization. It was, however, the place where the search for a 'native' German religion played a role in the starting phase of the conservation movement. The journalist and cultural historian, Wihelm Heinrich Riehl (1823–1897), was one of the first to develop a systematic critique and vision of the problems caused by untrammeled consumption and the increasing destruction of wild nature. Riehl based his environmental engagement on a Herderian notion of unity between landscape, culture, and nation. The ultra-conservative nationalist was driven by a longing for an idealized pre-modern society[19] and promoted an organicistic corporate state based on a traditional rural culture. He saw the materialist, foreign, and un-German Western civilization promoted by Jews at the root of the industrialization that destroyed German landscapes.[20] This Romantic anti-Semitic conception of *Volk* and state motivated his interest in the mythic and religious basis of German peasantry. A faithful adherent of Jacob Grimm, Riehl thought he had found the essence of German culture in rural customs and practices which, in his eyes, contained remnants of a pre-Christian, primordial German culture. This interest not only made him into an early representative of environmental protection, but also forged his reputation as the founder or forerunner of folklore, cultural history, and sociology.[21]

---

19   Frank Uekötter, *The Green and the Brown. A History of Conservation in Nazi Germany* (Cambridge: Cambridge University Press, 2006), 18.

20   See especially his four volume work Wilhelm Heinrich Riehl, *Naturgeschichte des Volkes als Grundlage einer deutschen Socialpolitik*, 4 vols. (Stuttgart/Augsburg: Cotta, 1851–1869) (Natural History of the German People as the Basis for a German Social Politics). Cf. Olsen, *Nature and Nationalism*, 64. The nationalist basis for Riehl's theories about nature become clear in the distinction he made between the "mythic German forest," which he saw as the essence of the German landscape, and the domesticated park and tilled soil that seemed characteristic for the merely aestheticist and economic quality of French and English landscapes. Cf. Hermann Bausinger, "Zwischen Grün und Braun. Volkstumsideologie und Heimatpflege nach dem Ersten Weltkrieg," in *Religions- und Geistesgeschichte der Weimarer Republik*, ed. Hubert Cancik (Düsseldorf: Patmos Verlag, 1982), 216.

21   Methodologically, Riehl proved important for these fields because he pointed to the necessity of studying folk life not through texts, but through immediate observation; an attitude he combined with a rejection of analytical 'rationalist' approaches. (Cf. Klaus v. See, *Die Ideen von 1789 und die Ideen von 1914. Völkisches Denken in Deutschland zwischen Französischer Revolution und Erstem Weltkrieg* (Frankfurt a.M.1975), 89, cf. 82–91) Riehl's influence on later environmental protection movements has been discussed in all histories of the green movement in Germany. The political assessment of Riehl differs in these accounts, but all agree on the fundamentally conservative nature of his social politics. Cf. Klaus Bergmann, *Agrarromantik und Großstadtfeindschaft* (Meisenheim a. Glan: Hain, 1970), 38–62; Jost Hermand, *Grüne Utopien in Deutschland. Zur Geschichte des ökolo-*

The issues of nature protection and the idealization of rural life, as they were first put forward by Riehl, gained momentum in Germany after 1870. This development was fuelled by the change from an agrarian to an industrialized society, which was accompanied by a quick urbanization, a rural exodus, and all the social and economic problems related to such processes. The motives behind this early environmentalism varied considerably, ranging from a Romantic aestheticization of national landscape and the conservative longing for a rootedness in an agrarian society, to economic attempts to ensure autarky.[22] This neo-Romantic environmentalist and conservationist constellation peaked around 1900, coinciding with the establishment of the *völkisch* movement and its religious branches.

In the spirit of Romantic holistic thought, environmental protection at the time included the protection of the *Heimat* – the mythical unity of landscape, the past, and rural culture for which 'homeland' is an insufficient translation.[23] Parts of the urban, bourgeois milieus in which this reaction to industrial modernization originated[24] adopted nationalist or *völkisch* sentiments. However, the movement as a whole became united with the politically diverse life reform and cultural reform associations described in chapter 1, and can be seen as an equivalent to the English *Arts and Craft* movement.[25] The first significant umbrella organization to have combined nature and *Heimat* protection efforts was the *Deutscher Bund Heimatschutz* (German Federation for the Protection of the Homeland), founded in 1904 by Ernst Rudorff and Paul Schultze-Naumburg, who became its first president (until 1913).[26] The architect, art

---

gischen Bewußtseins (Frankfurt a.M.: Fischer, 1991), 82f; Janet Biehl and Peter Staudenmaier, *Ecofascism. Lessons from the German Experience* (Edinburgh/San Francisco: AK Press, 1995), 6; Olsen, *Nature and Nationalism*, 63f.

22 Julius Langbehn, and others who promoted the hope of rejuvenating the German nation from mythical, cultural and spiritual sources, combined their cultural pessimist visions with a fear of losing agricultural autarky. Cf. Hermand, *Grüne Utopien in Deutschland*, 84.

23 Janet Biehl (Biehl and Staudenmaier, *Ecofascism*, 35) summarizes succinctly: "The word *Heimat* connotes as well a turn toward the past, an anti-urban mood, a familiar community, and proximity to nature."

24 Bergmann, *Agrarromantik und Großstadtfeindschaft*, 87.

25 Cf. Breuer, *Die Völkischen in Deutschland*, 99.

26 For a history of the *Heimat* and nature protection movement in Germany cf. Raymond H. III Dominick, *The Environmental Movement in Germany. Prophets & Pioneers 1871–1971* (Bloomington: Indiana University Press, 1992); ibid.; ibid., Karl Ditt and Jane Rafferty, "Nature Conservation in England and Germany 1900–1970. Forerunner of Environmental Protection?," *Contemporary European History* 5, no. 1 (1996), Rohkrämer, *Eine andere Moderne?* 127–140; "Bewahrung, Neugestaltung, Restauration? Konservative Raum- und Heimatvorstellungen in Deutschland 1900–1933," in *Ordnungen in der Krise*.

critic, painter, and later National Socialist politician saw the origin of contemporary environmental problems in a national and spiritual crisis, a sentiment that, as we have seen, was shared by many of his contemporaries in the early German Faith Movement as well as in Ariosophy. Guido von List is a case in point: prior to the development of his spiritual visions, he had been actively engaged in the Austrian Alpine Club and harbored great sympathies for the *Heimat* movement.[27]

Parts of the *Heimat* and nature protection movement, including its founding member Wihelm Bölsche and his collaborator Bruno Wille, were influenced by Ernst Haeckel (1834–1919), whose theories provided inspiration for modern environmentalism and nature spirituality. The immensely popular German anatomist and zoologist brought Darwin's evolutionary theory to Germany, and he was responsible for coining the term 'ecology' in his 1866 work, *"Generelle Morphologie der Organismen"* (General Morphology of Organisms).[28] Haeckel was heir to an anti-dualistic, pantheistic Romantic scientific tradition, which sees natural phenomena as expressions of universal aesthetic and spiritual forces.[29] His ideas about the inseparable union between nature and culture led him to apply scientific methods to the study of society as well. According to many critics, this 'biologizing of ethics' made him into one of the leading proponents of Social Darwinism. By turning this scientifically based holism into the veritable 'nature religion' of what he called 'monism,' he gave it a religious foundation.[30]

Zur politischen Kulturgeschichte Deutschlands 1900–1933, ed. Wolfgang Hardtwig (Munich: R. Oldenbourg Verlag, 2007).

27   Cf. Schnurbein, *Religion als Kulturkritik*, 240. For a discussion of the nationalist and *völkisch* politics of the German and Austrian Alpine associations cf. Corinna Peniston-Bird, Thomas Rohkrämer, and Felix Robin Schulz, "Glorified, Contested and Mobilized. The Alps in the 'Deutscher und Österreichischer Alpenverein' from the 1860s to 1933," *Austrian Studies* 18, no. 1 (2011).

28   For Haeckel, ecology denoted the "economy of nature" or, more aptly, the interactions of all organisms which live together in a place, their adaption to their environment as well as their transformation through their struggle for survival. Cf. Hermand, *Grüne Utopien in Deutschland*, 71f.

29   Robert J. Richards, *The Tragic Sense of Life. Ernst Haeckel and the Struggle over Evolutionary Thought* (Chicago: University of Chicago Press, 2008) made the attempt to rehabilitate Haeckel's legacy with this claim. While he is right in his reading of Haeckel as an heir to a Romantic pantheism, he tends to overlook the ambivalent legacy of Romanticism as such, and uses it to exculpate Haeckel in an apologetic manner.

30   Cf. Hermand, *Grüne Utopien in Deutschland*, 71f.

Monism created its organizational base in the *Monist League*, established in 1906. This "heterogenous alliance"[31] shows the ambivalence of Haeckel's theories, and it mirrors once again the contradictory legacy of Romantic organicistic thought. On the one hand, he and the *Monist League* promoted world peace, anti-militarism, international cooperation, and tolerance for homosexuals,[32] as well as a general pan-eroticism which allegedly ruled the collaborative principle in nature and should serve as a model for a better human society.[33] On the other hand, they foregrounded Social Darwinist teachings of natural differences and hierarchies between human races, scientific racism, and eugenics.[34] For our context, the promise to mend the split between science and religion is key. Haeckel first promoted this program in his famous 1892 lecture, "*Der Monismus als Band zwischen Religion und Wissenschaft*" (Monism as the Bond between Religion and Science) and elaborated it in the vastly popular book, "*Die Welträthsel*" (*The Riddle of the Universe*, 1899, English translation 1901).[35] The book offered an attractive program for the rising immanentist Neopagan religions of his era and proposed a scientific justification for including race hierarchies into these religious currents. Additionally, Haeckel's thought on evolutionary principles ruling cultural and spiritual matters was consistent

---

31   Richards, *The Tragic Sense of Life*, 372.
32   Ibid., 372.
33   Cf. Hermand, *Grüne Utopien in Deutschland*, 72.
34   Haeckel himself "increasingly pronounced support for aggressive foreign politics and German chauvinism" and strongly endorsed colonial politics (Mario A. Di Gregorio, *From Here to Eternity. Ernst Haeckel and Scientific Faith* (Göttingen: Vandenhoeck & Ruprecht, 2005), 508f). Daniel Gasman, *The Scientific Origins of National Socialism. Social Darwinism in Ernst Haeckel and the German Monist League* (New York: Science History Publications, 1971) was the first to forward the claim of a direct continuity between Haeckel's monism and National Socialist ideology (cf. also *Haeckel's Monism and the Birth of Fascist Ideology* (New York: Peter Lang, 1998)). While Richards, *The Tragic Sense of Life*, (6, 269f, and 448) has shown that it is largely unfounded to make Haeckel responsible for National Socialist racism and anti-Semitism, the totalitarian program of his monism was implicitly anti-liberal because it extended evolutionary principles to matters of the human spirit and culture. Richards (ibid., 269) correctly asserts that Haeckel was no supporter of a racial anti-Semitism, but that his anti-clericalism extended to orthodox Jews, whose assimilation Haeckel deemed impossible. However, as I have argued earlier (see chapter 4), such a clear distinction between a racist and a religious motivation of anti-Jewish thought has a tendency to obscure the multiple interactions and the mutual reliance of these argumentative patterns. Cf. Di Gregorio, *From Here to Eternity*, 497.
35   Ernst Haeckel, *Die Welträthsel. Gemeinverständliche Studien über Monistische Philosophie* (Bonn: E. Strauß 1899), *The Riddle of the Universe at the Close of the Nineteenth Century* (New York: Watts & Co, 1901).

with a specific variety of environmentalism. It laid the foundation for some versions of post-war environmental spirituality that also inherited some of the more problematic aspects of his monism, e.g., its illiberalism, as well as its potential for anti-democratic notions and racial thought.[36]

Protection and preservation of a rooted, national landscape, nature, and culture, along with the idea of nature as the normative model for human society, were on the agenda of various reform movements working toward a more natural organic modernity[37] – the same movements by which early Germanic Faith was inspired. The German youth movement, with its practical application of a 'back to nature' ethos (i.e., hiking in forests and unspoiled landscapes), promoted a 'nature spirituality' set in opposition to the mechanist logic of an alienated modernity.[38] Such a "cosmic worldview"[39] was celebrated in the essay "*Mensch und Erde*" (Man and Earth), which Ludwig Klages wrote for the memorable gathering of the youth movement at the Hoher Meissner in 1913.[40] Even Klages' most pronounced critics agree that the life-philosopher offered an astonishing anticipation of

> just about all of the themes of the contemporary ecology movement: It decried the extinction of species, disturbance of global ecosystemic balance, deforestation, destruction of aboriginal peoples and of wild habitats, urban sprawl, and the increasing alienation of people from nature. In emphatic terms, it disparaged Christianity, capitalism, economic utilitarianism, hyperconsumption, and the ideology of 'progress.' It even condemned the environmental destructiveness of rampant tourism and the slaughter of whales, and displayed a clear recognition of the planet as an ecological totality.[41]

As we have seen in chapter 5, Klages, as well as his followers then and today, did not limit themselves to a critique of instrumental reason. Rather, they completely rejected a logocentrism (the "*Geist*," as Klages puts it) whose origin

---

36 Di Gregorio, *From Here to Eternity*, 490.
37 Rohkrämer, *Eine andere Moderne?*, 124.
38 Cf. ibid., 141–156.
39 Winfried Mogge, "Religiöse Vorstellungen der deutschen Jugendbewegung," in *Religions- und Geistesgeschichte der Weimarer Republik*, ed. Hubert Cancik (Düsseldorf: Patmos Verlag, 1982), 102f.
40 Ulrich Linse, *Ökopax und Anarchie. Eine Geschichte der ökologischen Bewegungn in Deutschland* (Munich: dtv, 1986), 60, Biehl and Staudenmaier, *Ecofascism*, 11.
41 *Ecofascism*, 11.

they saw in Judeo-Christianity and Enlightenment thought. Klages wanted to replace it with 'bio-centrism,' a philosophy based on experience instead of scientific intersubjectivity.[42] Thus, the *Kosmiker's* Greek, Roman, and Germanic-based Neopagan worldview took on notions of a chthonic earth-and-blood-based spirituality. Also, in the cases of Klages, the *Kosmische Runde*, and the youth movement a deep ambiguity is at work between a profound insight into the consequences of a mechanistic modernity and instrumental reason, and a propagation of potentially totalitarian and not only anti-clerical, but also anti-Jewish, thought.[43]

The early German Faith Movement was clearly influenced by Romantic concepts of Pagan nature, earth, and fertility rites. In their cultic dramas, both Ludwig Fahrenkrog and Ernst Wachler depicted Norse gods, such as Baldur, as protagonists of seasonal myths.[44] The iconography of the German Faith Movement points in a similar direction. Ludwig Fahrenkrog painted the god Baldur blessing the fields in various versions. Hugo Höppener (alias Fidus), the star-artist of the life reform and youth movements, became famous with his paintings and drawings of naked, healthy, young, blond-haired and blue-eyed, muscular bodies celebrating a cult of light and air in open fields and mountain landscapes – the most famous and frequently reproduced being the "*Lichtgebet*" (Light Prayer).[45] Early promoters of a Germanic Faith also combined racist and eugenic ideals with the 'back to nature' ideology of alternative rural communities promoted by the settlement movement. The biologist and radical *völkisch* protagonist, Willibald Hentschel, developed the idea of a '*Mittgart*' colony for racial breeding.[46] To him and his followers, urbanization, industrialization, money, economy, and luxury appeared as signs of the Aryan race's degeneration, which had to be combated by a healthier and more natural life in rural colonies. This 'natural life' in the service of racial regeneration included the

---

42 Rohkrämer, *Eine andere Moderne?*, 175.

43 Joachim Radkau, *Die Ära der Ökologie. Eine Weltgeschichte* (Munich: C.H. Beck, 2011), 60–74, emphasizes the strong pacifist, non-aggressive, non-chauvinist tendencies in the life reform movement, and the anti-centralist, international strands within the *Heimat* protection movement. However, he fails to mention the simultaneously existing ideas of racial hierarchy and eugenicism, as well as the anti-Semitism characteristic of the Neopagan and neo-Germanic strands within these movements.

44 See for example Wachler, *Mittsommer. Trauerspiel mit Chören für die Bühne unter freiem Himmel*, Fahrenkrog, *Baldur*.

45 For an in-depth discussion of these aesthetic aspects of the German Faith Movement and Asatru see chapter 9.

46 Willibald Hentschel, *Varuna. Das Gesetz des aufsteigenden und sinkenden Lebens in der Geschichte* (Leipzig: Matthes, 1902).

so-called 'Mittgart-polygamy': a ratio of one male settler to ten women would ensure the quick and effective breeding of racially pure children.[47] Hentschel never put his ideas into practice, but they inspired the *Donnershag* settlement, which Ernst Hunkel, of the *Deutschgläubige Gemeinschaft*, founded in 1919 in Sontra. It combined such racial breeding ideas with the goal of economic autarky through agriculture and crafts, as well as cooperative land use.[48]

Spiritualized holistic ecology-cum-racial breeding and eugenics made an impression on the margins of National Socialism and policies as well, especially through the *Artamanen* movement. Inspired by Hentschel, as well as *völkisch* and *Heimatschutz* ideals, the *Artamanen* formed in the early 1920s, with the goal of colonizing Eastern Europe through agricultural settlements. By 1927, they had practically become a section of the National Socialist party, counting a number of future leaders of the National Socialist state among their members: the later head of the SS, Heinrich Himmler; Rudolf Höß, who was to become the commander of Auschwitz; the racial ideologue, Hans F.K. Günther; and future *Reichsbauernführer* (Reich Peasant Leader) Walter Darré, the infamous propagator of the catch-phrase "blood and soil."[49] *Heimatschutz* ideas of a *völkisch* conservationism thus exerted a certain influence on National Socialist politics and found their expression in laws on animal protection, small scale and organic farming, hunting, and landscape architecture.[50]

---

47   Cf. Dieter Löwenberg, "Willibald Hentschel (1858–1947), seine Pläne zur Menschenzüchtung, sein Biologismus und Antisemitismus" (Dissertation, Universität Mainz, 1978), 9–29; Ulrich Linse, *Zurück, o Mensch, zur Mutter Erde. Landkommunen in Deutschland 1890–1933* (Munich: dtv, 1983), 188f.

48   *Zurück, o Mensch, zur Mutter Erde*, 188–197.

49   Based on scant evidence from Darré's defence at the Nuremburg trials, Anna Bramwell has made out Walter Darré as a naïve and harmless early promoter of small scale farming and green thought (cf. Anna Bramwell, *Blood and Soil. Walther Darré and Hitler's Green Party* (Abbotsbrook: Kensal Press, 1985), *Ecology in the 20th Century. A History* (New Haven/London: Yale University Press, 1989)). Such claims have been thoroughly rebuked in later scholarship, which clarified that Darré was heavily involved in the NS policy of agrarian expansionism, cf. Gesine Gerhard, "Breeding Pigs and People for the Third Reich. Richard Walther Darré's Agrarian Ideology," in *How Green Were the Nazis? Nature, Environment and Nation in the Third Reich*, ed. Franz-Josef Brüggemeier, Martin Ciok, and Thomas Zeller (Athens, OH: Ohio University Press, 2005), Uekötter, *The Green and the Brown*, Rohrkrämer, "Bewahrung, Neugestaltung, Restauration?," 66.

50   Cf. Olsen, *Nature and Nationalism*, 73–80, see also Luc Ferry, *The New Ecological Order*, trans. Carol Volk (Chicago/London: University of Chicago Press, 1995), 104–107. In focusing mostly on biologist Walther Schoenichen's laws for animal protection, Ferry overstates his point of direct continuities between National Socialist views of environmentalism and contemporary deep ecology. But he is able to show the existence of an ethno-pluralist

Völkisch and National Socialist concepts of nature, conservationism and environmentalism were driven by two different, but intersecting, concepts of how to account for the 'nature' of the *Volk*, and consequently two different concepts of nature religion. One is the 'soil' idea of an outer nature: consisting of landscape, climate, vegetation, and fauna, which forms peoples and cultures, and which therefore must be preserved. This strand emphasizes the collaborative principle in ecosystems. It is conservative and anti-liberal in its political outlook, tending toward cultural anti-capitalist, xenophobic, and anti-Jewish attitudes, although usually lacking in outward aggression. The other strand emphasizes the 'blood' component. It posits an inner human nature, which is characterized by racial features that are formed by their habitats, resulting in certain races becoming expansionist 'by nature.' Such concepts of an inner nature tend toward a Social Darwinist ideology of a struggle for survival, in which the strongest and most enterprising races and peoples, which originate in the harsh Northern climates, 'naturally' subjugate the weaker peoples of the South and East.[51]

Nevertheless, already the agrarian Romanticism of the late 19th century combined elements of both concepts, for example by pointing out the significance of rural areas in preserving the resilience and military strength of a people. The diverging ideologies also share anti-Jewish sentiments, since they perceive the 'rootless' and 'landless' south-eastern Judaism as hostile to either version of 'nature.'[52] Furthermore, both promoted an anti-Christian Pagan

---

paradigm in National Socialist policies, which emphasized that peoples and races were just as worthy of preservation and in need of being kept pure and tied to their nature as animal and plant species. For a balanced assessment of the inconsistencies within National Socialist conservationism as the result of the NS state's "institutional anarchy," see Uekötter, *The Green and the Brown*, 9. The unresolved tension between a "blood and soil" ideology and the militarist-technological "reactionary modernism" (Jeffrey Herf, *Reactionary Modernism. Technology, Culture and Politics in Weimar and the Third Reich* (Cambridge: Cambridge University Press, 1984)), which also propelled National Socialist policies, was also never resolved and is another example of the multifaceted conglomerate of ideologies of which National Socialism was comprised.

51   Cf. Mark Bassin, "Blood or Soil? The *Völkisch* Movement, the Nazis, and the Legacy of Geopolitik," in *How Green Were the Nazis? Nature, Environment and Nation in the Third Reich*, ed. Franz-Josef Brüggemeier, Martin Ciok, and Thomas Zeller (Athens, OH: Ohio University Press, 2005); Uekötter, *The Green and the Brown*, 30f, who formulates pointedly: "Obviously, Hitler's nature did not require protection!" (31).

52   Friedemann Schmoll, "Die Verteidigung organischer Ordnungen. Naturschutz und Antisemitismus zwischen Kaiserreich und Nationalsozialismus," in *Naturschutz und Nationalsozialismus*, ed. Joachim Radkau and Frank Uekötter (Frankfurt a.M./New York:

spirituality as the more 'natural' version of religion and used it to substantiate their claims. Alfred Rosenberg's *"Der Mythus des 20. Jahrhunderts"* (The Myth of the 20th Century)[53] exemplifies the mythic foundation of nature spirituality's 'blood' strand. The Nazis' chief ideologist took up and expounded upon all the anti-clerical, anti-Semitic and anti-Christian ideas of *völkisch* religion. He promoted a 'Nordic' religion that allegedly affirmed life and immediate experience, overthrew dualisms, and upheld the belief in the creation of a 'New Man' through natural struggle.[54] Both concepts also spurred research in the humanities during the 'Third Reich.' A case in point is an encompassing research project initiated by the ss *Ahnenerbe* based on the idea of the forest as the embodiment of the Indo-European or Germanic religious essence.[55]

We can conclude that the idea of nature spirituality as an alternative to an allegedly anti-natural Judeo-Christianity becomes popularized in the politically ambiguous reform movements of the early 20th century. Through their proximity to the *völkisch* movement, and through shared ideas about a union between nature and a nation or *Volk*, such concepts formed more general ideas about the essence of Germanic spirituality. At the same time, Germanic religious ideas entered into general discourses on nature and spirituality. Thus, while we cannot say that all 'green' ideas and ecological politics originate in

---

Campus, 2003), 174–180, shows how the anti-Jewish tendency within the conservationist movement in Germany increased, especially after 1918.

53 Alfred Rosenberg, *Der Mythus des 20. Jahrhunderts* (Munich: Hoheneichen, 1930). English translation: *The Myth of the Twentieth Century. An Evaluation of the Spiritual-Intellectual Confrontations of our Age* (Torrance, CA: Noontide Press, 1982).

54 Robert A. Pois, *National Socialism and the Religion of Nature* (London/Sidney: Croom Helm, 1986) uses Rosenberg's religious ideas as central evidence for the Nazi "religion of nature" not recognizing the diverging concepts of nature either.

55 Cf. Bernd-A. Rusinek, "'Wald und Baum in der arisch-germanischen Geistes- und Kulturgeschichte' – Ein Forschungsprojekt des 'Ahnenerbe' der ss 1937–1945," in *Der Wald – ein deutscher Mythos? Perspektiven eines Kulturthemas*, ed. Albrecht Lehmann and Klaus Schriewer (Hamburg: Reimer, 2000). This project not only contributed to anchoring the general idea of the sacrality of the German forest even further in the popular imagination, but also firmly established the idea of the Christmas tree as an ancient Germanic practice. Cf. Hermann Bausinger, "Das Weihnachtsfest der Volkskunde. Zwischen Mythos und Alltag," in *Politische Weihnacht in Antike und Moderne. Zur ideologischen Durchdringung des Fests der Feste*, ed. Richard Faber and Esther Gajek (Würzburg: Königshausen & Neumann, 1997); Esther Gajek, "Nationalsozialistische Weihnacht. Die Ideologisierung eines Familienfestes durch Volkskundler," in *Politische Weihnacht in Antike und Moderne. Zur ideologischen Durchdringung des Fests der Feste*, ed. Richard Faber and Esther Gajek (Würzburg: Königshausen & Neumann, 1997).

this constellation, it is safe to claim that the idea of Germanic religion being an ecological religion has some of its roots here.[56]

The 'soil' and 'blood' elements of nature religion were carried over into early post-war green movements in Germany, where concepts of an indigenous Germanic or Nordic nature spirituality also played a role. In the 1980s, the emerging German Green Party had to battle right-wing extremist currents within their ranks. This was a result of the fact that the ideological heritage of *Heimatschutz* and *völkisch* conservationism was foundational to the network of cultural and religious associations in which former National Socialists and *völkisch* protagonists, under the guise of 'spirituality' and 'culture-work,' gathered in post-war Germany: the *Weltbund zum Schutz des Lebens*, the associated *Collegium Humanum*, and the *German Unitarians*.[57] Their environmental ideology included a strong stance against abortion, as well as nuclear power and weaponry. The anti-Christian and (Germanic) Neopagan tendency of this post-war right-wing ecological movement in Germany found its expression in a rejection of the "anti-natural" "Levantine moral codex" that had been "forced upon" the Europeans,[58] as well as in the promotion of a return to "European nature spirituality" or an "Occidental

---

56   Few authors who have investigated the roots of the German green movement in the *Heimat* and nature protection movements, the life reform movement, and early National Socialist environmental engagement have truly come to terms with the fundamental ambiguity of these intellectual and activist currents. The most differentiated discussions can be found in the seminal works of Ulrich Linse, *Zurück, o Mensch, zur Mutter Erde*; *Ökopax und Anarchie*. In English, Jonathan Olsen's investigations into "right-wing ecology" give the most balanced account. Biehl and Staudenmaier, *Ecofascism*, at times fall prey to an oversimplified theory of direct continuities of an all-encompassing "ecofascism," a stance which they justify and correct in the foreword to the book's new edition (cf. *Ecofascism Revisited. Lessons from the German Experience* (Porsgrunn: New Compass Press, 2011)). Anna Bramwell, *Ecology in the 20th Century* and Raymond Dominick, *The Environmental Movement in Germany*, on the other hand minimize the ideologically problematic aspects of the theories and activities of protagonists such as Haeckel, Darré, Klages etc.

57   See chapter 1. For the significance of these institutions and especially Werner Haverbeck, the leader of the WSL and founder of the *Collegium Humanum*, see Oliver Geden, *Rechte Ökologie. Umweltschutz zwischen Emanzipation und Faschismus*, 2. expanded ed. (Berlin: Elefanten Press, 1996), 113–120; Wölk, *Natur und Mythos. Ökologiekonzepte der 'Neuen' Rechten im Spannungsfeld zwischen Blut und Boden und New Age*, 6–42; Olsen, *Nature and Nationalism*, 92.

58   Peter Bahn, "'Natur-Religion.' Dem Leben begegnen," in *Zurück zur Natur-Religion? Wege zur Ehrfurcht vor allem Leben*, ed. Holger Schleip (Freiburg i.Br.: Hermann Bauer, 1986), 236: "[...] der bislang zutiefst der Natur und ihren Kreisläufen verbundene Europäer

pantheism."[59] In the 1970s and 80s, these positions of the German right-wing environmentalist milieu were formative for Alain de Benoist's and Henning Eichberg's ethno-pluralism.[60] Eichberg claimed that each culture's or "ethnos'" approach to nature is different, and that national sovereignty (which, according to National Revolutionaries and other right-wing thinkers in Germany, was not guaranteed for what they considered the still-"occupied" German nation) appears as a necessary precondition for environmental protection.[61] This implied anti-immigration policies, and impacted the programs of all parties to the political right of the Christian Democrats, such as the NPD, the DVU, and the *Republikaner* in the 1980s and early 90s, whose nationalist anti-immigration agendas were all motivated by ecological reasons.[62]

---

wurde unter einen weitgehend leibes – und naturfeindlichen Moralkodex vorderasiatischer Prägung gezwungen."

59 A central protagonist of this movement was Werner Georg Haverbeck, the leader of the WSL and founder of the *Collegium Humanum*. Together with his wife, he gathered a network of right-wing environmentalists which connected youth organizations such as the *Bund Heimattreuer Jugend* and the *Wiking Jugend* (which, as shown in chapter 2, were breeding grounds for future founders and members of the *Armanen Orden*). A connection to the *Artgemeinschaft* was facilitated through the intertwining of the WSL with the *Gesellschaft für biologische Anthropologie, Eugenik und Verhaltensforschung* (Society for Biological Anthropology, Eugenics and Etology), both of which were headed by the lawyer Jürgen Rieger. The Society promotes a scientific racism in the tradition of H.F.K. Günther, cf. Wölk, *Natur und Mythos. Ökologiekonzepte der 'Neuen' Rechten im Spannungsfeld zwischen Blut und Boden und New Age*, 15f; Geden, *Rechte Ökologie*, 114. Aside from Haverbeck himself, the main proponents of such a pantheistic return to European nature-spirituality were the former Catholic theologian and well-known church critic, Hubertus Mynarek, who in the 1980s had close contact to the DUR, (Hubertus Mynarek, *Ökologische Religion. Ein neues Verständnis der Natur* (Munich: Goldmann, 1986)) as well as the German Unitarian, Peter Bahn, and the co-founder of the Green party, the organic farmer Baldur Springmann, also German Unitarian, who also held contacts with the *Deutschgläubige Gemeinschaft*. Cf. Schnurbein, *Religion als Kulturkritik*, 250–252, Olsen, *Nature and Nationalism*, 92.

60 Cf. *Nature and Nationalism*, 95–97.

61 Ibid., 98f.

62 Cf. Thomas Jahn and Peter Wehling, *Ökologie von rechts. Nationalismus und Umweltschutz bei der Neuen Rechten und den 'Republikanern'* (Frankfurt a.M./New York: Campus, 1990); Alison Statham, "Ecology and the German Right," in *Green Thought in German Culture. Historical and Contemporary Perspectives*, ed. Colin Riordan (Cardiff: University of Wales Press, 1997).

Xenophobic right-wing ecologism had a certain influence on the early Green Party in the 1980s as well.[63] This was facilitated by a number of shared ideological convictions, such as the critique of mindless consumerism, moral pessimism, the rejection of Enlightenment (not only its progressive and technological bias, but its humanism and universalism as well), and sometimes even the call for authoritarian measures or dictatorial systems.[64] Most importantly though, both eco-left and eco-right harbor(ed) a tendency to consider nature also as a model for the social world, leading them to promote a variety of political systems ranging anywhere between democratic and authoritarian. They couched their ideas in a spiritual rhetoric of *Heimat*, belonging, and the 'protection of life' – a tendency that motivated them to embrace Ernst Haeckel and Ludwig Klages as early Greens.[65] Asatruers Géza von Neményi and Michael Pflanz, both founding members of the *Heidnische Gemeinschaft*, were actively

---

63   The conviction that Judeo-Christian monotheism and its dualism, which separated humans from nature, was the main culprit for the exploitation of the earth and the imminent ecological catastrophe, was a driving force behind the early green movement in Germany as well. Jost Hermand has analyzed such a reactivation of an older critique of religion in the name of the environment as a scapegoating of an "other" motivated by the inability to see oneself as profiting from this exploitation. This reactivation could occasionally be found on the left of the political spectrum. Examples include Carl Améry's passionate attack on the "merciless consequences of Christianity" (this is the subtitle of Carl Améry, *Das Ende der Vorsehung. Die gnadenlosen Folgen des Christentums* (Reinbek b. Hamburg: Rowohlt, 1972)) and Otto Ullrich's charges against the "Judeo-Christian religion" and its "disdain for the organic world" (Otto Ullrich, *Weltniveau. In der Sackgasse des Industriesystems* (Berlin: Rotbuch, 1979), 43). Améry later invoked "the old faith," which he thought had survived as a substratum in Bavarian Catholicism, as an effective immunization against the "pagan Conservatism" of Conservative Revolutionaries and racial theorists, such as Arthur Möller van den Bruck and Houston Stewart Chamberlain, cf. Carl Améry, "Deutscher Konservatismus und der faschistische Graben. Versuch einer zeitgeschichtlichen Bilanz," in *Neue soziale Bewegungen: Konservativer Aufbruch im bunten Gewand? Arbeitspapiere einer Diskussionsrunde*, ed. Wolf Schäfer (Frankfurt a.M.: Fischer Taschenbuch Verlag, 1983), 14.

64   The former GDR dissident and early member of the Green party, Rudolf Bahro, reasoned that an eco-dictatorship on spiritual (not Neopagan) grounds was the only means of avoiding the environmental catastrophe, cf. Peter Thompson, "New Age Mysticism, Postmodernism and Human Liberation," in *Green Thought in German Culture. Historical and Contemporary Perspectives*, ed. Colin Riordan (Cardiff: University of Wales Press, 1997), 109; Olsen, *Nature and Nationalism*, 101.

65   For a balanced and informed discussion of these commonalities between left and right-wing ecology in Germany see *Nature and Nationalism*, 100–108.

involved in the Berlin branch of the Green Party in the 1980s, a fact which caused a fierce public debate about right-wing infiltration of the party.[66]

We can conclude that there are clear continuities from *völkisch* and *Heimatschutz* ideas to post-war right-wing ecologism. Nevertheless, the fairly widespread idea in contemporary Asatru that Christianity or monotheism in general is detrimental to the natural environment, and that Paganism provides an ecologically sustainable spirituality, cannot be explained by an ideological-historical investigation into such German backgrounds alone.

Nature Religion in England and the United States

Modern nature spirituality also builds on English, and especially American, models that combined visions of a non-exploitative unity between humans and nature with political ideals ranging from democratic or socialist to conservative and nationalist. Some of their roots lie in the English garden city, the 19th century idealization of rural England,[67] or the Romantic socialism of William Morris, who imagined a classless society without private property based on agriculture and crafts. D.H. Lawrence's ideas regarding a worship of nature, which were inspired by Ernst Haeckel and the counter-cultural environment of Ascona, provided further stimulation.[68] Parts of the early 20th century back-to-nature movement in England combined their engagement for the environment and land reform with Anglo-Saxon or Teutonic spirituality. The *Kindred of the Kibbo Kifts*, a breakaway scout group that was in contact with factions of the German youth movement, combined pantheism and an interest in Eastern religions and Native American spirituality with Anglo-Saxon nationalism; socialist, pacifist, eugenic ideas; and an elitist government ideal.[69] Rolf Gardiner, a promoter of folk dance and dance reform with links to the German life reform movement, harbored dreams of a united Pagan England and Germany in the hope of their collective spiritual rebirth. Gardiner was actively involved with the international far right between the wars. His ideas on nature and spirituality led to his promotion of both organic farming

---

66 Cf. "Mythos der Edda," *Der Spiegel*, January 07, 1985.
67 Cf. Linse, *Ökopax und Anarchie*, 155.
68 Hermand, *Grüne Utopien in Deutschland*, 77; Bramwell, *Ecology in the 20th Century*, 107–112; Hutton, *The Triumph of the Moon*, 160.
69 Bramwell, *Ecology in the 20th Century*, 106–111, Hutton, *The Triumph of the Moon*, 163f.

and racial theory.⁷⁰ Such ideas also influenced the early Wicca movement's rites of fertility.⁷¹

The strongest impact on a spiritual vision within the ecological movement can be traced back to the legacy of the American transcendentalists, in particular Henry David Thoreau (1817–1862). The reflections he had during a two-year period spent in a small cabin in the woodlands, which he documented in his book *Walden* (1854) became a key text for the hippie, New Age, and environmental movements of the latter part of the 20th century. As Catherine L. Albanese has shown in her seminal work, *Nature Religion in America,* the transcendentalists' 'biocentric' Romanticism was characterized by a mostly unacknowledged confusion between two views of matter and nature: an idealistic one, which perceived matter as "illusion and unreality, ultimately a trap from which one needed to escape," and a pantheistic-vitalistic one, which saw matter and nature as the ultimate reality and thus the source of authentic spirituality.⁷² It is a similar contradiction to that of the 'outer' and 'inner' nature previously seen in the German tradition, which also spurred nature protection as well as life reform movements. This contradiction proved to be fairly productive, leading to the emergence of two seminal movements that remained entwined, and also contributed to different varieties of modern New Age and Neopagan nature spirituality: the preservationist movement; and the mind-cure movement, with its Romantic ideas about using the natural magnetic forces governing organisms for the healing of both body and soul.⁷³

Although the American preservationist movement, and especially its central protagonist John Muir (1838–1914), shared basic assumptions about the significance of nature with both German 19th century naturalists and English conservationists, their course of action differed due to different social and political conditions. The German *Heimat* and environmental protection movements focused on the necessity of anchoring humans in the landscape in which they reside, thus promoting a conservative, exclusionary, and xenophobic ideal of small-scale farming communities as well as anti-Enlightenment,

---

70   Bramwell, *Ecology in the 20th Century,* 113–116.
71   Cf. Gregorius, *Modern Asatro,* 181f.
72   Catherine L. Albanese, *Nature Religion in America. From the Algonkian Indians to the New Age,* ed. Martin E. Marty, Chicago History of American Religion (Chicago/London: University of Chicago Press, 1990), 82. It should be added that the same implicit contradiction was characteristic of German and English Romantic perceptions of nature. It is likely that some of the German idealist concepts of the sublime were transferred to the American transcendentalists via the mediation of English Romanticism.
73   Ibid., 108.

anti-French revolution, and anti-emancipatory ideas.[74] The English conservationists were motivated by an idealization of rural England. The American preservationists, however, were occupied with safeguarding the possibility of experiencing the sublime in nature, and thus were committed to the preservation of purportedly unspoiled wilderness areas[75] – ideals which led to the foundation of national parks as well as the wilderness association *Sierra Club*. In all three countries, increasing urbanization resulted in the desire to 'return to nature,' and in the inception of various youth movements and organizations. It seems significant that scouting organizations in both Great Britain and America promoted individualism and expansionism with military and imperialist overtones, relying strongly on a Christian basis. These political and social ideals stand in contrast to the far less centrally organized sections of the German youth movement and their pantheistic Neopaganism.[76]

Thoreau combined the preservationist and mind-cure rhetoric with his own version of an eclectic Hinduism, which led him to "confessions of paganism," while Muir started replacing "God" with "nature" and "beauty" in his writing. These anti-Christian notions notwithstanding, both preservationism and 'mind-cure,' which later influenced Neopaganism, relied mainly on a Calvinist and evangelical tradition (a relation similar to German Romanticism's debt to Pietist religiosity).[77] A more outspokenly anti-Christian impulse entered the

---

74 Linse, "'Fundamentalistischer' Heimatschutz. Die 'Naturphilosophie' Reinhard Falters," 158.
75 For a recent in depth discussion of the transcendentalists' influence on modern nature spirituality see Bron Taylor, *Dark Green Religion. Nature Spirituality and the Planetary Future* (Berkeley: University of California Press, 2010), 42–70.
76 Nevertheless, also in the United States xenophobic and anti-immigrant arguments gained traction within ecological and nature preservation rhetoric. In 1996, the Sierra Club discussed a "motion stating that environmental concerns called for restricted immigration" (Gardell, *Gods of the Blood*, 313). It was turned down by a small margin, cf. Olsen, *Nature and Nationalism*, 139f.
77 Albanese, *Nature Religion in America*, 89, 95, 99. This Christian tradition of nature religion goes back to early 19th century North America, where it was associated with the biblical paradigm of Eden, the original garden. Drawing on the aesthetic notion of the sublime, the transcendentalists in particular transformed this aesthetic category into a "Christianized mark of the Deity resident in nature," a fusion of the aesthetic and the religious which led to the "appropriation of the landscape for religious and ultimately [...] nationalist purposes," (Barbara Novak, *Nature and Culture. American Landscape and Painting 1825–1875*, 3. ed. (Oxford: Oxford University Press, 2007), 7). Accordingly, Thoreau as well as Muir have been criticized for anti-democratic attitudes, and Muir's misanthropic statements, often directed against the urban poor, Native Americans, and African slaves, have warranted skepticism, (Cf. Taylor, *Dark Green Religion*, 70). Considering the practice of

American environmental movement in the 1960s in the form of a seminal essay by Lynn White Jr. The UCLA professor of medieval history located "The Historical Roots of Our Ecologic Crisis" in the "activist" and pro-techonological mentality of medieval Christianity.[78] The argument was eagerly taken up by parts of the environmental movement both in America as well as Europe, which cited spiritual reasons for the current ecological crisis. The anti-clerical and anti-monotheist call for a "new story, a new myth, and a new religion" that "replace[s] anthropocentrism with biocentrism" and a holistic view which sees "the Earth, her ecosystems, and species as sacred"[79] became more prominent in parts of the green movement, in particular in deep ecology. The foundation for an ecological spirituality was sought in sources imagined to have originated outside the traditions of "Judeo-Christianity," Platonic dualism, and "Western civilization," i.e., in Western appropriations of Taoism, Zen Buddhisim, mysticism, as well as in the pantheist, polytheist, animist,[80] and allegedly "ecocentric religions and ways of life of primal peoples"[81] thought to be connected to the "roots of a regenerative spirituality grounded in the natural world."[82]

In this constellation, the 'nature religions' of Native Americans,[83] as well as neo-shamanism, gained significance and were promoted within New Age

---

displacing indigenous peoples from their land in order to create national parks, it does not seem far-fetched to claim that American nature Romanticism also followed a colonial logic (Cf. Joachim Radkau, *Natur und Macht. Eine Weltgeschichte der Umwelt* (Munich: C.H. Beck, 2000), 215; *Nature and Power. A Global History of the Environment* (Cambridge: Cambridge University Press, 2008), 234).

78   Cf. Ralph Metzner, "The Emerging Ecological Worldview," in *Worldviews and Ecology*, ed. Mary Evelyn Tucker and John A. Grim (Lewisburgh: Bucknell University Press, 1993), 167; George Sessions, "Deep Ecology as Worldview," in *Worldviews and Ecology*, ed. Mary Evelyn Tucker and John A. Grim (Lewisburgh: Bucknell University Press, 1993).

79   *Greenpeace* co-founder Paul Watson, quoted in Taylor, *Dark Green Religion*, 99.

80   Metzner, "The Emerging Ecological Worldview," 167.

81   Sessions, "Deep Ecology as Worldview," 210.

82   Metzner, "The Emerging Ecological Worldview," 167. For a systematic discussion of religious forms of environmentalism see Taylor, *Dark Green Religion*. In a chapter on the "Ecology of Religion," Joachim Radkau, *Nature and Power* (77–85), rejects the idea of a development of religions from immanence to transcendence, tracing it back to 19th century evolutionism. According to him, most religions contain elements of both, as well as of anthropocentrism. He also warns against confusing the history of religious ideas with the real history of the environment, pointing out that tree cults may well be prominent in societies which further deforestation and that mother cults co-exist with or even promote the exploitation of women. (79).

83   Karl-Heinz Kohl, "Coming Back to One's Own. What Happens to Tradition in Neo-Traditionalist Movements?," in *The Making and Unmaking of Differences. Anthropological,*

contexts. Neopagans, such as the prominent feminist witch Starhawk, gave their religious movements an activist direction by choosing environmentalism as their political forum.⁸⁴ This, along with growing concerns about neo-colonialist exploitation of native spirituality and culture, led to a search for ecological perspectives in 'indigenous Paganism.' Graham Harvey's dictum about an "elective affinity between paganism and ecology"⁸⁵ is thus quite precise, although he does not address the question of which conceptions of nature underlie this "affinity." The British Pagan and lecturer for religious studies instead perpetuates the argument that Neopaganism is a religion of pure immanence, invoking the idea that it is "nature itself" and an "intimacy with the land" that forms the basis of Paganism, and that the "chief sources of authority are in Nature," leading to a worldview of cyclical time and rooted spatiality.⁸⁶

Critics of an anti-humanist eco-spirituality have pointed out the political implications of a deep ecological spirituality of immanence that turns the biosphere into a quasi-divine entity combining Spinozean or Goethean pantheism with Nietzschean vitalism. They point out the parallels between *völkisch* and National Socialist biocentrism, and "the new ecological order which can lead to either an exclusionist, xenophobic policy or the call for an eco-dictatorship and even the elimination of humans."⁸⁷ As has been demonstrated, constructing

---

Sociological and Philosophical Perspectives, ed. Richard Rottenburg, Burkhard Schnepel, and Shingo Shimada (Bielefeld: transcript, 2006), 103f, has demonstrated that the "mother earth cult" of Native Americans has in fact European roots. See also Radkau, *Nature and Power*, 81.

84   Cf. Taylor, *Dark Green Religion*, 76.
85   Harvey, *Listening People, Speaking Earth*, 132.
86   Ibid., 186f. Harvey's interest for eco-Paganism has brought him to embrace what he calls 'bioregional animism,' a worldview in which the Cartesian gap between human and nature is supposedly overcome by seeing "the world or cosmos" as a "diverse community of living persons (only some of whom are human)." Cf. http://www.animism.org.uk/, last accessed January 14, 2013, as well as *Animism. Respecting the Living World* (London: Hurst, 2005).
87   Cf. Ferry, *The New Ecological Order*, as well as Michael E. Zimmermann, "Possible Political Problems of Earth-Based Religiosity," in *Beneath the Surface. Critical Essays in the Philosophy of Deep Ecology*, ed. Eric Katz, Andrew Light, and David Rothenberg (Cambridge, MA/London: The MIT Press, 2000). Michael Zimmermann had initially developed a deep ecological philosophy on the basis of Martin Heidegger's thought, which he revoked in an article from 2002, having realized the implications of Heidegger's anti-humanist philosophy. For a balanced discussion of Heidegger's views of the relations between community and nature, as well as his critique of modernity, see Thomas Rohkrämer, "German Cultural Criticism. The Desire for a Sense of Place and Community,"

direct lines between National Socialist ideas on nature and contemporary ecology is an over-simplification.[88] Nevertheless, it is no coincidence that a German intellectual tradition is invoked here, betraying the affinity between these versions of eco-spirituality, Romantic organicism, and *völkisch* thought, pointing to a fundamental philosophical problem in biocentric ideologies. The lack of a theory of the subject (and subjectivity) in deep ecology leads to the widespread conviction within environmentalism that scientific ecology not only offers a model to describe the world, but can and should also serve as a "prescriptive model of how we as humans ought to fit in."[89] Deep ecology does not search for new ways to conceptualize subjectivity and sociality in the wake of the Cartesian subject's demise. Instead, it creates a meta-narrative in which an original state of harmony between human and nature is followed by a 'fall' into disenchantment, which consequently has to be counteracted by 're-enchanting' the world and reestablishing the previous natural order. Such calls for a 'spiritual' solution oriented toward a deep past, in which the separation of human and nature can be dissolved and immediacy regained, does indeed bear similarities to German Romantic as well as *völkisch* thought.[90] It implies a naturalization of social life and neglects the fact that the laws of nature, to which everything is to be subjected, are themselves necessarily the result of cognition, and thus of the separation of human thought from what this thought constructs as 'nature.' What is conceptualized as 'nature' and becomes normative in this kind of nature philosophy cannot be anything but a projection of human values. The consequence is a naturalization of such values, an operation serving to immunize them from political critique, presenting them as irreducible and resistant to analysis. Consequently, the proposed political solutions are often undemocratic, sometimes leading to the call for an eco-dictatorship in the service of the higher goal of saving the earth.[91]

---

in *Making a New World. Architecture & Communities in Interwar Europe*, ed. Rajesh Heynickx and Tom Avermaete (Leuven: Leuven University Press, 2012).

88   For a discussion of this complex relation see Biehl and Staudenmaier, *Ecofascism Revisited*.

89   Peter C. van Wyck, *Primitives in the Wilderness. Deep Ecology and the Missing Human Subject* (New York: State University of New York Press, 1997), 48, cf. 6.

90   This is pointed out by van Wyck as well. (Ibid., 67–69).

91   Bron Taylor's discussion of elements of nature spirituality in Disney films is an interesting case in point. In his analysis of *Lion King*, he points to the message of the interconnectedness of all beings that the film espouses. We might raise the counterargument that the ideal here is one of a Social Darwinist kingdom in which a natural hierarchy is defended, according to which every creature has a pre-ordained place that it has to find and fulfill. (Taylor, *Dark Green Religion*).

Nature and National Identity in Scandinavia

So far, we can discern three major influences on Asatru conceptions of nature religion, all of which originate in Romantic conceptions of nature: (1) German discourse on *Heimat* and nature protection, which fused with a soil-and-forest-based natural and national spirituality and influenced the German(ic) Faith Movement; (2) American transcendentalist nature religion, which had a major impact on New Age and Neopagan spirituality in general; and (3) the English pastoral and rural tradition, which gave rise to the fertility cult of Wicca. In order to understand the specific views of nature in contemporary Heathenism, we also have to consider the Scandinavian countries and the way in which images of Northern nature merged with the reception of Nordic myth in the creation of European perceptions of the North, along with Scandinavian national self-perceptions.

The Nordic countries are traditionally seen as places with an abundance of unspoiled nature, with populations that build their mentality and culture on a special proximity to nature. Although images of landscape and nature have been formative for Norwegian and Swedish constructions of national identity,[92] such perceptions have not been systematically investigated. For our purposes, we can at least discern a few external and internal factors that have contributed to such images. Adding to pre-existing ideas on climate theory ideas that lent the North, its myths, and its culture a particular tinge of the melancholic, the heroic, and the sublime, 19th century German, Norwegian, and Swedish landscape painting cemented the idea of the North as the site of the sublime and the authentic in the imaginations of educated Europeans and Scandinavians alike.[93] Scandinavian artists trained in the

---

92   Cf. Gregorius, *Modern Asatro*, 184f.
93   See the contributions by Eva-Lena Bengtsson, "Die Schweden und Düsseldorf," in *Wahlverwandtschaft. Skandinavien und Deutschland 1800–1914*, ed. Bernd Henningsen, et al. (Berlin: Jovis, 1997); Helmut Börsch-Supan, "Dresden und der Norden I," in *Wahlverwandtschaft. Skandinavien und Deutschland 1800–1914*, ed. Bernd Henningsen, et al. (Berlin: Jovis, 1997); Peter Nørgaard Larsen, "Dänische Künstler in Düsseldorf – Düsseldorf in der dänischen Kunst," in *Wahlverwandtschaft. Skandinavien und Deutschland 1800–1914*, ed. Bernd Henningsen, et al. (Berlin: Jovis, 1997); and Magne Malmager, "Die Düsseldorfer Malerschule und ihre norwegischen Künstler," in *Wahlverwandtschaft. Skandinavien und Deutschland 1800–1914*, ed. Bernd Henningsen, et al. (Berlin: Jovis, 1997); "Dresden und der Norden II," in *Wahlverwandtschaft. Skandinavien und Deutschland 1800–1914*, ed. Bernd Henningsen, et al. (Berlin: Jovis, 1997). The most popular paintings of the era became national icons in their respective countries, e. g. the Norwegian painters' Adolph Tidemand and Hans Fredrik Gude's *Bridal*

German painting academies of Dresden and Düsseldorf brought German Romantic conceptions of landscape and nature with them as they returned to their respective countries.

Around 1900, interchanges between internal and external perceptions of a 'Nordic' relation to nature were intensified by the increase in tourism from England and Germany to Sweden and Norway.[94] The reshaping of nature in industrialized countries led to an interest in landscapes that were seen as unspoiled, and to the desire to experience the sublime and primordial in such landscapes. The subsequent development of tourism in the Alps[95] and parts of the Nordic countries is a result of such desires.[96] In the views of German tourists in particular, both the Alpine and the Scandinavian sublime and authentic landscape appeared as specifically Germanic and Nordic,[97] and a discourse on Nordic nature was easily folded into the discourse on Nordic mythic heroism.

Around the same time, modern Scandinavian art and literature were received enthusiastically in German intellectual circles, a reception which further solidified conceptualizations of the North as a source of authenticity, youth, and modernity. The painter Carl Larsson's idyllic interiors were published by Eugen Diederichs, who emphasized the unity between a healthy family life (represented by vigorous, blond-haired and blue-eyed children) and a modern rural interior architecture.[98] Larsson himself not only praised the

---

Procession in Hardanger (1848) depicting rowboats with peasants in national costumes on their way to a wedding in the spectacular fjord and mountain landscape of Hardanger. Reproductions adorn many Norwegian homes up until today. By placing scenes of Christian ritual, such as weddings and funerals, as well as national costumes, in fjord and mountain landscapes, they were both nationalized and sacralized.

94 In his history of environmentalism in Norway, Bredo Berntsen, *Grønne linjer. Natur- og miljøvernets historie i Norge* (Oslo: Grøndahl og Dreyer, 1994), 23, illustrates the fundamental significance of English nature tourism (especially for hunting and fishing) since the 1820s and the foundation of the Norwegian Tourist Association in 1868 for the emergence of this particular view of nature.

95 Cf. Peniston-Bird, Rohkrämer, and Schulz, "Glorified, Contested and Mobilized."

96 In the case of Norway, the fact that Emperor William II spent summers on his yacht in Norwegian fjords contributed greatly to popularizing the Norwegian coastal landscape as a touristic destination, at the same time emphasizing the perception of this landscape as Germanic. Cf. Birgit Marschall, *Reisen und Regieren. Die Nordlandfahrten Kaiser Wihelms II* (Heidelberg: Winter, 1991); Birgit Grimm, "Wilhelm II. und Norwegen," in *Wahlverwandtschaft. Skandinavien und Deutschland 1800–1914*, ed. Bernd Henningsen, et al. (Berlin: Jovis, 1997).

97 Cf. Peniston-Bird, Rohkrämer, and Schulz, "Glorified, Contested and Mobilized."

98 Cf. Cecilia Lengefeld, *Der Maler des glücklichen Heims. Zur Rezeption Carl Larssons im wilhelminischen Deutschland* (Heidelberg: Winter, 1993); "Der schwedische und der deutsche

FIGURE 6.1 *Carl Larsson's first sketch for Midvinterblot (1911)*
SOURCE: TORSTEN GUNNARSON, ED. *CARL LARSSON* (STOCKHOLM: WIKEN, 1992), 223. WORK IS IN THE PUBLIC DOMAIN.

Nordic home, childhood, and landscape, he also harbored a long-standing interest in Swedish pre-Christian ritual. His controversial monumental painting *Midvinterblot* (Midwinter Sacrifice, see Figure 6.1.), which has recently also attracted some Asatruers' attention,[99] bears witness to this interest and Larsson's particular take on nature spirituality. In a style that is reminiscent of Fidus' temple drafts, he interpreted the sacrifice of a mythic Swedish king as the expression of a cult of sacred kingship, fertility, and nature, explaining the first sketch for this painting with the following words in 1911:

> Here, a king is sacrificed for his people's welfare (to enable a good annual harvest). He is drowned in the sacred well located at the foot of the tree (according to Adam von Bremen there stood a tree in front of the temple which was green all year.)[100]

Carl Larsson," in *Wahlverwandtschaft. Skandinavien und Deutschland 1800–1914*, ed. Bernd Henningsen, et al. (Berlin: Jovis, 1997).

99   It has for example served as cover art for an album for Michael Moynihan's band *Blood Axis* (see chapter 9).

100 Georg Nordensvan, *Carl Larsson*, vol. I (1853–1890), vol. II (1890–1919), Sveriges Allmänna Konstförenings publikation (Stockholm: P.A. Norstedt, 1921), vol. II, 168: "Här offras en kung för folkets väl (för åstadkommande av god årsväxt). Han dränkes i den heliga källan

Images of rootedness and naturalness also formed the perception of Scandinavian early modernist literature in Germany. At the time, works by Henrik Ibsen and August Strindberg were not understood as inspired by French naturalism. Rather, their naturalist aspects were interpreted as an expression of a particular Nordic (human) nature.[101] Thus, while the German life reform movement in general might not have been driven by a particular enthusiasm for Northern nature,[102] artists and writers who were inspired by life reform ensured vivid exchanges of what we might call 'Nordic nature spirituality.' Such attitudes also fueled the reception of Knut Hamsun's (1859–1952) literary works. The Norwegian author and Nobel Prize winner's novel *Pan* (1894), about a former lieutenant who tries to find balance and spiritual regeneration in the forests of northern Norway, has been enthusiastically received as a manifesto of nature worship by both German contemporaries and, later on, deep ecologists.[103] Furthermore, his 1917 novel *Growth of the Soil* has been used as an example of the natural and simple yet fulfilled life of a peasant connected to his land. What is lacking from this picture of deep nature worship is Hamsun's contempt for modernity, his authoritarian political inclinations, his dreams of a great Germanic empire, and his active support for Hitler and the German occupation regime of the 1940s – a revealing omission which points at the very least to blind spots in the views of deep ecologists.[104]

---

vid trädets fot (framför templet stod enligt Adam von Bremen ett träd, som grönskade hela året)." The painting was highly controversial for its lack of historical accuracy and overly emphatic and operatic style and eventually rejected by the Swedish National Museum in Stockholm for which it was intended. Nevertheless, since 1997, it has been on display there.

101   Zernack, *Geschichten aus Thule*, 3, 215.

102   This argument was forwarded by Ulrich Linse, "Nordisches in der deutschen Lebensreformbewegung," who also pointed to the fact that the one exception from this was the nudist movement, which was driven by an admiration of the strong, natural, heroic "Nordic" body, an image which in turn inspired vitalist art of the era. See also Lill-Ann Körber, *Badende Männer. Der nackte männliche Körper in der skandinavischen Malerei und Fotografie des frühen 20. Jahrhunderts* (Bielefeld: transcript, 2013).

103   Cf. e.g. Peter Reed and David Rothenberg, eds., *The Norwegian Roots of Deep Ecology. Wisdom in the Open Air* (Minneapolis/London: University of Minnesota Press, 1993), 11.

104   A different reading of Hamsun's texts as deconstructions of such modern nature worship and its violent and inhuman consequences is possible and does more justice to his complex literary texts (cf. Stefanie v. Schnurbein, "Failed Seductions: Crises of Masculinity in Knut Hamsun's Pan and Knut Faldbakken's Glahn," *Scandinavian Studies* 73, no. 2 (2001); "Und ewig singen die Wälder. Trygve Gulbranssens Blut-und-Boden-Trilogie," in *Hundert Jahre deutsch-norwegische Begegnungen. Nicht nur Lachs und Würstchen*, ed. Bernd Henningsen (Berlin: Berliner Wissenschafts-Verlag, 2005); "Knut Hamsun's Narrative

We can summarize that the image of the nature-oriented Nordic mentality and culture emerged via a complex interplay between stereotypes formed by insiders and outsiders. It was constructed and exchanged in the arts and media, as well as in the emerging tourism industry and alternative life reform movements. The image became entrenched after World War II, through a similar interaction of an expanding mass tourism with the German film industry of the 1950s and 60s, which revived the image of *Heimat* as a site of a nostalgic and wholesome rural, natural world.[105] Eventually, the Scandinavian countries would employ such images of wholesomeness and unspoiled nature in the service of modern nation branding.

Right-Wing Ecologism and Asatru

As we have seen, the images of a spiritualized nature and naturalness emerging from Romantic thought and employed in and transformed by various national and temporal contexts are multi-faceted and contradictory. We thus now turn our attention to how Asatruers have made use of such widespread ideas to position themselves within mainstream thought, and if and how they share the ambiguous legacy of this tradition.

The 'brown' roots of ecologism notwithstanding, green ideology today is mostly perceived as leftist. It has been embraced by many a-racist Asatruers in an attempt to distance themselves from right-wing ideologies. Moreover, it has been rejected by ethnicist varieties of Asatru not wanting to be associated with allegedly socialist movements. American ethnicist Asatru also has an ambivalent attitude toward environmental issues, which no doubt stems from the impossibility of arguing for the rootedness of Norse gods and culture in the American landscape. Odinism and ethnicist Asatru have thus had a tendency to stress the 'blood' component of nature religion, arguing for

---

Fetishism," in *Knut Hamsun. Transgression and Worlding*, ed. Ståle Dingstad, et al., Acta Nordica. Studier i språk- og litteraturvitenskap (Trondheim: Tapir Press, 2011)). However, it is not relevant for my argument about its reception in deep ecology.

105   In this context it is interesting to note, that the German *Heimat*-film continued the conflation of Alpine and Nordic landscape, costume, and custom in order to re-create the abovementioned sentiment of an Arcadian world removed from modern civilization and the war-ravaged cities of the era. The popular German film, *Und ewig singen die Wälder* (Eternally Sing the Woods), which was loosely based on Norwegian author Tryggve Gulbransson's novels, is a case in point. It was shot in Norwegian as well as Austrian locations, and was quite obviously used to entice the budding post-war tourism to Norway (cf. "Und ewig singen die Wälder. Trygve Gulbranssens Blut-und-Boden-Trilogie").

the 'natural' expansionism of Nordic peoples. Nevertheless, within radical Odinism, there is considerable support for eco-terrorists, such as the Unabomber.[106] Asatru circles oriented toward the ethno-pluralism of the New Right, especially those around the 'radical traditionalist' journal *Tyr*, praise environmentalism as "the only high-profile 'mainstream' contemporary school of thought that might plausibly be termed anti-modern."[107] It is "interested in 'living in place' in an organic, homogeneous human community, as well as in an organic, regional ecosystem." From here, they derive the social ideal of "natural social hierarchy"[108] that they find most clearly developed in bio-regionalism.

Two of the strands of the ecology movement, deep ecology and bio-regionalism, strongly promote spiritual aspects of ecologism and are affiliated with Neopaganism.[109] Both promote a non-anthropocentric worldview similar to that of Ernst Haeckel's monism, in which humans are seen as merely a part of nature, and which aims at rescinding the separation of humans and nature by subjugating all beings to nature's laws. Deep ecology tends to speak of 'nature' and 'the earth' in a more global fashion, and thus appeals to universalist spiritual movements such as the New Age movement. Asatruers and other 'reconstructionist' Neopagans consider bio-regionalism the more attractive of the two radical ecological currents, because it places more emphasis on cultural specificity. Bio-regionalism originates in an anarchist model of ecological and cultural sustainability. It promotes decentralized political structures based on a network of small regions defined by the ecosystems they are embedded in and independence from arbitrary political borders. It is a holistic concept reminiscent of Herderian ideals, positing an organic unity between nature, landscape, culture, economy, aesthetics, and spirituality. This unity serves as the foundation for a renewed sense of space, belonging, and community.[110] Bio-regionalism's main theorist, Kirkpatrick Sale, recommends basing the arts and spirituality, which he deems indispensable for the creation of deep-rooted bio-regions, on the mythologies of archaic societies, such as the Greek, the

---

106 Cf. Gardell, *Gods of the Blood*, 312f.
107 Joshua Buckley, Collin Cleary, and Michael Moynihan, "Editorial Preface," *Tyr. Myth – Culture – Tradition* 1 (2002), 8.
108 Ibid., 9.
109 A third one is ecofeminism, which will be discussed in chapter 7.
110 Cf. Damian White, "Bioregionalism," in *International Encyclopedia of Environmental Politics*, ed. John Barry and E. Gene Frankland (London etc.: Routledge, 2002); Bernd Hamm and Barbara Rasche, *Bioregionalismus. Ein Überblick*, Schriftenreihe des Zentrums für Europäische Studien (Trier: Zentrum für europäische Studien, 2002).

Celtic, and the Germanic.[111] In contrast to social ecology, which favors a similarly decentralized, utopian model, bio-regionalism does not necessarily advocate democratic models in general. It tends to naturalize spiritual 'roots' as well as social systems as integral parts of bioregions, and thus has parallels to ethno-pluralistic models, which may suggest that "truly autonomous bioregions will very likely develop highly disparate political systems, some of which may not be democratic."[112]

In view of the ideological affinities between right-wing, ethno-pluralist thought and bio-regionalism, it comes as no surprise that parts of the postwar green-brown networks, as well as Asatruers and other reconstructivist Neopagans in Germany, would promote bio-regionalism as a spiritual ecological alternative.[113] In an attempt to regionalize theories imported from the USA and England, and to recover their 'own' bioregional traditions, the small German environmental party *Unabhängige Ökologen Deutschlands* (UÖD, Independent Ecologists of Germany),[114] a splinter organization from the conservative environmentalist *Ökologische Demokratische Partei* (ÖDP, Ecological Democratic Party), started reverting to theorists of the German *Heimatschutz* movement, such as Wihelm Heinrich Riehl, Ernst Rudorff, and Ludwig Klages. A leading member of the UÖD was Leif-Thorsten Kramps, an Asatruer affiliated with the *Germanische Glaubensgemeinschaft* and activist of the New Right.[115] He established a bio-regionalist working group, the *Arbeitskreis Bioregionalismus*

---

111   Kirkpatrick Sale, *Dwellers on the Land. The Bioregional Vision* (San Francisco: Secker and Warberg, 1985), 3–5.
112   White, "Bioregionalism," cf. Sale, *Dwellers on the Land*.
113   The initiative of bringing bio-regionalism to Germany and Austria goes back to a series of books and articles by Eduard Gugenberger and Roman Schweidlenka, two environmental and native spirituality activists. The authors had previously distinguished themselves with critical publications on right-wing esotericist currents within Neopaganism and New Age, while searching for an earth-friendly spirituality they now thought to have found in the American theories of bio-regionalism, cf. Eduard Gugenberger and Roman Schweidlenka, *Bioregionalismus. Bewegung für das 21. Jahrhundert* (Osnabrück: Packpapier Verlag, 1995).
114   The UÖD established itself as the official branch of bio-regionalism in Germany and joined bio-regionalism's international umbrella organization *Planet Drum Foundation* (founded in San Francisco in 1973) in 1996, cf. Hamm and Rasche, *Bioregionalismus*, 26.
115   Biographical information about Kramps was posted on the old homepage of the AK Bioregionalismus Sauerland which was still accessible in 2009: http://www.bioregionalismus.online.ms/ (printed July 07, 2009). The page currently only provides information about the dissolution of the AK (last accessed November 24, 2011). Kramps is currently listed as the regional contact for the GGG *Südwestfalen*, see http://www.ggg-world.net/index.php/regional-ggg-contacts, last accessed January 14, 2013. On the now defunct homepage of

Sauerland e.V. in the mid-1990s. The eclectic list of 'inspirators' listed leading German Faithlers and Asatruers Ludwig Fahrenkrog, Sveinbjörn Beinteinsson, and Géza von Neményi, together with *Heimatschutz* protagonist Paul Schultze-Naumburg, eco-anarchists Gustav Landauer and Paul Robien, and New Right theoreticians Alain de Benoist and Henning Eichberg. The fact that this webpage also provided a copy of the eco-terrorist *Unabomber Manifesto* points to the apocalyptic dimension of Kramps' philosophy as well as to his openness to violence in furthering bio-regionalist aims.

As is the case with the American journal *Tyr*, in German Asatru contexts, bio-regionalism is most enthusiastically promoted by the circle around *Tyr's* German equivalent, the *Heidnisches Jahrbuch*. Both of its editors, Holger Kliemannel and Daniel Junker, have long been promoting bio-regionalist ideals. Further, Kliemannel collaborated with Kramps on an alternative Pagan journal, *Stachelbeere* (Gooseberry), for a number of years. However, such engagements have brought to light underlying ideological differences within this network of Neopagan bio-regionalism as well. The anti-racist Neopagan network *Der Steinkreis* stopped distributing *Die Stachelbeere* once the ethno-pluralist predilections of Kramps were revealed. Furthermore, allegations of Kramps' "eco-fascism" contributed to the demise of his *Arbeitskreis Bioregionalismus*.[116]

Aside from bio-regionalism, 'geomancy,' another related blend of *Heimatschutz* and *völkisch* racial esotericist ecologism, has caught the attention of Asatru circles gathering around the journals *Tyr* and *Heidnisches Jahrbuch* as well as the Scandinavian online journal *Kulturorgan Skadinaujo*.[117] In Germany,

---

the *Arbeitskreis Bioregionalismus* he listed the GGG, the *Heidnische Gemeinschaft*, the *Odinic Rite*, and the WCER as recommended links.

[116] In an article which settled accounts with such "fascistoid" tendencies, Kliemannel's multiculturalism was explicitly distinguished from such "brown" tendencies: Theo, "'außen grün, innen braun, und zu allen Seiten offen?' Was ist los mit der 'Stachelbeere'?," *SteinKreis* 31 (200), 46f. A collection of Matthias Wenger's column "Schattenseiten," in which this article appeared, can be found at http://www.dersteinkreis.de/schattenseiten.htm, last accessed January 14, 2015.

[117] The Scandinavian organization and journal *Kulturorgan Skadinaujo* grew out of the milieu surrounding the defunct *Allgermanic Heathen Front*, (cf. Didrik Söderlind, "Diabolos in Musica. Om sort metall og et heller dystert livssyn," *Humanist* 3 (2008)). It promotes a similar blend of environmentalism, ethno-pluralism and geomancy, aligning nature protection with the protection of a native cultural and spiritual heritage in much the same way as the *völkisch Heimatschutz*. See Jørgen Exenberger, "Geomanti i Norge," KultOrg (KulturOrgan Skadinaujo, web page), http://www.kultorg.com/index.php?mact=News,cntnt01,detail,0&cntnt01articleid=175&cntnt01origid=51&cntnt01detailtemplate=ar

the link to geomancy is right-wing ecologist Reinhard Falter, whose ideas about "religions of experience" have been published in *Heidnisches Jahrbuch*.[118] Falter bases his ecological views, his "landscape racism" as Gerhard Hard has called it,[119] on a holistic unity of landscape, culture, myth, and mentality. He sees his ideal of a spiritually sustained nature protection realized in geomancy, which for him is an alternative to scientific reductionist views of nature as well as a means to "overcome the basic illnesses of traditional occidental esotericism."[120]

Geomancy is an esoteric theory derived from Western occultist speculations about correspondences between microcosm and macrocosm. Intersecting with environmental theories of Gaia, it is based on the idea that the Earth is a living organism, whose energy or power points (an equivalent to chakras) are connected by energy lines. Speculations that such "ley-lines" align the main holy sites of antiquity were first developed by British author Alfred Watkins in 1921.[121] It provided inspiration for German *völkisch* lay scholar Wilhelm Teudt, who saw the Externsteine as an ancient power point used by the Germanic

---

tikler.tpl&cntnto1dateformat=%25e.%25m.%25Y&cntnto1returnid=56, last accessed November 24, 2011 for a positive review of a book on geomancy and "Sarkofagsteinen i Externstein," KultOrg (KulturOrgan Skadinaujo, web page), http://www.kultorg.com/index.php?mact=News,cntnto1,detail,0&cntnto1articleid=213&cntnto1origid=58&cntnto1detailtemplate=artikler.tpl&cntnto1returnid=56, last accessed November 24, 2011 for an article on Externsteine.

118   Cf. chapter 5.

119   The term "landscape racism" was coined by Gerhard Hard, "'Hagia Chora.' Von einem neuerdings wieder erhobenen geomantischen Ton in der Geographie," *Erdkunde. Archiv für wissenschaftliche Geographie* 55, no. 2 (2001),178, and refers to a philosophy which assigns an absolute, fateful and lasting influence of a landscape on humans, nations (*Volk*) or races. Hard traces this figure of thought directly back to *völkisch* ideology.

120   "Überwindung der Grundkrankheiten der bisherigen abendländischen Esoterik," Reinhard Falter, *Natur neu denken. Erfahrung, Bedeutung, Sinn* (Klein Jasedow: Drachen Verlag, 2003), 98, cf. Linse, "'Fundamentalistischer' Heimatschutz. Die 'Naturphilosophie' Reinhard Falters," 169. Together with Jochen Kirchhoff, a "radical deep ecologist," self-appointed "redeemer" of National Socialism's "shadow," Falter is active in the German association for geomancy, *Hagia Chora*, and a regular contributor to its journal (http://www.geomantie.net/authors/925/view.html, last accessed January 19, 2015). In 1990, a book on "Nietzsche, Hitler, and the Germans" by Kirchhoff sparked discussions on a new eco-fascism. The book's subtitle was: "The Perversion of the New Age. The Unredeemed Shadow of National Socialism," Jochen Kirchhoff, *Nietzsche, Hitler und die Deutschen. Die Perversion des neuen Zeitalters. Vom unerlösten Schatten des Dritten Reiches* (Berlin: Edition Dionysos, 1990).

121   Cf. Harvey, *Listening People, Speaking Earth*, 147–150, for a discussion of geomancy as a branch of "sacred geographies."

tribes because of its exceptional earth energy.[122] The ley-line theory enjoyed a surge in popularity in the 1960s and 70s, in the wake of the hippie and other alternative movements.[123] It was picked up by Nigel Pennick, known in Asatru circles as an author of popular works on runes and Paganism.[124] Pennick has been promoting the 'experiential science' of geomancy since the 1960s. His *Institute of Geomantic Research* "also translated the works of neglected German geomantic writers of the 1930s and 40s."[125] Pennick has recently contributed several articles to the journal *Tyr*, and his homepage links to the German *Hagia Chora*. Through the activities of Pennick and others, geomancy's blend of the belief in 'earth power,' astronomy, and rune occultism has become one of the areas in which a German lay science, closely connected to the German Faith Movement and rune occultism of the early 20th century, was spread to a broader public, including sections of the environmental movement.

We can conclude that there is a network of groups, individuals and ideas that combine deep ecological engagement, ideas about the sacredness of earth and landscape, and an interest in Asatru with ethno-pluralist ideas, and the "cultural" and "landscape racisms"[126] found in New Right circles. It is in these circles that older ideas of German *Heimatschutz*, and especially its connections with the early German Faith Movement, have been revived. As the rejection of Kramps' theories within the a-racist Pagan group *Steinkreis* in Germany has shown, such obviously ethno-pluralist, anti-democratic, racist readings of an ecological spirituality within Asatru are also controversial.

Henrik Hallgren, the chair of SAS/SFS and one of the most outspoken and differentiated promoters of an ecological spirituality within Asatru, elicits further critical thought. In his recent book, titled *"Det gröna skiftet"* (The Green

---

122 For a further discussion of Teudt and the Externsteine see chapter 7 and 8.

123 Paul Devereux aligned it with neo-shamanism and considered the shaman's interaction with the land to be guided by such ley-lines and their intersections at megalithic sites, cf. Harvey, *Listening People, Speaking Earth*, 150.

124 For example Nigel Pennick, *Rune Magic* (London: The Aquarian Press, 1992), Nigel Pennick and Prudence Jones, *A History of Pagan Europe* (London/New York: Routledge Chapman & Hall, 1995).

125 http://www.nigelpennick.com/pb/wp_do4f1c1c/wp_do4f1c1c.html. Cf. Nigel Pennick, *Hitler's Secret Sciences* (Sudbury, Suffolk: Neville Spearman, 1985). See also Pennick's older website with additional links: http://www.nigelpennick.com/pb/wp_dae69759/wp_dae69759.html, last accessed November 24, 2011. For Pennick's promotion of Otto Sigfrid Reuter, Wilhelm Teudt, and other *völkisch* protagonists see *Einst war uns die Erde heilig. Die Lehre von den Erdkräften und Erdstrahlen* (Waldeck: Felicitas Hübner Verlag, 1987), 58, 69f, 123.

126 Cf. footnote 119.

Change, 2009),[127] he leaves no doubt that his environmental goals can and should exclusively be achieved by democratic means. He directs stern criticism against the potential xenophobia inherent in the static conception of culture, place, and belonging bio-regionalism promotes, as well as against its strong emphasis on cultural diversity at the cost of democratic ideals.[128]

Nevertheless, the Romantic idea of a sacred landscape in which nature, myth, and culture are embedded and mutually constitutive, and where spiritual forces are at work, remains an important aspect of ecologically minded Asatru. Hallgren calls for a re-mythologization of the world as a means of facilitating a shift of consciousness. Myth, as "the language of the soul,"[129] forms a gateway between human consciousness and landscape. With the concept of *chora* as a holistic, experiential space set against the reductive *topos* of industrialism, he invokes similar categories as Falter and other geomancers, just as he does when he promotes reviving indigenous myths as a spiritual alternative to both atheism and the "monotheistic religions, which often have a tendency to deny nature."[130] In England, ideas of a deified, animated nature and landscape (which includes ancient heritage sites) have motivated activism among English Pagans of all persuasions in recent years. For many of them, the protection of local landscape and remnants of the past has become an important facet of their religion.[131]

The examples show that neither environmental engagement nor its rejection within modern Asatru can be assigned to a specific political camp. We can, however, contend that spiritual environmentalism can cause troubling blind spots in the assessment of environmental measures within Paganism in general, and Asatru in particular.[132] Heathenism, as well as parts of the

---

127   Hallgren, *Det gröna skiftet*.
128   Ibid., 123.
129   Ibid., 233.
130   Ibid., 236: "ofta mer naturförnekande monoteistiska religioner." Cf. 223–236.
131   Cf. Blain and Wallis, *Sacred Sites – Contested Rites/Rights*; Blain, "Heathenry, the Past, and Sacred Sites in Today's Britain."
132   A case in point is Graham Harvey, who, as has been mentioned, now embraces bio-regional animism. In his discussion of Asatru, he mentions *Olgar Trust's* activities and the attempts at self-sufficiency pursued by *Hammarens Ordens Sällskap* (The Society of the Order of the Hammer) in one paragraph. What he completely fails to mention is that the groups have very different political goals: *Hammarens Ordens Sällskap* "considers multiculturalism and homosexuality to be the cause of confusion and problems, and seek an end to immigration since they believe that people's identity derives from the land," Jo Pearson, "Nature Religion," in *Encyclopedia of New Religious Movements*, ed. Peter B. Clarke (London/New York: Routledge, 2006), 393.

eco-spiritual movements that it relates to, perpetuates older ideas about a more 'natural' Germanic religion, also in its alleged opposition to Judeo-Christian or monotheist 'anti-natural' religion. At times, contradictory concepts of nature within these ideological traditions are overlooked, so that the 'blood' and 'soil' strands become conflated. This makes the varieties of nature spirituality that promote a return to 'indigenous' mythic traditions more vulnerable to racial thought. The example of Asatru as a nature religion is thus one prominent area in which Heathenism transposes residues of older *völkisch* ideas about Germanic myth and culture into our time, and often into quite varied political contexts. This is facilitated through the widespread use of the same terminology, in this case 'nature religion' or 'nature spirituality,' which spans a broad range of meanings, from the pure enjoyment of the outdoors or a well-reflected, spiritually based environmentalism, to ethno-pluralist bioregionalist ideas of separation and purification, or even to the celebration of the 'natural' superiority of the Indo-European or Germanic race.

CHAPTER 7

Gender and Sexuality

Together with deep ecology and bio-regionalism, eco-feminism is considered one of the strands of the ecology movement with the most prominent spiritual elements. Closely connected with feminist or women-centered varieties of Neopaganism, eco-feminism takes women's alleged proximity to nature and its cycles as its logical basis. The hope is that a spiritual approach of cooperation between (wo)man and nature will replace dominance and exploitation. Traditionally, alternative religions and spiritual movements, especially theosophy (which inspired many strands of Neopaganism), have provided opportunities for women to rise into influential positions. The opposite is the case for Germanic Faith in the early 20th century, as well as for contemporary Asatru. Whereas the former shared the outspoken masculinism of the *völkisch* movement and centered on warrior heroism, the latter, especially the North American Asatru revival in the 1970s, was initially borne out of an enthusiasm for the figure of the Viking, the male warrior, adventurer, and conqueror, and his war-gods Thor, Odin, and Tyr. Imagery of male physical power and violence still forms the external perception of Asatru and is reflected in the gender ratio of most groups, most commonly 60–70% men.[1] Nevertheless, women have been active in Germanic Neopaganism all along. By forging links to other, more women-centered varieties of earth and goddess spirituality and Neopaganism, such as Wicca, which puts an emphasis on female deities and priestesses, they have contributed to popular images of Asatru and its gods and goddesses.

As we have seen in the previous chapter, disillusionment with a destructive attitude toward the natural environment and human nature alike is a strong motivation to turn away from mainstream Christianity and search for alternative religious models. Women, femininity, corporeality, and sexuality have traditionally been equated with nature. Thus, another strong motive for the alienation from established religion is the desire to revalue these factors and search for arenas of equality, permission, and experimentation with regard to gender and sexuality in alternative spiritual movements. This search has been one of the driving forces in modern Western occultism and Neopaganism. Like ecologism, the related movements – feminism, libertarianism, and the queer movement – have a reputation for belonging to the political left. And just

---

1 *Bifrost* in Norway as well as the very small *Nornirs Ætt* in German and NTF in Denmark being significant exceptions with around 50% women amongst the members.

as with ecologism, this is one factor that has made women's spirituality and sexual experimentation an ambivalent issue for Germanic Neopaganism. Professing to spiritual equality between men and women, which allegedly is deeply rooted in the Germanic tradition, and to a freer attitude towards body and sexuality, helps Asatruers align themselves with accepted new social movements and thus gain respectability. At the same time, Asatru remains fairly conservative with regard to questions of gender, family, and sexuality, and tends to view forays into such alternative ideologies with great suspicion. But, as is the case with green spirituality, the picture is rather more complex than such ostensibly easy delineations may suggest. On the one hand, feminism, especially in its theological and spiritual varieties, has at times recalled conservative models of gender and sexuality, combining them with racist traditions. The same applies to parts of the queer movement today, just as it did for the sexual liberation and libertarian movements aligned with occultism around 1900.

Such ambivalences, and the significance of gendered images within Asatru and their partly contradictory nature, are reason enough to further investigate concepts of masculinity, femininity, and sexuality within Heathenism, as well as their transformations and alliances with other religious, social, and intellectual currents. Gender identity and sexualities have been contested fields in modernity, particularly in the new religious movements that appeared around 1900. In spite of its relative gender conservatism, Asatru has taken up a plethora of ideas from alternative movements on gender and sex, while forming conceptions of the 'Germanic,' which again entered into broader gender movements. It can therefore serve as a small and manageable field in which to study interdependencies between gender, sexuality, religion, race, ethnicity and nationality. It allows us to question the image of an absolutely masculinist or conservative family-oriented Heathenism and describe it as a field of tension between contradictory and competing concepts of gender and sexuality. Even more so, however, it will allow us to uncover some politically ambiguous strands within alternative movements and theories: feminism, the men's movement, and masculinity studies, as well as the queer movement and theory with their respective spiritual varieties.

The High Position of Germanic Women

The development of gender images within the early Germanic Faith Movement must be seen in the context of broader gender ideologies around 1900. The late 19th century's obsession with gender difference is well known and researched. It is an era in which gender complementarity, as well as an ideology of separate spheres and innate characteristics of men and women, were systematized in a joint effort of academic disciplines (among them biology, anthropology, cultural history) and dispersed through various media: the bourgeois novel, for example. This development reached both a climax and a crisis around 1900 and has been summarized in the famous 'war of the sexes' slogan. It is thus no surprise that the 'woman question' was also taken up by the *völkisch* movement. Since it was clearly male-dominated, it remained a discourse led "by men, amongst men, and predominantly for men. Women participated merely in the margins."[2] However, as we shall see, some of these women's core ideas would play a role in gender concepts of later Neopagan movements in Germany and beyond.

Two strands of thought became important for concepts of women and femininity within the *völkisch* religious movement. One was the idea of prehistoric matriarchies first presented by the Swiss classicist Johann Jacob Bachofen (1815–1887) in his seminal 1861 work, "*Das Mutterrecht*" ('Mother Right'). In suggesting that historical investigation be based on interpreting Greek and Roman myth, Bachofen joined contemporary attempts to find a science-based alternative to theological and biblical concepts of the origin of mankind. He concluded that pre-historic society had developed in three developmental stages: an original hetaric stage of promiscuity and chthonic chaos, which was briefly superseded by bands of warring amazons, to then be overcome by a gynaikocratic (i.e., women-dominated) phase. This first form of social order was eventually replaced by the superior 'father right,' which Bachofen saw as the final goal and zenith of human development. The concept was certainly not intended to be a nostalgic imagination of a better past by the outspokenly anti-liberal Bachofen. Rather, he saw it as proof of the superiority of a male, spiritual 'father right' over a social system bound to material nature, for which women supposedly stood.[3] Nevertheless, it contained a

---

2   "ein Diskurs von Männern, unter Männern und vornehmlich auch für Männer. Frauen nahmen daran nur am Rande teil." Uwe Puschner, "Völkische Diskurse zum Ideologem 'Frau,'" in *Völkische Bewegung – Konservative Revolution – Nationalsozialismus. Aspekte einer politisierten Kultur*, ed. Walter Schmitz and Clemens Vollnhals (Dresden: Thelem, 2005), 54. Nonetheless, Eva-Maria Ziege, *Mythische Kohärenz. Diskursanalyse des völkischen Antisemitismus* (Konstanz: UVK, 2002), 216–221, mentions contributions by women activists as well, who (seeing themselves as the guarantors for the preservation of the German or Nordic race) were particularly engaged in the areas of racial hygiene and eugenics.

3   For a discussion of Bachofen's idea cf. Beate Wagner-Hasel, *Matriarchatstheorien der Altertumswissenschaft*, Wege der Forschung (Darmstadt: Wissenschaftliche Buchgesellschaft, 1992); Claudia Bruns, *Politik des Eros. Der Männerbund in Wissenschaft, Politik und Jugendkultur (1880–1934)* (Cologne: Böhlau, 2008), 53–74; Brigitte Röder, Juliane Hummel, and

certain ambiguity, as it implicitly questioned the universality of static gender concepts. The linear-evolutionary model of history favored by Bachofen competed subliminally with a cyclical model of a permanent war of the sexes.[4] Together with anthropologists of his era, Bachofen's work thus questioned the function of family and reproduction and the nature of social and political structures in general.[5] This again allowed for its enthusiastic reception by conservative anti-feminists as well as socialist thinkers. Among the latter were Friedrich Engels and Paul Lafargue (Karl Marx' son-in-law), who imagined ancient classless and future socialist societies as matriarchal structures.[6] It was mainly this strand of reception that anchored the theory of matriarchy read as a social utopia in a broader public imagination.[7]

While Bachofen and the aforementioned socialist thinkers saw the shift from matriarchy to patriarchy as a universal evolutionary process, and thus a drive for social change, for better or worse, others perceived matriarchal and patriarchal social structures as characteristics of certain peoples, races, or cultures. They explained the expansion of patriarchy as the result of migrations and conquest.[8] This diffusionist model enabled racial readings of theories of matriarchy for which Bachofen's descriptions of the chthonic, oriental nature of gynaikocratic societies had already laid the groundwork. Depending on whether matriarchal systems were viewed as a welcome alternative to modernity or as a despicable sign of its degeneration, they were racialized in different ways. For representatives of the former, among them Ludwig Klages, matriarchy appeared as the basis of the ancient religion of the Aryans or Europeans, which was violently repressed by a despotic, monotheist father-god of Jewish origin.[9] For others, for example National-Socialist philosopher Alfred Bäumler, matriarchies appeared as Jewish-oriental systems curbed by

---

    Brigitta Kunz, *Göttinnendämmerung. Das Matriarchat aus archäologischer Sicht* (Munich: Droemer Knaur, 1996).

4 Bruns, *Politik des Eros*, 67.

5 Cf. ibid., 60; Röder, Hummel, and Kunz, *Göttinnendämmerung*, 30 f.

6 An elaborate discussion on the ambivalence of Bachofen's theories for concepts of gender and family in the 19th century can be found in Walter Erhart, *Familienmänner. Über den literarischen Ursprung moderner Männlichkeit* (Munich: Wilhelm Fink Verlag, 2001), 70–91.

7 Ziege, *Mythische Kohärenz*, 203.

8 Cf. Wagner-Hasel, *Matriarchatstheorien der Altertumswissenschaft*, 310–312, Peter Davies, "'Männerbund' and 'Mutterrecht.' Herman Wirth, Sophie Rogge-Börner and the *Ura-Linda-Chronik*," *German Life and Letters* 60, no. 1 (2007), 99.

9 Cf. Richard Faber, *Männerrunde mit Gräfin. Die 'Kosmiker' Derleth, George, Klages, Schuler, Wolfskehl und Franziska zu Reventlow. Mit einem Nachdruck des 'Schwabinger Beobachters'* (Frankfurt A.M.: Peter Lang, 1994), 51–84; Ziege, *Mythische Kohärenz*, 208.

the heroic Indo-Germanic warrior societies – a development that he saw repeated in the downfall of the 'mother right' which ruled the Weimar Republic and the rise of heroic Germanic National Socialists.[10]

The other strand was based on the assumption derived from Tacitus, and popularized by Jacob Grimm: that women enjoyed a particularly high position within Germanic societies, especially as priestesses and seeresses.[11] This idealizing image has not found much support in recent scholarship,[12] but it elicited considerable enthusiasm among 19th and 20th century scholars and Germanophiles who recognized their own ideal of the natural, primordial woman in it.[13] Jacob Grimm identified the women who were persecuted as witches in early modernity as the last representatives of these pre-Christian wise women. He thus provided another topos eagerly received and elaborated on by anti-Christian *völkisch* scholars and agitators, for whom the persecuted Germanic woman appeared as the ultimate victim of a violent, male racial Other.[14]

These two strands could be connected through the shared image of the natural, primordial woman and her male "Judeo-Christian" enemy – a constellation which at times culminated in the idea of Germanic women being persecuted and subjugated by Semitic men unable to curb their innate violent sexual drives, with those women being finally rescued by Aryan heroes. Obviously, the German Faith Movement could not avoid engaging with these questions. Ariosophy oscillated between two positions: Jörg Lanz von Liebenfels' violent anti-feminism, which saw women's inclination toward men of lower races as the main reason for the racial degeneration of the Aryans, consequently demanding their strict control; and Guido von List's idea of a Germanic order of maidens, a caste of priestesses. List adopted the idea of the high social position of Germanic women, stylizing their "inward unerring feeling for nature" as the basis for women's priesthood, which was to guarantee the preservation of the pure Aryan race. For him, witches thus appeared as the last

---

10   Cf. *Mythische Kohärenz*, 209. Regarding Bäumler, it is interesting to note that he started out as a supporter of Bachofen's 'mother right,' which for him appeared as the religion of the mother giving birth to the divine son.
11   Cf. Julia Zernack, "'Germanin im Hauskleid.' Bemerkungen zu einem Frauenideal deutscher Gelehrter," in *Kybele – Prophetin – Hexe. Religiöse Frauenbilder und Weiblichkeitskonzeptionen*, ed. Richard Faber and Susanne Lanwerd (Würzburg: Königshausen & Neumann, 1997), 214–224.
12   Cf. Reinhold Bruder, *Die germanische Frau im Lichte der Runeninschriften und der antiken Historiographie* (Berlin: de Gruyter, 1974).
13   Cf. Zernack, "'Germanin im Hauskleid,'" 224.
14   Cf. Felix Wiedemann, *Rassenmutter und Rebellin. Hexenbilder in Romantik, völkischer Bewegung, Neuheidentum und Feminismus* (Würzburg: Königshausen & Neumann, 2007).

representatives of these orders of race priestesses, bearers of a sex-magic fertility religion of racial breeding.[15]

The most pronounced *völkisch* reception of theories of matriarchy can be found in the work of the Dutch-born philologist, historian and musicologist Herman Wirth (1885–1981). His *Aufgang der Menschheit* (Rise of Mankind,[16] 1928) offered a grand imagination of an ancient Stone Age culture located in the area of today's arctic. This original anti-materialist, spiritual culture, from which all the world's cultural achievements were derived, was borne by the Arctic-Nordic or Atlantic race. Crucial for Wirth is the assumption that women and mothers played a central role in this Aryan high religion of an All-Mother Earth led by priestesses. A closer look at Wirth's theories reveals nevertheless that his ultimate interest is a "mythic redemption of masculinity,"[17] where the figure of the mother is merely considered the venerated source of origin; the eternal womb from which God the Father's son is created and to which he returns in an eternal cycle of birth, death, and rebirth. Wirth's phantasms of a matriarchal Aryan civilization found little support among Germanists and within the German Faith Movement.[18] However, as we shall see shortly, he gained recognition after World War II as the guru of an incipient Neopagan matriarchy in the 1980s.

---

15   Cf. List, *The Secret of the Runes*, 97f; more references can be found in Stefanie v. Schnurbein, "Weiblichkeitskonzeptionen im neugermanischen Heidentum und in der feministischen Spiritualität," in *Das neue Heidentum. Rückkehr zu den alten Göttern oder neue Heilsbotschaft?* ed. Otto Bischofberger (Freiburg (CH): Paulus Verlag, 1996), 48 and 67 f. See also Puschner, "Völkische Diskurse zum Ideologem 'Frau,'" 57; Wiedemann, *Rassenmutter und Rebellin*, 144. The close collaboration between the two Ariosophists points to the fact that they obviously did not see such differences as a grave cause for controversy.

16   The title is formulated as a programmatic alternative to Oswald Spengler's cultural pessimist *Decline of the West*.

17   Davies, "'Männerbund' and 'Mutterrecht,'" 107. Cf. ibid.; Herman Wirth, *Der Aufgang der Menschheit* (Jena: Diederichs, 1928), 16–23; Ingo Wiwjorra, "In Erwartung der 'Heiligen Wende.' Herman Wirth im Kontext der völkischen Bewegung," in *Utopien, Zukunftsvorstellungen, Gedankenexperimente. Literarische Konzepte von einer 'anderen' Welt im abendländischen Denken von der Antike bis zur Gegenwart*, ed. Klaus Geus (Frankfurt A.M.: Peter Lang, 2011); and Ziege, *Mythische Kohärenz*, 213. The emphasis on the birth of the divine son resembles Alfred Bäumler's early theories. According to Stefan Breuer, a similar ideological constellation can be found in the theories of Conservative Revolutionaries in general. Celebrating a masculinist, warrior heroism, they imagined the potential for a rebirth or regeneration of the nation in a "maternal soil, a pre- and super-individual unity of the feminine coded stream of life." Breuer, *Anatomie der konservativen Revolution*, 80.

18   Wirth's significance for academic thought will be discussed in Chapter 8.

The opposite is the case for another variety of the topos of an allegedly high social position of Germanic women. The idea that these women were both the equals of heroic men and mothers of heroes became popular in German research on saga literature from the early 20th century on. Arthur Bonus, the proponent of a 'Germanization of Christianity,' seems to have been the first to propose the idea that it is not the legal position of women (which appears as rather dismal in medieval Icelandic legal sources), but rather her high moral position which guaranteed equality of the sexes in Germanic history.[19] Germanist Bernhard Kummer in particular rejected Wirth's view of a mother earth cult as a construct with Semitic tendencies, postulating that Germanic society constituted neither a matriarchy nor a patriarchy. Downplaying gender difference and emphasizing racial difference, Kummer saw Germanic society as an agrarian idyll in which both men and women 'tilled the native soil' and defended it as 'heroes,' 'heroines,' and 'mothers of heroes,' thus securing the future of the pure Germanic race. This idealized old Germanic society served, for him, as proof that "mothers are most venerated, marriages bear most children and are most healthy, where the sexes stand in equal faith and equal morals before their gods and goddesses."[20] It furthermore seems significant that this ideal of "comradeship and equality"[21] was distinguished by a lack of eroticism and a 'natural' sense of chastity, values seen as the positive antitheses to French, Roman, and Jewish promiscuity and eroticism.[22]

In spite of these contradictory approaches, List, Wirth, and the saga researchers share a number of basic positions: First, the general idea of a veneration of women, who occupy a high social and religious position in Germanic societies. Second, the idea of men and women sharing values, but being responsible for separate, complementary spheres – an expression of the widespread ideas on gender complementarity of the era. Third, their agreement on the respective gender system's main purpose – the continuation of the Germanic or Nordic race. And finally, their vehement anti-Christian and

---

19 Zernack, "'Germanin im Hauskleid,'" 217 f.
20 Bernhard Kummer, *Die weibliche Gottheit bei den Germanen* (Leipzig: Adolf Klein, 1933), 32: "dort [sind] die Mütter am höchsten geehrt, dort die Ehen am kinderreichsten und gesündesten, wo die Geschlechter im gleichen Glauben und gleicher Sitte vor ihren Göttern und Göttinnen stehen."
21 "Die Bedeutung des altnordischen Schrifttums für Religionsgeschichte und Missionskunde," *Zeitschrift für Missionskunde und Religionswissenschaft* 43, no. 10, 11 (1928), 297
22 Cf. the more elaborate discussion in Zernack, "'Germanin im Hauskleid,'" 223–225.

anti-Jewish affect, which blamed Christianity for having destroyed this idealized system of gender harmony and racial purity.[23]

In Chapter 6, I argued that nature religion in contemporary Asatru has to be understood as an idiosyncratic blend of German Faith concepts of an immanent Germanic religion with general Neopagan and eco-spiritual ideas. There is a similar operation at play in the conceptions of gender and sexuality within modern Asatru. They have also been informed by more recent spiritual movements, not least spiritual feminist scholarship on matriarchies, as well as witchcraft and goddess worship, which all emerged as parts of second-wave feminism during the 1970s and 80s. The motives of feminists who turned their beliefs to ancient matriarchies, with their supposed worship of a great earth goddess or several female deities, are certainly quite different from the motives of the Germanic revival. However, the two movements share the desire to create a historical myth, an invented past in which a positive vision for the future can be anchored. And, as we shall see, the difference in motives does not immunize feminist spirituality against an echoing of Germanophile ideas.

Feminists of the 1970s began to look at theories of ancient matriarchies and their overthrow by patriarchal structures in order to find both "an adequate

---

[23] Julia Zernack and others have shown that the main motivation for the emergence of this idealized image of Germanic women seems to have been to prove the moral superiority of Germanic culture and religion over Christianity. Thus, the contradictory sources had to be interpreted in a selective way. The main problem which saga researchers in particular were faced with was the fact that legal documents from the Christian era showed a slight increase of women's rights to consent in marriage as well as self-determination in legal matters compared to earlier laws from pre-Christian times. At the same time, the literary descriptions of women in some of the Icelandic sagas indeed show an astonishing number of self-reliant, active women characters. Instead of reading these literary accounts as either literary topoi or projections of contemporary attitudes into the past, Gustav Neckel, for example, ignored such contradictions and insisted on reading the legal sources as normative documents, which had little to do with the actual conditions and practices that in his eyes had persisted from Tacitus' times well into the Middle Ages, until Christianity destroyed this system, Gustav Neckel, *Liebe und Ehe bei den vorchristlichen Germanen* (Leipzig: Teubner, 1932). For refutations of the myth of a better position of Germanic women before the advent of Christianity see e.g. Jenny Jochens, "Consent in Marriage. Old Norse Law, Life, and Literature," *Scandinavian Studies* 58 (1968), Rolf Heller, *Die literarische Darstellung der Frau in den Isländersagas* (Halle: Niemeyer, 1958), Judith Jesch, *Women in the Viking Age* (Woodbridge: Boydell Press, 1991), as well as Zernack, "'Germanin im Hauskleid,'" 222 f. For a discussion of theories of continuity and their employment within Germanic Neopaganism see Chapter 8.

explanation for the existence and persistence of male dominance,"[24] as well as a model of orientation for the creation of a better future, "a time of peace, ecological balance, and harmony between the sexes, with women either recovering their past ascendancy, or at last establishing a truly egalitarian society under the aegis of the goddess."[25] The feminist spirituality movement combined the idea of matriarchies with both the belief in a great goddess, who had supposedly been worshipped in pre-Christian times, and the belief in a version of modern witchcraft, which saw women as the guardians of such ancient cults due to women's supposed proximity to nature and its magic. Already during the re-emergence of such beliefs in the 1970s and 80s, these ideas had been widely dismissed by classicists and archaeologists.[26] Moreover, they were criticized for reproducing stereotypical 19th-century gender concepts, the purpose of which had been to stabilize their own era's ideology of gender complementarity. Nonetheless, the old idea of women's proximity to nature and materiality was embraced and revaluated as a positive (and eco-friendly) quality, a sign of superiority rather than inferiority. The same was true for women's alleged magical skills and irrationality. Critics rejected such concepts as a biologistic recurrence of a dangerous (menstrual) blood and earth mysticism.[27]

For our context, it seems important that notions of race and culture implicit in older theories were partially transferred to more recent feminist contexts. Many goddess worshippers and matriarchy theorists worked on the assumption that Judaism and its monotheistic successors had overthrown the original matriarchies and thus 'murdered the goddess' – a new variety of the old

---

24 Cynthia Eller, "Relativizing the Patriarchy. The Sacred History of the Feminist Spirituality Movement," *History of Religions* 30, no. 1 (1990), 281.

25 *The Myth of Matriarchal Prehistory. Why an Invented Past Won't Give Women a Future* (Boston: Beacon Press, 2000), 3.

26 For comprehensive summaries of such refutations from feminist perspectives see for example Wagner-Hasel, *Matriarchatstheorien der Altertumswissenschaft*; Eller, *The Myth of Matriarchal Prehistory*.

27 Cf. Schnurbein, "Neuheidnische Religionsentwürfe von Frauen"; Susanne Lanwerd, "Zur Bedeutung von 'Feministischer Spiritualität' in der Literatur des New Age," in *Die Religion von Oberschichten. Religion – Profession – Intellektualismus*, ed. Peter Antes and Donate Pahnke (Marburg: diagonal-Verlag, 1989); "Im Namen der Göttin? Überlegungen zur Faszinationskraft antiker Göttinnenbilder," in *Kybele – Prophetin – Hexe. Religiöse Frauenbilder und Weiblichkeitskonzeptionen*, ed. Richard Faber and Susanne Lanwerd (Würzburg: Königshausen & Neumann, 1997), Kerstin Lück, "Der Wunsch nach Verzauberung. Religionswissenschaftliche Überlegungen zur 'spirituellen Frauenbewegung,'" in *Kybele – Prophetin – Hexe. Religiöse Frauenbilder und Weiblichkeitskonzeptionen*, ed. Richard Faber and Susanne Lanwerd (Würzburg: Königshausen & Neumann, 1997).

Christian anti-Jewish stereotype of the Jews as 'god killers' with roots both in the small *völkisch* women's movement[28] as well as in the Socialist psychoanalyst and matriarchy theorist Otto Groß' ideas.[29] Anti-Jewish and racist ideas entered feminist spirituality through an uncritical adoption of ethnicist diffusionist theories of matriarchy as well. In her 1971 classic of feminist spirituality, *The First Sex*, American librarian Elizabeth Gould Davis drew on the theories of Bachofen and promoters of a Northern or Atlantic origin of culture to prove that a "blue-eyed, golden- or red-haired race of people"[30] originating in a "subarctic locale,"[31] whose last survivors she imagined to be the Celts, had spread matriarchal civilization across the world. This ancient "non-Aryan," "non-Semitic" race of unknown origin[32] was later overthrown by the "mammoths of masculinism – Teutonic barbarism and Semitic Christianity."[33]

This somewhat idiosyncratic combination of feminist anti-Indo-European and anti-Semitic theory relies on the work of Lithuanian archaeologist and Indo-Europeanist Marija Gimbutas (1921–94). From the 1950s on, Gimbutas combined Indo-European scholarship and theories of matriarchy to suggest that the peaceful matriarchal systems of "Old Europe" had been overrun by patriarchal Indo-European horsemen from the steppes north of the Caucasus, a culture she called 'Kurgan.'[34] Both traditional and feminist archaeologists tended to regard her theory as methodologically flawed, and as an unsupportable projection of current political values into a pre-historical past.[35] As she lost support within her academic field, from the 1980s on Gimbutas increasingly directed her work to an inexpert general public, "remodel[ing] the image

---

28 The idea of a Jewish origin of patriarchy, that "the Jewish man robbed woman of priesthood," existed already within the small *völkisch* women's movement in the early 20th century. Cf. Zlege, *Mythische Kohärenz*, 185–190, quote p. 188.
29 Cf. Faber, *Männerrunde mit Gräfin*, 42–50.
30 Elizabeth Gould Davis, *The First Sex* (New York: Putnam, 1971), 25 f.
31 Ibid., 22.
32 Ibid., 26.
33 Ibid., 207.
34 Cf. Lynne Meskell, "Goddesses, Gimbutas and 'New Age' Archaeology," *Antiquity* 69 (1995), Ronald Hutton, "The Neolithic Great Goddess. A Study in Modern Tradition," *Antiquity* 71 (1997), Arvidsson, *Aryan Idols*, 288–293.
35 As many of her critics have pointed out, her perception of violent Eastern hordes overrunning a peaceful Old Europe may well have been a reflection of her own experience of the Baltic States' occupation, first by the Germans, and then the Soviets. See e.g, Meskell, "Goddesses, Gimbutas and 'New Age' Archaeology," 78f; Stefan Arvidsson, *Ariska Idoler. Den indoeuropeiska mytologin som ideologi och vetenskap* (Stockholm/Stehag: Brutus Östlings Bokförlag Symposion, 2000), 291.

of [the great goddess] to conform with evolving feminist opinion."[36] Employing a "language of revelation,"[37] she ended her life as the "avatar of a rediscovered religion."[38] It is worth mentioning that Gimbutas also injected an anti-Jewish notion into her theories by claiming the genetic and cultural relatedness of Indo-Europeans and Semites (hence the idea of a "Teutonic-Semitic patriarchy"). It should therefore not come as a surprise that in the context of German feminist and eco-feminist spirituality, the work of Herman Wirth was also enthusiastically received.[39]

Ideas of matriarchy have always had a tense relationship to German Faith and Asatru, both because of their potential disruption of traditional gender orders, and more recently because of the monotheistic framework in which the cult of the 'one great goddess' operates. Nevertheless, there have been interactions, not only through the adoption of Germanic Neopagan ideas into feminist spirituality, but also vice versa. In the 1980s, this tendency was most pronounced in German Asatru. Sigrun von Schlichting, from the racial-religious *Armanen-Orden*, in particular based her renewal of Ariosophic doctrine on Herman Wirth's theories. She emphasized the significance of the Norse goddesses, to whom she assigned the areas of fertility, birth, and growth, as well as healing, family, and kin, reiterating the idea of Germanic woman being the preserver and guardian of a "pure Germanic race."[40]

Notions of an ideal gender balance in Heathenism were also promoted by other Asatru groups. For the *Heidnische Gemeinschaft*, the persecution of the witches, the "wise Germanic women," provided a welcome opportunity to formulate their radical anti-clericalism.[41] Adoptions of elements from Wicca and feminist spirituality became fairly frequent in other varieties of international Asatru as well. An influential figure has been Diana Paxson, long-term active member of *The Troth* in the USA, who also worked as an officer in the *Covenant of the Goddess* and founded the *Fellowship of the Spiral Path*

---

36 Hutton, "The Neolithic Great Goddess," 97.
37 Ibid., 89.
38 Ibid., 89.
39 Cf. Schnurbein, "Weiblichkeitskonzeptionen im neugermanischen Heidentum und in der feministischen Spiritualität," 62.
40 Cf. ibid., 50 f.
41 In the flyer "Hexen – weise Frauen" (Witches, wise women), the editor of the journal *Runenstein* propagated the practice of "our heathen religion" as an antidote to the "hatred of perverse, unnatural clerics against everything female." (Haß widernatürlich lebender Kleriker gegen alles Weibliche). Cf. http://www.runenstein-net.de/hexen.htm, last accessed August 25, 2014.

(a pan-Pagan association in California promoting different versions of reconstructed European Paganism, together with Earth and goddess spirituality).[42] Through her collaboration with feminist witch Zsuzsanna Budapest[43] and her sister-in-law Marion Zimmer Bradley,[44] Paxson's views on Paganism, women's rituals, and spirituality have exerted significant influence on the general perception of Asatru.

Consequently, adoptions of individual elements of women-centered spirituality can be found in most Asatru groups today. They are generally accepted as valid parts of Germanic spirituality, as long as they do not display their debts to Wicca too overtly. There is an almost unanimous, although rather vaguely formulated consensus that women indeed held a high social position in Nordic societies, that the influence of Christianity is to blame for that high regard's demise,[45] and that contemporary Western societies' principles of equality and justice are to be attributed to the survival of such Heathen traditions.[46] The reasons why these opinions are so rarely questioned within Asatru must be sought in the fact that they are also so widespread in other milieus, for example, in the spiritual women's movement or in eco-spirituality, and that they have found their way into idealizing (self-)perceptions of the Scandinavian countries. They have become part of a Scandinavian exceptionalism, according the North a particular tradition of equality and justice. It is thus easy to reconfigure the older stereotype of the high position of women in the pre-Christian North as a means of granting this modern exceptionalism a deep historical basis.[47] In his popular account of Scandinavian mythology, Lars Magnar Enoksen, a

---

42 Cf. http://www.thespiralpath.org/, last accessed August 25, 2014.

43 Cf. Zsuzsanna Budapest and Diana L. Paxson, *The Celestial Guide to Every Year of Your Life. Discover the Hidden Meaning of Your Age* (Newburyport, MA: Red Wheel/Weiser, 2003).

44 Paxson provided information about Pagan women's rituals (cf. Marion Zimmer Bradley, *The Mists of Avalon* (New York: Knopf, 1983), Acknowledgements) to Bradley's *The Mists of Avalon* and co-authored and later authored the sequels of the series.

45 Examples could be found in almost all the groups discussed here and in most of their publications, cf. for example Jennings, *The Norse Tradition*, 18; GardenStone, "Gleichberechtigung und Asatru," *Herdfeuer. Die Zeitschrift des Eldaring e.V.* 6, no. 20 (2008), 25.

46 Cf. Jennings, *The Norse Tradition*, 18.

47 For discussions of Nordic exceptionalism and its "regimes of goodness" see Christopher S Browning, "Branding Nordicity. Models, Identity and the Decline of Exceptionalism," *Cooperation and Conflict* 1 (2007); Lasse Koefoed and Kirsten Simonsen, "The Price of Goodness. Everyday Nationalist Narratives in Denmark," *Antipode* 2 (2007); Katarina Schough, *Hyperboré. Föreställningen om Sveriges plats i världen* (Stockholm: Carlsson Bokförlag, 2008); Mai Palmberg, "The Nordic Colonial Mind," in *Complying with Colonialism. Gender, Race and Ethnicity in the Nordic Region*, ed. Suvi Keskinen, et al. (Farnham/Burlington, VT: Ashgate, 2009); Nina Witoszek, *The Origins of the 'Regime of Goodness.' Remapping the Cultural History of Norway* (Oslo: Universitetsforlaget, 2011);

self-taught rune specialist and enthusiast of the Nordic pre-Christian Middle Ages, summarizes the images of women and gender which lie behind the idea that political ideals of equality and justice originate in Norse religion:

> But if we turn our gaze to the Scandinavian mainland, the biggest difference in relation to the rest of the world is that women's position here is stronger than any other place in public life. This fact has ancient ancestors and is something foreign religions of dominance have never been able to crush, in spite of persistent attempts throughout the centuries. In Pagan society, woman was equal with man on all levels, and in some areas, woman stood stronger than man. [...] Myth is always a direct reflection of the society it lives in, and the goddesses' unrestricted position and superiority in numbers can be seen as a mirror image of the social culture which gave rise to Norse mythology. Although woman's position in today's North is better than in many other countries and cultures, it is not as strong as it was in Pagan times.[48]

In this quote, we can find all the methodologically and historically problematic assumptions that had already vexed Germanophile scholarship in the 1930s and earlier, as well as feminist spirituality later on: The questionable idea that myth mirrors social structures, a lack of source criticism, unsupportable theories of continuity between pre-historic past and present society, not to mention the unfounded claims about the superiority of goddesses in the Norse pantheon.[49] It is also an example of how modern feminist ideas can be integrated into Asatru.

It thus makes sense that elements of 1930s scholarship, for example the bourgeois scholarly fantasies about Germanic women and their allegedly equal

---

Ebbe Volquardsen, *Die Anfänge des grönländischen Romans. Nation, Identität und subalterne Artikulation in einer arktischen Kolonie* (Marburg: Tectum, 2011), 37–43.

48 Lars Magnar Enoksen, *Norrøne guder og myter*, trans. Kåre A. Lie (Oslo: Schibsted Forlag, 2008), 211: "Men om vi vender blikket mot det skandinaviske fastlandet, er den største forskjellen i forhold til den øvrige verden at kvinnens stilling er sterkere her enn noe annet sted i det offentlige livet. Dette faktum har urgamle aner og er noe som utenlandske herskerreligioner aldri har klart å knuse, til tross for iherdige forsøk gjennom århundrene. I det hedenske samfunnet var kvinnen likestilt med mannen på alle plan, og på noen områder sto kvinnen sterkere enn mannen. [...] Myten er alltid en direkte gjenspeiling av det samfunnet den lever i, og gudinnenes uinnskrenkede stilling og overlegenhet i antall kan ses som et speilbilde av den samfunnskulturen som ga opphav til den norrøne gudelæren. Til tross for at kvinnens stilling i dagens Norden er bedre enn i mange andre land og kulturer, er den likevel ikke like sterk som den var i hedensk tid."

49 Such widespread methodological flaws are discussed in Chapter 8.

position in marriage and custom developed by writers such as Gustav Neckel and Bernhard Kummer, re-emerge in Asatru contexts. A case in point is the eighty-page discussion of Germanic conceptions of marriage and the legal position of women by *Eldaring* member Christian Brüning, published in *Heidnisches Jahrbuch*.[50] The author brazenly ignores all post-1945 scholarship demonstrating how the legal position of women improved with the arrival of Christianity. He points instead to the works of Neckel and Kummer and their thesis of morals (*Sitte*) predominating over legal texts. Matthias Wenger, another German Asatruer, started out as a supporter of the racial-religious *Armanenorden*, but then adopted an outspoken a-racist stance in the 1990s.[51] Nevertheless, he remains equally faithful to the ideas of both Bernhard Kummer and Herman Wirth, while omitting their affiliation to racist thought and National Socialism.[52] Herman Wirth's theories on Germanic matriarchies have made their way into American Asatru contexts as well. The *"Ura-Linda-Chronik,"* or *Oera Linda Book* as it is called in English, an allegedly ancient history of a Frisian family, which was uncovered as a forgery early on, and which Wirth used to support for his own ideas,[53] appears on several American Asatru sites.[54] Theories of a Germanic or pre-Indo-European matriarchy, on the other hand, have decreased in significance within contemporary Asatru. There are, however, exceptions on all sides of the spectrum. German Asatru author GardenStone, for example, supports the idea that Europe was ruled by

---

50 Christian Brüning, "Das Eheverständnis der Germanen und die rechtliche Stellung der Frau," *Heidnisches Jahrbuch* 3 (2008).

51 Matthias Wenger, "Meine politische Position und ihre Entwicklung in 30 Jahren – eine Dokumentation," Der HAIN – Das Magazin für natürliche Religion und gesellschaftliche Wandlung, http://www.derhain.de/, last accessed December 04, 2011.

52 Cf. Matthias Wenger, "Patriarchalische Ideologie oder matriarchalisches Wertsystem. Die Auseinandersetzung um Herman Wirth und die Ura-Linda-Chronik," Der HAIN – Das Magazin für natürliche Religion und gesellschaftliche Wandlung, http://www.derhain.de/WirthMatriarchat.htm, last accessed May 29, 2015, cf. also Chapter 8 regarding Wenger's reception of Wirth and Kummer.

53 Cf. Hunger, *Die Runenkunde im Dritten Reich*, 181; Davies, "'Männerbund' and 'Mutterrecht.'" Cf. also Chapter 8.

54 According to a Pagan Wiki, it "has been influential in the development of modern Paganism, and Odinism and Asatru in particular." http://pagan.wikia.com/wiki/Oera_Linda_Book, last accessed August 25, 2014. The page does not offer any evidence for this claim. However, on the eclectic homepage of the Alternative Religions Educational Network (AREN), the Asatru section lists links to the Oera Linda Book (http://www.aren.org/prison/documents/Asatru.htm). Prudence Priest, former member of the AFA, the *Ring of Troth*, and current head of *Yggdrasil*, refers to it as an important source in interviews. Cf. SilverWitch, "Just 'Wiccatru' Folk."

matriarchies until around 2200 BC, but warns against idealizing them, rejecting the thesis that women-centered societies, with their 'passionate,' 'emotional,' and possibly more fearsome Amazons, were more peaceful.[55] In contrast, Danish Starkad Storm, in his vicious attacks on monotheism's "enmity towards nature and life" discussed in Chapter 5, idealizes woman as the "life-giving and (most) natural" human, claiming: "In polytheistic and primordial cultures, woman was honored, respected and outright venerated as bearer of the sacred life – not to speak of regular matriarchies." In a manner that is fully compatible with Ariosophic, *völkisch* and biology-based feminist spirituality, he continues: "It has been decisive for world-negating monotheism to portray woman as bad and sinful, as she is the (most) sexual being, and due to menstruation as the physical expression of the lifecycle." Not surprisingly, his conclusion is anti-Islamist, as are his other invectives: "In the Muslim world, abuse of women is in some cases the duty of orthodoxes and is enforced fanatically."[56]

One effect of the consensus of a high religious position of Germanic woman is the equally widespread, unquestioned opinion that women can and should hold leading positions within Asatru groups and function as leaders of rituals.[57] At the same time, the alleged equality of the sexes in Asatru is very rarely based on an idea of equality. Most Asatruers assume natural differences between men and women, assign them separate areas of expertise and ability, and defend complementary gender relationships. This widespread attitude is mirrored in many descriptions of marriage and coming of age rituals. The Asatru manual *Our Troth* emphasizes the equality of the sexes in order to describe different rituals for 'man-making' and 'woman-making' that are based on assumptions of the different physical features of men and women. The chapter on woman-making concludes:

---

55 GardenStone, "Gleichberechtigung und Asatru," 23 f.
56 Stensgaard, "Om Monoteismens Uvæsen 2," 21: "Kvinden har i de polyteistiske og oprindelige kulturer været æret, respekteret og ligefrem tilbedt som bærer af det hellige liv – for ikke at tale om regulære matriarkater." "Som det (mest) seksuelle væsen og i kraft af menstruationen det kødelige udtryk for livscyklus, har det været afgørende for den verdensforsagende monoteisme at gøre kvinden ond og syndig." "I den muslimske verden er kvindemishandling i vise tilfælde de rettroendes pligt, som vogtes nidkært."
57 The only exception I have found is Theodism. Garman Lord agrees with Asatruers that "women are always understood to have the same natural rights as men have" and acknowledges the possibility that women can hold leading positions. Nevertheless, he considers it uncommon and problematic, because it is man who is "always theoretically an arms-bearer, and inherent in manhood is the principle of the potential use of force as an instrument as policy." Lord, *The Way of the Heathen*, 61.

It will be noticed that the woman-making seems less traumatic than the man-making, with less emphasis on the sharp change of status, the death and rebirth elements, and so forth. This is because all of these things are already going on inside the woman's body. Whereas the man-making is a single intense spiritual/social change, the woman-making is put forth as a somewhat slower and gentler spiritual/social change designed to integrate the single intense physical event which transforms a girl into a woman.[58]

The fact that one of the first acts of the newly initiated woman is to present the drinking horn to the men who re-enter the ritual space indicates that woman's role is also seen here in a fairly traditional way: as the symbolic nourisher of men and keeper of the house.

In his suggestion for a celebration of majority in the ethnicist German *VfgH*, Fritz Steinbock makes a similar argument. While he recommends identical ceremonies for both sexes, he suggests a different closure where a distinction is made between men's and women's realms: The father is supposed to speak a prayer for the young man, invoking male deities and emphasizing male tasks, such as providing for and protecting the family. The mother's prayer for the young woman is directed at female deities and invokes woman's role as lady of the house, wife, and mother, focused on home, kin, fertility, and healing.[59]

Danish Asatruer Viktoria Gotved discusses what it means that women receive a key in the wedding ceremony:

> This does not suggest that women should return to the meat pots, but it does entail an acknowledgment that the sexes are different and each have their strengths and weaknesses. How one then chooses to distribute labor in everyday life is everybody's own affair.[60]

The emphasizing of traditional gender differences, while simultaneously relegating alternative models to the private realm, is widespread in Asatru. It can be understood as a strategy to counter the undeniable fact that Asatru is still strongly dominated by men, with regard to both membership and leadership.

---

58   Gundarsson, *Our Troth*, vol. II, 263.
59   Steinbock, *Das heilige Fest*, 153.
60   Gotved, *Asatro. De gamle guder i moderne tid*, 68: "Det ligger ikke i dette, at kvinderne skal tilbage til kødgryderne, men dog en anerkendelse af, at kønnene er forskellige og hver har sine stærke og svage sider. Hvordan hver især vælger at fordele arbejdet i hverdagen, er deres egen sag."

An equal gender ratio can only be found in a-racist groups that strongly deemphasize natural differences between the sexes, such as the Norwegian *Bifrost*, the very small German *Nornirs Ætt*, and the Danish NTF. This points to the fact that the traditional gender concepts found within Asatru are not overly attractive for women, especially when one considers that women have a stronger presence in many other religious contexts, be they alternative, Christian, or Jewish.

Masculinity and *Männerbund*

The idea that natural differences between men and women are encoded in Norse myth or "Heathen mysteries,"[61] and that each sex can and should exercise their own modes of spirituality and ritual, has led to an interest in specifically male forms of Heathen religious practices. A programmatic example is found in the last chapter of Björn Ulbrich's 1990 book, "Cult and Rite of the Heathen Community."[62] Ulbrich, the founder of the German *Arun* publishing house,[63] ends his book with a chapter on women's moon rituals and men's male bonding and blood-brotherhood rituals. He ascribes these different modes of spirituality to physiological features and their alleged spiritual equivalents – an association which reverberates in many Asatru contexts today. He writes:

> We sense the nature of the moon only vaguely within us, and men seem to be less able to resonate with it than women. [...] The sun-cult is considered a manifestation of a masculine-influenced sun veneration, because it is in need of an intellectual spirituality in order to become institutionalized. [...] The gently hazy, but all the more sustainable, character of this [the moon's] planetarian energy finds its ideal complement and fulfillment of its nature in the female body. Female rites of consecration and initiation thus concentrate the mind on the cycle of the moon. In contrast to the male initiation, they require less of an orgiastic climax or outbreak of violent energy, but rather need steady and cyclical work in line with both nature's rhythm, and that of a specific femininity.[64]

---

61 Oertel, "Was ist Heidentum?"
62 Ulbrich, *Im Tanz der Elemente*.
63 See Chapter 2.
64 Ibid., 451f: "Wir spüren das Wesen des Mondes nur diffus in uns und Männer scheinen zu weniger Resonanz auf die Schwingungen fähig als Frauen [...] Der Sonnenkult gilt [...] als

During the 1920s and 30s, similar theoretical postulations led to the reception and transformation of German theories of all-male societies, the *Männerbünde*, which merge with ideas adopted from the spiritual men's movement in modern day Asatru.

The term *Männerbund* refers to all-male warrior associations in so-called primitive societies; it is rarely translated into other languages, but is used rather as an international ethnological term.[65] It was coined in 1902 by the German ethnologist Heinrich Schurtz, in his book *"Altersklassen und Männerbünde. Darstellung der Grundformen der Gesellschaft"*[66] ("Age-Classes and All-Male Associations. Presentation of the Basic Forms of Society"). Schurtz investigates various male-only phenomena, such as men's houses or boys' intitiation associations. His findings led him to claim that men have a stronger instinct for sociability (*Geselligkeitstrieb*) than women, and that boys need rites of initiation in order to ensure their separation from the mother and the maternally dominated realm of the family. This in turn allows them to be able to fulfill their role as creators of larger social formations.[67] In his analysis, Schurtz engaged with theories of matriarchy, offering an alternative explanation for the origin of society and the state, which placed men back at the center of academic attention.[68] Similar to Bachofen's theory of matriarchy, Schurtz's

---

Erscheinungsform einer männlich beeinflußten Sonnenverehrung, da er der intellektuellen Geistigkeit bedarf, um sich zu institutionalisieren. [...] Der zart-diffuse, aber umso nachhaltigere Charakter dieser planetarischen Kraft [des Mondes] findet im weiblichen Körper die ideale Ergänzung und Erfüllung seines Wesens. Weibliche Einweihungs- und Initiationsriten konzentrieren daher das Bewußtsein auf den Zyklus des Mondes und verlangen im Gegensatz zu männlichen Einweihung weniger einen orgiastischen Höhepunkt oder den Ausbruch gewalt-iger Energie, sondern bedürfen einer stetigen und zyklischen Arbeit im Rhythmus der Natur und der spezifisch eigenen Weiblichkeit."

65   The most comprehensive and up-to-date discussion of German theories of *Männerbund* between 1880 and 1934 can be found in Bruns, *Politik des Eros*, on which much of the following summarizing discussion is based.

66   Heinrich Schurtz, *Altersklassen und Männerbünde. Eine Darstellung der Grundformen der Gesellschaft* (Berlin: Reimer, 1902).

67   Rather than following this essentialist assumption of a basic 'nature' of masculinity, Schurtz's theory should be read as a "social new invention" (Ulrike Brunotte, "Der Männerbund zwischen Gemeinschaft und Gesellschaft. Communitas und Ritual um 1900" in *Diskurse des Theatralen*, ed. Erika Fischer-Lichte, et al. (Tübingen/Basle: A. Francke, 2005), 233) engaging with the contemporary theories of matriarchy discussed above in an explicitly anti-feminist manner, cf. Bruns, *Politik des Eros*, 62; see also See, *Barbar Germane Arier*, 318.

68   Bruns, *Politik des Eros*, 99; cf. also Brunotte, "Der Männerbund zwischen Gemeinschaft und Gesellschaft. Communitas und Ritual um 1900," 236.

approach can be read as both a cure for, and a symptom of, current social uncertainties and anxieties about gender identities and relations. A cure because it naturalized men's function as leaders of state and society, and a symptom because it implicitly demonstrated that masculinity needed to be produced through ritual and thus could not be as self-evidently natural as Schurtz himself assumed it to be.

Schurtz's ideas on male bonding had an impact on later theorists of the *Männerbund* in Germany. They manifested in the form of a rebellion against both patriarchal and maternal forces. In his idiosyncratic analysis of the German outdoor youth movement *Wandervogel*,[69] Hans Blüher (1888–1955), the foremost popularizer of *Männerbund*-theories in Germany, explained the attraction of this movement for young men through references to Schurtz, to Sigmund Freud's theory of the sexual drive, and to the misogynist writer Otto Weininger's concept of an original human bisexuality. Aligning theories of the *Männerbund* with the era's youth cult, he implicitly configured 'youth' as 'male.'[70]

According to Blüher, the youth movement was driven by a (sublimated) homoerotic eros projected onto the charismatic leader of the respective *Männerbund* – a savagely contested thesis, which nevertheless was able to fulfill two social needs at the time:

> The idea of a (homo)erotic bonding between men did not only help to develop forms of a modern and more emotional masculinity, but also to guarantee them a greater political influence. The discourse of the *Männerbund* defended an exclusively male understanding of the state and simultaneously effectively denied the right of political participation for women and Jews.[71]

By positing the homoerotically charged *Männerbund* instead of the family as the origin of the state, Blüher attempted to reevaluate homosexuality in a radical manner.[72] Contrary to similar developments in British and American

---

69   Hans Blüher, *Wandervogel. Geschichte einer Jugendbewegung*, 3 vols. (Berlin: Weise, 1912).
70   Bruns, *Politik des Eros*, 164.
71   From the back cover of ibid.: "Die Vorstellung vom (homo)erotischen Bündnis unter Männern half nicht nur, Formen einer modernen und gefühlvolleren Männlichkeit zu entwickeln, sondern diesen auch politisches Gewicht zu verleihen. Der Männerbunddiskurs verteidigte ein exklusiv männliches Staatsverständnis und sprach zugleich wirkungsvoll Frauen und Juden das Recht auf politische Partizipation ab."
72   Blüher's take on homosexuality was based on Adolf Brand's masculinist *Gemeinschaft der Eigenen* (Association of the Self-Owned), which sought an alternative to the then-influential Magnus Hirschfeld's medical and implicitly pathologizing approach.

masculinist homosexual movements, Blüher's ideas took an anti-egalitarian, anti-feminist, and Romantic nationalist turn.[73] His later works added an increasingly aggressive, militant, and anti-Semitic interpretation of the Aryan *Männerbund*, in which he now saw proof that homoeroticism was not a moral issue in Aryan society, but was condemned only after the arrival of Semitic monotheism.[74]

The focus on homoerotic forces made Blüher's theory highly controversial, and it solicited partially outraged reactions from supporters of the *völkisch* movement and religion, whose ideology was based on furthering the Aryan race.[75] Nevertheless, it captured the experience of bonding in the liminal space of nature that many young men of the youth movement shared, and which was also present in the German militant right-wing corps (the *Freikorps*),[76] as well as in other militant right-wing groups. The experience of World War I further emphasized the notions of sacrifice and death that had been present in theories of the *Männerbund* all along. These notions were now understood in a much less symbolic, but more concrete and contemporary way: as a cult of the union with fallen comrades, centered upon the cruel experience of the trenches. In this context, the *Männerbund* was seen as the militant answer to the despised democratic republic allegedly ruled by female, Jewish, and Bolshevik forces.

The idea of the *Männerbund* as the foundation for the modern state, with roots in a deep past, and as symbolic of the natural character of men, was thus cemented in the German public imagination after World War I. It is against this background that the folklorists and Germanists Lily Weiser and Otto Höfler developed their ideas about the existence of initiatory guilds and

---

73 Bruns, *Politik des Eros*, 164. For the reception of Blüher's ideas in general cf. ibid., 327–382.

74 Cf. especially Hans Blüher, *Die Rolle der Erotik in der männlichen Gesellschaft. Eine Theorie der menschlichen Staatsbildung nach Wesen und Wert.*, 2 vols., vol. I (Der Typus Inversus), vol. II (Familie und Männerbund) (Jena: Diederichs, 1919). Cf. Bruns, *Politik des Eros*, 324–330. For a reception of Blüher's ideas within Radical Traditionalism cf. also Robert Black, "Fidus, Brand, and Bluher. New Paths for Eroticism," *Living Traditions. A Magazine of Radical Traditionalism, Esotericism, Perennialism, Mysticism, Politics and Social Issues* 4, no. 2 (2011).

75 Cf. Bruns, *Politik des Eros*, 363. However, it seems significant that none of Blüher's critics questioned his demand to exclude women and girls from the *Wandervogel*; evidence that misogynist ideologies were at work on both sides of the spectrum. Ibid., 339.

76 The *Freikorps* were formed by German WWI veterans after the demilitarization of Germany and fought the Soviet republics which briefly emerged around 1918/19 in several parts of Germany.

male-only secret warrior bands in ancient Germanic societies. They based their concepts on Schurtz's theories, as well as on theories of religious experience developed by Jakob Wilhelm Hauer.[77] In this process, homoerotic notions were downplayed significantly. In his 1934 work, *"Kultische Geheimbünde der Germanen"* ("Cultic Secret Societies of the Teutons"), Höfler portrayed the belligerent ancestor worship of the *Männerbund*, centering on an 'ecstatic union' between the living and dead, as a universal Germanic phenomenon with great political significance. For him, the "social demonic" of the *Männerbund* formed the basis of "unmeasurable socio-political energies"[78] that supposedly survived in the all-important political institutions of the Germanic world up until the present day. The *Männerbund* was thus to be understood as the true carrier of sovereignty and of the forces forming the state.[79]

It was obvious to his contemporaries that using Höfler's theories of continuity, along with his portrayal of dedicated ecstatic and secret warrior bands as being the basis of the Germanic state, could serve as a means of historical legitimization for *Männerbund* formations within National Socialism, such as the paramilitary SA (*Sturmabteilung*), and the SS in particular.[80] Other National Socialists, such as the philosopher Alfred Bäumler, followed this line as well, declaring the *Männerbünde* as the basis of the state, while emphasizing their ability to defeat the chaos of a bourgeois, urban, feminized way of life.[81]

---

77   For a more systematic discussion of Weiser's and Höfler's methodology and theories of continuity see Chapter 8.

78   Otto Höfler, *Kultische Geheimbünde der Germanen* (Frankfurt a.M.: Diesterweg, 1934), 323, cf. VIII–IX: "Quelle unermeßlicher sozial-staatlicher Energien."

79   Helmut Birkhan, "Otto Höfler. Nachruf," *Almanach der Österreichischen Akademie der Wissenschaften* 138 (1988), 390.

80   Cf. Stefanie v. Schnurbein, "Geheime kultische Männerbünde bei den Germanen. Eine Theorie im Spannungsfeld zwischen Wissenschaft und Ideologie," in *Männerbande – Männerbünde. Zur Rolle des Mannes im Kulturvergleich*, ed. Gisela Völger and Karin v. Welck (Cologne: Rautenstrauch-Joest Museum, 1990); See, *Barbar Germane Arier*, 319–344. It is fairly undisputed that Höfler's membership in a precursor of the Austrian SA as a 21 year old and his early enthusiasm for National Socialism contributed to his fascination with military warrior associations (cf. Birkhan, "Otto Höfler. Nachruf," 401), and that his theories contain projections of his experiences and political convictions onto ancient ecstatic cults of male bonding, sacrifice, and union with the dead in the Germanic past, cf. Schnurbein, "Geheime kultische Männerbünde bei den Germanen"; See, *Barbar Germane Arier*.

81   Alfred Bäumler, *Männerbund und Wissenschaft* (Berlin: Junker und Dünnhaupt, 1934), 32–37.

While Hans Blüher's ideas gained influence in parts of the German(ic) Faith Movement, Höfler's and Bäumler's theories were productive in the realm of politics and political philosophy, but less so in religious contexts. As was the case for all *Männerbund* ideologues, Höfler's approach was clearly anti-feminist. He saw female witch cults, with their "cynical dinginess" and "licentious excess,"[82] as one of the main enemies of the firmly structured *Männerbund*. At the same time, he directed his theories against the blood-and-soil-based, family-oriented, ultimately bourgeois view of Germanic society, which Kummer, Hans F.K. Günther, and other race theorists favored.[83]

With respect to the post-war reception of the *Männerbund*, we can identify a line from the international conservative-revolutionary and fascist militant ideologies (as developed by Hans Blüher and later taken up by fascist traditionalist Julius Evola) through to present-day political and intellectual right-wing ideologies.[84] However, *Männerbund* theories had limited direct impact on modern Asatru.[85] In order to explain the function of images of male warriors in wider Asatru circles, we have to consider another tradition in which such images feature.

As was the case with 'Germanic' theories of matriarchy and second-wave feminism, the ground for a renewed reception of *Männerbund* concepts in modern Asatru was laid through the re-contextualization of such gender ideologies in a contemporary movement known as the international mythopoetic men's movement, which emerged in the 1980s around Robert Bly, a popular poet, translator, performer, leader of men's workshops, and author of the popular book *Iron John: A Book About Men*.[86] The men's movement was driven by a

---

82 Höfler, *Kultische Geheimbünde der Germanen*, 277: "zynische Schmutzigkeit" – "zügellose Ausschweifung."

83 See in particular the long footnote on Bernhard Kummer, *Midgards Untergang. Germanischer Kult und Glaube in den letzten heidnischen Jahrhunderten* (Leipzig: Adolf Klein, 1935) in Höfler, *Kultische Geheimbünde der Germanen*, 336–338.

84 It has lived on in traditional right-wing circles, such as the radical wing of German fraternities, the *Burschenschaften*, in militant right-wing extremist youth organizations, such as the *Wiking Jugend* in Germany, as well as in the intellectual New Right. One example, among many, is a book by Karlheinz Weißmann, *Männerbund* (Schnellroda: Edition Antaios, 2004), who uses Höfler's and Eliade's theories to advocate the necessity of such all-male associations in order to secure a natural, healthy gender order.

85 The links between Asatru groups and *Männerbund* theories include strongly ethnicist, male-oriented groups such as *Heffjendur* in Denmark, the now-defunct *Allgermanic Heathen Front*, and others that promote the neo-right ideas of male heroism.

86 Robert Bly, *Iron John. A Book About Men* (Vintage Books: New York, 1992 [1990]). Bly's workshops had a strong appeal for many spiritually interested men, who soon published

similar ambiguity as the pre-World War I *Männerbund* ideology, as well as the thoughts of a young Hans Blüher.[87] It rejected both a stifled authoritarian patriarchy and the allegedly overwhelming influence of feminism, considering them to be two of the forces enervating and stifling masculine initiative in modern Western societies. Moreover, it called for a rediscovery of male bonding and traditional masculine values as a remedy for these issues.[88] The fact that this lack of male strength was attributed to a lack of access to myth and ritual in modernity is important for tracing ideas of the *Männerbund* in contemporary contexts.[89] The proper path to a reconnection with "deep and instinctual *masculine* energies"[90] could be found through initiation rituals. These rituals were grounded in the ethnological tradition Schurtz had introduced; more specifically, the rite through which boys separated from mother and family in order to become accepted as proper men.

Affinities to pre-war *Männerbund* ideas can also be found in the emphasis on the archetype of the warrior[91] – the archaic embodiment of "greatness" and "proper aggressiveness"[92] – as well as the significance assigned to brotherhoods.[93] Ecstatic cults, and drumming in particular, play a central role in the mythopoetic men's movement. The integration of the individual man into a larger community and the connection with the power of "the ancestors"[94] or archetypes play a similarly important role as in Höfler's work. Keeping in line

---

their own books and started their own workshops. See for example Wayne Liebman, *Tending the Fire. The Ritual Men's Group* (St. Paul, MN: Ally Press, 1991); Michael Meade, *Men and the Water of Life. Initiation and the Tempering of Men* (New York: Harper San Francisco, 1993).

87   However, it was lacking Blüher's sexual radicalism and instead emphasized the heterosexual union as the natural, mature object choice, resembling Schurtz' and Höfler's ideas in this respect.

88   Bly, *Iron John*, 2 f. See also Schnurbein, "Kräfte der Erde – Kräfte des Blutes," 259.

89   Cf. Liebman, *Tending the Fire*, 6. Just as the feminist goddess movement, mytho-poetic men employed a model of archetypes as conceptualized by Carl Gustav Jung, as well as his most famous post-war adept, James Hillman, in order to explain the mythic structures on which the re-connection with archetypal 'natural' masculinities were to be based.

90   Robert Moore and Douglas Gillette, *King, Warrior, Magician, Lover. Rediscovering the Archetypes of the Mature Masculine* (New York: Harper San Francisco, 1991), XVIII.

91   "The warrior" is one of the four "archetypes of the mature masculine," which Jungian psychoanalyst Robert Moore and his co-author Douglas Gillette identify in their popular book, which has appeared in several new editions since its first publication in 1991. Cf. ibid.

92   Ibid., 26 and 80.

93   Cf. for example Meade, *Men and the Water of Life*, 310.

94   Ibid., 377.

with earlier propagators of the *Männerbund*, the figure of the leader has a central function in men's groups, as does the ability for "meaningful submission."[95] Robert Moore and Douglas Gillette associate the ability to be subordinate, which characterizes the good (spiritual) warrior, with his ability to create "new civilizations":

> He lives not to gratify his personal needs and wishes or his physical appetites but to hone himself into an efficient spiritual machine, trained to bear the unbearable in the service of the transpersonal goal. [...] And in the very act of destroying, often the Warrior energy is building new civilizations, new commercial, artistic, and spiritual ventures for humankind, new relationships.[96]

The idea that the "social demonic" of the *Männerbund* constitutes a historical continuity recurs in Wayne Liebman's accounts of "ritual men's group[s]." He writes: "I believe, that even as the old structures die, the psychic energies behind them remain. [...] They live on to find new forms in which to embody themselves."[97]

The parallels between these mythopoetic ideas about men and German concepts of the *Männerbund* from the early 20th century are quite striking. However, the former are not influenced directly by Blüher's or Höfler's ideas. Höfler's work in particular influenced two scholars of Indo-European myth and religion post-1945, George Dumézil and Mircea Eliade.[98] It was they and their students and followers, as well as students of C.G. Jung, who reintroduced concepts of the *Männerbund* into the Anglo-American context after 1945. Dumézil's concept of the warrior function, which is based on Höfler's

---

95 Ibid., 328.
96 Moore and Gillette, *King, Warrior, Magician, Lover*, 85 and 86.
97 Liebman, *Tending the Fire*, 41.
98 For a critical discussion of these scholars and Indo-European Studies in general see Chapter 8. My own claim in a previous publication, that scholarship on the *Männerbund* subsided in post-war years, cannot be upheld, as the works by Hans-Peter Hasenfratz, "Der indo-germanische Männerbund," *Zeitschrift für Religions- und Geistesgeschichte* 34 (1982); Joseph Harris, "Love and Death in the *Männerbund*. An Essay with Special Reference to the *Bjarkamál* and *The Battle of Maldon*," in *Heroic Poetry in the Anglo-Saxon Period. Studies in Honor of Jess B. Bessinger, Jr*, ed. Helen Damico and John Leyerle, Studies in Medieval Culture (Kalamazoo, MI: Medieval Institute Publications, Western Michigan University, 1993); and Wilhelm Heizmann, "Germanische Männerbünde," in *Geregeltes Ungestüm. Bruderschaften und Jugendbünde bei indogermanischen Völkern*, ed. Rahul Peter Das and Gerhard Meiser (Dresden: Hempen, 2002) show.

descriptions, surfaces in various writings in this context, for example in Robert Bly's *Iron John*:

> If Dumézil is right, one-third of the visions the Indo-European race has ever had in the near or far past amount to visions from the head of the warrior. We could say that a third of each person's brain is a warrior brain; a third of the instincts carried by our DNA relate to warrior behavior [...][99]

Just as feminist spirituality grounded their conception of gender in the biology of the female body, and their spirituality in the Old European "race," mythopoetic men drew upon Indo-European (formerly Aryan) ideology, as well as an essentialist reading of the male body's biology, in order to re-establish a social order based on an allegedly ancient and natural gender binary. Support for such tendencies, which naturalize belligerent male bonding as a universal characteristic of masculinity and reject the idea that both masculinity and femininity and the ideals surrounding them are constantly constructed and re-constructed in shifting social and historical contexts, is found in sociobiological theory. In *Men in Groups* (first edition 1969) as well as numerous articles, Lionel Tiger traced the dynamics of male bonding, which allegedly "characterizes human groups as varied as the Vatican Council, the New York Yankees, the Elks, the Masons, and the secret societies of Sierra Leone and Kenya"[100] back to human evolutionary history and humanity's origin in hunter and gatherer societies.[101]

Considering the broad popular success of Tiger's work and the impact on the mythopoetic men's and other gender-based movements in Western societies, it is unsurprising that theories surrounding the *Männerbund* were employed in academic discourse as well.[102] It is also no coincidence that the

---

99   Bly, *Iron John*, 150. Interestingly enough, Bly here draws upon a racial and genetic paradigm Dumézil himself rejected, emphasizing social dynamics instead. Dumézil's followers in the New Right, however, often overlooked this abstinence from biologist thought.
100 Lionel Tiger, *Men in Groups* (New York: Random House, 1969).
101 Ibid. Tiger's book has had a remarkable impact on sociobiological theories of gender and has been published in several new editions, the latest of which appeared in 2007.
102 A case in point is the extensive catalogue which the ethnological Rautenstrauch Joest museum in Cologne published in connection with an exhibition. Both catalogue and exhibition offered a critical approach to the universality of male dominance, which – much in the same way as Tiger claimed – was supposedly based on the influence of *Männerbünde*, and which affirmed the universality of the phenomenon while criticizing it as the singular cause for male dominance. Gisela Völger and Karin v. Welck, eds.,

most carefully argued and critical investigation, in terms of its sources, into the dynamics of *Männerbund* in Old Norse literature, carried out by Joseph Harris, drew upon Tiger's theses as a justification for the "timeless psychological context"[103] of male associations. The socio-biological approach allowed him to find an alternative explanation for the long-term continuity of, as well as the changes in, the dynamics of male bonding.

Mainstream ideas about naturalized traditional masculinities such as these form an inconspicuous ideological ground, distanced from the militant *Männerbund* ideologies of the political right, on which warrior and Viking masculinities can be developed. While the right-wing reception of *Männerbund* theories continues to focus on the importance of *Männerbünde* for state formation and politics,[104] Asatruers – to the extent that they rely on these theories – tend to emphasize the importance of a mythically grounded, archetypical masculinity of 'the warrior,' from which modern man may draw strength and a sense of belonging. If the *Bund* is mentioned, it is in the sense of an initiatory association responsible for the guiding of boys into a proper masculinity. A case in point is the German *Eldaring* member Alex Jahnke's call for the creation of "new *Bünde* and the revitalization of rites of passage as a central task for the future of Paganism."[105] This call reverberates with *Our Troth's* suggestions on "Man-Making," which refer extensively to Höfler's theories about the 'Wild Hunt' as a remnant of *Männerbund* activities, and recommends them as sources of inspiration for the appropriate rites of initiation.[106]

Contemporary aesthetic and academic manifestations foster this interpretation of the *Männerbund*. As we shall see in Chapter 9, metal and neofolk music scenes have embraced Höfler and other German and Austrian folklorists' readings of the Wild Hunt and its association with the *Männerbund* as a symbol for its aesthetics.[107] In her recent dissertation, *The One-eyed God: Odin*

       Männerbande – Männerbünde. Zur Rolle des Mannes im Kulturvergleich, 2 vols. (Cologne: Rautenstrauch-Joest Museum für Völkerkunde, 1990).

103   Harris, "Love and Death in the *Männerbund*," 78.

104   Cf. Weißmann, *Männerbund*.

105   Alex Jahnke, "Zieh mit den Wölfen. Krieger in der Vergangenheit und Gegenwart," *Herdfeuer. Die Zeitschrift des Eldaring e.V.* 7, no. 26 (2009), 14. "Hier neue Bünde zu schaffen und Übergangsriten wieder zu beleben, sehe ich als eines der zentralen Themen des Heidentums in der Zukunft."

106   Gundarsson, *Our Troth*, vol. II, 247–257.

107   Cf. Florian Heesch, "Die Wilde Jagd als Identitätskonstruktion im Black Metal," in *Eddische Götter und Helden. Milieus und Medien ihrer Rezeption. Eddic Gods and Heroes. The Milieux and Media of Their Reception*, ed. Katja Schulz (Heidelberg: Winter, 2011).

and the (Indo-) Germanic Männerbünde (2000),[108] the German translation of which was done by a German Asatruer and published in the Neopagan publishing house *Arun* in 2007, Kris Kershaw follows Höfler's argument closely, uncritically expanding it to encompass other Indo-European sources. In this way, she offers the first generally accessible account of Höfler's theses in English. In Asatru contexts, the book has been hailed as a long-desired academic justification of Höfler's theories, which were already established via the popular music scene, but lacked the academic credentials that are so important for a-racist Asatruers.[109]

These are the first indicators of a religious reception of Höfler's *Männerbund* thesis in Germanic Neopagan contexts. However, it should be noted that the notion of a binding, lifelong (secret) association of men is only very rarely mentioned. While the Danish ethnicist *Blotgroup Hefjendur's* self-conceptualization as a "brotherhood"[110] is an exception, generally speaking, the aspects pertaining to the 'spiritual warrior' and to male initiation play a more central role in Asatru. What is neglected in this mode of reception is the original context in which Höfler's theories originated and which formed their image of masculinity, namely, the violent post-WW I German rhetoric and practice of war and 'bloody revenge' of the 'horde of the dead' and their association with extreme right-wing politics.[111]

The tension between this foundational context and recent attempts to distance modern Asatru from its traditional focus on an exaggerated cult of war and the image of the warrior is rarely addressed directly, but can be gleaned from the reactions of some of my interview partners, who have been at pains to reassure me that the enthusiasm for Höfler's and Kershaw's theories are not related to images of gender, but rather to their methodology, which draws upon Indo-European continuities.[112] This claim is supported by the fact that there are a-racist Asatruers, especially in the USA and Great Britain, who have

---

108 Kris Kershaw, *The One-eyed God. Odin and the (Indo-) Germanic Männerbünde*, Journal of Indo-European Studies Monograph (Washington: Institute for the Study of Man, 2000), German translation: *Der einäugige Gott. Odin und die indogermanischen Männerbünde*, trans. Baal Müller (Engerda: Arun, 2007).

109 For details of this book, its publishing contexts, and methodological, as well as ideological problems around it, see Chapter 8.

110 Cf. http://www.hefjendur.dk/hefjendurs-profil, last accessed August 25, 2014.

111 Richard Faber, *'Wir sind Eines.' Über politisch-religiöse Ganzheitsvorstellungen europäischer Faschismen* (Würzburg: Königshausen & Neumann, 2005), 126 f.

112 Cf. Correspondence with Kurt Oertel (Eldaring). The problems of this methodological approach are discussed in Chapter 8.

used the practice of *seid* as a means of reevaluating conventional models of masculinity and rejecting their focus on violence.[113] Bil, one of the Heathen *seid* practitioners interviewed by Jenny Blain and Robert Wallis, emphasizes that the practice of *seid* has brought him to embrace a less normative masculinity, to his disavowal of "too much of a 'macho attitude,'" and towards an "eccentricity" that leads "folks often [to] wonder, now, if I am homosexual or not."[114] At the same time, he emphasizes his heterosexuality by rejecting the notion that alternative masculinity is automatically associated with homosexuality, which is strongly stigmatized in at least some Asatru contexts. Annette Høst, a Danish *seid* practitioner and teacher of shamanism,[115] makes a similar argument when she points to the ecstatic moments, the loss of control, and the powerful erotic energies which are set free in the practice of *seid*, which for her are unrelated to gender. She remarks that "this was what a 'real man' in the Viking society could not deal with socially, but that does not really need to concern us at all today."[116]

Queering Asatru? The Question of Sexuality

Such defensive statements point to the fact that *seid* is indeed associated with the contested site of homosexuality. In spite of Høst's comment that rejections of *seid* do not need to concern 'us' today, the alleged connections between *seid*, femininity, and sexually charged magic have led to the idea that *seid* is not a respectable activity for men. This causes some Asatruers to accuse male practitioners of *seid* of being *ergi* (perverted). In medieval Iceland, the terms *ergi*, *ragr* or *argr* denoted an insult so severe that those who used them against another man were legally punished by outlawry. The exact meanings of these insults are hard to determine, but indications point to their gendered and possibly sexualized nature, ranging from generally 'unmanly' and cowardly behavior to the specific insult referring to sexual relations between men, or even

---

113   Cf. Jenny Blain and Robert J. Wallis, "The 'Ergi' Seidman: Contestations of Gender, Shamanism and Sexuality in Northern Religion Past and Present," *Journal of Contemporary Religion* 15, no. 3 (2000).
114   Quote from ibid., 404.
115   Cf. Annette Høst and Karen Kelly, "Keep it Close to Nature. Karen Kelly Interviews Annette Høst on Seiðr, the Old Norse Way of Shamanic Magic," *Spirit Talk* 9 (1999). Annette Høst founded the *Scandinavian Center for Shamanic Studies* together with Jonathan Horowitz.
116   Ibid.

more specifically, the notion of one man being penetrated by another.[117] Some Asatruers use the debasement connected with *ergi* as proof of the fundamental rejection of (male) homosexuality in Germanic societies. They find further justification for this attitude in Chapter 12 of Tacitus' *"Germania"*, which refers to bog bodies as "corpores infames." This somewhat obscure passage has been read as referring to "sexual acts against nature," and has thus been employed as "proof" of the Germanic rejection and severe punishment of homosexuality by Heinrich Himmler and other National Socialists.[118]

In the wake of these homophobic theories, groups such as the ethnicist *Odinic Rite* consider homosexuality to be an unnatural "malady," which must be contained in order not to spread and 'infect' the community.[119] They despise "the hags of "women's lib" [...] and all the anti-life forces of homosexuality and the touters of abortion" as "part of Loki's Brood."[120] Theodist Garman Lord similarly deplores the "homosexualisation of modern American society, which turns normal people into misfits," and laments gays having 'taken over' Wicca.[121] Interviews with other Scandinavian and German groups, as well as a search of online forums, confirm that some Asatruers continue to consider homosexuality to be an 'unnatural' or even 'sinful' activity that cannot be reconciled with Heathenism's understanding of itself as a religion of nature (and thus natural reproduction) with a set of 'natural ethics.' This supports the observation that gender relations and reproduction within large parts of Asatru remain dependent on a traditional model based on the nuclear family, with an equally traditional division of labor and tasks.

117   The concept and its sexual and gendered connotations is most comprehensively discussed in Folke Ström, *Nið, Ergi and Old Norse Moral Attitudes* (London: Viking Society for Northern Research 1973), Preben Meulenkracht Sørensen, *The Unmanly Man. Concepts of Sexual Defamation in Early Northern Society* (Odense: Odense University Press, 1983), Carol J. Clover, "Regardless of Sex. Men, Women, and Power in Early Northern Europe," *Speculum* 68 (1993). Cf. also the discussion by anthropologist and Asatruer Jenny Blain, *Nine Worlds of Seid-Magic. Ecstasy and neo-Shamanism in North European Paganism*, 18, 115 f.

118   Cf. Karin Sanders, *Bodies in the Bog and the Archaeological Imagination* (Chicago/London: University of Chicago Press, 2009), 61–65.

119   WulfstanOR, "Odinic Values in Family Life & Personal Relationships," The Odinic Rite, http://www.odinic-rite.org/main/odinic-values-in-family-life-personal-relationships/, last accessed May 29, 2015.

120   The Circle of Ostara, "Loki," The Odinic Rite, http://www.odinic-rite.org/main/loki/, last accessed November 29, 2011.

121   Lord, *The Way of the Heathen*, 85f, 95.

At the same time, Germanic Neopagans past and present generally agree that Pagan attitudes toward sexuality are freer and "more natural" than those of Christianity and other monotheistic or "oriental" religions and cultures – an assessment which they share with other Neopagans, especially Wicca and Neoshamans. However, as we have seen in the previous chapter, the concrete meaning of 'natural' varies considerably. Attitudes toward the nature of sexuality within Germanic Neopaganism have always oscillated between an orientation toward family values and traditional morals, and the experiments with sexual magic characteristic of occult orders. The German Faith Movement saw Germanic sexual morals as characterized by a "natural" distance from "lasciviousness" and "artificial eroticism," setting them against the "lecherousness" of Romance morals.[122] The predominance of such attitudes left little room for deviant visions of sexual order, such as those of Willibald Hentschel and Ernst and Margart Hunkel, who advocated polygamy in the service of effective racial breeding.[123]

Ariosophist Guido List's esoteric system, which consists of a fundamental polarity which permeates the cosmos, and is the basis for a successful expansion of the Ario-Germanic race, has implicit sexual connotations. His breeding fantasies teem with sexual imagery. List's ideas are in part based on the work of Max Ferdinand Sebaldt von Werth (1859–1916). Combining ideas of nudism, occultism, and racial breeding, von Werth, the chair of a theosophical lodge and member of a Druid order, developed a veritable sexual religion of Aryan superiority in which "the distinct Nordic sense of polarity" and the "trinity of the highest powers" played a central role.[124] It is thus logical that Hunkel included more Ariosophic elements into the ideology of the *Order of the Nordungen*, which he founded later in his life. However, to my knowledge, there are no indications that Ariosophist circles practiced sex magic, or were involved in tantric activities to a

---

122 Cf. Zernack, "'Germanin im Hauskleid.'"
123 Hunkel was excluded from the *Deutscher Orden* and *Deutschgläubige Gemeinschaft* on the grounds of his promoting the "Mittgard polygamy." Cf. Chapters 1 and 6. Cf. also Breuer, *Die Völkischen in Deutschland*, 104.
124 Ellic Howe and Helmut Möller, *Merlin Peregrinus. Vom Untergrund des Abendlandes* (Würzburg: Königshausen & Neumann, 1986), 151; Maximilian Ferdinand Sebaldt von Werth, '*Wanidis.*' *Der Triumph des Wahns III: D.I.S. Die arische 'Sexualreligion' als Volks-Veredelung in Zeugen, Leben und Sterben. Mit einem Anhang über Menschenzüchtung von Carl du Prel* (Leipzig: Friedrich, 1897), 31: "ausgeprägter nordischer Sinn für Polarität" – "Dreiheit höchster Gewalten." Cf. also Bernd Wedemeyer-Kolwe, '*Der neue Mensch.' Körperkultur im Kaiserreiche und in der Weimarer Republik* (Würzburg: Königshausen & Neumann, 2004), 200.

similar extent as contemporary occultists, adherents of Aleister Crowley and Anglo-German occultist Theodor Reuss,[125] or the founders of Wicca, with their rituals of fertility steeped in sexual symbolism.[126]

The association between a general notion of Neopaganism and sexual magic is one reason why in recent years many members of sexual minorities, be they gay or lesbian, sado-masochistic or fetishist, have sought their spiritual home in Neopagan circles, and that the proximity between the queer- and BDSM[127] scenes and Neopaganism is relatively close.[128] Their association with sexual magic, Wicca, and neo-shamanism makes contemporary Asatruers who include sexuality in any form into their spiritual practices targets of suspicion within the community. The ensuing tensions around these issues are not easily attributed to any of the political camps within Asatru. As is the case with feminist spirituality, we can find overlaps between sexual libertarianism and racist or ethnicist ideologies. Stephen Flowers, alias Edred Thorsson, is an example of this. Although he shares the *Odinic Rite's* ethnicist outlook and embraces views of the New Right, his involvement with ritual sado-masochism and his foundation of the *Order of the Triskelion* in the 1980s based on Pauline Réage's *The Story of O*, the classic novel on sado-masochism, led to his exclusion from the *Odinic Rite* (OR) and to a minor scandal within the Heathen scene.[129] A-racist Asatruers are somewhat divided on the issue as well. The majority claim to be perfectly accepting of gays in their own ranks and avoid taking a strong stance on homosexuality by considering sexual preference to be an individuals' personal decision and thus not the community's affair, and therefore an issue that has nothing to do with religion.[130] Where legally possible,

---

125 Howe and Möller, *Merlin Peregrinus*, 136–170.
126 Cf Hutton, *The Triumph of the Moon*, 231–236.
127 The acronym stands for Bondage, Dominance, Submission, Sadism, and Masochism.
128 To mention just one prominent example: The prolific writer and sex educator, Pat(rick) Califia, who has written a great number of works on queer sado-masochism, radical sexual politics, and trans-gender issues, promotes an "indigenous paganism" as the way for white people who strive to avoid a cultural imperialism." (Pat Califia, *Public Sex. The culture of radical sex* (Pittsburgh: Cleis Press, 1994), 240). Califia is a member and priest of the *Fellowship of the Spiral Path* (Cf. Michael Manning, *Inamorata. The Erotic Art of Michael Manning* (San Francisco: Last Gasp, 2005): Information on contributors), which was founded by Marion Zimmer Bradley and is now headed by Diana Paxson and which Paxson.
129 Cf. Kaplan, *Radical Religion in America*, 26f; Edred, *History of the Rune-Gild*, III (The Reawakening of the Gild 1980–2005), 90–93.
130 Members of the German *VfgH* and *Eldaring* as well as the American *Troth* and all Scandinavian groups have professed this position.

Scandinavian groups have embraced same sex marriage. In fact, in Iceland, the *Ásatrúarfélagið* was the first religious community to officially wed same sex couples. In these groups, any dissent usually revolves around the fact that marriage and procreation are supposed to be closely linked. In most groups, the issue is resolved by letting individual *godis* and *gydjas* decide which rites they want to perform. Nevertheless, openly homosexual Asatruers remain a small minority. To my knowledge, the Swedish a-racist *Samfundet Forn Sed* is the only European group to count a very small homosexual/bisexual/transsexual or queer association among its *blotgroups*.[131]

The most radical practitioners, who work explicitly with the sexual nature of *seid, ergi*, or Northern shamanism, often do not identify explicitly as Heathen or Asatru, and do not feel connected to the Asatru community, but rather find it important to follow a "Northern way" within a more general Neopagan framework. Among them is Raven Kaldera, a queer "intersexed" and "transgendered" "author, shaman, and activist," who combines the spiritual ways of the "Northern ancestors" with the practices of polyamory and ritual sado-masochism.[132]

Other queer *seid* practitioners, including Jenny Blain and Robert Wallis, combine their anti-homophobic activities with a strong stance against racist or ethnicist tendencies within Asatru in their discussion of *seid*. Others, however, connect their support for sexual freedom and tolerance with the type of ethnicist and anti monotheist argument discussed in Chapter 5, and see sexual libertarianism as an integral part of Germanic culture. For example, Stephen Flowers/Edred Thorsson and his wife Crystal Dawn conceptualize sado-masochism as being a part of "our culture":

> Sexuality in all its forms, and most especially in this form, was suppressed (or sublimated) by the teachings of the medieval church, or pathologized by 19th century "professors." During the 20th century in European culture, however, the sacred power of sexuality is being rediscovered. The

---

131 *Bilröst* was founded in 2009 after "homo-Heathens" walked in the Stockholm Gay Pride Parade in 2008 with a statue of the god Freyr, as a reaction to anti-gay tendencies within Asatru, and with the hope of contributing to breaking the association between Asatru and racist and violent groups. Cf. Urban Johansson, "Innkalling til Pride," *Mimers Källa* 21 (2009), Håkan Lindh, "En HBT-hedning taler," *Mimers Källa* 21 (2009). As the example shows, "Homo-Heathens" orient their practices not only around *seid*, but also around the fertility god Freyr, whose Uppsala priests, according to Saxo Grammaticus, cross-dressed in ritual.

132 Cf. http://ravenkaldera.org/rumors.html, last accessed August 25, 2014.

apparently "new" interest in Sado-Masochistic sexuality is really just a renewal of something very ancient in our culture.[133]

Carl Johan Rehbinder, the chair of the Swedish SAS (now *Samfundet Forn Sed*) from 2000 to 2003 and teacher of tantric workshops in which he combines Nordic and other cultural elements,[134] stands for libertarian politics, with a critical stance toward Islam as well as Christianity.[135] Rehbinder has collaborated closely with sex educator Pia Struck and her *Orgasm Academy* in Denmark.[136] Struck has been a long-term member of *Harreskoven Blotgilde*, where she serves as a *gydja*, and has been partnered with Grølheim, co-founder of *Harreskoven Blotgilde* and *Forn Siðr*, and editor of the now-defunct journal, *Valravn*. Grølheim has shown active interest in issues of gender transgression and queerness, and has published an article in *Valravn* on the significance of *ergi*, gender, and homosexuality in Old Germanic and antique societies.[137] He has also publicly championed sexual and phallic aspects of the god Freyr at a mysticism fair (mytikmesse) in Denmark in 2000.[138]

The public activities of Struck and Rehbinder, which reach far beyond Asatru, point to the fact that their attitudes toward sexuality and ethnicity are compatible with at least parts of mainstream queer theory and activism. From a critical perspective, their standpoint can be compared to what has been termed "homonationalism" in recent years. "Homonationalism" describes a sexual politics in which

> claims to new or radical sexual freedoms are appropriated precisely by that point of view – usually enunciated from within state power – that would try to define Europe and the sphere of modernity as the privileged site where sexual radicalism can and does take place. Often, but not

---

133 Crystal Dawn and Stephen Flowers, *Carnal Alchemy. A Sado-Magical Exploration of Pleasure, Pain and Self-Transformation* (Smithville, TX: Runa-Raven Press, 1995), 11 f.
134 Ravn, "Interview med Carl Johan Rehbinder, en svensk hedning," 8. Cf. also Rehbinder's webpage http://www.cirkuseros.nu/sidor/om.html, last accessed August 25, 2014.
135 See, for example, his comments on Islam on http://ligator.wordpress.com/2010/08/28/fraga-till-sverigedemokraterna-om-islam-ar-som-nazismen-vad-gor-ni-med-muslimerna-da, last accessed Aug 25, 2014. Rehbinder has otherwise been active in the small party *Piratparti*, as well as in the new party of the Liberal Democrats. (Cf. his blog http://tantrikblog.wordpress.com, last accessed August 25, 2014).
136 http://www.orgasmeakademiet.dk, last accessed August 25, 2014.
137 Grølheim, "Køn, Sex og Ergi," *Valravn. Hedensk tidskrift om samfund og kultur* 24 (2008).
138 Photos of his presentation can be found on his facebook page at https://www.facebook.com/Grolheim/photos, last accessed August 25, 2014.

always, the further claim is made that such a privileged site of radical freedom must be protected against the putative orthodoxies associated with new immigrant communities.[139]

In other words, Western societies' inclusion of (some) 'proper' homosexual subjects in the realm of the nation is taken as proof of the progressive and tolerant nature of these 'modern' societies and is set against allegedly illiberal, homophobic Islamic or Asian traditions. A certain form of secularism indicated by sexual freedom is thus turned into an absolute value that characterizes 'good' societies, while at the same time foreclosing religious tolerance or the negotiation of differences in pluralistic societies.[140]

Asatruers who embrace such ideals combine them with ethnicist positions, turning the praiseworthy tolerance of 'modernity' into a timeless marker of the 'Germanic' or 'Nordic' cultural tradition or essence. Instead of representing state power, they give the homonationalist argument an ethnicist twist by projecting the notion of modern libertarianism onto the pre-Christian past, and by configuring its current emergence as a recovery of an ethnic or cultural essence destroyed by Christianity and currently threatened by monotheistic Islam. We could interpret this as an ethnic essentializing of homonationalism, secured through a spiritualized ethnic identity rooted in a deep past.

This kind of 'homo-ethnicism' is not the sole preserve of Asatruers, but is shared by academic theories which utilize aspects of queer theory for innovative interpretations of Norse mythology and society. In turn, these are employed by Asatruers to support their beliefs. A case in point is Norwegian archeologist Brit Solli's book about the otherness of Viking society and the queer character of its main god, Odin, published in 2002 under the title "*Seid – Myter, sjamanisme og kjønn i vikingenes tid*" (Seid – myths, shamanism, and gender in the Viking age). Solli sets out to refute once and for all nationalist or National Socialist appropriations of Viking culture. She rejects the notion of cultural or ethnic identity and asserts the shamanistic, sexual, and queer nature of Viking society's most prominent god, Odin. At the same time, she uses theories of otherness derived from queer and postcolonial studies to make an antimonotheistic claim, stating that the Heathen worldview is fundamentally different from any monotheism. Her anti-Islamic agenda is revealed in her attack on Muslims during a passage on the 'deplorable' influence of Christianity on

---

139   Butler, "Sexual Politics, Torture, and Secular Time," 2.
140   Cf. Puar, *Terrorist Assemblages*.

Viking culture, which has absolutely nothing to do with Viking culture's encounters with Arab and Islamic cultures.[141]

Such incidents are examples of Asatru's increasing tendency to align itself with alternative, yet respectable social movements, and of Asatruers' tendencies to adopt ethnicist and cultural essentialist positions within such movements. They point to the important intersection of academic theory with Asatru, which will be discussed in the following chapter.

---

141   Cf. Brit Solli, *Seid. Myter, sjamanisme og kjønn i vikingenes tid* (Oslo: Pax, 2002), 76 and 232.

CHAPTER 8

Asatru – An Academic Religion?

The relation between Germanic Neopaganism and academia is highly ambiguous. While knowledge of primary sources as well as academic theory plays a foundational role for a-racist and many ethnicist Asatruers, the majority of these Heathens have little first-hand knowledge of those sources and the Old Norse or Latin languages that they are written in. Their knowledge comes mostly from fictional literature,[1] Neopagan popular interpretations, and other popularized accounts of Norse mythology, as well as from Internet sources.[2] Asatruers who are able to cite sources and discuss academic theories about them are imbued with considerable symbolic capital within the Asatru community. Most importantly, though, references to scholarship have served to successfully repudiate allegations of any right-wing political involvement of Asatru. This strategy of immunization against the political instrumentalization of Asatru has been fairly effective in recent years. At the same time, we cannot overlook the fact that certain strands of scholarship dealing with Old Norse mythology and culture have themselves been deeply involved in various political or ideological identity projects. Germanic philology, folklore, history of religion, anthropology, and pre-historic archaeology were all concerned with the search for pure, pre-historical origins and have contributed to the mythologizing of scholarship and

---

1 A former board member of the Danish *Forn Siðr* thinks that the information he received from the popular children's book series on *Erik Menneskesøn* (Erik, Son of Man) by Lars-Henrik Olsen sufficed for him to become a Goði. Cf. Interview II.
2 René Gründer, *Blótgemeinschaften* (128f) observes, with regard to German Asatru, that the knowledge of basic Eddic texts constitutes a hidden norm for the social acceptance as an Asatruer within the community, but that most of his interview partners name Heathen interpretations of the sources and popular retellings as the immediate foundations of their knowledge and beliefs. Looking back at "Three Decades of the Ásatrú Revival" Stephen McNallen lists a number of mistakes, including "Lack of philosophical depth": "[...] until we can hold our own in debate with the Jesuits or the pages of the *New York Times Review of Books*, we will not be taken seriously. [...] verses from the *Hávamál* will not suffice to express our beliefs to a sophisticated world." (McNallen, "Three Decades of the Ásatrú Revival in America," 217f.) And Kurt Oertel, Warden of the Lore in the German *Eldaring*, compares Neopagans' ignorance of translation problems and source criticism with the attitudes of "self-proclaimed lay preachers in evangelical communities.": ("Selbsternannte Laienprediger evangelikaler Gemeinschaften," Kurt Oertel, "'Denn es steht geschrieben...' Neue Heiden und die Quellenkunde," *Heidnisches Jahrbuch* 2 (2007), 37).

the 'scientification' of myth.[3] While we have already discussed some 19th century contributions to the widespread popular image of Germanic myth and religion in Chapter 1, and a few particular interactions between theories of religion and the formation of new religions in Chapter 5, this chapter focuses on the use Asatruers make of primary sources and investigates the interfaces between Germanic Neopaganism and the disciplines that have contributed to 20th and 21st century notions of a Germanic or Nordic faith.

How Heathens Relate to their Sources

"The Edda" is the most frequent spontaneous answer Asatruers in just about any country offer when asked about the main 'original' sources for their belief. The two most-quoted Eddic poems attracted much attention during the Romantic era, and have remained central to popular ideas about Norse mythology ever since. The poem *Völuspá* is renowned for its cosmological vision of the origin and order of the world, and its decline in the oft-cited *Ragnarök*. The wisdom-poem *Hávamál* is cherished for its practical advice, upon which Asatruers like to build their ethics. Its account of Odin hanging in a tree and attaining runic knowledge contributes to its popularity in Pagan circles.[4] Depending on their country of origin and the availability of translations, some also include the most well-known ancient and medieval renderings of pre-Christian Germanic mythology and history in their source list, namely Tacitus' "*Germania*," Saxo Grammaticus' "*Gesta Danorum*," and Bede's *Ecclesiastical History of the English People*.[5] Others stress the importance of folklore, as well as material sources such as archaeological finds. In any case, sources do not speak in unmediated ways. This warrants the question: through which lense is the mythological knowledge perceived?

---

3 Cf. Ingo Wiwjorra, "Germanenmythos und Vorgeschichtsforschung im 19. Jahrhundert," in *Religion und Nation, Nation und Religion. Beiträge zu einer unbewältigten Geschichte*, ed. Michael Geyer and Hartmut Lehmann (Göttingen: Wallstein, 2004).

4 All of the field research done on Asatru in different countries in the last years comes to the conclusion that the Hávamál in particular is considered an almost sacred text in modern Asatru, regardless of ideological variety. See e.g. Jonsson, "Ásatrú á Íslandi við upphaf 21. aldar," 142; Gregorius, *Modern Asatro*, 135–137; Blain and Wallis, "Heathenry," 418. The same is true for Asatruers themselves who write about the basis of their faith, such as Jennings, *The Norse Tradition*, 51, who claims "one must live as closely as possible to the Havamal," and the interviews I conducted with Norwegian and Icelandic Asatruers.

5 See Chapter 1.

The significance Asatruers ascribe to written, folkloristic, and material sources varies widely. It ranges from the conviction that a hidden continuity of Heathen traditions once existed, which had been transmitted orally or through practices for generations, particularly in rural areas, and which simply needs to be re-discovered and revived; to the realization that the available sources are highly unreliable, and can only serve as a starting point for the creation of a new, contemporary religion. The attitudes toward different sources vary from country to country as well. This indicates that the construction of modern Asatru is closely connected to the role that Old Icelandic literature and an interest in a pre-Christian past have played in the media and institutions of the nations in question since the 19th century.

Of the countries studied here, Iceland is the one where the idea that Asatru continues an existing, albeit multiply broken tradition, is most widespread.[6] An older Asatruer takes exception to the claim that Asatru is a reconstructed faith:

> Asatru has always lurked underneath the surface. It has always been there. It was life-threatening to profess to it, earlier. But it has never disappeared. One can see it in 'low religion' in particular, which has existed side-by-side with Christianity. It has been frowned upon, but the church has not succeeded in extinguishing it.[7]

Icelandic Asatruers display a strong confidence that it is possible to build directly upon the available sources, connect them to a coherent whole, and tie these readings to a living tradition.[8] Icelandic Asatruers are generally in

---

6 This observation aligns well with an argument Piotr Wiench, "A Postcolonial Key to Understanding Central and Eastern European Neopaganisms," makes regarding Central Eastern European Neopaganism. He explains the tendency to resort to the founding myths of allegedly "native religions" in post-Soviet states with these countries' quasi-post-colonial status. Having reached independence from Danish rule only in 1942, of the countries discussed in this book, Iceland is the one which comes closest to exhibiting features of a post-colonial condition.

7 Interview U: "Asatroen har altid luret lige under overfladen. Den har altid været der. Det har været livsfarligt at bekende sig til den. Tidligere, ikke? Så den er aldrig forsvundet. Man kan se det på lavreligionen specielt. Som har eksisteret side om side med kristendommen. Den har været ugleset, men det har ikke lykkedes kirken at få det udryddet helt."

8 Hence the widespread sentiment that the *Hávamál* in particular can easily be related to by old and young people. Cf. Interview with Jóhanna Harðardóttir (Ásatrúarfélagið). This text is even used to spread information about Asatru actively: The *Ásatrúarfélagið* contributed to the edition of the poem that appeared with Iceland's premier publisher *Íslenska bókmenntafélagið* in 2007.

agreement with leading scholars in their country when they assume the existence of Pagan remnants in medieval sources.[9] Furthermore, the idea that Iceland is the only country where Pagan practices have survived in an unbroken manner has in fact become a stereotype that is confirmed even by otherwise highly critical scholars, such as the historian of religion Friedrich H. Tenbruck, who contends in a footnote: "Only in Iceland, where religion remained a private matter, was the Germanic religion preserved up until today."[10]

The reception of scholarship in Icelandic Asatru follows a pattern applicable to Asatru groups in other countries as well, and for which René Gründer, in his analysis of German Heathenism, has identified two different strategies of authenticity: the alleged historical authenticity of the written sources, and the authenticity of subjective experience. In the case of Iceland, these strategies merge and support one another. This allows Asatruers to acknowledge that "the roots are in this primitive religion," but that it has to be "further created: We don't want to go [back] there, we are living today."[11]

Claims to a more or less unbroken religious continuity also exist in other Scandinavian countries. Danish Asatruer Gudrun Victoria Gotved assumes that Asatru has survived in folklore and customs up until today, claiming that:

> the faith has never been dead, it has at most been dormant. Now we have taken it up again in full force, we are no longer ashamed to admit that Odin and Thor are close to us. Neither are we embarrassed of that which used to be called superstition, because it is something natural.[12]

---

[9] Among them are, to name just a few recent examples, the late folklorist Jón Hnefill Aðalsteinsson and his successor Terry Gunnell, who have tried to identify descriptions in the Eddas and sagas as reverberations of older religious practices. Cf. Jón Hnefill Aðalsteinsson, *Under the Cloak. A Pagan Ritual Turning Point in the Conversion of Iceland*, 2. extended ed. (Reykjavík: Háskólaútgáfan, 1999). An article by Terry Gunnell on Icelandic Folkloristics can be found on the prison outreach site for the "Alternative Religions Educational Network," http://www.aren.org/prison/documents/Asatru/iceland.pdf, last accessed August 27, 2014.

[10] Tenbruck, "Die Religion im Maelstrom der Reflexion," 55: "Nur in Island, wo die Religion Privatsache blieb, hielt sich die germanische Religion bis heute." Unfortunately, he neither cites evidence for this claim, nor does he question the problematic assumption of a "Germanic religion" or address the question of how he uses the term 'private' here.

[11] Interview T.

[12] Gotved, *Asatro. De gamle guder i moderne tid*, 20: "Alt dette viser, at troen aldrig har været død, den har højest været slumrende. Nu har vi taget den op for fuld kraft igen, vi er ikke længere flove over at indrømme, at Odin og Thor står os nær. Heller ikke det, der før blev kaldt overtro, er vi flove over, for det er noget naturligt."

The sense of an accessible and palpable unity of pre-Christian traditional heritage with one's own experience goes hand-in-hand with the popular acknowledgment that Christian influences play at least a minor role in the poetic Edda. Downplaying the fact that the preserved manuscript dates back to the 13th century, more than 250 years after Iceland's Christianization, most Icelandic and some Scandinavian Asatruers consider it a genuine source, free of Christian influences.[13] Others proceed a little more cautiously when asked about the role Old Norse texts play in their belief, such as this Norwegian Asatruer:

> They are pretty important to me, but at the same time, I don't stare myself blind on them, because I have studied some of this, and I know that the majority is written in the 12th and 13th century, and by then, Christianity had dominated for a hundred or two hundred years and there is nobody who had had to deal with Paganism in a concrete way, it has just become oral tradition. Nevertheless I think there is a core of truth.[14]

Skeptical attitudes like this can have two consequences. They can either lead to a confident, eclectic handling of medieval sources, an attitude that is denounced by others as an arbitrary and frivolous "anything goes" approach.[15] Or, the Eddas and sagas remain central and binding fundaments, "the scriptures," as one Danish Asatruer put it, which are used to keep beliefs and practices "pure" through the application of a "rigorous source criticism" – a phrase which, in this case, implies the identification of any Christian influence and its subsequent removal, the source thus arriving at a Pagan essence.[16]

In Norway, and particularly in Sweden, there has at times been a more overt split between those who take their inspiration from written sources as well as from academic and literary writings on those sources, and those who believe in

---

13   Frequently, it is contrasted with Snorri's Edda, which holds a somewhat more contested place, being considered the concoction of a Christian scribe by some (Interview U) and a valid basis by others (Interview T).

14   Interview Q: "For meg så er de ganske viktige, [...] men samtidig ser jeg meg ikke blind på dem, fordi at jeg har jo studert en del av dette her, og jeg vet jo at mesteparten er jo skrevet på elleve – og tolvhundretallet og da er det jo...da har jo kristendommen dominert i hundre – tohundre år og det er ingen som lever da som har hatt noe med hedendommen på kroppen, lissom, det er bare blitt muntlige overleveringer, men likevel tror jeg at det er en del kjerne av sannhet der."

15   Interview I.

16   Interview V, with a Danish Asatruer, July 2010, Denmark.

a line of rural folk customs and traditions they perceive to be more authentic and reliable. The Swedish group *Samfälligheten för Nordisk Sed* here appears as the most radical in its complete rejection of alternative religious and New Age approaches.[17] Generally speaking, however, the trend in Norway and Sweden tends more toward a reconciliation between the two factions of a-racist Asatru. The renaming of *Sveriges Asatrosamfund's* to *Samfundet Forn Sed*, and the growing understanding between Norwegian *Bifrost* and *Foreningen Forn Sed*, are institutional indicators that a compromise has been reached between the different interpretations of the sources.

The notion that Norse mythology is an integral part of a Scandinavian cultural and religious heritage, and that Scandinavians thus have a more legitimate claim to the Old Norse sources, periodically leads to the devaluation of other countries' claims, in particular those of American Asatruers. Some Scandinavian Heathens blame their American counterparts for integrating obscure esoteric readings of Norse mythology into their beliefs, of being too heavily influenced by Wicca, or of "having seen the light in Asatru," leading them to "therefore gorge on all imaginable source materials."[18] This quote points to an awareness in Scandinavian Asatru of the existing sources' unreliability. It also highlights that, in countries outside of Scandinavia, Asatru cannot use Norse mythology as an integral, self-evident part of a national cultural heritage. In England, for example, Celtic myth (or what is considered as such) and Arthurian legend have been much more foundational for a national mythology, and the Wicca movement dominates modern Neopaganism in England and America to a much larger degree than in the Scandinavian countries.[19] Sure enough, Asatruers in these countries cite the same sources as their Scandinavian counter-parts. In order to justify the use of Scandianavian sources as part of their own national mythological heritage, they rely mostly on the construction of an Anglo-Saxon and partly Viking legacy. Pete Jennings, co-founder of the a-racist English *Odinshof* and long-standing, now-retired president of the *Pagan Federation*,

---

17 Cf. Gregorius, *Modern Asatro*, 111–113.
18 Jannik Thalbitzer Thiberg, "Hvad skal vi udbrede? Hvad står man for i asatro?," *Valravn. Hedensk tidskrift om samfund og kultur* 11 (2004), 15: "de nyreligiøse amerikanere, som åbenbart har set lyset i asatroen, og derfor æder alt kildematerialet råt."
19 The debates about authenticity, continuity and the use of sources is a problem Asatru shares with other Neopagan denominations, for example Wicca, which had originally claimed to revive a pre-Christian, old-European mystery and fertility religion that allegedly existed in an oral and initiatory lineage since before the Christianization of Europe. The majority of Wicca has by now abandoned this claim of an unbroken line of tradition. This is discussed at length in Hutton, *The Triumph of the Moon*.

asserts that the Anglo-Saxons brought a "religion of Teutonic origins" to England, and that Icelandic sources can therefore be used as a basis for this religion.[20] Jennings implicitly relies on the assumption of a 'Germanic' or 'Teutonic' unity. He claims that folk customs can be used to supplement this written evidence because they preserve a knowledge of Heathen beliefs and practices that is otherwise lost.[21] As mentioned in Chapter 1, both Anglo-Saxon ideology in the 19th century and Neopaganism (including Wicca) in general rely heavily on the Romantic theories of a pre-Christian folk heritage that were developed by Jacob and Wilhelm Grimm and others. This is true for Scandinavian Asatru as well. Here, however, the idea that one can take up one's own tradition by examining Norse mythology is much more naturalized, as this mythology forms an integral part of the respective Scandinavian national histories. Therefore, the constructed nature of such concepts is less visible.[22] Asatruers in other countries have to invest more into theoretical explanations of their choice of source material and its applicability. Hence, it comes as no surprise that American and German Asatru both depend strongly on Jacob Grimm's *Teutonic Mythology*. It is considered to be an almost primary source because it integrates Scandinavian, Continental, and Anglo-Saxon written, linguistic, and folkloristic evidence in the holistic construction of a German(ic) mythology.

In German Asatru, the discussions about the status of the various sources hover around similar topics. Here, different groups stand for different attitudes towards the same basic sources, namely Old Icelandic literature, folklore, and archaeological finds. In Ariosophic groups such as the *Armanen-Orden*, the Edda in particular is read in the tradition of Guido List and his followers, as a revelation of secret truths that can be decoded with the help of esoteric and occult knowledge by initiates.[23] The ethnicist *Germanische*

---

20   Jennings, *The Norse Tradition*, 7–9.
21   Ibid., 40f.
22   Nevertheless, Scandinavian Asatruers share the underlying dilemmas in many ways. We might, for example, ask if the perception of the medieval Icelandic sources as 'Nordic,' and as immediate reflections of a 'national' or 'native' Swedish or Danish mythological heritage, is not the expression of a cultural imperialist move as well, which could be compared to the German appropriation of Scandinavian sources as Germanic for a construction of a German national mythology. (Cf. Maja Hagerman, *Det rena landet. Om konsten att uppfinna sine förfäder* (Stockholm: Prisma, 2006)). And we could ask where the idea that Asatru can build on a quasi-natural "cultural current" – as one Asatruer from Denmark put it – actually comes from. Cf. Interview K.
23   The *Armanen-Orden* insists that the Edda originated between the last Ice Ages, and that it was recorded in an encrypted form by the Icelandic Heathen priest Saemundr, who only pretended to be a Christian priest in order to protect his knowledge and save it from

Glaubensgemeinschaft attests to the status of Eddic literature as an authentic and ancient source as well, saying "we take the Eddas seriously as religious sources and do not see any Christian influence in them."[24] This claim is countered by a member of the a-racist *Eldaring*, who emphasizes both the validity of taking a certain cultural context seriously and basing one's modern faith on a dialogue with both the sources themselves, and the academic theories surrounding them:

> We scarcely have secure sources for how a blot was held back then. And we live in the twenty-first century. [...] We do not play with certain historical periods, but live our faith today. On the other hand, 'traditional' can maybe also mean to take our faith seriously, to try to live up to it in a certain sense, to consider it a closed system that originates in a specific cultural context and doesn't avail itself arbitrarily as it seems fit, to appreciate the discourse with the surviving sources but also with the current research on them. In this way we would very much like to be traditional.[25]

In the *Eldaring*, there is a theoretical consensus, which has been adopted from the American mother organization *The Troth*, supporting the use of Eddic sources as a "system of orientation and reference,"[26] and supplemented by readings of popularized academic summaries.[27]

---

persecution and elimination. This theory allows for the conclusion to consider the Edda as Germanic, and most of all, German property. Schnurbein, *Religion als Kulturkritik*, 43, cf. 40–43.

24 Géza von Neményi in an interview, see Ravn, "Interview med Géza von Neményi den Tyske Allherjargode," 10.

25 "Interview med Tim Peters fra Eldaring," *Valravn. Hedensk tidskrift om samfund og kultur* 14 (2005), 8: "Vi har næppe sikre kilder for, hvordan et blot foregik den gang. Og som sagt lever vi i det 21. århundrede. Et nutidigt ritual må imødekomme nutidsmenneskers behov. Vi leger ikke med bestemte historiske perioder, men lever vores tro i dag. På den anden side kan 'traditionel' måske også forstås på den måde, at vi tager vores tro alvorlig, at vi forsøger at leve efter den i den beskrevne mening, at betragte den som et lukket system, som stammer fra en ganske bestemt kulturel kontekst og ikke betjener sig på må og få, som det nu passer, – at vi sætter stor pris på diskursen med de overleverede kilder, men også med den aktuelle forskning dertil. På den måde vil vi meget gerne være traditionelle."

26 "Orientierungs- und Bezugssystem," Correspondence with Kurt Oertel (Eldaring).

27 For example by Maier, *Die Religion der Germanen*; Simek, *Religion und Mythologie der Germanen*, Jan de Vries, *Altgermanische Religionsgeschichte* (Berlin/Leipzig: de Gruyter, 1935–37).

In recent years, we can identify a shift in emphasis from Scandinavian to continental sources within German and American Asatru.[28] This shift has led to a renewed interest in folkloristic, as well as archeological, evidence. The latter in particular is considered more reliable by some Asatruers, because it seems older and less tainted by Christian influences than the textual evidence.[29] However, the usefulness of folkloristic evidence as proof of the survival of pre-Christian beliefs and practices seems to be more contested in German Asatru than in other countries. Kurt Oertel, the Warden of *Eldaring*, generally rejects the use of folkloristic sources, claiming them to be unreliable,

> because they tell us nothing about Germanic traditions, and they do not give any corroboration that modern traditions reach back into a pre-Christian past. [...] The way one arbitrarily explained festivals and customs whose Christian origin was not immediately visible as 'Pagan-Germanic' and took for granted an unbroken continuity, had nothing whatsoever to do with any scholarly standard.[30]

Another member of the *Eldaring* asserts the contrary:

> An essential part of the old traditions go back to pre-Christian roots. Also in our region, continuities are likely. For me, the cautious reserve of some folklorists towards this approach has always been astonishing. Especially because with some scholars it takes on the dimension of a fanatic denial. [...] Apparently, what must not be, cannot be. Of course, in this connection there is never offered a conclusive explanation of what such customs might go back to instead.[31]

---

28   See for example McNallen, "Three Decades of the Ásatrú Revival in America," 216.
29   Cf. for example Interview F.
30   Correspondence with Kurt Oertel (Eldaring): "weil sie [...] keinerlei Bestätigung dafür erbringen kann, dass neuzeitliches Brauchtum in vorchristliche Zeit zurückreichen würde. [...] die Selbstverständlichkeit, mit der man dort vor 1945 Feste und Bräuche, deren christlicher Ursprung nicht sofort ins Auge sprang, willkürlich als ‚heidnisch-germanisch' zu erklären und eine ungebrochene Kontinuität vorauszusetzen versuchte, hatte mit Wissenschaftlichkeit nichts zu tun."
31   Tiurik Alvisson, "Brauchtum und Heidentum – eine Annäherung," *Herdfeuer. Die Zeitschrift des Eldaring e.V.* 3, no. 9 (2005), 6: "dass ein wesentlicher Teil alten Brauchtums auf vorchristliche Wurzeln zurückgeht. Auch bei uns sind [...] Kontinuitäten wahrscheinlich. Die vorsichtige Zurückhaltung einiger Volkskundler gegenüber diesem Ansatz ist für mich immer wieder erstaunlich. Vor allem, da sie bei vielen Wissenschaftlern das Ausmaß

Although the attitudes towards specific sources vary between countries and groups, we can conclude that they share similar patterns and an interest in finding some measure of unity and continuity for their faith and convictions.

This warrants a closer investigation into the scholarly sources Asatruers make use of, as well as into their historical contexts and the interactions between scholarship and new religions in (re)constructions of 'Germanic' or 'Nordic' religion and culture. After all, as the previous chapters have already shown, Asatruers were not the first to invest in the business of historical reconstruction in the service of a cultural and religious renewal.

Völkisch Scholarship and Germanic Faith

Germanic Neopagan adaptations of scholarship can be understood as popularizations of academic approaches in the tradition of Romanticism, with which Neopagans have at times shared goals, dreams, and convictions. Such approaches strongly emphasize intuition and psychology. They bear witness to the desire to spur a national spiritual rebirth by going back to ancient sources in which an untainted origin is sought. This method and ideology has not been limited to Germany. It also appears in both the construction of a Nordic Viking Age[32] and of an Anglo-Saxon past for England.[33] As Allen J. Frantzen has so astutely observed, the underlying method "relies on a belief in the fragment, or part, as that from which the system of the whole can be reconstructed."[34] This type of holism obviously lends itself to Reconstructionist religions and has in fact a mythic quality itself.[35]

The first wave of productivity in the search for a national identity in Germany and other European countries unfolded in the 19th century, when,

---

von fanatischer Verneinung annimmt. [...] Anscheinend kann nicht sein, was nicht sein darf. Freilich wird in diesem Zusammenhang auch nie eine schlüssige Erklärung angeboten, auf was diese Bräuche denn sonst zurück gehen könnten." The author overlooks a whole strand of research that has been able to demonstrate interactions between high culture and folk culture in modern eras and thus explain the origin of folk beliefs and customs in similar, considerably more recent, interactions. Cf. Amy Gazin-Schwartz and Cornelius Holtorf, "'As long as ever I've known it...' On Folklore and Archaeology," in *Archaeology and Folklore*, ed. Amy Gazin-Schwartz and Cornelius Holtorf (London/New York: Routledge, 1999), 12f.

32   Cf. Hagerman, *Det rena landet. Om konsten att uppfinna sine förfäder*.
33   Frantzen, *Desire for Origins*; Allen J. Frantzen and John D. Niles, *Anglo-Saxonism and the Construction of Social Identity* (University Press of Florida, 1997).
34   Frantzen, *Desire for Origins*, 110.
35   Wiwjorra, "Germanenmythos und Vorgeschichtsforschung im 19. Jahrhundert," 368f.

in the wake of Herder and the brothers Grimm in particular, a collection of new scholarly disciplines emerged, including *Germanistik*, Anglo-Saxon-Studies, and folklore. A second wave took off in the late 19th century with the emergence of the *völkisch* study of the Germanic, which gained its strongest momentum in the 1930s and early 40s in Germany. From the outset, the study of 'Germanic antiquity' was an interdisciplinary endeavor, to which the established fields of Germanic linguistics, philology, and history contributed. It also provided opportunities for new disciplines to move from the margins of academia to the center. One of them was German archaeology, or prehistory,[36] which tried to establish itself in competition with the archeology of Greek and Roman antiquity in the late 19th century. Its central proponent, Gustaf Kossina (1858–1931), attempted to prove that independent Teutonic and Indo-European culture had its origins in Northern regions and spread from there.[37] Other new disciplines which managed to establish themselves around the same time were physical anthropology, in particular its incarnation as 'race science,'[38] folklore, cultural anthropology, and the history of religions. This interdisciplinary *Germanenkunde* (literally: Lore of the Germanic), or *Germanische Altertumskunde* (Lore of Germanic antiquity), was set in opposition to the study of Roman and Greek antiquity, which dominated not only the universities but also the curricula of the *Gymnasium*, the German classical high school. Ingo Wiwjorra points to the ideological origin of this field and identifies three central issues that were at stake in this

---

36 Cf. Heiko Steuer, ed. *Eine hervorragend nationale Wissenschaft. Deutsche Prähistoriker zwischen 1900 und 1995*, Ergänzungsbände zum Reallexikon der Germanischen Altertumskunde (Berlin/New York: de Gruyter, 2001).

37 Cf. Ingo Wiwjorra, *Der Germanenmythos. Konstruktion einer Weltanschauung in der Altertumsforschung des 19. Jahrhunderts* (Darmstadt: Wissenschaftliche Buchgesellschaft, 2006); Heinz Grünert, *Gustaf Kossina (1858–1931). Vom Germanisten zum Prähistoriker. Ein Wissenschaftler im Kasiserreich und in der Weimarer Republik*, vol. 22, Vorgeschichtliche Forschungen (Rahden (Westf.): Verlag Marie Leidorf, 2002) (see also the critical review by Ingo Wiwjorra, "Review of Heinz Grünert: Gustaf Kossina (1858–1931)," *Ethnographisch-Archäologische Zeitschrift* 44 (2003)). Heiko Steuer, "Das 'völkisch' Germanische in der deutschen Ur- und Frühgeschichtsforschung," in *Zur Geschichte der Gleichung 'germanisch-deutsch.' Sprache und Namen, Geschichte und Institutionen*, ed. Heinrich Beck, et al., RGA Sonderband (Berlin/New York: de Gruyter, 2004), 383f, draws attention to the fact that archaeology was considered to be an eminently national science, also in other European countries, including Scandinavia, and that the intertwinement with racial science could be found amongst Swedish archaeologists of the era as well.

38 Cf. Wiwjorra, *Der Germanenmythos. Konstruktion einer Weltanschauung in der Altertumsforschung des 19. Jahrhunderts*, 28f.

"construction of a *Weltanschauung*."[39] This multidisciplinary enterprise aimed at proving the great antiquity of a Germanic culture, its high level of development, and its origin in either Germany, Northern Europe, or even Atlantis – all of which are located in the North as opposed to the Orient, from where Christianity had supposedy brought "the light" or spiritual enlightenment.[40]

One source of inspiration for both Scandinavian (in particular Danish) and German scholarship on Germanic myth and culture was the Danish historian of religion Vilhelm Grønbech, with his book *The Culture of the Teutons* (1909–1912).[41] Grønbech used a particular interpretation of the Icelandic sagas to offer a panoptic reconstruction of the mentality of "the Germanic peoples," beginning with the era of Tacitus and tracing through to the late Middle Ages. With his German contemporaries, he shared the goal of proving the existence of a highly developed, independent, ancient Germanic culture. He thus hoped to gain insight into the 'reality' of 'the ancestors' through the reconstruction of their ethics, cosmology, anthropology, and culture.[42] In Grønbech's eyes, this past can and should be re-constructed in order to identify the roots that gave 'our ancestors' their strength, perhaps providing inspiration for contemporary cultural life. Peace,[43] honor, kin and clan, *hamingja*, revenge, and fate emerge as key concepts in his writing.

Vilhelm Grønbech was inspired by late 19th century historians of religion and their interest in 'primitive' religion and animism, particularly James George Frazer. Just as Frazer provided the impetus for research into pre-Christian religion and practices of English Paganism, especially Wicca,[44] Grønbech's theories served as an inspiration for scholars and enthusiasts of a

---

39 "Germanenmythos und Vorgeschichtsforschung im 19. Jahrhundert."
40 For academic and esoteric speculations about Atlantis and the north or the ice as the cradle for all higher culture see, for example, Joscelyn Godwin, *Arktos. The Polar Myth in Science, Symbolism, and Nazi Survival* (Kempton, IL: Adventures Unlimited Press, 1996); Franz Wegener, *Das atlantidische Weltbild. Nationalsozialismus und Neue Rechte auf der Suche nach der versunkenen Atlantis* (Gladbeck: KFVR – Kulturförderverein Ruhrgebiet e.V., 2001).
41 Cf. Grønbech, *Vor Folkeæt i Oldtiden*. The English translation appeared in 1931, cf. *The Culture of the Teutons*.
42 *Vor Folkeæt i Oldtiden*, 151.
43 Peace appears as a "hard" ideal, which works inwards towards one's kin; it is an activist concept that calls for blood revenge against anybody who threatens it from outside the clan.
44 Cf. Hutton, *The Triumph of the Moon*; Lanwerd, *Mythos, Mutterrecht und Magie*.

neo-Germanic religion.[45] In contrast to many of his followers' overt Germanophile political predilections, Grønbech's holistic imagination is untainted by direct political agendas. This fact, allied with the accessibility of English and German translations of his work after 1945, enabled the enthusiastic reception of his work, not only in Scandinavian but also American and German Asatru as well. Although he makes an honest attempt to envision Old Norse society with the help of an intuitive grasp of the sagas' essence, his texts are nonetheless permeated by the life-philosophy of his own era. By basing his interpretations on categories such as experience (including mystical experience), wholeness, and authenticity, he gives his readers the chance to alloy their own life-philosophical ideals with the *Weltanschauung* of 'their ancestors.' The ensuing mirror effect of recognition gives contemporary Pagans the illusion of being able to connect with the historical depths of their ancestral religion.

Vilhelm Grønbech's work inspired a number of scholars, who turned from Eddic literature to saga literature as central sources for mythology in the first third of the 20th century. For them, as for Grønbech, these texts seemed to provide an authentic and realistic depiction of their Germanic ancestors' lives and worldviews. Central protagonists of this school were Swiss scholar Andreas Heusler (1865–1940), who served as chair of Germanic Philology at Berlin University from 1914–1919, and afterwards at the University of Basel; Gustav Neckel (1878–1940), Heusler's successor in Berlin; and Bernhard Kummer (1897–1962), Neckel's temporary colleague and assistant.[46] Together with other enthusiasts for the renewal of a Germanic faith, such as Arthur Bonus, the eloquent supporter of a "Germanization of Christianity,"[47] and Otto Siegfried Reuter, the founder of the *Deutschgläubige Gemeinschaft*, the three scholars depicted Germanic religion as an immanent religion in which the divine manifests in man, nature, folk, or race. Claiming that "gods and men form a

---

45 This has also to do with Frazer's and Grønbech's rejection of an evolutionism which depicted the 'primitives' as backward. Cf. Jørgen Prytz-Johansen, *Religionshistorikeren Vilhelm Grønbech* (Copenhagen: Gyldendal, 1987), 107. The immense impact of Grønbech's ideas and categories for 20th century Scandinavian literature (for example on Johannes V. Jensen and Aksel Sandemose) are well known, although considerably under-researched.

46 The following arguments on Heusler, Neckel, and Kummer are further developed in Schnurbein, "Religionsforskning og religionsfornyelse i 'nordisk' ånd i Tyskland etter første verdenskrig" and "Nordisten und Nordglaube. Wechselwirkungen zwischen akademischen und religiösen Konzepten von germanischer Religion," in *Germanentum im Fin de siècle. Wissenschaftsgeschichtliche Studien zum Werk Andreas Heuslers* ed. Jürg Glauser and Julia Zernack (Basle: Schwabe, 2005).

47 Bonus, *Von Stoecker zu Naumann*.

community of fate" and that the "Nordic gods are ideal images of Nordic man,"[48] the works incorporated images of Germanic heroism, individualism, fatalism, and the *fulltrúi* belief of Germanic fealty discussed in Chapter 3.

Before addressing the common background to the striking similarities between the concepts of these in fact quite ideologically and temperamentally divergent scholars, some of the fundamental differences in their views of Germanic religion must be addressed. Andreas Heusler was strictly and often controversially opposed to any attempt at reviving a Germanic religion. He dismissed any alleged national sentiment in Germanic mentality that, according to his description, distinguished itself by its anti-state individualism.[49] While both Neckel and Kummer worked actively for the establishment of a neo-Germanic religion,[50] their views of the god Odin could not have been more different from each other. For Neckel, Odin appeared as a Dionysian character, the embodiment of a dynamic spirit of war and poetry.[51] Kummer, in his cultural pessimist dissertation *"Midgards Untergang"* (Midgard's Decline), described the cult of Odin as a symptom of the deterioration of Germanic culture, as a foreign influence pioneering degenerate Christian morals of sin and redemption.[52]

All of these concepts are idealized and ideological images of a Germanic antiquity that was set against an allegedly degenerate (Christian) modernity. All the aforementioned scholars also directed their criticism against

---

48   Bernhard Kummer, *Die germanische Weltanschauung nach altnordischer Überlieferung. Vortrag, gehalten im Auftrag der 'Vereinigung der Freunde germanischer Vorgeschichte' in Detmold am 10. Juni 1930* (Leipzig: Adolf Klein, 1933), 29: "Götter und Menschen bilden eine Schicksalsgemeinschaft" ... "die nordischen Götter sind Idealbilder nordischer Menschlichkeit".

49   Cf. Andreas Heusler, *Germanentum. Vom Lebens- und Formgefühl der alten Germanen* (Heidelberg: Winter, n.d. (ca. 1942)), 38, where he claims: "There was no Germanic sense of community" – "Es gab kein germanisches Gemeinschaftsgefühl."

50   Kummer was a member of the *Nordisch-religiöse Arbeitsgemeinschaft* (cf. Fritz Heinrich, *Die deutsche Religionswissenschaft und der Nationalsozialismus. Eine ideologiekritische und wissenschaftsgeschichtliche Untersuchung* (Petersberg: Michael Imhof Verlag, 2002), 186–200; "Bernhard Kummer (1897–1962). The Study of Religions Between Religious Devotion for the Ancient Germans, Political Agitation, and Academic Habitus," in *The Study of Religion under the Impact of Fascism*, ed. Horst Junginger (Leiden/Boston: Brill, 2008)), and Neckel joined the appeal to found the *Deutsche Glaubensbewegung* in 1933. Cf. Breuer, *Die Völkischen in Deutschland*, 259.

51   Gustav Neckel, *Die altgermanische Religion*, Zeitfragen deutscher Kultur Heft 2 (Berlin: Wendt, 1932), 11.

52   Kummer, *Die germanische Weltanschauung nach altnordischer Überlieferung*, 36.

well-known 'enemies' who, according to widespread popular right-wing opinions, were made responsible for this downfall of Germanic values: the Roman world, revolutionary France, the Socialist workers' movement, the Capitalist West, as well as the Jews, who were suspected to lurk behind all of the above. They also shared the goal of a Germanic rebirth: a mostly spiritual notion for German Faithlers, but understood as a revival of German national self-confidence by Germanists and Scandinavianists. A volume edited by Hermann Nollau in 1926[53] summarizes this popularized academic agenda in its title – *"Germanische Wiedererstehung: Ein Werk über die germanischen Grundlagen unserer Gesittung"* ("Germanic Revival: A Study of the Germanic Foundation of our Culture"). In his preface, Nollau denounced the plight of the German people, attributing it to the "excessive permeation of our original nature by foreign cultural thoughts." He then called on German scholars to assist in the "revival of the Germanic past in our people's knowledge."[54]

The concept of religion with which both Neckel and particularly Kummer operated was provided by Jakob Wilhelm Hauer (1881–1962). Hauer was chair of the department for the history of religions at the University of Marburg, and was one of the founding fathers of this discipline, which provided a sustainable academic impetus for the formation of an institutionalized neo-Germanic religion. The indologist and student of Rudolf Otto (1869–1937) shared with his teacher the belief that all religion originates in inner, non-rational experiences, and that the study of religion can only be approached properly through a scholar's own religious feelings.[55] In order to explain the major differences

---

53   Hermann Nollau, ed. *Germanische Wiedererstehung. Ein Werk über die germanischen Grundlagen unserer Gesittung* (Heidelberg: Winter, 1926). It is the volume in which Andreas Heusler's above-quoted essay was published.

54   Ibid.: "übermäßige[.] Durchsetzung unseres ursprünglichen Wesens durch fremde Kulturgedanken" – "Wiedererstehung der germanischen Vergangenheit in dem Wissen unseres Volkes."

55   The early promoters of the field of history of religions and the phenomenology of religion, such as Rudolf Otto, Jakob Wilhelm Hauer, and Mircea Eliade were subsumed by what Rainer Flasche has aptly called a "prophecy-syndrome." Cf. Burkhard Gladigow, "Religionsgeschichte des Gegenstandes – Gegenstände der Religionsgeschichte," in *Religionswissenschaft. Eine Einführung*, ed. Hartmut Zinser (Berlin: Dietrich Reimer Verlag, 1988), 7; Heinrich, *Die deutsche Religionswissenschaft und der Nationalsozialismus*, 105. In this context, it would be interesting to follow the trajectory Peter van Rooden has suggested in his critical discussion of concepts of secularization. He put forward the thesis that what has been called "secularization" in the early 19th century could more aptly be described as a "relocation of religion," which is related to the replacement of confessional states with nation-states. "Whereas the social and political practices of the confessional state had located religion in a visible and hierarchical social order, the practices of the

between religions, which, according to these theories, were all based on fundamental ecstatic experiences, Hauer turned to racial anthropology, in particular to the ideas of Hans F.K. Günther (1891–1968).[56]

Their common interests in a national revival occasionally motivated the aforementioned scholars to collaborate with religously motivated lay scholars, sometimes involving themselves actively in the Germanic Faith Movement. Even the a-religious, anti-nationalist Heusler was captured by the spirit of Germanic revival and inspired by the dilettante Arthur Bonus, a former Protestant minister and active promoter of a "Germanized Christianity."[57] Bernhard Kummer embodied both the academic and the religious activist. He served as editor of several *völkisch* religious journals, including *Nordische Stimmen* (Nordic Voices), and also as a leading member of the *Nordisch-religiöse Arbeitsgemeinschaft* (Nordic religious work association), which was incorporated by the *Deutsche Glaubensbewegung* (German Faith Movement) in 1933. However, these activities, as well as his speculative theories, soon brought him the rejection of his academic colleagues.[58] Heusler's successor, Gustav Neckel, frequently quoted Herman Wirth and Wihelm Teudt, two lay scholars whose work he initially publicly endorsed and who have remained important references for Germanic Neopagans up until today.[59]

---

       nation-state located religion in the inner selves of the members of the moral community of the nation." (Peter van Rooden, "Secularization and the Trajectory of Religion in the West," in *Post-Theism. Reframing the Judeo-Christian Tradition*, ed. Henri A. Krop (Leuven: Peeters, 2000), 181). The study of the particular relation he posits between nation-state and protestant introspection could be fruitful not only for the study of historians of religions but also their Neopagan followers.

56   Günther was to become a leading race-theorist of the National Socialist era. Günther was engaged in the revival of Germanic religion on racial grounds as well, and he supported the existence of a 'racial soul' as the prime form-giving category or *Gestalt-Idee*. Cf. Nanko, *Die Deutsche Glaubensbewegung*, Horst Junginger, *Von der philologischen zur völkischen Religionswissenschaft. Das Fach Religionswissenschaft an der Universität Tübingen von der Mitte des 19. Jahrhunderts bis zum Ende des Dritten Reiches*, vol. 51, Contubernium. Tübinger Beiträge zur Universitäts- und Wissenschaftsgeschichte (Stuttgart: Franz Steiner Verlag, 1999), 57, 166f; Emberland, *Religion og rase*, 55–57.

57   Cf. Zernack, *Geschichten aus Thule*, 3, for a discussion of Bonus and his engagement for the popularization of saga literature. For a discussion of Bonus' religious ideas and activities see Lächele, "Germanisierung des Christentums." See also Chapter 1.

58   Cf. Heinrich, *Die deutsche Religionswissenschaft und der Nationalsozialismus*, 186–200; "Bernhard Kummer."

59   Cf. Hunger, *Die Runenkunde im Dritten Reich*, 333.

Herman Wirth (1885–1981) was a Dutch-born philologist, historian, musicologist, and national-Romantic enthusiast for a pan-German 'matriarchal' ideology,[60] as well as author of the cultural-pessimist *"Der Aufgang der Menschheit"* ("The Rise of Mankind").[61] He dedicated his life to the study of a supposed ancient Atlantic civilization, which had, he claimed, inspired all the world's cultures. Wirth was especially interested in this culture's symbols, in particular the runes, which he thought to be the origin of all other symbolic systems. With his growing collection of signs and ornaments from all over the world, he aimed to spur a "rebirth of the Nordic race" and with it the liberation of mankind from the curse of civilization.[62] Wirth's method did not show a single trace of source criticism, and when he insisted on the authenticity of the so-called *"Ura-Linda-Chronik"* (also known as the "Oera-Linda-Book"), his status as both an academic charlatan and a cultural icon became firmly established.[63] Ousted by academic colleagues, Wirth found supporters in leading circles of the National Socialist party after 1933, and co-founded the SS research institution *Deutsches Ahnenerbe* (Ancestral Heritage) together with Heinrich Himmler and Walter Darré in 1935.[64] Prior to his removal from his post as *Ahnenerbe* director in 1937, he was able to organize an expedition to Sweden and Norway, where he was able to disseminate his ideas in extreme nationalist, racist, and anti-Semitic circles in Sweden, especially through his lectures held at the neo-Gothicist *Manhems* Association.[65]

---

60 See Chapter 7.
61 Wirth, *Der Aufgang der Menschheit*.
62 Cf. Hunger, *Die Runenkunde im Dritten Reich*, 186–191; Michael H. Kater, *Das 'Ahnenerbe' der SS 1935–1945. Ein Beitrag zur Kulturpolitik des Dritten Reiches* (Stuttgart: Deutsche Verlags-Anstalt, 1974), 12f.
63 The Oera-Linda-Book is an allegedly ancient history of a Frisian family, published in the Netherlands in 1872 and exposed as a forgery shortly after. It presents a "racially pure and matriarchal" utopian society, "which is credited with the creation of European culture," and constitutes a "curious combination of Germanophile racism, a Romantic ideology of motherhood, and liberal constitutional concerns." Davies, "'Männerbund' and 'Mutterrecht,'" 89f. Wirth used this allegedly "oldest testament of the North" as support for his own ideas. Cf. also Hunger, *Die Runenkunde im Dritten Reich*, 181.
64 For Wirth's brief activities in the *Ahnenerbe* see Kater, *Das 'Ahnenerbe' der SS 1935–1945*, 11–42; Hunger, *Die Runenkunde im Dritten Reich*, 180–202; Anka Oesterle, "The Office of Ancestral Inheritance and Folklore Scholarship," in *The Nazification of an Academic Discipline. Folklore in the Third Reich*, ed. James R. Dow and Hansjost Lixfeld (Bloomington/Indianapolis: Indiana University Press, 1994), 202–205.
65 Cf. Luitgard Löw, "På oppdrag for Himmler. Herman Wirths ekspedisjoner til Skandinavias helleristninger," in *Jakten på Germania. Fra nordensvermeri til SS-arkeologi*, ed. Terje

Another lay scholar promoted by Heinrich Himmler was the former protestant minister and *völkisch* folklorist Wilhelm Teudt (1860–1942). Teudt combined his Germanophile religious interest with speculative theories about an ancient Germanic high culture. In the 1920s, he took up a number of older, unfounded speculations about the peculiar rock formation known as *Externsteine* near Detmold and the Teutoburg Forest.[66] Teudt claimed to have found the site of a "Germanic Stonehenge," the location of the sacred Saxon column, Irminsul, and the center for an ancient Germanic sun cult destroyed by Charlemagne.[67] Excavations were undertaken in 1932, but no traces of an ancient observatory or of its destruction by Charlemagne were found that could have confirmed Teudt's theories.[68] During the National Socialist regime, Heinrich Himmler adopted Teudt's ideas about *Externsteine* and developed plans to re-install a site of worship there.[69] Himmler initiated another

---

Emberland and Jorunn Sem Fure (Oslo: Humanist forlag, 2009). From 1952 on, Wirth used his Swedish contacts to establish himself in this country after his two-year internment as a collaborator. Cf. Roland Häke, *Der Fall Herman Wirth – 1978–1981 – im Landkreis Kusel oder: Das verschüttete Demokratiebewußtsein* (Frauenberg b. Marburg: Mutter-Erde-Verlag, 1981); Kater, *Das 'Ahnenerbe' der SS 1935–1945*, 63; Luitgard Löw, "Völkische Deutungen prähistorischer Sinnbilder. Herman Wirth und sein Umfeld," in *Völkisch und national. Zur Aktualität alter Denkmuster im 21. Jahrhundert*, ed. Uwe Puschner and G. Ulrich Großmann (Darmstadt: WBG, 2009).

66   The bizarre and impressive rock formation contains a medieval Christian chapel. Speculations about the existence of a pre-Christian site of worship go back to the 19th century, but have still not been verified up until today. Schockenhoff, "'Stonehenge' contra 'Störrische Kuh'"; Uta Halle, *'Die Externsteine sind bis auf weiteres germanisch!' Prähistorische Archäologie im Dritten Reich* (Steinhagen: Verlag für Regionalgeschichte, 2003).

67   Cf. *'Die Externsteine sind bis auf weiteres germanisch!,'* 116–125. As mentioned in Chapter 6, Teudt was inspired by the theory of ley lines advanced by the founder of geomancy Alfred Watkins in the early 1920s, and promoted the idea of the Externsteine being the crossing point of "cultic lines" connecting major ancient religious sites in Europe and Egypt.

68   Cf. ibid., 118–122; "Die Externsteine/Kr. Lippe. Ein Natur- und Kulturdenkmal im Spannungsfeld rechter und esoterischer Ideologie Stuttgart," in *Das Denkmal als Fragment – Das Fragment als Denkmal. Denkmale als Attraktionen. Jahrestagung der Vereinigung der Landesdenkmalpfleger (VdL) und des Verbandes der Landesarchäologen (VdLA) und 75. Tag für Denkmalpflege 10.-13. Juni 2007 in Esslingen a. N.*, ed. Regierungspräsidium Stuttgart – Landesamt für Denkmalpflege (Stuttgart: Landesamt für Denkmalpflege, 2008), 122.

69   Cf. Erich Kittel, *Die Externsteine als Tummelplatz der Schwarmgeister und im Urteil der Wissenschaft* (Detmold: Naturwissenschaftlicher Verein Detmold, 1965).

excavation during 1934/35 under Teudt's mentorship, which interpreted the findings as proof of Teudt's theories.[70]

Kummer, Wirth, Teudt, and others who moved in their circles were inspired by the ideal of an agrarian, rural, family-centered racial Germanic society in the 1930s. An altogether different vision was developed by the Scandinavianist and Germanist Otto Höfler (1901–1987), the supporter of the *Männerbund* theory discussed in Chapter 7. Like his antagonist Bernhard Kummer, Höfler's multi-disciplinary holistic approach to Germanic cult and culture was inspired by Vilhelm Grønbech, with whom he shared an interest in the application of contemporary ethnological research into the minds of 'the primitives' to matters Germanic. Höfler developed this holistic concept further into what he called 'cultural morphology,' a method that allegedly allowed him to grasp the *Gestalt* of Germanic culture.[71] In contrast to Grønbech, he did not reject folklore as a valid source for such inquiries, but instead included research on folk customs, in particular those of the alpine region, together with analyses of linguistic, textual, and pictorial evidence, into his set of methodologies.[72] He followed in the footsteps of Jacob Grimm and Wilhelm Mannhardt, whose Romantic ideas of an imagined continuity between "Germanic antiquity" and contemporary folklore were taken to new heights by the Vienna school of *Germanistik*. Within this academic school, two factions competed for

---

70 The archaeologist Julius Andree, the head of the excavation, never managed to present satisfactory material proof for these conclusions. In later years, this has led to speculations that the state museum in Detmold was deliberately suppressing and distorting evidence of a Pagan site of worship. Cf. Halle, *'Die Externsteine sind bis auf weiteres germanisch!,'* 507, as well as "Die Externsteine/Kr. Lippe," 122. Today, the site is popular amongst Neopagan groups of all persuasions. This is not the least due to a popular book on alleged ancient ritual sites by Gisela Graichen, *Das Kultplatzbuch. Ein Führer zu den alten Opferplätzen, Heiligtümern und Kultstätten in Deutschland* (Hamburg: Hoffmann & Campe, 1988). Cf. Martin Schmidt and Uta Halle, "On the Folklore of the Externsteine – or a Centre for Germanomaniacs," in *Archaeology and Folklore*, ed. Amy Gazin-Schwartz and Cornelius Holtorf (London/New York: Routledge, 1999), 161–164.

71 Cf. Julia Zernack, "Kontinuität als Problem der Wissenschaftsgeschichte," in *Kontinuität in der Kritik. Zum 50jährigen Bestehen des Münchner Nordistikinstituts: Historische und aktuelle Perspektiven der Skandinavistik*, ed. Klaus Böldl and Miriam Kauko, Rombach Wissenschaften – Reihe Nordica (Freiburg i.Br.: Rombach, 2005), 68f.

72 For the fundamental methodological differences between Grønbech and Höfler see Heinrich Beck, "Zur Rezeption von Vilhelm Grønbechs Werk im deutschen Sprachraum," in *Verschränkung der Kulturen. Der Sprach- und Literaturaustausch zwischen Skandinavien und den deutschsprachigen Ländern*, ed. Oskar Bandle, Jürg Glauser, and Stefanie Würth (Tübingen/Basle: Francke, 2004), 341.

authority of interpretation. One side saw its roots in myth, and the other focused on ritual as the source of religious and *völkisch* cultural continuity.[73] Belonging to the 'ritualists,' together with his teacher Rudolf Much and his colleague Lily Weiser, Höfler also made use of theories developed in a branch of German folklore studies (*Volkskunde*) in the 1920s which had an acute interest in religion. This variant of folklore explicitly understood itself not merely as an antiquarian endeavor. Rather, it formulated its goal as being "to glimpse the divine power which is eternal and leads man time and again to the same original experiences."[74]

Höfler's theories were not utilized by proponents of a Germanic religion initially, and Höfler himself connected his ideas less to a religious renewal than to political and cultural goals.[75] His work inspired a considerable number of other scholars in Germany and Scandinavia, among them Stig Wikander (1908–1983), of Sweden. Wikander further developed Höfler's ideas in his thesis on the Aryan *Männerbund*[76] and harbored fascist sympathies himself.[77]

---

[73] Olaf Bockhorn, "The Battle for the 'Ostmark.' Nazi Folklore in Austria," in *The Nazification of an Academic Discipline. Folklore in the Third Reich*, ed. James R. Dow and Hansjost Lixfeld (Bloomington/Indianapolis: Indiana University Press, 1994).

[74] Eugen Fehrle in his series editor's preface to Lily Weiser, *Altgermanische Jünglingsweihen und Männerbünde. Ein Beitrag zur deutschen und nordischen Altertums- und Volkskunde*, ed. Eugen Fehrle, Bausteine zur Volkskunde und Religionswissenschaft 1 (Bühl (Baden): Konkordia, 1927): "die göttliche Macht zu erschauen, die ewig ist und den Menschen immer wieder zu denselben Urerlebnissen führt." Fehrle was one of the first to introduce Hans F.K. Günther's concept of race into the discipline and later became the 'chief ideologist' of national socialist folklore. Peter Assion, "Eugen Fehrle and 'The Mythos of Our Folk,'" in *The Nazification of an Academic Discipline. Folklore in the Third Reich*, ed. James R. Dow and Hansjost Lixfeld (Bloomington/Indianapolis: Indiana University Press, 1994), 113–115.

[75] Höfler's willing and active participation in a political instrumentalization of his theories in the 1930s and 40s is reflected, among other things, in his report about the "Development of the intellectual situation in Scandinavia," which he wrote for the German Secret Service (the *Sicherheitsdienst*) in 1942. See Julia Zernack, "Nordische Philologie," in *Kulturwissenschaften und Nationalsozialismus*, ed. Jürgen Elvert and Jürgen Nielsen-Sikora (Stuttgart: Franz Steiner Verlag, 2008), 702.

[76] Stig Wikander, *Der arische Männerbund. Studien zur indo-iranischen Sprach- und Religionsgeschichte* (Lund: Gleerup, 1938). Two Austrian scholars who worked in a similar line as Höfler were his "ritualist" colleagues, Richard Wolfram, *Schwerttanz und Männerbund* (Kassel: Bärenreiter Verlag, 1935) and Robert Stumpfl, *Kultspiele der Germanen als Ursprung des mittelalterlichen Dramas* (Berlin: Junker und Dünnhaupt, 1936).

[77] Cf. Lincoln, *Theorizing Myth*, 126; Stefan Arvidsson, "Stig Wikander och forskningen om ariska mannaförbund," CHAOS. *Dansk-norsk tidsskrift for religionshistoriske studier* 38 (2002); Mihaela Timuş, "'Quand l'Allemange était leur Mecque...' La science des religions

Höfler's method is a prime example of the close collaboration between the disciplines of ancient history, archaeology, folklore, and (Germanic) philology[78] that characterized National Romantic scholarship. It was revitalized in early 20th century (German) scholarship, and subsequently turned into official state-doctrine during the 1930s. It privileged a paradigm of continuity as well as the search for a unity of *völkisch* essence in the past and in customs of rural life. Not only did this approach lead to the exclusion of Continental Jewish folklore,[79] urban life, and workers' lives from the material to be studied, the field also developed a decidedly anti-Christian slant.[80]

Höfler's theories also influenced the Swiss scholar Martin Ninck. Ninck's theories, which interpret Wodan as the expression of the Germanic racial soul, were one of the primary sources of inspiration for C.G. Jung's essay, "Wotan."[81] Ninck found a theoretical-aesthetic framework in the life-philosophy of Ludwig Klages[82] and followed a holistic approach similar to that of his forerunners, promising his readers a comprehensive overview (*Gesamtüberschau*), which would combine "science and life," and consider philology a mere auxiliary method in this process of reconstruction.[83] Reworking the concept of a Germanic fatalism, Ninck considered Wodan the "God in which the fate of a

---

chez Stig Wikander (1935–1941)," in *The Study of Religion under the Impact of Fascism*, ed. Horst Junginger (Leiden/Boston: Brill, 2008).

78 This was pointed out already by Hermann Bausinger in the 1960s in his critical discussion of National Socialist folklore. Bausinger's seminal article is available in an English translation: Hermann Bausinger, "Nazi Folk Ideology and Folk Research," in *The Nazification of an Academic Discipline. Folklore in the Third Reich*, ed. James R. Dow and Hansjost Lixfeld (Bloomington/Indianapolis: Indiana University Press, 1994).

79 Cf. Christoph Daxelmüller, "Nazi Conception of Culture and the Erasure of Jewish Folklore," in *The Nazification of an Academic Discipline. Folklore in the Third Reich*, ed. James R. Dow and Hansjost Lixfeld (Bloomington/Indianapolis: Indiana University Press, 1994).

80 In spite of the continual competition and controversy between the SS *Ahnenerbe* and the *Amt Rosenberg*, the main institutional bearers of folklore, archaeology, and historical studies outside the universities during Hitler's rule, the ideas of *völkisch* unity and continuity united the two factions and facilitated collaborations between researchers in both institutions. Cf. Wolfgang Emmerich, *Zur Kritik der Volkstumsideologie* (Frankfurt a.M.: Suhrkamp, 1971), "The Mythos of Germanic Continuity," in *The Nazification of an Academic Discipline. Folklore in the Third Reich*, ed. James R. Dow and Hansjost Lixfeld (Bloomington/Indianapolis: Indiana University Press, 1994), 46, who points to the significance of Alfred Rosenberg's anti-Christian, anti-Jewish ideology in this context.

81 Carl Gustav Jung, "Wotan," *Neue Schweizer Rundschau* III (Neue Folge), no. 11 (1936), 665.

82 For Klages cf. also Chapter 6.

83 Martin Ninck, *Wodan und germanischer Schicksalsglaube* (Jena: Diederichs, 1935).

race, *our* race, has been decided."⁸⁴ He attributed to the Germanic peoples two essential characteristics: male heroism, and *Wanderlust*, which led to numerous migrations and campaigns of conquest throughout the ages.⁸⁵ Deviating from Höfler and following Klages, he considered the "organic" fatalism that forms the core of Germanic religion to be a female force.⁸⁶ The polar opposition between the Roman and the Germanic is decisive for Ninck, and he makes sure to emphasize that this type of fatalism has nothing whatsoever to do with the "Jewish Jahve-religion" which he conceptualizes as completely alien to Germanic religion.⁸⁷ Ninck supposes the survival of a Pagan belief in Wodan and fate in Gothic and other 'Germanic' architecture, joining his German colleagues in fashioning another of the theories of continuity and unity of Germanic culture that are so appealing to Neopagans.⁸⁸

The main components of the image of an ancient Germanic religion, including heroic fatalism; the idea of an immanent, worldly faith; concepts of fealty; and the idea of strong women and ecstatic warrior bands, which continue to shape large parts of the religious ideas of German and Anglo-American Asatruers, were thus formulated within and by a network of mainly German and Austrian scholars during the 1920s and 30s. In spite of their differences and controversies, they agreed that it was both possible and desirable to reconstruct an 'Old Germanic' worldview, religion, and social structure from written, folkloristic, and material sources. They were united by their sympathy for, if not their active support of, contemporary fascist regimes and ideologies. Höfler, Wikander, and other scholars contributing to these ideas could thus be called parts of what Cristiano Grottanelli has called "a vast European front," a "cultural and trans-national *Männerbund*" of the totalitarian right, which

---

84   Ibid., 3: "eines Gottes, in dem sich das Schicksal einer Rasse, unserer Rasse entschieden hat."
85   Ibid., 108.
86   Although Ninck relies strongly on Höfler, and Höfler reviews Ninck quite favorably, he criticizes Ninck's emphasis on trance and the idea of the soul leaving the body in ecstatic states, because it can only capture the element of poetry and prophecy in Odin, but not the aspect of war which requires a much more orderly type of ecstasy. Cf. Otto Höfler, "Zwei Grundkräfte im Wodankult," in *Otto Höfler: Kleine Schriften. Ausgewählte Arbeiten zur germanischen Altertumskunde und Religionsgeschichte, zur Literatur des Mittelalters, zur germanischen Sprachwissenschaft sowie zur Kulturphilosophie und -morphologie*, ed. Helmut Birkhan (Hamburg: Helmut Buske Verlag, 1992 [1974]).
87   Ninck, *Wodan und germanischer Schicksalsglaube*, 334.
88   For a critique of such theories of "Germanic continuity," which employ continuity as a "seeming answer" instead of questioning it critically in each case, see Kellner, *Grimms Mythen*, 9f.

furthermore "kept in contact or re-contacted each other" after the war and continued to influence the study of religion after 1945.[89]

Remnants of *Völkisch* Scholarship after 1945

Many of the scholars working at the fringe of official academia, such as Herman Wirth, Wilhelm Teudt, and to a certain degree also Bernhard Kummer, had already been discredited by their more established colleagues by the mid to late 1930s. This did not prevent their continued religious productivity after the war. The right-wing subcultural network of associations and publishing houses that emerged in post-war Germany[90] ensured a largely unbroken continuity of *völkisch* myth.[91] Groups such as the *Deutschgläubige Gemeinschaft* and the *Artgemeinschaft* continued to quote Kummer and Neckel,[92] and Kummer himself remained active in Germanic religious circles.[93] The works by Teudt and Wirth had even more impact on the formation of the worldview of more recent Asatru groups in countries other than Germany as well.

After 1945, and contrary to evidence, Herman Wirth and his followers often presented him as having been persecuted by National Socialism.[94] This allowed him to pick up the threads of his pre-war activities after his return from Sweden. In 1954 he founded the *Gesellschaft für europäische Urgemeinschaftskunde/Herman-Wirth-Gesellschaft* (today called *Ur-Europa e.V.*) in Marburg and tried to raise money to establish a museum intended to hold his symbol collection.[95] In the 1970s and 80s, the aging Herman Wirth gained new

---

89 Cristiano Grottanelli, "War-time Connections: Dumézil and Eliade, Eliade and Schmitt, Schmitt and Evola, Drieu La Rochelle and Dumézil," in *The Study of Religion under the Impact of Fascism*, ed. Horst Junginger (Leiden/Boston: Brill, 2008), 313.

90 Cf. Chapter 1.

91 Wiwjorra, *Der Germanenmythos. Konstruktion einer Weltanschauung in der Altertumsforschung des 19. Jahrhunderts*, 19.

92 The *Artgemeinschaft* sold the quoted essay by Andreas Heusler, as well as works by Neckel (*Germanisches Heldentum*), together with publications of their own authors (http://asatru.de/versand/main_bigware_29.php?bigPfad=22, last accessed September 13, 2014), and quotes Kummer in several articles published on their homepage www.asatru.de.

93 Kummer collaborated with Jakob Wilhelm Hauer in the *Arbeitsgemeinschaft für freie Religionsforschung und Philosophie*, resp. the *Freie Akademie*. Cf. Nanko, "Religiöse Gruppenbildungen vormaliger 'Deutschgläubiger' nach 1945," 131.

94 Cf. Häke, *Der Fall Herman Wirth – 1978–1981 – im Landkreis Kusel oder: Das verschüttete Demokratiebewußtsein*; Kater, *Das 'Ahnenerbe' der SS 1935–1945*, 63; Eduard Gugenberger and Roman Schweidlenka, *Mutter Erde, Magie und Politik. Zwischen Faschismus und neuer Gesellschaft* (Vienna: Verlag für Gesellschaftskritik, 1987), 119.

95 Löw, "Völkische Deutungen prähistorischer Sinnbilder," 221–224.

supporters in green-alternative circles, who were drawn to his theories about Germanic matriarchy, as well as his ecological ideas.[96] After World War II, Wilhelm Teudt's theories were continually promoted by members of Germanic and *völkisch* religious groups. In the 1950s, Teudt's former assistant, Ulrich von Motz, espoused his theories in guided tours at the Externsteine rocks, where he also sold brochures published by the infamous right-wing company *Hohe Warte*, run by the *Ludendorff Gesellschaft*. Another lay scholar of the post-war era, Elisabeth Neumann-Gundrum, connected Teudt's and Wirth's theories with the phantasms of Jürgen Spanuth, who claimed that the German island Helgoland is identical to Atlantis.[97] Teudt's and Neumann-Gundrum's work on the Externsteine has been continually promoted by a working group founded by Walther Machalett, who was also active in the circles around the *Armanen-Orden* and proponent of Guido List's ideas.[98] In 2010, Matthias Wenger was elected president of the association known today as the *Forschungskreis Externsteine e.V.*[99] Wenger has been a long-term activist in German Asatru. In the mid-2000s, he publicly renounced his right-wing past.[100] At the same time, he has been writing for the research group's journal on a regular basis since

---

96 These contacts were facilitated by the fact that Wirth had considered Native Americans as the inheritors of the lost high Atlantic culture. One of Wirth's adherents, Andreas Lentz, a supporter of Native American spirituality in Germany, became active in the *Armanen-Orden*, whose Ariosophic and racial esoteric teachings he adopted. Today, Lentz runs the publishing company *Neue Erde* specialising in "spiritual ecology and nature philosophy." Cf. Davies, "'Männerbund' and 'Mutterrecht,'" 105; Gugenberger and Schweidlenka, *Mutter Erde, Magie und Politik. Zwischen Faschismus und neuer Gesellschaft*, 125–128. http://www.neueerde.de/der-verlag, last accessed August 27, 2014.

97 Neumann-Gundrum was a member of the *Herman-Wirth-Gesellschaft* (*Ureuropa e.V.*) to which she left all her property after her death in 2002. She contributed to the *völkisch* Externstein research with the idea that the natural rock formations actually were giant megalithic sculptures and thus witnesses of the high culture of 'our ancestors.' Halle, "Die Externsteine/Kr. Lippe"; "'Treibereien wie in der NS-Zeit.'"

98 Cf. Schnurbein, *Religion als Kulturkritik*, 218.

99 The original *Walther Machalett-Forscherkreis für Vor- und Frühgeschichte der Externsteine im Teutoburger Wald* was renamed once before into *Arbeits- und Forschungskreis Walther Machalett*.

100 Wenger was the co-founder of the right-wing radical *Asgardbund*, former member of the *Armanen-Orden* and founder of the *Gemeinschaft für heidnisches Leben* in Berlin. Cf. Schnurbein, *Religion als Kulturkritik*, 176. He later supported the German *Rabenclan* in laying bare the right-wing esotericist connections within Ariosophy and Germanic Neopaganism.See http://www.rabenclan.de/index.php/Magazin/MatthiasWengerGezavon Nemenyi, last accessed August 26, 2014, and Matthias Wenger, "Meine politische Position und ihre Entwicklung in 30 Jahren."

1996, as well as for the yearbook of *Ur-Europa e. V.*[101] More recently, Wenger has started to promote the work of Teudt and others through the *Forschungskreis Externsteine*. In his online journal, *Der Hain*, he endorses theories by Herman Wirth and Bernhard Kummer, whom he considers pioneers of an alternative, matriarchal view of the Germanic past.[102] Wirth's and Teudt's theories have also found supporters in the European New Right,[103] as well as American and English Asatru contexts.[104]

These examples notwithstanding, their theories are contested in contemporary Asatru. Asatruers are increasingly aware of the political implications of such connections and tend to distance themselves accordingly. Instead, they rely on academic and popularized academic works available in the languages of their respective countries to shape their imaginaries of Germanic religion, in the hope of not falling prey to racist and *völkisch* distortions of their beliefs. However, such works are themselves frequently based on scholarship which emerged as a continuation of the Höfler school after 1945. Two other controversial scholars closely connected to him loom large within the fields of Scandinavian studies, Indo-European studies, and the history of

---

101 http://www.forschungskreis-externsteine.de/: "Rückschau" (last accessed March 24, 2011 – the link has since been removed from the Forschungskreis' homepage). Cf. also Halle, "Die Externsteine/Kr. Lippe," 129.

102 Cf. Wenger, "Patriarchalische Ideologie oder matriarchalisches Wertsystem." For recent controversies around the activities of the *Forschungskreis Externsteine*, as well as the association *Ur-Europa*, which promotes the work of Herman Wirth, see http://www.hiergeblieben.de/pages/textanzeige.php?limit=10&order=datum&richtung=DESC&z=1&id=32603 (last accessed August 26, 2014).

103 See Jakob Christiansen Senholt, "Radical Politics and Political Esotericism. The Adaptation of Esoteric Discourse within the Radical Right," in *Contemporary Esotericism*, ed. Egil Asprem and Kennet Granholm (London: Equinox, 2012).

104 In an online article from 2008, the *Odinic Rite* wrote about the location of the Irminsul at the Externsteine, although without making direct mention of Wilhelm Teudt. (http://www.odinic-rite.org/main/the-irminsul-and-the-externsteine-from-yggdrasil-to-the-irminsul, last accessed August 26, 2014). The Norwegian site *Kulturorgan Skadinaujo* discusses Teudt's work on the Externsteine favorably. (Cf. Jørgen Exenberger, "Sarkofagsteinen i Externstein," *KultOrg* (*KulturOrgan Skadinaujo*) 8, no. 1 (2008)). American Asatruers occasionally mention the forged *Ura-Linda-Chronik* or *Oera-Linda-Book*, which Herman Wirth promoted so adamantly as a testimony for his ancient 'Atlantic' religion. A list of Asatru prison resources (http://aren.org/prison/documents/Asatru.htm, last accessed August 26, 2014) contains a link to "Oera Linda Book Extracts (pub 1876, but derives from a diary between the periods of 560–558 BC, but written in 1256 AD)": http://earth-history.com, last accessed August 26, 2014. A google search for "Oera Linda Asatru" gave 63.800 results in December 2011.

religions – Georges Dumézil (1898–1986) and Mircea Eliade (1907–1986). Together with their collaborators, students, and followers, including Jan de Vries and Edgar Polomé, Dumézil and Eliade were to become important for both post-war Germanic studies as well as later Asatru constructions of Germanic religion. In the 1930s and 40s, Höfler, Dumézil, and Eliade all belonged to the "vast European front" of right-wing totalitarianism, and the foundations for their lifelong network of collaboration and friendship were already laid in this era.[105]

Höfler's post-war career started with his dismissal from his position at the University of Munich by the American military government in 1945. Although he was classified as a mere follower and nominal member of the National Socialist party (*Mitläufer*), the controversy around his person, activities, and theories continued until 1954. That year, a new chair position was created for him in Munich, which he held until he was appointed at the University of Vienna in 1957.[106] Höfler remained an authority in the study of Germanic myth up until his death in 1987, and continued to investigate the "consistency and continuity of state-building instincts and

---

105 The relationship between Höfler and Dumézil goes back as far as 1931, when the young French language instructor Dumézil met his German colleague Höfler and Stig Wikander at the University of Uppsala in Sweden. Cf. Bruce Lincoln, "Dumézil, Georges," Encyclopaedia Iranica, http://www.iranica.com/articles/dumezil, last accessed February 06, 2015. Eliade's contact to Dumézil was probably initiated some time before 1940, but the friendship between the two scholars of myth commenced in Eliade's years in Paris after 1945. Beck, "Zur Rezeption von Vilhelm Grønbechs Werk im deutschen Sprachraum" (341) discusses Höfler's debt to Eliade's idea of epiphany and his anti-historicist thesis of man's liberation from history through the repetition of archetypical actions. For a laudatory discussion of the close intellectual and personal connections between the three, from the perspective of a German historian who himself belongs to the New Right, see Karlheinz Weißmann, "Das Heilige ist eine unverlierbare Größe," *Junge Freiheit*, March 09, 2007. Cf. Arvidsson, *Aryan Idols*; Grottanelli, "War-time Connections: Dumézil and Eliade, Eliade and Schmitt, Schmitt and Evola, Drieu La Rochelle and Dumézil." See also Otto Höfler's favorable review of Jan de Vries' *Altgermanische Religionsgeschichte* from 1959 where he makes positive references to both Dumézil and Eliade. Otto Höfler, "Rez.: Jan de Vries, Altgermanische Religionsgeschichte," in *Otto Höfler: Kleine Schriften. Ausgewählte Arbeiten zur germanischen Altertumskunde und Religionsgeschichte, zur Literatur des Mittelalters, zur germanischen Sprachwissenschaft sowie zur Kulturphilosophie und -morphologie*, ed. Helmut Birkhan (Hamburg: Helmut Buske Verlag, 1992 [1959]).

106 Zernack, "Kontinuität als Problem der Wissenschaftsgeschichte," 49–55.

state-building institutions"[107] which he now saw embodied in traditions of sacral kingship.[108]

The fundamental innovation in the post-1945 study of Indo-European myth came from the French structuralist theorist of myth, Georges Dumézil. He aimed to shed light on the basic structures of thought which distinguished Indo-European religion and society. Following Höfler's assessment that religion and social order were closely intertwined,[109] Dumézil understood religion as a "coherent vision defined by a conceptual system that both organized [the social order] and informed the social body and the priestly class."[110] Dumézil's analysis of myths from different parts of the Indo-European world brought him to the conclusion that a tripartite structure of a priestly, a sovereign, and a fertility function was characteristic of Indo-European religions and societies. In his post-war work,[111] Dumézil took much more care than Höfler to point out the limits of his analyses. He called attention to the fact that his methods were helpful in identifying structures of thought, but not in reconstructing (pre)historical events or social systems as such, nor were they suitable for informing or legitimizing a contemporary political program.[112] He lacked the enthusiasm for Indo-European 'greatness' that motivated some of

---

107 Weißmann, "Das Heilige ist eine unverlierbare Größe": "Konstanz und Kontinuität der staatenbildenden Instinkte [...] staatenbildenden Institutionen".

108 Otto Höfler, *Germanisches Sakralkönigtum* (Tübingen: Niemeyer, 1952). Höfler continued to pay tribute to Vilhelm Grønbech as well by promoting a German translation of *Culture of the Teutons* with the academic publishing house *Wissenschaftliche Buchgesellschaft*, for which he also wrote a new preface. For a scathing critique of the renowned academic publishing houses' policy in this matter see Wolfgang Behringer, "Das 'Ahnenerbe' der Buchgesellschaft. Zum Neudruck einer Germanen-Edition des NS-Ideologen Otto Höfler," *Sowi* 27 (1998). For general critical discussions of Höfler's career and theories of continuity see also Harm-Peer Zimmermann, "Männerbund und Totenkult. Methodologische und ideologische Grundlinien der Volks- und Altertumskunde Otto Höflers 1933–1945," *Kieler Blätter zur Volkskunde* 26 (1994); Esther Gajek, "Germanenkunde und Nationalsozialismus. Zur Verflechtung von Wissenschaft und Politik am Beispiel Otto Höflers," in *Völkische Bewegung – Konservative Revolution – Nationalsozialismus. Aspekte einer politisierten Kultur*, ed. Walter Schmitz and Clemens Vollnhals (Dresden: Thelem, 2005).

109 Cf. Bruce Lincoln, "Dumézil, Ideology, and the Indo-Europeans," *ZfR. Zeitschrift für Religionswissenschaft* 6, no. 2 (1998), 221.

110 Maurice Olender, *Race and Erudition*, trans. Jane Marie Todd (Cambridge, MA/London: Harvard University Press, 2009), 35.

111 According to Lincoln, "Dumézil, Ideology, and the Indo-Europeans," 221, a change in perspective in Dumézil's work occurred in the 1950s.

112 Cf. Olender, *Race and Erudition*, 35, 181.

his colleagues and followers, and remained the most complicated and complex thinker among the scholars discussed here.[113] While insisting on the purely linguistic nature of what he called Indo-European reality, he nevertheless supported a linguistic essentialism, claiming that "language involves much more than itself: it entails both a representation of the universe and the civilization that results from it."[114]

Such ambiguous assertions reflect the ambiguity of Dumézil's involvement with right-wing politics, as well as the ambivalence of the discussions around these topics. Dumézil admired Charles Maurras; the right-wing extremist, anti-Semitic, royalist *Action Française*; and Mussolini's fascism; but was critical of German National Socialism.[115] What remains highly disputed is the question of how extensively such political sympathies formed his theories, and how Dumézil's post-war involvement with protagonists and organizations of the French New Right, such as Alain de Benoist and *G.R.E.C.E.*, as well as the journal *Nouvelle Ecole*, should be assessed.[116] What is clear is that the French New Right took inspiration from Dumézil's comparative method and used his theories to justify their metapolitical visions of an Indo-European re-awakening, which would work against Judaism, Christianity, and Enlightenment ideals.[117]

---

113   Cf. Lincoln, "Dumézil, Ideology, and the Indo-Europeans," 146.
114   Dumézil in an interview with Maurice Olender, *Race and Erudition*, 73.
115   In the 1980s, Arnaldo Momigliano, *Studies on Modern Scholarship* (Berkeley: University of California Press, 1994) and Carlo Ginzburg, *Clues, Myths, and the Historical Method* (Baltimore: Johns Hopkins University Press, 1989) accused Dumézil of harboring sympathies for National Socialism, which was effectively rebuked by Didier Eribon, *Faut-il brûler Dumézil ? Mythologie, science et politique* (Paris: Flammarion, 1992), Guy G. Stroumsa, "Georges Dumézil, Ancient German Myths, and Modern Demons," *ZfR. Zeitschrift für Religionswissenschaft* 6, no. 2 (1998), and Lincoln, "Dumézil, Ideology, and the Indo-Europeans" who, on the other hand produced ample proof of Dumézil's sympathies for the French and Italian extreme right.
116   Olender, *Race and Erudition*, 46–48, mentions that Dumézil resigned from the sponsorship board of the *Nouvelle Ecole* after the publication of a special volume on him in winter 1972/73 apparently because he was troubled by the vision for the future which Benoist derived from his work. Olender insists that Dumézil cannot be made responsible for promoting such theories of continuity and visions for the future. Bruce Lincoln, *Theorizing Myth*, 123 and 259, on the other hand, points out Dumézil's ongoing fascination and involvement with right-wing movements and protagonists.
117   Olender, *Race and Erudition*, 40–66 mentions Jean-Louis Tristani, who combined an anti-monotheist, anti-Jewish ideology with his reading of Dumézil, who he thought provided "access to our first religious tradition" (ibid., 51) and Jean Haudry's theses on the racial implications of an Indo-European continuity. Haudry and Jean Varenne were also involved with the right-wing French *Front National*. Haudry in particular is popular

The third scholar in this trio, Mircea Eliade, joined the others in a search for "the source of the universally human phenomenon of the religious in an original relation of the human spirit to the Holy," as Otto Höfler put it. He stressed the "significance of the archetypical, of the relations between culture and the original spiritual forms (*geistige Urformen*), of the entry of the cult into the transtemporal, and the ritual commitment of the historical orders of life to the numinous, the Holy and extra-temporal."[118] Like Höfler, Eliade was politically engaged on the far right (in the Romanian fascist *Iron Guard*, for example) in his early years.[119] Whereas Höfler and Dumézil focussed on social and political structure in their readings of myth, Eliade's scholarly work was centered around symbolism and esotericism.[120] He was influenced by theorists of the

---

in Asatru circles with affinities to the New Right. The American AFA sells his book, *The Indo-Europeans*, in its online store (cf. http://www.runestone.org/store/index.htm, last accessed August 27, 2014). Stefan Björn and Romana Ulbrich, of the German *Arun-Verlag*, quote him in a recent book on name-giving ceremonies (Björn Ulbrich and Romana Ulbrich, *Dein Name sei... Rituale und Zeremonien zu Geburt und Namensgebung* (Engerda: Arun, 2009), 30), where they also refer positively to a work by Richard v. Kienle, *Germanische Gemeinschaftsformen*, ed. Forschungs- und Lehrgemeinschaft 'Das Ahnenerbe,' vol. 4, Reihe B: Fachwissenschaftliche Untersuchungen. Abteilung: Arbeiten zur Germanenkunde (Stuttgart: Kohlhammer, 1939) on "Germanic Forms of Community," which appeared in a series edited by the *Ahnenerbe*. To Haudry see also Lincoln, *Theorizing Myth*, 121 and 285. In this context it seems significant as well that Stig Wikander, Höfler and Dumézil's colleague from their time in Uppsala, who seems to have shared Dumézil's appreciation of European fascism, although not necessarily of German National Socialism during the war, appears amongst the supporters of *Nouvelle Ecole* in the 1970s. Cf. Arvidsson, "Stig Wikander och forskningen om ariska mannaförbund."

118 The quotes are by Höfler, cited in Weißmann, "Das Heilige ist eine unverlierbare Größe": "Quelle der gesamtmenschlichen Erscheinung des Religiösen in einer Ur-Beziehung des Menschengeistes zum Heiligen zu suchen" – "Über die Bedeutung des Archetypischen, über die Zusammenhänge der Kultur mit den geistigen Urformen, über das Hineintreten des Kultes in das Überzeitliche und die rituelle Bindung der historischen Lebensordnungen an das Numinose, das Heilige und Zeitentrückte, hat Eliade Einsichten eröffnet, die ihn in die Reihe der bahnbrechenden Erschließer der historisch-überhistorischen Glaubensformen stellen."

119 For Eliade's involvement with Romanian fascism see Wasserstrom, *Religion after Religion*, 306 and 308, as well as Norman Manea, "Happy Guilt. Mircea Eliade, Fascism, and the Unhappy Fate of Romania," *New Republic*, August 05, 1991 and Adriana Berger, "Mircea Eliade. Romanian Fascism and the History of Religions in the United States," in *Tainted Greatness. Antisemitism and Cultural Heroes*, ed. Nancy Harrowitz (Philadelphia: Gemple University Press, 1994).

120 Until the 1920s, he was involved with theosophy and occultism, an interest that he shared with the traditionalists René Guénon and Julius Evola. In the 1930s, he settled for

German Conservative Revolution, and he remained in close contact with Ernst Jünger, with whom he edited the journal *Antaios* between 1959 and 1971.[121]

Most admirers of Eliade consider that he broke with his early political convictions and devoted his later academic life to an a-political study of religion, establishing the discipline history of religions in its unique form in the United States. However, critics identify continuities between his early political convictions and his later work[122] as a respected professor at the prestigious University of Chicago and author of the widely praised book, *The Myth of the Eternal Return*,[123] as well as other influential publications. Eliade's "covert theology"[124] followed the line of Rudolf Otto and other promoters of the primacy of experience, and considered inward experience and a Heideggerian '*Ergriffenheit*' to be constitutive for all religion. *Ergriffenheit* in Heidegger's sense denotes a kind of "primal ontic seizure" and is a key philosophical concept which includes the submission to the authority of someone or something that seizes.[125] Eliade shares his affinity for the notion of *Ergriffenheit* with C.G. Jung,[126] another theorist of "ontic depths."

While Eliade's scholarly work on Germanic matters remains contested,[127] his ideas on 'continual hierophanies' as the positive driving force for mankind

---

the more exalted elitism of traditionalism, which entailed a strong anti-historicism, a planetary pessimism, and cosmic catastrophism, and saw the present age as the *Kali Yuga*, the low point of cosmic development. Cf. Wasserstrom, *Religion after Religion*, 48.

121 Cf. ibid., 320.

122 Wasserstrom and Benavides point to the continued rhetoric of violence in his work, and to the militant metaphors connected to his "rebirth model of sacrality." They remind us of Eliade's agitation for a "New Man" in the Romanian Legionary Movement, the *Iron Guard*. (Cf. Gustav Benavides, "Heroic Deeds and the Extraction of Surplus," in *The Study of Religion under the Impact of Fascism*, ed. Horst Junginger (Leiden/Boston: Brill, 2008), 266f) For a brief analysis of the fascist ideology of the Romanian Legionary Movement *Iron Guard* see Valentin Šandulescu, "Fascism and its Quest for the 'New Man.' The Case of the Romanian Legionary Movement," *Studia Hebraica* 4 (2004). It found its continuation in his later writings on the rebirth of a New Man, and his "suspension of ethics in favor of ontic depths" implied in his model of totality (Wasserstrom, *Religion after Religion*, 225, see also 18 and 132).

123 Mircea Eliade, *Cosmos and History. The Myth of the Eternal Return* (Princeton, NJ: Princeton University Press, 1954).

124 Wasserstrom, *Religion after Religion*, 25.

125 Cf. ibid., 29–31.

126 Cf. Petteri Pietikäinen, "C.G. Jung, anti-Semitism, and racial psychology," *Psykologia* 31, no. 2 (1996).

127 Eliade draws on Höfler and Dumézil in his analysis of the role of ecstasy and shamanism in Germanic contexts. See Mircea Eliade, *Shamanism. Archaic Techniques of Ecstasy* (London: Routledge and Kegan Paul, 1964).

and his assertion that the goal of the study of religion should be the "liberation of man from history"[128] have had a considerable impact, both on the study of religion in general as well as on modern esotericism, New Age spirituality, alternative religion, and Neopaganism.[129] It is most likely due to Eliade's writings and activities that the ideas of his correspondent and collaborator Otto Höfler were so widely disseminated in American contexts.[130]

We can conclude that scholarship of Germanic and Indo-European myth not only incorporates earlier oppositions of 'Aryan versus Semitic' religion,[131] but also has direct ties to German *völkisch*, Conservative Revolutionary, and National Socialist scholarship, which was institutionalized in the ss research institution *Ahnenerbe*. The unifying element between the various academic attempts to understand Germanic or Indo-European myth and religion is their use of fragmented and temporally and spatially scattered sources of evidence, with the goal of reconstructing a common pre-Christian, Germanic, Nordic, or Indo-European worldview, mentality, religion, or social structure. Such attempts at constructing identity academically are dependent on the creation and exclusion of an 'other,' which in many cases is 'the Jew' or the Semite. They thus align themselves all too easily with an overt or latent anti-Judaism or anti-Semitism.[132] Furthermore, they lead to a biased selection of sources from the respective eras, and to the de-contextualization of these sources from the eras in which they originated. Thus, in the case of medieval Icelandic literature, mythological texts are held in high regard and taken as expressions of an ancient Germanic essence, whereas the abundant hagiographic or Christian literature of the same era is more or less ignored as

---

128   Gladigow, "Religionsgeschichte des Gegenstandes – Gegenstände der Religionsgeschichte," 12.
129   This impact is probably only superseded by the influence of C.G. Jung with whom Eliade shared a number of interests and with whom he was connected through the *Eranos* conference group. (Cf. Wasserstrom, *Religion after Religion*).
130   To the contact between Höfler and Eliade see Timuş, "'Quand l'Allemange était leur Mecque...'"; Weißmann, "Das Heilige ist eine unverlierbare Größe." Weißmann's and others' treatment of the relations between Höfler, Dumézil and Eliade shows that such connections today are actively propagated by the European and American intellectual New Right in order to give their way of thought a respectable academic foundation.
131   Cf. Arvidsson, *Aryan Idols*.
132   Dumézil is the only one of the scholars discussed here who has never been accused of anti-Semitism. Cf. Stroumsa, "Georges Dumézil, Ancient German Myths, and Modern Demons," 131. For a discussion of the anti-Semitic implications of Eliade's as well as de Vries' thought cf. Stefan Arvidsson, *Draksjukan. Mytiska fantasier hos Tolkien, Wagner och de Vries* (Lund: Nordic Academic Press, 2007), 84, 94, 97.

secondary and derivative. The sagas of the Icelanders serve as testimonies of a Nordic or Germanic mentality, while the large number of sagas on knights and saints, as well as those dealing with fantastic material, are considered to be dependent on Continental, courtly literature and are thus also dismissed.[133] This type of reconstructive scholarship lends itself to the belief that combining de-contextualized fragments from vastly different eras and regions can in fact lead to the identification of deep structures of a deep past in which the origin of one's identity can be found. Such a reconstruction can then supposedly explain the present or help one's own nation or group to regain a proper identity or essence. In other words: it is the construction of a unified, naturalized ethnic identity, which is set against a devalued 'other.' It is thus not surprising that scholars critical of this ideology have concluded that the whole discourse surrounding Indo-Europeans, as well as notions of a Germanic or Nordic wholeness, ought to be considered a "web of scientific myths."[134] Scholarship on Indo-European or Germanic myth has, in turn, lent itself to myth-making. Many of the scholars who have investigated this area harbor mythological, religious, political, or ideological agendas themselves. They have been primarily interested in the relevance of their historical findings for their respective societies' identity projects. This explains the intellectual affinities and the personal, as well as institutional, connections between these scholars and political movements, which are interested both in constructing society on the basis of such essences, and in 'curing' or 'purifying' contemporary societies of the aberrations of a complex and 'degenerate' modernity.[135]

Reconstructive approaches, including Dumézil's work, are generally well received within Asatru contexts, with which they share a basic interest in reconstruction and religious or social renewal on the basis of ancient 'truths' or 'essences.' But this is certainly not the only, and perhaps not even the main, means by which Dumézil's theories reach the majority of Asatru groups today. His influence can be attributed to his impact on other leading post-war Scandinavianists in the Netherlands, Scandinavia, and the

---

[133] The selection chosen for the German saga translations in the *Sammlung Thule* are a good example for this kind of discriminatory procedure. For a critical discussion see Zernack, *Geschichten aus Thule*, 3.

[134] This is a position which has been supported by Poliakov, *The Aryan Myth*; Colin Renfrew, *Archaeology and Language. The Puzzle of the Indo-European Origins* (London: Jonathan Cape, 1987); Lincoln, *Theorizing Myth* and others. For a systematic summary and inquiry into the backgrounds of such criticism see Arvidsson, *Aryan Idols*.

[135] Cf. also Stroumsa, "Georges Dumézil, Ancient German Myths, and Modern Demons," 134.

English-speaking world, who are in turn consulted by Asatruers in their search for reliable popular academic sources. Among them are a number of scholars who used Dumézil's theories to write comprehensive overviews of Germanic religion. One of them was the Dutch historian of religion, Jan de Vries (1890–1964), who himself belonged to a network of scholars with a strong connection to National Socialism during the 1930s and 40s.[136] His comprehensive standard reference work, "*Altgermanische Religionsgeschichte*" (Old Germanic history of religions), a "model of encyclopedic learning,"[137] owes a debt to Grønbech,[138] and was influential for Georges Dumézil's view of Germanic myth and society. Its second edition, from 1956/7, was in turn inspired by Dumézil's theory of the tripartite structure of Indo-European myth. The American and English Scandinavianists and historians of religion who popularized their summaries of Norse or Germanic religion, such as Gabriel Turville-Petre[139] and Hilda Ellis Davidson,[140] have relied heavily on Dumézil, employing his theories to work out extensive summations of Northern religion, which are widely read and remain well-respected today. They are still used extensively as basic Asatru readings as well.

Edgar Polomé (1920–2000) is another author frequently referred to by Asatruers. Polomé was an Indo-Europeanist of Belgian origin who served as a professor for comparative religion and languages at the University of Austin from the 1960s until 1997. His work is characterized by a tendency to idealize Indo-European culture and religion. Through his work as editor for the *Journal for Indo-European Studies* from its inception in 1973, and as the co-editor for *The Mankind Quarterly*, he has been actively involved in American-European right-wing and racist scholarship. Both journals were published by the Institute for the Study of Man funded by the Pioneer Fund, an institution dedicated to the financing of research on race difference and eugenics. The Fund's founder, South African Roger Pearson, is a white supremacist, eugenicist, and ideologist of "Aryan purity" and "racial hygiene" who bases his ideas "largely on the

---

136 de Vries collaborated with the *Deutsches Ahnenerbe*, Otto Höfler and others. Cf. Arvidsson, *Draksjukan*, 72–98.
137 Lincoln, *Theorizing Myth*, 125; de Vries, *Altgermanische Religionsgeschichte*.
138 Cf. Beck, "Zur Rezeption von Vilhelm Grønbechs Werk im deutschen Sprachraum," 339.
139 Gabriel Turville-Petre, *Myth and Religion of the North* (London: Weidenfeld and Nicolson, 1964).
140 Ellis Davidson has written a number of books on Northern religion between the 1960s and 1990s. See, for example, Hilda Roderick Ellis Davidson, *Gods and Myths of Northern Europe* (Middlesex: Penguin, 1964), Hilda Ellis Davidson, *The Lost Beliefs of Northern Europe* (London: Routledge, 1993).

thinking of notorious Nazi theorist Hans F.K. Günther."[141] As director of the Institute for the Study of Man he headed three important journals, among them *Mankind Quarterly*, in the 1960s.[142] The latter overtly promoted race science and eugenics and developed a stronger interest in pre-history, religion, and myth under Pearson's leadership.[143] The *Journal for Indo-European Studies*, edited by Polomé and Indo-Europeanist Maria Gimbutas,[144] was and still is considered to be the more reputable academic face of *Mankind Quarterly*.[145] In recent years, the connections between the *Journal for Indo-European Studies* and *Mankind Quarterly* have been further concealed, possibly due to the extensive criticism their association has drawn.[146] We can conclude that the field of

---

141 William H. Tucker, *The Funding of Scientific Racism. Wickliffe Draper and the Pioneer Fund* (Urbana/Chicago: University of Illinois Press, 2002), 159. In the 1950s, Pearson launched a "Pan-Nordic" campaign in Britain through his *Northern League* and subsequently took his activities to the United States.

142 *Mankind Quarterly* was initially founded as the result of "new alliances between segregationists and racial scientists" (Gavin Schaffer, "'Scientific Racism Again?' Reginald Gates, the *Mankind Quarterly* and the Question of 'Race' in Science after the Second World War," *Journal of American Studies* 41, no. 2 (2007), 269) and "churned out a steady stream of justifications for racism." (William H. Tucker, *The Cattell Controversy. Race, Science, and Ideology* (Urbana/Chicago: University of Illinois Press, 2009), 121).

143 *Mankind Quarterly* is also connected with *Neue Anthropologie*, the journal of the German eugenicist and racist *Gesellschaft für biologische Anthropologie, Eugenik und Verhaltensforschung*, which was chaired by Jürgen Rieger, the head of the German Neopagan *Artgemeinschaft*. Cf. Wetzel, "Die Maschen des rechten Netzes," 171.

144 See Chapter 7.

145 The two journals were furthermore intertwined through an elaborate citation policy. Thus, articles in *Mankind Quarterly* regularly cite *JIES* articles to provide objective, scholarly, reputable, scientific support for their views. The citation traffic rarely goes in the opposite direction and the fiction of independence is maintained. Cf. Tucker, *The Funding of Scientific Racism*; *The Cattell Controversy*, 120–128; Lincoln, *Theorizing Myth*, 123.

146 Currently, *Mankind Quarterly* is published under the umbrella of the *Council for Social and Economic Studies*, which also publishes the *Journal for Social, Political, and Economic Studies*, the third of Pearson's journals from the 1970s. The latter aims for more direct political intervention (Cf. http://www.mankindquarterly.org/about.html, last accessed August 27, 2014). *The Institute for the Study of Man* does not appear here anymore, but on the website of the *Journal of Indo-European Studies* it is given as the address to which copies of manuscripts are to be sent. The Washington D.C. mailing address given here is the same as the one for the *Council for Social and Economic Studies*. In J.P. Mallory, from the University of Queens in Belfast, JIES has found a well-reputed scholar as an editor. At the same time, Mallory has also authored at least one article for *Mankind Quarterly*. (J.P. Mallory, "Human populations and the Indo-European problem," *Mankind Quarterly* 33, no. 2 (1992))

Indo-European studies and its organs of distribution have remained in precarious proximity to right-wing politics and racial science. Indirectly, this applies to the Swedish historian of religion Åke Ström as well, whose Dumézil-inspired overviews of Germanic and Indo-European religion have been widely used as textbooks in Swedish schools, as well as by Asatruers. In his interpretation of Germanic religion, Ström insists on a polar opposition between Indo-European and Semitic religion. His main goal is to demonstrate that Germanic faith and its ethics were bearers of "true piety or religiosity" (echte Frömmigkeit), a claim for which he made ample use of Vihelm Grønbech's ideas as well.[147] He polemically labels "hypercritical" source criticism, which denies the existence of a unified Indo-European culture, a "disease."[148]

These examples notwithstanding, such political and religious dimensions do not play an overt role in the popular textbooks used as points of reference by Asatruers – a fact which makes them all the more useful for current a-racist Asatruers in their attempts to distinguish themselves from right-wing associations.[149]

---

[147] Cf. Åke v. Ström and Haralds Biezais, *Germanische und baltische Religion* (Stuttgart etc.: Kohlhammer, 1975), 11. For a critical discussion see Arvidsson, *Aryan Idols*, 109f.

[148] For a discussion on the anti-Semitic cultural-protestant ideology of Ström's colleague Haralds Biezais with whom he wrote the synopsis on Germanic and Baltic religion, cf. Iveta Leitane, "Haralds Biezais (1909–1995). Ein Religionshistoriker zwischen Theologie und Religionswissenschaft," in *The Study of Religion under the Impact of Fascism*, ed. Horst Junginger (Leiden/Boston: Brill, 2008).

[149] Much-used works are, for example, René Derolez' overview over Norse myths and deities (René Derolez, *Les dieux et la religion des germains* (Paris: Payot, 1962)) and, even more so, Paul Bauschatz, *The Well and the Tree*. The latter is popular among Asatruers due to its attempt to reconstruct the worldview and concepts of time of "early Germanic culture." The Belgian professor of English and Old Germanic philology, René Derolez (1921–2005), wrote a synopsis of the Germanic gods and myths in 1959, which was translated into French and German. (Derolez, *Les dieux et la religion des germains*; *Götter und Mythen der Germanen* (Einsiedeln: Benzinger, 1963)) Although relying on de Vries and Höfler as well, he is rather more careful in his conclusions regarding grand syntheses and theories of continuity, such as Höfler's. (Cf. ibid., 102). Of the standard works currently used by Scandinavian Heathens as inspiration in their construction of Asatru, that of Swedish Britt-Mari Näsström is the most favorable towards Dumézil's approach. (Britt-Mari Näsström, *Freyja. The Great Goddess of the North* (Lund: Department of History of Religions, 1995), 29f) Näsström is primarily interested in the female deities of the Nordic pantheon, and she criticizes Dumézil mainly for his neglect of the goddesses. She suggests a combination of structuralist, comparative, and linguistic methods in her own effort to reconstruct the significance of Freyja as the "Great Goddess of the North." Folke

Asatru Uses of Scholarship

Germanic Neopaganism has always been concerned with academic theories about the Nordic past, and there have long been regular exchanges between (lay) scholars and religionists. Post-1970, such exchanges were most intense in the Anglo-American world, where internationally read Asatruers also moved in academic contexts. The internationally influential a-racist group *The Troth* was founded by an academic, and it emphatically nurtured the idea of Asatru being 'the religion with homework,' of having to base one's beliefs on 'the lore,' i.e., the available sources as well as academically acknowledged secondary literature. The reception of pre-1945 *völkisch*-tainted scholarship on Germanic antiquity and its transformation into scholarship on Indo-European antiquity has been most marked in Anglo-American Asatru contexts. From here, these concepts found their way back to Germany and, to an extent, Scandinavia as well.

The direct dissemination of these concepts of a Germanic antiquity, which were promoted by German scholars between 1910 and 1940, and later on by Höfler, Dumézil, Eliade, and their followers, can be attributed to the activities and writing of Stephen Flowers (aka Edred Thorsson), the circle around his *Rune Gild*, and the early *Ring of Troth*, to which Stephan Grundy/Kveldulf Gundarsson belonged as well. These two men, who were instrumental in the creation of the 'lore' of *The Troth*, can be considered central mediators between the fringes of the academic world and Asatru since the 1980s.

In his writings, Flowers frequently pays homage to his dissertation advisor, Edgar Polomé,[150] as well as to Jan de Vries and Vilhelm Grønbech, who provided him with the holistic methodology required to reconstruct an allegedly ancient religion and understanding of the world:

> Ström's (not to be confused with the Åke Ström!) standard work on "Nordic Heathenism" calls Dumézil's tripartite system an "imaginative construction" ("fantasifull konstruktion" Ström, *Nordisk hedendom*, 105). Ström is convinced of the existence of a foundational fatalism in Norse religion, but is far from connecting it with the militant heroism so typical for German readings of it. Such a fairly matter of fact, non-idealizing treatment of Nordic myth and religion is characteristic of Norwegian Gro Steinsland's overview as well. (Gro Steinsland, *Norrøn religion. Myter, riter, samfunn* (Oslo: Pax, 2005)).

150   In a presentation of his esoteric as well as his scholarly development, Flowers also attributes his first acquaintance with the European New Right to Edgar Polomé, who had pointed him to the French Scandinavianist François-Xavier Dillmann, "an adherent of the so-called French New Right, whose chief exponent was Alain de Benoist" – incidentally a point of evidence for Polomé's own right-wing connections as well. (Edred, *History of the Rune-Gild*, III (The Reawakening of the Gild 1980–2005), 73).

To understand an archaic culture one must learn to think as they did – this involves primarily learning of the culture's cosmology (view of the world/environment) and psychology (view of one's own self, or being). This psycho-cosmology is then applied to real artifacts (literary or otherwise) of the archaic culture.[151]

The quote illustrates the circular reasoning from which such methods emerge. The knowledge of the psycho-cosmology that is to be applied to the 'real artifacts' is first and foremost derived from these same artifacts, namely the source texts, which are separated from their medieval context.[152]

Having failed at building an academic career parallel to his engagement in Asatru, Flowers established the independent *Woodharrow Institute* to further his own version of Germanic Studies.[153] However, his main influence on Asatru dates back to his more popular esoteric publications on runes from the 1980s and 90s. Flowers also had a considerable influence on the young Stephan Grundy/Kveldulf Gundarsson, himself a student of Germanic Studies. Through his writings on runes, ecstasy, magic, and Odin/Wotan, Grundy/Gundarsson contributed to the espousal of Jan de Vries'[154] and other scholars' ideas to a broader Asatru audience. A chapter in *Our Troth* he edited sketches the (pre-)history of Asatru from the Stone Age, through Indo-European times, the Viking Age, and finally the "rebirth," starting with Romanticism. This article is an instructive example of how reconstructionist, holistic assumptions are transferred into Asatru. It claims a "relationship between genetics, language, and culture" which together form "the heritage," although "the nature of such connections is not entirely clear or indisputed."[155] Consequently, "by studying this reconstructed [Indo-European] language, we can begin to understand how the Holy was regarded among our earliest cultural ancestors."[156]

---

151   Ibid., 70.
152   Harm-Peer Zimmermann, "Männerbund und Totenkult," 14, criticizes a similar circular reasoning and muddled relation between empirical evidence and "intuition" in Otto Höfler's theories and concludes: "The insistence on 'intuition' as a basis for his research as a methodological trick to conceal and effectually launch ideological intentions." ("Das Insistieren auf der 'Intuition' erweist sich als methodischer Kunstgriff, um ideologische Absichten zu kaschieren und wirkungsvoll zu lancieren").
153   http://www.woodharrow.com/woodharrow.html, last accessed August 27, 2014.
154   Correspondence with Stephan Grundy.
155   Gundarsson, *Our Troth*, vol. I, 5.
156   Ibid., 23. This approach reverberates Edred Thorsson's ideas of a "culture grid" (see Chapter 4).

The guiding intellectuals, who were initially responsible for the attempt and demand to build modern Asatru on an academic basis and provided the material for this, emerged from an academic milieu with ties to the New Right and with roots in German and European *völkisch* scholarship. However, in the past fifteen years, the awareness of the problems underlying such methodologies has grown.[157] Many of the new approaches within the study of pre-Christian Germanic religion have been gaining currency within Asatru in recent years. Jenny Blain, a British academic and *Troth* member who has been actively involved with Diana Paxson's a-racist *Hrafnar* in California, has been introducing more modern academic perspectives into the worldviews and practices of Asatru. The anthropologist is the first academic who has gone public about being a Heathen practitioner.[158] Her book, *Nine Worlds of Seid-Magic. Ecstasy and Neo-Shamanism in North European Paganism*, appeared with the publisher Routledge in English, while the German translation was published by the alternative religious *Arun-Verlag*.[159] This attests to her ability to bridge the space between (popular) scholarship and new religion. Together with Robert Wallis, Blain positions herself differently to her forebears with regard to the existence and possibility of an access to a deep past on which to build modern Asatru. She emphasizes the creative, forward-looking processes Neopagans employ to construct religious identities. The two scholars criticize approaches that conflate "'peoples,' languages, and geography – an 'us versus them' model that relies on apparently authoritative [...] interpretations of culture and conflict."[160] At the same time, Blain's heavy involvement with an outspokenly anti-racist and 'queer' variety of Asatru leads her at times to underestimate the broader impact of theories and ideologies that originate within the more racially or ethnicist-oriented spectrum and the New Right.[161] Blain's work could be characterized as that of a theologian invested in informing a broader public about

---

157 *Our Troth*, for example, makes positive references to Vilhelm Grønbech's and Otto Höfler's premises it also alerts to some of the problematic sides of the Dumézilian method. (See ibid., 30, 129ff, 150ff) However, it does not go as far as to claim that a reconstruction of Indo-European myth or religion is methodologically unsound.
158 Blain teaches anthropology at Sheffield Hallam University and has published extensively on modern constructions of *seid* in academic as well as Asatru circles. Cf. http://home.freeuk.net/jenny.blain/, last accessed September 13, 2014.
159 See Chapter 2.
160 Blain and Wallis, "Heathenry," 425.
161 Thus, while she strongly objects to racist groups within Asatru, aiming her critique mainly at the British *Odinic Rite*, she mentions Stephen Flowers/Edred Thorsson quite neutrally as one of the formative scholars for *The Troth* a couple of pages later. (Cf. ibid., 422 and 424).

her religion, creating a space for it in her society, and at the same time working to create a critical sense within her own religion – an illuminating approach which nevertheless leads to its own blind spots. Thus, she partially neglects problematic aspects of the history of scholarship behind central articles of creed in Asatru.

In recent years, another American Asatruer, Bil Linzie, has come forward with a critique of the misperceptions the Heathen community has about Germanic religion. He points out that neither the idea of a unified 'Germanic' culture nor 'religion' are concepts that can be applied to the old Heathen religion. Reconstruction for him "is an experiment pure and simple," and he continues:

> The basis of reconstructionism is to reconstruct the 'worldview' of any group of people and apply it to gain experience. [...] what the reconstructionist is seeking to experience is not the religion, but the worldview, the mindset of the people in question, which gave birth to certain specific spiritual practices. [...] The reconstructionist is looking not for a religion but for that which underlies spiritual practice.[162]

A similar sentiment reverberates within Scandinavian Asatru. In the Scandinavian countries in general, the sense that Norse myth and the Viking Age are an integral part of one's own cultural heritage, which one is connected to almost naturally, leads to a less urgent relation to academic research. Generally speaking, Asatruers here are as uninterested and uninvested in detailed academic disputes as their counterparts in other countries. They simply refer to the available comprehensive overviews of Norse religion written by respectable university professors, such as Gro Steinsland from Norway, and Folke Ström and Britt-Mari Näsström from Sweden.[163] They also turn to more

---

162   Bil Linzie, "Reconstructionism's Role in Modern Heathenry," Seidhman, http://www.angelfire.com/nm/seidhman/reconstruction-c.pdf, last accessed December 06, 2011.

163   Steinsland, *Norrøn religion*; Ström, *Nordisk hedendom*; Näsström, *Freyja. The Great Goddess of the North*; *Blot. Tro och offer i det förkristna Norden* (Stockholm: Norstedt, 2002). While Steinsland's work is an important source of inspiration for many reconstructionist Asatruers in Norway, she offered a negative expert comment during the process of Asatru's acknowledgement as an official religious association in Norway in the late 1990s. According to her, Asatru constitutes "a historical falsification," and its acknowledgement would have "negative consequences for all serious activities concerning the Viking Age." (Asprem, "Heathens Up North," 58). This is an indicator of the fear that the field of history of religions would be devaluated by such official acknowledgements.

popular representations of Norse mythology, which directly aim at keeping "the old myths alive."[164] As in other countries, many Asatruers in Norway, Sweden, Denmark, and Iceland use academic knowledge as a basis and combine it with an experiential and experimental (re)constructionist approach. A founding member of the Norwegian *Bifrost* puts it this way:

> Well, we have to [use research], we cannot go and do research ourselves, we don't have time for that. So we have to have permission to skim the cream of that which others have used hours and hours to find out. But we don't take everything any scholar writes at face value, because one knows that academics have their own agendas, they have their theories and their hobbyhorses, and they are not always right.[165]

At the same time, an increasing number of students choose their field of study, mainly Norse philology, archaeology, or history of religion, because of their spiritual interests, using academic theory to develop their own faith. It remains to be seen what the consequences will be for both Asatru and these students' respective academic fields if any should undertake academic careers.[166]

For German Asatruers, the referencing of academic research has taken on a greater importance. Frequently, a-racist Heathens in this country use the fact of American, English, and Scandinavian Asatru claims to a basis in academic findings as a means of creating distance from the overt racial esotericism of

---

164   The quote is by Lars Magnar Enoksen, *Norrøne guder og myter*, 223, a Swedish-Norwegian author, illustrator, punk musician, glima wrestler (an Icelandic variety of wrestling whose adherents claim it has Heathen roots), and autodidactic runologist, whose work on runes is used in university courses. In a lavish volume on Nordic myths and gods, Enoksen promotes imaginations of a united ancient pre-Christian culture in the Scandinavian countries that has been suppressed by "foreign religions of dominance" ("utenlandske herskerreligioner," ibid.).

165   Interview O: "Ja, vi må jo det, vi kan ikke sitte og forske sjøl, vi har ikke tid til det. Så vi må jo få lov til å skumme fløten litt av det andre har brukt timevis til å finne ut av. Men vi tar det ikke for god fisk det enhver forsker skriver, for man vet jo at forskere har sine agendaer, de har sine teorier og sine hester å kjøre, og det er ikke alltid de har rett."

166   The first Scandinavianist to draw the field's attention to "students whose religious practices are rooted in extrapolated (re-constructed) pre-Christian *European* rituals" was Sandra Ballif Straubhaar, "Rezension: Hilda Ellis Davison. *Roles of the Northern Goddess*," *Scandinavian Studies* 7, no. 3 (1999). My own observations from Scandinavian departments in Germany, as well as conversations with colleagues in other fields (for example archaeology or history of religion) and other countries, point to the fact that an increasing number of students combine religious and academic interests in this way.

Ariosophic groups, and to gain respectability in the eyes of a critical public. The reference to scholarship serves two goals. Firstly, it helps avert allegations of political agendas lurking behind Asatru religion. Secondly, it allows the groups to participate to a certain degree in the prestige of acknowledged scholarship, while simultaneously taking pride in their own contributions. *Eldaring* warden Kurt Oertel emphasizes the obligations that in his opinion derive from the problematic German history of reception of Germanic myth. He appeals to contemporary German Asatruers to consider accepting post-1945 scholarship into Asatru, along with an "enlightening and de-mythifying" approach to sources such as Tacitus' *Germania*. For Oertel, not only "contributions and book presentations in the journals of the associations and other Heathen publications such as the *Heidnisches Jahrbuch*, but also [...] lectures and workshops at the big meetings"[167] are means of honoring this obligation. This pride in an active engagement with the study of sources and relevant scholarship is shared by other German groups, for example the a-racist *Nornirs Ætt*, as well as the ethnicist *VfgH*, and is foundational for their group identities. Haimo Grebenstein, of the *VfgH*, claims:

> At least a third, maybe even half, of our members have above-average knowledge regarding the actual state of academic theory, what scholarship is doing. We have people who do their own Edda-translations etc., who really have worked themselves into this as non-experts [...] with or without having studied Scandinavian Studies or related literature...that is indeed enormous.[168]

The need to navigate between their insight into the necessity of a critical review of *völkisch* conceptions of the Germanic and a desire to find an accessible and more or less solid basis for their own religion leads to a number of contradictions within Asatru, and also within individuals themselves

---

167   Correspondence with Kurt Oertel (Eldaring): "Aufklärung und Entmythisierung [...] Die erfolgt in Form von Beiträgen und Buchvorstellungen in den Vereinszeitschriften sowie anderen heidnischen Eigenpublikationen wie z.B. dem *Heidnischen Jahrbuch*, aber auch in Vorträgen und Workshops auf den großen Vereinstreffen."
168   Interview with Haimo Grebenstein (VfgH): "Mindestens ein Drittel, eventuell sogar die Hälfte, unserer Mitglieder hat eine überdurchschnittlich hohe Kenntnis, was [der] tatsächliche Stand der Wissenschaft [ist], was Forschung macht. Wir haben Leute, die machen eigene Edda-Übersetzungen usw., die sich wirklich als Laien da eingearbeitet haben, [...] mit oder ohne begleitendes Studium der Skandinavistik oder einer verwandten Literatur...das ist schon enorm."

regarding the use of certain types of scholarship. On the one hand, scholarly approaches emphasizing the Christian origin of, and Christian influence on, the written sources are heavily criticized by many.[169] On the other hand, Asatruers can display an almost naïve trust in academic works that offer even minimal outlines of a pre-Christian worldview. Those who concern themselves with the academic foundations of the faith tend to receive books like these enthusiastically and promote them to 'common' believers in the groups. This leads to the downplaying of differences between divergent scholarly positions and the eclectic use of isolated results from comprehensive textbooks, or even a total disregard of academic controversies and differing schools.[170] The reception of a recent book by Bernhard Maier in German Asatru is an instructive example. Maier deconstructs both the existence of "the Teutons" (*die Germanen*) as a unified ethnic entity and adamantly rejects the idea of a Germanic fatalism, a Germanic *Männerbund,* or other holistic, reconstructive concepts, such as those proposed by Vilhelm Grønbech. Fritz Steinbock, of the *VfgH*, partially embraces Maier's skepticism, and recommends his book to everybody who is in danger of succumbing to an overly naïve zeal for Germanic culture and religion.[171] However, he also reads Maier as someone who has been able to shed light on "inner" aspects of Germanic religion[172] and cites Grønbech, whom Maier rejects, as an author who does

---

169 Unless they acknowledge such limits of written sources and consequently turn to archaeological sources as allegedly more reliable – an approach which creates rather more problems than it solves with regard to the reconstruction of religious aspects.

170 An instructive example of such more or less neglected differences is the use of two authors recommended by both the *Eldaring* (see http://asawiki.de/index.php?title=Porta l:Gesamtdarstellungen, last accessed August 27, 2014), the *VfgH* (see thread "Grimm: Germanische Mythologie" in the forum at www.vfgh.de, last accessed August 27, 2014) and *Nornirs Ætt* (see Interview with six members of Nornirs Ætt): Klaus Bemmann and Rudolf Simek. These two are currently the most successfully popularizing German-language writers on 'Germanic religion.' However, their approaches are as different as can be. In his book, which in the first edition appeared under the speaking title *Der Glaube der Ahnen* (The Faith of the Ancestors, Klaus Bemmann, *Der Glaube der Ahnen. Die Religion der Deutschen bevor sie Christen wurden.* (Essen: Phaidon, 1990)), Bemmann uncritically assumes the identity of contemporary Germans and "the Teutons," to then present ideas about a unified Indo-European religion and its continuity, making frequent references to Vilhelm Grønbech's image of a cohesive Germanic worldview, which he presents as unanimously affirmed academic knowledge. Simek, on the other hand, frequently and vehemently points to Christian influences in Old Norse mythological sources.

171 Cf. Steinbock, "Die Freiheit eines Heidenmenschen."

172 *Das heilige Fest*, 20.

something similar, without addressing this apparent contradiction.[173] The example shows that although they are at pains to integrate skeptical approaches like Maier's into their own religious system, Asatruers remain dependent on supplementing the meagre findings of recent critical scholarship on a pre-Christian Germanic past by resorting to holistic academic theories about Indo-European culture and myth derived from Dumézil, de Vries, Höfler, Polomé, Eliade, or Grønbech – names which show up on all comprehensive bibliographical lists of German Asatruers. Inadvertently, they help to sustain and spread a type of scholarship characterized by problematic ideological backgrounds and implications.[174]

We can conclude that the 'theorists' within Asatru make ample use of holistic ideas of a Germanic or Indo-European antiquity. This is one reason why they at times share a precarious proximity to Conservative Revolutionary or New Right thought. Obviously, this does not imply that Asatruers who revert to dated or questionable scholarship can be accused of adhering to right-wing ideologies, simply because of their intellectual interests. On the contrary, some are quite aware of such problematic intellectual alliances. The desire to have academically sound, popular, accessible, and affordable works at hand is widespread among Asatruers, but certainly not limited to Asatru. As the title of a recent examination of popular uses of history in Germany correctly tells us,

---

173   Ibid., 21.
174   The most recent instructive example of the reception of such older, holistic scholarship is the career which one book has made, within Asatru and beyond: Kris Kershaw's aforementioned book on *Männerbünde*. (Kershaw, *The One-eyed God. Odin and the (Indo-) Germanic Männerbünde*.) Kershaw follows Höfler's argument closely and uncritically, avoiding discussing the vastly different natures of the various sources in much the same way as Höfler did, and expands it to encompass other Indo-European sources. In this way, she offers the first generally accessible account of Höfler's theses in English. The book has been enthusiastically welcomed by German Asatruers as a long-desired rehabilitation of Otto Höfler's theories of continuity, as well as of Martin Ninck's concept of a Germanic fatalism connected to Odin. For them, the fact that this book appeared in the monograph series of the "acclaimed *Journal of Indo-European Studies*" serves as an argument for the academic soundness of both Kershaw and Höfler. (Cf. http://www.nornirsaett.de/asatru_forum/index.php?action=posts&fid=5&tid=146&hl=1&site=2, and Kurt Oertel's thorough review on http://www.amazon.de/Odin-ein%C3%A4ugige-Gott-indogermanischen-M%C3%A4nnerb%C3%BCnde/dp/3866630190/ref=sr_1_1?ie=UTF8&qid=1300270855&sr=1-1, last accessed August 27, 2014). The abovementioned history of this journal warrants a less sanguine assessment, as does the fact that the German edition appeared courtesy of *Arun Verlag* in a translation by Baal Müller. (For Baal Müller's activities see Chapter 5.)

"History sells."[175] The following quote by *Eldaring* member Christian Brüning concludes an article on *völkisch* esotericism and Germanic Paganism. It contains not only the common defensive appeal to other Heathens along with their academic observers and critics, but it also points out similarities between Asatru and popular, experimental approaches to history and archeology.

> It makes sense that polytheistic Asatru, in all its experimental freedom, has agreed to build on experience based in scholarship. It is absolutely necessary as both support and a corrective, and this is how it is largely understood in Asatru circles. Academic scholarship should thus support Asatru, instead of excluding the new, polytheistic Heathenism rashly and undifferentiatedly as an occult, right-wing extremist current – if nothing else, then for the interest of scholarship itself. To attempt an analogy, today's Germanic paganism is a kind of experimental archaeology, an experimental religion of experience, which has already understood much of the mythological knowledge through several generations.[176]

Rather than singling out Asatruers as particularly prone to reconstructionist scholarly approaches, it is worth looking at the interest in the reconstruction of an 'own' pre-Christian religion and culture in general which they share with a broader public as well as with academics.

---

175 Wolfgang Hardtwig, ed. *History Sells! Angewandte Geschichte als Wissenschaft und Markt* (Stuttgart: Steiner, 2009). This puts scholarly authors who cater to such general demands in a predicament – at least those who accept the idea that reconstructing a pre-Christian Germanic religion from the existing sources is next to impossible. It leads to somewhat ironic effects, as in the case of German Bernhard Maier. Maier adamantly rejects the existence of a Germanic unity, but, writing for a market which wants to be fed with identity-founding, holistic images of 'our' past, titles his book *Die Religion der Germanen*. (The Religion of the Teutons).

176 Christian Brüning, "Völkische Esoterik und germanisches Heidentum," *Heidnisches Jahrbuch* 2 (2007), 350: "Es ist [...] sinnvoll, daß das polytheistische Asatru von heute bei aller experimentellen Freiheit sich darauf verständigt hat, auf wissenschaftsorientierte Erfahrung zu bauen. Sie ist als Rückhalt und Korrektiv absolut notwendig und das wird in Asatrukreisen weitgehend auch so verstanden. Die akademische Forschung sollte Asatru daher unterstützen statt das neue polytheistische Heidentum vorschnell und undifferenziert als okkulte und rechtsextreme Strömung aussperren zu wollen – nicht zuletzt im Interesse der Forschung selbst. Im Versuch einer Analogie stellt das heutige germanische Heidentum, eine Art experimenteller Archäologie dar, eine experimentelle Erfahrungsreligion, die bereits über mehrere Generationen viel vom mythologischen Wissen begriffen hat."

Practices at museums for cultural history and pre-history are a case in point. Since the 19th century, such museums have been institutions working at the intersection of science, education, and performance or public entertainment. Combining research with its presentation, they often employ theatrical elements.[177] In 1920s' and 30s' German reconstructionist open-air museums, the outspokenly germanophile ideological content of attempts to create "holistic impressions of an ideological projection as a 'culture image'" led to a "transgression of serious scholarly standards."[178] In Germany, the approach was therefore abandoned, and not taken up again until the 1970s. In Scandinavia in particular, such a break never occurred, and Scandinavian open-air and cultural historical museums, including the archeological site in Lejre, Denmark, which has existed since the 1950s, have been at the forefront of creating and popularizing myths of national pasts continuously.[179] Today, they are the locations of experiential archaeological endeavors attempting to re-create objects and artisanal techniques of the past. They also collaborate with re-enactment groups in order to attract, communicate with, and educate a broader public in an entertaining way.

Museums, folklorists, and archeologists themselves participate actively in popularizing the past, often in order to garner public acceptance and thus

---

177 Cf. Erika Sandström, *På den tiden, i dessa dagar. Föreställningar om och bruk av historia under medeltidsveckan på Gotland och Jamtli Historieland* (Jamtli: Jamtli Förlag, 2005), 96; Lotten Gustafsson, *Den förtrollade zonen. Lekar med tid, rum och identitet under medeltidsveckan på Gotland* (Nora: Nya Doxa, 2002), 77f. What is called Living History today originated in the military historical re-enactment movement in the USA and Britain (cf. Nils Kagel, "Geschichte leben und erleben. Von der Interpretation historischer Alltagskultur in deutschen Freilichtmuseen," in *Living History in Freilichtmuseen. Neue Wege der Geschichtsvermittlung*, ed. Heike Duisberg (Ehestorf: Förderverein des Freilichtmuseums am Kiekeberg, 2008), 10) as well as in the first open air museum, Skansen in Stockholm, Sweden, founded by philologist and folklorist Artur Immanuel Hazelius in 1891. It was the first of its kind, and it initiated a whole movement of popular museums presenting the rural life of the past as part of the creation of national identities. (Cf. for example Stefan Bohman, *Historia, museer och nationalism* (Stockholm: Carlsson, 1997)).

178 Frank Andraschko, "Wikinger, Römer und Co. Living History in archäologischen Freilichtmuseen und ihrem weiteren Umfeld," in *Living History in Freilichtmuseen. Neue Wege der Geschichtsvermittlung*, ed. Heike Duisberg (Ehestorf: Förderverein des Freilichtmuseums am Kiekeberg, 2008), 39: "Mit dieser auf Schaffung eines 'ganzheitlichen Eindrucks' ausgerichteten ideologischen Projektion als 'Kulturbild' wurden in Deutschland in den 1930er Jahren die Grenzen seriöser Wissenschaftlichkeit zugunsten 'germanophiler Volkserziehung' überschritten."

179 Cf. ibid., Bodil Pettersson, *Föreställningar om det förflutna. Arkeologi och rekonstruktion* (Lund: Nordic Academic Press, 2003).

funding for their research. Evidently, the ideals behind such popularizations change according to the respective contemporary values through which the past is perceived. Thus, as Erika Sandström writes with regards to Swedish museums, while a hundred years ago encounters with a venerable history were meant to incite patriotism, today they are meant to nurture empathy, engagement, and equality. They at times revive older holistic (national-)Romantic identity projects in the process.[180]

While some Heathens are against re-enactment because they believe it blurs the boundary between life and fantasy, many others have recognized their affinity for experiential history and archeology, or are involved in re-enactment themselves. One prominent example is Pete Jennings, from England's *Odinshof*, who helps run a re-enactment group called *Ealdfaether*, where the majority of members are Heathens. *Ealdfaether* is active at the museum site of Sutton Hoo, an Anglo-Saxon burial ground near Suffolk.[181] The same ambivalence is brought to Heathens' participation in the more general historical event culture of medieval markets or creative live re-enactment organizations such as the *Society for Creative Anachronism* (co-founded by Asatruer Diana Paxson) and role-play groups.[182] While they are seen by some as frivolous players wanting to nostalgically immerse themselves in a fictional past, it remains true that many Asatruers come from re-enactment, role-playing, and medieval scenes, and continue to be connected to them.

These scenes are characterized by a sometimes contradictory, but often creative mix of a confident embracing of fiction with the search for authenticity: of creative play with identities and nostalgic identification with the past.[183] Scientific reconstructive attempts and aesthetic appropriation of sources, ideas, and images of the past intersect in a multitude of ways. They are suspended in a field of tension between the transference of tainted or dated knowledge, its rejection where it is recognized, and the enjoyment of the

---

180   Cf. Sandström, *På den tiden, i dessa dagar*, 100; Pettersson, *Föreställningar om det förflutna*, 122–206, describes how contemporary nation branding around archaeological reconstructions of Viking ships and archaeological sites harks back to Romantic Nordic 'archetypes,' such as the Viking and the self-reliant peasant.
181   Correspondence with Pete Jennings (Odinshof), and http://www.ealdfaeder.org/v03/programme.html, last accessed September 13, 2014.
182   While historical re-enactment is usually seen as an attempt to reconstruct events as close to historical reality as possible, Live Action Role Playing (LARP), as well as groups such as the SCR, take inspiration from the positive aspects of the past (often the Middle Ages) and create role plays out of this.
183   Cf. Sandström, *På den tiden, i dessa dagar*, 56.

freedom to imaginatively (re-)create. Fragments of tainted knowledge are utilized together with critical approaches, and Asatruers are active participants in all facets of this entangled web of scholarship, creative arts, pop culture, esotericism, religion, and politics. We can draw three preliminary conclusions from such associations: 1) Asatruers are not alone in reviving potentially problematic paradigms of the holistic, rooted nature of cultures that can be associated with exclusionary identity politics. Rather, they are participants in a broader trend of contemporary politics of history and identity, and they lend this trend a particular religious flavor. 2) Many Heathens claim that academic theory is foundational for their faith. They use such claims to protect themselves against political misuses of their religion, and to achieve a more respectable public standing. Nevertheless, Asatru, even in its reconstructionist variety, is an aesthetic endeavor based on creativity and experience. This aesthetic dimension also drives the contemporary historical reconstruction scene, which has equally deep roots in 19th-century Romantic nationalism and its holistic academic views of culture. 3) The holistic cultural academic theories and methodologies which can be traced back to Romanticism and which fueled historians of religion, such as Vilhelm Grønbech, Jakob Wilhelm Hauer, Rudolf Otto, and Mircea Eliade; folklorists and Scandinavianists, such as Eugen Fehrle, Otto Höfler, and Bernhard Kummer; and archeologists, such as Gustav Kossina, are much more easily incorporated into Neopagan religion than medievalist methods. The latter attempt to contextualize texts within the textual traditions and the social and political conditions of their era, and they try to locate the sources within a high-medieval clerical and scholarly philosophical tradition. This has to do with the fact that scholarly constructions of wholeness and coherence are themselves dependent on operations which belong to the realm of the aesthetic: imaginations of a whole, a *Gestalt*, and experiential intuition, through which the fragments are held together and the gaps between them filled.

These entanglements make it seem productive to conclude this book with a final chapter that considers the interfaces between aesthetics, religion, and politics that have governed the reception of Germanic myth.

CHAPTER 9

Germanic Neopaganism – A Nordic Art-Religion?

Aesthetic imaginaries in stories, paintings, film, and music, ranging from Wagnerian opera to contemporary black metal, Viking metal, Pagan metal, and neofolk music have had a strong impact on Asatru as well as on popular images of Nordic myth and religion. They have even shaped academic contributions to the discourse of Nordic myth. In spite of their professed commitment to academic knowledge, many Asatruers mention fictional books as their main sources of inspiration and knowledge of Nordic religion. Furthermore, Asatruers often perceive their own religious practices as aesthetic activities. All of this can be attributed to the specific appeal of art and fiction in modernity. They are modes that bring to life the historical past, speak to the senses, and allow emotional identification. Artworks can create a sense of identity and community (be it national or otherwise) which goes beyond a purely fact-oriented and intellectual level; they allow the creation of coherent worlds beyond the meager and scattered, often contradictory primary sources. This widespread popularity has turned certain aesthetic genres – popular literature and music in particular – into privileged media in Asatru's path toward respectability. They are media Asatruers themselves use to disseminate their thoughts and connect themselves with broader ideas about culture and identity. In addition, they are mainstream media that provide material for the construction of Heathen religion. At the same time, aesthetic approaches lend themselves to a more playful, individualized manner of conducting a spiritual life. Contemporary Neopagan religions in particular tend to perceive their spirituality as a creative process, and to assign art, music, literature, and performance spiritual qualities.

All of these observations can be contextualized within a concept that originated around 1800 in German Romanticism: the concept of art-religion (*Kunstreligion*). Generally speaking, and perhaps surprisingly for many, it is in modernity rather than in ancient or pre-modern times that religion and art, the spiritual and the aesthetic, appear to be most closely related. 19th-century thought, and particularly that of German idealist theologian Friedrich Schleiermacher (1768–1834), conceptualizes religion as a realm of aesthetic experience. Schleiermacher was the first to tie religion explicitly to emotion, experience, interiority, and the private sphere, the fields in which modern art is located as well. At the same time, art is increasingly assigned religious functions: the artwork is seen as capable of creating transcendent meaning; the process of artistic creation is perceived as a religiously inspired act; the artist is assigned the role of a prophet, priest, or savior; and art itself is celebrated in cultic ways.[1]

Germanist Heinrich Detering has recently argued that the historical precondition for this constellation of art-religion, for the adoption of religious functions in art and vice versa, is a differentiation of the spheres of art and religion in modern society into two clearly distinguishable realms. It is the perception of, or a conscious suffering from, this differentiation that leads to the nostalgic yearning for a restoration of an imagined lost unity, the emphatic invocation of a future unification or a synthesis of both.[2] What is compelling for our context is the fact that this art-religion paradigm and the discourse on Nordic myth originate in the same era and in the same intellectual constellation, and that they are so closely entwined from the beginning.[3]

This chapter demonstrates that the rediscovery of Norse mythology and its functionalization for various national, cultural, and religious renewals in different countries (most prominently Germany and the Nordic countries) is set within an art-religious context. It concludes that Germanic Neopagan beliefs and practices, as well as the discourses from which they emerge, to which they contribute and which have been at the center of the previous chapters, are best understood as the popularization of the discourse of Nordic myth, as well as of art-religion itself and its transformation into alternative spiritual practice.

Nineteenth Century Concepts of Germanic Art-Religion

If we look at the Romantic context in which the German and Scandinavian Romantic revival of Norse myth and the literary discovery of the Eddic lays

---

1 For a summarizing discussion of art-religion see Heinrich Detering, "Was ist Kunstreligion? Systematische und historische Bemerkungen," in *Kunstreligion. Ein ästhetisches Konzept der Moderne in seiner historischen Entfaltung. Vol. 1 (Der Ursprung des Konzepts um 1800)*, ed. Albert Meier, Allesandro Costazza, and Gérard Laudin (Berlin: De Gruyter, 2011) and "Religion," in *Handbuch Literaturwissenschaft. Vol. 1 (Gegenstände – Konzepte – Institutionen)*, ed. Thomas Anz (Stuttgart/Weimar: Metzler, 2007).

2 Cf. "Was ist Kunstreligion?" and "Religion," as well as Williamson, *The Longing for Myth in Germany*, 15. He argues not only that the discourse on myth emerged in secular institutions, mainly in scholarship, art, and literature, but that its claim to sacred status and – we might add – the formation of new religions based on such myths have their origins in such secular institutions as well.

3 This might also have to do with the fact that, since the Renaissance, the arts appear as the realm where the depiction of non-Christian myth is permitted. We might even go so far as to say that one of the main sources for Nordic myth, Snorri's Edda, follows a similar pattern, as it is written as a reference book for poets.

were set, we encounter the same authors who also laid the ground for the modern sacralization of art. During his twenty years in the Danish court, German writer Friedrich Gottlieb Klopstock (1724–1803) developed a vision of the artist as a seer-priest, and of religious texts as works of poetry.[4] During this time he made use of the first translations of the Eddic lays. He fused them with Ossianic elements in order to create an art form inspired by then-current conceptions of 'national' mythology. For Johann Gottfried Herder, who further developed this approach, the search for a national mythology was first and foremost an aesthetic endeavor as well, or more precisely, a literary one. For him, folk songs in particular represented the purest embodiment of national folk poetry. His essayistic dialogue *"Iduna, oder der Apfel der Verjüngung"* ("Iduna, or the Apple of Rejuvenation"), which appeared in Friedrich Schiller's monthly literary journal *Die Horen* in 1796,[5] outlines the pros and cons of employing the newly available Eddic myths for a renewal of German poetry as a didactic dialogue. It took up the then-recent fashion of Bardic poetry in the spirit of Macpherson's Ossian and melded it with Herder's own ideas about the unity of myth, landscape, and nation. However, in contrast to many of his contemporaries, Herder insisted on the fundamental difference between the "soft, sad sentiments" of the Celts and the deed-oriented songs of the Nordic peoples, with whom he identified the Germans.[6] Herder's targeted course was clearly literary and aesthetic, but in a way which imbues fictional narrative with a sacral aura. He saw literature as the privileged medium conveying transcendent universal truth and meaning. In order to be effective, understandable, vital, capable of development, and thus apt for modernity, universal ideas need forms that are organically connected to the past (the childhood of the nation) and an equally organically developed language with roots in national myth. Herder hoped to find compensation for the lack of "a mythology rooted in their own mentality and language"[7] and the lack of a developed heroic poetry in the "mythology of a neighboring people."[8] Refined in the meters of classical Greek poetry, this mythology would lay the foundations for the rejuvenation of national literature and culture. Herder formulated two principles that were to have great impact on the future development of theories of myth and nation both in Germany and abroad. One of these principles was the notion of a *Kulturnation*, a nation built on an organic culture and not defined by a state apparatus. This idea was to influence German nationalism in the 19th century and laid the

---

4 Detering, "Religion," 391f, see also "Was ist Kunstreligion?" 15.
5 Johann Gottfried Herder, "Iduna, oder der Apfel der Verjüngung," *Die Horen* 5, no. 2 (1796).
6 Ibid., 30 [26].
7 Ibid., 2 [8]: "eine in ihrer eigenen Denkart und Sprache entsproßene Mythologie."
8 Ibid., 8 [14]: "Mythologie eines benachbarten Volkes."

foundation for the formulation of a national art-religion in other countries. The notion of a *Kulturnation* implied the assumption that Scandinavian mythological texts actually stem from the same sources as the lost German mythology, and can thus be employed to reconstruct a German literary and mythical national heritage.

Herder's impact on the rediscovery of Norse mythological themes in Germany, as well as in Anglo-American thought and the Gothic and Nordic revivals of Scandinavian Romanticism, can hardly be over-estimated, although the reception of his work in the Nordic countries and in English-language contexts is as yet under-researched.[9] What is clear is that the aesthetic works of the Nordic or Gothic revival in Swedish and Danish Romanticism provided an arsenal of literary topoi, ideas, and images of Norse mythology and religion which spread widely and became firmly established, not only in their respective national imaginations but also internationally. In Denmark as well as in Sweden, the Romantic literary movements were set in the context of the national defeats connected with the Napoleonic and other early 19th-century wars. Also here, the turn to literature as a privileged medium to create access to a national heroic past and thus a feeling of unity and identity became an important part of the attempt to consolidate national identities in times of political crisis and military decline. It inspired the popularizations of medieval materials in poetry, drama, and later, in painting as well. Among them were the immensely popular heroic historical dramas by the Dane Adam Oehlenschläger (1779–1850). With his early poem *"Guldhornene"* ("The Gold-Horns," 1802), this author had previously provided a poetic myth of national loss and rebirth through the search for roots in a mythological past still living in Danish soil, nature, and rural people.[10] Another Danish writer, Nikolai Frederik Severin Grundtvig (1783–1872), succeeded in firmly tying poetical imaginaries of Nordic deities to a sense of a national Christian identity.[11] As a result, Nordic myth

---

9   First reflections on the topic can be found in Bernd Henningsen, "Johann Gottfried Herder and the North. Elements of a Process of Construcion," in *Northbound. Travels, Encounters, and Constructions 1700–1830*, ed. Karen Klitgaard Poulsen (Aarhus: Aarhus University Press, 2007).

10   Adam Oehlenschläger, *Digte* (Copenhagen: Andreas Seidelin, 1803).

11   See in particular Nikolai Frederik Severin Grundtvig, "Nordens Mytologi, eller Udsigt over Eddalæren for dannede Mænd, der ei selv ere Mytologer," in *N.F.S. Grundtvig, Værker i udvalg*, ed. Georg Christensen and Hal Koch (Copenhagen: Gyldendal, 1940 [1810]). Cf. also Lars Lönnroth, "The Academy of Odin. Grundtvig's Political Instrumentalization of Old Norse Mythology," in *Idee – Gestalt – Geschichte. Studien zur europäischen Kulturtradition. Festschrift für Klaus von See*, ed. Gerd Wolfgang Weber (Odense: Odense University Press, 1988); Lundgreen-Nielsen, "Gundtvig's Norse Mythological Imagery."

came to be seen as such an integral part of the Danish nation, culture, and even mainstream Protestant religion throughout the 19th and 20th centuries that a need for the foundation of Asatru groups did not arise until the late 1990s.[12] In Sweden, poems by Erik Gustaf Geijer (1783–1847) established the Viking and the independent peasant as archetypical images of the great Swedish nation.[13] The single most influential text on an international scale was an epic poem by Esaias Tegnér (1782–1846) about the hero Frithiof, which was loosely inspired by an Icelandic saga.[14] *Frithiofs Saga* was soon translated into English and German and became widely popular in both countries as well as in Scandinavia. It shaped ideas about Nordic heroism, which was depicted as an equivalent of modern bourgeois European ideals, and claimed a fundamental affinity between Nordic pagan and Christian values.[15]

The Nordic aesthetic revival in the Scandinavian countries provided sacralized images of Nordic history that were reconcilable with the sense that Lutheranism was the national religion. The implicit logic of this idea is similar to that of the German case: while Mediterranean culture and Greek and Roman antiquity are alleged to hold a strong appeal for the Northerners, they should nevertheless be perceived as ultimately foreign. Catholicism is then aligned with these 'foreign,' 'Southern' Greek and Roman traditions, while Lutheran Protestantism is perceived to be a continuation of the Nordic traditions celebrated in Romantic poetry. A similar argument was made for the Church of England in the mid-19th century, as the following quote by the novelist and historian Charles Kingsley shows:

> I say that the Church of England is wonderfully and mystically fitted for the souls of free Norse-Saxon race; for men whose ancestors fought by the side of Odin, over whom a descendant of Odin now rules.[16]

Also in England, knowledge about and imagery of Norse gods, Anglo-Saxon, and Viking culture were disseminated in literary works, for example those by

---

12   Cf. Schnurbein, *Religion als Kulturkritik*, 211f.
13   For Oehlenschläger's and Geijer's debt to Macpherson's Ossian cf. Bo Jansson, "Nordens poetiska reception av Europas reception av det nordiska," in *The Waking of Angantyr. The Scandinavian Past in European Culture – Den nordiske fortid i europæisk kultur*, ed. Else Roesdahl and Preben Meulengracht Sørensen (Aarhus: Aarhus University Press, 1996).
14   Esaias Tegnér, *Frithiofs saga*, ed. Åke K.G. Lundquist, 7 vols., vol. 4, Esaias Tegnérs samlade dikter (Lund: Gleerup, 1986).
15   Cf. Wawn, *The Vikings and the Victorians*, 117–141.
16   Quoted in ibid., mottos.

Walter Scott. His *The Pirate* (1821) borrowed heavily from saga literature,[17] and *Ivanhoe* "inspired a whole generation with a vision of Saxon freedom and honesty."[18] Most important for the spread of Nordic myth and heroic poetry in England was William Morris' retelling of the Norse *Nibelungen* material.[19] A plethora of late 19th-century Viking novels, including *Eric Brighteyes* (1891) by H. Rider Haggard, projected a vision of the "white race's" imperial conquest onto the Vikings[20] – a vision which still reverberates in 20th century English and American literary and filmic Viking imagery, and which inspired some of the early Asatruers in the United States.

Morris, along with later Viking enthusiasts, followed another German source of inspiration: Richard Wagner. In his *The Ring of the Nibelung* (first staged in Bayreuth in 1876), the Nordic constellation of art-religion reached its climax. Anti-clerical in outlook, Wagner's work popularized the idea that a Pagan Germanic religion that was preserved in the far north should form the basis for the national renewal of Germany, and he assigned the artist the role of the herald of this ancient, yet new message. Wagner was the first German artist to make use of medieval Scandinavian sources of the Nibelungen material, because he found them to be more original and thus apt to express myth's timeless character than the German *Nibelungenlied*, which is located in a courtly and Christian setting.[21] He drew on contemporary scholarship in German philology, including Jacob Grimm's "*Deutsche Mythologie*," in order to give his ideas on myth and art a foundation in canonical themes and motives. In his theoretical texts, particularly in *The Artwork of the Future*,[22] he developed a revolutionary political vision: a "political economy of love," based on the revolutionary notion of the *Volk* itself as the artist who was to bring about

---

17 David M. Wilson, "The Viking Age in British Literature and History in the Eighteenth and Nineteenth Centuries," in *The Waking of Angantyr. The Scandinavian Past in European Culture – Den nordiske fortid i europæisk kultur*, ed. Else Roesdahl and Preben Meulengracht Sørensen (Aarhus: Aarhus University Press, 1996), 64f.

18 Horsman, *Race and Manifest Destiny*, 40.

19 Wilson, "The Viking Age in British Literature and History," 67; Wawn, *The Vikings and the Victorians*, 245–281; Paola Spinozzi, "The Topos of Ragnarök in the Utopian Thought of William Morris," in *Eddische Götter und Helden. Milieus und Medien ihrer Rezeption. Eddic Gods and Heroes. The Milieux and Media of Their Reception*, ed. Katja Schulz (Heidelberg: Winter, 2011).

20 Cf. Wawn, *The Vikings and the Victorians*, 332–335.

21 For Wagner's treatment of the Nordic sources see for example Böldl, *Der Mythos der Edda*, 271–277.

22 Richard Wagner, "The Art-Work of the Future," in *The Art-Work of the Future. Richard Wagner's Prose Works* (London: Keegan Paul, Trench, Trübner, 1895 [1849]).

the "new myth." Wagner certainly supported Romantic ideas of the unity of nature, humanity, myth, and art as the basis of the people, for example, in his description of art as a process by which nature "grows conscious of herself in man, the artist."[23] The *Volk* for Wagner was constituted through a shared need. Only those who felt this need belonged to the *Volk*, while the "egoists," basking in luxury and empty fashionable aestheticism, were excluded. Consequently, the artist, who is to give the eternal myth its appropriate form to counter such present "need," is the one who feels and embodies this need most strongly.

Wagner's model for the renewed unity of *Volk* and art is Greek tragedy in its idealized version as promoted by German classicists such as Johann Joachim Winckelmann (1717–1768) and Friedrich Schiller (1759–1805). For him, it appears as an art form which emerged directly from the people, celebrated its unity in a simultaneously religious and artistic act, and united all the individual arts including song, poetry, dance, and visual art in a grand *Gesamtkunstwerk* (total art work). In contrast to Schiller and Winckelmann however, Wagner did not consider Greek myth to be the appropriate form for the new holistic artwork that was meant to unite the German people of his time. Instead of using Greek myth as the basis for his work, Wagner merged ideas about a 'pure' Christianity (i.e., uncorrupted by church institutions) with Nordic myth. The result is an immanent concept of religion centered on "human nature in its naked essence, before it had been corrupted by succeeding layers of religion, history, and convention."[24] Wagner took his inspiration from Ludwig Feuerbach's (1804–1872) critical theory of religion. The philosopher saw the essence of human nature in "material activity *(Handlung)*" rather than abstract concepts. He despised Christianity, considering it as a decline from the ancient Greek polytheism, which, due to its connection between humans and nature, had furthered the development of art and science.[25] Feuerbach and Wagner thus laid the foundation for later ideas about pre-Christian religions as religions of deed *(Tatreligion)*, discussed in Chapter 3. Feuerbach's theory also provided Wagner with a justification for his anti-Semitic critique of both religion and contemporary art.[26] Wagner's attitude toward Jews, along with his

---

23   Ibid., 70; "Das Kunstwerk der Zukunft," in *Sämtliche Schriften und Dichtungen*, ed. Richard Wagner (Leipzig: Breitkopf und Härtel, 1911 [1849]).
24   Williamson, *The Longing for Myth in Germany*, 196.
25   This argument is developed by Williamson, ibid., 193.
26   Cf. Lincoln, *Theorizing Myth*, 57f; Williamson, *The Longing for Myth in Germany*, 205; Hildegard Chatellier, "Wagnerismus in der Kaiserzeit," in *Handbuch zur 'Völkischen Bewegung' 1871–1918*, ed. Uwe Puschner, Walter Schmitz, and Justus H. Ulbricht (Munich etc.: K.G. Saur, 1996), 577 and 583.

fierce anti-Semitic diatribes, especially in his infamous essay *"Das Judentum in der Musik"* (*"Judaism in Music,"* 1850),[27] have given rise to much controversial discussion that cannot be addressed in detail here.[28] Two facets are pertinent in this respect. Firstly, many of Wagner's theoretical writings place the concept of art-religion in an anti-Semitic context. In combination with the aforementioned blend of a "pure" Christianity and Nordic myth, they lend themselves easily to *völkisch* (art-)religious interpretations. Secondly, Wagner's operatic work itself does not make open mention of Jews, neither does his seminal essay, "Artwork of the Future." However, his antagonists, such as Alberich and Mime in *The Ring*, display characteristics that are typical of contemporary anti-Semitic stereotypes and can be decoded as allusions to the negative influence of 'capitalist Jews' by an audience that shares these codes.[29]

With regards to the popularization of Wagnerian images of Nordic myth and the establishment of a neo-Germanic religion, the reception of Wagner is even more influential than his theoretical concept of art-religion proper. His art-religious ideas were taken up by his followers in the *Bayreuther Kreis* (Bayreuth Circle), under the leadership of Hans von Wolzogen between 1878 and 1938. Wolzogen, the *Bayreuther Kreis*, and its journal, *Bayreuther Blätter*, were responsible for an increasingly *völkisch* reading of Wagner, for a concentration on national heritage and the art of the past, which for them culminated in Wagner and did not include contemporary avant-gardes. Although the majority of the *Bayreuther Kreis* itself remained within a German-Christian

---

27 Richard Wagner, "Das Judentum in der Musik," in *Sämtliche Schriften und Dichtungen*, ed. Richard Wagner (Leipzig: Breitkopf und Härtel, 1911 [1850]); "Judaism in Music," in *The Theatre. Richard Wagner's Prose Works* (London: Keegan Paul, Trench, Trübner, 1894 [1850]).

28 The most prominent accusations against Wagner's anti-Semitism have been forwarded by Hartmut Zelinsky, *Richard Wagner – ein deutsches Thema. Eine Dokumentation zur Wirkungsgeschichte Richard Wagners 1876–1976* (Frankfurt a.M.: Zweitausendeins, 1976); Rose, *Revolutionary Antisemitism in Germany from Kant to Wagner*; and Marc A. Weiner, *Richard Wagner and the Anti-Semitic Imagination* (Lincoln: University of Nebraska Press, 1995). For counterarguments see for example Dieter Borchmeyer, "Wagner und der Antisemitismus," in *Richard-Wagner-Handbuch*, ed. Ulrich Müller and Peter Wapnewski (Stuttgart: Kröner, 1986).

29 The contemporary reception of Wagner by many anti-Semites bears witness to this possibility. However, the opposite is true as well: a reception of Wagner's work ignoring these elements is possible and has certainly contributed to its continuing popularity. For a differentiated discussion of the latently anti-Semitic uses of language in Wagner's *Ring* see David Levin, *Richard Wagner, Fritz Lang, and the Nibelungen. The Dramaturgy of Disavowal* (Princeton, NJ: Princeton University Press, 1998), 30–95.

religious paradigm, its influence on the German Faith and the Ariosophic movement was considerable, as will be discussed shortly.[30]

In addition to Wagner, there were two other theorists and popularizers of art-religion in Germany around 1900 whose legacies for the *völkisch* religious movement were instrumental, namely Friedrich Nietzsche (1844–1900) and Julius Langbehn (1851–1907). These two thinkers are vastly different from each other in sophistication and long-term international impact, but equally influential for German art-religion of the early 20th century.

Friedrich Nietzsche's philosophy did not shape popular images of Nordic deities and myth as directly as Wagner's artistic work did. However, his anti-monotheist, non-idealistic, tragic-heroic, aristocratic view of humanity contributed to alternative-religious, Neopagan, and Conservative Revolutionary worldviews to a degree which cannot be understated, and which was not limited to Germany. It is impossible here to do justice to the complex and changing attitudes toward the aesthetic in Nietzsche's philosophy and its extensive and diverse reception.[31] Many Nietzscheans plainly ignored the fierce antagonisms that drove his work and understood his philosophy of 'life' as a holistic worldview, which based life as a whole on aesthetic values and thus excluded ethics not only from art, but from politics as well.

The immense popularity of nationalist readings of Nietzschean art-religion is confirmed indirectly by the reception of Julius Langbehn's culturally critical, nationalist manifesto, "*Rembrandt als Erzieher*" (Rembrandt as Educator, 1890). When the work first appeared anonymously, it stated only that it was written "by a German" ("von einem Deutschen").[32] Speculations ran wild that Nietzsche (whose "*Schopenhauer als Erzieher*" inspired the title) was behind this emphatic appeal for a spiritual renewal of the German nation.[33] According to Langbehn, national rebirth was to be facilitated with the help of the German aesthetic heritage, by artists, as the "leading spirits," in search of a truly "national style,"[34]

---

30 For a discussion of the *Bayreuther Kreis* and the *völkisch* movement see Chatellier, "Wagnerismus in der Kaiserzeit," 585–595.

31 For an overview of the popular reception of Nietzsche in Germany see Aschheim, *The Nietzsche Legacy in Germany 1890–1990*. For a comprehensive discussion of Nietzsche's view of myth and his shifting concepts of art-religion see Lincoln, *Theorizing Myth*, 101–120, and Williamson, *The Longing for Myth in Germany*, 234–284.

32 Julius Langbehn, *Rembrandt als Erzieher. Von einem Deutschen* (Leipzig: Hirschfeld, 1890).

33 Others imagined Paul de Lagarde or even Bismarck to be behind the anonymous author. Cf. Ingrid Oberndorfer, "Antisemitismus im 19. Jhdt. – August Julius Langbehn," *David. Jüdische Kulturzeitschrift* 57 (2003).

34 Peter Ulrich Hein, *Die Brücke ins Geisterreich. Künstlerische Avantgarde zwischen Kulturkritik und Faschismus* (Reinbek b. Hamburg: Rowohlt, 1992), 83f.

the models and heroes of which were to be canonized artists such as Rembrandt, Dürer, and Goethe.

Both Nietzsche's and Langbehn's ideas permeated the life reform movement and its emphatic identification of 'natural' beauty and health, as well as the avant-garde aesthetic and elitist right-wing movements, and helped to forge links between them.[35] Langbehn's enthusiastically received and widely read manifesto influenced a great number of art-reform associations in early 20th-century Germany, among them the *Deutscher Werkbund* (German Association of Craftsmen, founded in 1907),[36] the cultural reform journal *Kunstwart* (founded and edited by Ferdinand Avenarius),[37] the art-education movement (*Kunsterziehungsbewegung*),[38] and the *Werdandi-Bund* – named after one of the three norns (or fates) of Norse mythology, the norn of the present, or

---

35   According to Peter Ulrich Hein, the 'Germanization' and politicization of the Nietzschean version of art-religion should be understood in the context of a longing for a strong leader, a *Führer*, amongst German intellectuals in the early 20th century, and especially after WW I. This *Führer* was seen as a "potentiation of the *Volk*'s characteristics." The German concept of *Kulturnation* saw the specific German character in the ability to unite essence and appearance in a higher form. Thus, this *Führer* came to resemble the ideal image of the artist. Ibid., 29. Such potentially totalitarian ideas were virulent in both expressionist circles as well as in the extreme right of the Weimar Republic, which tended to see the state, and politics itself, as an aesthetic institution. On the potential for totalitarianism of such art-religious ideas see Cornelia Klinger, *Flucht Trost Revolte. Die Moderne und ihre ästhetischen Gegenwelten* (Munich: Hanser, 1995), especially ch. 6. Hein, *Die Brücke ins Geisterreich*, 63 alerts to the fact that Armin Mohler, the apologetic theorist of the Conservative Revolution conceptualizes the movement as an aesthetic project himself: Mohler, *Die konservative Revolution in Deutschland 1918–1932*, 109. The disputed theories by George L. Mosse, *The Crisis of German Ideology. Intellectual Origins of the Third Reich* (New York: Grosset & Dunlap, 1964); Roger Griffin, *The Nature of Fascism*; and Zev Sternhell, "Von der Gegenaufklärung zu Faschismus und Nazismus," who consider international fascism in the 20th century as a predominantly cultural phenomenon are immensely helpful for an understanding of the right-wing art-religious ideas discussed in this chapter. For a summary of the controversies around these theories see Umland, Loh, and Griffin, *Fascism Past and Present, West and East*.

36   This umbrella organization sought to professionalize the numerous dilettante cultural associations in Germany and formed the cradle for the *Bauhaus* idea.

37   Cf. Hein, *Die Brücke ins Geisterreich*, 91–96; Marina Schuster, "Die Bildwelt der Völkischen," in *Völkische Religion und Krisen der Moderne. Entwürfe 'arteigener' Glaubenssysteme seit der Jahrhundertwende*, ed. Stefanie v. Schnurbein and Justus H. Ulbricht (Würzburg: Königshausen & Neumann, 2001), 254f.

38   Hein, *Die Brücke ins Geisterreich*, 97–103. This movement promoted an organological model of art, saw the expression of mythic essences in a national art, and aimed at cultivating one's own myth and type as purely as possible.

'becoming' – the umbrella organization for various strands of the *völkisch* art movement.[39] Through figures like Wagner, Nietzsche, and Langbehn, as well as Felix Dahn, historian and author of the popular nationalist novel *A Struggle for Rome* (*"Ein Kampf um Rom"*) and other nationalist poetry,[40] along with their followers, the connections between 'Germanic' mythology, German aesthetic and intellectual heritage, national rebirth, and the leading role of art and the artist became firmly established in this modern 'Germanic' art-religion.

J.R.R. Tolkien and the Nordic Art-Religion of Middle-Earth

These protagonists of a Nordic art-religious tradition were immensely important for the emerging Germanic Neopaganism in the German Faith Movement after 1900, and thus for later Asatru. However, another novelist, J.R.R. Tolkien

---

39 Cf. Rolf Parr, "Der 'Werdandi-Bund'," in *Handbuch zur 'Völkischen Bewegung' 187–1918*, ed. Uwe Puschner, Walter Schmitz, and Justus H. Ulbricht (Munich etc.: K.G. Saur, 1996), 317. Inspired by Richard Wagner's idea of the total artwork, the *Werdandi-Bund* sought to unite religion, philosophy, and art in a new "German" folk-culture. It took an independent position between the *Heimatschutz* movement and its purely preservationist approach to German folk-culture, and the *Werkbund*, with its search for a national form of industrialized art and craft. The wide range of prominent members from all cultural spheres, including many activists of the *Bayreuther Kreis*, Paul Schultze-Naumburg of the *Bund Heimatschutz*, *Kunstwart*-editor Ferdinand Avenarius, Felix Dahn, Otto Höfler's father Alois Höfler, and even Theodor Heuss, the first liberal president of the Federal Republic of Germany after the war, testifies to the ideological breadth and influence of the *Werdandi-Bund*. Cf. also Chatellier, "Wagnerismus in der Kaiserzeit," 608.

40 Felix Dahn was an accomplished professor of jurisprudence and legal history when he published his four-volume novel, *A Struggle for Rome* (Felix Dahn, *Ein Kampf um Rom*, English translations by Lily Wolffsohn (A Struggle for Rome – The Ostrogoths and Belisarius, 1878) and Herb Parker (A Struggle for Rome, 2005) (Leipzig: Breitopf & Sartel, 1876–1878)), which is set in Italy in the two decades after the death of the Gothic king Theoderic in 493 AD. In his fictional account, the fights between east and west Rome serve to convey a message of the degeneration and future restoration of the Gothic people and are given an implicit (national) religious or mythic content. Dahn makes a young warrior-poet into one of the last princely survivors of these struggles and lets him quite anachronistically be rescued by Vikings. Transferred to the North he and his young wife, an innocent child of nature, will assure the rebirth of this great nation in the future. Quite obviously, Felix Dahn ascribes a similarly national prophetic role to himself and assigns literature and poetry a prominent place in the national renewal which bears "Pagan" traits as well. Cf. Bernhard Viel, *Utopie der Nation. Ursprünge des Nationalismus im Roman der Gründerzeit* (Berlin: Matthes & Seitz, 2009).

(1892–1973), influenced the perception of European myth and folk belief after the 1960s in an unprecedented way and set the terms for the genre of fantasy literature. The fantastic world of his *The Lord of the Rings* trilogy has provided material for a whole industry of media, film, and games.[41] In many aspects, Tolkien can be seen as a direct heir to the Anglo-Saxonist and Romantic constellation discussed above, with its characteristic merging of scholarship, myth, and aesthetic revival of myth.[42] Philological theories of myth strongly influenced his literary work, and he supported the idea that myth can be reconstructed on the basis of a philological study of languages. His seeing languages as bearers of ancient mythological and cultural essences motivated his more activist, rather than antiquarian, relation to Old Norse material.[43]

---

41 Tolkien has received both immense praise as the "author of the [20th] century" (Tom Shippey, *J.R.R. Tolkien. Author of the Century* (Boston/New York: Houghton Mifflin Company, 2002)), who lucidly anticipated green and alternative ideas, and equally outspoken scorn, as having written trivial, immature boys' stories with racist and misogynist undertones (see e.g. Guido Schwarz, *Jungfrauen im Nachthemd – blonde Krieger aus dem Westen. Eine motivpsychologisch-kritische Analyse von J.R.R. Tolkiens Mythologie und Weltbild* (Würzburg: Königshausen & Neumann, 2003)), while his work has been largely ignored by academic literary criticism. The following discussion of Tolkien is based on Schnurbein, "Kontinuität durch Dichtung" and supplemented with arguments from Stefan Arvidsson's analysis, the most lucid interpretation of Tolkien's concept of myth currently available. Cf. Arvidsson, *Draksjukan*, 142–198.

42 Tolkien is another example of an accomplished academic-turned-mythmaker. He taught as a professor of Germanic philology at Oxford University, his main contribution to the field being a still-relevant essay on Beowulf. (Cf. J.R.R. Tolkien, "Beowulf. The Monsters and the Critics," *Proceedings of the British Academy* 22 (1936), reprinted in *The Monster and the Critics and Other Essays* (London: George Allen & Unwin, 1983)). At the same time, he was a member of a circle of intellectual male friends, 'the Inklings.' They discussed and brought to life the mythical worlds they studied by identifying with figures from Old Norse or Old English literature. For a still authoritative and detailed biography of Tolkien see Humphrey Carpenter, *J.R.R. Tolkien: A Biography* (London: George Allen & Unwin, 1977), for the Inklings see also Ronald Hutton, *Witches, Druids and King Arthur* (London/New York: Hambledon and London, 2003), 215–238. Shippey, *J.R.R. Tolkien. Author of the Century* (XIV–XVI) compares Tolkien's academic and literary activities with those of Jacob and Wilhelm Grimm, particularly their literary and linguistic reconstructions of Germanic grammar, law, mythology, and fairy tales; with those of Elias Lönnrot who reconstructed the Finnish "national epos," the *Kalevala*, from disparate sources; and of Nikolai Frederik Severin Grundtvig, and his project of the reconstruction of a national Danish identity. See also T.A. Shippey, "Goths and Huns. The Rediscovery of the Northern Cultures in the Nineteenth Century," in *The Medieval Legacy. A Symposium*, ed. Andreas Haarder, et al. (Odense: Odense University Press, 1982), 64f.

43 See Arvidsson, *Draksjukan*, 150.

Tolkien deplored the lack of an original English mythology, which he sought to compensate for in his literary work.[44] The choice of an aesthetic genre in this process of reconstruction points to an aesthetic attitude toward a critique of contemporary society, and the potential for its healing through ancient myth – not unlike that of Richard Wagner. Tolkien engaged extensively with Wagner's *Ring of the Nibelung*, although he claimed to detest him and rejected any such influence.[45]

A Herderian worldview, and its central assumption of a unity of landscape, language, and nation, resonates in the descriptions of the relations between the many creatures, peoples, and 'races' of Middle-earth in *The Lord of the Rings*. For Herder as for Tolkien, myth is fundamental for the formation of a people. It reflects a people's attachment to its landscape and history, transmitting ancestral traditions and forming its customs and morals. Neither Herder nor Tolkien submitted to a reductive blood-and-soil ideology,[46] rather, their works are marked by an unresolved tension between universalism and cultural relativism. For Tolkien, the struggle between good and evil is universal and unites all races. Through this alliance, these various races also become aware of their common ancestral roots. The ideal state after the victory, however, is different: here, each race or species lives peacefully on its own native soil, mostly separated from other races. Migration, cultural exchange, and interbreeding are rare, and not seen as desirable. The only exception is the marriage between elves and men in the future class of rulers of the new monarchic order. This has more to do with the arrival of a new age in which the race of men leads Middle-earth after the departure of the elves. The new ruling class is thus legitimized as the bearer of ancient wisdom, religion, and art, which the elves stand for in Tolkien's work. Søren Staal Balslev has thus argued convincingly that paradigms of racial hygiene and concern over the degeneration of bloodlines

---

44   Cf. Bradley J. Birzer, *J.R.R. Tolkien's Sanctifying Myth. Understanding Middle-Earth* (Wilmington, DE: ISI Books, 2003), 41f; Patrick Curry, *Defending Middle-Earth. Tolkien: Myth and Modernity* (London: HarperCollins, 1998), 30f; Hutton, *Witches, Druids and King Arthur*, 227, claims that Tolkien started out by constructing such a mythology, which was in place by 1920, and that his further literary work builds upon it.

45   For a good overview of the parallels between Wagner's and Tolkien's "Rings" see Arvidsson, *Draksjukan*, 148f. It is above all the main symbol – the ring as a sign of the misuse of power – that unites the two works. It also deserves attention that Tolkien, in contrast to Wagner, did not combine his cultural critique with anti-Semitic sentiments, although his work is not otherwise free from racist imagery.

46   Ibid., 151, draws attention to the fact that Tolkien's idealization of a seafaring imperialist patriotism has left traces in *Lord of the Rings*.

pervade the book.⁴⁷ The racial stereotyping found in *The Lord of the Rings* resembles that of Herder (and the general colonial imagination), with dark-skinned, slant-eyed evil creatures residing in the arid, hot, southern regions and infertile eastern regions, whereas heroic peoples, like the riders of Rohan, are blond, blue-eyed, and reside in the North-West.⁴⁸ In Tolkien's world, however, evil or degeneration is not caused by an unfortunate climate, but is the result of processes of degeneration caused by an untrammeled hunger for power. This process is accompanied by both the darkening of physical features and linguistic degeneration.⁴⁹

But what about religion in Middle-earth? While Tolkien describes the languages, mentalities, and cultural peculiarities of his 'races' in great detail, neither their religious practices nor beliefs are mentioned directly. Himself a devout Catholic, Tolkien claimed to have refrained from putting "anything like 'religion' or cults or practices in the imaginary world," in order to let the work as a whole stand out as "fundamentally religious and Catholic," religion being "absorbed into the story and the symbolism."⁵⁰ As a result, the literary work itself appears as a great myth, or, as we might say in the context of our argument, as an emphatic expression of art-religion. A closer look at *The Lord of the Rings* shows that Tolkien amalgamates Christian⁵¹ elements with the images and ethics of the medieval Northern European tradition he taught all his life, and which he, in accordance with the spirit of his era and academic practice,

---

47 Cf. Søren Staal Balslev, "Blodsaristokrati i *Ringenes herre* og *Det mørke tårn*," *Kritik* 202 (2011), 94–97.

48 This does not imply that such Nordic-heroic peoples are without flaw – quite the contrary: their blind heroism and atavistic concept of honor is set negatively against the hobbits Frodo's and Sam's unassuming, humble, and altruistic heroism.

49 Thus, the orks are elves converted to evil, trolls were ents, Gollum is originally a hobbit etc. The distorted speech of Gollum and the Orks are examples of such linguistic degeneration. The fear of a degeneration and impoverishment of speech through institutions of political power such as the church, the court and the legal system are also a concern of Herder, who hoped for a renewal of language and literature through the vital impulses of folk song and Nordic poetry. Arvidsson, *Draksjukan*, 163, alerts to the Zoroastrian implications of this philosophy: the enemy creates evil through the perversion of the good.

50 J.R.R. Tolkien, quoted in: ibid., 237.

51 Some of the most prominent examples are Gandalf's resurrection, the ethics of compassion and humility, Frodo's ordeal which leads to the redemption of the world, and not least, the reinstatement of an idealized king in the spirit of an equally idealized Christian medieval sacral kingdom. For a comprehensive discussion of Tolkien's work's Christian message see Birzer, *J.R.R. Tolkien's Sanctifying Myth*.

considered originally pre-Christian.⁵² This synthesis mirrors his conviction that Paganism needs to be sanctified by Christianity, but also that the Christianity of the present is in need of the values which, in Tolkien's eyes, characterize Nordic Paganism, in particular courage, strength, and will.⁵³ A quote from Tolkien's essay on *Beowulf* shows that he assigned this heroic, courageous attitude characteristic of the "Northern mythological imagination" a continued strength and vitality in the present:

> So potent is it [the Northern mythological imagination], that while the older southern imagination has faded forever into literary ornament, the northern has power, as it were, to revive its spirit even in our times. It can work, even as it did work with the *goðlauss* Viking, without gods: martial heroism as its own end.⁵⁴

The quote is from 1936, and betrays a similar fascination with contemporary 'Germanic' revivals as C.G. Jung's "Wotan" essay, which assigns a very similar archetypal force to the Nordic gods. We could thus argue that the 'Nordic Christianity' which Birzer correctly identifies as Tolkien's program, and which originates in Anglo-Saxonism, shows certain parallels to ideas of German(ic) Christianity propagated in early 20th century Germany.⁵⁵

The antagonists are similar in both Tolkien and the Germanic religious revival in Germany: contemporary decadence, untrammeled materialism and industrialism, represented by the utterly destructive nature found in Tolkien's gloomy descriptions of the land of Mordor.⁵⁶ Positive and functional worlds in

---

52 One example is the imagery of the wanderer Gandalf as an Odin-figure. His name is taken from the Edda, as are the dwarves' names. The depiction of heroes resembles narrative patterns from the Icelandic sagas.
53 See Birzer, *J.R.R. Tolkien's Sanctifying Myth*, XXIII.
54 Quoted in Arvidsson, *Draksjukan*, 150. See Tolkien, *The Monster and the Critics and Other Essays*, 159f.
55 Cf. Arvidsson, *Draksjukan*, 159f. This is not an argument against Tolkien's fundamental and passionate opposition to National Socialism, which he thought had perverted the original Nordic values still very much alive in the English tradition. There is, however, a fundamental difference between the self-redemptive worldviews of Germanic Faith and German Christianity and Tolkien's ethics: for him, not the heroic deeds of an individual, but rather collaboration and compassion, are the character traits necessary to bring about redemption.
56 Again, we should note that in the case of Tolkien, and opposed to the often rabid anti-Semitism of the Germanic revival in Germany, Jews are not made the culprits. At the most, a trace of a Christian anti-Jewish topos could be identified in the depiction of the

The Lord of the Rings are characterized as being in tune with the natural world and nature itself, and plants and trees in particular are depicted as animated. This has motivated Patrick Curry, another defender of Tolkien, to describe the religious ideas at the base of *The Lord of the Rings* as a kind of nature religion modified by Christianity. He identifies animist and polytheistic elements in Tolkien's conception of myth, and emphasizes that conception's proximity to contemporary forms of nature-religiosity in Neopagan groups.[57] The enthusiastic reception of Tolkien in different green spiritual movements (to which Curry himself belongs)[58] confirms this analysis, and the proximity between Tolkien's Herderian worldview and bio-regionalism, "'green' or 'brown' decentralism, and small-scale conservatism"[59] cannot be dismissed.[60] Neither can Niels Werber's claim that the worldview in *The Lord of the Rings* mirrors German pre-war geopolitical ideology.[61] Rather, Tolkien appears to be a herald for a Nordic art-religion. In his essay "On Fairy Stories" (1947),[62] Tolkien assigns fairy tales the capacity to open "a door on Other Time," which resembles Mircea Eliade's "jargonizing speech about *in illo tempore*,"[63] talking about story-telling as a way for fallen man to return 'home,' to find a way to Eden.[64] Through his literary work, Tolkien fashioned himself as a poetic genius capable of creating myth and thus conveying a religious message.[65]

---

dwarves (who are portrayed as 'Jewish' in a mostly favorable way). The dwarves awaken the creature Balrog who is to kill Gandalf later. This passage evokes the mythic guilt of killing a savior figure.

57 Curry, *Defending Middle-Earth*, 28f, 108–111, 122f.
58 See for example his *Ecological Ethics. An Introduction* (Cambridge: Polity Press, 2006).
59 Arvidsson, *Draksjukan*, 164.
60 See ibid., 164. German Asatru bio-regionalist Thorsten Kramps referred to Tolkien as one important source of inspiration as well. See Chapter 6.
61 Niels Werber, "Geo- and Biopolitics of Middle-Earth. A German Reading of Tolkien's The Lord of the Rings," *New Literary History* 36, no. 2 (2005), 230, investigates the following dimensions of geopolitical discourse in *The Lord of the Rings*: "the construction of the other as an absolute foe in total warfare (section 2), the function in this construction of biopolitics (3), the belief that every nation takes part in a "clash" of ethnically shaped "greater regions" (4), that a politicized nature itself is mobilizing in a global and total war to end all wars (5), and that a secure international order could be expected only from a strict separation of nations (6)."
62 Re-published in J.R.R. Tolkien, *The Tolkien Reader*, 2. ed. (New York: Del Rey, 1986).
63 Arvidsson, *Draksjukan*, 173.
64 Ibid., 154.
65 Ibid., 172. At the same time, there is an ambivalence in Tolkien's conception of free artistic creation, a never-quite resolved uncertainty as to whether it is a breach of God's plan or its realization. See ibid., 175.

Religious and Ideological Art in the German Faith Movement

Long before Tolkien-mania set in during the first decade of the 2000s, converting Tolkienian worlds into popular games and religious practice, and any conceivable post modern hybrid of the two, leading figures of the German Faith Movement forged their own versions of the Nordic art-religious tradition. Quite a few of them were artists themselves. They considered art to be a religious medium and the artist to be a prophetic figure, quite literally assigning the poet a "sacred, almost priestly calling."[66] Furthermore, they conceptualized the "national, great, modern" drama as a religious means of counteracting the "bloody victories of Roman ecclesiasticism"[67] and a way to combine "art and devotion."[68] Before becoming the prophet of the Germanic occultist revival of Ariosophy, Guido von List (see Figure 9.1) had won some notoriety as the author of historical novels, short stories, dramas, and sacral plays teeming with equally sentimental and bloody imaginations of national rebirth through sacrifice and self-sacrifice.[69] Remaining an ardent supporter of Wagner, List continued to style himself as a genius and prophet in Wagnerian fashion. More relevant still was Ernst Wachler (1871–1945), one of the first promoters of a German Faith and a leading figure in Ludwig Fahrenkrog's *Germanische Glaubensgemeinschaft*. To the broader public he was known as an influential literary critic, author, promoter of theater reform, and initiator of the German open-air theatre movement.[70] In his 1897 pamphlet, *"Läuterung deutscher Dichtkunst im Volksgeiste"* ("Purification of German poetry in the spirit of the

---

66   Ernst Wachler, *Läuterung deutscher Dichtkunst im Volksgeiste. Eine Streitschrift* (Berlin-Charlottenburg: Richard Heinrich, 1897), 16: "heiligen, fast priesterlichen Beruf."
67   Ibid., 20: "nationale, große, moderne" – "blutigen Siege des römischen Kirchentums."
68   *Die Freilichtbühne. Betrachtungen über das Problem des Volkstheaters unter freiem Himmel* (Leipzig: Fritz Eckhardt, 1909), 11: "Kunst und Andacht."
69   The only academic author who has addressed List's literary work in detail is Inge Kunz, "Herrenmenschentum, Neugermanen und Okkultismus," 14–90, in her unpublished dissertation.
70   The following is developed more fully in Schnurbein, "Religiöse Ikonographie – religiöse Mission. Das völkische Weihespiel um 1910," as well as in "Gjenbruken av edda-diktningen i 'völkisch-religiöses Weihespiel' rundt århundreskiftet i Tyskland." For the broader background of Wachler's literary program and his theater projects see Puschner, "Deutsche Reformbühne und völkische Kultstätte," and Justus H. Ulbricht, "Die Geburt der Deutschen aus dem Geist der Tragödie. Weimar als Ort und Ausgangspunkt nationalpädagogischer Theaterprojekte," in *Wege nach Weimar. Auf der Suche nach der Einheit von Kunst und Politik*, ed. Hans Wilderotter and Michael Dorrmann (Berlin: Jovis, 1999).

FIGURE 9.1
Portrait photograph of Guido von List
(probably 1909/10)
PUBLISHED WITH PERMISSION FROM
THE GERMAN FEDERAL ARCHIVES
(BUNDESARCHIV). BARCH, BILD 183-
2007-0705-500/CONRAD H. SCHIFFER

Volk"),[71] he criticized the lack of a patriotic poetry for the new German Empire.[72] He rejected the "elitism" of the classicist tradition as well as the "decadence" of naturalism, while promoting a regional poetry based in folk customs and literature. The dramatic genre for him constituted the only living, public, literary genre which truly existed in and for the Volk,[73] as long as it succeeded in leaving behind the urban "theatre of luxury" and was made accessible to all classes in open-air theaters or in great halls. Another key condition was that it be based on traditional material such as myths and (fairy) tales, patriotic history, and folk custom[74] originating in a "homogeneous," "cohesive" culture.[75] The new theater

71 Wachler, *Läuterung deutscher Dichtkunst im Volksgeiste*.
72 Here, Wachler adopted the central position of the *völkisch* literary movement and its most prominent promoter Adolf Bartels (1862–1945). On Bartels cf. Thomas Rösner, "Adolf Bartels," in *Handbuch zur 'Völkischen Bewegung' 1871–1918*, ed. Uwe Puschner, Walter Schmitz, and Justus H. Ulbricht (Munich etc.: K.G. Saur, 1996).
73 Wachler, *Läuterung deutscher Dichtkunst im Volksgeiste*, 51.
74 Ibid., 42.
75 Ibid., 163: "einheitlichen" – "in sich geschlossenen." With this program, Wachler posits himself explicitly within the tradition of the 19th century German national political festival play (Festspiel). See, for example, Uwe-K. Ketelsen, "Das völkisch-heroische Drama," in *Handbuch des deutschen Dramas*, ed. Walter Hinck (Düsseldorf: Bagel, 1980); Bruno

was to serve as the "solemn shrine of the whole people,"[76] thus recreating the "religious, national, and popular fundament of the theatre"[77] modeled on Greek tragedy.[78]

In order to realize his lofty ambitions, Wachler founded the *Harzer Bergtheater* in 1903, a 25-by-20-meter open-air stage, with seating for 1200 people, on a forest clearing in the Harz mountains. This location was chosen with a specifically religious purpose in mind, as the Harz was considered a pre-Christian site of worship.[79] Not only was the stage to become an altar, but the location of the theater itself was also turned into a place of worship, in synchronicity with the powers of nature and landscape. The *Harzer Bergtheater* was used for the activities of German Faith organizations such as the *Deutschreligiöse Gemeinschaft* and *Germanische Glaubensgemeinschaft*. At their gatherings, myth-inspired plays by Wachler and the organizations' founder, Ludwig Fahrenkrog, were performed as well.[80] Thematically, the dramas often

---

Fischli, *Die Deutschen-Dämmerung. Zur Genealogie des völkisch-faschistischen Dramas und Theaters (1897–1933)* (Bonn: Bouvier, 1976); Georg Kreis, "Das Festspiel – ein antimodernes Produkt der Moderne," in *Das Festspiel. Formen, Funktionen, Perspektiven*, ed. Bernd Engler and Georg Kreis (Willisau: Theaterkultur-Verlag, 1988); Klaus Sauer and German Werth, *Lorbeer und Palme. Patriotismus in deutschen Festspielen* (Munich: dtv, 1971). Not surprisingly, Wachler praises Wagner as the "last great master" ("letzte große Meister" Wachler, *Die Freilichtbühne*, 16), with one important reservation: He explicitly rejects the late Wagner's Christian ideas as well as the primacy of song, which he considered a "bastard," while praising the "purity" of the spoken word. (*Läuterung deutscher Dichtkunst im Volksgeiste*, 110).

76 *Die Freilichtbühne*, 13: "festliche Heiligtum des ganzen Volkes."
77 Ibid., 20: "religiöse, nationale und volkstümliche Grundlage des Theaters."
78 With this, he placed his program in the German tradition of the quasi-religious celebration of Greek tragedy spanning from Romanticism to Nietzsche. Cf. Manfred Frank, "Vom 'Bühnenweihefestspiel' zum 'Thingspiel'. Zur Wirkungsgeschichte der 'Neuen Mythologie' bei Nietzsche, Wagner und Johst," in *Das Fest*, ed. Walter Haug and Rainer Warning (Munich: Wilhelm Fink Verlag, 1989), 611.
79 In another programmatic appeal, Wachler recommended to look for "old national sites of worship" for the new stages. Ernst Wachler, *Sommerspiele auf vaterländischer Grundlage* (Berlin: Vaterländischer Schriftenverband, 1910), 17.
80 Fahrenkrog's plays, *Baldur* and *Wölund*, served this purpose. Fahrenkrog, *Baldur; Wölund*. Cf. Puschner, "Deutsche Reformbühne und völkische Kultstätte," 780. See also the recent discussion of the uses of Eddic material in *völkisch* theater by Sven Neufert, "'Aus dunklen Tiefen empor zu lichten Höhen.' Die Edda-Rezeption in der völkischen Theater- und Festkultur," in *Eddische Götter und Helden. Milieus und Medien ihrer Rezeption. Eddic Gods and Heroes. The Milieux and Media of Their Reception*, ed. Katja Schulz (Heidelberg: Winter, 2011).

revolved around the topic of a new age: a turning point in history announcing a decline, to be followed by a new awakening of the national spirit (mirrored in the cycles of nature). They propagated a new religion of knowledge and deed, where the god-like hero poses as an artist and *Übermensch* in the spirit of Nietzsche(-anism).[81]

The performances of these religious dramas served a dual purpose and were directed at two audiences simultaneously. On the one hand, they ministered to what could be called a missionary goal, namely to entertain a broader public and win it over to the religious and ideological messages of German Faith. On the other hand, they were directed at members and sympathizers of German Faith groups, who were able to decode their messages and experience them as an immediate expression of their own religious convictions and thus as a religious ritual.

The same is true for the *Gesinnungskunst* (art of conviction and persuasion) of visual artists associated with the German Faith Movement of the era. Their work was aimed directly at religious experience, conveying *völkisch* religious messages and thus contributing to the creation of 'congregations' of like-minded followers.[82] Ludwig Fahrenkrog, the Wagnerian and *Bayreuther Kreis* member Franz Stassen (1869–1949), Hermann Hendrich (1854–1931), and Hugo Höppener (alias Fidus, 1868–1948) produced paintings and easily reproducible graphic art. Their visual work was inspired by *Jugendstil*, and typically combined Wagnerian and Nietzschean themes with nature-religious impulses, merging them with symbols of national or racial purity, such as runes, swords, hammers, and the

---

81   This is most prominent in Fahrenkrog's figures of *Baldur* and *Wölund*, who unite features of the then-popular super-humans and *Tatmenschen* (Men of Deed) Lucifer and Prometheus. Friedrich Nietzsche used the figure of Prometheus, who steals the fire from the gods to give it to man, as a heroic (masculine) contrast figure to the "oriental" Eve of Genesis which is configured as a shameful (and feminine-coded) "fall from grace." See Lincoln, *Theorizing Myth*, 65 and Williamson, *The Longing for Myth in Germany*, 241. A comprehensive discussion of the reception of the figure of Lucifer around 1900 can be found in Ernst Osterkamp, *Lucifer. Stationen eines Motivs* (Berlin/ New York: de Gruyter, 1979). In contemporary theories of religion, both figures are associated with an alleged Germanic fire and sun cult, an idea put forward by Adalbert Kuhn on whose theories Nietzsche built his argument. Cf. Williamson, *The Longing for Myth in Germany*, 14f.

82   Marina Schuster, "Bildende Künstler als Religionsstifter. Das Beispiel der Maler Ludwig Fahrenkrog und Hugo Höppener genannt Fidus," in *Kunst und Religion. Studien zur Kultursoziologie und Kulturgeschichte*, ed. Richard Faber and Volkhard Krech (Würzburg: Königshausen & Neumann, 1999), 276f.

swastika. By far the most popular among the works of these graphic artists is Fidus' piece, *Lichtgebet* (Light Prayer, see Figure 9.2). It consists of the rear view of a muscular, young, androgynous, naked man on a rock in the mountains, reaching his arms and face toward the rising sun in a simultaneously contained and ecstatic gesture.[83] It was not only the content of their work that turned these *völkisch* artists into true popularizers of Nordic art-religion, but also the distribution of their work through mass media. Fidus' and others' works were used as illustrations, vignettes, and ornaments in *völkisch* religious publications, such as the later editions of Wilhelm Schwaner's *Germanenbibel*, and Fidus himself traveled with slide presentations to promote his temple designs.[84]

Along with Fidus, Fahrenkrog and Hendrich also attempted to expand their religious artwork into architecture, and harbored plans for Germanic Faith temples. As Fahrenkrog's and Fidus' plans never materialized due to the lack of sufficient funds and supporters, the theater in Thale remained the only site where the German Faith art-religion found an actual location. This was also due to the work of Hermann Hendrich, co-founder of the *Werdandi-Bund*, an ardent Wagnerian and, as a member of the *Deutschgläubige Gemeinschaft*, supporter of a renewal of Germanic religion.[85] In 1901, Hendrich realized his first architectural project in Thale. The *Walpurgishalle*, a blockhouse with 'old Germanic' elements inspired by stave churches and Viking architecture, was built by Bernhard Sehring according to Hendrich's design. (See Figure 9.3) In the hall, five monumental paintings of motifs from Goethe's *Faust* are exhibited. They merge Nordic imagery with allegedly Pagan witchcraft rituals,[86] as well as the German classical tradition and the cult of the national genius, which Goethe had come to personify during the course of 19th-century German nationalism. Its location in nature, close to alleged ancient Pagan sites of

---

83   Höppener drew and painted the Light Prayer in several versions, and it was widely distributed through postcards and affordable prints, serving as an icon for the youth movement in particular, whose cult of youth, health, and nature it seemed to summarize in a compelling way. Cf. "Fidus – ein Gesinnungskünstler der völkischen Kulturbewegung," in *Handbuch zur 'Völkischen Bewegung' 1871–1918*, ed. Uwe Puschner, Walter Schmitz, and Justus H. Ulbricht (Munich etc.: K.G. Saur, 1996), 640; Y, *Fidus, der Tempelkünstler*.

84   Cf. Janos Frecot, Johann Friedrich Geist, and Diethart Kerbs, *Fidus 1868–1948. Zur ästhetischen Praxis bürgerlicher Fluchtbewegungen* (Munich: Rogner & Bernhard, 1972).

85   Puschner, *Die Völkische Bewegung im wilhelminischen Deutschland*, 228f.

86   In the folklore of the region, the Harz and the Brocken mountains were believed to be the location of the witches' Sabbath, celebrated on the night to May 1. Goethe used this idea in *Faust*.

FIGURE 9.2 *Fidus,* Lichtgebet (*1894/1924*)
© VG BILD-KUNST, BONN 2014

FIGURE 9.3 *Painting by Hermann Hendrich, "Walpurgishalle," Hexentanzplatz, printed on postcard by Meisenbach, Riffarth & Co., Berlin*
PUBLISHED WITH PERMISSION FROM GEORG JÄGER, WWW.GOETHEZEITPORTAL.DE.

worship, is characteristic of this new art-religion, being both regional and close to nature. It was thus mere coincidence that Wachler would then seize the opportunity to establish his *völkisch* religious theater project at this overdetermined location a few years later.[87]

---

87 Hendrich continued to realize similar projects celebrating a unity between a regional and mythic folk art in a second hall dedicated to German folk legends, the *Sagenhalle* in the

Emphatic nationalist art-religious attitudes, which promoted the idea that the core of the German nation is to be found in its art, and which culminates in the idea that the *Volk* itself is the artwork and its leader the artist, permeate both the avant-garde and expressionism, *völkisch* (religious) and Conservative Revolutionary thought.[88] Differences are found in the intellectual level and the grade of abstraction: *völkisch* art criticism and theory tend to turn to concrete symbols and images of the Germanic, and are characterized by a "tendency towards the trivial."[89] This, however, does not necessarily mean that Conservative Revolutionary thinkers did not employ Nordic images, as the case of Ernst Jünger (1895–1998) shows. His images of the male hero, the figure of the warrior, and also that of the *Waldgänger* (forest walker) are taken directly from an intertextual engagement with Icelandic saga literature. His self-stylization as an author-prophet-seer, who alone is able to access myth and essential form, must be read within this context as well.[90]

Heirs of Wagner and Tolkien: Asatru Novelists

Modern Asatru recalls Romantic as well as *völkisch* art-religious traditions on a number of different levels. Asatruers tend to experience art as religion or religious inspiration, or they appeal emphatically to the spiritual quality of art itself and to the artist as a prophet, in stark contrast to adherents of Christianity, which is seen as a religion of legal codification rather than living inspiration, as is evidenced by this quote by Fritz Steinbock, of the German *VfgH*:

> In Paganism, poetry is a sacred art, the profession of the poet a religious task. Deities inspire the poets. In the Germanic tradition, it is none other than Allfather Wodan/Odin himself. Poetry thus stands in an immediate relation to prophecy. [...]

Riesengebirge in 1903. In 1913, on Richard Wagner's 100th birthday, his *Nibelungenhalle* was opened in Königswinter at the Rhine river, where he exhibited paintings inspired by the Nibelungen cycle.

88 This theses is put forward by Hein, *Die Brücke ins Geisterreich* and "Völkische Kunstkritik," in *Handbuch zur 'Völkischen Bewegung' 1871–1918*, ed. Uwe Puschner, Walter Schmitz, and Justus H. Ulbricht (Munich etc.: K.G. Saur, 1996).
89 "Völkische Kunstkritik," 616.
90 This has been been shown by Niels Penke, *Ernst Jünger und der Norden – Eine Inszenierungsgeschichte*, Frankfurter Beiträge zur Germanistik (Heidelberg: Universitätsverlag Winter, 2012).

Pagan poems have the character of mythic prophecies [...], of revelations – albeit not in the sense of immutable dogmas which are equally binding for everybody – these we search for in vain in Pagan poetry – but in the sense of a free and personal vision of divine reality, which in Paganism never declares itself in an authoritarian way nor requires blind faith. The gods do not proclaim who they are, but they *show* themselves and want to be experienced personally. [...] Heathen tradition is based on this understanding of poetry as a sacred art, given by the gods, in which the gods speak themselves. Poetry is not fiction but truth – a truth that goes beyond mere actuality and lies in the nature of things themselves. It is the truth of the gods which speaks in poetry, because it is the language of the gods. The poet is the one who knows how to hear it and mediate it.[91]

Theodist Garman Lord goes a step further. He makes a strong ethnicist argument, claiming that it is the poet's task to see and point to the significance of the "organic processes" that form Germanic society and religion.[92] According to him, true poetry is made possible by the characteristics of the Indo-European language, the roots of which he imagines to lie in the Ice Age.[93]

---

91   Fritz Steinbock, "Die heilige Kunst – Dichtung und Wahrheit," VfgH e.V., http://www.vfgh .de/, last accessed November 04, 2011: "Die Dichtung ist im Heidentum eine heilige Kunst, der Beruf des Dichters eine religiöse Aufgabe. Gottheiten inspirieren die Dichter. In der germanischen Tradition ist es kein geringerer als Allvater Wodan/Odin selbst. Die Dichtkunst wird damit in unmittelbaren Zusammenhang mit dem Sehertum gestellt [...]. Heidnische Dichtungen [...] haben den Charakter von seherischen Kündungen, von Offenbarungen – allerdings nicht im Sinn unveränderlicher, für alle gleich verbindlicher Lehrsätze, die man in der heidnischen Dichtung vergeblich sucht, sondern im Sinn einer freien und persönlichen Schau der göttlichen Wirklichkeit, die sich im Heidentum niemals autoritär deklariert und blinden Glauben fordert. Die Götter verkünden nicht, wer sie sind, sondern *zeigen* sich und wollen persönlich erfahren werden. [...].
     Auf diesem Verständnis der Dichtung als heilige, von den Göttern gegebene Kunst, in der letztlich die Götter selbst sprechen, beruht die heidnische Überlieferung. Dichtung ist nicht Fiktion, sondern Wahrheit – eine über die bloße Tatsächlichkeit hinausgehende Wahrheit, die im Wesen der Dinge selbst liegt. Es ist die Wahrheit der Götter, die in der Dichtung spricht, denn sie ist die Sprache der Götter. Der Dichter ist derjenige, der sie zu hören und weiterzugeben versteht."
92   Lord, *The Way of the Heathen*, 66.
93   Many Scandinavian Asatruers share the Romantic art-religious view of poetry as an important means of gaining access to the content and spirit of their religion. A long-term member of Danish *Forn Siðr* appreciates the fact that Asatru, from its beginnings, i.e. already in the medieval sources, is mediated in poetic form. Cf. for example Interview

GERMANIC NEOPAGANISM

Völkisch religious artists such as Fahrenkrog, Fidus, Stassen, and Hendrich are promoted in the parts of Heathenism that align themselves with Conservative Revolutionary ideas and the New Right, the circles around the journal *Tyr* in particular. Here, illustrations by Fidus, Fahrenkrog, and other *völkisch* artists, such as Hans Thoma (1839–1924) and Franz von Stuck (1863–1928), are employed.[94] *Tyr* published a comprehensive article about Ludwig Fahrenkrog by Markus Wolff,[95] as well as reviews of a Hendrich biography[96] and a CD honoring Hermann Hendrich.[97] The *Heidnisches Jahrbuch* also contains a long article on Hendrich's work.[98] The author, Thomas Lückewerth, is active in occultist circles[99] and in an association called *Nibelungenhort*, whose purpose is to promote Hendrich's work today.[100] The only recent monography available on Ludwig Fahrenkrog's life and work was written by Claus Wolfschlag[101] and was released by the publishing house *Zeitenwende* (Turn of

---

I. Eggert Solberg Jonsson, "Ásatrú á Íslandi við upphaf 21. aldar," 117f, in his Master's thesis on the Icelandic Heathen revival, claims that Romantic literature, plays, and art have great importance for current imaginations of the life and religion of the Heathen era.

94 Cf. *Tyr* I, 15, 26; *Tyr* II, 134; *Tyr* III, 122.
95 Wolff, "Ludwig Fahrenkrog and the Germanic Faith Community."
96 "Review of 'Hermann Hendrich: Leben und Werk' by Elke Rohling."
97 *Tyr* I, 271f.
98 Lückewerth, "Hermann Hendrich – Mythenmaler und Tempelkünstler."
99 He appears as an author in *Shekinah*, a journal for "shamanism, occultism, parapsychology and magic" edited by Holger Kliemannel (see also Chapter 6).
100 Cf. http://www.nibelungen-hort.de, last accessed September 02, 2014. Lückewerth, who prepares a monograph on Hendrich as well, praises Hendrich unequivocally as an artist-leader, calling him a "tool" which "myth itself" has chosen and "through which it seeks incarnation" – a "willing tool of European transcendence," who "erected a temple for the *Volk* for its own old myths" and "leads us back to our own source." Lückewerth, "Hermann Hendrich – Mythenmaler und Tempelkünstler," 195: "errichtet er dem Volk einen Tempel für seine ureigenen Mythen;" and 229: "führt uns zurück zu unserer eigenen Quelle." Ibid., 229: "Der Mythos selbst hat Hendrich zum Werkzeug auserkoren und sucht durch ihn die Fleischwerdung. Die tiefe Sehnsucht nach dem Nordischen, den Sagas, den Märchen und Mythen, läßt Hendrich zum allzu willigen Werkzeug der europäischen Transzendenz werden." He follows the romanticizing idea that the *Walpurgishalle* is located at a Heathen site of worship and that *Faust* is a "Germanic" myth, and he praises the *Werdandi-Bund* as a promoter of "the healthy and life-affirming elements in art" as a "counterweight to the decadent and modern art-scene." Ibid., 196: "das Gesunde und Lebensbejahende in der Kunst zu stärken und ein Gegengewicht zur dekadenten und modernen Kunstszene zu liefern."
101 Claus Wolfschlag, *Ludwig Fahrenkrog. Das goldene Tor. Ein deutscher Maler zwischen Jugendstil und Germanenglaube* (Dresden: Verlag Zeitenwende, 2006).

the Ages) in Dresden, which at least initially promoted New Right ideas and continues to collaborate closely with *Arun Verlag*.[102]

While the reception of *völkisch* art remains confined to a small circle within Heathenism, Richard Wagner and J.R.R. Tolkien constitute important sources for Asatruers in all countries.[103] Although many Heathens today consider Wagner's "version of the religion [...] slightly warped," he is seen as a "deeply inspired man,"[104] whose musical technique of *leitmotifs* are experienced by one author from the American *The Troth* as a "deeply spiritual element" reminiscent for him of the web of the *wyrd*.[105] Tolkien's work is enthusiastically received by many Heathens. Pagan authors[106] refer to him as part of exactly this neo-Romantic mythic tradition, and thus as an important contributor to the revival of Germanic faith. In this context, he is appreciated for his stance against the National Socialist appropriation of Germanic myth.[107] This enthusiasm is part of the more general post-war atmosphere in which the constellation of a Romantic art-religious mythical revival and (national) history continued to thrive in popular literary genres, namely historical and fantasy novels. Popular books and films claiming to bring to life ancient rites and customs in the guise of either wholly imagined or fictional historical worlds are among the most regularly mentioned sources of inspiration for contemporary Asatruers. By now, the market for

---

102   Wolfschlag himself is involved with the German New Right, writing in the right-wing journal *Junge Freiheit*, and has published a book on anti-Hitler Conservative Revolutionaries with *Arun Verlag*, which contains a section about Fidus. Cf. Thomas Grumke and Bernd Wagner, *Handbuch Rechtsradikalismus* (Cologne: Leske & Budrich, 2002), 458. According to the owner, Zeitenwende has published exclusively esoteric books since 2003, among which Wolfschlag's publication on Fahrenkrog is obviously counted. Cf http://www.netz-gegen-nazis.de/artikel/verlag-zeitenwende, last accessed September 02, 2104. Other publications include a book on Rune Qui Gong (http://www.verlag-zeitenwende.de/epages/64479676.sf/de_DE/?ObjectPath=/Shops/64479676/Products/63-8) and Julius Evola's *Revolt against the modern world*. (http://www.amazon.de/Cavalcare-tigre-Den-Tiger-reiten/dp/3934291228/ref=sr_1_2?s=books&ie=UTF8&qid=1409663285&sr=1-2&keywords=Julius+Evola. Both links last accessed September 02, 2014.)

103   Scandinavian Heathens, however, tend to rely more on their own countries' Romantic traditions and numerous re-tellings of Norse mythology.

104   Gundarsson, *Our Troth*, vol. I, 97.

105   Ben Waggoner, "Wagners Ring. Übersetzung aus dem Englischen und Literaturanhang von Kurt Oertel," *Herdfeuer. Die Zeitschrift des Eldaring e.V.* 2, no. 4 (2004).

106   A member of German *Nornirs Ætt* claims to have been inspired by Tolkien in his religious search. Cf. Interview with six members of Nornirs Ætt.

107   Gundarsson, *Our Troth*, vol. I, 107.

fantasy and historical literature with 'Germanic' or 'Nordic' themes has expanded to an extent that makes it almost impossible to keep an overview of the relevant works and authors. The same applies to the film industry. I shall therefore limit myself to a more detailed discussion of a few texts and authors that have had close interactions with the contemporary Asatru scene. These include books which are produced by Asatruers and have reached a certain level of public recognition, books which have been produced in collaboration with Asatruers, and books which are widely read in Asatru circles, and thus significantly shape Asatruers' perception of their religion. Four novelistic sub-genres stand out here: historical fantasy, alternate history, historical novels about national icons, and urban fantasy.

Ever since Marion Zimmer Bradley's immensely successful best-selling novel *The Mists of Avalon*[108] appeared in 1983, these genres have served not only as escapist entertainment. They have also been received as models for religious orientation in present day life beyond or alongside Christianity. They are formulaic genres, whose easily accessible narrative structure seems apt for providing spiritual orientation. Historical fantasy in particular is a genre that lends itself to the purpose of envisioning what pre-Christian belief and practices might have looked like, and gives ample room for identification with the protagonists, whose psychological characteristics are portrayed in detail. They thus invite the modern reader to relate to their spiritual struggles and adversities. This explains the genre's popularity not only among Heathen readers, but also Asatru authors. Two of the most publicly visible a-racist North American Asatruers, Diana Paxson and Stephan Grundy/Kveldulf Gundarsson, make their living as authors of fantasy novels and have authored trilogies about the Nibelungen material. They make explicit references to the Romantic art-religious tradition by listing Wagner, Grimm, and Tolkien among their sources.[109] They portray themselves as the heralds of Nordic art-religion, imbuing their own work with a religious message – a self-stylization mirrored in the role the poet or story is assigned in the novels themselves.

Paxson relates her fictional writing directly to her religious development when she says that she found her way into Paganism at the same time as she

---

108 Bradley, *The Mists of Avalon*.
109 Diana L. Paxson, *The Wolf and the Raven* (*Wodan's Children*, Book 1) (New York: William Morrow, 1993), 313f, lists Jacob Grimm as one of her main sources, and uses a quote from Richard Wagner's *Siegfried* libretto as a motto for the third volume of *Wodan's Children*, cf. *The Lord of the Horses* (*Wodan's Children*, Book 3) (New York: William Morrow, 1996), XIV. Grundy, *Rhinegold*, v, dedicates his book to Wagner and Tolkien.

began writing.[110] Her trilogy, *Wodan's Children*, in which she re-counts the Nibelungen material mostly from the perspective of women, focusing particularly on their role in religion and magic,[111] is her greatest success in Germany and in Asatru circles in both North America and Europe. The novel's setting provides the opportunity to depict two aspects of an imagined Pagan spiritual world – a fertility religion centered on the sacred marriage between sacred king and land (in the figure of the queen), and a shamanic magic religion. Bearers of the latter are Sigfrid, with his 'wolf magic,' and Brunahild, who is a member of the 'valkyries,' a Pagan order of 'wise women.' In the novels, Wodan is a god continually in search of wisdom, which he gains through accessing human experience. In this way, ritual and magic, as well as poetry, are depicted as means of gaining insight into the hidden connections of fate, which are not merely historical, but eternal. The novel ends with a prophecy about the return of the gods:

> Wodan still walks the world, though men no longer recognize him, learning, experiencing, testing the new ways of thinking to which they turned when they abandoned their old gods. He is very curious, that one, and will follow the path to its end. When that time comes, perhaps he will seek a new way of knowing, and take up his conversation with Erda once more. [...] The ravens still fly, and to whom do they report, if not to the god? In every word that you speak and thought that you

---

110 Cf. V. Vale and John Sulak, *Modern Pagans. An Investigation of Contemporary Pagan Practices* (San Francisco, CA: Re/Search Publications, 2001), 23f. This happened in the circle around Marion Zimmer Bradley, her brother Paul Edwin Zimmer, and their adopted brother, whom Paxson married and with whom Paxson experimented around magical and Pagan rituals in the 1970s. At the time of writing, Bradley herself experimented with occultism and esoteric magic, and co-founded a Wiccan group centered on the Goddess, the *Dark Moon Circle*. Cf. ibid., 22. Paxson participated in Bradley's bestselling success *The Mists of Avalon* for which she provided information about Pagan women's rituals (cf. Bradley, *The Mists of Avalon*, Acknowledgements), and the sequels of which she co-authored and later authored individually. By now, the Avalon series contains the following titles: *The Fall of Atlantis* (1987), *The Forest House* (1993, with Diana L. Paxson), *Lady of Avalon* (1997, with Diana L. Paxson), *Priestess of Avalon* (2000, with Diana L. Paxson), *Ancestors of Avalon* (2004, written by Diana L. Paxson), *Ravens of Avalon* (2007, written by Diana L. Paxson), *Sword of Avalon* (2009, written by Diana L. Paxson).
111 Paxson, *The Wolf and the Raven* (*Wodan's Children, Book 1*); *The Dragons of the Rhine* (*Wodan's Children, Book 2*) (New York: William Morrow, 1995); *The Lord of the Horses* (*Wodan's Children, Book 3*).

think, in the ecstasy of every new idea he is there, whether or not you know his name...[112]

The direct address to the reader makes it clear that this prophetic ending is written with the purpose of convincing readers that this story and its religious message are relevant for the present as well. Considering the fact that the rituals depicted in the novel are based on the author's own experience,[113] it becomes clear that Paxson directs her writing at a two audiences simultaneously, in a manner similar to that of Ernst Wachler's sacral plays: a general audience that might be won over to Paganism , and an 'initiated' audience that will recognize their own beliefs and practices in the text, or perhaps draw inspiration for the design of their own religious practices from it.

A similar combination of references to a Romantic tradition of myth revival and art-religion based in personal religious experience can be found in the work of Stephan Grundy. Stephan Grundy's *Rhinegold* was first published in a German translation in 1992,[114] became an immediate bestseller in Germany, and was equally popular in German Heathen circles.[115] Grundy uses his own religious experience (which in turn is influenced by the academic knowledge gained through his simultaneous studies in German and English philology) in his descriptions of the ritual, magical, and religious plot of the novel. In accordance with Grundy's interest in runes and magic, Wodan appears as the god of the runes, which are understood as an expression of cosmic forces weaving together earth, gods, humans, and fate – a view which recalls the rune magical theories of Edred Thorsson. Thorsson advised Grundy to use the Nibelungen material for a novel and, according to Grundy, served as "a mentor of mine and a crucial influence on my writing and my interest in approaching Norse magic and religion from an academic viewpoint."[116]

---

112   *The Lord of the Horses* (*Wodan's Children, Book 3*), 366f.
113   Cf. Correspondence with Stephan Grundy (*The Troth*), who writes: "A number of the rituals that she describes were taken directly from rituals practiced by her divinatory group Hrafnar."
114   Several English and American publishers had turned down the manuscript. The German translation by the same translators who had worked on *The Mists of Avalon*, Manfred Ohl and Hans Sartorius, was published by Wolfgang Krüger Verlag, an established publisher of popular literature.
115   See for example *Rabenclan's* journal *Heidenarbeit*, 2 (1995), 37 as well as Correspondence with Kurt Oertel (Eldaring).
116   Correspondence with Stephan Grundy, 2014.

The human part of the magic runic web upon which *Rhinegold's* world is based is cast in metaphors of blood and earth. It is Wodan's blood which courses through the Wälsungen's veins. It serves as the store for ancient genealogical and magical knowledge, and roots its members in the holy earth.[117] The prophetic vision Grundy provides at the end of his novel is based on blood and genealogy as well. After Gudrun has sunk the last parts of the dragon's treasure in the Rhine, she hears Wodan's voice ringing "through her skull":

> 'Though the new ways may seem to bode the death of our kin, I have wrought so that our foes' work shall not last for ever, nor our voices be for ever stilled. Do not weep, but watch and learn.' [...] She could feel the rushing of her blood in the riverways of her body, the might running unseen through her, flowing unbroken from him who had named himself Mannaz to father the first of humankind. The same might whispered in every breath she drew, as she know it always had, though she had never marked nor thought of it till now; and she knew that no Christian dewsprinkling nor Latin prayers could still Wodan's gift in her children, or the children who would come of her folk, though the god's own kin forsook his memory.[118]

Wodan then prophesizes that the stories just told will not be forgotten, and indeed "live through the long northern nights, even to the very doors of the White Christ's church."[119] Grundy's art-religious prophecy is thus directly connected with the cosmic web of ancestral blood and runic power.[120] The author implicitly ascribes such a prophetic function to himself, thus counting himself among those "who first in our time brought the gold forth from the dragon's mound and

---

117 For a more detailed discussion of these elements in *Rhinegold* see Schnurbein, "Kontinuität durch Dichtung."
118 Grundy, *Rhinegold*, 853.
119 Ibid., 854.
120 In spite of such associations to a blood and ancestry, and some examples of racial stereotyping in the novel, Grundy is certainly not a supporter of racial theories in Asatru. In the sequel to *Rhinegold*, 1996's *Attila's Treasure*, the blood metaphors and racial stereotypes have all but vanished from the descriptions of magical practices. They are replaced by reflections on different systems of gender and sexuality and by the focus on protagonist Hagan's shamanic experiences, with which the author quite obviously identifies, and which are situated in a realm between genders and human and non-human worlds, making space for Hagan's bisexual leanings as well.

the dark waters of the Rhine to awaken our memories of our northern forebears"[121] – Richard Wagner and J.R.R. Tolkien, to whom he dedicates his book.

Alternate history, otherwise known as historiographic metafiction, is a popular genre that allows for creative imaginations of a different historical outcome due to the changing of crucial historical details. Harry Harrison and John Holm's 1990's trilogy, *Hammer and Cross,* explores the consequences of such a fictitious historical development. Instead of the church, a coalition of English insurgents and Pagan Vikings have gained power over Northwestern Europe in the years between 865 AD and the reign of King Alfred (who is depicted as an honorable, tolerant Christian and remains an admirable figure in the book). The spread of the concept of the *fulltrúi,* or patron deity, in American Asatru (see Chapter 3), has been attributed to these novels.[122] Referring to church history, Old Icelandic sources, and the legend of the Holy Grail, the novels center on the protagonist Shef, a former slave who rises to become 'the one king' of Norse Heathen prophecies. Shef defeats the Christian army and the cruel, fascistoid Knights of the Lance, is crucified, rescued, and then survives in hiding and finally withdraws from political power.

Co-author John Holm is a pseudonym for Tom Shippey, the eminent Tolkien scholar and linguist. The worldview advanced in the novels can be attributed to a modernized Tolkien-inspired view of Nordic mentality and ethics. The novel's perspective on history is Anglo-Saxonist, and its message firmly anticlerical, rejecting organized religion altogether as both unnecessary and as an impediment to natural inventiveness, resourcefulness, and vigor. The novel ascribes the latter features mainly to the peoples of the North-West. They are initially embodied in the religion of "Asgard's Way," in which the protagonist finds his own destiny. Reminiscent of Tolkien, the ideal is a secularized merging of non-dogmatic Christian values, such as compassion, with the inspired, heroic, yet pragmatic Paganism, accompanied by a skepticism towards corruptive political power. The third volume of the trilogy is set in the Mediterranean, and shows the contributions of all existing religions to the Enlightenment, which starts about 800 years earlier than in factual history. Despite its claim about the positive forces in all religions, the volume is infused with common stereotypes, particularly those of an overly refined, decadent, and cruel Islam,

---

121 Grundy, *Rhinegold,* v.
122 Cf. Harry Harrison and John Holm, *The Hammer and the Cross* [Der Hammer des Nordens (2001)] (New York: Tor Books, 1993); *One King's Way* [Der Pfad des Königs (2001)] (New York: Tor Books, 1995); *King and Emperor* [König und Imperator (2001)] (New York: Tor Books, 1996). Many discussions on www.asatrulore.org (last accessed September 02, 2014) give this information.

which in the universe of the novel lacks any kind of creativity, and merely preserved the book-knowledge of antiquity the vigorous Northerners make productive use of.[123] Transcendent religions appear as incapable of innovation, and serve as a negative backdrop for the inventive brilliance, democratic-mindedness, and psychological maturity of Shef, under whose genial leadership all the world's progressive forces gather. Implicitly, it is Anglo-Saxon individualism that is assigned benevolent leadership over the rest of the world and its less independently thinking and acting inhabitants.

Not only alternate history sells in Asatru-circles[124] and among the general public. As we have seen, popular historical fantasies have an abundant market, be it in the shape of re-enactment, experiential archaeology, role-play, or computer games. This trend is accompanied by an ever-increasing number of historical novels and films,[125] among them those that re-tell national myths for contemporary audiences. An example which has been resonant in Heathen circles in England and Germany is Bernard Cornwell's book series on King Alfred,[126] the 'founder' of united Anglo-Saxon England. Its success among Heathens is related to Cornwell's choice of narrator and figure of identification. The fictional character Uhtred, King Alfred's most important and successful warrior and commander, is born Christian but raised by Danes in the Pagan faith, to which he remains true all his life. This allows the author to present a skeptical view of the Christian religion, whose theological convictions remain

---

123 As we have seen in Chapter 5, such stereotypes origin in Enlightenment thought itself.
124 A Swedish example is the crime novel *Odens öga* (Odin's eye) by Håkan Strömberg, *Odens øga* (Stockholm: Ordfront, 2002), which takes place in a contemporary Sweden in which Christianisation and reformation have not been completely successful. Thus, religious conflict involving marginalized and discriminated Heathen groups, which have militant factions as well, dominate the political scene. The book was fairly well received by Asatruers for its inspiring descriptions of ritual and the overall imagination of how a Pagan tradition might function in the contemporary world. Cf. for example discussions in *Samfundet Forn Sed's* internet forum http://forum.samfundetfornsed.se/, last accessed September 15, 2014.
125 Films that are frequently mentioned by Asatruers include *Conan the Barbarian* (1982) and *The Thirteenth Warrior* (1999). Taking inspiration from Norse sources and scholarship, such films blend Wagnerian aesthetics with historical, mythic, fantasy, and horror elements, and create fantastic worlds that distribute images of 'Germanic' barbarians and heroes more widely.
126 Bernard Cornwell, *The Last Kingdom* (London: Harper Collins, 2004); *The Pale Horseman* (London: Harper Collins, 2005); *The Lords of the North* (London: Harper Collins, 2006); *Sword Song* (London: Harper Collins, 2007); *The Burning Land* (London: Harper Collins, 2009); *Death of Kings* (London: Harper Collins, 2011).

as incomprehensible and foreign to Uhtred as they might be to the intended reader, the 'secularized' male youth of today. On the other hand, it portrays Uhtred's and the Danes' Paganism as a straightforward warrior religion, characterized by an ethics of valiant struggle and worldly pleasures, which remains grounded and avoids exaggerated heroism.

The books are quite obviously intended for an audience interested in the technicalities of medieval warfare and battle. They teem with detailed descriptions of weaponry and battle techniques. However, the underlying message of this re-imagination of the origin of the English nation seems to be that England has its roots not only in the activities and grand visions of a Christian king, as the chronicles and official historical records would have it. It is also based on a Pagan warrior spirit, which is rendered much more admirable and accessible to the reader than its Christian counterpart. Furthermore, the author ties Uhtred into his own line of ancestors and alludes to his own identification with this Paganism. He writes in the "Historical Note" to one of his books: "There was an Uhtred involved in those years, and he is my direct ancestor, but the tales I tell of him are pure invention. The family held Bebbanburg (now Bamburgh Castle in Northumberland) from the earliest years of the Anglo-Saxon invasion of Britain until the Norman Conquest."[127]

A German equivalent to this re-imagination of the origin of the English nation is Iris Kammerer's trilogy, which recounts the defeat of the Roman legions under Varus by Arminius[128] – the historical event that has been considered foundational for German nationalism since the Germanic renaissance in humanism. The protagonist is a fictional Roman centurion, who for a period after the battle lives as a captive of a Germanic tribe, eventually eloping with and marrying the chieftain's daughter. The author succeeds in simultaneously portraying the Germanic "barbarians" and their struggle against Roman imperialism sympathetically and with understanding, and characterizing the 'national hero' Arminius as a cruel, deceptive traitor to his own people. Consequently, the clashes and mixes of cultures in the frontier area are depicted as formative for the later development of the region. Combined with the outspoken skepticism towards militarism and male heroism (the protagonist is an accomplished officer and fighter, but he is also depicted as suffering from severe war trauma) the trilogy's message is a far cry from the German national heroic myth of Hermann. The novels' success among German Asatruers is

---

127   *Death of Kings*, 333.
128   Iris Kammerer, *Der Tribun* (Munich: Heyne, 2004); *Die Schwerter des Tiberius* (Munich: Heyne, 2004); *Wolf und Adler* (Munich: Heyne, 2007). The books thus appeared in good time before the 2000-year anniversary of the battle in the Teutoburg forest in 2009.

related to the fact that their author sought help from *Eldaring* members for the depiction of ritual and customs, and according to Kurt Oertel, contributed significantly to a more differentiated view of Arminius within Asatru.[129]

In Scandinavia, nearly each generation of authors and readers has had their favorite re-telling of Scandinavian mythology in the spirit of their respective era, some of which – in contrast to the aforementioned popular novels in the US and Germany – found their way into the canon of high literature. In Norway, Vera Henriksen's historical novels[130] remain popular reading and have inspired Asatruers, as have Tor Åge Bringsværd's creative imaginations of the Norse deities' adventures and morals.[131] In Denmark, the children's books on *Erik Menneskesøn* by Lars-Henrik Olsen and the immensely popular *Valhalla* cartoons,[132] both of which continue to form younger Asatruers' worldviews, work with a similar concept: the insertion of human children into the mythological plots, like the looming decline of the world in *Ragnarok*.[133] These Danish texts can be considered as belonging to another genre that has been important for the popularization of Norse mythology and served as inspiration for Asatru, namely, fantasy novels set in contemporary, often urban, contexts, in which deities make their appearance. Similar to the *völkisch* sacral plays at the beginning of the 20th century, and to the historical novels that are often located in the era of the religious shift of Christianization, they make use of the idea of a shift in eras, the potential for the beginning of a new age in our times. Diana Paxson's second novel, *Brisingamen*,[134] is an example of such an urban fantasy. It features a vision quest in which listening to a Wagnerian opera plays a key role. It ends in a wild, magical battle between humans who embody the Norse gods and their adversaries. Not only does this novel portray the lives of

---

129 Kammerer thanks Oertel, with whom she collaborated closely, working out the details of Germanic religious practice for the first volume for an "intensive academic exchange." *Der Tribun*, 576. She also consulted with *Eldaring* co-founder Alex Jahnke regarding military knowledge for her novel *Varus*, which appeared in 2009. Correspondence with Kurt Oertel (Eldaring).

130 Vera Henriksen, "Historiske romaner," (Oslo: Aschehoug, 1980).

131 Tor Åge Bringsværd, "Vår gamle gudelære," ed. Dagny Hald and Thorstein Rittun (Oslo: Gyldendal, 1985–1992).

132 Peter Madsen, *Valhalla*, 15 vols. (Copenhagen: Carlsen Comics, 1979–2009). The German translations are popular with German Asatruers as well.

133 One of the authors of *Valhalla*, Henning Kure, is connected with Danish Asatru and has authored a number of articles in *Forn Siðr*'s journal *Vølse*. Cf. International Asatru-Summer camp 2009, "We Proudly Present: The Programme!," IASC Herald, http://www.asatru-summercamp.eu/docs/IASC_Herald-June-09.pdf, last accessed January 02, 2012, 2.

134 Diana L. Paxson, *Brisingamen* (New York: Berkley, 1984).

some of the early members of the AFA, which was then active in Northern California,[135] Paxson also casts her alter ego, Karen, as the bearer of a reawakened magical tradition harking back to the Viking age. A more widely known and complex example is American author Neil Gaiman's humorous novel, *American Gods*,[136] published in 2001, in which the gods are alive as long as people believe in them. The novel imagines gods as traveling and migrating with their believers. Many different kinds of deities now reside in America leading marginalized lives, on the brink of disappearance. Wednesday – or Odin – is the leader of the coalition of old gods struggling for their survival and return.[137] The idea that gods exist only as long as there are believers gives literature about them a religious function: Writing about gods implicitly becomes an act of keeping them alive.

The award-winning Norwegian novel, Cornelius Jakhelln's *"Gudenes fall"* ("The Fall of the Gods")[138] takes up almost all of the themes, motives, and philosophies discussed in this chapter in a complex and often humorous way, giving them a postmodern twist. The novel is well liked by Norwegian Asatruers,[139] although its innovative form makes it much less accessible than the traditional and often formulaic fiction mentioned earlier. *Gudenes fall* plays with contemporary Norwegian slang (in which the sections by Odin are written), different Norwegian dialects, as well as contemporary Danish (Loki's language), which are all rendered in phonetic transcription. The plot is convoluted. Since the Christianization of Iceland in the year 1000, the Norse gods have resided in a second Valhalla *Valhall* underground. Odin plans their return to the surface and the extinction of mankind for the coming millennium. This plan is compromised by two factors. The first is Odin's admiration for some men's (no women among them!) creative genius. The other factor is the expelled dwarf Regin's successful attempt to build a totalitarian system of 'bionts': Genetically modified and perfected chimeras who serve as loyal, cruel, uniform, fascistoid fighting machines, killing almost all humans and fighting the gods in the millennial battle. The third relevant group of players in the final battle are the gods' traditional enemies and trade partners,

---

135 Prudence Priest claims in an interview to have been "written up anonymously" together with Steven McNallen in this novel. Cf. SilverWitch, "Just 'Wiccatru' Folk."
136 Neil Gaiman, *American Gods* (New York: W. Morrow, 2001).
137 Cf. Fulvio Ferrari, "Gods of Dreams and Suburbia. Old Norse Deities in Neil Gaiman's Polymythical Universe," in *Eddische Götter und Helden. Milieus und Medien ihrer Rezeption. Eddic Gods and Heroes. The Milieux and Media of Their Reception*, ed. Katja Schulz (Heidelberg: Winter, 2011).
138 Cornelius Jakhelln, *Gudenes fall* (Oslo: Cappelen, 2007).
139 Cf. for example Interview O.

the giants, who are slightly ridiculous creatures known for their poor memory. They went underground a few centuries after the gods, and accompany them back up to the surface. Their leader erects one totalitarian, monotheistic religious system after the other, starting from Christianity, through "sintologi" (a parody of Scientology), and finally "maxism" (Stalinism), an atheism-turned-religion.

The political message of this wild dystopian fantasy is undermined by irony and ambiguities. Odin and his best friend, the dwarf Hornbore, share the cultural pessimist outlook of artists and thinkers like Wagner, Nietzsche, and Heidegger, as interpreted by the Conservative Revolution and the contemporary New Right. This becomes especially clear in their contempt for the uncontrolled breeding of the human masses and their simultaneous admiration for the genius of the few. The result is a political aestheticism, for which the German prophets of an art-religion stand. This depiction of a Nietzschean *Übermensch* is ironically disrupted by the fact that Odin appears as an unreliable narrator, a failing spouse and distant father; he is far from the perfect embodiment of ideal values, and rather human. However, the self-stylization of the narrator as a knowledgeable, divine philosopher and an unpredictable, divine jester mirrors the cultural pessimist outlook of other modernist and post-modernist writers. Some of these writers (Knut Hamsun, for example) operated in close political proximity to nationalist, anti-Semitic, Conservative Revolutionary or even National Socialist ideology.[140]

In this context, the novel's debt to art-religious discourse is important. It is mainly tied to music, to which Odin shows a particular attachment, and which ranges from Richard Wagner to Norwegian composer Geirr Tveitt, a supporter of the Norwegian radical National Socialist (but anti-Hitler) Pagan group around Hans S. Jacobsen.[141] Norwegian (black) metal plays an ambiguous role here as well. Like the book itself, this musical genre, and the subculture surrounding it, combines an apocalyptic aesthetic, a fascination with war and warrior ethics, a misanthropic and misogynistic attitude, and the rejection of modern capitalist society with an interest for an ancient mythic heritage and its revival. Jakhelln is also a musician, who mostly works within in the metal

---

140   For a discussion of Hamsun's reactionary modernism see for example Schnurbein, "Knut Hamsun's Narrative Fetishism."
141   Cf. Emberland, *Religion og rase*, 311–353; "Im Zeichen der Hagal-Rune," 519–522. Tveitt set to music old Norse materials and texts, as well as nature themes. The most consequent realization of such Norse Neopagan ideas can be found in his *Baldrs Draumr*, which Odin frequently listens to in the novel.

genre. He plays in the bands *Solefald* and *Sturmgeist*,[142] and characterizes his music, which combines Norse mythological motives with Goethe's poetry, as "grim Germanic thrash metal."[143] Having flirted with Satanism and Odinism as a teenager in the mid 1990s, Jakhelln turned to German and Norse material. Jakhelln traces his project of aesthetic violence back to two experiences of discrimination: His being bullied in school, and some events from the Parisian suburb where he lived while studying philosophy and where a confrontation with what he saw as 'anti-white racism' motivated him to embrace anti-Islamist and racist ideologies. The experience of being threatened because of being middle-class, bookish, and white – in other words, because of a position in society which is commonly perceived as entitling one to privilege – led to his wanting "to find out what suited my own heritage. Play black metal with a Germanic edge. So it became poems by Goethe; a fascination with German military history; singing in German."[144] His aesthetic is influenced by his search for a Northern, white, male identity rooted in myth, tradition, and heritage – a search that fails to question the assumption that German military history,

---

142   The names of the bands are taken from the context of a 'Germanic' art-religion as well. *Solefald* is the name of a painting by national-Romantic Norwegian artist Theodor Kittelsen, and *Sturmgeist* is inspired by Goethe's early ballads. Cf. Cornelius Jakhelln, *Raseri. En hvitings forsøk på en selvbiosofi* (Oslo: Cappelen Damm, 2011), 132.

143   Ibid., 227. The quote is taken from an article Jakhelln published in the Norwegian weekly, *Morgenbladet*, shortly after the bombing and killings in Oslo and the island of Utøya on July 22, 2011, and which is reprinted in his book *Raseri* (Rage) from the same year. It is a (self-)critical investigation into the ideology and emotions of the perpetrator Anders Behring Breivik, with whom the author discovers similarities. The difference, however, is, that Jakhelln feels he has found an outlet for his own rage in literature and music, a strategy he strongly recommends to counter the turn to manifest violence.

144   From an interview with Jakhelln in Håvard Rem, *Innfødte skrik. Norsk svartmetall* (Oslo: Schibsted, 2010), 243: "Jeg var rett og slett interessert i å finne ut hva som passet til min egen arv. Spille black metal med germansk *edge*. Da ble det for eksempel dikt av Goethe, en fascinasjon for tysk militærhistorie, å synge på tysk." This type of personal experience, which individuals who are in a privileged situation in a system, but do not have the personal experience of being so are subject to, is structurally typical for the many crises of modernity, including the "crisis of masculinity" which Jakhelln performs in his work. Here, the crisis and its conquering through art or intellectual activity can be interpreted as a reinstitution of the allegedly threatened position. This logic is explored with regard to Scandinavian and German literature in Stefanie v. Schnurbein, *Krisen der Männlichkeit. Schreiben und Geschlechterdiskurs in skandinavischen Romanen seit 1890* (Göttingen: Wallstein, 2001), and with regard to English literature and a colonial logic in Yekani Elahe Haschemi, *The Privilege of Crisis. Narratives of Masculinities in Colonial and Postcolonial Literature, Photography and Film* (Frankfurt/New York: Campus, 2011).

Goethe's writing, and Norse myth belong to the same "heritage." With his turn from Satanism to Odinism, and later to a more philosophical and literary based interest in Germanic and Norse heritage, Jakhelln is a typical representative of the contemporary music scene of metal and neofolk, in which European, mainly 'Germanic' or 'Nordic' Pagan, themes play a prominent role.[145]

Jakhelln has acknowledged such political implications in his book, "*Raseri*" (Rage, 2011), an idiosyncratic collage of older essays and articles and more recent multi-faceted reflections on them. Here, he promotes a philosophical Heathenism that combines a Spinozean pantheistic reading of the Norse gods with neo-Darwinist theories of genetics, breeding, survival of the fittest, and the transfer of cultural 'memes,' taken from Richard Dawkins.[146] At the same time, he continues with his project of self-stylization as an 'angry white man' and avant-garde artist – a stylization in which the "Viking memes" that have survived a "thousand years of Christianity" play an identity-forming role.[147] In this sense, he has turned himself into a prophet of a Nordic art-religion, who follows a philosophical and artistic Heathenism without being affiliated with any Asatru group.[148]

Dark Heirs of Wagner and Tolkien: Metal and Neofolk

Since the 1960s, rock music has made use of counter-cultural imagery of the Satanic and occult.[149] The origin of modern Satanism lies in Romanticism. Artistic genres that employ it can be understood as heirs to the 'dark side' of Romanticism and its art-religious impulse. The figure of Mephisto in Goethe's

---

145   Up until 2011, Jakhelln perceived his own project as a primarily artistic and religious one, denying any interest in politics. However, the aesthetic and religious, or rather, art-religious concepts he employs, always already have (meta-)political implications; for example, through the aesthetisation of totalitarian political ideologies. Cf. Sandra Lillebø, "Dr. Jakhelln og Mr. Hyde," *Klassekampen*, December 02, 2011.
146   Cf. Jakhelln, *Raseri*, 48–50.
147   Ibid., 50.
148   He did, however, have contact with the Icelandic *Ásatrúarfélagið*, and Jörmundur Ingi features on *Solefald*'s CD *Red for Fire – An Icelandic Odyssey* from 2005 with a recitation from the Eddic poem, 'Lokasenna.'
149   A major inspiration came from Aleister Crowley and the anti-egalitarian, radically individualist and hedonist ethics of Anton LaVey, the founder of the Californian *Church of Satan*. Cf. Gardell, *Gods of the Blood*, 287f; Christian Dornbusch and Hans-Peter Killguss, *Unheilige Allianzen. Black Metal zwischen Satanismus, Heidentum und Neonazismus* (Hamburg/Münster: Unrast, 2005), 84f.

Faust, the embodiment of a longing for freedom and power and its destructive potential, is a prominent source of inspiration, as are the literary characters of E.T.A. Hoffmann and Charles Baudelaire. Authors such as Lord Byron, Percy Bysshe Shelley, and William Blake "disembedded the Devil, Satan, Lucifer from the narrow constraints of Christianity and re-embedded the figure in an aesthetic and classical context," merging it with other mythical figures, such as Prometheus and Pan.[150] Together with the Nietzschean influence, the literary roots of modern Satanism draw attention to the aesthetic character of this movement. Satanic, anti-Christian, anti-egalitarian, and mythological imagery played a significant role in the deliberately shocking and anti-bourgeois aesthetic of heavy metal bands of the 1970s as well. Around 1990, the Swedish Metal group *Bathory* replaced Satan with the equally anti-Christian imagery of Viking warriors and Heathen mythology in their 'Asatru trilogy,' *Blood Fire Death* (1988), *Hammerheart* (1990), and *Twilight of the Gods* (1991). The imagery, lyrics, and musical language of these albums contained tributes to the Nordic art-religious constellation. The cover of *Blood Fire Death* featured an 1872 Romantic painting of the Scandinavian version of the Wild Hunt, *Oskorei*, by Peter Nicolai Arbo (see Figure 9.4); *Hammerheart* mentions Richard Wagner in the credits; and *Twilight of the Gods* uses lyrical themes from Nietzsche, as well as veiled references to the SS. It thus "deliberate[ly] flirt[s] with the iconography of fascism and National Socialism."[151]

Other Scandinavian bands, such as *Unleashed, Riger, Menhir, Enslaved, Einherjer, Bifrost*, and *Helheim* followed in this newly established tradition, and gained popularity as well as notoriety in the first part of the 1990s. The Norwegian black metal scene became notorious due to Varg Vikernes', of *Burzum*, and others' involvement in church burnings and two murder cases in the early 1990s.[152] Vikernes later turned to an explicit anti-Semitic, racist, Germanic Paganism and founded the *Norwegian Heathen Front* – an organization that added other national chapters throughout the years

---

150 Petersen, "Introduction: Embracing Satan," 11. These mythological figures also became central icons for alternative religious movements around 1900, including for the *völkisch* religious movement. Ludwig Fahrenkrog for example merged Promothean and Luciferian traits in his *Wölund* character (cf. Fahrenkrog, *Wölund*). For the enthusiasm around Pan cf. Aleida Assmann, "Pan, Paganismus und Jugendstil," in *Antike Tradition und Neuere Philologien. Symposium zu Ehren des 75. Geburtstags von Rudolf Sühnel*, ed. Hans-Joachim Zimmermann (Heidelberg: Winter, 1984).

151 Michael Moynihan and Didrik Søderlind, *Lords of Chaos. The Bloody Rise of the Satanic Metal Underground*, Revised and expanded ed. (Port Townsend, WA: Feral House, 2003), 21 (cf. also 18–21).

152 The events are documented in ibid. and Rem, *Innfødte skrik*.

FIGURE 9.4 *Peter Nikolai Arbo, Åsgårdsreien* (1872)
PUBLISHED WITH PERMISSION FROM THE NATIONAL MUSEUM OF ART, ARCHITECTURE AND DESIGN IN NORWAY

under the umbrella organization *Allgermanic Heathen Front* (AHF).[153] Vikernes is a fairly marginal figure in Asatru today, and thus only of indirect importance for my investigations of the entanglements between current Asatru and music.

In order to understand the relationship between Asatru and the "Euro-Pagan"[154] music scene, it is worth taking a closer look at the book from which much of the information on Heathen and Viking themes in black metal referred to here is gleaned: *Lords of Chaos* (first published in 1998), by Norwegian journalist Didrik Søderlind and Michael Moynihan. Moynihan has been a member of the *Asatru Alliance*, as well as of Stephen Flowers'/Edred Thorsson's *Rune Gild*, co-editor of *Tyr* and translator of Karl Maria Wiligut's work. (See Chapter 2) The authors themselves take a "mythic" approach to

---

153 Cf. Gardell, *Gods of the Blood*, 307.
154 The term stems from Stéphane François, "The Euro-Pagan Scene. Between Paganism and Radical Right," *Journal for the Study of Radicalism* 1, no. 2 (2007) and indicates that it is an aesthetic formation which is not held together by a particular musical style but by common references to 'Germanic' and 'Nordic' Pagan themes, or, to put it in the frame of this discussion, by the Nordic art-religious tradition.

their subject. Beyond simply documenting the black metal scene, they want to identify its "metaphysical and spiritual underpinnings,"[155] and they read it as the "return of an atavism."[156] Moynihan and Søderlind attribute the fact that this "atavism" or archetype breaks through in Scandinavia today to Northern Europe's late Christianization.[157] Furthermore, they point to the important role which the barren Northern landscape and harsh climate play in black, Viking, and Pagan metal,[158] and claim that the "gods of the North seem particularly prone to stirring feelings which may unexpectedly resurge among the descendants of those who once worshipped them."[159] They thus use the 'blood and soil' framework, which is constitutional for ethnicist Asatru, to explain the emergence of Heathen themes in music, the resurfacing of Asatru, and Vikernes' and others' crimes.[160]

As we have seen, such ideas of a mythic continuity were supported by scholars of the Romantic school and their followers around the turn of the century. They culminated in the 1920s and 30s in the theories of C.G. Jung and Otto Höfler, for example. Instead of talking about ancient mythic continuities, we can read *Lords of Chaos* as an appropriation of this type of holistic scholarship and its theories of *völkisch* unity and continuity, as discussed in Chapter 8. It is no coincidence that Höfler's theories, depicting the Wild Hunt in the Alpine area and its Nordic equivalent, *Oskorei*, as expressions of a ritual and social formation with roots in a deep Germanic past, inform both the music scene and Moynihan's and Søderlind's approach. The resurgence of the theme can already be found on *Bathory's* first album. Vikernes took it up in his fascination for, and identification with, the "werewolf warriors of the Oskorei"[161] – a fascination that was soon shared by the Austrian musician Gerhard Petak, of the band *Allerseelen*, who at the time called himself Kadmon. His 1995 essay on the parallels between *Oskorei* and black metal quotes Otto Höfler frequently, and it became the primary avenue for the dissemination of Höfler's ideas in the

---

155 Moynihan and Søderlind, *Lords of Chaos*, 196.
156 They borrow the term from Nietzsche and C.G. Jung, the latter of whom uses the concept in his essay 'Wotan.'
157 Moynihan and Søderlind, *Lords of Chaos*, 195.
158 Ibid., 203.
159 Ibid., 204.
160 By referring to Stephen McNallen's observation of an 'organic' and synchronized revival of Asatru in the 1970s, they indirectly endorse Vikernes' own claims that the Norse gods are the archetypes of the Nordic race that break through, again quasi-naturally. Ibid., 204f.
161 Ibid., 196f.

Alpine black metal scene.[162] The wider distribution of Kadmon's essay can be attributed to Moynihan's and Søderlind's decision to add an English translation of it to the appendix of *Lords of Chaos*. Both Kadmon, as well as Moynihan/Søderlind's book, thus contribute to a mythisation not only of black metal music, which Kadmon sees as a direct expression of Nordic cosmology,[163] but of the church burnings as well, which they see as reflections of ancient European fire myths spun out of control.[164]

There is still another conclusion to be drawn from this. Moynihan makes frequent positive references to black metal musicians who seriously devote themselves to the study and revival of Norse myth. Kadmon does the same in his article when he praises musicians who, contrary to those using Nordic cosmology as "cosmetic make-up, decoration," take it "seriously, linking Ariosophic mythology together in their work with a mental attitude of self-respect and resistance, uniting them in a Nordic Nietzscheanism...Here Black Metal becomes a Pagan avant-garde, a Nordic 'occulture' reconciling both myth and modern world."[165]

With the combination of Ariosophy and a Nietzschean ethic of self-reliance, Kadmon evokes the spiritual world of modern Asatru and links this version of Heathenism directly to the idea of an aesthetic avant-garde. Kadmon/Gerhard Petak and Moynihan themselves are younger members of a music scene

---

162   I here follow Florian Heesch's elaborate argument, cf. Florian Heesch, "Metal for Nordic Men. Amon Amarth's Representations of Vikings," in *The Metal Void. First Gatherings*, ed. Niall W.R. Scott and Imke v. Helden (Oxford: Inter-Disciplinary Press, 2010).
163   Kadmon in Moynihan and Søderlind, *Lords of Chaos*, 376.
164   Kadmon in ibid., 377. Moynihan/Søderlind even ascribe a prophetic quality to Vikernes' legal change of Kristian (meaning Christian in Norwegian) to Varg. They are reminiscent of allegedly obscure medieval and folkloristic uses of the term 'Varg' or 'Varg Veum' (old Norse for 'wolf in temple' as well as 'outlawed criminal'), which is associated with crimes like arson, grave robbery, treason, theft, and manslaughter, all crimes of which Vikernes was eventually accused or found guilty. However, there is no need to construct such esoteric connections about a sub-conscious prophetic application of this name. The term "Varg Veum" is quite well known in Norwegian and it was further popularized in the 1970s and 1980s by Gunnar Staalesen, an author from Vikernes' hometown Bergen, whose Norwegian version of hard-boiled crime novels centred on a detective with this name. The first book in the series appeared in 1977. The eighth novel, *Falne Engler* (Fallen Angels), published in 1989, deals with Varg Veum's youth in the 1960s milieu of rock music. Cf. Gunnar Staalesen, *Bukken til havresekken* (Oslo: Gyldendal, 1977); *Falne engler* (Oslo: Gyldendal, 1989).
165   Kadmon in Moynihan and Søderlind, *Lords of Chaos*, 387.

labelled neofolk, apocalyptic folk, Euro-Pagan music, or apoliteic music.[166] They share its appropriation of a Pagan art-religious philosophy in the spirit of the German Conservative Revolution and European fascisms and fascist occultism.[167]

The collaboration of the Euro-Pagan music subculture in the USA and Great Britain with Asatru goes back as far as the 1970s. Neofolk's "ancestor,"[168] Robert N. Taylor, of the band *Changes*, was one of the very few folk singers of the era to be involved with right-wing political organizations, including the paramilitary *Minutemen*, as well as with the *Asatru Free Assembly* and the *Asatru Alliance*.[169] Neofolk proper emerged as part of the so-called "extreme culture" scene around punk/industrial/noise music of the 1970s. Part of this scene

---

166 Anton Shekhovtsov, "Apoliteic Music. Neo-Folk, Martial Industrial and 'Metapolitical Fascism'," *Patterns of Prejudice* 43, no. 5 (2009).

167 Moynihan and Petak collaborated in several projects within this context, including the album *Gotos = Kalanda* (1995), based on twelve poems that Karl Maria Wiligut (alias Weisthor) wrote for Heinrich Himmler. Cf. Andreas Diesel and Dieter Gerten, *Looking for Europe. Neofolk und Hintergründe* (Zeltingen-Rachtig: Index Verlag, 2007), 236; Thomas Naumann and Patrick Schwarz, "Von der CD zur 'Lichtscheibe.' Das Kulturmagazin Sigill," in *Ästhetische Mobilmachung. Dark Wave, Neofolk und Industrial im Spannungsfeld rechter Ideologien*, ed. Andreas Speit (Hamburg/Münster: Unrast Verlag, 2002), 181. Wiligut's racial esotericism or National Socialist occultism has been a topic for both as writers as well. As mentioned earlier, Moynihan worked with Stephen Flowers on an English edition of Wiligut's texts, and Petak took up his theories in his journal *Aorta* (later *Ahnstern*). Cf. Diesel and Gerten, *Looking for Europe*, 243.

168 François, "The Euro-Pagan Scene," 37.

169 Having been a member of several occult and Satanic groups from the late 1960s on, he and his wife Karen started to look for an alternative to these "elitist cults" as well as "witchcraft (Wicca) with its heavy post-hippie influences and its growing feminist and multi-cultural slant." (FluxEuropa, "Changes. Interview with Robert Taylor," Changes, http://www.nmia.com/~thermite/interviews/flux97.html, last accessed January 02, 2012) They founded the *Northernway* and, after a schism in the 1970s, *The House of Wulfings* and *Wulfing Kindred*, which became part of the *Asatru Free Assembly*, and after its demise, the *Asatru Alliance*. It was here that he met Michael Moynihan, whose label *Storm* first released *Changes'* songs recorded between 1969 and 1974 in 1996, and thus contributed to the renewed popularity of Taylor beyond Asatru circles. Taylor remains an active presence both within the music scene and American ethnicist Asatru up until today. Stephen McNallen's e-mail newsletter, *AFA-Update*, reports that "our long-time friend and musician" Taylor and *Changes* "entertained us with beautiful and stirring songs in the 'apocalyptic folk' genre" at the "Folkish Summer Hallowing, hosted by the Irminfolk in Pennsylvania." Stephen A. McNallen, "Folkish Summer Hallowing – an Asatru Affirmation!," Newsletter, *AFA Update* 150, August 24 (2011).

centered around Asatruers and rune occultists such as Freya Aswynn[170] and, a little later, Ian Read, the current leader of the initiatory, Ariosophically inspired *Rune Gild* in Britain. It took a turn from a provocative anarchism toward the revolutionary right during the 1980s. It started to embrace the idea of the artist as a Nietzschean *Übermensch* and turned to a more affirmative, although often ambiguous use of fascist, Satanist, and militant imagery.[171] This change was accompanied by a gradual move away from synthetic sound and toward the use of more 'natural' acoustic instruments, and included medieval and Pagan themes that merged with fascist and occult, and increasingly also Ariosophic, elements. Aswynn herself appeared as a guest on several music productions with her runic chanting,[172] as did other prominent Asatruers such as Heimgest, leader of the ethnicist British *Odinic Rite,* who performed a recitation of the runic alphabet on *Sol Invictus*' CD *The Blade* in 1997,[173] and whose article on runes was published in the booklet for the band's production *Three Nine* in 2000.[174]

Collaborations between music and religion extended to leaders of the Icelandic *Ásatrúarfélagið* as well. Gerhard Petak's *Allerseelen* used Sveinbjörn Beinteinsson's lyrics on his album *Neuschwabenland* in 2000.[175] Nine years earlier, the Icelandic composer Hilmar Örn Hilmarsson, who was later to become *allsherjargodi* for the a-racist *Ásatrúarfélagið,* had moved in the extreme culture circles around performance artist Genesis P-Orridge's ironic sexual magic *Temple Ov Psychick Youth*. He collaborated with David Tibet from *Current 93* on

---

170 It was in her London house that the members of what was to become the inner circle of early apocalyptic folk, the so-called "family" around Douglas Pearce and his act *Death In June,* connected in the mid 1980s, amongst them Tony Wakeford (Sol Invictus), David Tibet (Current 93), and Boyd Rice (NON), as well as Ian Read of Tony Wakeford's band, *Sol Invictus,* who later founded his own act, *Fire and Ice*. (Cf. Christian Dornbusch, "Von Landsertrommeln und Lärmorgien. Death In June und Kollaborateure," in *Ästhetische Mobilmachung. Dark Wave, Neofolk und Industrial im Spannungsfeld rechter Ideologien,* ed. Andreas Speit (Hamburg/Münster: Unrast Verlag, 2002), 147).

171 Cf. Gardell, *Gods of the Blood,* 296; François, "The Euro-Pagan Scene," 38; Andreas Speit, ed. *Ästhetische Mobilmachung. Dark Wave, Neofolk und Industrial im Spannungsfeld rechter Ideologien* (Hamburg/Münster: Unrast Verlag, 2002), 11; Shekhovtsov, "Apoliteic Music," 441f; Kennet Granholm, "'Sons of Northern Darkness.' Heathen Influences in Black Metal and Neofolk Music," *Numen* 58 (2011), 531–534.

172 Cf. Diesel and Gerten, *Looking for Europe,* 125.

173 Ibid., 112.

174 Ibid., 119.

175 Ibid., 236.

the album *Island* (1991) – a production for which Tibet's and Hilmar Örn's friend, the famous Icelandic singer Björk, provided backing vocals.[176]

As the links between Moynihan and Gerhard Petak have already shown, these musico-religious collaborations extended as far as central Europe as well. In this context, the activities of German musician Markus Wolff, from *Waldteufel*, are important. Wolff lives in the United States and has been actively transferring information from the German(ic) Faith scene to English-speaking audiences, not only through his music, but also through articles in *Tyr*[177] and in the journal *Vor Tru*, of the ethnicist *Asatru Alliance*.[178] Michael Moynihan, of *Blood Axis*, is a prominent Asatruer who is involved in the occultist and 'left-hand path' (i.e., Satanist) community, as well as in neofolk, in a myriad of ways: as a musician, writer, and owner of his own label and publishing series.[179]

We can preliminarily conclude that the parts of the neofolk scene which have been connected to Asatru milieus can be mainly, but not exclusively, found around the groups that take a decidedly ethnicist or racial-religious approach to Asatru and/or are actively interested in Ariosophic and occult aspects of the religion as well as in 'Satanism.' Most prominent among them are the *Rune Gild*, the *Asatru Alliance*, the *Odinic Rite*, and, to a certain degree, the *Asatru Folk Assembly*. Neofolk's take on Asatru is reflected in the content which these bands spread in word and image, and which they share with black, Viking, and Pagan metal, namely a combination of nature mysticism, a fascination for war-imagery, fascist aesthetics,[180] an aestheticized Social Darwinism,

---

176 Ibid., 66. Musical performances of *seid* and Galdr also appear in ex-*Death In June* member Patrick Leaga's records, not only through his collaboration with Freya Aswynn, but also through his marriage to Amodali, of *Mother Destruction* – a musician who understands her own music as part of her involvement with female mysteries and *seid* shamanism. (cf. ibid., 126f). Northern shamanism and witchcraft are interests she shares with another former member of the circle around Freya Aswynn and Ian Read, Andrea Haugen, alias Nebelhexe or Andréa Nebel. The German musician, painter, writer, and performance artist resides in Norway and has played in groups such as *Aghast* and *Hagalaz Runedance*, and considers it her "heritage and birthright to keep the faith and traditions of my Germanic ancestors alive." Chad Hensley, "Wails from a Haunted Winter. Interview with Aghast," in *Esoterra. The Journal of Extreme Culture*, ed. Chad Hensley (s.l.: Creation Books, 2011), 259. Cf. http://www.andreanebel.com/, last accessed September 02, 2014.

177 See for example Wolff, "Ludwig Fahrenkrog and the Germanic Faith Community."

178 Diesel and Gerten, *Looking for Europe*, 428.

179 Cf. http://heathenharvest.org/2014/02/25/harvest-history-month-pt-xii-an-interview-with-michael-moynihan-between-birds-of-prey/, last accessed September 15, 2014.

180 One example is the band name *Blood Axis* which refers to the alliance between Hitler and Mussolini, the "axis Berlin-Rome."

and the occultist traditionalism of Italian fascist philosopher Julius Evola (1898–1974),[181] one of the most revered authors of the neofolk scene next to Ernst Jünger and Friedrich Nietzsche.[182] Entwined with the lionization of these authors are references to German Faith and Ariosophic ideas, protagonists, and works.[183]

The use of *völkisch*, fascist, and Ariosophic imagery and ideology has earned the neofolk scene fierce political critique, especially from anti-fascist individuals and organizations within and without the subcultures of metal and dark wave.[184] Most of these critical authors agree that the political intentions behind these projects are not outright National Socialist or fascist. Rather, they share a number of interests and values with the political or meta-political approach of the Conservative Revolution and the New Right. Less critical explorers of the neofolk scene advocate taking the music and its overall presentation in word and image seriously as an aesthetic, and not as a political program. Consequently, the ambiguities with which many of the artists surround their own production should be understood as a "legitimate strategy of obscuring" which creates an "ambiguous legibility."[185]

---

181   The term *Sol Invictus* is taken from Evola's hallowing of the Roman sun god.
182   For the role of these thinkers within the music scene see the article by Patrick Achermann in the appendix of Diesel and Gerten, *Looking for Europe*, 461–487.
183   Illustrations by Fidus and Ludwig Fahrenkrog are used, for example, by the bands Strength Through Joy and Blood Axis. Cf. ibid., 135; Jan Raabe and Andreas Speit, "L'art du mal. Vom antibürgerlichen Gestus zur faschistoiden Ästhetik," in *Ästhetische Mobilmachung. Dark Wave, Neofolk und Industrial im Spannungsfeld rechter Ideologien*, ed. Andreas Speit (Hamburg/Münster: Unrast Verlag, 2002), 87, 92. In 2001, a number of Euro-Pagan bands contributed to a whole album honoring Herman Hendrich, which was produced to raise money for the *Nibelungenhort e.V.* Cf. ibid., 121. Furthermore, Blood Axis set to music a text by Jörg Lanz von Liebenfels,' about the 'electric' organs of the original Aryan *Übermenschen* in their song, *Electricity*. Their logo, the *Kruckenkreuz*, which can be read as a combination of two swastikas turning in different directions, is the same as that which Ariosophist Jörg Lanz von Liebenfels used for his *Neutempler-Orden*. Cf. ibid., 91; Diesel and Gerten, *Looking for Europe*, 177.
184   The anthology by Speit, *Ästhetische Mobilmachung*, and the volume by Dornbusch and Killguss, *Unheilige Allianzen*, as well as the work by Stéphane François, *La musique Européenne. Ethnographie politique d'une subculture de droite* (Paris: L'Harmattan, 2006); "The Euro-Pagan Scene," and Shekhovtsov, "Apoliteic Music" are examples of outside, politically critical, or anti-fascist perspectives on Neofolk, while the activities of groups like *Grufties gegen Rechts* or bands like *Goethes Erben* bear witness to the anti-fascist engagement of insiders.
185   Diesel and Gerten, *Looking for Europe*, 25, cf. 105.

It is true that an aesthetic product needs to be approached on its own terms. Many artists within the broader scene of 'dark' music indeed work with modernist artistic means, which deliberately leave their audiences in an ambiguous space: They are confronted with the uncertainty as to whether the display of totalitarian themes, Germany's "brown past," and the occult[186] is meant as a provocation or subversion, or whether it is supposed to convey a deeper truth. Mattias Gardell characterizes this deliberate obscurity of the "Asatrú/Satanic underworld" as a projection of "different faces, [a] mix [of] seriousness with pose, and use [of] smoke screens and distorting mirrors to enact a Nietzschean masquerade."[187]

Anton Shekovtsov interprets this mix of fascist worldview and abstinence from calls to "outright violence," political parties, and "recruitment to any political tendency"[188] in the framework of Roger Griffin's theory of post-war fascism. This "third form" of fascism, and its main theorists, Julius Evola and Armin Mohler, sought neither to establish political parties nor enter into an alliance with revolutionary ultra-nationalism. Instead, it chose a kind of "right-wing 'inner emigration'" after 1945, in order to save the idea of "the true State, the hierarchical and organic State"[189] in the era of the "interregnum" of the despised liberal democracy. These concepts of "interregnum" and *apoliteia* influenced the New Right's concept of metapolitics as well, along with its attempts to "modify the dominant political culture and make it more susceptible to a non-democratic mode of politics."[190]

From a social scientific point of view, it might seem reductionist to view fascism in general to be predominantly a cultural phenomenon. Nevertheless, it remains useful to consider the cultural and aesthetic aspects of international fascism and the Conservative Revolution in order to understand the nature of some black metal and neofolk groups,' as well as some Heathens' *apoliteic* strategies. It might very well serve the purpose that Cornelia Klinger[191] describes when she claims that the merit of modern aesthetics is the synthesis of a simultaneous orientation toward the past and toward modernity. It is a synthesis, an attempt at reconciliation which acts as a surrogate for material gratification and social emancipation or participation. It offers of a sense of totality, unity, and meaning, the yearning for which modernity excludes and

---

186 Ibid., 33–35.
187 Gardell, *Gods of the Blood*, 284.
188 Shekhovtsov, "Apoliteic Music," 432.
189 Julius Evola, quoted in ibid., 437.
190 Ibid., 438.
191 Klinger, *Flucht Trost Revolte*.

illegitimizes. Klinger goes on to argue that fascism offers a dangerous answer to this most-important blind spot of modernity – dangerous, because it enables an adaption to modernity on the aesthetic level, while excluding social modernization and justifying social and economic inequality as eternal laws. She suggests that fascism should not be understood as a surrogate religion, because in modernity, religious elements are already aestheticized. Rather, she investigates the mechanisms at work within this kind of a totalitarian aesthetic, in which politics themselves are aestheticized, and where the artist becomes the perfect embodiment of the political leader. This is a logic pursued by Julius Langbehn, for example, who understands 'German' artists, such as Rembrandt and Dürer, as the perfect models for future educators and leaders of their people. In this sense, the invocation of an ancient past is not to be taken as a wish to return to it, but rather as an expression of the conviction that one's own values are eternal and thus directed at an ideal future.[192]

The aesthetic strategies found in neofolk can be understood as a return to such an ideologically ambiguous art-religious constellation. This thesis is supported by the fact that neofolk invokes exactly the protagonists of this formation, from Wagner and Nietzsche to Ernst Jünger, Ludwig Fahrenkrog, Fidus, Hermann Hendrich, and Ariosophy. Occasionally, the race-theoretical implications of *völkisch* religion are invoked as well. Ian Read, of the *Odinic Rite* and the *Rune Gild*, promotes his music as part of his esoteric rune magic activities. He relates this musico-religious activity directly to ancestry and genetic make up when he calls "folk music [a part of] our sacred way" which has "a deeper resonance for those of common European descent [as:] DNA will out, as it were."[193]

The musician and history of religions student, Joshua Gentzke, of the band *Lux Interna* (Inner Light), makes an elaborate and obscure argument; he emphasizes the difficulty of accessing the divine under the ambiguous "post-apocalyptic" condition characterized by a simultaneous longing for the presence of god or the gods and the fact of the absence of gods in today's world. He claims:

> In art forms which reflect this struggle, this struggle itself is happening. It is not merely an event and the representation of this event. Here, we are not on the terrain which one usually calls 'aesthetics.' For me, the creation of music which deals with these questions is a real participation in this struggle.

---

192 Ibid., 201–216.
193 Joshua Buckley, "The Saxon Songwriter. An Interview With Fire & Ice's Ian Read," *Tyr. Myth – Culture – Tradition* 1 (2002), 164f.

This is certainly a most emphatic affirmation of the religious purpose of art, which consequently is granted a privileged place in the process of learning to be open and to nurture and protect a place that could make such a return of the divine possible. The "inner light" after which his band is named is thus to be understood in a religious way. "With creative work, we elevate life to a higher plane, gather and let shine the light which is hidden in the essence of the world in which we live."[194]

Art-Religion – An Encompassing Paradigm?

The last example illustrates once more that the aesthetic and creative processes, scholarship, (meta-)politics, and religion are closely interwoven in these holistic, postmodern varieties of Conservative Revolutionary, Germanic Neopagan, and *völkisch* art-religion. This network can mostly be found on the side of contemporary artists who continue the *apoliteic* approach of the Conservative Revolutionary or fascist avant-garde. Some of them have been influential in the development of international Asatru. This does not mean, however, that their musical productions have had resounding success among the majority of a-racist Asatruers, who seem to have as eclectic musical tastes as their non-Asatru contemporaries. However, the part of this music scene which has made the mainstream, in particular Scandinavian and Eastern European metal bands, have become important conveyors of elements of the discourse on Nordic myth, and of the constellation of Nordic art-religion to a broader international public.

The close examination of Asatruers involved in neofolk, and their affinities to racial thought or ethnic essentialism, points to a fundamental ambiguity that has plagued Nordic art-religion from its beginnings up until the present day. In all the transformations and disparate political alliances, some central problems connected with this constellation have remained rather constant:

---

194   All quotes: Joshua Gentzke in Diesel and Gerten, *Looking for Europe*, 457–459: "In Kunstformen, die dieses Ringen reflektieren, findet dieses Ringen *selbst statt*. Es handelt sich hier nicht bloß um ein Ereignis und die Darstellung dieses Ereignisses. Wir befinden uns hier nicht auf dem Terrain dessen, was man für gewöhnlich mit dem Begriff 'Ästhetik' bezeichnet. Für mich ist das Schaffen von Musik, die sich mit diesen Fragen auseinander setzt, eine tatsächliche Teilnahme an diesem Ringen." – "Mit schöpferischer Arbeit heben wir das Leben auf eine höhere Ebene, versammeln und lassen das Licht strahlen, das im Wesen der Welt, in der wir leben, verborgen liegt."

(1) There is a tendency to connect myth, poetry, and art to seemingly stable entities anchored in a deep mythic past, such as nature, landscape, ethnicity, and race. (2) There is a tendency to see art and culture, as well as aesthetic proficiency, as expressions of deep *völkisch* essences, and not as evolving and transforming practices shaped in constant, contingent exchanges. (3) Finally, there is a tendency to focus on aesthetics as a kind of compensation for social and economic modernization.

These central problems, however, are not limited to constellations of Nordic art-religion. Rather, as the previous chapters have shown, they constitute the whole discourse on Nordic myth, as well as its surrounding discourses on ethnicity, religion, nature, gender, and scholarship. As theories about art-religion and modernism inform us,[195] the argument can be turned around as well. Aesthetics play a key role in modern(ist) attempts at a renewal of the arts, as well as of society, politics, and religion. Taking this into perspective, the art-religious logic is relevant for all the facets of modern Asatru discussed in this book, its forerunners in Germanic Faith, and Ariosophy, as well as their sources of inspiration in social movements and academic theory. They are all suspended in the characteristic field of tension between essentialist mechanisms of exclusion and the experience of the free play of autonomous creativity.

We have seen that the creation of ritual discussed in Chapter 3, which is so typical for modern alternative religions, is experienced as a genuinely aesthetic creativity and can entail more or less elaborate theories of the aesthetic. On one end of the spectrum, in racial-religious and ethnicist Asatru, we find imaginations of ritual as a means to re-create the nation or give the state a ritual foundation, as is the case with fascist or Conservative Revolutionary movements. On the other end, and mainly in a-racist Asatru, there is the contemporary variety of the aesthetic search for totality, unity, and meaning, which is ruled by a late-modern logic of taste and choice.[196] Here, the aesthetic has moved from art into life in a thoroughly post-Nietzschean way, into a psychotherapeutic culture which projects the experience of religious ritual

---

195   For example, Klinger, *Flucht Trost Revolte*; Klaus Lichtblau, "'Innerweltliche Erlösung vom Rationalen' oder 'Reich diabolischer Herrlichkeit'? Zum Verhältnis von Kunst und Religion bei Georg Simmel und Max Weber," in *Kunst und Religion. Studien zur Kultursoziologie und Kulturgeschichte*, ed. Richard Faber and Volker Krech (Würzburg: Königshausen & Neumann, 1999); Roger Griffin, *Modernism and Fascism. The Sense of a Beginning under Mussolini and Hitler* (London: Palgrave Macmillan, 2007).

196   Cf. Klinger, *Flucht Trost Revolte*, 222–236.

as a creative, aesthetic, and therapeutic process onto a pre-Christian romanticized past. Aesthetic dimensions play a role in race theories and the ethnic and cultural essentialisms discussed in Chapter 4, just as they do for imaginations of polytheism and constructed oppositions of the Semitic versus the Indo-European (or Aryan) analyzed in Chapter 5. In most of these theories, the higher-valued races, ethnicities, cultures, and religions are imbued with the aura of creativity and the inclination toward artistic talent, or are at least seen as being more conducive to the development of aesthetic expression than their respective counterparts, 'the Jews,' 'Semites,' and 'Orientals.' As shown in Chapter 6, concepts of a nature religion or spirituality are highly dependent on the aestheticized modern view of nature that reaches its first climax in Romanticism. This applies equally to the models of gendered spirituality discussed in Chapter 7. Women's and matriarchal spirituality are closely associated with specific forms of artistic expression. Prominent figures of the feminist and women's spirituality or the goddess movement, such as Heide Göttner-Abendroth, with her theories of a matriarchal aesthetic,[197] and the Swedish-born British painter, Monica Sjöö,[198] promote their religion in aesthetic terms, rejecting the modern divide between art and ritual. Theories of the *Männerbund* provide academic foundations for the aestheticization of the (military) state and war. In the mythopoetic men's movement, such aestheticism is shifted from the collective to the individual, but it is still characterized by aestheticized images of the warrior. And finally, the academic theories employed to reconstruct a pre-Christian Germanic or Nordic religion, which we considered in Chapter 8, are dependent on a methodology that dates back to Romanticism and is driven by aesthetic concerns. From Danish poet and antiquarian N.F.S. Grundtvig's attempts to re-create a broad vision of Norse myth to the 19th- and early 20th-century theories of folklorists and historians of religions, a hermeneutics of a 'contemplation of the whole,' of 'poetic vision,' 'enthusiasm' (*Begeisterung*), and spiritual experience has constituted the preconditions for the understanding of religion as well as art. And, as I have argued, all attempts to reconstruct a pre-Christian Norse religion up until today ultimately have had to employ such aesthetic imaginations of wholeness and authenticity.

---

197   Heide Göttner-Abendroth, *Die tanzende Göttin. Prinzipien einer matriarchalen Ästhetik*, 5. ed. (Munich: Frauenoffensive, 1991 [1982]); *The Dancing Goddess. Principles of a Matriarchal Aesthetic*, trans. Maureen T. Krause (Boston: Beacon Press, 1991).

198   Cf. Monica Sjöö and Barbara Mor, *The Great Cosmic Mother. Rediscovering the Religion of the Earth* (San Francisco: Harper Collins, 1987).

The results of this last chapter on Nordic art-religion raise broader questions about the relation between ideas about Nordic or Germanic myth, literary and aesthetic movements, contemporary spirituality, and their shifting political functions. From this perspective, art-religion can indeed serve as a useful, all-encompassing paradigm for understanding Germanic Neopaganism and its ambiguous location in modern societies.

CHAPTER 10

Instead of a Conclusion

"How could that happen to me?" More than two decades have passed after the key scene at the *Armanen-Orden's* Ostara Thing described at the very beginning of my introduction, which led to this question. During this entire period, my work on Germanic Neopaganism was motivated and guided by the righteous indignation spurred by such moments of disillusion. Twenty-five years later, I am still driven by it, but something has changed as well. Three experiences from my research round between 2010 and 2012 capture this change.

(1) *It is around Easter 2010, and Ostara is still popular amongst German Heathens. I am invited to a castle turned youth hostel to celebrate this fictional goddess and the arrival of spring once again. The invitation was extended to me after I conducted the first interviews with members of the German a-racist Eldaring. After considerable apprehension from both sides, a dialogue had been established. I am to speak at the event, to give a talk about Heathens' concepts of religion, putting forth the argument that is now developed in Chapter 5. I was hesitant to put myself in a situation where I had to talk about my research in front of my research subjects, but I finally decided that I wanted to meet this challenge head on. The talk seems to go well, the ensuing discussion is open, lively. We do not agree on every point; to the contrary. But I am impressed by my audience's openness and willingness to reflect on their own positions. Afterwards I receive compliments for my courage to "enter the lion's den."*

Later that evening, I realize that my ambivalence around these Asatruers is still there, as is their defensiveness. At the dinner table I have a peculiar encounter with a young man, who tries somewhat frantically to convince me that they could not possibly be right-wingers. I am somewhat puzzled by this unsolicited revelation. Later on, when I see the selection of books for sale at the event, I begin to understand this defensiveness: there are a number of titles that clearly hark back to a völkisch *tradition. The duplicity that characterizes Germanic Neopaganism is still there, and yet my main impression remains that something in the atmosphere has changed. There is an increased openness and friendliness, and the defensiveness is less aggravated, at least in this and other a-racist groups. They seem to cherish their friendships and their community more than they need to insist on their status as ostracized outsiders.*

(2) *I am sitting in a spacious meadow somewhere in Northern Germany. I am surrounded by young people and families; there are about twenty people hanging out on the grounds of an old farmhouse that now serves as a modest group retreat*

and self-catering seminar center. The day before has been spent in preparation of an elaborate self-designed ritual involving an anonymous gift exchange. We were all supposed to bring an object that was meaningful to us, but that we were also ready to part with. I had brought a small crystal cube with a carving of a koala bear inside, the type you get at souvenir stores all over the world. This one was given to my by an Australian Odinist whom I had met in California a few years earlier. I had kept it on my desk since then as reminder of my ambivalent involvement with Asatru. It seems like a good time to part with it, to pass it on. During the ritual we weave and knot together numerous strands of multicolored fabric into a convoluted web. There is chatter and laughing and sighs of exasperation. We have moved in a circle, or maybe rather in an elipse, then in a spiral. The gifts have been gathered in a large sack, and at the end of the ritual we each draw one. I end up with a small, dome-shaped bluish rock, covered in dots and ridges like those of a fossil. A part of the top and one of its sides is broken off, revealing a smooth, marble-like inside. It has now replaced the crystal on my desk and reminds me of my journey of discovery within Asatru – a journey which has involved the violent breaking away of petrified layers of defense, and the uncovering of equally petrified and persistent remnants of völkisch *thought, along with unexpected discoveries.*

Yet another one of those unexpected, memorable events takes place in the afternoon of the same day. The small group Nornirs Ætt is gathering for its annual meeting – an event that combines a decision-making assembly with ritual. I am invited to participate as a non-member, which is a rare event. After long discussions about members, workshops, offices, and responsibilities, a surprise topic is called. A long-term member of the group stands up and talks about the book I published in 1992. He recalls how a bunch of rather unorganized but enthusiastic Pagans set out in the early nineties to rid the scene of its racial esoteric and völkisch *ideological baggage. He says, "Sure, we could have done this research on our own and completed the process independently. But this book has certainly saved us a lot of time and effort." With a grand gesture he raises a drinking horn and offers it to me as a gift, honoring my contribution to Asatru's turn towards respectability. I am flabbergasted and a little flattered. I accept the gift in a manner I hope is somewhat graceful and am honestly moved. In a flash, I realize how complicated my relationship to these 'reform-Asatruers' really is. Sure enough, this gesture can be construed as a calculated move to forestall my fundamental critique. But I sense an honest connection between their wish to live as decent, politically reflective, and observant human beings, while following their Neopagan convictions and appreciating my attempts to enlighten them as to the scene's involvement with right-wing machinations.*

(3) A year and a half later I have finished my manuscript and am working on my proposal, with this last chapter yet to be written. I am sitting at lunch with a

younger colleague, who is a medievalist. I tell her that there is one fundamental question this book project has not been able to resolve, and that leaves me ambivalent. I feel torn between two forces. On the one hand, I harbor sympathy towards many of the younger a-racist Heathens, the metal fans, and the enthusiastic admirers of myth and ancient religions and rituals. On the other hand, I cannot let go of this deep-seated unease in face of the circulating discourse on Norse myth, with all its ideological ballast. My colleague exclaims, "I know the feeling, I know it exactly." She is one of the few medievalists who share my opinion that attempts to reconstruct any kind of pre-Christian Norse thought, religion, or culture are futile and methodologically flawed, hence her deep skepticism. But I am amazed that she shares the sense of sympathy that I feel, and that she agrees that many of her students who harbor an enthusiastic interest in reconstructionist approaches, and also practical aesthetic engagements with Norse myth, are intelligent, deliberate, and engaged people. After a while, we come to the conclusion that it is impossible to resolve the contradiction and eliminate the feeling of being torn.

I realize now that all I have done in the chapters of this book was to circle around and to explore this ambivalence, to look for clues, for possibilities of distinction, and for clear-cut delineations. I have not been able to pinpoint them clearly. Rather, I have performed them over and over again in various contexts. It could be that the not-quite resolved oscillation between an ideologically critical discourse analysis and hermeneutic approaches that run through the argumentation of this book has to do with these ambivalences.

These three instances show how intricately interwoven my work has been with the Germanic Neopagan communities I have researched. The honoring of my book by younger Asatruers has made it clear to me that my work has had a very real impact, at least on the struggles within German Asatru. In my earlier books I focused on the *Armanen-Orden* and its affiliates, which alerted other Pagans to their racial-esoteric agenda. It also gave them an easy target, and the chance to distance themselves and their own groups from racist thought by simply rejecting the *Armanen-Orden* and its teachings. The existence of my book might have kept groups like the *Armanen-Orden* and the *Germanische Glaubensgemeinschaft* at the center of attention much longer than their actual influence in the scene lasted, while other, equally complicated strands of thought were less scrutinized.

The influence has been mutual. Reflecting on these encounters now, I realize how much they have changed me. They have provided me with new answers to my question, "how could this happen to me?" During my interviews and conversations, I have felt time and again that I do in fact share interests and desires with some Asatruers. The surprise during my research process was indeed that I am not the only one to criticize Asatru as potentially ethnicist and culturally essentialist, while simultaneously acknowledging its continual creative productivity. Some Asatruers actually harbor similar sentiments and concerns.

This acknowledgment of a kinship with some of my research subjects carries with it a certain disappointment. My book has turned out to be much less sensationalist and not as immediately politically urgent as I had intended it to be. What this does give me, however, is space to look, to listen, to explore, and to find the more subtle connections between Asatru and the fields of discourse, ideas, and topics that are dear to me, such as feminist and queer theory, ecology, art and literature, and scholarly discourse. Thus, my own person, my own thought, is involved in the field that I research to a much larger degree. In my previous work, I tried to distance myself from the scene by demarcating my investigative position. However, lines of connection between myself and my subject began emerging more frequently. My encounters with Asatruers have made this sense of connection more concrete, anchoring it in lived experience. Seeing and meeting people who ask themselves questions that resemble those I am asking makes for a changed dynamic. Also, it changes my perspective in a way that brings my own thinking into focus, and not just the thoughts of 'others.'

The initial motive that drove my research in the 1980s was to show the world how dangerous a religion that bases itself on racial-esoteric ideas could become. Implicit in my research was the wish to 'rescue' that which was 'good' and 'untainted' within the discourse of Nordic myth, which had become fascinating for me during my studies of medieval and modern Scandinavian literature. It was the same motivation that leads many of my students to choose Scandinavian studies as a field today as well.

From the 1990s onwards, my desire to identify areas that employed discourses on (Nordic) myth, but were untainted by ethnic or cultural essentialism, was continually disappointed. This process of disillusionment with alternative religion, feminism and feminist spirituality, ecology, and, finally, my own academic fields of Scandinavian and literary studies is mirrored in the chapters of this book. Increasingly, the realization that there is no clear-cut outside to this problematic discourse reshaped my own position as a researcher. More than ever before, during my most recent field studies, conducted between 2008 and 2012, I met Asatruers who seemed to be considerably more informed about and critical toward the problems inherent in a naïve application of Old Icelandic and ancient sources to contemporary religion than their contemporaries from other alternative religions or social movements. Conversations with non-specialists who asked about my work showed something else as well:

namely that a strong cultural essentialism, unfounded assumptions about the age of Nordic myths, and the survival of these myths in modern customs and tales are all deeply ingrained in common perceptions of 'the Nordic,' and reach far beyond the Asatru community. The Romantic paradigm is still very much alive. These shared ideas are strongly related to a broader tendency, which I have described as the conflation of ethnicity, culture, and religion, or, the culturalization of religion and the sacralization of culture and ethnicity. This kind of new holism, the assumption that there is an uncomplicated continuity between heritage, culture, land, climate, and spirituality, has become naturalized again in recent years. It appears as almost a matter of fact in parts of mainstream discourse. In this context, 'culture' indeed acquires a function that 'race' held previously, connoting an essence that has to be 'preserved' and 'kept pure.'

While I continually point to the perpetuation of ethnicist or *völkisch* thought in and beyond Asatru, I am also aware that this thinking can be changed. These ideas are intertwined with contemporary concerns, attitudes, and discourses, and they are employed in order to make sense of a contemporary world. It is thus not the purpose of this book to label all individuals who are fascinated with Asatru or the world of Nordic myth as 'racists.' My critique is in fact rarely directed against individuals. Rather, my interest has been to show that certain religious or reconstructionist attitudes have racist, ethnicist, or cultural essentialist implications. Their critical analysis is necessary, as reconstructionism can prove fecund for politics of exclusion and domination. As George S. Williamson wrote in the conclusion to his analysis of *The Longing for Myth in Germany* in the 19th century, the discourse on myth tended to "harden already existing divisions of class, religion, and ethnicity. In doing so, [it] ignored not only the potential for human communities that crossed such lines but the very possibility of meaningful cultural transfer or translation from one epoch, nation or 'race' to another."[1]

Ethnicist, cultural essentialist, and racist ideas are indeed closely intertwined with the history of my field and my own academic predilections. Scandinavian studies, Germanic studies, and Indo-European studies have all contributed to the formation of the discourse which has been fashioned into religion by Asatruers, and to which they remain attached today. It is therefore no wonder that some of my colleagues in Scandinavian studies, as well as my students, seem to find it hard to let go of the desire to reconstruct pre-Christian Nordic or Germanic beliefs, mentality, and culture – at the price of neglecting the fascinating political, theological, and literary connections between the

---

1 Williamson, *The Longing for Myth in Germany*, 299.

North and the rest of the continent during the High Medieval Period. As much as both sides hate to acknowledge this kinship, Asatru and reconstructive Old Norse studies remain connected by the desire to reconstruct pre-Christian religion, culture, thought, and practice.

Two questions remain to be addressed:

(1) What constitutes the ongoing attraction of the discourse on Nordic myth?

At its core, it comes down to the combination of the thrill of exoticism and the safety of familiarity or alleged ownership. The imagined return to 'the old Gods,' to 'the gods of the ancestors,' implies that the 'innocent native,' the 'noble savage,' and the 'repressed origin' are located not in a repressed other, but in the individual itself. Identifying with these positions implies that one is not a perpetrator or profiteur of imperial conquest, colonial despotism, or violent proselytizing. Rather, one counts oneself among those subject to cultural extinction. Thus, the drive toward Asatru is as much an identification with a position of innocent victimhood, which supposedly relieves one of historical guilt, as it is a fantasy of superiority. This speculation leads to the second core question:

(2) Where does the acute defensiveness and awareness of Asatruers with regard to their religion and its ideological implications come from?

Although their defensiveness is exacerbated by outside allegations of National Socialist sympathies, such outside attacks are not the only, and probably not even the core, reason. It rather seems to be a more or less conscious unease with the political, ethical, or ideological implications of neo-Germanic religion, which are based on a Romantic fiction of unity, wholeness, and origin. From this defensive and precarious position stem the numerous attempts to 'purify' Asatru, a desire that manifests itself on many different levels. Most prominent is the desire to rid oneself of Christian elements or influences, along with any *völkisch* ones, as well as any ties to the National Socialist tradition.

The nine chapters of this book have explored the manifold ways in which this Romantic fiction develops, unfolds, and manifests itself, and have illuminated them from different perspectives. My investigations also demonstrate the remarkable persistence and equally remarkable malleability of the discourse on Nordic myth. Its individual elements, which I have discussed at length in this book, have been astonishingly stable since their inception and their more systematic compilation in Romanticism. They have also inspired various movements and ideologies from quite different sides of the political spectrum, and they have become productive in the arts, in music, literature, and religious thought in various eras and contexts.

As I struggle to complete this fragmented collage of a conclusion, a small text by Birna Bjarnadóttir comes my way, entitled *a book of fragments*.[2] The author is an Icelandic literary critic who for the last ten years has chaired the only Icelandic studies department outside of Iceland, in Winnipeg, Manitoba, the location where a large group of Icelandic immigrants settled in the late 19th century. Her short text circles around the past and present connections between Iceland and Western Iceland, as this part of Manitoba is referred to. The book locates these connections firmly in European historical and contemporary global contexts, weaving together themes, motives, and images that have shown up in the book you hold in your hands now, including German Romanticism, (Icelandic) nature, religion and conversion, aesthetics and its decline, pictures from films, and more. But maybe it does not really weave them togther, but rather lets these strands and ribbons of thought blow in the wind. They tangle and untangle, forming unstable patterns of unexpected beauty. And they elicit skepticism.

The foreword of the book, written by Winnipeg film scholar George Tole, reflects on the beauty and effects of the fragment. Together with Birna Bjarnadóttir's fragments, his text brings to life the aesthetic revolutionary spirit of the early Jena Romanticists, as well as a contemporary search for "connection, fuller belonging."[3] Tole finds a Zen-like quality in these Romantics' life and writings. In Birna Bjarnadóttir's texts, their experiments with love and togetherness, and their 'symphilosophic' literary experiments connect with Old Norse saga literature, especially with the figure of Sigurd from the *Völsunga* saga. She associates his desire to be taught "mighty things," and his tragic, yet necessary, forgetting with contemporary twenty-first century sentiment. "There is no eternal bliss in sight. The knowledge gained is also knowledge lost."[4] Tole elaborates on this in his foreword:

> Bjarnadóttir knows better than Sigurdur that we are meant to forget [the mighty things] as soon as we begin to grasp what they are. Or if we are not meant to, that we almost surely will. Let us be forgiven each and every time for our need to know and our need to forget. With any luck we will come round upon these 'mighty things' again, as though (always) for the first time.[5]

---

2 Birna Bjarnadóttir, *a book of fragments* (Winnipeg, MB: KIND Publishing, 2010).
3 Tole in ibid., xviii.
4 Ibid., 61.
5 Tole in ibid., xviii.

Has this book done the same, just the other way round? Have I written it so that the dark sides of the Romantic constellation and of the tradition of Norse myth will not be forgotten? And if we remember those, do we lose the 'mighty things' (whatever they might be) once and for all? Birna Bjarnadóttir writes a fragment titled "rivers full of gods":

> Where she comes from, the rivers are full of gods. When the conversion to Christianity took place, they threw the Nordic Olympus into a waterfall, knowing that whatever happened in life, the old religion would be passed around the table. Christianity was never a threat, nor was any other religion for that matter.[6]

I wonder if there is a way to pass the gods around the table all the same – albeit never an unambiguous one? I somehow still doubt it. Yet, I don't know.

The problem remains that the discourse on Germanic myth, as I have demonstrated, has always been dependent on the idea of national, racial, or ethnic essences. In order to read the mythological sources as messages from a pre-Christian era, one has to employ these ideas of ethnic essences. Therefore, any attempt at a mythological revival will necessarily be tainted by essentialist operations. This is also true for the diverse artistic appropriations of this discourse on Nordic or Germanic myth, to the extent that they take the idea of a principally accessible pre-Christian past as their starting point. In this sense, the discourse and its religious or aesthetic actualization can never be innocent. The gods passed around the table will always carry with them a tinge of nationalism, racism, or ethnic and cultural essentialism. This is why an elective affinity between this discourse on Nordic myth and right-wing thought is always immanent – a connection that can never be completely eschewed by well-intentioned a-racist Heathenism.

The problem lies in the temptations attached to this discourse on myth, a discourse which has itself turned into mythology: Romantic aestheticism; ideas of creative unfolding; a less alienated, more authentic life; a sustainable life at peace with what is seen as 'nature.' In keeping these yearnings alive, we keep the gods alive, or vice versa: keeping the gods alive promises to keep us tied to these yearnings.

But does a historical-critical engagement with mythological sources really have to lead to a merciless disenchantment of the world of Nordic myth? Again, the answer would be 'yes' and 'no.' Yes, in the sense that it would mean one has to acknowledge that the 'beliefs of our ancestors' prior to the advent of

---

6 Ibid., 31.

Christianity necessarily remain obscure, inaccessible due to a lack of valid sources. No, in that a historical-critical approach can open our eyes to fascinating and creative medieval engagements by Christian writers in the North, with their own *imaginations* of their forefathers' lives and beliefs, as well as to the continued productivity of such engagements. Moreover, it can also open our eyes to the fact that these engagements are entangled in their own ambiguities and political agendas, i.e., that they themselves have probably contributed to laying the ground for the essentialist thinking criticized in this book.

Interviews Conducted by Author

Interview A, with an American Asatruer, 2004.
Interview B, with an American Asatruer, 2004.
Interview C, with an American Asatruer, 2004.
Interview D, with a German Asatruer, 2010.
Interview E, with a German Asatruer, 2010.
Interview F, with a German Asatruer, 2010.
Interview G, with a Danish Asatruer, 2010.
Interview H, with a Danish Asatruer, 2010.
Interview I, with a Danish Asatruer, 2010.
Interview J, with a Danish Asatruer, 2010.
Interview K, with Danish Asatruers, 2010.
Interview L, with a German Asatruer, 2010.
Interview M, with a German Asatruer, 2010.
Interview N, with a German Asatruer, 2010.
Interview O, with a Norwegian Asatruer, 2010.
Interview P, with two Norwegian Asatruers, 2010.
Interview Q, with a Norwegian Asatruer, 2010.
Interview R, with a Norwegian Asatruer, 2010.
Interview S, with an Icelandic Asatruer, 2010.
Interview T, with an Icelandic Asatruer, 2010.
Interview U, with an Icelandic Asatruer, 2010.
Interview V, with a Danish Asatruer, 2010.
Interview W, with a Swedish Asatruer, 2010.
Interview with Uwe Ehrenhöfer (Eldaring), March 11, 2010.
Interview with Søren Fisker and Lars Irenessøn (Forn Siðr), April 13, 2010.
Interview with Haimo Grebenstein (VfgH), May 04, 2010.
Interview with Henrik Hallgren (Samfundet Forn Sed), August 28, 2010.
Interview with Jóhanna Harðardóttir (Ásatrúarfélagið), August 12, 2010.
Interview with Ivar Hille (Foreningen Forn Sed), February 25, 2010.
Interview with Óttar Ottóson (Ásatrúarfélagið), August 11, 2010.
Interview with Arne Sjöberg (Breidablikk-Gildet), 1991.
Interview with Egil Stenseth (Bifrost), February 22, 2010.
Interview with six members of Nornirs Ætt, May 9, 2010.

Correspondences with Author

Correspondence with Stephan Grundy (The Troth), 2011 and 2014.
Correspondence with Hilmar Örn Hilmarsson (Ásatrúarfélagið), 2012.
Correspondence with Pete Jennings (Odinshof), 2010.
Correspondence with Duke Meyer (Nornirs Ætt), 2010
Correspondence with Alan Nash (Kith of Yggdrasil), 2010.
Correspondence with Kurt Oertel (Eldaring), 2010.

Bibliography

Aðalsteinsson, Jón Hnefill. *Under the Cloak. A Pagan Ritual Turning Point in the Conversion of Iceland.* 2. extended ed. Reykjavík: Háskólaútgáfan, 1999.

Adler, Margot. *Drawing Down the Moon. Witches, Druids, Goddess-Worshippers, and Other Pagans in America Today* 4. ed. New York: Penguin, 2006 [1979].

Agrell, Sigurd. *Runornas talmystik och dess antika förebild.* Lund: Gleerup, 1927.

Albanese, Catherine L. *Nature Religion in America. From the Algonkian Indians to the New Age.* Chicago History of American Religion, edited by Martin E. Marty. Chicago/London: University of Chicago Press, 1990.

Alvisson, Tiurik. "Brauchtum und Heidentum – eine Annäherung." *Herdfeuer. Die Zeitschrift des Eldaring e.V.* 3, no. 9 (2005): 4–8.

Améry, Carl. *Das Ende der Vorsehung. Die gnadenlosen Folgen des Christentums.* Reinbek b. Hamburg: Rowohlt, 1972.

———. "Deutscher Konservatismus und der faschistische Graben. Versuch einer zeitgeschichtlichen Bilanz." In *Neue soziale Bewegungen: Konservativer Aufbruch im bunten Gewand? Arbeitspapiere einer Diskussionsrunde*, edited by Wolf Schäfer, 11–19. Frankfurt a.M.: Fischer Taschenbuch Verlag, 1983.

Amm, Bettina. "Die Ludendorff-Bewegung im Nationalsozialismus – Annäherung und Abgrenzungsversuche." In *Die völkisch-religiöse Bewegung im Nationalsozialismus. Eine Beziehungs- und Konfliktgeschichte*, edited by Uwe Puschner and Clemens Vollnhals, 127–148. Göttingen: Vandenhoeck & Ruprecht, 2012.

Andraschko, Frank. "Wikinger, Römer und Co. Living History in archäologischen Freilichtmuseen und ihrem weiteren Umfeld." In *Living History in Freilichtmuseen. Neue Wege der Geschichtsvermittlung*, edited by Heike Duisberg, 37–54. Ehestorf: Förderverein des Freilichtmuseums am Kiekeberg, 2008.

Anonymous. "'Gott in uns'. Völkische Religiosität in Deutschland." *Ringhorn. Gemeinschaftsanzeiger des Vereins für germanisches Heidentum e.V.* 41 (2004): 5–6.

Arvidsson, Stefan. *Ariska Idoler. Den indoeuropeiska mytologin som ideologi och vetenskap.* Stockholm/Stehag: Brutus Östlings Bokförlag Symposion, 2000.

———. "Stig Wikander och forskningen om ariska mannaförbund." *CHAOS. Dansknorsk tidsskrift for religionshistoriske studier* 38 (2002): 55–68.

———. *Aryan Idols. Indo-European Mythology as Ideology and Science.* Translated by Sonia Wichmann. Chicago: University of Chicago Press, 2006.

———. *Draksjukan. Mytiska fantasier hos Tolkien, Wagner och de Vries.* Lund: Nordic Academic Press, 2007.

Asad, Talal. "Europe Against Islam. Islam in Europe." *The Muslim World* 87, no. 2 (1997): 183–195.

"Åsatrofellesskapet Bifrost." published by Åsatrufellesskapet Bifrost, 2002.

Aschheim, Steven E. *The Nietzsche Legacy in Germany 1890–1990*. Berkeley: University of California Press, 1992.

Asfrid. "Ahnen." *Ringhorn. Gemeinschaftsanzeiger des Vereins für germanisches Heidentum e.V.* 42 (2004): 3–8.

———. "Warum Asatru?" *Ringhorn. Gemeinschaftsanzeiger des Vereins für germanisches Heidentum e.V.* 48 (2006): 3–7.

———. "Heidnische Grundbegriffe." *Ringhorn. Gemeinschaftsanzeiger des Vereins für germanisches Heidentum e.V.* 51 (2007): 10–11.

———. "Religion der dritten Sorte." *Ringhorn. Gemeinschaftsanzeiger des Vereins für germanisches Heidentum e.V.* 55 (2008): 10–11.

Asprem, Egil. "Heathens Up North. Politics, Polemics, and Contemporary Norse Paganism in Norway." *The Pomegranate* 10, no. 1 (2008): 41–69.

Assion, Peter. "Eugen Fehrle and 'The Mythos of Our Folk'." In *The Nazification of an Academic Discipline. Folklore in the Third Reich*, edited by James R. Dow and Hansjost Lixfeld, 112–134. Bloomington/Indianapolis: Indiana University Press, 1994.

Assmann, Aleida. "Pan, Paganismus und Jugendstil." In *Antike Tradition und Neuere Philologien. Symposium zu Ehren des 75. Geburtstags von Rudolf Sühnel*, edited by Hans-Joachim Zimmermann, 177–195. Heidelberg: Winter, 1984.

Assmann, Jan. *Die Mosaische Unterscheidung oder der Preis des Monotheismus*. Munich: Carl Hanser Verlag, 2003.

———. *Monotheismus und die Sprache der Gewalt*. Vienna: Picus Verlag, 2006.

———. *The Price of Monotheism*. Translated by Robert Savage. Stanford: Stanford University Press, 2010.

Aswynn, Freya. *Leaves of Yggdrasil. Runes, Gods, Magic, Feminine Mysteries, and Folklore*. St. Paul, MN: Llewellyn, 1990.

———. *Die Blätter von Yggdrasil. Runen, Götter, Magie. Nordische Mythologie & weibliche Mysterien*. Translated by Lionel Snell. Vienna: Edition Ananael, 1998.

———. *Northern Mysteries and Magic. Runes and Feminine Powers*. St. Paul, MN: Llewellyn, 2002.

Atkinson, Jane M. "Shamanisms Today." *Annual Review of Anthropology* 21 (1992): 307–330.

Attri, Sarrinder P. "Striden om et tempel – historien bag AYODHYA." *Valravn. Hedensk tidskrift om samfund og kultur* 1 (2002): 4–5.

"Aufruf: Was will die Germanisch-deutsche Religionsgemeinschaft?" *Der Volkserzieher* 26 (1912)

Backes, Uwe, ed. *Rechtsextreme Ideologien in Geschichte und Gegenwart*. Schriften des Hannah-Arendt-Instituts für Totalitarismusforschung, vol. 23, edited by Gerhard Besier. Cologne/Weimar/Vienna: Böhlau, 2003.

Bahn, Peter. "'Natur-Religion'. Dem Leben begegnen." In *Zurück zur Natur-Religion? Wege zur Ehrfurcht vor allem Leben*, edited by Holger Schleip, 234–242. Freiburg i. Br.: Hermann Bauer, 1986.

BIBLIOGRAPHY

Balibar, Étienne. "Is there a 'New Racism'?" In *Race, Nation, Class. Ambiguous Identities*, edited by Étienne Balibar and Immanuel Wallerstein, 17–28. London/New York: Verso, 1991.

Balslev, Søren Staal. "Blodsaristokrati i *Ringenes herre* og *Det mørke tårn*." *Kritik* 202 (2011): 93–101.

Balzli, Johannes. *Guido von List. Der Wiederentdecker uralter arischer Weisheit. Sein Leben und Schaffen.* Vienna etc.: Guido-von-List-Gesellschaft, 1917.

Bar-On, Tamir. *Where Have all the Fascists Gone?* Aldershot-Hamshire: Ashgate, 2007.

Bartsch, Heinz. *Die Wirklichkeitsmacht der Allgemeinen Deutschen Glaubensbewegung der Gegenwart.* Breslau: Ludwig, 1938.

Bassin, Mark. "Blood or Soil? The *Völkisch* Movement, the Nazis, and the Legacy of Geopolitik." In *How Green Were the Nazis? Nature, Environment and Nation in the Third Reich*, edited by Franz-Josef Brüggemeier, Martin Ciok and Thomas Zeller, 204–242. Athens, OH: Ohio University Press, 2005.

Bates, Brian. *The Way of Wyrd. Tales of an Anglo-Saxon Sorcerer.* 2. ed. Carlsbad, CA: Hay House, 2005 [1983].

Bäumler, Alfred. *Männerbund und Wissenschaft.* Berlin: Junker und Dünnhaupt, 1934.

Bauschatz, Paul. *The Well and the Tree. World and Time in Early Germanic Culture.* Amherst: University of Massachusetts Press, 1982.

Bausinger, Hermann. "Zwischen Grün und Braun. Volkstumsideologie und Heimatpflege nach dem Ersten Weltkrieg." In *Religions- und Geistesgeschichte der Weimarer Republik*, edited by Hubert Cancik, 176–214. Düsseldorf: Patmos Verlag, 1982.

———. "Nazi Folk Ideology and Folk Research." In *The Nazification of an Academic Discipline. Folklore in the Third Reich*, edited by James R. Dow and Hansjost Lixfeld, 11–33. Bloomington/Indianapolis: Indiana University Press, 1994.

———. "Das Weihnachtsfest der Volkskunde. Zwischen Mythos und Alltag." In *Politische Weihnacht in Antike und Moderne. Zur ideologischen Durchdringung des Fests der Feste*, edited by Richard Faber and Esther Gajek, 169–181. Würzburg: Königshausen & Neumann, 1997.

Beck, Heinrich. *Zur Geschichte der Gleichung "germanisch – deutsch." Sprache und Namen, Geschichte und Institutionen* Ergänzungsbände zum Reallexikon der germanischen Altertumskunde. Berlin: de Gruyter, 2004a.

———. "Zur Rezeption von Vilhelm Grønbechs Werk im deutschen Sprachraum." In *Verschränkung der Kulturen. Der Sprach- und Literaturaustausch zwischen Skandinavien und den deutschsprachigen Ländern*, edited by Oskar Bandle, Jürg Glauser and Stefanie Würth, 331–350. Tübingen/Basle: Francke, 2004b.

Behrendt, Bernd. "August Julius Langbehn, der 'Rembrandtdeutsche'." In *Handbuch zur 'Völkischen Bewegung' 1871–1918*, edited by Uwe Puschner, Walter Schmitz and Justus H. Ulbricht, 94–113. Munich etc.: K.G. Saur, 1996.

Behringer, Marcel. "Naturreligion und ökologisches Bewusstsein." *Herdfeuer. Die Zeitschrift des Eldaring* e.V. 5, no. 18 (2007): 9–14.
Behringer, Wolfgang. "Das 'Ahnenerbe' der Buchgesellschaft. Zum Neudruck einer Germanen-Edition des NS-Ideologen Otto Höfler." *Sowi* 27 (1998): 283–289.
Beinteinsson, Sveinbjörn. *Correspondence with the Icelandic Ministry of Justice and Church*. Reykjavík: Archive Pétur Pétursson, 1972.
Bemmann, Klaus. *Der Glaube der Ahnen. Die Religion der Deutschen bevor sie Christen wurden*. Essen: Phaidon, 1990.
Benavides, Gustav. "Heroic Deeds and the Extraction of Surplus." In *The Study of Religion under the Impact of Fascism*, edited by Horst Junginger, 263–282. Leiden/Boston: Brill, 2008.
Bengtsson, Eva-Lena. "Die Schweden und Düsseldorf." In *Wahlverwandtschaft. Skandinavien und Deutschland 1800–1914*, edited by Bernd Henningsen, Janine Klein, Helmut Müssener and Solfrid Söderlind, 313–319. Berlin: Jovis, 1997.
Berger, Adriana. "Mircea Eliade. Romanian Fascism and the History of Religions in the United States." In *Tainted Greatness. Antisemitism and Cultural Heroes*, edited by Nancy Harrowitz, 51–74. Philadelphia: Gemple University Press, 1994.
Berger, Helen A. *A Community of Witches. Contemporary Neo-Paganism and Witchcraft in the United States*. Columbia, SC: University of South Carolina Press, 1999.
Bergmann, Klaus. *Agrarromantik und Großstadtfeindschaft*. Meisenheim a. Glan: Hain, 1970.
Berntsen, Bredo. *Grønne linjer. Natur- og miljøvernets historie i Norge*. Oslo: Grøndahl og Dreyer, 1994.
Besser, Joachim. "Die Vorgeschichte des Nationalsozialismus im neuen Licht." *Die Pforte* 2 (1950): 763–784.
Biehl, Janet, and Peter Staudenmaier. *Ecofascism. Lessons from the German Experience*. Edinburgh/San Francisco: AK Press, 1995.
———. *Ecofascism Revisited. Lessons from the German Experience*. Porsgrunn: New Compass Press, 2011.
Birkhan, Helmut. "Otto Höfler. Nachruf." *Almanach der Österreichischen Akademie der Wissenschaften* 138 (1988): 385–406.
Birzer, Bradley J. *J.R.R. Tolkien's Sanctifying Myth. Understanding Middle-Earth*. Wilmington, DE: ISI Books, 2003.
Bjarnadóttir, Birna. *A book of fragments*. Winnipeg, MB: KIND Publishing, 2010.
Black, Robert. "Fidus, Brand, and Bluher. New Paths for Eroticism." *Living Traditions. A Magazine of Radical Traditionalism, Esotericism, Perennialism, Mysticism, Politics and Social Issues* 4, no. 2 (2011): 14–17.
Blain, Jenny. *Nine Worlds of Seid-Magic. Ecstasy and Neo-Shamanism in North European Paganism*. London etc.: Routledge, 2002.

———. "Heathenry, the Past, and Sacred Sites in Today's Britain." In *Modern Paganism in World Cultures. Comparative Perspectives*, edited by Michael Strmiska, 181–208. Santa Barbara, CA: ABC-Clio, 2005.

Blain, Jenny, Douglas Ezzy, and Graham Harvey, eds. *Researching Paganism*. Walnut Creek etc.: Altamira Press, 2004.

Blain, Jenny, and Brian Wallis. *Sacred Sites – Contested Rites/Rights*. Brighton: Sussex Academic Press, 2007.

Blain, Jenny, and Robert J. Wallis. "The 'Ergi' Seidman: Contestations of Gender, Shamanism and Sexuality in Northern Religion Past and Present." *Journal of Contemporary Religion* 15, no. 3 (2000): 395–411.

———. "Heathenry." In *Handbook of Contemporary Paganism*, edited by James R. Lewis and Murphy Pizza, 413–431. Leiden/Boston: Brill, 2009.

Blüher, Hans. *Wandervogel. Geschichte einer Jugendbewegung*. 3 vols. Berlin: Weise, 1912.

———. *Die Rolle der Erotik in der männlichen Gesellschaft. Eine Theorie der menschlichen Staatsbildung nach Wesen und Wert.*, 2 vols., vol. I (Der Typus Inversus), vol. II (Familie und Männerbund). Jena: Diederichs, 1919.

Bly, Robert. *Iron John. A Book about Men*. Vintage Books: New York, 1992 [1990].

Bockhorn, Olaf. "The Battle for the 'Ostmark'. Nazi Folklore in Austria." In *The Nazification of an Academic Discipline. Folklore in the Third Reich*, edited by James R. Dow and Hansjost Lixfeld, 135–155. Bloomington/Indianapolis: Indiana University Press, 1994.

Bogdan, Henrik. "The Influence of Aleister Crowley on Gerald Gardner and the Early Witchcraft Movement." In *Handbook of Contemporary Neopaganism*, edited by James R. Lewis and Murphy Pizza, 81–107. Leiden/Boston: Brill, 2009.

Bohman, Stefan. *Historia, museer och nationalism*. Stockholm: Carlsson, 1997.

Böldl, Klaus. *Der Mythos der Edda. Nordische Mythologie zwischen europäischer Aufklärung und nationaler Romantik*. Tübingen etc.: Francke, 2000.

Bönisch Michael. "Die 'Hammer'-Bewegung." In *Handbuch zur 'Völkischen Bewegung' 1871–1918*, edited by Uwe Puschner, Walter Schmitz and Justus H. Ulbricht, 341–365. Munich etc.: K.G. Saur, 1996.

Bonus, Arthur. *Von Stoecker zu Naumann. Ein Wort zur Germanisierung des Christentums*. Heilbronn: Eugen Salzer, 1896.

Borchmeyer, Dieter. "Wagner und der Antisemitismus." In *Richard-Wagner-Handbuch*, edited by Ulrich Müller and Peter Wapnewski, 137–161. Stuttgart: Kröner, 1986.

Börsch-Supan, Helmut. "Dresden und der Norden I." In *Wahlverwandtschaft. Skandinavien und Deutschland 1800–1914*, edited by Bernd Henningsen, Janine Klein, Helmut Müssener and Solfrid Söderlind, 284–287. Berlin: Jovis, 1997.

Boyer, Régis. "Vikings, Sagas and Wasa Bread." In *Northern Antiquity. The Post-medieval Reception of Edda and Saga*, edited by Andrew Wawn, 69–82. Middlesex: Hisarlik, 1994.

Bradley, Marion Zimmer. *The Mists of Avalon*. New York: Knopf, 1983.

Bramwell, Anna. *Blood and Soil. Walther Darré and Hitler's Green Party*. Abbotsbrook: Kensal Press, 1985.

―――. *Ecology in the 20th Century. A History*. New Haven/London: Yale University Press, 1989.

Braun, Stephan, and Daniel Hörsch. *Rechte Netzwerke – eine Gefahr*. Wiesbaden: VS Verlag, 2004.

Breuer, Stefan. "Die 'Konservative Revolution' – Kritik eines Mythos." *Politische Vierteljahresschrift* 31, no. 4 (1990): 585–607.

―――. *Anatomie der konservativen Revolution*. Darmstadt: Wissenschaftliche Buchgesellschaft, 1993.

―――. *Die Völkischen in Deutschland. Kaiserreich und Weimarer Republik*. Darmstadt: Wissenschaftliche Buchgesellschaft, 2008.

Bringsværd, Tor Åge. *Vår gamle gudelære*. Edited by Dagny Hald and Thorstein Rittun, 12 vols. Oslo: Gyldendal, 1985–1992.

Bronder, Dietrich. *Bevor Hitler kam. Eine historische Studie*. 2. expanded ed. Geneva: Pfeiffer, 1975.

Browning, Christopher S. "Branding Nordicity. Models, Identity and the Decline of Exceptionalism." *Cooperation and Conflict* 1 (2007): 27–51.

Bruder, Reinhold. *Die germanische Frau im Lichte der Runeninschriften und der antiken Historiographie*. Berlin: de Gruyter, 1974.

Brüning, Christian. "Völkische Esoterik und germanisches Heidentum." *Heidnisches Jahrbuch* 2 (2007): 271–352.

―――. "Das Eheverständnis der Germanen und die rechtliche Stellung der Frau." *Heidnisches Jahrbuch* 3 (2008): 221–301.

―――. "Zum Unterschied von Monotheismus und Kosmotheismus." *Heidnisches Jahrbuch* 5 (2011): 217–276.

Brunotte, Ulrike. "Der Männerbund zwischen Gemeinschaft und Gesellschaft. Communitas und Ritual um 1900." In *Diskurse des Theatralen*, edited by Erika Fischer-Lichte, Christian Horn, Sandra Umathum and Matthias Warstat, 231–246. Tübingen/Basle: A. Francke, 2005.

Bruns, Claudia. *Politik des Eros. Der Männerbund in Wissenschaft, Politik und Jugendkultur (1880–1934)*. Cologne: Böhlau, 2008.

Buckley, Joshua. "Relativizing the Patriarchy. The Sacred History of the Feminist Spirituality Movement." *History of Religions* 30, no. 1 (1990): 279–295.

―――. "The Saxon Songwriter. An Interview with Fire & Ice's Ian Read." *Tyr. Myth – Culture – Tradition* 1 (2002): 159–166.

BIBLIOGRAPHY

Buckley, Joshua, Collin Cleary, and Michael Moynihan. "Editorial Preface." *Tyr. Myth – Culture – Tradition* 1 (2002): 7–10.
Budapest, Zsuzsanna, and Diana L. Paxson. *The Celestial Guide to Every Year of Your Life. Discover the Hidden Meaning of Your Age.* Newburyport, MA: Red Wheel/Weiser, 2003.
Butler, Judith. "Sexual Politics, Torture, and Secular Time." *The British Journal of Sociology* 59, no. 1 (2008): 1–23.
Califia, Pat. *Public Sex. The Culture of Radical Sex.* Pittsburgh: Cleis Press, 1994.
Campbell, Colin. "The Cult, the Cultic Milieu and Secularization." *A Sociological Yearbook of Religion in Britain* 5 (1972): 119–136.
Carpenter, Humphrey. *J.R.R. Tolkien: A Biography.* London: George Allen & Unwin, 1977.
Carstensen, Christoph. *Der Volkserzieher. Eine historisch-kritische Untersuchung über die Volkserzieherbewegung Wilhelm Schwaners.* Diss. Jena 1939. Würzburg-Aumühle: Konrad Triltsch, 1941.
Carter, Adam. "Packaging Hate – the New Right Publishing Network." Online Article, *Searchlight*, (2012). Published electronically March 01, 2012. http://www.searchlightmagazine.com/archive/packaging-hate-%E2%80%93-the-new-right-publishing-networks.
Chatellier, Hildegard. "Rasse und Religion bei Houston Stewart Chamberlain." In *Völkische Religion und Krisen der Moderne. Entwürfe 'arteigener' Glaubenssysteme seit der Jahrhundertwende*, edited by Stefanie v. Schnurbein and Justus H. Ulbricht, 184–207. Würzburg: Königshausen & Neumann, 2001.
———. "Wagnerismus in der Kaiserzeit." In *Handbuch zur 'Völkischen Bewegung' 1871–1918*, edited by Uwe Puschner, Walter Schmitz and Justus H. Ulbricht, 575–612. Munich etc.: K.G. Saur, 1996.
Christiansen, Ingolf, Rainer Fromm, and Hartmut Zinser. *Brennpunkt Esoterik. Okkultismus, Satanismus, Rechtsradikalismus.* Hamburg: Behörde für Inneres, 2004.
Christoffersen, Lisbet. "Religion and State. Recognition of Islam and Related Legislation." In *Islam in Denmark. The Challenge of Diversity*, edited by Jørgen S. Nielsen, 57–80. Lanham etc.: Lexington Books, 2010.
Clover, Carol J. "Regardless of Sex. Men, Women, and Power in Early Northern Europe." *Speculum* 68 (1993): 363–387.
———. *The Medieval Saga.* Ithaca, NY: Cornell University Press, 1982.
Cornwell, Bernard. *Death of Kings.* London: Harper Collins, 2011.
———. *The Burning Land.* London: Harper Collins, 2009.
———. *Sword Song.* London: Harper Collins, 2007.
———. *The Lords of the North.* London: Harper Collins, 2006.
———. *The Pale Horseman.* London: Harper Collins, 2005.
———. *The Last Kingdom.* London: Harper Collins, 2004.
Curry, Patrick. *Ecological Ethics. An Introduction.* Cambridge: Polity Press, 2006.

———. *Defending Middle-Earth. Tolkien: Myth and Modernity.* London: HarperCollins, 1998.

Dahl, Göran. "Den 'nya högern' och nyhedendommen." In *Myter om det nordiska – mellan romantik och politik*, edited by Catharina Raudvere, Anders Andrén and Kristina Jennbert. Vägar till Midgård, 127–152. Lund: Nordic Academic Press, 2001.

Dahn, Felix. *Ein Kampf um Rom*. English translations by Lily Wolffsohn (A Struggle for Rome – The Ostrogoths and Belisarius, 1878) and Herb Parker (A Struggle for Rome, 2005). Leipzig: Breitopf & Sartel, 1876–1878.

Daim, Wilfried. *Der Mann der Hitler die Ideen gab. Jörg Lanz von Liebenfels.* 3. ed. Vienna: Überreuter, 1994.

Davidson, Hilda Ellis. *The Lost Beliefs of Northern Europe.* London: Routledge, 1993.

Davidson, Hilda Roderick Ellis. *Gods and Myths of Northern Europe.* Middlesex: Penguin, 1964.

Davies, Peter. "'Männerbund' and 'Mutterrecht'. Herman Wirth, Sophie Rogge-Börner and the *Ura-Linda-Chronik*." *German Life and Letters* 60, no. 1 (2007): 98–115.

Davis, Elizabeth Gould. *The First Sex.* New York: Putnam, 1971.

Dawn, Crystal, and Stephen Flowers. *Carnal Alchemy. A Sado-Magical Exploration of Pleasure, Pain and Self-Transformation.* Smithville, TX: Runa-Raven Press, 1995.

Daxelmüller, Christoph. "Nazi Conception of Culture and the Erasure of Jewish Folklore." In *The Nazification of an Academic Discipline. Folklore in the Third Reich*, edited by James R. Dow and Hansjost Lixfeld, 69–86. Bloomington/Indianapolis: Indiana University Press, 1994.

de Vries, Jan. *Altgermanische Religionsgeschichte.* Berlin/Leipzig: de Gruyter, 1935–37.

Derolez, René. *Götter und Mythen der Germanen.* Einsiedeln: Benzinger, 1963.

———. *Les dieux et la religion des germains.* Paris: Payot, 1962.

Detering, Heinrich. "Was ist Kunstreligion? Systematische und historische Bemerkungen." In *Kunstreligion. Ein ästhetisches Konzept der Moderne in seiner historischen Entfaltung. Vol. I (Der Ursprung des Konzepts um 1800)*, edited by Albert Meier, Allesandro Costazza and Gérard Laudin, 11–27. Berlin: De Gruyter, 2011.

———. "Religion." In *Handbuch Literaturwissenschaft. Vol. I (Gegenstände – Konzepte – Institutionen)*, edited by Thomas Anz, 382–395. Stuttgart/Weimar: Metzler, 2007.

Di Gregorio, Mario A. *From Here to Eternity. Ernst Haeckel and Scientific Faith.* Göttingen: Vandenhoeck & Ruprecht, 2005.

"Die Religionen der 'Völker'." *Ringhorn. Gemeinschaftsanzeiger des Vereins für germanisches Heidentum e.V.* 41 (2004): 3–4.

Diederichsen, Diedrich. "Der Anarch, der Solitär und die Revolte. Rechte Poststrukturalismus-Rezeption in der BRD." In *Rechtsextremismus. Ideologie und Gewalt*, edited by Richard Faber, Hajo Funke and Gerhard Schoenberner, 241–258. Berlin: Edition Hentrich, 1995.

BIBLIOGRAPHY

Diesel, Andreas, and Dieter Gerten. *Looking for Europe. Neofolk und Hintergründe.* Zeltingen-Rachtig: Index Verlag, 2007.

Diesel, Anja A. "Primäre und sekundäre Religion(serfahrung) – das Konzept von Th. Sundermeier und J. Assmann." In *Primäre und sekundäre Religion als Kategorie der Religionsgeschichte des Alten Testaments*, edited by Andreas Wagner. Beihefte zur Zeitschrift für die alttestamentliche Wissenschaft, 23–44. Berlin: Walter de Gruyter, 2006.

Ditt, Karl, and Jane Rafferty. "Nature Conservation in England and Germany 1900–1970. Forerunner of Environmental Protection?" *Contemporary European History* 5, no. 1 (1996): 1–28.

Dominick, Raymond H. III. *The Environmental Movement in Germany. Prophets & Pioneers 1871–1971.* Bloomington: Indiana University Press, 1992.

Dornbusch, Christian. "Von Landsertrommeln und Lärmorgien. Death In June und Kollaborateure." In *Ästhetische Mobilmachung. Dark Wave, Neofolk und Industrial im Spannungsfeld rechter Ideologien*, edited by Andreas Speit, 123–160. Hamburg/Münster: Unrast Verlag, 2002.

Dornbusch, Christian, and Hans-Peter Killguss. *Unheilige Allianzen. Black Metal zwischen Satanismus, Heidentum und Neonazismus.* Hamburg/Münster: Unrast, 2005.

Dörr, Georg. *Muttermythos und Herrschaftsmythos. Zur Dialektik der Aufklärung um die Jahrhundertwende bei den Kosmikern, Stefan George und in der Frankfurter Schule.* Würzburg: Königshausen & Neumann, 2007.

Dronke, Ursula. *The Poetic Edda: Mythological Poems.* Oxford: Clarendon Press, 1997.

———. *The Poetic Edda: Heroic Poems.* Oxford: Clarendon Press, 1969.

Dudek, Peter, and Gerd Jaschke. *Entstehung und Entwicklung des Rechtsextremismus in der Bundesrepublik. Zur Tradition einer besonderen politischen Kultur.* 2 vols., vol. 1. Opladen: Leske und Budrich, 1984.

Dundzila, Vilius Rudra. "Baltic Lithuanian Religion and Romuva." *Tyr. Myth – Culture – Tradition* 3 (2007): 279–360.

Düwel, Klaus. *Runenkunde.* Sammlung Metzler. 4. ed. Stuttgart: Metzler, 2004.

Eatwell, Roger. "The Nature of 'Generic Fascism'. The 'Fascist Minimum' and the 'Fascist Matrix'." In *Comparative Fascist Studies. New Perspectives*, edited by Constantin Iordachi, 134–164. London: Routledge, 2009.

Ebach, Jürgen. "Amputierte Antike. Über Ursachen und Folgen des Antijudaismus in deutscher Altertumswissenschaft und Theologie." In *Antike heute*, edited by Richard Faber and Bernhard Kytzler, 183–196. Würzburg: Königshausen & Neumann, 1992.

Edred. *History of the Rune-Gild.* vol. III (The Reawakening of the Gild 1980–2005). Smithville, TX: The Rune-Gild, 2007. Typskript.

———. *A Book of Troth. Runa-Raven Yrmin-Edition.* Smithville, TX: Runa-Raven Press, 2003.

Ehrentreich, Alfred. "Wilhelm Schwaner (1863-1944) und die Volkserzieherbewegung." *Jahrbuch des Archivs der deutschen Jugendbewegung* 7 (1975): 75-97.

Eibensang. "Ariosophie – was ist das und wo kommt sie her? (Basiert auf: "Ariosophie – ein Überblick" von Hans Schuhmacher 1996. Textliche Neufassung samt Erweiterungen von Duke Meyer 2004)." Accessed November 14, 2011. Nornirs Ætt (web page), http://www.nornirsaett.de/ueberblick-uber-ariosophie/.

Eliade, Mircea. *Shamanism. Archaic Techniques of Ecstasy.* London: Routledge and Kegan Paul, 1964.

———. *Cosmos and History. The Myth of the Eternal Return.* Princeton, NJ: Princeton University Press, 1954.

Eller, Cynthia. *The Myth of Matriarchal Prehistory. Why an Invented Past Won't Give Women a Future.* Boston: Beacon Press, 2000.

Ellwood Jr., Robert S. "Polytheism: Establishment or Liberation Religion." *Journal of the American Academy of Religion* 42 (1974): 344-349.

Emberland, Terje. "Im Zeichen der Hagal-Rune. 'Arteigene' Religion und nationalsozialistischer Aktivismus in Norwegen." In *Die völkisch-religiöse Bewegung im Nationalsozialismus. Eine Beziehungs- und Konfliktgeschichte*, edited by Uwe Puschner and Clemens Vollnhals, 509-526. Göttingen: Vandenhoeck & Ruprecht, 2012.

———. *Religion og rase. Nyhedenskap og nazisme i Norge 1933-1945.* Oslo: Humanist forlag, 2003.

Emmerich, Wolfgang. *Zur Kritik der Volkstumsideologie.* Frankfurt a.M.: Suhrkamp, 1971.

———. "The Mythos of Germanic Continuity." In *The Nazification of an Academic Discipline. Folklore in the Third Reich*, edited by James R. Dow and Hansjost Lixfeld, 34-54. Bloomington/Indianapolis: Indiana University Press, 1994.

Enoksen, Lars Magnar. *Norrøne guder og myter.* Translated by Kåre A. Lie. Oslo: Schibsted Forlag, 2008.

Erhart, Walter. *Familienmänner. Über den literarischen Ursprung moderner Männlichkeit.* Munich: Wilhelm Fink Verlag, 2001.

Eribon, Didier. *Faut-il brûler Dumézil ? Mythologie, science et politique.* Paris: Flammarion, 1992.

Espseth, Astrid. "'Stemplingens konsekvens? En studie av nynazistiske grupperinger'. Master's thesis, University of Oslo, 2007.

Exenberger, Jørgen. "Geomanti i Norge." Accessed November 24, 2011. KultOrg (KulturOrgan Skadinaujo, web page), http://www.kultorg.com/index.php?mact=News,cntnto1,detail,0&cntnto1articleid=175&cntnto1origid=51&cntnto1detailtemplate=artikler.tpl&cntnto1dateformat=%25e.%25m.%25Y&cntnto1returnid=56.

———. "Sarkofagsteinen i Externstein." Accessed November 24, 2011. KultOrg (KulturOrgan Skadinaujo, web page), http://www.kultorg.com/index.php?mact=News,cntnto1,detail,0&cntnto1articleid=213&cntnto1origid=58&cntnto1detailtemplate=artikler.tpl&cntnto1returnid=56.

———. "Sarkofagsteinen i Externstein." *KultOrg (KulturOrgan Skadinaujo)* 8, no. 1 (2008).

Faber, Richard. *'Wir sind Eines.' Über politisch-religiöse Ganzheitsvorstellungen europäischer Faschismen*. Würzburg: Königshausen & Neumann, 2005.

———. *Männerrunde mit Gräfin. Die 'Kosmiker' Derleth, George, Kiages, Schuler, Wolfskehl und Franziska zu Reventlow. Mit einem Nachdruck des 'Schwabinger Beobachters'*. Frankfurt a.M.: Peter Lang, 1994.

Fahrenkrog, Ludwig. *Wölund*. Stuttgart: Greiner und Pfeiffer, 1914.

———. *Baldur*. Stuttgart: Greiner und Pfeiffer, 1908.

———. "Germanentempel III." *Der Volkserzieher* 10 (1908): 77–78.

———. "Germanentempel II." *Der Volkserzieher* 6 (1908): 41–42.

———. "Germanentempel I." *Der Volkserzieher* 6 (1907): 42–43.

Falter, Reinhard. *Natur prägt Kultur. Der Einfluß von Landschaft und Klima auf den Menschen. Zur Geschichte der Geophilosophie*. Munich: Telesma-Verlag, 2006.

———. "Die Götter der Erfahrungsreligion wieder verstehen. Das griechische Beispiel und die heutige Situation." *Heidnisches Jahrbuch* 1 (2006): 90–146.

———. *Natur neu denken. Erfahrung, Bedeutung, Sinn*. Klein Jasedow: Drachen Verlag, 2003.

Faulkes, Anthony. "Introduction." In *Snorri Sturluson: Edda. Prologue and Gylfaginning*, edited by Anthony Faulkes, xi–xxxi. London: Viking Society for Northern Research, 2005.

Ferrari, Fulvio. "Gods of Dreams and Suburbia. Old Norse Deities in Neil Gaiman's Polymythical Universe." In *Eddische Götter und Helden. Milieus und Medien ihrer Rezeption. Eddic Gods and Heroes. The Milieux and Media of Their Reception*, edited by Katja Schulz, 129–142. Heidelberg: Winter, 2011.

Ferry, Luc. *The New Ecological Order*. Translated by Carol Volk. Chicago/London: University of Chicago Press, 1995.

Fink, Gonthier-Louis. "Diskriminierung und Rehabilitierung des Nordens im Spiegel der Klimatheorie." In *Imagologie des Nordens. Kulturelle Konstruktionen von Nördlichkeit in interdisziplinärer Perspektive*, edited by Astrid Arndt, Andreas Blödorn, David Fraesdorff, Annette Weisner and Thomas Winkelmann, 45–107. Frankfurt a.M. etc.: Peter Lang, 2004.

Fischli, Bruno. *Die Deutschen-Dämmerung. Zur Genealogie des völkisch-faschistischen Dramas und Theaters (1897–1933)*. Bonn: Bouvier, 1976.

Flowers, Stephen. "Magic." In *Medieval Scandinavia. An Encyclopedia*, edited by Phillipp Pulsiano, 399–400. New York/London: Garland Publishing, 1993.

———. *Johannes Bureus and Adalruna*. Smithville, TX: Runa-Raven Press, 1998.

Flowers, Stephen E. *Runes and Magic. Magical Formulaic Elements in the Older Runic Tradition*. New York: Peter Lang, 1986.

———. *The Northern Dawn. A History of the Reawakening of the Germanic Spirit*, vol. I (From the Twilight of the Gods to the Sun at Midnight). Smithville, TX: Runa-Raven Press, 2006.

Flowers, Stephen Edred. "The Idea of Integral Culture. A Model for a Revolt against the Modern World." *Tyr. Myth – Culture – Tradition* 1 (2002): 11–21.

Flowers, Stephen, and Michael Moynihan. *The Secret King. The Myth and Reality of Nazi Occultism*. Los Angeles: Feral House, 2007.

FluxEuropa. "Changes. Interview with Robert Taylor." Accessed January 02, 2012. Changes (web page), http://www.nmia.com/~thermite/interviews/flux97.html.

François, Stéphane. "Les paganismes de la Nouvelle Droite (1980–2004)." Doctoral thesis, Université de Lille II- Droit et santé, 2005.

———. *La musique Européenne. Ethnographie politique d'*Harmattan, 2006.

———. "The Euro-Pagan Scene. Between Paganism and Radical Right." *Journal for the Study of Radicalism* 1, no. 2 (2007): 35–54.

Frank, Manfred. "Vom 'Bühnenweihefestspiel' zum 'Thingspiel'. Zur Wirkungsgeschichte der 'Neuen Mythologie' bei Nietzsche, Wagner und Johst." In *Das Fest*, edited by Walter Haug and Rainer Warning, 610–638. Munich: Wilhelm Fink Verlag, 1989.

Frantzen, Allen J. *Desire for Origins. New Language, Old English, and Teaching the Tradition*. New Brunswick/London: Rutgers University Press, 1990.

Frantzen, Allen J., and John D. Niles. *Anglo-Saxonism and the Construction of Social Identity*. University Press of Florida, 1997.

Franz, Sandra. *Die Religion des Grals. Entwürfe arteigener Religiosität im Spektrum von völkischer Bewegung, Lebensform, Okkultismus, Neuheidentum und Jugendbewegung (1871–1945)*. Edition Archiv der deutschen Jugendbewegung. Schwalbach Ts.: Wochenschau-Verlag, 2009.

Frecot, Janos, Johann Friedrich Geist, and Diethart Kerbs. *Fidus 1868–1948. Zur ästhetischen Praxis bürgerlicher Fluchtbewegungen*. Munich: Rogner & Bernhard, 1972.

Fries, Jan. *Helrunar. Ein Handbuch der Runenmagie*. Bad Ischl: Ananael, 1997.

Gaier, Ulrich. "Herder als Begründer des modernen Kulturbegriffs." *Germanisch-Romanische Monatsschrift* 57, no. 4 (2007): 5–18.

Gaiman, Neil. *American Gods*. New York: W. Morrow, 2001.

Gajek, Esther. "Nationalsozialistische Weihnacht. Die Ideologisierung eines Familienfestes durch Volkskundler." In *Politische Weihnacht in Antike und Moderne. Zur ideologischen Durchdringung des Fests der Feste*, edited by Richard Faber and Esther Gajek, 183–205. Würzburg: Königshausen & Neumann, 1997.

———. "'Feiergestaltung' – Zur planmäßigen Entwicklung eines 'aus nationalsozialistischer Weltanschauung geborenen, neuen arteigenen Brauchtums' am Amt Rosenberg." In *Völkische Religion und Krisen der Moderne. Entwürfe 'arteigener' Glaubenssysteme seit der Jahrhundertwende*, edited by Stefanie v. Schnurbein and Justus H. Ulbricht, 386–408. Würzburg: Königshausen & Neumann, 2001.

———. "Germanenkunde und Nationalsozialismus. Zur Verflechtung von Wissenschaft und Politik am Beispiel Otto Höflers." In *Völkische Bewegung – Konservative Revolution – Nationalsozialismus. Aspekte einer politisierten Kultur*, edited by Walter Schmitz and Clemens Vollnhals, 325–356. Dresden: Thelem, 2005.

Gallagher, Anne-Marie. "Weaving a Tangled Web? Pagan Ethics and Issues of History, 'Race' and Ethnicity in Pagan Identity." In *Handbook of Contemporary Neopaganism*, edited by James R. Lewis and Murphy Pizza, 577–626. Leiden/Boston: Brill, 2009.

Gardell, Mattias. *Gods of the Blood. The Pagan Revival and White Separatism*. Durham/London: Duke University Press, 2003.

———. *Islamofobi*. Stockholm: Leopard, 2011.

GardenStone. *Germanische Magie*. Engerda: Arun, 2001.

———. *Germanischer Götterglaube. Asatru – eine moderne Religion aus alten Zeiten*. Engerda: Arun, 2003.

———. "Gleichberechtigung und Asatru." *Herdfeuer. Die Zeitschrift des Eldaring e.V.* 6, no. 20 (2008): 22–29.

Gasman, Daniel. *Haeckel*'ve known it...' On Folklore and Archaeology." In *Archaeology and Folklore*, edited by Amy Gazin-Schwartz and Cornelius Holtorf, 1–25. London/New York: Routledge, 1999.

Geden, Oliver. *Rechte Ökologie. Umweltschutz zwischen Emanzipation und Faschismus*. 2. expanded ed. Berlin: Elefanten Press, 1996.

Gerdmar, Anders. "Germanentum als Überideologie. Deutsch-schwedischer Theologenaustausch unter dem Hakenkreuz." In *Die völkisch-religiöse Bewegung im Nationalsozialismus. Eine Beziehungs- und Konfliktgeschichte*, edited by Uwe Puschner and Clemens Vollnhals, 265–284. Göttingen: Vandenhoeck & Ruprecht, 2012.

Gerhard, Gesine. *Rhinegold*. New York: Bantam, 1994.

———. "Breeding Pigs and People for the Third Reich. Richard Walther Darré's Agrarian Ideology." In *How Green Were the Nazis? Nature, Environment and Nation in the Third Reich*, edited by Franz-Josef Brüggemeier, Martin Ciok and Thomas Zeller, 129–146. Athens, OH: Ohio University Press, 2005.

Gerstner, Alexandra. *Rassenadel und Sozialaristokratie. Adelsvorstellungen in der völkischen Bewegung (1890–1914)*. Berlin: SuKuLTuR, 2003.

Ginzburg, Carlo. *Clues, Myths, and the Historical Method*. Baltimore: Johns Hopkins University Press, 1989.

Gladigow, Burkhard. "Polytheismus und Monotheismus. Zur historischen Dynamik einer europäischen Alternative." In *Polytheismus und Monotheismus in den Religionen des Vorderen Orients*, edited by Manfred Krebernik and Jürgen van Oorschot, 3–21. Münster: Unrast Verlag, 2002.

———. "Polytheismen der Neuzeit." In *Religion und Wahrheit. Religionsgeschichtliche Studien. Festschrift für Gernot Wießner zum 65. Geburtstag*, edited by Bärbel Köhler, 45–59. Wiesbaden: Harrassowitz, 1998.

———. "Religionsgeschichte des Gegenstandes – Gegenstände der Religionsgeschichte." In *Religionswissenschaft. Eine Einführung*, edited by Hartmut Zinser, 6–37. Berlin: Dietrich Reimer Verlag, 1988.

Globisch, Claudia. "'Deutschland uns Deutschen, Türkei den Türken, Israelis raus aus Palästina.' Ethnopluralismus und sein Verhältnis zum Antisemitismus." In *Die Dynamik der europäischen Rechten. Geschichte, Kontinuitäten, Wandel*, edited by Claudia Globisch, Agnieszka Pufelska and Volker Weiß, 203–226. Wiesbaden: VS Verlag, 2011.

Godwin, Joscelyn. *Arktos. The Polar Myth in Science, Symbolism, and Nazi Survival*. Kempton, IL: Adventures Unlimited Press, 1996.

Goodrick-Clarke, Nicholas. *Helena Blavatsky*. Berkeley, CA: North Atlantic Books, 2004.

———. *The Occult Roots of Nazism. The Ariosophists of Austria and Germany 1890–1935*. Wellingborough, Northamptonshire: Aquarian Press, 1985.

Gorsleben, Rudolf John. *Hoch-Zeit der Menschheit. Das Welt-Gesetz der Drei oder Entstehen – Sein – Vergehen in Ursprache – Urschrift – Urglaube. Aus den Runen geschöpft*. Leipzig: Koehler & Amelang, 1930.

Göttner-Abendroth, Heide. *The Dancing Goddess. Principles of a Matriarchal Aesthetic*. Translated by Maureen T. Krause. Boston: Beacon Press, 1991.

———. *Die tanzende Göttin. Prinzipien einer matriarchalen Ästhetik*. 5. ed. Munich: Frauenoffensive, 1991 [1982].

Gotved, Gudrun Victoria. *Asatro. De gamle guder i moderne tid*. Copenhagen: Aschehoug, 2001.

Graf, Friedrich Wilhelm. *Die Wiederkehr der Götter. Religion in der modernen Kultur*. Munich: C.H. Beck, 2004.

———. "Das Laboratorium der Moderne. Zur 'Verlagsreligion' des Eugen Diederichs Verlags." In *Versammlungsort moderner Geister. Der Eugen Diederichs Verlag – Aufbruch ins Jahrhundert der Extreme*, edited by Gangolf Hübinger, 243–298. Munich: Diederichs, 1996.

Graichen, Gisela. *Das Kultplatzbuch. Ein Führer zu den alten Opferplätzen, Heiligtümern und Kultstätten in Deutschland*. Hamburg: Hoffmann & Campe, 1988.

Granholm, Kennet. "'Sons of Northern Darkness.' Heathen Influences in Black Metal and Neofolk Music." *Numen* 58 (2011): 514–544.

———. *Embracing the Dark. The Magic Order of Dragon Rouge – Its Practice in Dark Magic and Meaning Making*. Åbo: Åbo Akademi University Press, 2005.

Graus, František. *Lebendige Vergangenheit. Überlieferung im Mittelalter und in den Vorstellungen vom Mittelalter*. Cologne/Vienna: Böhlau, 1975.

Greer, John Michael. *A World Full of Gods. An Inquiry into Polytheism*. Tucson: ADF Publishing, 2005.

Gregorius, Fredrik. *Modern Asatro. Att konstruera etnisk och kulturell identitet*. Lund: Lunds Universitet, 2008.

Griffin, Roger. *Modernism and Fascism. The Sense of a Beginning under Mussolini and Hitler*. London: Palgrave Macmillan, 2007.
———. *The Nature of Fascism*. London/New York: Routledge, 1991.
Grillo, Ralph D. "Cultural Essentialism and Cultural Anxiety." *Anthropological Theory* 3, no. 2 (2003): 157–173.
Grimm, Birgit. "Wilhelm II. und Norwegen." In *Wahlverwandtschaft. Skandinavien und Deutschland 1800–1914*, edited by Bernd Henningsen, Janine Klein, Helmut Müssener and Solfrid Söderlind, 100–112. Berlin: Jovis, 1997.
Grølheim. "Køn, Sex og Ergi." *Valravn. Hedensk tidskrift om samfund og kultur* 24 (2008): 12–18.
———. "Mangfoldighed og tolerance." *Vølse* 11 (2000): 16–17.
Grølsted, Morten. "Den mosaiske skelnen." *Vølse* 55 (2011): 31–34.
Grønbech, Vilhelm. *The Culture of the Teutons*. 2 vols. London: Oxford University Press, 1931.
———. *Vor Folkeæt i Oldtiden*. 4 vols. Copenhagen: Pìos, 1909–12.
Grottanelli, Cristiano. "War-time Connections: Dumézil and Eliade, Eliade and Schmitt, Schmitt and Evola, Drieu La Rochelle and Dumézil." In *The Study of Religion under the Impact of Fascism*, edited by Horst Junginger, 303–314. Leiden/Boston: Brill, 2008.
Grumke, Thomas, and Bernd Wagner. *Handbuch Rechtsradikalismus*. Cologne: Leske & Budrich, 2002.
Gründer, René. *Blótgemeinschaften. Eine Religionsethnografie des 'germanischen Neuheidentums'*. Würzburg: Ergon, 2010.
———. *Germanisches (Neu-)Heidentum in Deutschland. Entstehung, Struktur und Symbolsystem eines alternativreligiösen Feldes*. Berlin: Logos Verlag, 2008.
Grundtvig, Nikolai Frederik Severin. "Nordens Mytologi, eller Udsigt over Eddalæren for dannede Mænd, der ei selv ere Mytologer." In *N.F.S. Grundtvig, Værker i udvalg*, edited by Georg Christensen and Hal Koch. Copenhagen: Gyldendal, 1940 [1810].
Grundy, Stephan. *Attila's Treasure*. New York: Bantam, 1996.
Grünert, Heinz. *Gustaf Kossina (1858–1931). Vom Germanisten zum Prähistoriker. Ein Wissenschaftler im Kasierreich und in der Weimarer Republik*. Vorgeschichtliche Forschungen, vol. 22. Rahden (Westf.): Verlag Marie Leidorf, 2002.
Gugenberger, Eduard, and Roman Schweidlenka. *Mutter Erde, Magie und Politik. Zwischen Faschismus und neuer Gesellschaft*. Vienna: Verlag für Gesellschaftskritik, 1987.
———. *Bioregionalismus. Bewegung für das 21. Jahrhundert*. Osnabrück: Packpapier Verlag, 1995.
Gullestad, Marianne. *Plausible Prejudice. Everyday Experiences and Social Images of Nation, Culture and Race*. Oslo: Universitetsforlaget, 2006.
Gundarsson, Kveldulf. *Teutonic Magic. The Magical and Spiritual Practices of the Germanic People*. St. Paul, MN: Llewellyn, 1990.

———. *Teutonic Religion. Folk Beliefs & Practices of the Northern Tradition.* St. Paul, MN: Llewellyn, 1993.

———, ed. *Our Troth, by Members of the Troth and Other True Folk.* 2. ed. 2 vols. Vol. I (History and Lore), vol. II (Living the Troth). North Charleston, SC: BookSurge, 2006.

Gundarsson, Kveldúlf Hagan. *Ásatrú. Die Rückkehr der Götter. Zusammengestellt von Kveldúlf Hagan Gundarsson. Deutsche Ausgabe erweitert und herausgegeben von Kurt Oertel.* Rudolstadt: Edition Roter Drache, 2012.

———. *Wotan: The Road to Valhalla.* E-book www.aswynn.co.uk. s.l., n.d.

Gustafsson, Lotten. *Den förtrollade zonen. Lekar med tid, rum och identitet under medeltidsveckan på Gotland.* Nora: Nya Doxa, 2002.

Haeckel, Ernst. *Die Welträthsel. Gemeinverständliche Studien über Monistische Philosophie.* Bonn: E. Strauß 1899.

———. *The Riddle of the Universe at the Close of the Nineteenth Century.* New York: Watts & Co, 1901.

Hagerman, Maja. *Det rena landet. Om konsten att uppfinna sine förfäder.* Stockholm: Prisma, 2006.

Häke, Roland. *Der Fall Herman Wirth – 1978–1981 – im Landkreis Kusel oder: Das verschüttete Demokratiebewußtsein.* Frauenberg b. Marburg: Mutter-Erde-Verlag, 1981.

Halbmayr, Alois. *Lob der Vielheit. Zur Kritik Odo Marquards am Monotheismus.* Salzburger Theologische Studien, vol. 13. Innsbruck: Tyrolia, 2000.

Halle, Uta. *'Die Externsteine sind bis auf weiteres germanisch!' Prähistorische Archäologie im Dritten Reich.* Steinhagen: Verlag für Regionalgeschichte, 2003.

———. "Die Externsteine/Kr. Lippe. Ein Natur- und Kulturdenkmal im Spannungsfeld rechter und esoterischer Ideologie Stuttgart." In *Das Denkmal als Fragment – Das Fragment als Denkmal. Denkmale als Attraktionen. Jahrestagung der Vereinigung der Landesdenkmalpfleger (VdL) und des Verbandes der Landesarchäologen (VdLA) und 75. Tag für Denkmalpflege 10.–13. Juni 2007 in Esslingen a.N.*, edited by Regierungspräsidium Stuttgart – Landesamt für Denkmalpflege, 121–132. Stuttgart: Landesamt für Denkmalpflege, 2008.

———. "'Treibereien wie in der NS-Zeit'. Kontinuitäten des Externsteine-Mythos nach 1945." In *Völkisch und national. Zur Aktualität alter Denkmuster im 21. Jahrhundert*, edited by Uwe Puschner and G. Ulrich Großmann, 195–213. Darmstadt: WBG, 2009.

Hallgren, Henrik. *Det gröna skiftet. Från industrialism till ekologism.* Borås: Recito, 2009.

Halmi, Nicholas. *The Genealogy of the Romantic Symbol.* Oxford: Oxford University Press, 2007.

Hamm, Bernd, and Barbara Rasche. *Bioregionalismus. Ein Überblick.* Schriftenreihe des Zentrums für Europäische Studien. Trier: Zentrum für europäische Studien, 2002.

Hanegraaff, Wouter J. *New Age Religion and Western Culture. Esotericism in the Mirror of Secular Thought.* Leiden/New York/Cologne: Brill, 1996.

Hanke, Edith, and Gangolf Hübinger. "Von der 'Tat'-Gemeinde zum 'Tat'-Kreis. Die Entwicklung einer Kulturzeitschrift." In *Versammlungsort moderner Geister. Der Eugen Diederichs Verlag – Aufbruch ins Jahrhundert der Extreme*, edited by Gangolf Hübinger, 299–334. Munich: Diederichs, 1996.

Hansen, Martin P. "Blótets liturgi, før og nu." *Vølse* 45 (2008a): 20–22.

———. "Politik og religion." *Vølse* 44 (2008b): 23–24.

Hard, Gerhard. "'Hagia Chora'. Von einem neuerdings wieder erhobenen geomantischen Ton in der Geographie." *Erdkunde. Archiv für wissenschaftliche Geographie* 55, no. 2 (2001): 172–198.

Hardtwig, Wolfgang, ed. *History Sells! Angewandte Geschichte als Wissenschaft und Markt*. Stuttgart: Steiner, 2009.

Harris, Joseph. "Love and Death in the *Männerbund*. An Essay with Special Reference to the *Bjarkamál* and *The Battle of Maldon*." In *Heroic Poetry in the Anglo-Saxon Period. Studies in Honor of Jess B. Bessinger, Jr.*, edited by Helen Damico and John Leyerle. Studies in Medieval Culture. Kalamazoo, MI: Medieval Institute Publications, Western Michigan University, 1993.

Harrison, Harry, and John Holm. *One King's New Religion*, edited by Wilhelm Hauer, Karl Heim and Karl Adam. New York: The Abingdon Press, 1937.

———. *King and Emperor* [König und Imperator (2001)]. New York: Tor Books, 1996.

Heesch, Florian. *Metal for Nordic Men. Amon Amarth's Guide*. London: Hodder & Stoughton, 1998.

———. *One King's Way* [Der Pfad des Königs (2001)]. New York: Tor Books, 1995.

———. *The Hammer and the Cross* [Der Hammer des Nordens (2001)]. New York: Tor Books, 1993.

Hartwich, Wolf-Daniel. *Romantischer Antisemitismus. Von Klopstock bis Richard Wagner*. Göttingen: Vandenhoeck & Ruprecht, 2005.

———. *Deutsche Mythologie. Die Erfindung einer nationalen Kunstreligion*. Berlin/Vienna: Philo, 2000.

Harvey, Graham. *Animism. Respecting the Living World*. London: Hurst, 2005.

———. *Listening People, Speaking Earth. Contemporary Paganism*. London: Hurst & Company, 1997.

Haschemi, Yekani Elahe. *The Privilege of Crisis. Narratives of Masculinities in Colonial and Postcolonial Literature, Photography and Film*. Frankfurt/New York: Campus, 2011.

Hasenfratz, Hans-Peter. "Der indo-germanische Männerbund." *Zeitschrift für Religions- und Geistesgeschichte* 34 (1982): 148–163.

Hauer, Wilhelm. "Origin of the German Faith Movement. An Alien or a German Faith? The Semitic Character of Christianity." In *Germany's New Religion*, edited by Wilhelm Hauer, Karl Heim and Karl Adam. New York: The Abingdon Press, 1937.

Heesch, Florian. "Die Wilde Jagd als Identitätskonstruktion im Black Metal." In *Eddische Götter und Helden. Milieus und Medien ihrer Rezeption. Eddic Gods and*

Heroes. The Milieux and Media of Their Reception, edited by Katja Schulz, 335–366. Heidelberg: Winter, 2011.

———. "Metal for Nordic Men. Amon Amarth's Representations of Vikings." In *The Metal Void. First Gatherings*, edited by Niall W.R. Scott and Imke v. Helden, 71–80. Oxford: Inter-Disciplinary Press, 2010.

Heidenreich, Gert, and Juliane Wetzel. "Die organisierte Verwirrung. Nationale und internationale Verbindungen im rechtsextremistischen Spektrum." In *Rechtsextremismus in der Bundesrepublik. Voraussetzungen, Zusammenhänge, Wirkungen*, edited by Wolfgang Benz, 151–168. Frankfurt a.M., 1989.

Heimgest CG. "Continuing Tradition." Accessed April 18, 2014. The Odinic Rite (web page), http://www.odinic-rite.org/main/continuing-tradition/.

Hein, Peter Ulrich. "Völkische Kunstkritik." In *Handbuch zur 'Völkischen Bewegung' 1871–1918*, edited by Uwe Puschner, Walter Schmitz and Justus H. Ulbricht, 613–633. Munich etc.: K.G. Saur, 1996.

———. *Die Brücke ins Geisterreich. Künstlerische Avantgarde zwischen Kulturkritik und Faschismus*. Reinbek b. Hamburg: Rowohlt, 1992.

Heinrich, Fritz. "Bernhard Kummer (1897–1962). The Study of Religions Between Religious Devotion for the Ancient Germans, Political Agitation, and Academic Habitus." In *The Study of Religion under the Impact of Fascism*, edited by Horst Junginger, 229–262. Leiden/Boston: Brill, 2008.

———. *Die deutsche Religionswissenschaft und der Nationalsozialismus. Eine ideologiekritische und wissenschaftsgeschichtliche Untersuchung*. Petersberg: Michael Imhof Verlag, 2002.

Heizmann, Wilhelm. "Germanische Männerbünde." In *Geregeltes Ungestüm. Bruderschaften und Jugendbünde bei indogermanischen Völkern*, edited by Rahul Peter Das and Gerhard Meiser, 117–138. Dresden: Hempen, 2002.

Heller, Rolf. *Die literarische Darstellung der Frau in den Isländersagas*. Halle: Niemeyer, 1958.

Henderson, Peter. "Frank Browne and the Neo-Nazis." *Labour History* 89 (2005): http://www.historycooperative.org/journals/lab/89/henderson.html.

Hengest/OR. "In Memory of John Yeowell – 'Stubba.'" Accessed October 24, 2011. The Odinic Rite (web page), http://www.odinic-rite.org/main/in-memory-of-john-yeowell-%e2%80%9cstubba%e2%80%9d/.

Henningsen, Bernd. "Johann Gottfried Herder and the North. Elements of a Process of Construcion." In *Northbound. Travels, Encounters, and Constructions 1700–1830*, edited by Karen Klitgaard Poulsen, 129–150. Aarhus: Aarhus University Press, 2007.

Henriksen, Vera. *Historiske romaner*. 10 vols. Oslo: Aschehoug, 1980.

Hensley, Chad. "Wails from a Haunted Winter. Interview with Aghast." In *Esoterra. The Journal of Extreme Culture*, edited by Chad Hensley, 256–260. s.l.: Creation Books, 2011.

Hentschel, Willibald. *Varuna. Das Gesetz des aufsteigenden und sinkenden Lebens in der Geschichte.* Leipzig: Matthes, 1902.

Herder, Johann Gottfried. "Iduna, oder der Apfel der Verjüngung." *Die Horen* 5, no. 2 (1796): 1–29.

Herf, Jeffrey. *Reactionary Modernism. Technology, Culture and Politics in Weimar and the Third Reich.* Cambridge: Cambridge University Press, 1984.

Hermand, Jost. *Grüne Utopien in Deutschland. Zur Geschichte des ökologischen Bewußtseins.* Frankfurt a.M.: Fischer, 1991.

Hethey, Raimund, and Peter Kratz. *In bester Gesellschaft. Antifa-Recherche zwischen Konservativismus und Neo-Faschismus.* Göttingen: Die Werkstatt, 1991.

Heusler, Andreas. *Germanentum. Vom Lebens- und Formgefühl der alten Germanen.* Heidelberg: Winter, n.d. (ca. 1942).

Hieronimus, Ekkehard. "Jörg Lanz von Liebenfels." In *Handbuch zur 'Völkischen Bewegung' 1871–1918*, edited by Uwe Puschner, Walter Schmitz and Justus H. Ulbricht, 131–148. Munich etc.: K.G. Saur, 1996.

Hirsch, Kurt. *Rechts von der Union. Personen, Organisationen, Parteien seit 1945. Ein Lexikon.* Munich: Knesebeck & Schuler, 1989.

Höfler, Otto. "Zwei Grundkräfte im Wodankult." In *Otto Höfler: Kleine Schriften. Ausgewählte Arbeiten zur germanischen Altertumskunde und Religionsgeschichte, zur Literatur des Mittelalters, zur germanischen Sprachwissenschaft sowie zur Kulturphilosophie und -morphologie*, edited by Helmut Birkhan, 17–28. Hamburg: Helmut Buske Verlag, 1992 [1974].

———. "Rez.: Jan de Vries, Altgermanische Religionsgeschichte." In *Otto Höfler: Kleine Schriften. Ausgewählte Arbeiten zur germanischen Altertumskunde und Religionsgeschichte, zur Literatur des Mittelalters, zur germanischen Sprachwissenschaft sowie zur Kulturphilosophie und -morphologie*, edited by Helmut Birkhan, 308–343. Hamburg: Helmut Buske Verlag, 1992 [1959].

———. *Germanisches Sakralkönigtum.* Tübingen: Niemeyer, 1952.

———. *Kultische Geheimbünde der Germanen.* Frankfurt a.M.: Diesterweg, 1934.

Hoppál, Mihály. "Urban Shamans. A Cultural Revival." In *Studies on Shamanism*, edited by Anna-Leena Siikala and Mihály Hoppál, 197–209. Helsinki/Budapest: Finnish Anthropological Society, 1992.

Horsman, Reginald. *Race and Manifest Destiny. The Origins of American Racial Anglo-Saxonism.* Cambridge, MA: Harvard University Press, 1981.

Høst, Annette, and Karen Kelly. "Keep it Close to Nature. Karen Kelly Interviews Annette Høst on Seiðr, the Old Norse Way of Shamanic Magic." *Spirit Talk* 9 (1999): Republished 2010 on http://www.shamanism.dk/closetonature.htm.

Howe, Ellic, and Helmut Möller. *Merlin Peregrinus. Vom Untergrund des Abendlandes.* Würzburg: Königshausen & Neumann, 1986.

Hoyningen-Huene, Stefan v. *Religiosität bei rechtsextrem orientierten Jugendlichen.* Münster/Hamburg/London: LIT Verlag, 2003.

Hufenreuter, Gregor. *Philipp Stauff. Ideologe, Agitator und Organisator im völkischen Netzwerk des Wilhelminischen Kaiserreichs. Zur Geschichte des Deutschvölkischen Schriftstellerverbandes, des Germanen-Ordens und der Guido-von-List-Gesellschaft.* Frankfurt a.M.: Peter Lang, 2011.

Hume, David. *The Natural History of Religion. Edited with an introduction by H.E. Root.* London: Adam and Charles Black, 1956.

Hundseder, Franziska. *Wotans Jünger. Neuheidnische Gruppen zwischen Esoterik und Rechtsradikalismus.* Munich: Heyne, 1998.

Hunger, Ulrich. *Die Runenkunde im Dritten Reich. Ein Beitrag zur Wissenschafts- und Ideologiegeschichte des Nationalsozialismus.* Frankfurt a.M. : Lang, 1984.

Huntington, Samuel P. *The Clash of Civilizations and the Remaking of World Order.* New York: Simon and Schuster, 1996.

Hutton, Ronald. *Witches, Druids and King Arthur.* London/New York: Hambledon and London, 2003.

———. *The Triumph of the Moon. A History of Modern Pagan Witchcraft.* Oxford/New York: Oxford University Press, 1999.

———. "The Neolithic Great Goddess. A Study in Modern Tradition." *Antiquity* 71 (1997): 91–99.

International Asatru-Summer camp 2009. "We Proudly Present: The Programme!" Accessed January 02, 2012. IASC Herald, http://www.asatru-summercamp.eu/docs/IASC_Herald-June-09.pdf.

Jacobsen, Brian Arly. "Muslims in Denmark. A Critical Evaluation." In *Islam in Denmark. The Challenge of Diversity*, edited by Jørgen S. Nielsen, 31–56. Lanham etc.: Lexington Books, 2010.

Jahn, Thomas, and Peter Wehling. *Ökologie von rechts. Nationalismus und Umweltschutz bei der Neuen Rechten und den 'Republikanern'.* Frankfurt a.M./New York: Campus, 1990.

Jahnke, Alex. "Zieh mit den Wölfen. Krieger in der Vergangenheit und Gegenwart." *Herdfeuer. Die Zeitschrift des Eldaring e.V.* 7, no. 26 (2009): 8–17.

Jakhelln, Cornelius. *Raseri. En hvitings forsøk på en selvbiosofi.* Oslo: Cappelen Damm, 2011.

———. *Gudenes fall.* Oslo: Cappelen, 2007.

Jakobsen, Merete Demant. *Shamanism. Traditional and Contemporary Approaches to the Mastery of Spirits and Healing.* New York/Oxford: Berghahn Books, 1999.

Jansson, Bo. "Nordens poetiska reception av Europas reception av det nordiska." In *The Waking of Angantyr. The Scandinavian Past in European Culture – Den nordiske fortid i europæisk kultur*, edited by Else Roesdahl and Preben Meulengracht Sørensen, 192–208. Aarhus: Aarhus University Press, 1996.

Jennings, Pete. *The Norse Tradition. A Beginner's Guide*. London: Hodder & Stoughton, 1998.
Jensen, Jack. "Om æren, freden og lykken." *Valravn. Hedensk tidskrift om samfund og kultur* 12 (2005): 4–7.
Jesch, Judith. *Women in the Viking Age*. Woodbridge: Boydell Press, 1991.
Jochens, Jenny. "Consent in Marriage. Old Norse Law, Life, and Literature." *Scandinavian Studies* 58 (1968): 142–176.
Johansson, Urban. "Innkalling til Pride." *Mimers Källa* 21 (2009): 12.
Jonsson, Eggert Solberg. "Ásatrú á Íslandi við upphaf 21. aldar. Uppruni, heimsmynd og helgiathafnir." Master's thesis, University of Iceland, 2010.
Jung, Carl Gustav. "Wotan." *Neue Schweizer Rundschau* III (Neue Folge), no. 11 (1936): 657–669.
Junginger, Horst. *Von der philologischen zur völkischen Religionswissenschaft. Das Fach Religionswissenschaft an der Universität Tübingen von der Mitte des 19. Jahrhunderts bis zum Ende des Dritten Reiches*. Contubernium. Tübinger Beiträge zur Universitäts- und Wissenschaftsgeschichte, vol. 51. Stuttgart: Franz Steiner Verlag, 1999.
Junker, Daniel. *Gott in uns! Die Germanische Glaubens-Gemeinschaft. Ein Beitrag zur Geschichte völkischer Religiosität in der Weimarer Republik*. Hamburg: Verlag Daniel Junker, 2002.
Kagel, Nils. "Geschichte leben und erleben. Von der Interpretation historischer Alltagskultur in deutschen Freilichtmuseen." In *Living History in Freilichtmuseen. Neue Wege der Geschichtsvermittlung*, edited by Heike Duisberg, 9–22. Ehestorf: Förderverein des Freilichtmuseums am Kiekeberg, 2008.
Kalmar, Ivan Davidson. "Anti-Semitism and Islamophobia. The Formation of a Secret." *Human Architecture. Journal of the Sociology of Self-Knowledge* VII, no. 2 (2009): 135–144.
Kammerer, Iris. *Wolf und Adler*. Munich: Heyne, 2007.
———. *Der Tribun*. Munich: Heyne, 2004.
———. *Die Schwerter des Tiberius*. Munich: Heyne, 2004.
Kaplan, Jeffrey, ed. *Encyclopedia of White Power. A Sourcebook on the Radical Racist Right*. Walnut Creek: Altamira Press, 2000.
———. *Radical Religion in America. Millenarian Movements from the Far Right to the Children of Noah*. New York: Syracuse University Press, 1997.
Karlsson, Thomas. *Uthark. Nightside of the Runes*. Sundbyberg: Ouroboros Productions, 2002.
Kater, Michael H. *Das 'Ahnenerbe' der SS 1935–1945. Ein Beitrag zur Kulturpolitik des Dritten Reiches*. Stuttgart: Deutsche Verlags-Anstalt, 1974.
Kellner, Beate. *Grimms Mythen. Studien zum Mythosbegriff und seiner Anwendung in Jacob Grimms Deutscher Mythologie*. Frankfurt a.M.: Peter Lang, 1994.

Kerbs, Diethart, and Jürgen Reulecke. *Handbuch der deutschen Reformbewegungen 1880–1933*. Wuppertal: Peter Hammer Verlag, 1998.

Kershaw, Kris. *Der einäugige Gott. Odin und die indogermanischen Männerbünde*. Translated by Baal Müller. Engerda: Arun, 2007.

———. *The One-eyed God. Odin and the (Indo-) Germanic Männerbünde*. Journal of Indo-European Studies Monograph. Washington: Institute for the Study of Man, 2000.

Ketelsen, Uwe-K. "Das völkisch-heroische Drama." In *Handbuch des deutschen Dramas*, edited by Walter Hinck, 418–430. Düsseldorf: Bagel, 1980.

Kienle, Richard v. *Germanische Gemeinschaftsformen*. Reihe B: Fachwissenschaftliche Untersuchungen. Abteilung: Arbeiten zur Germanenkunde, edited by Forschungs- und Lehrgemeinschaft 'Das Ahnenerbe', vol. 4. Stuttgart: Kohlhammer, 1939.

Kippenberg, Hans Gerhard. *Die Entdeckung der Religionsgeschichte. Religionswissenschaft und Moderne*. Munich: Beck, 1997.

Kirchhoff, Jochen. *Nietzsche, Hitler und die Deutschen. Die Perversion des neuen Zeitalters. Vom unerlösten Schatten des Dritten Reiches*. Berlin: Edition Dionysos, 1990.

Kittel, Erich. *Die Externsteine als Tummelplatz der Schwarmgeister und im Urteil der Wissenschaft*. Detmold: Naturwissenschaftlicher Verein Detmold, 1965.

Klinger, Cornelia. *Flucht Trost Revolte. Die Moderne und ihre ästhetischen Gegenwelten*. Munich: Hanser, 1995.

Koch, Klaus. "Monotheismus als Sündenbock?" In *Die Mosaische Unterscheidung oder der Preis des Monotheismus*, edited by Jan Assmann, 221–238. Munich: Carl Hanser Verlag, 2003.

Koefoed, Lasse, and Kirsten Simonsen. "The Price of Goodness. Everyday Nationalist Narratives in Denmark." *Antipode* 2 (2007): 310–330.

Kohl, Karl-Heinz. "Coming Back to One's Own. What Happens to Tradition in Neo-traditionalist Movements?" In *The Making and Unmaking of Differences. Anthropological, Sociological and Philosophical Perspectives*, edited by Richard Rottenburg, Burkhard Schnepel and Shingo Shimada, 97–107. Bielefeld: transcript, 2006.

Körber, Lill-Ann. *Badende Männer. Der nackte männliche Körper in der skandinavischen Malerei und Fotografie des frühen 20. Jahrhunderts*. Bielefeld: transcript, 2013.

Kotowski, Elke-Vera. "Verkünder eines 'heidnischen' Antisemitismus. Die Kosmiker Ludwig Klages und Alfred Schuler." In *'Verkannte Brüder'? Stefan George und das deutsch-jüdische Bürgertum zwischen Jahrhundertwende und Emigration*, edited by Gert Mattenklott, Michael Philipp and Julius H. Schoeps. Hildesheim: Georg Olms Verlag, 2001.

Kratz, Peter. *Die Götter des New Age. Im Schnittpunkt von 'Neuem Denken', Faschismus und Romantik*. Berlin: Elefanten Press, 1994.

Krautkrämer, Felix. "Wachwechsel in Coburg. Politische Publizistik: Der Verleger Dietmar Munier hat offenbar das Traditionsmagazin 'Nation & Europa' gekauft." *Junge Freiheit* 42, no. 09 (2009): http://www.jf-archiv.de/archiv09/200942100922.htm.

Kreis, Georg. "Das Festspiel – ein antimodernes Produkt der Moderne." In *Das Festspiel. Formen, Funktionen, Perspektiven*, edited by Bernd Engler and Georg Kreis, 186–208. Willisau: Theaterkultur-Verlag, 1988.

Kühne-Spicer, Berna. "Der Odinic Rite Deutschland – Neuheidentum im Spannungsfeld neurechter Religiosität." Accessed February 26, 2014. Rabenclan e.V. (web page), http://www.rabenclan.de/index.php/Magazin/KuehneSpicerORDKap1.

Kummer, Bernhard. "Die Bedeutung des altnordischen Schrifttums für Religionsgeschichte und Missionskunde." *Zeitschrift für Missionskunde und Religionswissenschaft* 43, no. 10, 11 (1928): 289–306, 321–334.

———. *Die germanische Weltanschauung nach altnordischer Überlieferung. Vortrag, gehalten im Auftrag der 'Vereinigung der Freunde germanischer Vorgeschichte' in Detmold am 10. Juni 1930*. Leipzig: Adolf Klein, 1933a.

———. *Die weibliche Gottheit bei den Germanen*. Leipzig: Adolf Klein, 1933b.

———. *Midgards Untergang. Germanischer Kult und Glaube in den letzten heidnischen Jahrhunderten*. Leipzig: Adolf Klein, 1935.

Kummer, Siegfried Adolf. *Rune Magic*. Edited and translated by Edred Thorsson. Smithville, TX: Runa Raven, 1993.

Kunz, Inge. "Herrenmenschentum, Neugermanen und Okkultismus. Eine soziologische Bearbeitung der Schriften von Guido List." Unpublished doctoral thesis, Universität Wien, 1961.

Lächele, Rainer. "Germanisierung des Christentums – Heroisierung Christi: Arthur Bonus – Max Bewer – Julius Bode." In *Völkische Religion und Krisen der Moderne. Entwürfe 'arteigener' Glaubenssysteme seit der Jahrhundertwende*, edited by Stefanie v. Schnurbein and Justus H. Ulbricht, 165–183. Würzburg: Königshausen & Neumann, 2001.

Langbehn, Julius. *Rembrandt als Erzieher. Von einem Deutschen*. Leipzig: Hirschfeld, 1890.

Lanwerd, Susanne. "Zur Bedeutung von 'Feministischer Spiritualität' in der Literatur des New Age." In *Die Religion von Oberschichten. Religion – Profession – Intellektualismus*, edited by Peter Antes and Donate Pahnke, 269–278. Marburg: diagonal-Verlag, 1989.

———. *Mythos, Mutterrecht und Magie. Zur Geschichte religionswissenschaftlicher Begriffe*. Berlin: Dietrich Reimer, 1993.

———. "Im Namen der Göttin? Überlegungen zur Faszinationskraft antiker Göttinnenbilder." In *Kybele – Prophetin – Hexe. Religiöse Frauenbilder und Weiblichkeitskonzeptionen*, edited by Richard Faber and Susanne Lanwerd, 147–160. Würzburg: Königshausen & Neumann, 1997.

Larsen, Peter Nørgaard. "Dänische Künstler in Düsseldorf – Düsseldorf in der dänischen Kunst." In *Wahlverwandtschaft. Skandinavien und Deutschland 1800–1914*, edited by Bernd Henningsen, Janine Klein, Helmut Müssener and Solfrid Söderlind, 320–323. Berlin: Jovis, 1997.

Leitane, Iveta. "Haralds Biezais (1909–1995). Ein Religionshistoriker zwischen Theologie und Religionswissenschaft." In *The Study of Religion under the Impact of Fascism*, edited by Horst Junginger, 511–542. Leiden/Boston: Brill, 2008.

Lengefeld, Cecilia. *Der Maler des glücklichen Heims. Zur Rezeption Carl Larssons im wilhelminischen Deutschland*. Heidelberg: Winter, 1993.

———. "Der schwedische und der deutsche Carl Larsson." In *Wahlverwandtschaft. Skandinavien und Deutschland 1800–1914*, edited by Bernd Henningsen, Janine Klein, Helmut Müssener and Solfrid Söderlind, 413–418. Berlin: Jovis, 1997.

Levin, David. *Richard Wagner, Fritz Lang, and the Nibelungen. The Dramaturgy of Disavowal*. Princeton, NJ: Princeton University Press, 1998.

Lichtblau, Klaus. "'Innerweltliche Erlösung vom Rationalen' oder 'Reich diabolischer Herrlichkeit'? Zum Verhältnis von Kunst und Religion bei Georg Simmel und Max Weber." In *Kunst und Religion. Studien zur Kultursoziologie und Kulturgeschichte*, edited by Richard Faber and Volker Krech, 51–78. Würzburg: Königshausen & Neumann, 1999.

Liebman, Wayne. *Tending the Fire. The Ritual Mens Group*. St. Paul, MN: Ally Press, 1991.

Lillebø, Sandra. "Dr. Jakhelln og Mr. Hyde." *Klassekampen*, December 02, 2011.

Lincoln, Bruce. *Theorizing Myth. Narrative, Ideology, and Scholarship*. Chicago/London: University of Chicago Press, 1999.

———. "Dumézil, Ideology, and the Indo-Europeans." *ZfR. Zeitschrift für Religionswissenschaft* 6, no. 2 (1998): 221–230.

———. "Dumézil, Georges." Accessed February 06, 2015. Encyclopaedia Iranica, http://www.iranica.com/articles/dumezil.

Lindh, Håkan. "En HBT-hedning taler." *Mimers Källa* 21 (2009): 13.

Lindqvist, Galina. *Shamanic Performances on the Urban Scene. Neo-Shamanism in Contemporary Sweden*. Stockholm Studies in Social Anthropology, vol. 39. Stockholm: Department of Social Anthropology, 1997.

Linse, Ulrich. "Der Chiemsee-Goldkessel – ein völkisch-religiöses Kultobjekt aus der NS-Zeit? The State of the Affairs." In *Die völkisch-religiöse Bewegung im Nationalsozialismus. Eine Beziehungs- und Konfliktgeschichte*, edited by Uwe Puschner and Clemens Vollnhals, 527–595. Göttingen: Vandenhoeck & Ruprecht, 2012.

———. "'Fundamentalistischer' Heimatschutz. Die 'Naturphilosophie' Reinhard Falters." In *Völkisch und national. Zur Aktualität alter Denkmuster im 21. Jahrhundert*, edited by Uwe Puschner and G. Ulrich Großmann, 156–178. Darmstadt: WBG, 2009.

———. "Nordisches in der deutschen Lebensreformbewegung." In *Wahlverwandtschaft. Skandinavien und Deutschland 1800–1914*, edited by Bernd Henningsen, Janine Klein, Helmut Müssener and Solfrid Söderlind, 397–407. Berlin: Jovis, 1997.

BIBLIOGRAPHY

———. *Ökopax und Anarchie. Eine Geschichte der ökologischen Bewegungn in Deutschland*. Munich: dtv, 1986.

———. *Zurück, o Mensch, zur Mutter Erde. Landkommunen in Deutschland 1890–1933*. Munich: dtv, 1983.

Linzie, Bil. "Germanic Spirituality." Accessed December 06, 2011. Temple of Our Heathen Gods (web page), http://heathengods.com/library/bil_linzie/germanic_spirituality.pdf.

———. "Reconstructionism's Role in Modern Heathenry." Accessed December 06, 2011. Seidhman (web page), http://www.angelfire.com/nm/seidhman/reconstruction-c.pdf.

List Guido v. *The Secret of the Runes*. Edited and translated by Stephen E. Flowers. Rochester, VT: Destiny Books, 1988.

Löchte, Anne. *Johann Gottfried Herder. Kulturtheorie und Humanitätsidee der Ideen, Humanitätsbriefe und Adrastea*. Würzburg: Königshausen & Neumann, 2005.

Lönnroth, Lars. "The Academy of Odin. Grundtvig's Political Instrumentalization of Old Norse Mythology." In *Idee – Gestalt – Geschichte. Studien zur europäischen Kulturtradition. Festschrift für Klaus von See*, edited by Gerd Wolfgang Weber, 339–354. Odense: Odense University Press, 1988.

Lord, Garman. *The Way of the Heathen. A Handbook of Greater Theodism*. Watertown, NY: Theod, 2000.

———. "The Evolution of Theodish Belief. Part I." *THEOD Magazine* Lammas (1995).

———. "The Evolution of Theodish Belief. Part II." *THEOD Magazine* Hallows (1995).

Losehand, Joachim. "'The Religious Harmony in the Ancient World.' Vom Mythos religiöser Toleranz in der Antike." *Göttinger Forum für Altertumswissenschaft* 12 (2009): 99–132.

Löw, Luitgard. "På oppdrag for Himmler. Herman Wirths ekspedisjoner til Skandinavias helleristninger." In *Jakten på Germania. Fra nordensvermeri til SS-arkeologi*, edited by Terje Emberland and Jorunn Sem Fure, 180–201. Oslo: Humanist forlag, 2009.

———. "Völkische Deutungen prähistorischer Sinnbilder. Herman Wirth und sein Umfeld." In *Völkisch und national. Zur Aktualität alter Denkmuster im 21. Jahrhundert*, edited by Uwe Puschner and G. Ulrich Großmann, 214–232. Darmstadt: WBG, 2009.

Löwenberg, Dieter. "Willibald Hentschel (1858–1947), seine Pläne zur Menschenzüchtung, sein Biologismus und Antisemitismus." Dissertation, Universität Mainz, 1978.

Lück, Kerstin. "Der Wunsch nach Verzauberung. Religionswissenschaftliche Überlegungen zur 'spirituellen Frauenbewegung.'" In *Kybele – Prophetin – Hexe. Religiöse Frauenbilder und Weiblichkeitskonzeptionen*, edited by Richard Faber and Susanne Lanwerd, 271–287. Würzburg: Königshausen & Neumann, 1997.

Lückewerth, Thomas. "Hermann Hendrich – Mythenmaler und Tempelkünstler." *Heidnisches Jahrbuch* 1 (2006): 190–231.

Lundgreen-Nielsen, Flemming. "Gundtvig's Norse Mythological Imagery – An Experiment That Failed." In *Northern Antiquity. The Post-medieval Reception of Edda and Saga*, edited by Andrew Wawn, 41–68. Middlesex: Hisarlik, 1994.

Madsen, Peter. *Valhalla* [in Danish]. 15 vols. Copenhagen: Carlsen Comics, 1979–2009.

Maes, Jochen. *Dokumentation: 'Völkische' Ideologien und Gruppierungen*. Berlin: PREMA-Presseagentur, 1983.

Magliocco, Sabina. *Witching Culture. Folklore and Neo-Paganism in America*. Philadelphia: University of Pennsylvania Press, 2004.

Maidenbaum, Aryeh, and Stephen A. Martin, eds. *Lingering Shadows. Jungians, Freudians, and Anti-semitism*. Boston/London: Shambala, 1991.

Maier, Bernhard. *Die Religion der Germanen. Götter – Mythen – Weltbild*. Munich: C.H. Beck, 2003.

Mallory, J.P. "Human populations and the Indo-European problem." *Mankind Quarterly* 33, no. 2 (1992): 131–154.

Malmager, Magne. "Die Düsseldorfer Malerschule und ihre norwegischen Künstler." In *Wahlverwandtschaft. Skandinavien und Deutschland 1800–1914*, edited by Bernd Henningsen, Janine Klein, Helmut Müssener and Solfrid Söderlind, 305–312. Berlin: Jovis, 1997a.

———. "Dresden und der Norden II." In *Wahlverwandtschaft. Skandinavien und Deutschland 1800–1914*, edited by Bernd Henningsen, Janine Klein, Helmut Müssener and Solfrid Söderlind, 288–295. Berlin: Jovis, 1997b.

Manea, Norman. "Happy Guilt. Mircea Eliade, Fascism, and the Unhappy Fate of Romania." *New Republic*, August 05, 1991, 27–36.

Manning, Michael. *Inamorata. The Erotic Art of Michael Manning*. San Francisco: Last Gasp, 2005.

Marquard, Odo. "Lob des Polytheismus. Über Monomythie und Polymythie." In *Abschied vom Prinzipiellen. Philosophische Studien*, edited by Odo Marquard, 91–116. Stuttgart: Philipp Reclam jun., 1991.

———. "Lob des Polytheismus. Über Monomythie und Polymythie." In *Zukunft braucht Herkunft. Philosphische Essays*, edited by Odo Marquard, 46–71. Stuttgart: Philipp Reclam jun., 2003.

Marschall, Birgit. *Reisen und Regieren. Die Nordlandfahrten Kaiser Wihelms II*. Heidelberg: Winter, 1991.

Martin, M. "Ostara – oder: dem Fest ist es egal, ob eine Göttin so heißt." Accessed October 31, 2011. Nornirs Ætt (web page), http://www.nornirsaett.de/ostara-oder-dem-fest-ist-es-egal-ob-eine-gottin-so-heist/.

McNallen, Stephen A. *Rituals of Ásatrú. I Major Blots*. Breckenridge, TX: The Ásatrú Free Assembly, 1985.

———. "Genetics & Beyond. Metagenetics – An Update." *The Runestone* 26 (1999): Republished on http://www.runestone.org/index.php?option=com_content&view

=article&id=144:genetics-a-beyond-metagenetics-an-update&catid=182:articles&It emid=571.

———. "Metagenetics." Accessed January 12, 2015. Asatru Folk Assembly (web page), http://www.runestone.org/index.php?option=com_content&view=article&id=143: metagenetics&catid=82:articles&Itemid=571.

———. "Three Decades of the Ásatú Revival in America." In *Tyr. Myth – Culture – Tradition II*, edited by Joshua Buckley and Michael Moynihan, 203–219. Atlanta: Ultra, 2003/04.

———. "Folkish Summer Hallowing – An Asatru Affirmation!" Newsletter, *AFA Update* 150, August 24 (2011).

McOisdealbhaigh, Garadyn. "Metagenetics: The Fear of Penetration and the Penetration of Fear." Accessed January 12, 2015. Irminsul Ættir (web page), http://www.irminsul.org/arc/008gm.html.

Meade, Michael. *Men and the Water of Life. Initiation and the Tempering of Men.* New York: Harper San Francisco, 1993.

Mertens, Dieter. "Die Instrumentalisierung der 'Germania' des Tacitus durch die deutschen Humanisten." In *Zur Geschichte der Gleichung 'germanisch – deutsch'. Sprache und Namen, Geschichte und Institutionen*, edited by Heinrich Beck, Dieter Geuenich, Heiko Steuer and Dietrich Hakelberg. Ergänzungsbände zum Reallexikon der germanischen Altertumskunde, 37–102. Berlin: de Gruyter, 2004.

Meskell, Lynne. "Goddesses, Gimbutas and 'New Age' Archaeology." *Antiquity* 69 (1995): 74–86.

Metzner, Ralph. "The Emerging Ecological Worldview." In *Worldviews and Ecology*, edited by Mary Evelyn Tucker and John A. Grim, 163–180. Lewisburgh: Bucknell University Press, 1993.

Miller, David L. *The New Polytheism. Rebirth of the Gods and Goddesses.* with a prefatory letter by Henry Corbin, appendix by James Hillman. 2. ed. Dallas, TX: Spring Publications, 1981.

Mills, Alexander Rud. *The Odinist Religion. Overcoming Jewish Christianity.* Melbourne: Ruskin Press, 1939.

Minkenberg, Michael. *Die neue radikale Rechte im Vergleich. USA, Frankreich, Deutschland.* Opladen/Wiesbaden: Westdeutscher Verlag, 1998.

———. "Die radikale Rechte in Europa heute. Profile und Trends in Ost und West." In *Die Dynamik der europäischen Rechten. Geschichte, Kontinuitäten, Wandel*, edited by Claudia Globisch, Agnieszka Pufelska and Volker Weiß, 111–132. Wiesbaden: VS Verlag, 2011.

Mogge, Winfried. "Religiöse Vorstellungen der deutschen Jugendbewegung." In *Religions- und Geistesgeschichte der Weimarer Republik*, edited by Hubert Cancik, 90–103. Düsseldorf: Patmos Verlag, 1982.

———. "Wandervogel, Freideutsche Jugend und Bünde. Zum Jugendbild der bürgerlichen Jugendbewegung." In *'Mit uns zieht die neue Zeit'. Der Mythos Jugend*, edited by

Thomas Koebner, Rolf-Peter Janz and Frank Trommler, 174–198. Frankfurt a.M.: Suhrkamp, 1985.

———. "'Wir lieben Balder, den Lichten...' Völkisch-religiöse Jugendbünde vom Wilhelminischen Reich zum 'Dritten Reich'." In *Die völkisch-religiöse Bewegung im Nationalsozialismus. Eine Beziehungs- und Konfliktgeschichte*, edited by Uwe Puschner and Clemens Vollnhals, 45–64. Göttingen: Vandenhoeck & Ruprecht, 2012.

Mohler, Armin. *Die konservative Revolution in Deutschland 1918–1932. Grundriss ihrer Weltanschauungen*. Stuttgart: Vorwerk, 1950.

———. *Die konservative Revolution in Deutschland 1918–1932. Ein Handbuch*. 6. revised and expanded ed. Graz: Ares, 2005.

Momigliano, Arnaldo. *Studies on Modern Scholarship*. Berkeley: University of California Press, 1994.

Moore, Robert, and Douglas Gillette. *King, Warrior, Magician, Lover. Rediscovering the Archetypes of the Mature Masculine*. New York: Harper San Francisco, 1991.

Mørch, Martin. "Om politik og religion." *Vølse* 46 (2008): 18.

Mosse, George L. *The Crisis of German Ideology. Intellectual Origins of the Third Reich*. New York: Grosset & Dunlap, 1964.

Moynihan, Michael. "Wisdom for the Wolf-Age. A Conversation with Dr. Stephen Flowers." *New Dawn Magazine* 77, no. March–April (2003): non-paginated internet source.

Moynihan, Michael, and Didrik Søderlind. *Lords of Chaos. The Bloody Rise of the Satanic Metal Underground*. Revised and expanded ed. Port Townsend, WA: Feral House, 2003.

Müller, Baal. "Was ist Neopaganismus?" *Heidnisches Jahrbuch* 1 (2006): 11–40.

Mund, Rudolf J. *Jörg Lanz v. Liebenfels und der Neue Templer Orden. Die Esoterik des Christentums*. Stuttgart: Spieth, 1976.

Mynarek, Hubertus. *Ökologische Religion. Ein neues Verständnis der Natur*. Munich: Goldmann, 1986.

"Mythos der Edda." *Der Spiegel*, January 07, 1985, 71–74.

Nanko, Ulrich. *Die Deutsche Glaubensbewegung. Eine historische und soziologische Untersuchung*. Marburg: diagonal-Verlag, 1993.

———. "Von 'Deutsch' nach 'Frei' und zurück? Jakob Wilhelm Hauer und die Frühgeschichte der Freien Akademie." In *Das evangelische Württemberg zwischen Weltkrieg und Wiederaufbau*, edited by Rainer Lächele and Jörg Thierfelder, 214–233. Stuttgart, 1995.

———. "Religiöse Gruppenbildungen vormaliger 'Deutschgläubiger' nach 1945." In *Antisemitismus, Paganismus, Völkische Religion – Antisemitism, Paganism, Voelkisch Religion*, edited by Hubert Cancik and Uwe Puschner, 121–134. Munich: K.G. Saur, 2004.

Näsström, Britt-Mari. *Freyja. The Great Goddess of the North.* Lund: Department of History of Religions, 1995.

———. *Blot. Tro och offer i det förkristna Norden* Stockholm: Norstedt, 2002.

Naumann, Thomas, and Patrick Schwarz. "Von der CD zur 'Lichtscheibe'. Das Kulturmagazin Sigill." In *Ästhetische Mobilmachung. Dark Wave, Neofolk und Industrial im Spannungsfeld rechter Ideologien,* edited by Andreas Speit, 161–194. Hamburg/Münster: Unrast Verlag, 2002.

Neckel, Gustav. *Die altgermanische Religion.* Zeitfragen deutscher Kultur Heft 2. Berlin: Wendt, 1932a.

———. *Liebe und Ehe bei den vorchristlichen Germanen.* Leipzig: Teubner, 1932b.

Nederveen Pieterse, Jan. *Empire and Emancipation. Power and Liberation on a World Scale.* London: Pluto Press, 1989.

Neményi, Géza v. *Heidnische Naturreligion. Altüberlieferte Glaubensvorstellungen, Riten und Bräuche.* Bergen a.d. Dumme: Johanna Bohmeier Verlag, 1988.

———. *Heidentum und NS-Ideologie.* Werbig: Germanische Glaubensgemeinschaft, 1997.

———. *Heilige Runen. Zauberzeichen des Nordens.* Berlin: Ullstein, 2004.

———. "Rune Song or Magic Charms? An Investigation of the 'Hávamál'." *Tyr. Myth – Culture – Tradition* 3 (2007): 183–192.

Neufert, Sven. "'Aus dunklen Tiefen empor zu lichten Höhen'. Die Edda-Rezeption in der völkischen Theater- und Festkultur." In *Eddische Götter und Helden. Milieus und Medien ihrer Rezeption. Eddic Gods and Heroes. The Milieux and Media of Their Reception,* edited by Katja Schulz, 267–292. Heidelberg: Winter, 2011.

Nielsen, Jørgen S., ed. *Islam in Denmark. The Challenge of Diversity.* Lanham etc.: Lexington Books, 2010.

Ninck, Martin. *Wodan und germanischer Schicksalsglaube.* Jena: Diederichs, 1935.

Noll, Richard. *The Jung Cult. Origins of a Charismatic Movement.* New York etc.: Free Press Paperbacks, 1994.

Nollau, Hermann, ed. *Germanische Wiedererstehung. Ein Werk über die germanischen Grundlagen unserer Gesittung.* Heidelberg: Winter, 1926.

Nordensvan, Georg. *Carl Larsson.* Sveriges Allmänna Konstförenings publikation, vol. I (1853–1890), vol. II (1890–1919). Stockholm: P.A. Norstedt, 1921.

Novak, Barbara. *Nature and Culture. American Landscape and Painting 1825–1875.* 3. ed. Oxford: Oxford University Press, 2007.

Oberndorfer, Ingrid. "Antisemitismus im 19. Jhdt. – August Julius Langbehn." *David. Jüdische Kulturzeitschrift* 57 (2003): Republished on http://david.juden.at/kulturzeitschrift/57-60/58-Oberndorfer-50.htm.

Oehlenschläger, Adam. *Digte.* Copenhagen: Andreas Seidelin, 1803.

Oertel, Kurt. "Die Angeln. Teil 2: Die neue Heimat." *Herdfeuer. Die Zeitschrift des Eldaring e.V.* 3, no. 10 (2005): 4–14.

———. "'Denn es steht geschrieben...' Neue Heiden und die Quellenkunde." *Heidnisches Jahrbuch* 2 (2007): 34–75.

———. "Was ist Heidentum? Wie kann man den Begriff verstehen." Accessed November 14, 2011. Eldaring e.V. (web page), http://www.eldaring.de/pages/germanisches-heidentum/was-ist-heidentum.php.

Oesterle, Anka. "The Office of Ancestral Inheritance and Folklore Scholarship." In *The Nazification of an Academic Discipline. Folklore in the Third Reich*, edited by James R. Dow and Hansjost Lixfeld, 189–246. Bloomington/Indianapolis: Indiana University Press, 1994.

Olender, Maurice. *The Languages of Paradise. Aryans and Semites. A Match Made in Heaven.* Translated by Arthur Goldhammer. New York: Other Press, 1992.

———. *The Languages of Paradise. Aryans and Semites – A Match Made in Heaven.* Translated by Arthur Goldhammer. 2nd revised and augmented ed. New York: Other Press, 2002.

———. *Race and Erudition.* Translated by Jane Marie Todd. Cambridge, MA/London: Harvard University Press, 2009.

Olsen, Jonathan. *Brisingamen.* New York: Berkley, 1984.

———. *The Languages of Paradise. Aryans and Semites. A Match Made in Heaven.* Translated by Arthur Goldhammer. New York: Other Press, 1992.

Olsen, Jonathan. *Nature and Nationalism. Right-Wing Ecology and the Politics of Identity in Contemporary Germany.* New York: St. Martin's Press, 1999.

Opitz, Reinhard. *Faschismus ud Neofaschismus.* 2 vols., vol. II (Neofaschismus in der Bundesrepublik). Cologne: Pahl-Rugenstein, 1988.

Osterkamp, Ernst. *Lucifer. Stationen eines Motivs.* Berlin/New York: de Gruyter, 1979.

Palmberg, Mai. "The Nordic Colonial Mind." In *Complying with Colonialism. Gender, Race and Ethnicity in the Nordic Region*, edited by Suvi Keskinen, Salla Tuori, Sari Irni and Diana Mulinari, 35–50. Farnham/Burlington, VT: Ashgate, 2009.

Parr, Rolf. "Der 'Werdandi-Bund'." In *Handbuch zur 'Völkischen Bewegung' 1871–1918*, edited by Uwe Puschner, Walter Schmitz and Justus H. Ulbricht, 316–327. Munich etc.: K.G. Saur, 1996.

Paul, Ina-Ulrike. "Paul Anton de Lagarde." In *Handbuch zur 'Völkischen Bewegung' 1871–1918*, edited by Uwe Puschner, Walter Schmitz and Justus H. Ulbricht, 45–93. Munich etc.: K.G. Saur, 1996.

Pauwels, Louis, and Jacques Bergier. *The Morning of the Magicians.* London: Mayflower, 1971.

Paxson, Diana L. *Essential Asatrú. Walking the Path of Norse Paganism.* New York: Citadel Press, 2006.

———. *The Lord of the Horses (Wodan's Children, Book 3).* New York: William Morrow, 1996.

———. *The Dragons of the Rhine (Wodan's Children, Book 1).* New York: William Morrow, 1993.

Pearson, Jo. "Nature Religion." In *Encyclopedia of New Religious Movements*, edited by Peter B. Clarke, 392–393. London/New York: Routledge, 2006.

Peniston-Bird, Corinna, Thomas Rohkrämer, and Felix Robin Schulz. "Glorified, Contested and Mobilized. The Alps in the 'Deutscher und Österreichischer Alpenverein' from the 1860s to 1933." *Austrian Studies* 18, no. 1 (2011): 141–158.

Penke, Niels. *Ernst Jünger und der Norden – Eine Inszenierungsgeschichte*. Frankfurter Beiträge zur Germanistik. Heidelberg: Universitätsverlag Winter, 2012.

Pennick, Nigel. *Einst war uns die Erde heilig. Die Lehre von den Erdkräften und Erdstrahlen*. Waldeck: Felicitas Hübner Verlag, 1987.

———. *Rune Magic*. London: The Aquarian Press, 1992.

———. *Hitler's Secret Sciences*. Sudbury, Suffolk: Neville Spearman, 1985.

Pennick, Nigel, and Prudence Jones. *A History of Pagan Europe*. London/New York: Routledge Chapman & Hall, 1995.

Petersen, Jesper Aagaard. "Introduction: Embracing Satan." In *Contemporary Religious Satanism. A Critical Anthology*, edited by Jesper Aagaard Petersen, 1–24. Farnham/Burlington: Ashgate, 2009.

Pettersson, Bodil. *Föreställningar om det förflutna. Arkeologi och rekonstruktion*. Lund: Nordic Academic Press, 2003.

Pétursson, Pétur. *Asasamfundet på Island och massmedia*. Forskningsrapport, edited by Religionssociologiska Institutet, vol. 185:1. Stockholm: Religionssociologiska Institutet, 1985.

———. *Church and Social Change. A Study of the Secularization Process in Iceland 1830–1930*. Studies in Religious Experience and Behavior, vol. 4. Helsingborg: Plus Ultra, 1983.

Pfahl-Traughber, Armin. *"Konservative Revolution" und "Neue Rechte". Rechtsextremistische Intellektuelle gegen den demokratischen Verfassungsstaat*. Opladen: Leske + Budrich, 1998.

Pietikäinen, Petteri. "C.G. Jung, anti-Semitism, and racial psychology." *Psykologia* 31, no. 2 (1996): 9–103.

Piper, Ernst. "'Der Nationalsozialismus steht über allen Bekenntnissen.' Alfred Rosenberg und die völkisch-religiösen Erneuerungsbestrebungen." In *Die völkisch-religiöse Bewegung im Nationalsozialismus. Eine Beziehungs- und Konfliktgeschichte*, edited by Uwe Puschner and Clemens Vollnhals, 337–354. Göttingen: Vandenhoeck & Ruprecht, 2012.

Poewe, Karla. *New Religions and the Nazis*. New York: Routledge, 2006.

Pöhlmann, Matthias. "Trügerischer 'Heidenspass'? Das '1. Berliner Heiden- und Hexenfest' im Spiegel interner Kritik." *Materialdienst Evangelische Zentralstelle für Weltanschauungsfragen* 11 (2004): 434–435.

Pöhlmann, Matthias "Streit um Heiden-Papst – Géza von Neményi erhebt Führungsanspruch innerhalb des Neuheidentums." *Materialdienst Evangelische Zentralstelle für Weltanschauungsfragen* 66, no. 11 (2003): 424–428.

Pois, Robert A. *National Socialism and the Religion of Nature*. London/Sidney: Croom Helm, 1986.

Poliakov, Léon. *The Aryan Myth. A history of racist and nationalist ideas in Europe*. New York: Basic Books, 1974.

Pross, Wolfgang. "Herder und die moderne Geschichtswissenschaft." *Germanisch-Romanische Monatsschrift* 57, no. 4 (2007): 19–44.

Prytz-Johansen, Jørgen. *Religionshistorikeren Vilhelm Grønbech*. Copenhagen: Gyldendal, 1987.

Puar, Jasbir K. *Terrorist Assemblages. Homonationalism in Queer Times*. Durham/London: Duke University Press, 2007.

Puschner, Uwe. "Mittgart – Eine völkische Utopie." In *Utopien, Zukunftsvorstellungen, Gedankenexperimente. Literarische Konzepte von einer 'anderen' Welt im abendländischen Denken von der Antike bis zur Gegenwart*, edited by Klaus Geus, 155–185. Frankfurt a.M.: Peter Lang, 2011.

———. "Völkische Bewegung und Jugendbewegung." In *Ideengeschichte als politische Aufklärung. Festschrift für Wolfgang Wippermann zum 65. Geburtstag*, edited by Stefan Vogt, Ulrich Herbeck, Ruth Kinet, Susanne Pocai and Bernard Waiderny, 54–70. Berlin: Metropol, 2010.

———. "Katholisches Milieu und alldeutsch-völkische Bewegung. Die Münchner Zeitschrift 'Odin' (1899–1901)." In *Le milieu intellectuel catholique en Allemagne, sa presse et ses réseaux (1871–1960)/Das katholische Intellektuellenmilieu in Deutschland, seine Presse und seine Netzwerke (1871–1960)*, edited by Michel Grunewald and Uwe Puschner, 143–167. Berne: Peter Lang, 2006.

———. "Völkische Diskurse zum Ideologem 'Frau'." In *Völkische Bewegung – Konservative Revolution – Nationalsozialismus. Aspekte einer politisierten Kultur*, edited by Walter Schmitz and Clemens Vollnhals, 45–76. Dresden: Thelem, 2005.

———. "Deutschchristentum. Eine völkisch-christliche Weltanschauungsreligion." In *Der Protestantismus – Ideologie, Konfession oder Kultur?*, edited by Richard Faber and Gesine Palmer, 93–122. Würzburg: Königshausen & Neumann, 2003.

———. "'One People, One God, One Reich.' The 'Völkisch Weltanschauung' and Movement." *German Historical Institute London Bulletin* 24, no. 1 (2002): 5–27.

———. *Die Völkische Bewegung im wilhelminischen Deutschland. Sprache – Rasse – Religion*. Darmstadt: Wissenschaftliche Buchgesellschaft, 2001.

———. "Deutsche Reformbühne und völkische Kultstätte. Ernst Wachler und das Harzer Bergtheater." In *Handbuch zur 'Völkischen Bewegung' 1871–1918*, edited by Uwe Puschner, Walter Schmitz and Justus H. Ulbricht, 762–796. Munich etc.: K.G. Saur, 1996.

Raabe, Jan, and Andreas Speit. "L'art du mal. Vom antibürgerlichen Gestus zur faschistoiden Ästhetik." In *Ästhetische Mobilmachung. Dark Wave, Neofolk und Industrial*

Im Spannungsfeld rechter Ideologien, edited by Andreas Speit, 65–122. Hamburg/Münster: Unrast Verlag, 2002.

Radkau, Joachim. *Natur und Macht. Eine Weltgeschichte der Umwelt.* Munich: C.H. Beck, 2000.

———. *Nature and Power. A Global History of the Environment.* Cambridge: Cambridge University Press, 2008.

———. *Die Ära der Ökologie. Eine Weltgeschichte.* Munich: C.H. Beck, 2011.

Rainer, Y. *Fidus, der Tempelkünstler. Interpretation im kunsthistorischen Zusammenhang mit Katalog der utopischen Architekturentwürfe.* 2 vols. Göppingen: Kümmerle, 1985.

Ravenscroft, Trevor. *The Spear of Destiny.* London: Samuel Weiser, 1972.

Ravn, Valdemar. "Interview med en vølve." *Valravn. Hedensk tidskrift om samfund og kultur* 7 (2003): 10–11.

———. "Interview med Carl Johan Rehbinder, en svensk hedning." *Valravn. Hedensk tidskrift om samfund og kultur* 15 (2005a): 6–10.

———. "Interview med Tim Peters fra Eldaring." *Valravn. Hedensk tidskrift om samfund og kultur* 14 (2005b): 8–10.

———. "Interview med Géza von Neményi den Tyske Allherjargode." *Valravn. Hedensk tidskrift om samfund og kultur* 13 (2005c): 10–13.

———. "Interview med Mikael Perman." *Valravn. Hedensk tidskrift om samfund og kultur* 12 (2005d): 8–12.

Reed, Peter, and David Rothenberg, eds. *The Norwegian Roots of Deep Ecology. Wisdom in the Open Air.* Minneapolis/London: University of Minnesota Press, 1993.

Rehbinder, Carl Johann. "Multikulturell andlig konferens in Indien – en omtumlande resa på många sätt." *Mimers Källa* 13 (2006): 6–7.

Reid, Sían. "'A Religion without Converts' Revisited. Individuals, Identity and Community in Contemporary Paganism." In *Handbook of Contemporary Neopaganism*, edited by James R. Lewis and Murphy Pizza, 171–191. Leiden/Boston: Brill, 2009.

Rem, Håvard. *Innfødte skrik. Norsk svartmetall.* Oslo: Schibsted, 2010.

Renfrew, Colin. *Archaeology and Language. The Puzzle of the Indo-European Origins.* London: Jonathan Cape, 1987.

Richards, Robert J. *The Tragic Sense of Life. Ernst Haeckel and the Struggle over Evolutionary Thought.* Chicago: University of Chicago Press, 2008.

Riedel, Katrin. "Von Gott und Göttern. Eine komparative Untersuchung der neuheidnischen Germanischen Glaubens-Gemeinschaft(en)." *Zeitschrift für Religions- und Geistesgeschichte* 66, nos. 3/4 (2014): 270–294.

Riehl, Wilhelm Heinrich. *Naturgeschichte des Volkes als Grundlage einer deutschen Socialpolitik.* 4 vols. Stuttgart/Augsburg: Cotta, 1851–1869.

Ritter, Hermann. "Zaubern ohne Gott?" *Herdfeuer. Die Zeitschrift des Eldaring e.V.* 6, no. 22 (2008): 11–20.

Röbel, Sven. "NPD-Vizechef Rieger ist tot." Accessed January 05, 2015. Spiegel Online, 29.09.2009, http://www.spiegel.de/politik/deutschland/prominenter-rechtsextremist-npd-vizechef-rieger-ist-tot-a-658206.html.

Röder, Brigitte, Juliane Hummel, and Brigitta Kunz. *Göttinnendämmerung. Das Matriarchat aus archäologischer Sicht*. Munich: Droemer Knaur, 1996.

Rohkrämer, Thomas. *Eine andere Moderne? Zivilisationskritik, Natur und Technik in Deutschland 1880–1933*. Paderborn etc.: Ferdinand Schöningh, 1999.

———. "Bewahrung, Neugestaltung, Restauration? Konservative Raum- und Heimatvorstellungen in Deutschland 1900–1933." In *Ordnungen in der Krise. Zur politischen Kulturgeschichte Deutschlands 1900–1933*, edited by Wolfgang Hardtwig, 47–68. Munich: R. Oldenbourg Verlag, 2007.

———. "German Cultural Criticism. The Desire for a Sense of Place and Community." In *Making a New World. Architecture & Communities in Interwar Europe*, edited by Rajesh Heynickx and Tom Avermaete, 43–56. Leuven: Leuven University Press, 2012.

Römer, Ruth. *Sprachwissenschaft und Rassenideologie in Deutschland*. Munich: Wilhelm Fink Verlag, 1989.

Rooden, Peter van. "Secularization and the Trajectory of Religion in the West." In *Post-Theism. Reframing the Judeo-Christian Tradition*, edited by Henri A. Krop, 168–188. Leuven: Peeters, 2000.

Rose, Paul Lawrence. *Revolutionary Antisemitism in Germany from Kant to Wagner*. Princeton, NJ: Princeton University Press, 1990.

Rosenberg, Alfred. *Der Mythus des 20. Jahrhunderts*. Munich: Hoheneichen, 1930.

———. *The Myth of the Twentieth Century. An Evaluation of the Spiritual-Intellectual Confrontations of Our Age*. Torrance, CA: Noontide Press, 1982.

Rösner, Thomas. "Adolf Bartels." In *Handbuch zur 'Völkischen Bewegung' 1871–1918*, edited by Uwe Puschner, Walter Schmitz and Justus H. Ulbricht, 874–896. Munich etc.: K.G. Saur, 1996.

Ross, Margaret Clunies. *Prolonged Echoes. Old Norse Myths in Medieval Northern Society: The Myths*. The Viking Collection, Studies in Northern Civilization, vol. 7. Odense: Odense University Press, 1994.

Rusinek, Bernd-A. "'Wald und Baum in der arisch-germanischen Geistes- und Kulturgeschichte' – Ein Forschungsprojekt des 'Ahnenerbe' der SS 1937–1945." In *Der Wald – ein deutscher Mythos? Perspektiven eines Kulturthemas*, edited by Albrecht Lehmann and Klaus Schriewer, 267–359. Hamburg: Reimer, 2000.

Sale, Kirkpatrick. *Dwellers on the Land. The Bioregional Vision*. San Francisco: Secker and Warberg, 1985.

Salomonsen, Jone. *Enchanted Feminism. Ritual, Gender and Divinity among the Reclaiming Witches of San Francisco*. London/New York: Routledge, 2002.

Samuels, Andrew. "National Socialism, National Psychology, and Analytical Psychology." In *Lingering Shadows. Jungians, Freudians, and Anti-Semitism*, edited by Aryeh Maidenbaum and Stephen A. Martin, 177-209. Boston/London: Shambala, 1991.

Sanders, Adrienne. "Group Claims White Victims." *San Francisco Examiner*, June 05, 2002

Sanders, Karin. *Bodies in the Bog and the Archaeological Imagination*. Chicago/London: University of Chicago Press, 2009.

Sandström, Erika. *På den tiden, i dessa dagar. Föreställningar om och bruk av historia under medeltidsveckan på Gotland och Jamtli Historieland*. Jamtli: Jamtli Förlag, 2005.

Šandulescu, Valentin. "Fascism and Its Quest for the 'New Man'. The Case of the Romanian Legionary Movement." *Studia Hebraica* 4 (2004): 349-361.

Sauer, Klaus, and German Werth. *Lorbeer und Palme. Patriotismus in deutschen Festspielen*. Munich: dtv, 1971.

Sauerland, Karol. "'Die fremden Völker in Europa'. Herders unpolitische Metaphern und Bilder zu den höchst politischen Begriffen Volk und Nation." In *Unerledigte Geschichten. Der literarische Umgang mit Nationalität und Internationalität*, edited by Gesa von Essen and Horst Turk, 57-71. Göttingen: Wallstein, 2000.

Schaffer, Gavin. "'Scientific Racism Again?' Reginald Gates, the *Mankind Quarterly* and the Question of 'Race' in Science after the Second World War." *Journal of American Studies* 41, no. 2 (2007): 253-278.

Schleswig-Holstein, Ministry of Interior of Land, ed. *Verfassungsschutzbericht 2008* [*Report on the Protection of the Constitution*]. Kiel: The Ministry of Interior of Land Schleswig-Holstein, 2008.

Schmidt, Martin, and Uta Halle. "On the Folklore of the Externsteine – or a Centre for Germanomaniacs." In *Archaeology and Folklore*, edited by Amy Gazin-Schwartz and Cornelius Holtorf, 158-174. London/New York: Routledge, 1999.

Schmitz, Walter, and Uwe Schneider. "Völkische Semantik bei den Münchner 'Kosmikern' und im George-Kreis." In *Handbuch zur 'Völkischen Bewegung' 1871-1918*, edited by Uwe Puschner, Walter Schmitz and Justus H. Ulbricht, 711-746. Munich etc.: K.G. Saur, 1996.

Schmoll, Friedemann. "Die Verteidigung organischer Ordnungen. Naturschutz und Antisemitismus zwischen Kaiserreich und Nationalsozialismus." In *Naturschutz und Nationalsozialismus*, edited by Joachim Radkau and Frank Uekötter, 169-182. Frankfurt a.M./New York: Campus, 2003.

Schneider, Tobias. "Sektierer oder Kampfgenossen? Der Klages-Kreis im Spannungsfeld der NS-Kulturpolitik." In *Völkische Bewegung – Konservative Revolution – Nationalsozialismus. Aspekte einer politisierten Kultur*, edited by Walter Schmitz and Clemens Vollnhals, 299-323. Dresden: Thelem, 2005.

Schnurbein, Stefanie v. "Knut Hamsun's Pan and Knut Faldbakken'außen grün, innen braun, und zu allen Seiten offen?'Allemange était leur Mecque...' La science des religions chez Stig Wikander (1935–1941)." In *The Study of Religion under the Impact of Fascism*, edited by Horst Junginger, 205–228. Leiden/Boston: Brill, 2008.

———. "The Use of Theories of Religion in Contemporary Asatru." In *Nordic Ideology between Religion and Scholarship*, edited by Horst Junginger and Andreas Åkerlund, 225–246. Frankfurt a.M.: Lang, 2013.

———. "Germanic Neo-Paganism – A Nordic Art Religion?" In *Religion, Tradition and the Popular. Transcultural Views from Asia and Europe*, edited by Judith Schlehe and Evamaria Sandkühler. History in Popular Cultures, 243–260. Bielefeld: transcript 2014.

———. "Tales of Reconstruction. Intertwining Germanic Neo-Paganism and Old Norse Scholarship." *Critical Research on Religion* 3, no. 1 (2015).

———. "Knut Hamsun's Narrative Fetishism." In *Knut Hamsun. Transgression and Worlding*, edited by Ståle Dingstad, Ylva Frøjd, Elisabeth Oxfeldt and Ellen Rees. Acta Nordica. Studier i språk- og litteraturvitenskap, 47–64. Trondheim: Tapir Press, 2011.

———. "Kontinuität durch Dichtung. Moderne Fantasyromane als Mediatoren völkisch-religiöser Denkmuster." In *Völkisch und national. Zur Aktualität alter Denkmuster im 21. Jahrhundert*, edited by Uwe Puschner and G. Ulrich Großmann, 245–265. Darmstadt: WBG, 2009.

———. "Neuheidentum und Fantasyroman." In *Bilder vom Mittelalter. Eine Berliner Ringvorlesung*, edited by Volker Mertens and Carmen Stange, 137–154. Göttingen, 2007.

———. "Schamanismus in der altnordischen Überlieferung – eine wissenschaftliche Fiktion zwischen den ideologischen Lagern." In *Kontinuität in der Kritik. Zum 50jährigen Bestehen des Münchener Nordistikinstituts: Historische und aktuelle Perspektiven der Skandinavistik*, edited by Klaus Böldl and Miriam Kauko, 149–175. Freiburg i.Br., 2005.

———. "Und ewig singen die Wälder. Trygve Gulbranssens Blut-und-Boden-Trilogie." In *Hundert Jahre deutsch-norwegische Begegnungen. Nicht nur Lachs und Würstchen*, edited by Bernd Henningsen, 284–286. Berlin: Berliner Wissenschafts-Verlag, 2005.

———. "Nordisten und Nordglaube. Wechselwirkungen zwischen akademischen und religiösen Konzepten von germanischer Religion." In *Germanentum im Fin de siècle. Wissenschaftsgeschichtliche Studien zum Werk Andreas Heuslers* edited by Jürg Glauser and Julia Zernack, 309–325. Basle: Schwabe, 2005.

———. "Religiöse Ikonographie – religiöse Mission. Das völkische Weihespiel um 1910." In *Kunst, Fest, Kanon. Inklusion und Exklusion in Gesellschaft und Kultur*, edited by Hermann Danuser, Herfried Münkler and in cooperation with the Staatsoper Unter den Linden, 85–97. Schliengen: Edition Argus, 2004.

BIBLIOGRAPHY

———. "Religion of Nature or Racist Cult? Contemporary Neogermanic Pagan Movements in Germany." In *Antisemitismus, Paganismus, Völkische Religion – Antisemitism, Paganism, Voelkisch Religion*, edited by Hubert Cancik and Uwe Puschner, 135–150. Munich: K.G. Saur, 2004.

———. *Krisen der Männlichkeit. Schreiben und Geschlechterdiskurs in skandinavischen Romanen seit 1890*. Göttingen: Wallstein, 2001.

———. "Religionsforskning og religionsfornyelse i 'nordisk' ånd i Tyskland etter første verdenskrig." In *Myter om det nordiska – mellan romantik och politik*, edited by Catharina Raudvere, Anders Andrén and Kristina Jennbert. Vägar till Midgård, 111–126. Lund: Nordic Academic Press, 2001.

———. "Transformationen völkischer Religion seit 1945." In *Völkische Religion und Krisen der Moderne. Entwürfe 'arteigener' Glaubenssysteme seit der Jahrhundertwende*, edited by Stefanie v. Schnurbein and Justus H. Ulbricht, 409–429. Würzburg: Königshausen & Neumann, 2001.

———. "Failed Seductions: Crises of Masculinity in Knut Hamsun's Pan and Knut Faldbakken's Glahn." *Scandinavian Studies* 73, no. 2 (2001): 147–164.

———. "Kräfte der Erde – Kräfte des Blutes. Elemente völkischer Ideologie in Marion Zimmer-Bradley: Die Nebel von Avalon und Diana Paxson: Der Zauber von Erin." *Weimarer Beiträge* 44, no. 4 (1998): 600–614.

———. "Mütterkult und Männerbund. Über geschlechtsspezifische Religionsentwürfe." In *Kybele – Prophetin – Hexe. Religiöse Frauenbilder und Weiblichkeitskonzeptionen*, edited by Richard Faber and Susanne Lanwerd, 249–270. Wurzburg: Königshausen & Neumann, 1997.

———. "Neuheidnische Religionsentwürfe von Frauen." In *Das neue Heidentum. Rückkehr zu den alten Göttern oder neue Heilsbotschaft?*, edited by Otto Bischofberger, 72–103. Freiburg (CH): Paulus Verlag, 1996.

———. "Weiblichkeitskonzeptionen im neugermanischen Heidentum und in der feministischen Spiritualität." In *Das neue Heidentum. Rückkehr zu den alten Göttern oder neue Heilsbotschaft?*, edited by Otto Bischofberger, 42–71. Freiburg (CH): Paulus Verlag, 1996.

———. "Die Suche nach einer 'arteigenen' Religion in 'germanisch'- und 'deutschgläubigen' Gruppen." In *Handbuch zur 'Völkischen Bewegung' 1871–1918*, edited by Uwe Puschner, Walter Schmitz and Justus H. Ulbricht, 172–185. Munich etc.: K.G. Saur, 1996.

———. "Gjenbruken av edda-diktningen i 'völkisch-religiöses Weihespiel' rundt århundreskiftet i Tyskland." *Nordica Bergensia* 3 (1994): 87–102.

———. "Fornyet naturreligion eller rasistisk kult. Moderne åsatrogrupper i Tyskland og Norden." *CHAOS. Dansk-norsk tidsskrift for religionshistoriske studier* 22 (1994): 117–129.

———. *Göttertrost in Wendezeiten. Neugermanisches Heidentum zwischen New Age und Rechtsradikalismus*. Munich: Claudius, 1993.

———. *Religion als Kulturkritik. Neugermanisches Heidentum im 20. Jahrhundert.* Heidelberg: C. Winter, 1992.

———. "Geheime kultische Männerbünde bei den Germanen. Eine Theorie im Spannungsfeld zwischen Wissenschaft und Ideologie." In *Männerbande – Männerbünde. Zur Rolle des Mannes im Kulturvergleich*, edited by Gisela Völger and Karin v. Welck, 97–102. Cologne: Rautenstrauch-Joest Museum, 1990.

Schockenhoff, Volker. "'Stonehenge' contra 'Störrische Kuh'." In *Wir zeigen Profil. Aus den Sammlungen des Staatsarchivs Detmold. Ausstellung des Nordrhein-Westfälischen Staatsarchivs Detmold*. Detmold: NW Staatsarchiv, 1990.

Scholz, Robert, and Mathias Brodkorb. "Über Habitus, Ideologie und Praxis. Im Gespräch mit Henning Eichberg." Accessed November 11, 2011. Endstation Rechts (web page), http://www.endstation-rechts.de/index.php?option=com_k2&view=item&id=4971.

Schough, Katarina. *Hyperboré. Föreställningen om Sveriges plats i världen*. Stockholm: Carlsson Bokförlag, 2008.

Schuhmacher, Hans. "'Das Heilige Fest' – ein Grundlagenwerk?" Accessed January 21, 2015. Rabenclan e.V. (web page), www.rabenclan.de/index.php/Magazin/HansSchuhmacherDasheiligeFest3.

Schuler, Alfred. *Cosmogonische Augen. Gesammelte Schriften*. Edited, commented and with an introduction by Baal Müller. Paderborn: Igel Verlag, 1997.

Schurtz, Heinrich. *Altersklassen und Männerbünde. Eine Darstellung der Grundformen der Gesellschaft*. Berlin: Reimer, 1902.

Schuster, Marina. "Die Bildwelt der Völkischen." In *Völkische Religion und Krisen der Moderne. Entwürfe 'arteigener' Glaubenssysteme seit der Jahrhundertwende*, edited by Stefanie v. Schnurbein and Justus H. Ulbricht, 254–267. Würzburg: Königshausen & Neumann, 2001.

———. "Bildende Künstler als Religionsstifter. Das Beispiel der Maler Ludwig Fahrenkrog und Hugo Höppener genannt Fidus." In *Kunst und Religion. Studien zur Kultursoziologie und Kulturgeschichte*, edited by Richard Faber and Volkhard Krech, 275–288. Würzburg: Königshausen & Neumann, 1999.

———. "Fidus – ein Gesinnungskünstler der völkischen Kulturbewegung." In *Handbuch zur 'Völkischen Bewegung' 1871–1918*, edited by Uwe Puschner, Walter Schmitz and Justus H. Ulbricht, 634–650. Munich etc.: K.G. Saur, 1996.

Schwarz, Guido. *Jungfrauen im Nachthemd – blonde Krieger aus dem Westen. Eine motivpsychologisch-kritische Analyse von J.R.R. Tolkiens Mythologie und Weltbild*. Würzburg: Königshausen & Neumann, 2003.

Sebaldt von Werth, Maximilian Ferdinand. *'Wanidis'. Der Triumph des Wahns III: D.I.S. Die arische 'Sexualreligion' als Volks-Veredelung in Zeugen, Leben und Sterben. Mit einem Anhang über Menschenzüchtung von Carl du Prel*. Leipzig: Friedrich, 1897.

See, Klaus v. *Barbar Germane Arier. Die Suche nach der Identität der Deutschen.* Heidelberg: Universitätsverlag C. Winter, 1994.

———. *Die Ideen von 1789 und die Ideen von 1914. Völkisches Denken in Deutschland zwischen Französischer Revolution und Erstem Weltkrieg.* Frankfurt a.M.1975.

———. *Deutsche Germanen-Ideologie vom Humanismus bis zur Gegenwart.* Frankfurt a.M.: Athenäum-Verlag, 1970.

Seibert, Wolfgang. *Deutsche Unitarier-Religionsgemeinschaft. Entwicklung, Praxis und Organisation.* Stuttgart: Quell-Verlag, 1989.

Senholt, Jakob Christiansen. "Radical Politics and Political Esotericism. The Adaptation of Esoteric Discourse within the Radical Right." In *Contemporary Esotericism*, edited by Egil Asprem and Kennet Granholm, 244–264. London: Equinox, 2012.

Sessions, George. "Deep Ecology as Worldview." In *Worldviews and Ecology*, edited by Mary Evelyn Tucker and John A. Grim, 207–227. Lewisburgh: Bucknell University Press, 1993.

Shastri, Dhirendra Nath. *Monotheism and the Western Pathology. Causes, Development and Impact of the Western Drive for World Domination from the 1st Millennium BCE to the Present.* http://www.hindurevolution.org/01/monotheism-and-the-western-pathology-contents.htm, 2009.

Shekhovtsov, Anton. "Apoliteic Music. Neo-Folk, Martial Industrial and 'Metapolitical Fascism'." *Patterns of Prejudice* 43, no. 5 (2009): 431–457.

Shippey, T.A. "Goths and Huns. The Rediscovery of the Northern Cultures in the Nineteenth Century." In *The Medieval Legacy. A Symposium*, edited by Andreas Haarder, Iorn Pio, Reinhold Schröder and Preben Meulengracht Sørensen. Odense: Odense University Press, 1982.

Shippey, Tom. *J.R.R. Tolkien. Author of the Century.* Boston/New York: Houghton Mifflin Company, 2002.

SilverWitch, Sylvana. "Just 'Wiccatru' Folk. A Word With Prudence Priest." Accessed November 01, 2011. Widdershins (web page), http://www.widdershins.org/vol3iss6/y9702.htm.

Simek, Rudolf. *Religion und Mythologie der Germanen.* Darmstadt: WBG, 2003.

Simonsen, Jørgen Bæk. "Denmark, Islam and Muslims. Socioeconomic Dynamics and the Art of Becoming." In *Islam in Denmark. The Challenge of Diversity*, edited by Jørgen S. Nielsen, 13–30. Lanham etc.: Lexington Books, 2010.

Sjöö, Monica, and Barbara Mor. *The Great Cosmic Mother. Rediscovering the Religion of the Earth.* San Francisco: Harper Collins, 1987.

Skott, Fredrik. *Asatro i tiden.* Göteborg: Språk och folkminnesinstitutet, 2000.

Sloterdijk, Peter. *Gottes Eifer. Vom Kampf der drei Monotheismen.* Frankfurt a.M.: Verlag der Weltreligionen, 2007.

Söderlind, Didrik. "Diabolos in Musica. Om sort metall og et heller dystert livssyn." *Humanist* 3 (2008): 18–37.

Solli, Brit. *Seid. Myter, sjamanisme og kjønn i vikingenes tid.* Oslo: Pax, 2002.

Sørensen, Øystein. "Drømmen om det storgermanske rike. Pangermanismen i Norge ca. 1850–1945." In *Jakten på Germania. Fra nordensvermeri til SS-arkeologi*, edited by Terje Emberland and Jorunn Sem Fure, 61–81. Oslo: Humanist forlag, 2009.

Sørensen, Preben Meulengracht. *The Unmanly Man. Concepts of Sexual Defamation in Early Northern Society.* Odense: Odense University Press, 1983.

Speit, Andreas, ed. *Ästhetische Mobilmachung. Dark Wave, Neofolk und Industrial im Spannungsfeld rechter Ideologien.* Hamburg/Münster: Unrast Verlag, 2002.

Spiesberger, Karl. *Runenmagie. Handbuch der Runenkunde.* Berlin: Schikowski, 1955.

Spilker, Annika. *Geschlecht, Religion und völkischer Nationalismus. Die Ärztin und Antisemitin Mathilde von Kemnitz-Ludendorff (1877–1966).* Frankfurt a.M.: Campus, 2013.

Spinozzi, Paola. "The Topos of Ragnarök in the Utopian Thought of William Morris." In *Eddische Götter und Helden. Milieus und Medien ihrer Rezeption. Eddic Gods and Heroes. The Milieux and Media of Their Reception*, edited by Katja Schulz, 187–198. Heidelberg: Winter, 2011.

Staalesen, Gunnar. *Falne engler.* Oslo: Gyldendal, 1989.

———. *Bukken til havresekken.* Oslo: Gyldendal, 1977.

Stanley, Eric Gerald. *The Search for Anglo-Saxon Paganism.* Cambridge: Brewer, 1975.

Statham, Alison. "Ecology and the German Right." In *Green Thought in German Culture. Historical and Contemporary Perspectives*, edited by Colin Riordan, 125–138. Cardiff: University of Wales Press, 1997.

Stauf, Renate. "'Was soll überhaupt eine Messung aller Völker nach uns Europäern?' Der Europagedanke Johann Gottfried Herders." *Germanisch-Romanische Monatsschrift* 57, no. 4 (2007): 45–60.

Stegemann, Wolfgang. "Wie 'christlich' ist das Judentum? Zur Kritik an einigen seiner (protestantischen) Konstruktionen." In *Zwischen Affirmation und Machtkritik. Zur Geschichte des Protestantismus und protestantischer Mentalitäten*, edited by Richard Faber, 141–164. Zurich: Theologischer Verlag Zürich, 2005.

Steinbock, Fritz. *Das heilige Fest. Rituale des traditionellen germanischen Heidentums in heutiger Zeit.* 2. ed. Hamburg: Verlag Daniel Junker, 2008.

———. "Die Freiheit eines Heidenmenschen. Inhalt und Gründe der 'Leitidee freies Heidentum' des ORD." *Heidnisches Jahrbuch* 1 (2006): 147–165.

———. "Die heilige Kunst – Dichtung und Wahrheit." Accessed November 04, 2011. VfgH e.V. (web page), http://www.vfgh.de/.

Steinsland, Gro. *Norrøn religion. Myter, riter, samfunn.* Oslo: Pax, 2005.

Stenseth, Egil. "Nyhedendom i Norge." *Humanist* 2 (2003).

Stensgaard, Starkad Storm. "Om Monoteismens Uvæsen. Religiøs Begrebsbefrielse, del 3." *Valravn. Hedensk tidskrift om samfund og kultur* 16 (2006): 13–17.

———. "Om Monoteismens Uvæsen. Religiøs Begrebsbefrielse, del 2." *Valravn. Hedensk tidskrift om samfund og kultur* 15 (2005): 20–24.

———. "Om Monoteismens Uvæsen. Religiøs Begrebsbefrielse, del 1." *Valravn. Hedensk tidskrift om samfund og kultur* 14 (2005): 18–19.

Stern, Fritz. *The Politics of Cultural Despair. A Study in the Rise of the Germanic Ideology.* Berkeley, CA: University of California Press, 1961.

Sternhell, Zeev. "Von der Gegenaufklärung zu Faschismus und Nazismus. Gedanken zur europäischen Katastrophe des 20. Jahrhunderts." In *Die Dynamik der europäischen Rechten. Geschichte, Kontinuitäten, Wandel,* edited by Claudia Globisch, Agnieszka Pufelska and Volker Weiß, 19–40. Wiesbaden: VS Verlag, 2011.

Steuer, Heiko. "Das 'völkisch' Germanische in der deutschen Ur- und Frühgeschichtsforschung." In *Zur Geschichte der Gleichung 'germanisch-deutsch'. Sprache und Namen, Geschichte und Institutionen,* edited by Heinrich Beck, Dieter Geuenich, Heiko Steuer and Dietrich Hakelberg. RGA Sonderband, 357–502. Berlin/New York: de Gruyter, 2004.

———, ed. *Eine hervorragend nationale Wissenschaft. Deutsche Prähistoriker zwischen 1900 und 1995.* Ergänzungsbände zum Reallexikon der Germanischen Altertumskunde, vol. 29, edited by Heinrich Beck, Dieter Geuenich and Heiko Steuer. Berlin/New York: de Gruyter, 2001.

Storm, Starkad. "Politisk Polyteisme og Antimonoteistisk Selvforsvar." *Vølse* 45 (2008): 24–29.

Straubhaar, Sandra Ballif. "Rezension: Hilda Ellis Davison. *Roles of the Northern Goddess.*" *Scandinavian Studies* 7, no. 3 (1999): 360–362.

Strauß, Botho. "Anschwellender Bocksgesang." In *Die selbstbewusste Nation. 'Anschwellender Bocksgesang' und weitere Beiträge zu einer deutschen Debatte,* edited by Heimo Schwilk and Ulrich Schacht, 19–42. Frankfurt a.M.: Ullstein, 1994.

Strmiska, Michael. "Romuva Looks East. Indian Inspiration in Lithuanian Paganism." In *Religious Diversity in Post-Soviet Society. Ethnographies of Catholic Hegemony and the New Pluralism in Lithuania,* edited by Milda Alisauskiene and Ingo W. Schröder, 125–151. Farnham/Burlington: Ashgate, 2012.

———, ed. *Modern Paganism in World Cultures. Comparative Perspectives.* Santa Barbara, CA: ABC-Clio, 2005.

———. "Modern Paganism in World Cultures. Comparative Perspectives." In *Modern Paganism in World Cultures. Comparative Perspectives,* edited by Michael Strmiska, 1–54. Santa Barbara, CA: ABC-Clio, 2005.

———. "The Evils of Christianization. A Pagan Perspective on European History." In *Cultural Expressions of Evil and Wickedness,* edited by Terry Waddell, 59–72. New York: Rodopi, 2003.

Strmiska, Michael, and Vilius Rudra Dundzila. "Romuva. Lithuanian Paganism in Lithuania and America." In *Modern Paganism in World Cultures. Comparative Perspectives,* edited by Michael Strmiska, 241–298. Santa Barbara, CA: ABC-Clio, 2005.

Strmiska, Michael, and Baldur A. Sigurvinsson. "Asatru: Nordic Paganism in Iceland and America." In *Modern Paganism in World Cultures. Comparative Perspectives*, edited by Michael Strmiska, 127–180. Santa Barbara, CA: ABC-Clio, 2005.

Ström, Åke v., and Haralds Biezais. *Germanische und baltische Religion*. Stuttgart etc.: Kohlhammer, 1975.

Ström, Folke. *Nið, Ergi and Old Norse Moral Attitudes*. London: Viking Society for Northern Research 1973.

———. *Nordisk hedendom. Tro och sed i förkristen tid.* 2. ed. Göteborg: Akademiförlaget, 1967.

Strömbäck, Dag. *Seijd. Textstudier i Nordisk Religionshistoria*. Stockholm/Copenhagen: Levin & Munksgaard, 1935.

Strömberg, Håkan. *Odens øga*. Stockholm: Ordfront, 2002.

Stroumsa, Guy G. "Georges Dumézil, Ancient German Myths, and Modern Demons." *ZfR. Zeitschrift für Religionswissenschaft* 6, no. 2 (1998): 125–136.

Stubba. *The Book of Blots. Ceremonies, Rituals & Invocations of the Odinic Rite*. London: Odinic Rite, 1991.

Stuckrad, Kocku von. *Western Esotericism. A Brief History of Secret Knowledge*. London: Equinox, 2005.

Stumpfl, Robert. *Kultspiele der Germanen als Ursprung des mittelalterlichen Dramas*. Berlin: Junker und Dünnhaupt, 1936.

Sundermeier, Theo. *Was ist Religion? Religionswissenschaft im theologischen Kontext*. Gütersloh: Gütersloher Verlagshaus, 1999.

———. "The Meaning of Tribal Religions for the History of Religion. Primary Religious Experience." *Scriptura* 10 (1992): 1–9.

Sutcliffe, Steven. "Between Apocalypse and Self-realisation. 'Nature' as an Index of New Age Religiosity." In *Nature Religion Today. Paganism in the Modern World*, edited by Joanne Pearson, Richard H. Roberts and Geoffrey Samuel, 33–44. Edinburgh: Edinburgh University Press, 1998.

Sveriges Asatrosamfund. "Snart är de nya stadgarna här!" *Mimers Källa* 21 (2009): 5–6.

Szczudlo, Andrzej. "Schlichtingsheim. Das 'Feenschloss' Rothenhorn der Frfr. Sigrun v. Schlichting." *Neuer Glogauer Anzeiger*, September, 2005.

Taguieff, Pierre-André. *The Force of Prejudice. On Racism and its Doubles*. Minneapolis: University of Minnesota Press, 2001.

———. *La Force du préjugé. Essai sur le racisme et ses doubles*. Paris: La Découverte, 1988.

Taubes, Jacob. "Mythos und Moderne. Begriff und Bild einer Rekonstruktion." In *Mythos und Moderne. Begriff und Bild einer Rekonstruktion*, edited by Karl Heinz Bohrer, 457–470. Frankfurt a.M.: Suhrkamp, 1983.

Taylor, Bron. *Dark Green Religion. Nature Spirituality and the Planetary Future*. Berkeley: University of California Press, 2010.

Tegnér, Esaias. *Frithiofs saga*. Esaias Tegnérs samlade dikter, edited by Åke K.G. Lundquist, 7 vols., vol. 4. Lund: Gleerup, 1986. 1825.

Tenbruck, Friedrich H. "Die Religion im Maelstrom der Reflexion." In *Religion und Kultur*, edited by Jörg Bergmann, Alois Hahn and Thomas Luckmann. Kölner Zeitschrift für Soziologie und Sozialpsychologie, Sonderheft 33, 31–67. Opladen: Westdeutscher Verlag, 1993.

The Circle of Ostara. "Loki." Accessed November 29, 2011. The Odinic Rite (web page), http://www.odinic-rite.org/main/loki/.

Theo. "'außen grün, innen braun, und zu allen Seiten offen?' Was ist los mit der 'Stachelbeere'?" *SteinKreis* 31 (200): 46–47.

Thiberg, Jannik Thalbitzer. "Hvad skal vi udbrede? Hvad står man for i asatro?". *Valravn. Hedensk tidskrift om samfund og kultur* 11 (2004): 14f.

Thompson, Peter. "New Age Mysticism, Postmodernism and Human Liberation." In *Green Thought in German Culture. Historical and Contemporary Perspectives*, edited by Colin Riordan, 107–124. Cardiff: University of Wales Press, 1997.

Thorsson, Edred. *The Nine Doors of Midgard. A Curriculum of Rune-Work*. Smithville, TX: Runa Raven, 2003 [1991].

———. *Northern Magic. Rune Mysteries & Shamanism*. St. Paul, MN: Llewellyn, 1998.

———. *Rune Might. Secret Practices of the German Rune Magicians*. St. Paul, MN: Llewellyn, 1989.

———. *Runelore. A Handbook of Esoteric Runology*. Wellingborough, Northamptonshire: Llewellyn, 1987.

———. *Futhark. A Handbook of Rune Magic*. Wellingborough, Northamptonshire: Llewellyn, 1984.

Tiger, Lionel. *Men in Groups*. New York: Random House, 1969.

Timuş, Mihaela. "'Quand l'Allemange était leur Mecque...' La science des religions chez Stig Wikander (1935–1941)." In *The Study of Religion under the Impact of Fascism*, edited by Horst Junginger, 205–228. Leiden/Boston: Brill, 2008.

Tolkien, J.R.R. "Beowulf. The Monsters and the Critics." *Proceedings of the British Academy* 22 (1936): 245–295.

———. *The Monster and the Critics and Other Essays*. London: George Allen & Unwin, 1983.

———. *The Tolkien Reader*. 2. ed. New York: Del Rey, 1986.

Tönnies, Ferdinand. *Community and Civil Society*. Cambridge University Press, 2001.

Trinkunas, Jonas. "Revival of the ancient Baltic religions. Presented at the First International Gathering and Conference of Elders of Ancient Traditions and Cultures in Mumbay, India. Presentation sponsored by the Infinity Foundation." Accessed February 26, 2014. Infinity Foundation (web page), http://www.infinityfoundation.com/mandala/h_es/h_es_trink_j_baltic.htm.

Trommler, Frank. "Mission ohne Ziel. Über den Kult der Jugend im modernen Deutschland." In *'Mit uns zieht die neue Zeit'. Der Mythos Jugend*, edited by Thomas Koebner, Rolf-Peter Janz and Frank Trommler, 14–49. Frankfurt a.M.: Suhrkamp, 1985.

Tucker, William H. *The Funding of Scientific Racism. Wickliffe Draper and the Pioneer Fund*. Urbana/Chicago: University of Illinois Press, 2002.

———. *The Cattell Controversy. Race, Science, and Ideology*. Urbana/Chicago: University of Illinois Press, 2009.

Turville-Petre, Gabriel. *Myth and Religion of the North* London: Weidenfeld and Nicolson, 1964.

Tveito, Lill-Hege. "Judaism in Music." Translated by William Ashton Ellis. In *The Theatre. Richard Wagner's The Lord of the Rings." New Literary History* 36, no. 2 (2005): 227–246.

———. "Kampen for den Nordiske rases overlevelse. Bruken av den norrøne mytologien innenfor Vigrid." Master's thesis, University of Tromsø, 2007.

Uekötter, Frank. *The Green and the Brown. A History of Conservation in Nazi Germany*. Cambridge: Cambridge University Press, 2006.

Ulbrich, Björn. *Im Tanz der Elemente. Kult und Ritus der heidnischen Gemeinschaft*. Vilsbiburg: Arun, 1990.

Ulbrich, Björn, and Romana Ulbrich. *Dein Name sei...Rituale und Zeremonien zu Geburt und Namensgebung*. Engerda: Arun, 2009.

Ulbricht, Justus H. "Die Geburt der Deutschen aus dem Geist der Tragödie. Weimar als Ort und Ausganspunkt nationalpädagogischer Theaterprojekte." In *Wege nach Weimar. Auf der Suche nach der Einheit von Kunst und Politik*, edited by Hans Wilderotter and Michael Dorrmann, 127–142. Berlin: Jovis, 1999.

———. "'Meine Seele sehnt sich nach Sichtbarkeit deutschen Wesens.' Weltanschauung und Verlagsprogramm von Eugen Diederichs im Spannungsfeld zwischen Neuromantik und 'Konservativer Revolution'." In *Versammlungsort moderner Geister. Der Eugen Diederichs Verlag – Aufbruch ins Jahrhundert der Extreme*, edited by Gangolf Hübinger, 335–374. Munich: Diederichs, 1996.

———. "Völkische Erwachsenenbildung. Intentionen, Programme und Institutionen zwischen Jahrhundertwende und Weimarer Republik." In *Handbuch zur 'Völkischen Bewegung' 1871–1918*, edited by Uwe Puschner, Walter Schmitz and Justus H. Ulbricht, 252–276. Munich etc.: K.G. Saur, 1996.

———. "Wider das 'Katzenjammergefühl der Enwurzelung.' Intellektuellen-Religion im Eugen Diederichs Verlag." *Buchhandelsgeschichte* 76 (1996): B111–B120.

———. "'Heil Dir, Wittekinds Stamm.' Verden, der "Sachsenhain" und die Geschichte völkischer Religiosität in Deutschland, Teil 1 und 2." In *Heimatkalender für den Landkreis Verden: Verdener Sachsenhain, Jahrbuch 1995 und 1996*, edited by Landkreis Verden, 69–123; 224–267. Verden: Landkreis Verden, 1995/96.

Ullrich, Otto. *Weltniveau. In der Sackgasse des Industriesystems.* Berlin: Rotbuch, 1979.

Umland, Andreas, Werner Loh, and Roger Griffin, eds. *Fascism Past and Present, West and East. An International Debate on Concepts and Cases in the Comparative Study of the Extreme Right.* Stuttgart: ibidem, 2006.

Vale, V., and John Sulak. *Modern Pagans. An Investigation of Contemporary Pagan Practices.* San Francisco, CA: Re/Search Publications, 2001.

Viel, Bernhard. *Utopie der Nation. Ursprünge des Nationalismus im Roman der Gründerzeit.* Berlin: Matthes & Seitz, 2009.

Völger, Gisela, and Karin v. Welck, eds. *Männerbande – Männerbünde. Zur Rolle des Mannes im Kulturvergleich.* 2 vols. Cologne: Rautenstrauch-Joest Museum für Völkerkunde, 1990.

Volquardsen, Ebbe. *Die Anfänge des grönländischen Romans. Nation, Identität und subalterne Artikulation in einer arktischen Kolonie.* Marburg: Tectum, 2011.

Wachler, Ernst. *Sommerspiele auf vaterländischer Grundlage.* Berlin: Vaterländischer Schriftenverband, 1910.

———. *Die Freilichtbühne. Betrachtungen über das Problem des Volkstheaters unter freiem Himmel.* Leipzig: Fritz Eckhardt, 1909.

———. *Mittsommer. Trauerspiel mit Chören für die Bühne unter freiem Himmel.* Munich/Leipzig: Georg Müller, 1905.

———. "Über die Zukunft des deutschen Glaubens." *Irminsul. Schriftenreihe für Junggermanische (eddische) Religion und Weltanschauung* 44 (1930 [1900]): 1–25.

———. *Walpurgis. Ein Festspiel zur Frühlingsfeier.* Leipzig: C.F. Amelangs Verlag, 1903.

———. *Läuterung deutscher Dichtkunst im Volksgeiste. Eine Streitschrift.* Berlin-Charlottenburg: Richard Heinrich, 1897.

Waggoner, Ben. "Wagners Ring. Übersetzung aus dem Englischen und Literaturanhang von Kurt Oertel." *Herdfeuer. Die Zeitschrift des Eldaring e.V.* 2, no. 4 (2004): 18–22.

Wagner-Hasel, Beate. *Matriarchatstheorien der Altertumswissenschaft.* Wege der Forschung. Darmstadt: Wissenschaftliche Buchgesellschaft, 1992.

Wagner, Richard. "Das Judentum in der Musik." In *Sämtliche Schriften und Dichtungen*, edited by Richard Wagner, 66–85. Leipzig: Breitkopf und Härtel, 1911 [1850].

———. "Das Kunstwerk der Zukunft." In *Sämtliche Schriften und Dichtungen*, edited by Richard Wagner, 194–206. Leipzig: Breitkopf und Härtel, 1911 [1849].

———. "The Art-Work of the Future." Translated by William Ashton Ellis. In *The Art-Work of the Future. Richard Wagner's Prose Works*, 69–213. London: Keegan Paul, Trench, Trübner, 1895 [1849].

———. "Judaism in Music." Translated by William Ashton Ellis. In *The Theatre. Richard Wagner's Prose Works*, 79–100. London: Keegan Paul, Trench, Trübner, 1894 [1850].

Walser, Martin. *Ich vertraue. Querfeldein.* Frankfurt a.M.: Suhrkamp, 2000.

Walthard, Peter. "Die alte Sitte." *Herdfeuer* 2, no. 3 (2004): 4–6.

Warneck, Igor. *Ruf der Runen. Eine Einführung in die Welt der Runen.* Darmstadt: Schirner, 2005.

Wasserstrom, Steven M. *Religion after Religion. Gershom Scholem, Mircea Eliade, and Henry Corbin at Eranos.* Princeton, NJ: Princeton University Press, 1999.

Wawn, Andrew. *The Vikings and the Victorians. Inventing the Old North in 19th-Century Britain.* Cambridge: Brewer, 2000.

Webb, James. *The Occult Establishment.* La Salle, IL: Open Court, 1976.

Wedemeyer-Kolwe, Bernd. "Völkisch-religiöse Runengymnastiker im Nationalsozialismus." In *Die völkisch-religiöse Bewegung im Nationalsozialismus. Eine Beziehungs- und Konfliktgeschichte*, edited by Uwe Puschner and Clemens Vollnhals, 459–472. Göttingen: Vandenhoeck & Ruprecht, 2012.

———. *'Der neue Mensch.' Körperkultur im Kaiserreiche und in der Weimarer Republik.* Würzburg: Königshausen & Neumann, 2004.

Wegener, Franz. *Das atlantidische Weltbild. Nationalsozialismus und Neue Rechte auf der Suche nach der versunkenen Atlantis.* Gladbeck: KFVR – Kulturförderverein Ruhrgebiet e.V., 2001.

Weiner, Marc A. *Richard Wagner and the Anti-Semitic Imagination.* Lincoln: University of Nebraska Press, 1995.

Weiser, Lily. *Altgermanische Jünglingsweihen und Männerbünde. Ein Beitrag zur deutschen und nordischen Altertums- und Volkskunde.* Bausteine zur Volkskunde und Religionswissenschaft 1, edited by Eugen Fehrle. Bühl (Baden): Konkordia, 1927.

Weißmann, Karlheinz. "Das Heilige ist eine unverlierbare Größe." *Junge Freiheit*, March 09, 2007

———. *Männerbund.* Schnellroda: Edition Antaios, 2004.

Wenger, Matthias. "Meine politische Position und ihre Entwicklung in 30 Jahren – eine Dokumentation." Accessed December 04, 2011. Der HAIN – Das Magazin für natürliche Religion und gesellschaftliche Wandlung (web page), http://www.derhain.de/.

———. "Patriarchalische Ideologie oder matriarchalisches Wertsystem. Die Auseinandersetzung um Herman Wirth und die Ura-Linda-Chronik." Accessed November 28, 2011. Der HAIN – Das Magazin für natürliche Religion und gesellschaftliche Wandlung (web page), http://www.derhain.de/WirthMatriarchat.htm.

Werber, Niels. "Geo- and Biopolitics of Middle-Earth. A German Reading of Tolkien's The Lord of the Rings." *New Literary History* 36, no. 2 (2005): 227–246.

Werner, Meike G. "Die Erneuerung des Lebens durch ästhetische Praxis. Lebensreform, Jugend und Festkultur im Eugen Diederichs Verlag." In *Versammlungsort moderner Geister. Der Eugen Diederichs Verlag – Aufbruch ins Jahrhundert der Extreme*, edited by Gangolf Hübinger, 222–242. Munich: Diederichs, 1996.

Wetzel, Juliane. "Die Maschen des rechten Netzes. Nationale und internationale Verbindungen im rechtsextremen Spektrum." In *Rechtsextremismus in Deutschland. Voraussetzungen, Zusammenhänge, Wirkungen*, edited by Wolfgang Benz, 154–178. Frankfurt a.M.: Fischer, 1994.

White, Damian. "Bioregionalism." In *International Encyclopedia of Environmental Politics*, edited by John Barry and E. Gene Frankland. London etc.: Routledge, 2002

Wiedemann, Felix. *Rassenmutter und Rebellin. Hexenbilder in Romantik, völkischer Bewegung, Neuheidentum und Feminismus*. Würzburg: Königshausen & Neumann, 2007.

Wien Ulrich Andreas. "Interview mit Géza von Neményi, dem Allsherjargoden (Stammespriester) der Germanischen Glaubens-Gemeinschaft." *Materialdienst der Evangelischen Zentralstelle für Weltanschauungsfragen* 60, no. 4 (1997): 114–121.

Wiench, Piotr. "A Postcolonial Key to Understanding Central and Eastern European Neopaganisms." In *Modern Pagan and Native Faith Movements in Central and Eastern Europe*, edited by Scott Simpson and Kaarina Aitamurto. Studies in Contemporary and Historical Paganism, 10–26. Durham: Acumen, 2013.

Wikander, Stig. *Der arische Männerbund. Studien zur indo-iranischen Sprach- und Religionsgeschichte*. Lund: Gleerup, 1938.

Williamson, George S. *The Longing for Myth in Germany. Religion and Aesthetic Culture from Romanticism to Nietzsche*. Chicago: University of Chicago Press, 2004.

Wilson, David M. "The Viking Age in British Literature and History in the Eighteenth and Nineteenth Centuries." In *The Waking of Angantyr. The Scandinavian Past in European Culture – Den nordiske fortid i europæisk kultur*, edited by Else Roesdahl and Preben Meulengracht Sørensen, 58–71. Aarhus: Aarhus University Press, 1996.

Winterbourne, Anthony. *When the Norns Have Spoken. Time and Fate in Germanic Paganism*. Madison/Teaneck: Fairleigh Dickinson University Press, 2004.

Wirth, Herman. *Der Aufgang der Menschheit*. Jena: Diederichs, 1928.

Wistrich Robert S. "Radical Antisemitism in France and Germany (1840–1880)." *Modern Judaism* 15, no. 2 (1995): 109–135.

Witoszek, Nina. *The Origins of the 'Regime of Goodness'. Remapping the Cultural History of Norway*. Oslo: Universitetsforlaget, 2011.

Wiwjorra, Ingo. "Review of Heinz Grünert: Gustaf Kossina (1858–1931)." *Ethnographisch-Archäologische Zeitschrift* 44 (2003): 141–148.

———. "Germanenmythos und Vorgeschichtsforschung im 19. Jahrhundert." In *Religion und Nation, Nation und Religion. Beiträge zu einer unbewältigten Geschichte*, edited by Michael Geyer and Hartmut Lehmann, 367–386. Göttingen: Wallstein, 2004.

———. *Der Germanenmythos. Konstruktion einer Weltanschauung in der Altertumsforschung des 19. Jahrhunderts*. Darmstadt: Wissenschaftliche Buchgesellschaft, 2006.

———. "In Erwartung der 'Heiligen Wende'. Herman Wirth im Kontext der völkischen Bewegung." In *Utopien, Zukunftsvorstellungen, Gedankenexperimente. Literarische Konzepte von einer 'anderen' Welt im abendländischen Denken von der Antike bis zur Gegenwart*, edited by Klaus Geus, 399–416. Frankfurt a.M.: Peter Lang, 2011.

Wodans, Erben. *Gemeinschaftsblatt*. vol. Ausgabe 2010. Berlin: Wodans Erben e.V., 2010.

Wodening, Eric. *We are Our Deeds. The Elder Heathenry. Its Ethic and Thew*. Watertown, NY: Theod, 1998.

Wolbert, Klaus. "Die Lebensreform – Anträge zur Debatte." In *Die Lebensreform. Entwürfe zur Neugestaltung von Leben und Kunst um 1900*, edited by Kai Buchholz, Rita Latocha, Hilke Pcekmann and Klaus Wolbert, 13–21. Darmstadt: haeusser, 2001.

Wolff, Markus. "Review of 'Hermann Hendrich: Leben und Werk' by Elke Rohling." *Tyr. Myth – Culture – Tradition* 1 (2002): 218–219.

———. "Ludwig Fahrenkrog and the Germanic Faith Community. Wodan Triumphant." *Tyr. Myth – Culture – Tradition* 2 (2003/04): 221–242.

Wolfram, Richard. *Schwerttanz und Männerbund*. Kassel: Bärenreiter Verlag, 1935.

Wolfschlag, Claus. *Ludwig Fahrenkrog. Das goldene Tor. Ein deutscher Maler zwischen Jugendstil und Germanenglaube*. Dresden: Verlag Zeitenwende, 2006.

Wölk, Volkmar. *Natur und Mythos. Ökologiekonzepte der 'Neuen' Rechten im Spannungsfeld zwischen Blut und Boden und New Age*. Natur und Mythos ed. Duisburg: DISS-Texte, 1992.

Woods, Roger. *Germany's New Right as Culture and Politics*. London: Palgrave Macmillan, 2007.

Wulfstan, O.R. "Odinic Values in Family Life & Personal Relationships." Accessed November 29, 2011. The Odinic Rite (web page), http://www.odinic-rite.org/main/odinic-values-in-family-life-personal-relationships/.

Wyck, Peter C. van. *Primitives in the Wilderness. Deep Ecology and the Missing Human Subject*. New York: State University of New York Press, 1997.

Zander, Helmut. *Rudolf Steiner. Die Biographie*. Munich: Piper, 2011.

Zelinsky, Hartmut. *Richard Wagner – ein deutsches Thema. Eine Dokumentation zur Wirkungsgeschichte Richard Wagners 1876–1976*. Frankfurt a.M.: Zweitausendeins, 1976.

Zernack, Julia. *Geschichten aus Thule. Íslendingasögur in Übersetzungen deutscher Germanisten*. Berliner Beiträge zur Skandinavistik, vol. 3. Berlin: Freie Unversität Berlin, 1994.

———. "Fulltrúi." In *Reallexikon der Germanischen Altertumskunde*, edited by Heinrich Beck, Dieter Geuenich and Heiko Steuer, 243–245. Berlin/New York: Walter de Gruyter, 1996.

———. "'Germanin im Hauskleid'. Bemerkungen zu einem Frauenideal deutscher Gelehrter." In *Kybele – Prophetin – Hexe. Religiöse Frauenbilder und Weiblichkeitskonzeptionen*, edited by Richard Faber and Susanne Lanwerd, 213–232. Würzburg: Königshausen & Neumann, 1997a.

———. "Germanische Restauration und Edda-Frömmigkeit." In *Politische Religion – religiöse Politik*, edited by Richard Faber, 143–160. Würzburg: Königshausen & Neumann, 1997b.

———. "Fulltrúi." In *Reallexikon der germanischen Altertumskunde*, edited by Heinrich Beck, Heiko Steuer and Dieter Timpe, 243–245. Berlin: de Gruyter, 1997c.

———. "Germanische Altertumskunde, Skandinavistik und völkische Religion." In *Völkische Religion und Krisen der Moderne. Entwürfe 'arteigener' Glaubenssysteme seit der Jahrhundertwende*, edited by Stefanie v. Schnurbein and Justus H. Ulbricht. Würzburg: Königshausen & Neumann, 2001.

———. "Kontinuität als Problem der Wissenschaftsgeschichte." In *Kontinuität in der Kritik. Zum 50jährigen Bestehen des Münchner Nordistikinstituts: Historische und aktuelle Perspektiven der Skandinavistik*, edited by Klaus Böldl and Miriam Kauko. Rombach Wissenschaften – Reihe Nordica. Freiburg i.Br.: Rombach, 2005.

———. "Nordische Philologie." In *Kulturwissenschaften und Nationalsozialismus*, edited by Jürgen Elvert and Jürgen Nielsen-Sikora, 691–713. Stuttgart: Franz Steiner Verlag, 2008.

Ziege, Eva-Maria. *Mythische Kohärenz. Diskursanalyse des völkischen Antisemitismus*. Konstanz: UVK, 2002.

Zimmermann, Harm-Peer. "Männerbund und Totenkult. Methodologische und ideologische Grundlinien der Volks- und Altertumskunde Otto Höflers 1933–1945." *Kieler Blätter zur Volkskunde* 26 (1994): 5–27.

Zimmermann, Michael E. "Possible Political Problems of Earth-Based Religiosity." In *Beneath the Surface. Critical Essays in the Philosophy of Deep Ecology*, edited by Eric Katz, Andrew Light and David Rothenberg, 169–194. Cambridge, MA/London: The MIT Press, 2000.

Index

14 Word Press   73, 74

Adam von Bremen   206, 207
Allerseelen (band)   339, 342
Allgermanic Heathen Front (AHF, Norway and Sweden, racial-religious)   63, 66, 211, 237, 338
American Vinland Association (USA, a-racist)   59, 72, 111
Amt Rosenberg   46, 271
Anaximander   175
Anglecyn Church of Odin   48
Aquino, Michael   72, 126
Arbeitsgemeinschaft Deutsche Glaubensbewegung   45
Arbeitsgemeinschaft naturreligiöser Stammesverbände Europas (ANSE, Germany, racial-religious)   57, 74, 75, 78, 79, 81
Arbeitskreis Bioregionalismus   210, 211
Arizona Kindred   72
Armanen-Orden (Germany, racial-religious)   55–57, 70, 74, 75, 78, 79, 81, 99, 110, 113, 116, 117, 124, 125, 129, 139, 226, 257, 274, 351, 353
Arminius   331, 332
Artamanen   192
Artgemeinschaft (Germany, racial-religious)   49, 56, 105, 196, 273, 284
Asatrofællesskabet (Denmark, ethnicist)   68
Asatrofællesskabet Yggdrasil (Denmark, a-racist)   67, 109, 185
Asatru Alliance (USA, ethnicist)   59, 72, 73, 78, 128, 338, 341, 343
Asatru Folk Assembly (AFA, USA, ethnicist)   59, 73, 148, 343
Asatru Free Assembly (AFA, USA, ethnicist)   58, 59, 72, 73, 78, 79, 83, 86, 110, 111, 113, 128, 131, 135, 139, 163, 229, 279, 333, 341
Ásatrúarfélagið (Iceland, a-racist)   59, 60, 69, 70, 78, 79, 101, 108–110, 247, 253, 336, 342
Ásatrúarmenn 126. *See also* Ásatrúarfélagið
Asbjørnsen, Peter Christen   26
Asfrid. *See* Steinbock, Fritz

Asgardbund (Germany, racial-religious)   274
Assmann, Jan   164–166, 170
Aswynn, Freya   71, 78, 83, 111, 117, 342, 343
Australia First   48
Avenarius, Ferdinand   307, 308

Bachofen, Johan Jakob   51, 218–220, 225, 233
Bahn, Peter   196
Bainbridge, William   128
Bartels, Adolf   315
Bathory (band)   337, 339
Baudelaire, Charles   337
Bäumler, Alfred   219–221, 236, 237
Bede   97, 252
Beinteinsson, Sveinbjörn   60, 69, 184, 211, 342
Benn, Gottfried   172
Benoist, Alain de   137–139, 163, 169, 174, 196, 211, 278, 286
Bifrost (band)   337
Bifrost (Norway, a-racist)   62, 64, 66, 86, 101, 113, 140, 143, 144, 182, 216, 232, 256, 290
Bismarck, Otto von   306
Bjarnadóttir, Birna   357, 358
Blain, Jenny   12, 72, 105, 120, 121, 143, 243, 244, 247, 288
Blake, William   337
Blavatsky, Helena Petrovna   34, 51
Blood Axis (band)   343, 344
Blüher, Hans   234, 235, 237–239
Bly, Robert   237, 240
Bölsche, Wilhelm   188
Bonus, Arthur   29–31, 178, 222, 263, 266
Bradley, Marion Zimmer   227, 246, 325, 326
Brand, Adolf   234
Breidablikk-Gildet (Sweden, ethnicist)   61, 65, 79
Breivik, Anders Behring   179, 335
Bringsværd, Tor Åge   332
Broughton, John   71
Brüning, Christian   229, 294
Budapest, Zsuzsanna   227
Bund für Persönlichkeitskultur   39
Bund Heimattreuer Jugend   50, 55, 56, 196
Bureus, Johannes   19, 115, 118
Burzum (band)   337

INDEX

Califia, Pat   246
Castaneda, Carlos   61, 119
Chamberlain, Houston Stewart   29, 197
Changes (band)   341
Charlemagne   108, 268
Chisholm, James   72
Christensen, Else   58, 72, 73, 77
Collegium Humanum   50, 195, 196
Cornwell, Bernard   330
Council for Social and Economic Studies   284
Council for the Hindu Revolution or *Hindu Kranti Parishad* (HKP)   166
Covenant of the Goddess   111, 226
Crowley, Aleister   34, 41, 112, 246, 336
Current 93 (band)   342

Dahn, Felix   308
Darré, Walter   192, 195, 267
Däubler, Theodor   172
Davidson, Hilda Ellis   283
Davis, Elizabeth Gould   225
Dawkins, Richard   336
De negen verelden (Netherlands, a-racist)   86
Der Steinkreis   211
Detering, Heinrich   299
Deutschbund   37
Deutsche Erneuerungsgemeinde   37
Deutsche Glaubensbewegung   45, 47, 49, 264, 266
Deutsche Unitarier Religionsgemeinschaft (DUR)   49, 50, 195, 196
Deutscher Bund Heimatschutz   187
Deutscher Orden   40, 45, 245
Deutscher Werkbund   307
Deutsches Kulturwerk europäischen Geistes (DKEG)   50
Deutschgläubige Gemeinschaft (Germany, racial-religious)   40, 44, 45, 47, 49, 57, 76, 113, 192, 196, 245, 263, 273, 318
Deutschreligiöse Gemeinschaft   40, 316
Deutschreligiöser Bund   37
Devereux, Paul   213
Diederichs, Eugen   31, 205
Dragon Rouge   83, 118
Dumézil, George   239, 240, 276–283, 285, 286, 293
Dürer, Albrecht   307, 346

Ealdfaether   296
Eckart, Dietrich   125
Eichberg, Henning   127, 136, 137, 196, 211
Einherjer (band)   337
Eldaring (Germany, a-racist)   76, 80, 81, 84, 86, 96, 107, 113, 120, 127, 143, 149, 164, 170, 172, 183, 229, 241, 246, 251, 258, 259, 291, 292, 294, 332, 351
Eliade, Mircea   139, 159, 172, 173, 237, 239, 265, 276, 279–281, 286, 293, 297, 313
Engels, Friedrich   219
Enoksen, Lars Magnar   227, 290
Enslaved (band)   337
Eriksson, Jörgen I.   62
European Congress of Ethnic Religions (ECER)   81
Evans, Sir Arthur   51
Evola, Julius   77, 80, 237, 279, 324, 344, 345

Fahrenkrog, Ludwig   39, 44, 56, 76, 83, 103, 104, 109, 112, 113, 126, 150, 191, 211, 314, 316–318, 323, 324, 337, 344, 346
Falter, Reinhard   172, 173, 176, 212, 214
Fehrle, Eugen   270, 297
Fellowship of the Spiral Path   226, 246
Feuerbach, Ludwig   152, 157, 304
Fidus   109, 191, 206, 317, 318, 323, 324, 344, 346
First Church of Odin   48
Fisker, Søren   85, 86
Flowers, Stephen. *See* Thorsson, Edred
Foreningen Forn Sed (FFS, Norway, a-racist)   64, 80, 105, 113, 184, 256
Forn Siðr (Denmark, a racist with an ethnicist faction)   67
Forn Siðr (Denmark, a-racist with ethnicist faction)   67, 68, 79, 86, 107, 112, 113, 132, 133, 154, 168, 248, 251, 322
Fortune, Dion   51
Fraternitas Saturni   116
Frazer, James   51, 52, 262, 263
Freie Akademie   49, 273
Freud, Sigmund   35, 234
Friðriksson, Friðrik Þór   69
Frisksportrörelsen   61
Fritsch, Theodor   37

Gaiman, Neil   333
Gardiner, Rolf   198

Gardner, Gerald 52, 112
Gaup, Ailo 121
Geijer, Erik Gustaf 26, 302
Gemeinschaft für heidnisches Leben (Germany, ethnicist) 56, 274
George, Stefan 172, 173
Germanen-Ring 47
Germanisch-deutsche Religions-Gemeinschaft 39, 40
Germanische Glaubensgemeinschaft (Germany, ethnicist) 39, 44, 56, 57, 75, 76, 79, 81, 82, 104, 112, 113, 126, 155, 181, 210, 258, 314, 316, 353
Gesellschaft für biologische Anthropologie, Eugenik und Verhaltensforschung 56, 196, 284
Gesellschaft für freie Publizistik (GfP) 50
Gesellschaft Wodan 39, 40
Gibbs-Bailey, John 57
Gimbutas, Marija 225, 226, 284
Gimle 61, 62, 65
Gobineau, Arthur de 29
Goden-Orden (Germany, ethnicist) 49, 55, 113
Goethe, Johann Wolfgang 157–159, 307, 318, 335, 336
Goethes Erben (band) 344
Gorsleben, Rudolf John 44, 115, 116
Göttner-Abendroth, Heide 349
Graf, Friedrich Wilhelm 175
Gramsci, Antonio 138
Graves, Robert 51
Grebenstein, Haimo 111, 291
GRECE 137
Grimm, Jacob and Wilhelm 17, 23–26, 97, 186, 220, 257, 261, 269, 292, 303, 309, 325
Grimsson, Atrid. See Eriksson, Jörgen I.
Grønbech, Vilhelm 101, 262, 263, 269, 277, 283, 285, 286, 288, 292, 293, 297
Groß, Otto 225
Grundtvig, Nikolai Frederik Severin 25, 301, 309, 349
Grundy, Stephan 84, 118, 120, 286, 287, 325, 327, 328
Gude, Hans Fredrik 204
Guðjónsson, Þorsteinn 60, 79
Guénon, René 279
Gugenberger, Eduard 210
Guido-von-List-Gesellschaft 41, 43, 49, 55
Gulbransson, Tryggve 208

Gundarsson, Kveldulf. *See* Grundy, Stephan
Günther, Hans F. K. 192, 196, 237, 266, 270, 284
Gylfiliten (Germany, racial-religious) 124

Haeckel, Ernst 33, 34, 188, 189, 195, 197, 198, 209
Haggard, Rider 51, 303
Hagia Chora 212, 213
Hallgren, Henrik 144, 148, 184, 213, 214
Hammarens Ordens Sällskap 214
Hamsun, Knut 207, 334
Hannerz, Nils 47
Hansen, Jörmundur Ingi 69, 79, 336
Harner, Michael 61, 119
Harrison, Harry 96, 329
Harrison, Jane Ellen 51
Harry Schmidt. *See* Radegeis, Harry
Hartmann, Eduard von 33
Haudry, Jean 278, 279
Hauer, Jakob Wilhelm 45–47, 49, 128, 236, 265, 266, 273, 297
Haugen, Andrea 343
Haverbeck, Werner 50, 195, 196
Hazelius, Artur Immanuel 295
Heffendur (Denmark, ethnicist) 237, 242
Hegel, Georg Wilhelm Friedrich 156
Heidegger, Martin 202, 280, 334
Heidnische Gemeinschaft (Germany, ethnicist) 56, 79, 197, 210, 226
Heimgest 70, 78, 153, 342
Helheim (band) 337
Hendrich, Hermann 83, 317, 318, 320, 323, 344, 346
Henriksen, Vera 332
Hentschel, Willibald 37, 45, 191, 192, 245
Herder, Johann Gottfried 17, 21–26, 136, 138, 141, 157, 158, 186, 209, 261, 300, 301, 310, 311, 313
Heß, Rudolf 125
Het Rad (Netherlands, a-racist) 86
Heusler, Andreas 263–266, 273
Heuss, Theodor 308
Hicker, Bernd (alias Thorbern) 78
Hille, Ivar 184
Hillman, James 94, 159, 238
Hilmarsson, Hilmar Örn 69, 80, 342, 343
Himmler, Heinrich 46, 125, 192, 244, 267, 268, 341
Hirschfeld, Magnus 234

Hoffmann, E.T.A. 337
Höfler, Alois 308
Höfler, Otto 235–239, 241, 242, 269–272, 275–277, 279–281, 283, 285–288, 293, 297, 308, 339
Hoher Armanen Orden 42
Hölderlin, Friedrich 156, 157
Höppener, Hugo. *See* Fidus
Horowitz, Jonathan 243
Höß, Rudolf 192
Høst, Annette 121, 243
Hrafnar (USA, a-racist) 120, 288, 327
Hübner, Kurt 172
Hume, David 155, 158
Hunkel, Ernst 45, 192, 245
Hunkel, Margart 245
Hyltén-Cavallius, Gunnar Olof 26

Ibsen, Henrik 178, 207
Institute for the Study of Man 283, 284
International Asatru/Odinist Alliance (IAOA) 78
Irenessøn, Lars 86
Iron Guard 279, 280

Jacobsen, Hans S., 47 334
Jahnke, Alex 241, 332
Jakhelln, Cornelius 333–336
Järnåldersföreningen Birka 65
Jennings, Pete 71, 256, 257, 296
Jensen, Johannes V. 263
John Holm. *See* Shippey, Tom
Jordanes 19
Julius Cesar 18
Jung, Carl Gustav 35, 45, 58, 74, 94, 95, 130, 139, 159, 172, 238, 239, 271, 280, 281, 312, 339
Jünger, Ernst 280, 321, 344, 346
Junker, Daniel 83, 211

Kadmon 339, 340
Kaldera, Raven 247
Kammerer, Iris 331, 332
Karlsson, Thomas 83, 118
Kershaw, Kris 242, 293
Kindir (Denmark, a-racist online board) 68, 148
Kindred of the Kibbo Kifts 198
Kipling, Rudyard 51
Kith of Yggdrasil (Great Britain, a-racist) 71

Klages, Ludwig 33, 45, 158, 162, 172–174, 190, 191, 195, 197, 210, 219, 271, 272
Kliemannel, Holger 83, 211, 323
Klopstock, Friedrich Gottlieb 300
Kosmische Runde 173, 191
Kossina, Gustaf 261, 297
Kramps, Leif-Thorsten 210, 211, 213, 313
Krebs, Pierre 137
Kummer, Bernhard 222, 229, 237, 263–266, 269, 273, 275, 297
Kummer, Siegfried Adolf 44, 82, 115–117
Kusserow, Wilhelm 49, 56

Lafargue, Paul 219
Lagarde, Paul de 28, 29, 31, 38, 306
Landauer, Gustav 211
Lane, David 74
Lane, Katja 73, 74
Langbehn, Julius 29, 187, 306, 308, 346
Lanz von Liebenfels, Jörg 42–44, 115, 117, 128, 151, 220, 344
Larsson, Carl 205
LaVey, Anton 336
Lawrence, D.H. 51, 198
Leeuw, Gerardus van der 159
Leland, Charles G. 52
Liebman, Wayne 239
Linzie, Bil 121, 289
List, Guido (von) 41–44, 55, 81, 82, 94, 114–118, 125, 130, 151, 188, 220, 222, 245, 257, 274, 314
Lönnrot, Elias 26, 309
Lord Byron 337
Lord, Garman 153, 230, 244, 322
Ludendorff, Erich 47
Ludendorff, Mathilde 47
Lux Interna (band) 346

Machalett, Walther 274
Macpherson, James 302
Maier, Bernhard 96, 292, 294
Mallet, Paul Henri 21
Mannhardt, Wilhelm 24, 269
Marby, Friedrich Bernhard 44, 115–117
Marquard, Odo 160, 162, 163
Maurras, Charles 278
McNallen, Stephen 58, 59, 72, 73, 76, 78, 83, 86, 110, 129–132, 135, 139, 148, 251, 333, 339, 341

McVan, Ron 73
Menhir (band) 337
Merlinorden 62
Miller, David L. 159
Mills, Alexander Rud 10, 48, 57, 58, 72, 77, 127
Minutemen 341
Moe, Jørgen 26
Mohler, Armin 36, 307, 345
Möller van den Bruck, Arthur 197
Monistenbund 33, 189
Montesquieu 20
Morris, William 198, 303
Mosley, Oswald 57
Motz, Ulrich von 274
Moynihan, Michael 82, 206, 338–341, 343
Much, Rudolf 270
Muir, John 199, 200
Müller, Baal 172–174, 293
Murray, Margaret 51, 52
Murray, Valgard 72
Musfeldt, Hermann 49
Mussolini, Benito 278, 343

Näsström, Britt-Mari 285, 289
Natur og ungdom 184
Nätverket Forn Sed (Sweden) 65
Nebel, Andréa. *See* Haugen, Andrea
Nebelhexe. *See* Haugen, Andrea
Neckel, Gustav 223, 229, 263–266, 273
Neményi, Géza von 56, 57, 75, 76, 79, 82, 113, 115, 126, 131, 155, 181, 197, 211, 258
Neumann-Gundrum, Elisabeth 274
Nibelungenhort 323, 344
Nietzsche, Friedrich 33, 45, 103, 104, 150, 152, 157–162, 172, 202, 212, 306–308, 315, 317, 334, 337, 339, 340, 342, 344–346, 348
Ninck, Martin 271, 272, 293
Nollau, Hermann 265
Nordische Glaubensgemeinschaft 45, 49
Nordisch-Religiöse Arbeitsgemeinschaft 45
Nordisk Tingsfællig (NTF, Denmark, a-racist) 68, 109, 168, 216, 232
Nordiska Ringen 65
Norges Åsatrolag 79
Nornirs Ætt (Germany, a-racist) 74–76, 91, 104, 105, 114, 144, 216, 232, 291, 292, 324, 352

Norrœnt Mankyn 60
Norröna Samfundet (Sweden, ethnicist) 65
Norwegian Heathen Front 63, 337
Norwegian Nature Protection Society 184
Nýalssinna 59, 60, 79, 99

Odinic Rite (OR, Great Britain, ethnicist) 48, 57, 70–73, 77–79, 110, 111, 153, 210, 244, 246, 275, 288, 342, 343, 346
Committee for the Restoration of the Odinic Rite 57
Odinic Rite Deutschland (ORD, now VfgH, Germany, ehtnicist) 75, 77, 78, 83, 111, 172
Odinist Fellowship (USA, racial-religious) 58, 70, 72, 86
Odins Hird 67
Odinshof (Great Britain, a-racist) 71, 185, 256, 296
Oehlenschläger, Adam 301, 302
Oertel, Kurt 84, 143, 170, 251, 259, 291, 293, 332
Olgar Trust 109, 185, 214
Olsen, Lars-Henrik 251, 332
Orden der Nordungen 45, 245
Order of the Golden Dawn 34, 41, 51, 52
Order of the Triskelion 246
Ordo Novi Templi 43
Otto, Rudolf 265, 280, 297
Otto, Walter F. 172

Pagan Federation 71, 256
Pannwitz, Rudolf 172
Paxson, Diana 120, 160, 226, 227, 246, 288, 296, 325–327, 332, 333
Pearson, Roger 283
Pennick, Nigel 213
Petak. *See* Kadmon
Péturss, Helgi 59, 60
Planet Drum Foundation 210
Polomé, Edgar 276, 283, 284, 286, 293
P-Orridge, Genesis 342
Priest, Prudence 59, 72, 111, 229, 333
Proudhon, Pierre-Joseph 156

Quisling, Vidkun 47
Rabenclan 74, 75, 78, 136, 274, 327
Radegeis, Harry 139
Ragnarsson, Thorbjørn 79

INDEX

Rask, Rasmus   25
Ratatosk   120
Read, Ian   71, 342, 343, 346
Reclaiming Witches   52, 53
Rehbinder, Carl Johan   120, 248
Rembrandt van Rijn   29, 306, 307, 346
Renan, Ernest   33, 152, 153, 156–158
Reuss, Theodor   34, 41, 246
Reuter, Otto Siegfried   40, 44, 45, 76, 113, 213
Rieger, Jürgen   56, 196, 284
Riehl, Wilhelm Heinrich   186, 187, 210
Riger (band)   337
Rilke, Rainer Maria   172
Ring of Troth. See The Troth
Robien, Paul   211
Romuva   74, 79
Rosenberg, Alfred   29, 46, 125, 194, 271
Rudbeck, Olaus   19
Rudorff, Ernst   187, 210
Rune Gild (Great Britain, ethnicist)   59, 71, 72, 78, 81–83, 113, 116, 117, 126, 139, 286, 342, 343, 346

Sale, Kirkpatrick   209
Samfälligheten för Nordisk Sed (Sweden)   66, 256
Samfundet Forn Sed (SFS, Sweden, a-racist)   66, 107, 113, 120, 143, 148, 182, 213, 256, 330
Samfundet Manhem   47
Sandemose, Aksel   263
Saxo Grammaticus   247, 252
Schelling, Friedrich Wilhelm   156
Schiller, Friedrich   156, 300, 304
Schjelderup, Kristian   47
Schleiermacher, Friedrich   298
Schleipfer, Adolf   55, 117, 124
Schleipfer, Sigrun   55, 79, 115, 117. *See also* Schlichting, Sigrun von
Schlichting, Sigrun von   57, 74, 79, 81, 110, 226
Schmitz, Hermann   172
Schoenichen, Walther   192
Schopenhauer, Arthur   33, 157, 158
Schuhmacher, Hans   136
Schuler, Alfred   158, 162, 172–174
Schultze-Naumburg, Paul   187, 211, 308
Schurtz, Heinrich   233, 234, 236, 238
Schwaner, Wilhelm   38, 39, 318

Schweidlenka, Roman   210
Scott, Walter   25, 303
Sebaldt von Werth, Max Ferdinand   41, 245
Sebottendorf, Rudolf von   117, 125
Sehring, Bernhard   318
Shelley, Percy Bysshe   337
Shippey, Tom   329
Sierra Club   200
Sjöberg, Arne   61, 79
Sjöö, Monica   349
Society for Creative Anachronism   296
Søderlind, Didrik   338–340
Sol Invictus (band)   342
Solefald (band)   335, 336
Spanuth, Jürgen   274
Spiesberger, Karl   116, 117
Spieth, Rudolf Arnold   116
Springmann, Baldur   196
SS *Ahnenerbe*   194, 267, 271, 279, 281, 283
Stassen, Franz   317, 323
Steinbock, Fritz   75, 106, 135, 136, 140, 170, 171, 174, 175, 231, 292, 321
Steinsland, Gro   286, 289
Stenseth, Egil   140, 144
Stensgaard, Starkad Storm   167, 168, 176, 230
Strauß, Botho   161, 162, 164
Strauß, David Friedrich   33, 152
Strength Through Joy (band)   344
Strindberg, August   207
Ström, Folke   96, 119, 285, 286, 289
Strömbäck, Dag   119
Struck, Pia   248
Stuck, Franz von   323
Sturluson, Snorri   19, 20
Sturmgeist (band)   335
Sundermeier, Theo   164, 165, 170
Sveinsson, Brynjolfr   19
Svensk Hednisk Front   66
Sveriges Asatrosamfund (SAS, Sweden, a-racist)   62, 65, 66, 86, 108, 120, 144, 256. *See also Samfundet Forn Sed*

Tacitus   18, 20, 114, 220, 223, 244, 252, 262, 291
Tannenberg Bund   47
Taubes, Jacob   162, 163
Taylor, Martyn   71
Taylor, Robert N.   72, 341
Tegnér, Esaias   26, 302

Telge Fylking 65
Temple of Set 72, 126
Temple of Wotan 74
Teudt, Wilhelm 212, 213, 266, 268, 269, 273–275
The Troth 59, 72, 73, 76, 83, 113, 120, 128, 132, 143, 177, 182, 226, 258, 286, 288, 324
Theosophical Society 34
Thoma, Hans 323
Thoreau, Henry David 199, 200
Thorsson, Edred 57, 59, 71, 72, 78, 81–84, 98, 99, 110, 111, 113, 116–118, 120, 125, 126, 132, 139, 149, 163, 246, 247, 286–288, 327, 338, 341
Thule Seminar 137
Thule-Gesellschaft 125
Tidemand, Adolph 204
Tiger, Lionel 240, 241
Tolkien, J.R.R. 309–314, 324, 325, 329
Trinkunas, Jonas 79
Turville-Petre, Gabriel 283
Tveitt, Geirr 334
Tylor, Edward Burnett 24

Ulbrich, Stefan Björn 77, 169, 170, 232, 279
Unabhängige Ökologen Deutschlands (UÖD) 210
Unleashed (band) 337

Varenne, Jean 278
Verein für germanisches Heidentum VfgH 75–78, 83, 86, 94, 106, 107, 111, 113, 114, 127, 134, 135, 140, 170, 172, 178, 231, 246, 291, 292, 321
Vigrid 63, 129
Vikernes, Varg 63, 337–340
Viking Brotherhood 58
Vishva Hindu Parisad (VHP) 80
Volkmann, Volkert 78, 111
Voltaire 156

Vries, Jan de 276, 281, 283, 285–287, 293
Wachler, Ernst 38, 39, 41, 112, 150, 191, 314–316, 320, 327
Wagner, Richard 1, 24, 29, 157, 298, 303–305, 308, 310, 314, 315, 317, 318, 320, 324, 325, 329, 330, 332, 334, 337
Waldteufel (band) 343
Wallis, Robert 243, 247, 288
Walser, Martin 162, 164
Wandervogel 32, 234, 235
Watkins, Alfred 212, 268
Watson, Paul 201
Weiser, Lily 235, 270
Weißleder, Karl 39
Weltbund zum Schutz des Lebens (WSL) 50, 195
Wenger, Matthias 56, 211, 229, 274, 275
Werdandi-Bund 307, 308, 318, 323
Wikander, Stig 270, 272, 276, 279
Wiking Jugend 50, 196, 237
Wiligut, Karl Maria 46, 125, 338, 341
Wille, Bruno 188
Winckelmann, Johann Joachim 304
Wirth, Herman 221, 222, 226, 229, 266, 267, 269, 273–275
Wodening, Eric 104
Wolff, Markus 83, 323, 343
Wolzogen, Hans von 305
Woodharrow Institute 82, 287
World Congress of Ethnic Religions (WCER) 79–81, 210
Worm, Ole 19
Wotansvolk 73, 74
Wulfing Kindred 72, 341

Yeats, Richard 51
Yeowell, John 57, 70
Yggdrasil 61, 62, 65, 118–120, 182, 229
Yggdrasil Kreis 78, 111
Yockey, Francis Parker 58